Teach Yourself VISUALLY™ Windows® 2000 Server

by
Michael Toot
Eric Butow

Visual

From
maranGraphics™

&

IDG Books Worldwide, Inc.
An International Data Group Company
Foster City, CA • Indianapolis • Chicago • New York

Teach Yourself VISUALLY™ Windows® 2000 Server

Published by
IDG Books Worldwide, Inc.
An International Data Group Company
919 E. Hillsdale Blvd., Suite 400
Foster City, CA 94404
www.idgbooks.com (IDG Books Worldwide Web Site)

Library of Congress Control Number: 00-109410

ISBN: 0-7645-3428-9

Printed in the United States of America
10 9 8 7 6 5 4 3 2 1

1K/RQ/RR/QQ/IN

Distributed in the United States by IDG Books Worldwide, Inc.

Distributed by CDG Books Canada Inc. for Canada; by Transworld Publishers Limited in the United Kingdom; by IDG Norge Books for Norway; by IDG Sweden Books for Sweden; by IDG Books Australia Publishing Corporation Pty. Ltd. for Australia and New Zealand; by TransQuest Publishers Pte Ltd. for Singapore, Malaysia, Thailand, Indonesia, and Hong Kong; by Gotop Information Inc. for Taiwan; by ICG Muse, Inc. for Japan; by Intersoft for South Africa; by Eyrolles for France; by International Thomson Publishing for Germany, Austria and Switzerland; by Distribuidora Cuspide for Argentina; by LR International for Brazil; by Galileo Libros for Chile; by Ediciones ZETA S.C.R. Ltda. for Peru; by WS Computer Publishing Corporation, Inc., for the Philippines; by Contemporanea de Ediciones for Venezuela; by Express Computer Distributors for the Caribbean and West Indies; by Micronesia Media Distributor, Inc. for Micronesia; by Chips Computadoras S.A. de C.V. for Mexico; by Editorial Norma de Panama S.A. for Panama; by American Bookshops for Finland.

For corporate orders, please call maranGraphics at 800-469-6616.

For general information on IDG Books Worldwide's books in the U.S., please call our Consumer Customer Service department at 800-762-2974. For reseller information, including discounts and premium sales, please call our Reseller Customer Service department at 800-434-3422.

For information on where to purchase IDG Books Worldwide's books outside the U.S., please contact our International Sales department at 317-572-3993 or fax 317-572-4002.

For consumer information on foreign language translations, please contact our Customer Service department at 1-800-434-3422, fax 317-572-4002, or e-mail rights@idgbooks.com.

For information on licensing foreign or domestic rights, please phone +1-650-653-7098.

For sales inquiries and special prices for bulk quantities, please contact our Order Services department at 800-434-3422 or write to the address above.

For information on using IDG Books Worldwide's books in the classroom or for ordering examination copies, please contact our Educational Sales department at 800-434-2086 or fax 317-572-4005.

For press review copies, author interviews, or other publicity information, please contact our Public Relations department at 650-653-7000 or fax 650-653-7500.

For authorization to photocopy items for corporate, personal, or educational use, please contact Copyright Clearance Center, 222 Rosewood Drive, Danvers, MA 01923, or fax 978-750-4470.

Screen shots displayed in this book are based on pre-released software and are subject to change.

Trademark Acknowledgments

FOR PURPOSES OF ILLUSTRATING THE CONEPTS AND TECHNIQUES DESCRIBED IN THIS BOOK, THE AUTHOR HAS CREATED VARIOUS NAMES, COMPANY NAMES, MAILING ADDRESSES, E-MAIL ADDRESSES AND PHONE NUMBERS, ALL OF WHICH ARE FICTITIOUS. ANY RESEMBLANCE TO THESE FICTITIOUS NAMES, COMPANY NAMES, MAILING ADDRESSES, E-MAIL ADDRESSES AND PHONE NUMBERS TO ANY ACTUAL PERSON, COMPANY AND/OR ORGANIZATION IS UNINTENTIONAL AND PURELY COINCIDENTAL.

Permissions

maranGraphics

U.S. Corporate Sales
Contact maranGraphics at (800) 469-6616 or Fax (905) 890-9434.

U.S. Trade Sales
Contact IDG Books at (800) 434-3422 or (650) 655-3000.

ABOUT IDG BOOKS WORLDWIDE

Welcome to the world of IDG Books Worldwide.

IDG Books Worldwide, Inc., is a subsidiary of International Data Group, the world's largest publisher of computer-related information and the leading global provider of information services on information technology. IDG was founded more than 30 years ago by Patrick J. McGovern and now employs more than 9,000 people worldwide. IDG publishes more than 290 computer publications in over 75 countries. More than 90 million people read one or more IDG publications each month.

Launched in 1990, IDG Books Worldwide is today the #1 publisher of best-selling computer books in the United States. We are proud to have received eight awards from the Computer Press Association in recognition of editorial excellence and three from Computer Currents' First Annual Readers' Choice Awards. Our best-selling *...For Dummies®* series has more than 50 million copies in print with translations in 31 languages. IDG Books Worldwide, through a joint venture with IDG's Hi-Tech Beijing, became the first U.S. publisher to publish a computer book in the People's Republic of China. In record time, IDG Books Worldwide has become the first choice for millions of readers around the world who want to learn how to better manage their businesses.

Our mission is simple: Every one of our books is designed to bring extra value and skill-building instructions to the reader. Our books are written by experts who understand and care about our readers. The knowledge base of our editorial staff comes from years of experience in publishing, education, and journalism — experience we use to produce books to carry us into the new millennium. In short, we care about books, so we attract the best people. We devote special attention to details such as audience, interior design, use of icons, and illustrations. And because we use an efficient process of authoring, editing, and desktop publishing our books electronically, we can spend more time ensuring superior content and less time on the technicalities of making books.

You can count on our commitment to deliver high-quality books at competitive prices on topics you want to read about. At IDG Books Worldwide, we continue in the IDG tradition of delivering quality for more than 30 years. You'll find no better book on a subject than one from IDG Books Worldwide.

John Kilcullen
Chairman and CEO
IDG Books Worldwide, Inc.

Eighth Annual Computer Press Awards 1992

Ninth Annual Computer Press Awards 1993

Tenth Annual Computer Press Awards 1994

Eleventh Annual Computer Press Awards 1995

IDG is the world's leading IT media, research and exposition company. Founded in 1964, IDG had 1997 revenues of $2.05 billion and has more than 9,000 employees worldwide. IDG offers the widest range of media options that reach IT buyers in 75 countries representing 95% of worldwide IT spending. IDG's diverse product and services portfolio spans six key areas including print publishing, online publishing, expositions and conferences, market research, education and training, and global marketing services. More than 90 million people read one or more of IDG's 290 magazines and newspapers, including IDG's leading global brands — Computerworld, PC World, Network World, Macworld and the Channel World family of publications. IDG Books Worldwide is one of the fastest-growing computer book publishers in the world, with more than 700 titles in 36 languages. The "...For Dummies®" series alone has more than 50 million copies in print. IDG offers online users the largest network of technology-specific Web sites around the world through IDG.net (http://www.idg.net), which comprises more than 225 targeted Web sites in 55 countries worldwide. International Data Corporation (IDC) is the world's largest provider of information technology data, analysis and consulting, with research centers in over 41 countries and more than 400 research analysts worldwide. IDG World Expo is a leading producer of more than 168 globally branded conferences and expositions in 35 countries including E3 (Electronic Entertainment Expo), Macworld Expo, ComNet, Windows World Expo, ICE (Internet Commerce Expo), Agenda, DEMO, and Spotlight. IDG's training subsidiary, ExecuTrain, is the world's largest computer training company, with more than 230 locations worldwide and 785 training courses. IDG Marketing Services helps industry-leading IT companies build international brand recognition by developing global integrated marketing programs via IDG's print, online and exposition products worldwide. Further information about the company can be found at www.idg.com. 1/26/00 maranGraphics is a family-run business located near Toronto, Canada.

At **maranGraphics**, we believe in producing great computer books — one book at a time.

maranGraphics has been producing high-technology products for over 25 years, which enables us to offer the computer book community a unique communication process.

Our computer books use an integrated communication process, which is very different from the approach used in other computer books. Each spread is, in essence, a flow chart — the text and screen shots are totally incorporated into the layout of the spread. Introductory text and helpful tips complete the learning experience.

maranGraphics' approach encourages the left and right sides of the brain to work together —resulting in faster orientation and greater memory retention.

Above all, we are very proud of the handcrafted nature of our books. Our carefully-chosen writers are experts in their fields, and spend countless hours researching and organizing the content for each topic. Our artists rebuild every screen shot to provide the best clarity possible, making our screen shots the most precise and easiest to read in the industry. We strive for perfection, and believe that the time spent handcrafting each element results in the best computer books money can buy.

Thank you for purchasing this book. We hope you enjoy it!

Sincerely,

Robert Maran
President
maranGraphics
Rob@maran.com
www.maran.com
www.idgbooks.com/visual

CREDITS

Acquisitions, Editorial, and Media Development

Development Editor
Kyle Looper

Project Editor
Jade L. Williams

Acquisitions Editor
Martine Edwards

Technical Editor
Allen L. Wyatt, Discovery Computing, Inc.

Product Development Supervisor
Lindsay Sandman

Editorial Managers
Kyle Looper, Rev Mengle

Media Development Manager
Laura Carpenter

Editorial Assistant
Sarah Shupert

Production

Book Design
maranGraphics™

Project Coordinator
Maridee Ennis

Layout
Joe Bucki, Barry Offringa,
Kristin Pickett, Kathie Schutte

Editorial Graphics Production
Ronda David-Burroughs, Craig Dearing,
Dave Gregory, Mark Harris, Jill Johnson,
Suzana Miokovic, Steve Schaerer

Proofreaders
Laura Albert, Marianne Santy,
Jeannie Smith, Charles Spencer

Indexer:
York Production Services, Inc.

Special Help
Microsoft Corporation, Mary Corder,
Amanda M. Foxworth, Clint Lahnen, Rus Marini,
Darren Meiss, Shelley Norris, Ryan Roberts,
Brent Savage, Rebecca Senninger

ACKNOWLEDGMENTS

General and Administrative

IDG Books Worldwide, Inc.: John Kilcullen, CEO; Bill Barry, President and COO; John Ball, Executive VP, Operations & Administration; John Harris, CFO

IDG Books Technology Publishing Group: Richard Swadley, Senior Vice President and Publisher; Mary Bednarek, Vice President and Publisher; Walter R. Bruce III, Vice President and Publisher; Joseph Wikert, Vice President and Publisher; Mary C. Corder, Editorial Director; Andy Cummings, Publishing Director, General User Group; Barry Pruett, Publishing Director

IDG Books Manufacturing: Ivor Parker, Vice President, Manufacturing

IDG Books Marketing: John Helmus, Assistant Vice President, Director of Marketing

IDG Books Online Management: Brenda McLaughlin, Executive Vice President, Chief Internet Officer; Gary Millrood, Executive Vice President of Business Development, Sales and Marketing

IDG Books Packaging: Marc J. Mikulich, Vice President, Brand Strategy and Research

IDG Books Production for Branded Press: Debbie Stailey, Production Director

IDG Books Sales: Roland Elgey, Senior Vice President, Sales and Marketing; Michael Violano, Vice President, International Sales and Sub Rights

The publisher would like to give special thanks to Patrick J. McGovern, without whom this book would not have been possible.

ABOUT THE AUTHORS

Michael Toot lives in Seattle, Washington and is a senior program manager with a local software company. As a certified MCSE and MCP+I, Michael has been working with Microsoft operating systems since 1992. When he's not working or playing with software, he can be found reading, sailing, and writing fiction and nonfiction works.

Eric Butow is the owner of E.E. Butow Services, a technical communications company based in Roseville, California. He has over 15 years experience using Intel compatible computers in the programming, graphic design, Web design, and technical writing fields.

Butow has documented a wide variety of computer-related products and methods, including networking procedures, telecommunications hardware, software quality-assurance practices, and Java networking software. From 1997 to 1999, Butow was editor of Sacra Blue, the monthly magazine of the Sacramento Personal Computer Users Group.

Butow holds a bachelor and master degree in speech communication from California State University, Fresno. He is currently studying for his A+ and MCSE+I computing certifications.

AUTHOR'S ACKNOWLEDGMENTS

The first round of thanks goes to Andy Levy and Tracy Anthony who started me down the road with IDG Books Worldwide.

The second round belongs to the tireless, ever-helpful folks at IDG. Martine Edwards, Jade Williams, Kyle Looper, and Lindsay Sandman, all of whom went above and beyond the call in helping publish this book.

Another round belongs to the folks at IDG and maranGraphics whom I have not met, but who have labored to create the artwork, screenshots, and page layout.

My co-author Eric Butow also gets a curtain call for his hard work and source material.

The loudest and grandest applause of all goes to my wife and best friend Victoria, who always knew when it was the right time for me to turn off the computer and come to bed. I love ya, hon.

Michael Toot

TABLE OF CONTENTS

Chapter 1 — INTRODUCING WINDOWS 2000 SERVER

Chapter 2 — ACQUIRING WINDOWS 2000 SERVER BASICS

Chapter 3

EXPLORING THE CONTROL PANEL

Chapter 4

SETTING UP NETWORK SERVICES

TABLE OF CONTENTS

Chapter 

CONFIGURING YOUR SERVER'S SECURITY

Chapter 

CONNECTING TO THE INTERNET

Chapter 7

MANAGING THE MICROSOFT MANAGEMENT CONSOLE

Chapter 8 

MANAGING PEOPLE AND GROUPS ON YOUR NETWORK

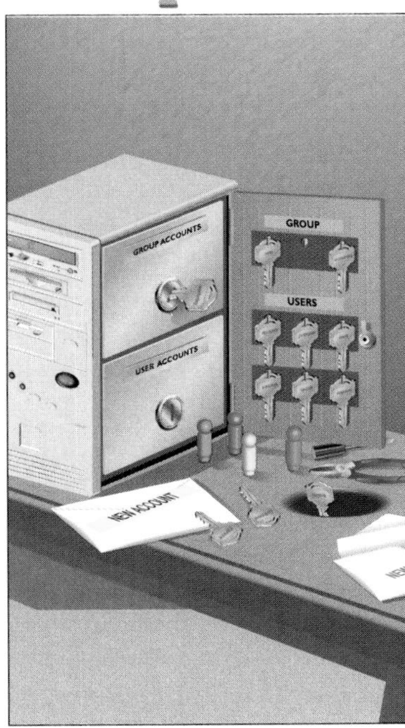

Chapter 9 

OVERSEEING COMPUTERS ON YOUR NETWORK

Chapter 10 MANAGING FILES AND DISKS

Chapter 11 CONFIGURING PRINTERS

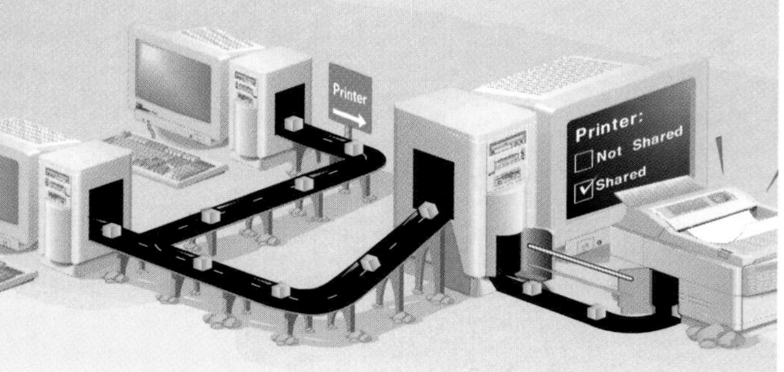

Chapter 12 USING INTERNET APPLICATIONS

Chapter 13 RUNNING YOUR WEB SERVER

Chapter 14 USING RECOVERY TOOLS

Chapter 15

BACKING UP AND RESTORING FILES

Chapter 16

MONITORING YOUR SERVER

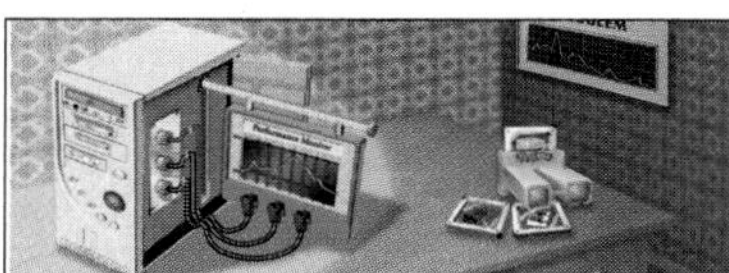

Chapter 17

TROUBLESHOOTING YOUR SERVER

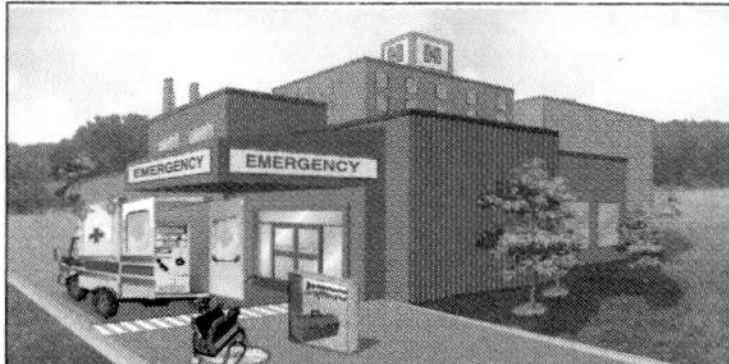

Appendix

INSTALLING WINDOWS 2000 SERVER

My Documents
My Computer
My Network Places
Recycle Bin
Internet Explorer
Connect to the Internet
Start
12:00
Microsoft Windows 2000 Server
Microsoft
Built on NT Technology
Windows 2000
Microsoft Windows 2000 Server

CHAPTER 1

Introducing Windows 2000 Server

This chapter covers the basics that you need to know about operating Windows 2000 Server.

DISCOVER WINDOWS 2000 SERVER

Microsoft Windows 2000 Server is an operating system that controls your computer and the network it belongs to.

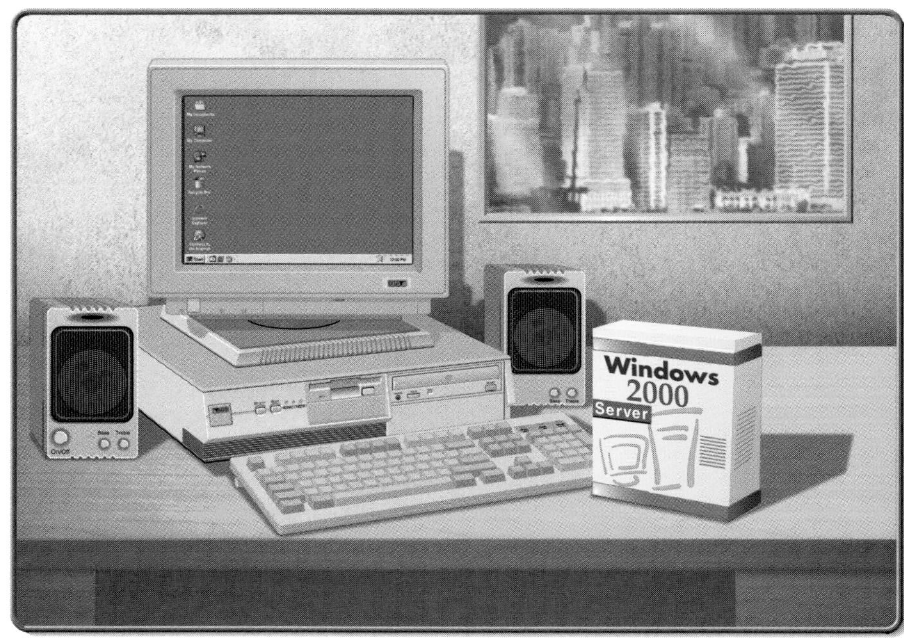

The operating system ensures that the various pieces of hardware and software on the network function seamlessly for the network's users.

CUSTOMIZE WINDOWS 2000 SERVER

You can customize Windows 2000 Server in many ways. You can fit more information on the screen, change the appearance of your desktop, or change the way your mouse works.

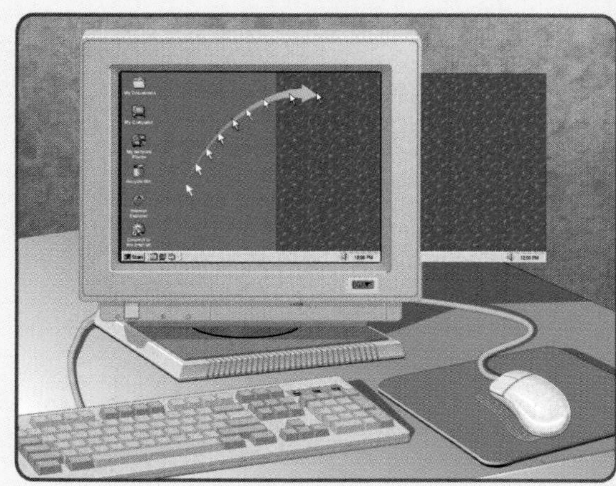

WORK WITH ACCESSORIES

You can quickly create files using Windows 2000 Server's accessories. These include a word processing program (WordPad), a drawing program (Paint), a quick notetaking program (Notepad), and a calculator program (Calc).

WORK WITH FILES

Windows 2000 Server acts as a file server for you and others on your network. You can make files available to others, store files for backup, and encrypt files so that they cannot be read without a password.

MANAGE YOUR NETWORK

Networks allow you to manage people and computers from a central location. You can set up user and computer accounts, control access to printers, and enforce security policies that restrict access to sensitive data.

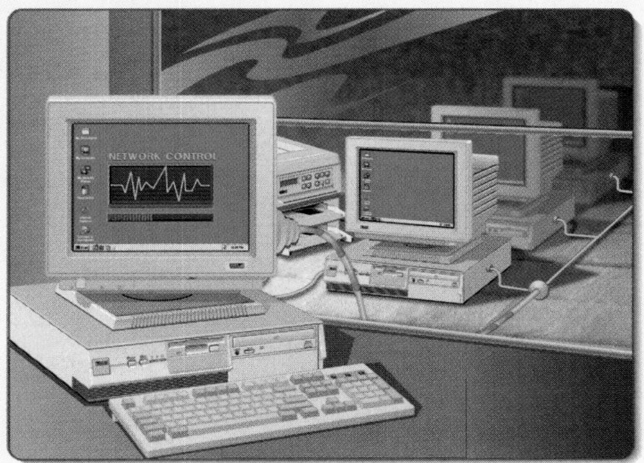

CONNECT TO THE INTERNET

You can set up access to the Internet for all computers on your network and run a Web server that gives others access to your Web site. You can also allow users to connect to your network while on the road or at home.

PROTECT AGAINST DISASTER

You can protect your server from accidents and misfortune by using disaster protection tools on your server. These tools allow you to make backups of your data, run an uninterruptible power supply, and add extra hard drives for fault tolerance.

EXPLORE THE WINDOWS 2000 SERVER DESKTOP

The Windows 2000 desktop allows you quick access to programs, depending on how your server is set up.

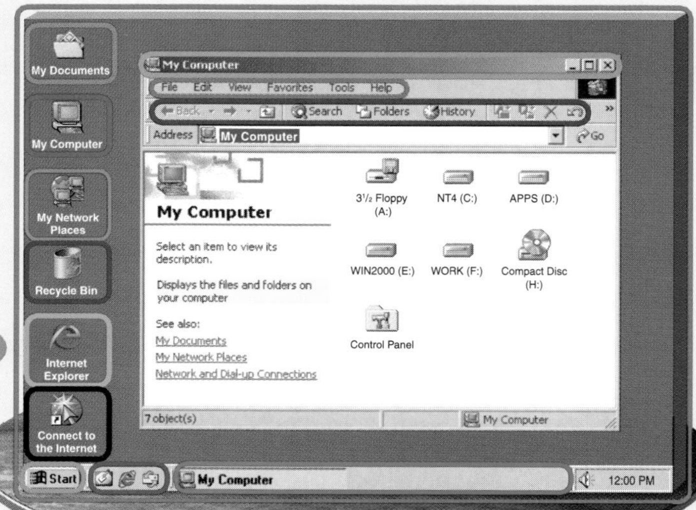

TITLE BAR

Displays the window name.

MENU BAR

Provides a command list for a window.

TOOLBAR

Toolbar buttons provide quick access to menu commands.

MY DOCUMENTS

Provides a convenient place to store your documents.

MY COMPUTER

Lets you view all the information stored on your computer.

MY NETWORK PLACES

Lets you view all the information and resources available on your network.

RECYCLE BIN

You can recover files from the Recycle Bin if you deleted them by mistake.

INTERNET EXPLORER

Launches your Web browser so you can view information on the Internet.

WINDOW

Provides a window frame that displays information from your computer or programs running on your computer.

TASKBAR

You can see which windows are open and switch between them quickly using the buttons on the taskbar.

CONNECT TO THE INTERNET

Lets you quickly configure your desktop's Internet access settings.

START BUTTON

Gives you quick access to programs, files, and Windows 2000 Server Help.

QUICK LAUNCH TOOLBAR

Gives you quick access to commonly used features, including Internet Explorer, Outlook Express, and the desktop.

USING THE MOUSE

A mouse is a device on your desk shaped like a bar of soap that moves an arrow-shaped cursor on your screen.

Your hand rests lightly on the mouse, with your first two fingers over the two mouse buttons. Use your hand to move the mouse around the desktop. Try adjusting your hand on the mouse until you find a hand position that feels comfortable for you.

MOUSE ACTIONS

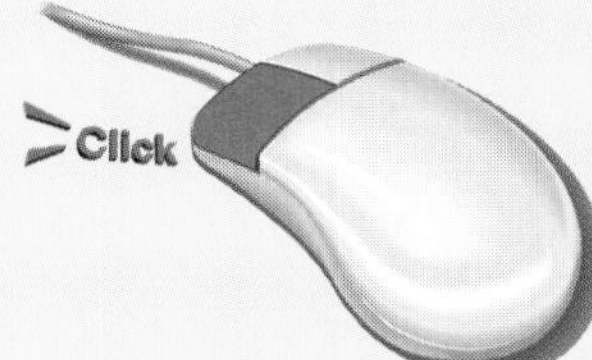

Click

Press and release the left mouse button. A click selects an item on the screen.

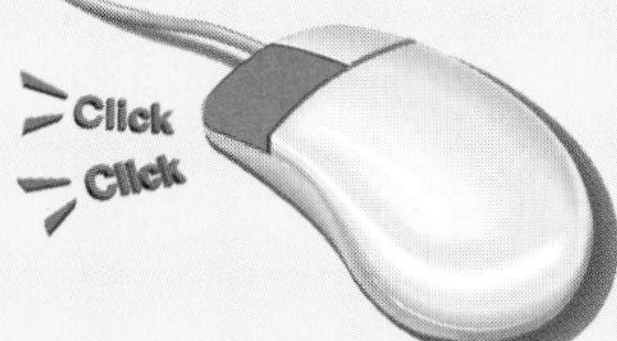

Double-Click

Quickly press and release the left mouse button twice. A double-click opens a document or starts a program.

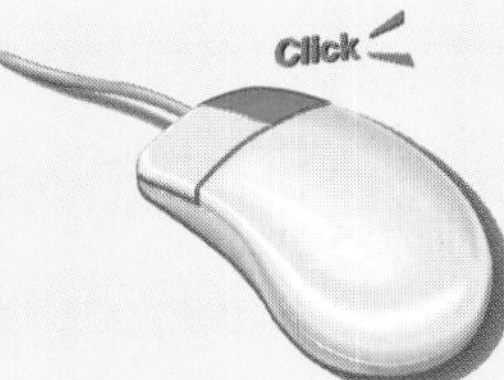

Right-Click

Press and release the right mouse button. A right-click displays a list of commands you can use to work with an item.

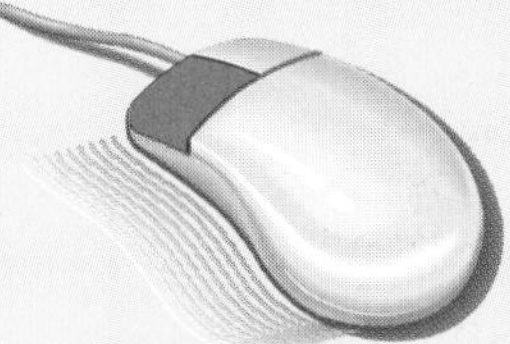

Drag and Drop

Dragging and dropping makes it easy to move an item to a new location. Position the mouse pointer over an object on the screen and then press and hold the left mouse button. While holding down the button, move the mouse to the item's destination and then release the button.

START WINDOWS 2000 SERVER

Windows 2000 Server is set to start when you first turn on the computer. You need to log on to Windows 2000 before you can work with the operating system and its programs.

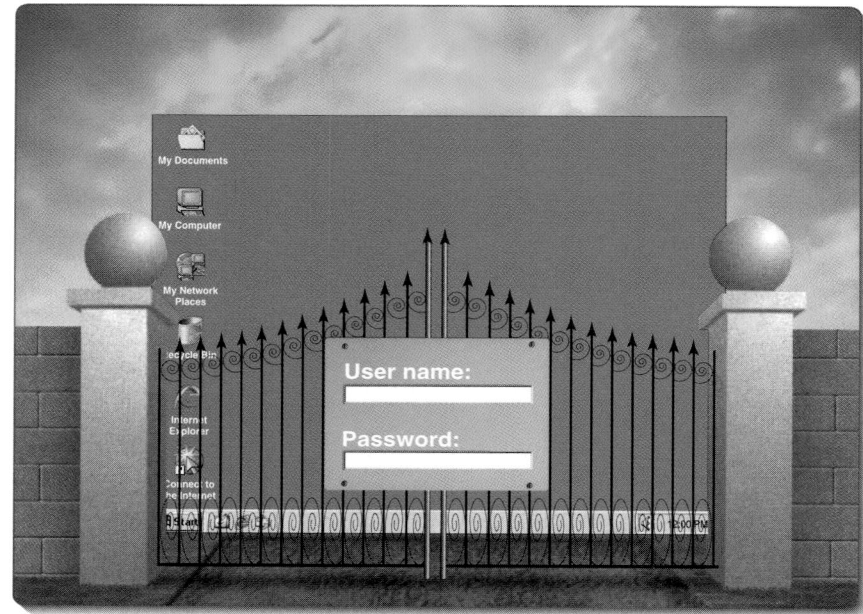

START WINDOWS 2000 SERVER

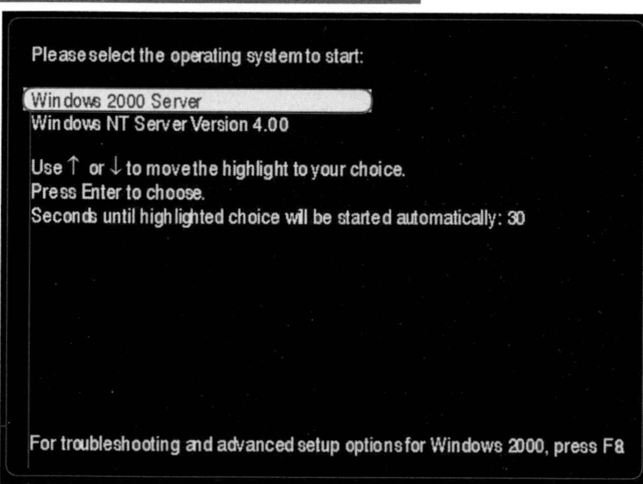

Please select the operating system to start:
Windows 2000 Server
Windows NT Server Version 4.00
Use ↑ or ↓ to move the highlight to your choice.
Press Enter to choose.
Seconds until highlighted choice will be started automatically: 30
For troubleshooting and advanced setup options for Windows 2000, press F8

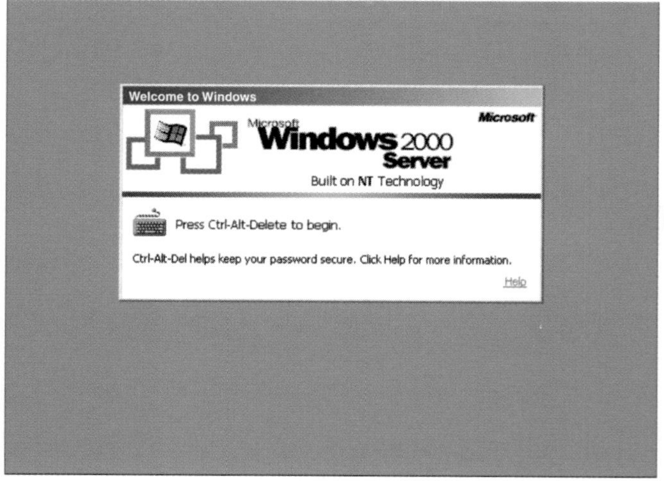

1 Turn on your computer and monitor.

■ Windows 2000 Server starts.

■ If your server has more than one operating system, the Windows 2000 OS Loader starts.

CHOOSE BETWEEN SYSTEMS

1 Press ↑ or ↓ to move up or down the list.

2 Select **Windows 2000 Server** and press **Enter**.

■ The Welcome to Windows dialog box appears.

LOG ON TO THE SERVER

1 To log on to the server, press and hold down **Ctrl** and **Alt** as you press the **Delete** key.

■ The Log On to Windows dialog box appears.

What is a domain?

A domain is a collection of computers or users that you manage as a group. This arrangement allows you to create security policies that define who may access your computers, programs, and information. You can log on to a domain or a local computer; for most tasks, you will want to log on to a domain.

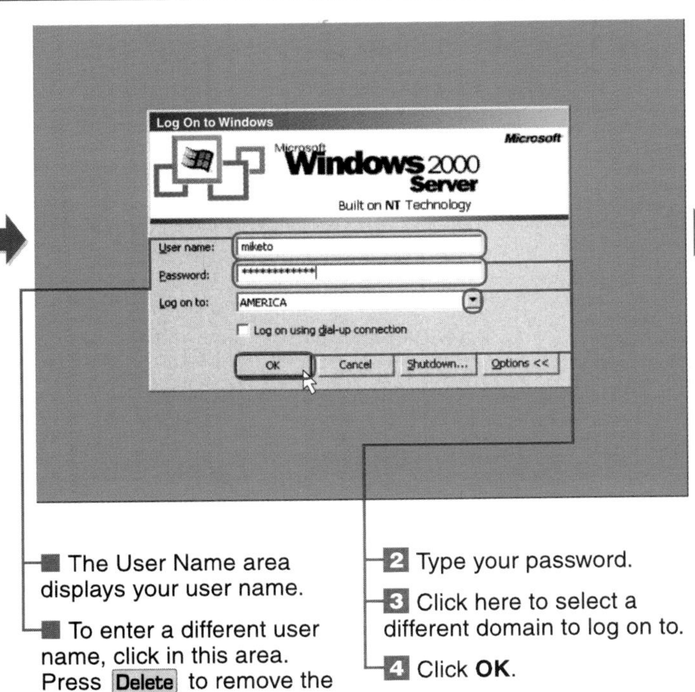

- The User Name area displays your user name.
- To enter a different user name, click in this area. Press Delete to remove the old name. Type a new name.

2 Type your password.

3 Click here to select a different domain to log on to.

4 Click **OK**.

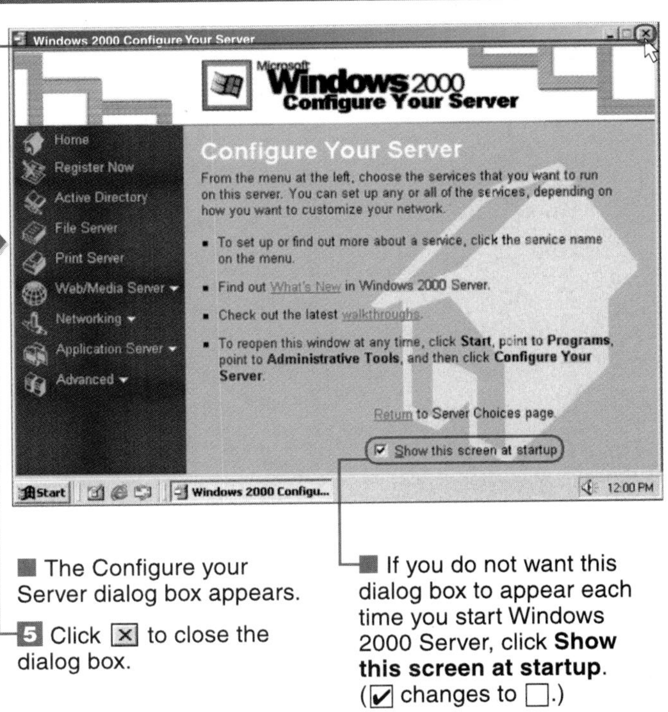

- The Configure your Server dialog box appears.

5 Click ☒ to close the dialog box.

- If you do not want this dialog box to appear each time you start Windows 2000 Server, click **Show this screen at startup**. (☑ changes to ☐.)

LOCK YOUR COMPUTER

If you are leaving your computer unattended, you can lock your computer so others cannot access information.

LOCK YOUR COMPUTER

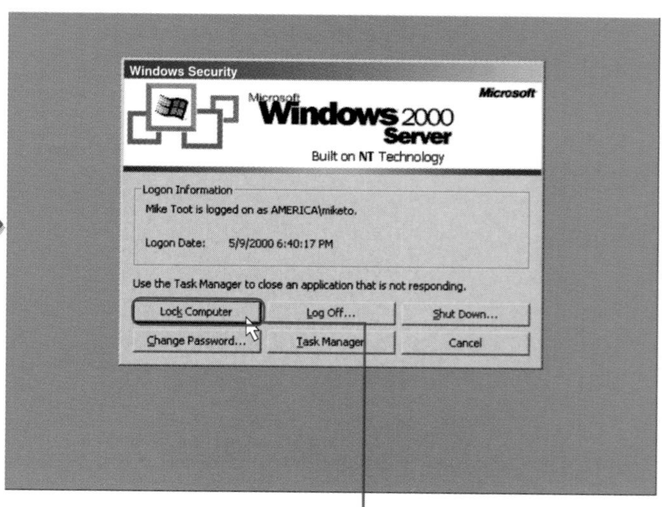

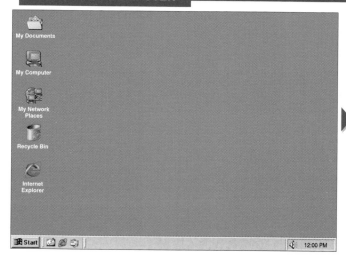

1 Press and hold down Ctrl and Alt and then press Delete.

■ The Windows Security dialog box appears.

2 Click **Lock Computer**.

Can I hide my information without locking my computer?

Yes. You can use your screensaver to hide the desktop so that others can't see your information. You can require a password to unlock the screen saver and regain access to your information. To set up a screensaver, see Chapter 2.

■ The Computer Locked dialog box appears.

UNLOCK YOUR COMPUTER

1 Press and hold down Ctrl and Alt and then press Delete.

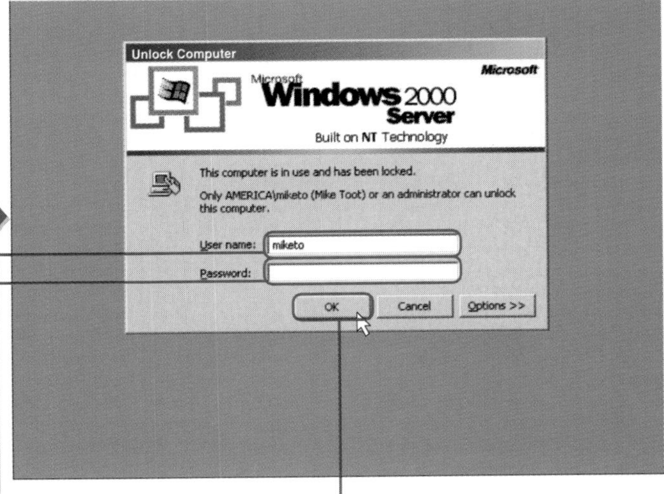

■ The Unlock Computer dialog box appears.

■ This area displays your name.

2 Type your password.

■ Asterisks appear in place of each character so that others can't see your password.

3 Click **OK**.

LOG OFF YOUR COMPUTER

When you finish using the computer, you can log off so that others can use it.

Don't forget to save your information and close your programs before logging off. Try to save your files regularly, not just when you log off your computer.

LOG OFF YOUR COMPUTER

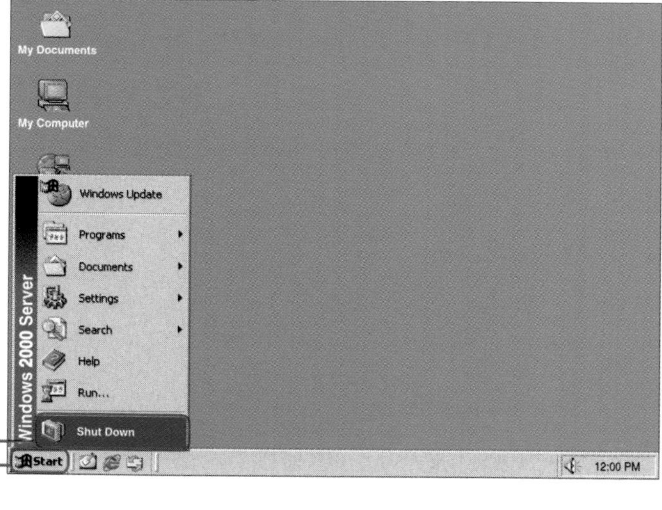

1 Click **Start**.

2 Click **Shut Down**.

■ The Shut Down Windows dialog box appears.

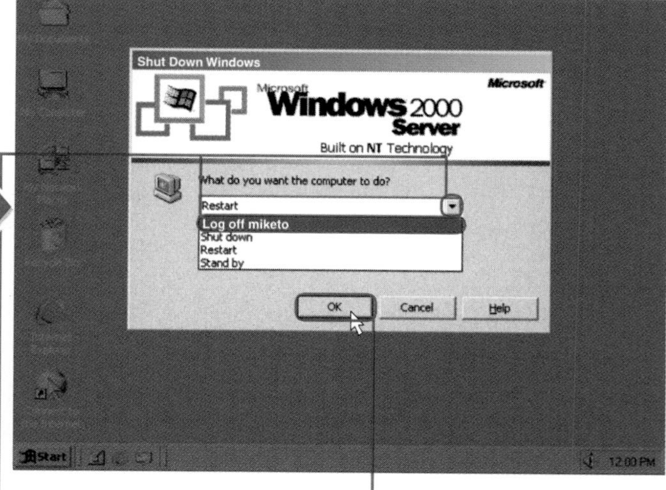

3 Click ▼.

4 Click **Log off** (example: **Log off miketo**).

5 Click **OK**.

■ The Welcome to Windows dialog box appears.

Why does everyone need a user name and password before they can use Windows 2000?

The user name and password help provide security in two ways. First, they keep unauthorized people from getting access to information on the computer and the network. Second, they determine which domain and organizational units users belong to. Depending on which group a user belongs to, the user may have different rights than someone else.

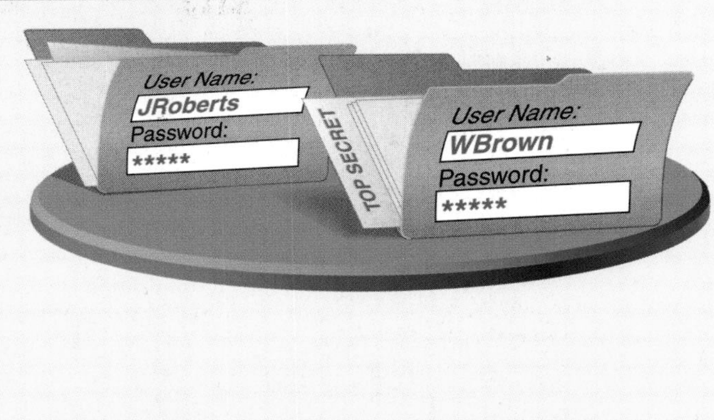

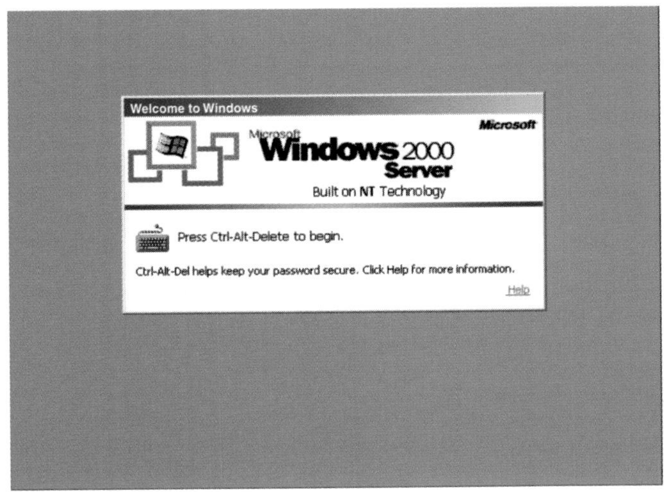

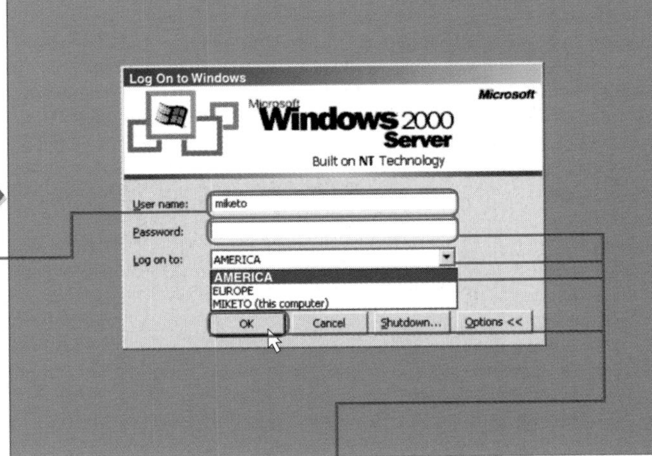

LOG ON AS A DIFFERENT USER

1 Press and hold down Ctrl and Alt and then press Delete.

■ The Log On to Windows dialog box appears.

2 Click the current user name (example: **miketo**) to highlight it.

3 Press Delete.

4 Type a user name.

5 Type the password.

■ You can select a different domain by clicking ▼ and then clicking the domain (example: **AMERICA**).

6 Click **OK**.

Windows 2000 Server has extensive help files, checklists, and wizards. If you get stuck or need more information, you should use the Help features to get information.

GET HELP

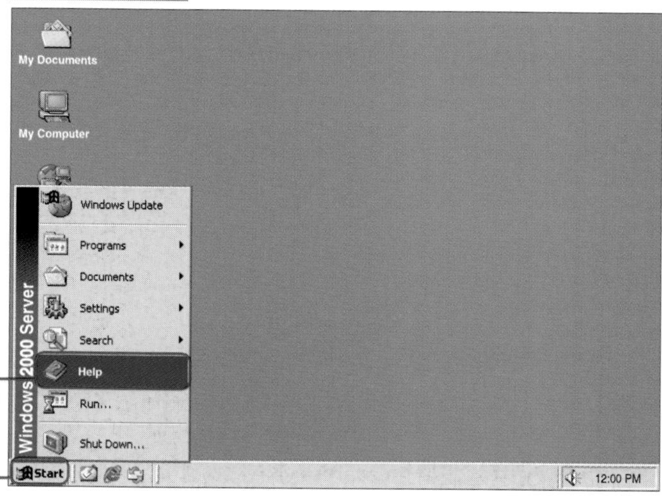

1 Click **Start**.

2 Click **Help**.

■ The Windows 2000 Help appears.

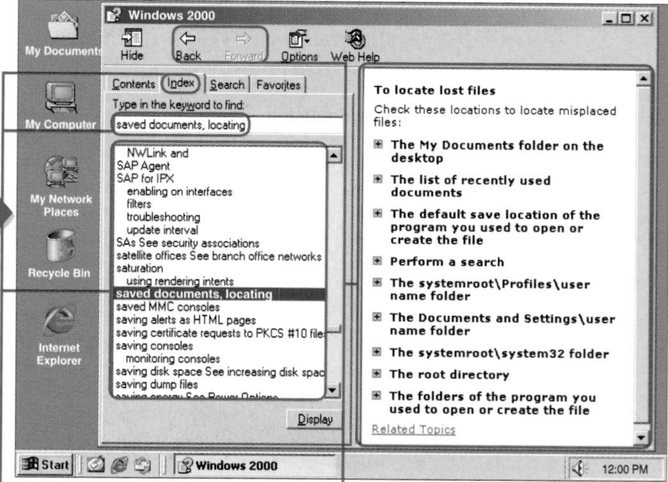

3 Click **Index**.

4 Type a few letters of the topic.

5 Double-click the help topic that sounds like what you're looking for (example: **saved documents, locating**).

■ The help topic information appears here.

6 Click a ⊞ to expand the topic for more help.

■ Click **Back** or **Forward** to move through the help topics you have viewed.

If you are finished using the server and no one else needs it, you should shut down Windows 2000 Server before turning off the power to your computer.

When you shut down Windows 2000 Server, you may be keeping others from using its services, such as using a printer or accessing files on the hard drive. You should generally leave a server running unless you know for sure it will not be needed by others.

SHUT DOWN WINDOWS 2000 SERVER

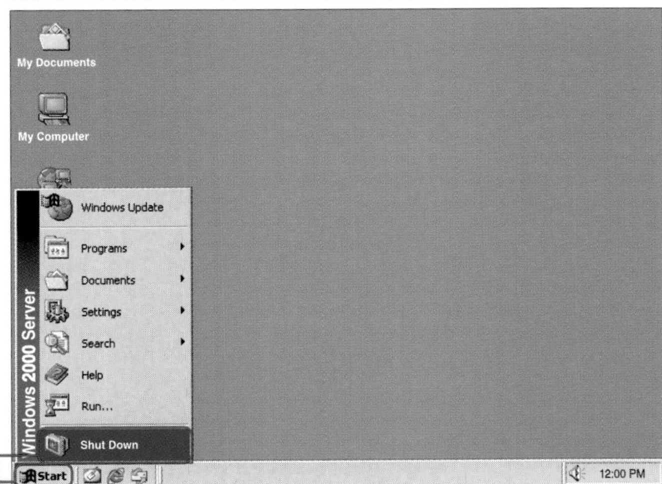

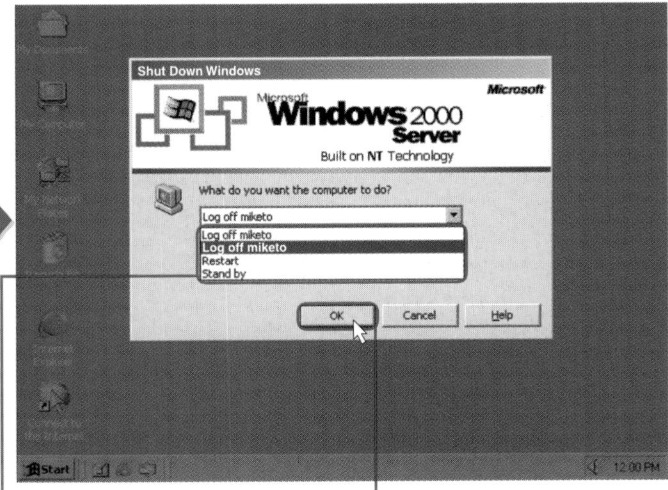

1 Click **Start**.

2 Click **Shut Down**.

■ The Shut Down Windows dialog box appears.

3 Click the shut down option you want from the list.

4 Click **OK**.

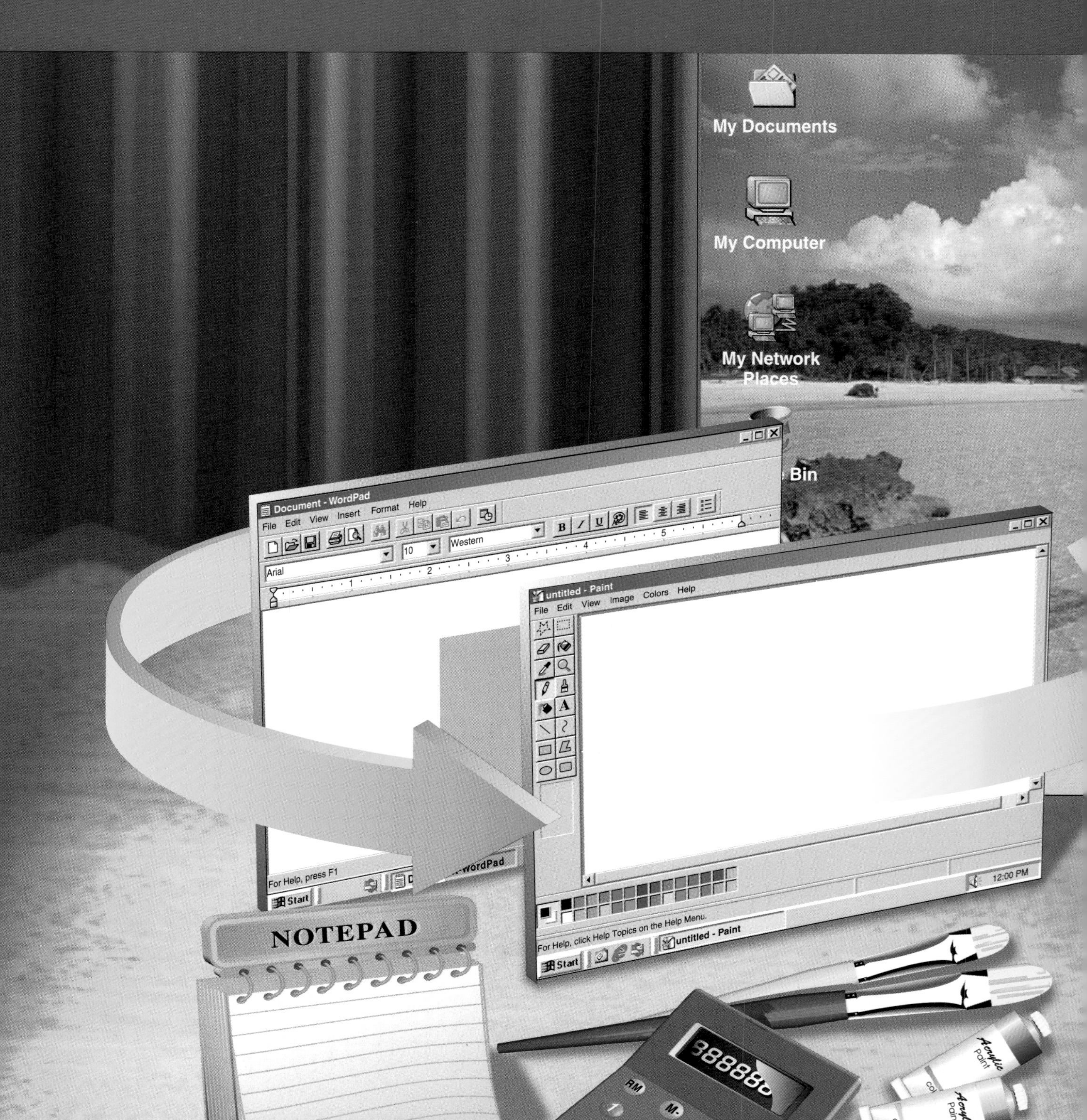
My Documents
My Computer
My Network Places
Document - WordPad
File Edit View Insert Format Help
Arial
Western
For Help, press F1
Start
untitled - Paint
File Edit View Image Colors Help
For Help, click Help Topics on the Help Menu.
untitled - Paint
12:00 PM
NOTEPAD
Acrylic Paint

CHAPTER 2

Acquiring Windows 2000 Server Basics

In this chapter you will gain experience with Windows 2000 Server and Windows applications.

The Start button is the starting point for launching programs in Windows 2000.

START A PROGRAM

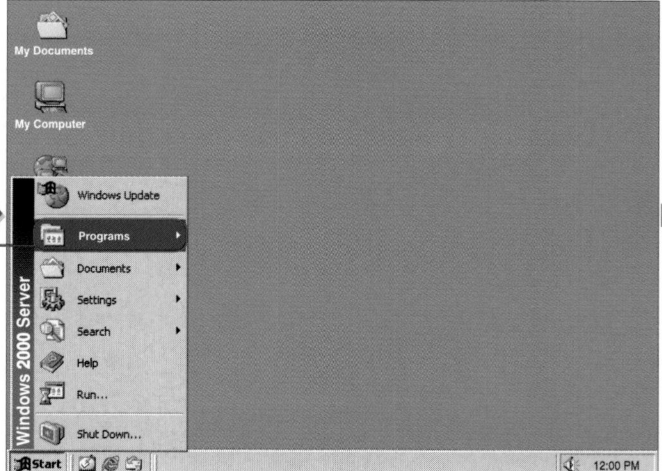

1 Click **Start**.

Note: To display the Start menu using the keyboard, press and hold down **Ctrl** *and then press* **Esc**.

■ The Start menu appears.

2 Click **Programs** to see which programs are on your computer.

Note: You can use the keyboard to select a menu item. Press the key with the underlined letter (example: ***P*** *for* ***Programs****) to select that item.*

Does Windows 2000 Server have other programs that I can use?

Windows 2000 Server comes with many programs that let you get work done.

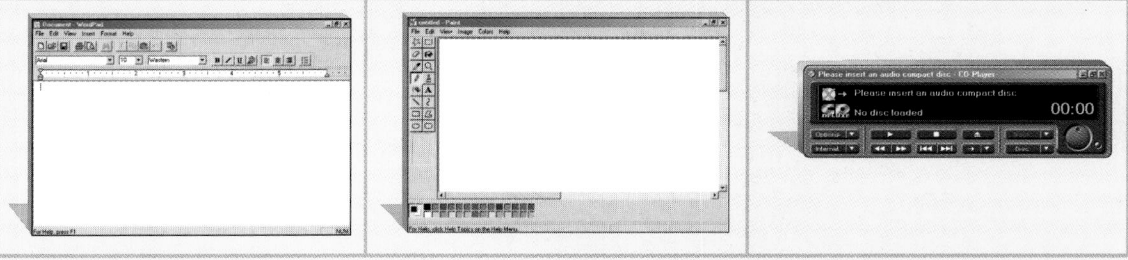

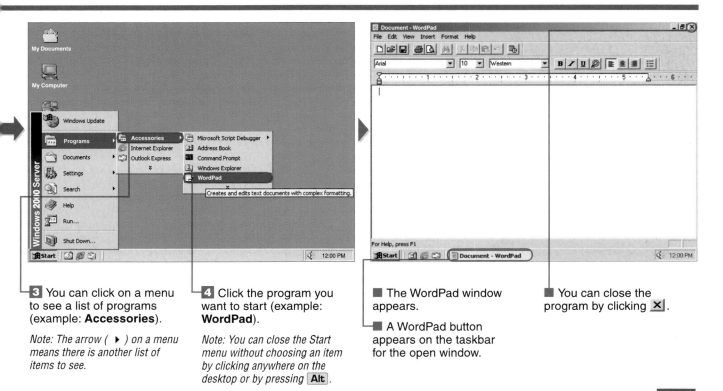

3 You can click on a menu to see a list of programs (example: **Accessories**).

Note: The arrow (▸) on a menu means there is another list of items to see.

4 Click the program you want to start (example: **WordPad**).

Note: You can close the Start menu without choosing an item by clicking anywhere on the desktop or by pressing **Alt**.

■ The WordPad window appears.

■ A WordPad button appears on the taskbar for the open window.

■ You can close the program by clicking **X**.

LAUNCH NOTEPAD

Notepad is a simple text editor that can be used to create, edit, and print text files. Text files are files that do not have any formatting information in them, like margins, fonts, or graphics.

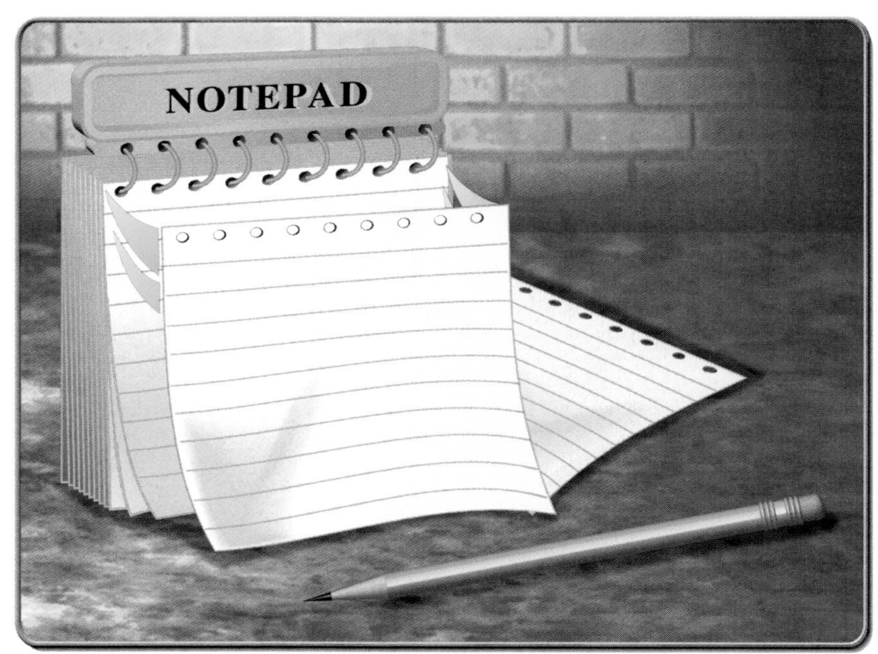

Windows 2000 uses some system files that are text files. Notepad is used to view and edit these files.

LAUNCH NOTEPAD

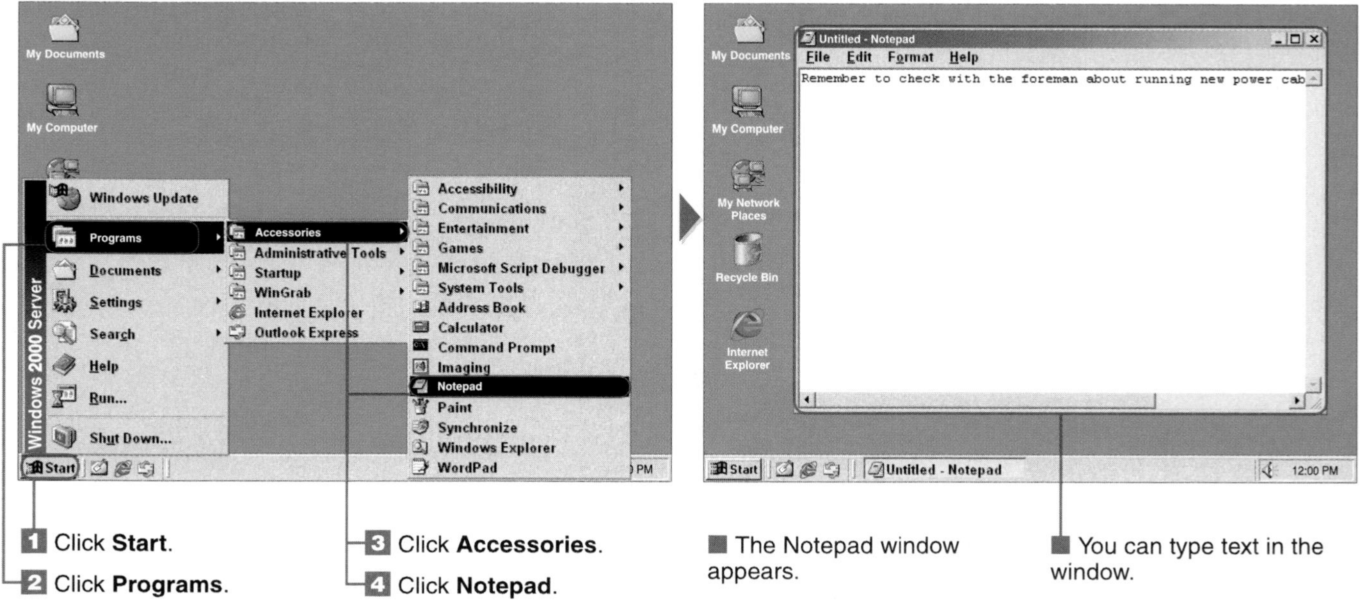

1 Click **Start**.

2 Click **Programs**.

3 Click **Accessories**.

4 Click **Notepad**.

■ The Notepad window appears.

■ You can type text in the window.

How do I tell which files are text files?

Most text files use `.txt` as part of the filename. Windows 2000 keeps a list of other files that are also text files, such as ones with `.ini` or `.log` as part of the filename.

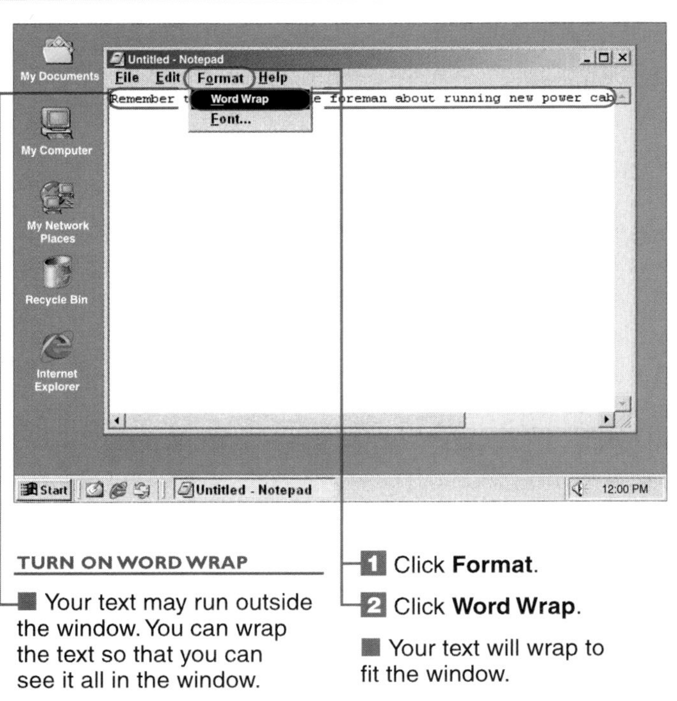

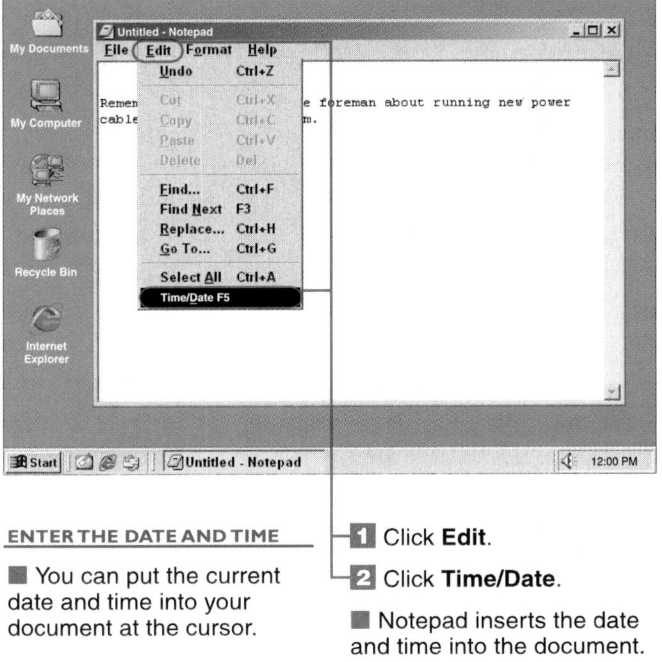

TURN ON WORD WRAP

■ Your text may run outside the window. You can wrap the text so that you can see it all in the window.

1 Click **Format**.

2 Click **Word Wrap**.

■ Your text will wrap to fit the window.

ENTER THE DATE AND TIME

■ You can put the current date and time into your document at the cursor.

1 Click **Edit**.

2 Click **Time/Date**.

■ Notepad inserts the date and time into the document.

WordPad is a word processor that you can use to create, edit, and print documents. It has more features than Notepad and can be used for more professional-looking documents.

USING WORDPAD

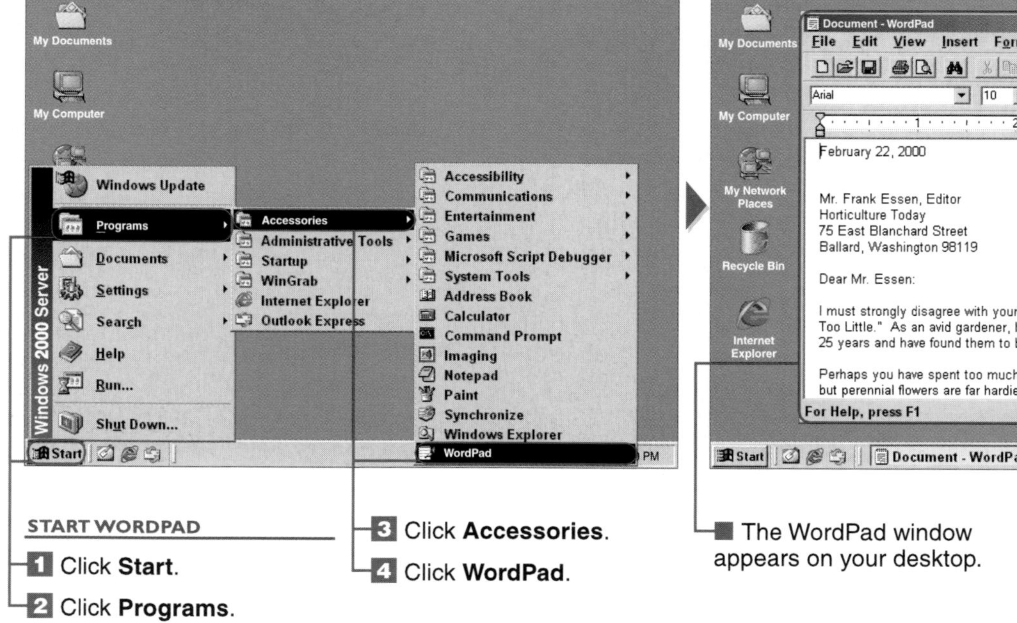

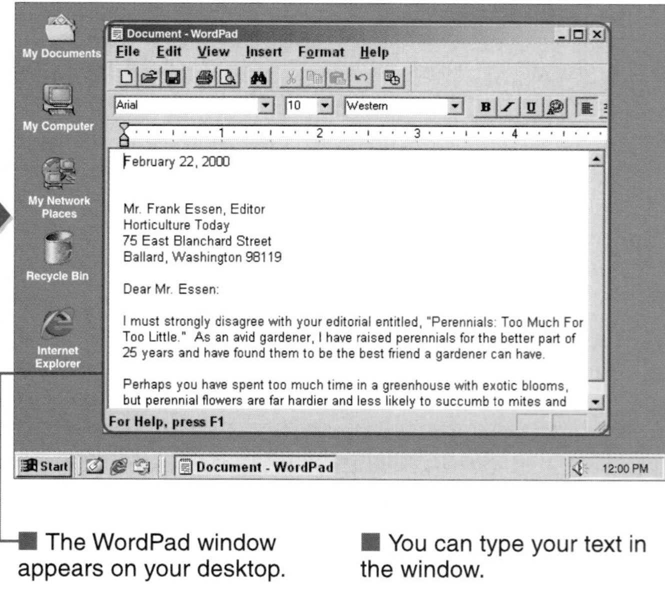

START WORDPAD

1. Click **Start**.
2. Click **Programs**.
3. Click **Accessories**.
4. Click **WordPad**.

- The WordPad window appears on your desktop.

- You can type your text in the window.

Can I use WordPad for all the documents I want to work on?

You can; however, WordPad has only basic word processing abilities. If you will be working on more complex documents such as newsletters or business reports, you will want to purchase a dedicated publishing or word processing program.

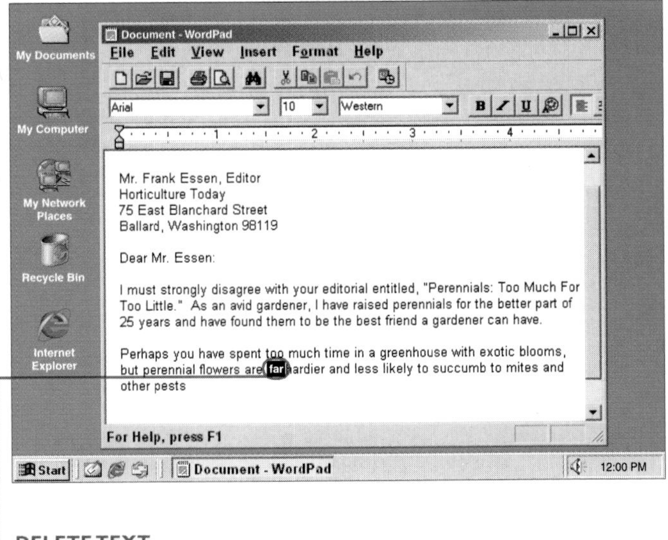

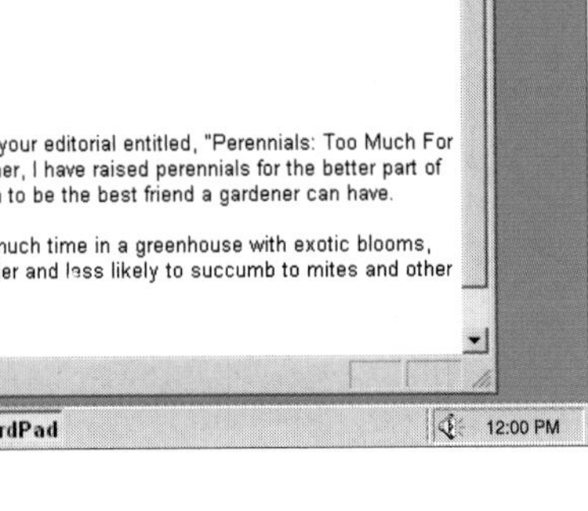

DELETE TEXT

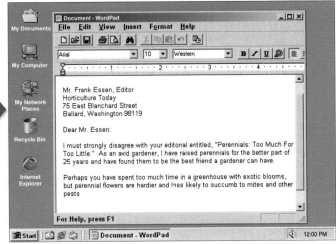

1 Drag the mouse over the text you want to remove.

2 Press Delete to remove the text.

Note: You can also press ←Backspace *to remove text.*

CONTINUED

You can print your WordPad documents whenever you want to have a paper copy available.

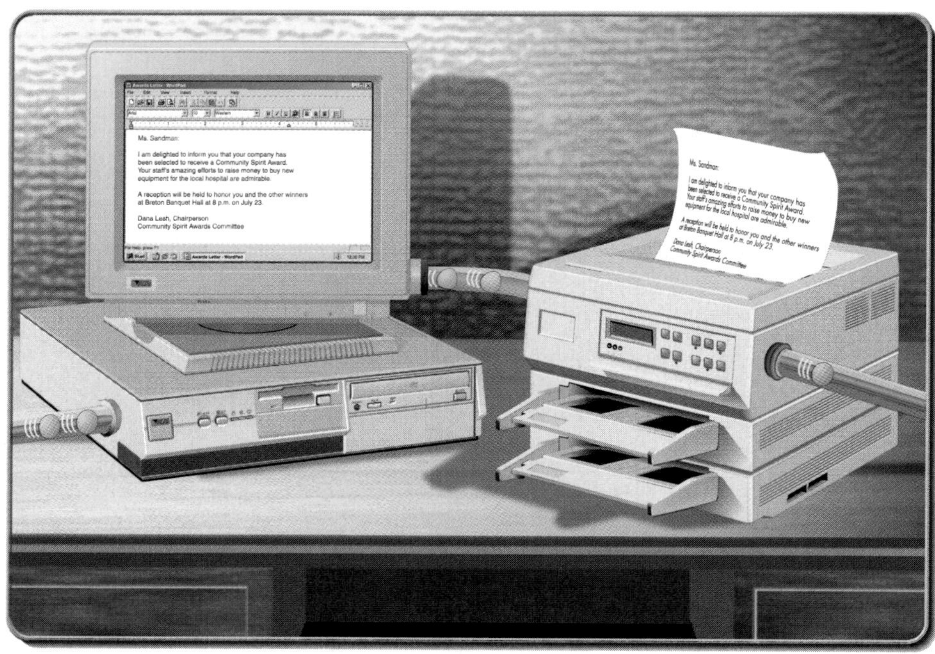

In order to print a document, you must have a printer available, either attached to your server or available on your network.

USING WORDPAD (CONTINUED)

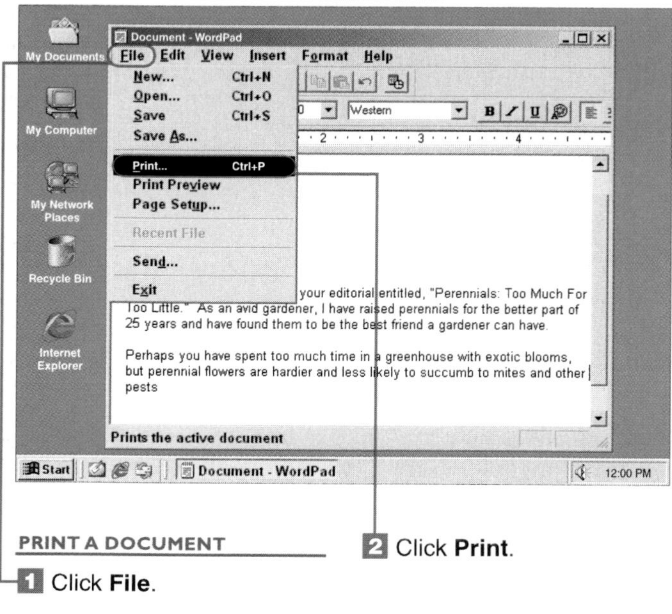

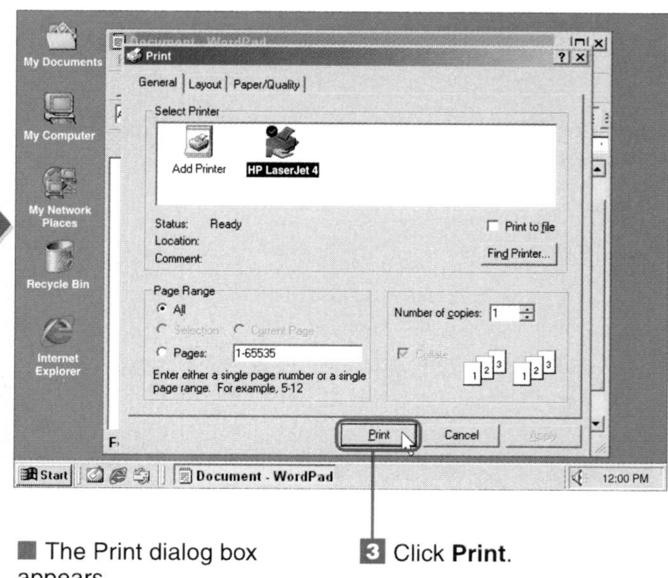

PRINT A DOCUMENT

1 Click **File**.

2 Click **Print**.

■ The Print dialog box appears.

3 Click **Print**.

What file types can be saved using WordPad?

WordPad can save files in several different formats. You can save files in Microsoft Word 6.0 format, using the `.doc` extension. Files using the Rich Text Format have the `.rtf` extension and are frequently used over the Internet or with non-Windows users. You can also save files as text files, using the `.txt` extension.

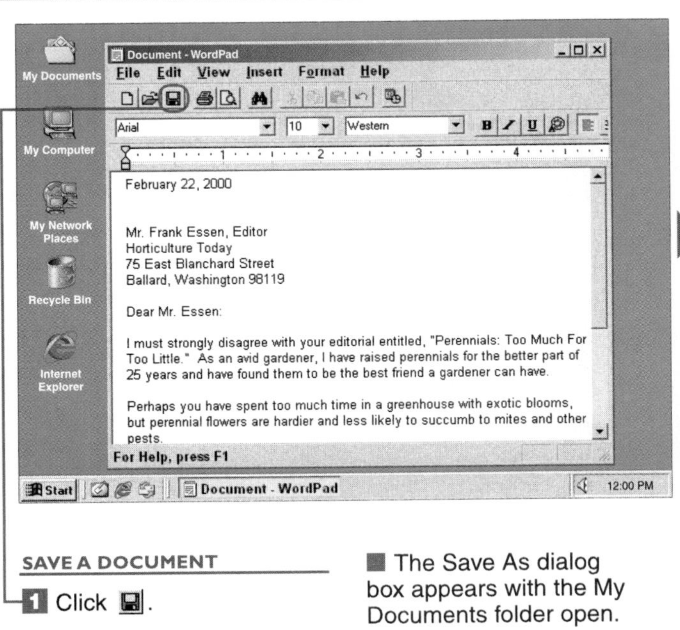

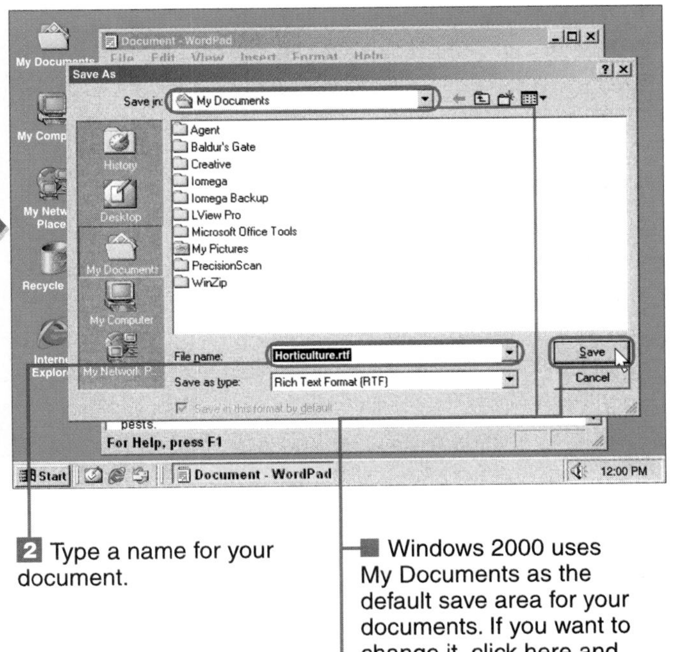

SAVE A DOCUMENT

1 Click 💾.

■ The Save As dialog box appears with the My Documents folder open.

2 Type a name for your document.

■ Windows 2000 uses My Documents as the default save area for your documents. If you want to change it, click here and choose a different location.

3 Click **Save**.

USING PAINT

You can use Paint to create artwork for your documents, such as illustrations or letterhead.

USING PAINT

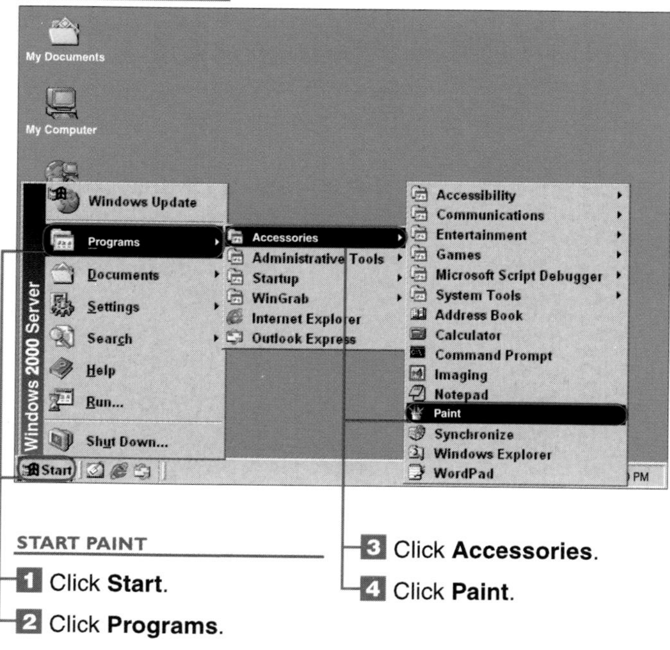

START PAINT

1 Click **Start**.

2 Click **Programs**.

3 Click **Accessories**.

4 Click **Paint**.

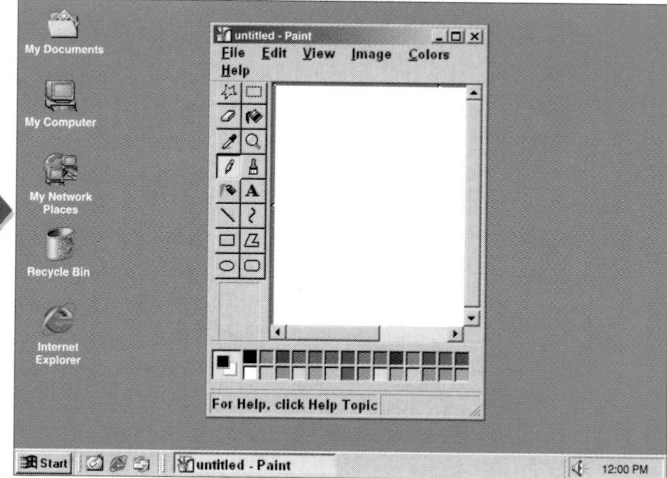

■ The Paint window appears on your desktop.

■ If the Paint window is not full size, you can click ☐ to maximize it.

What kinds of pictures can I create with Paint?

You can create many kinds of pictures or illustrations with Paint. For example, you can create a company letterhead that you can use in letters or other business documents.

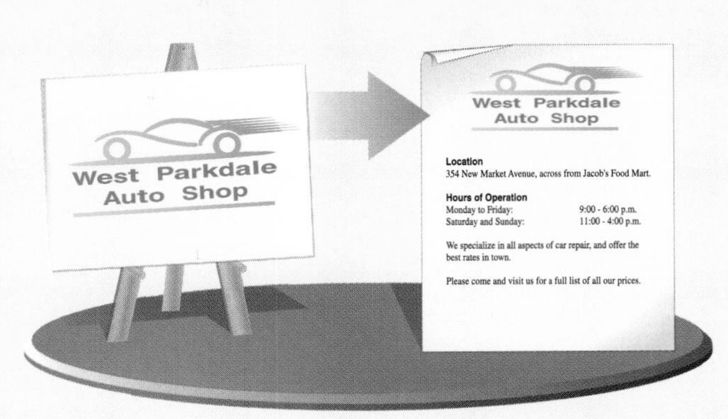

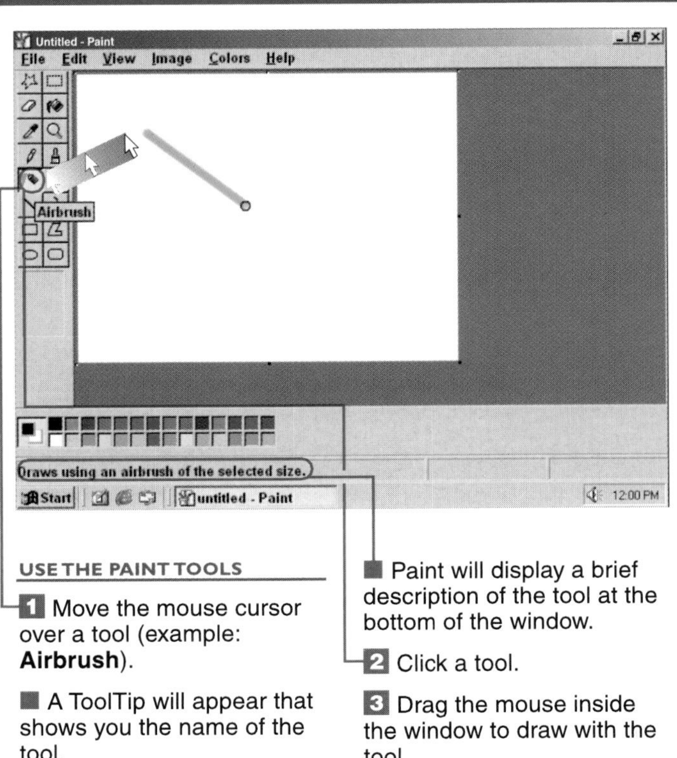

USE THE PAINT TOOLS

1 Move the mouse cursor over a tool (example: **Airbrush**).

■ A ToolTip will appear that shows you the name of the tool.

■ Paint will display a brief description of the tool at the bottom of the window.

2 Click a tool.

3 Drag the mouse inside the window to draw with the tool.

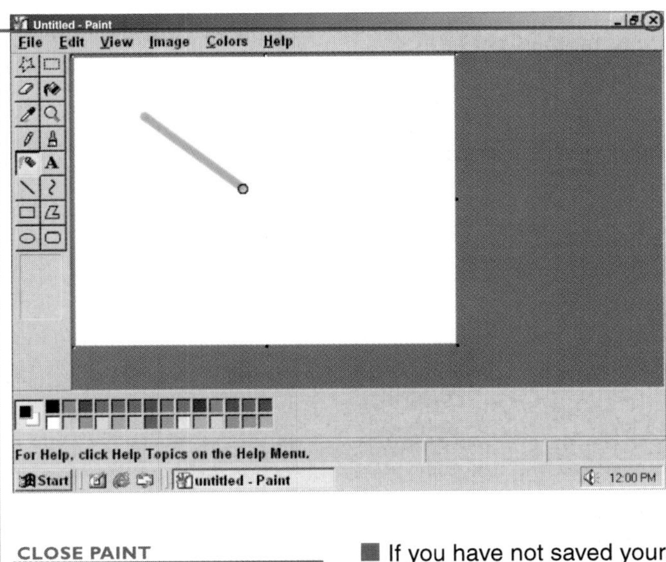

CLOSE PAINT

■ When you finish with Paint, you can close the window and return to the desktop.

1 Click ✕ to close Paint.

■ If you have not saved your picture, you will be asked to save it.

CONTINUED

You can print your pictures and illustrations that you've created with Paint.

USING PAINT (CONTINUED)

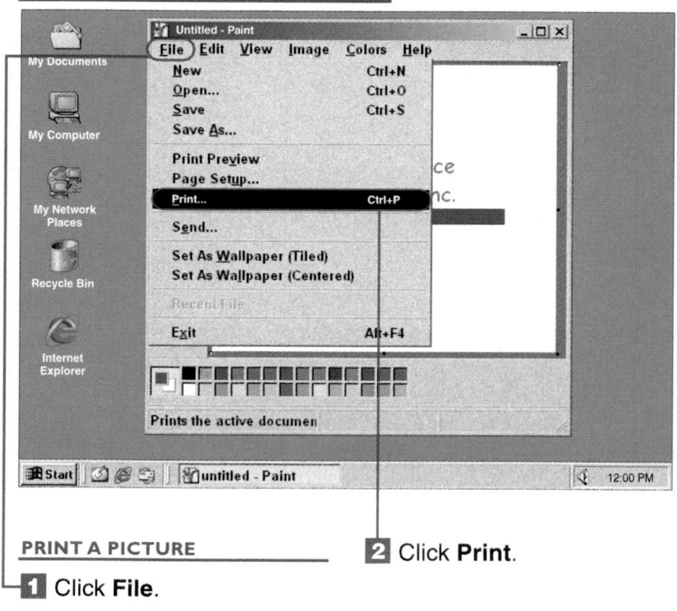

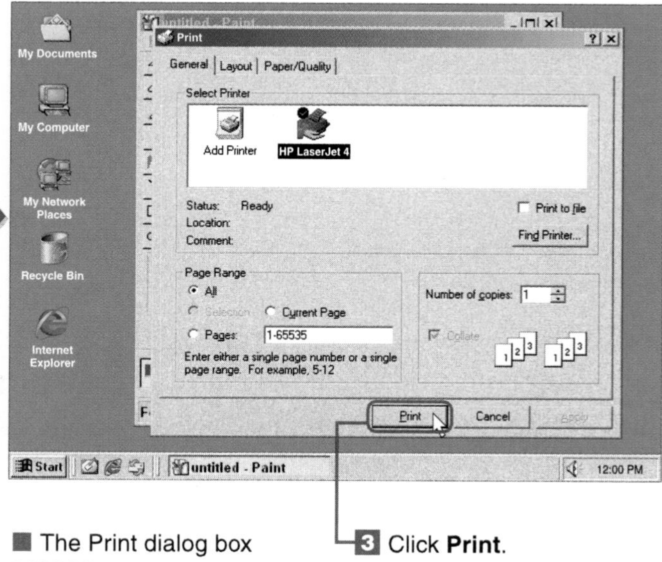

PRINT A PICTURE

1 Click **File**.

2 Click **Print**.

■ The Print dialog box appears.

3 Click **Print**.

When should I save my document?

You should always save your documents every few minutes so you don't accidentally lose all your work.

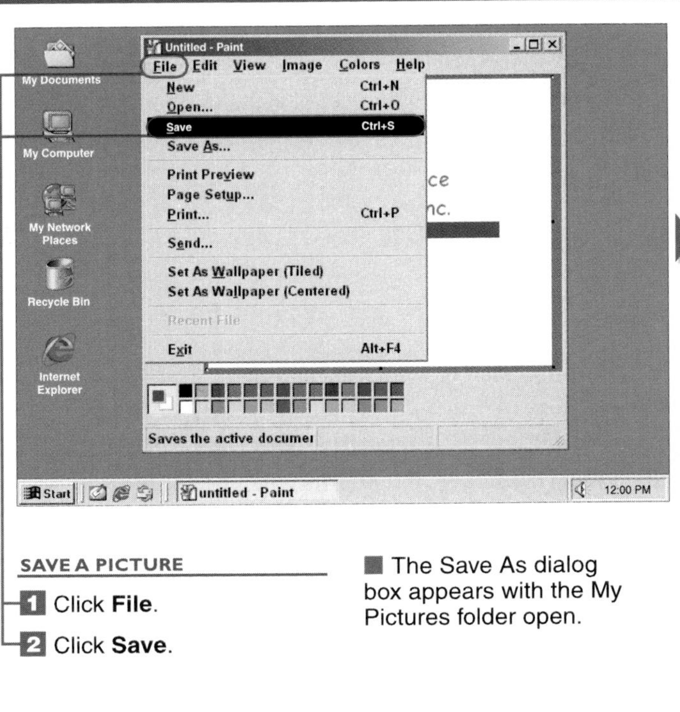

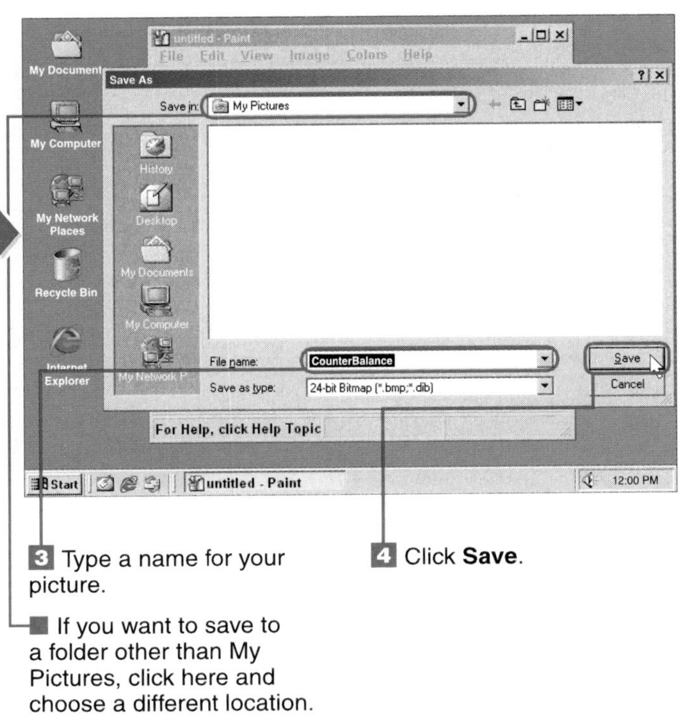

SAVE A PICTURE

1 Click **File**.

2 Click **Save**.

■ The Save As dialog box appears with the My Pictures folder open.

3 Type a name for your picture.

■ If you want to save to a folder other than My Pictures, click here and choose a different location.

4 Click **Save**.

OPEN THE CALCULATOR

Windows 2000 includes a calculator so you can do simple and advanced calculations.

OPEN THE CALCULATOR

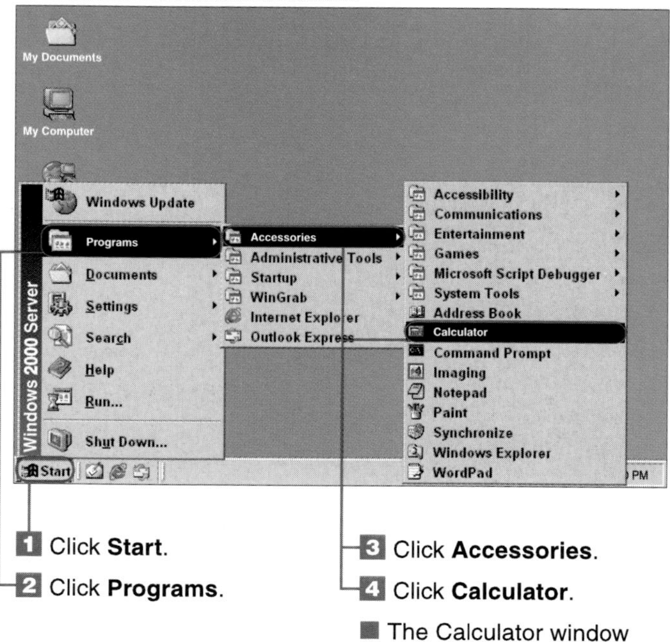

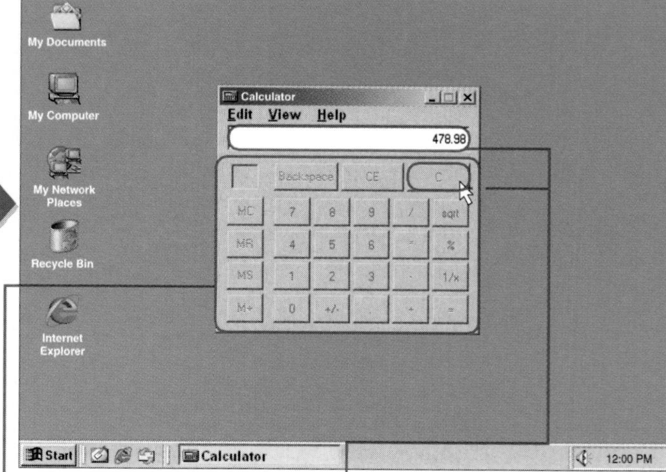

1 Click **Start**.

2 Click **Programs**.

3 Click **Accessories**.

4 Click **Calculator**.

■ The Calculator window appears.

5 Click the buttons on the screen, just as you would press the buttons on a regular calculator.

■ The display shows you the numbers you've entered and the results of your calculations.

6 Click C to clear the display and start a new calculation.

Can I use the keypad on the right side of my keyboard to enter numbers?

Yes. You can use the numeric keypad to enter numbers and do calculations. Make sure the Numeric Lock (Num Lock) light is on by pressing the Num Lock key on the keypad.

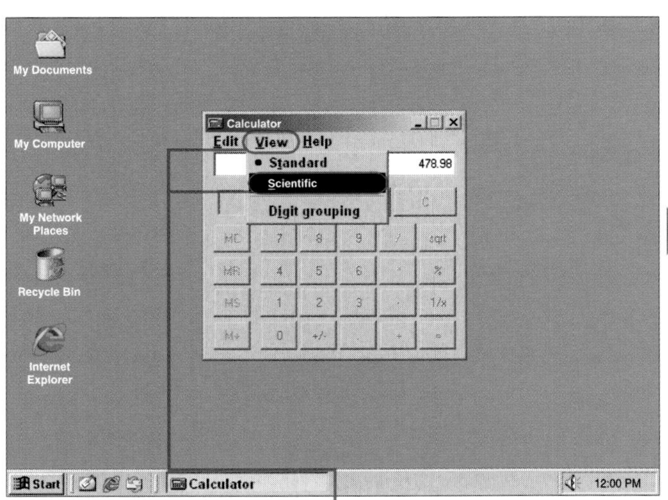

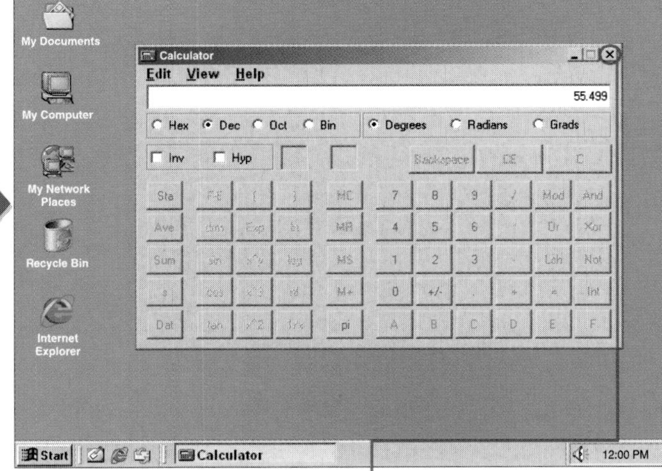

USE SCIENTIFIC MODE

■ You can switch to Scientific mode, which performs more complex calculations than Standard mode.

1 Click **View**.

2 Click **Scientific**.

■ The Scientific view appears.

*Note: To return to Standard view, repeat steps 1 and 2 and click **Standard** in step 2.*

■ Click ☒ if you want to quit the Calculator.

MAXIMIZE OR MINIMIZE A WINDOW

You can make windows larger or smaller, depending on what works best for you. This capability lets you view more of the window's contents at once, or see more windows at a time.

MAXIMIZE OR MINIMIZE A WINDOW

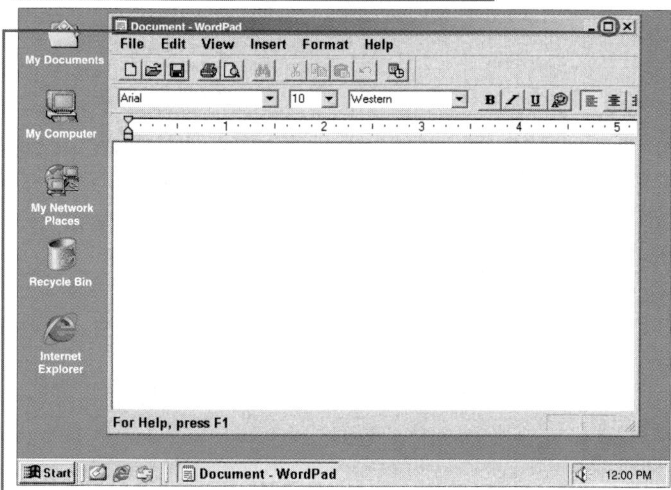

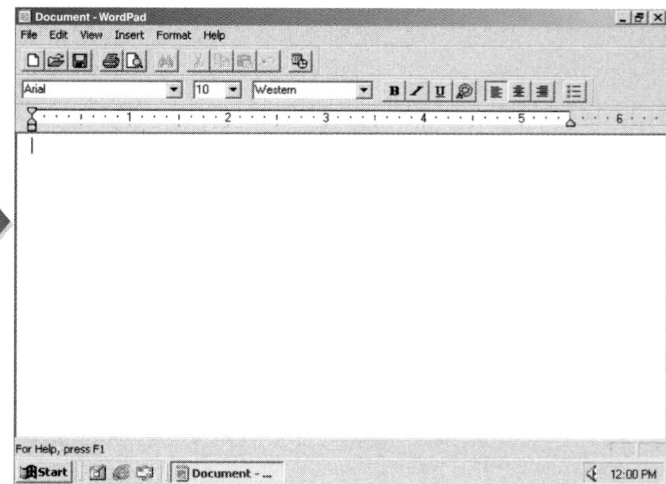

MAXIMIZE A WINDOW

1 Click □ to maximize a window.

■ The window fills the whole screen.

■ To shrink the window back to its previous size, click 🗗.

What is the Minimize button useful for?

If you are not using a window, you can minimize the window to remove it from your screen. You can redisplay the window at any time.

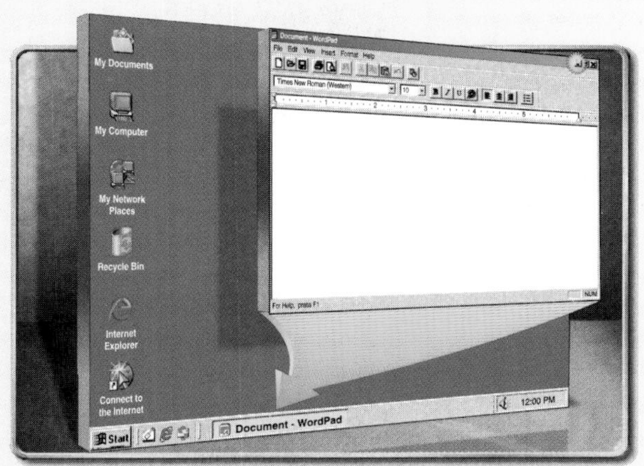

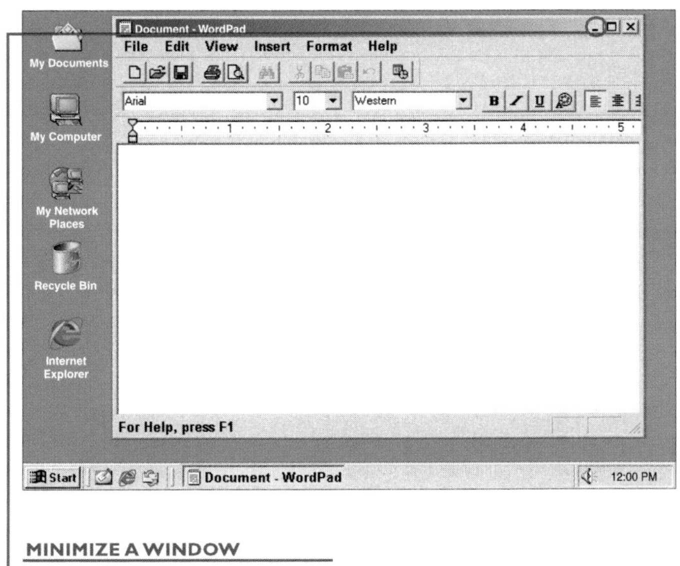

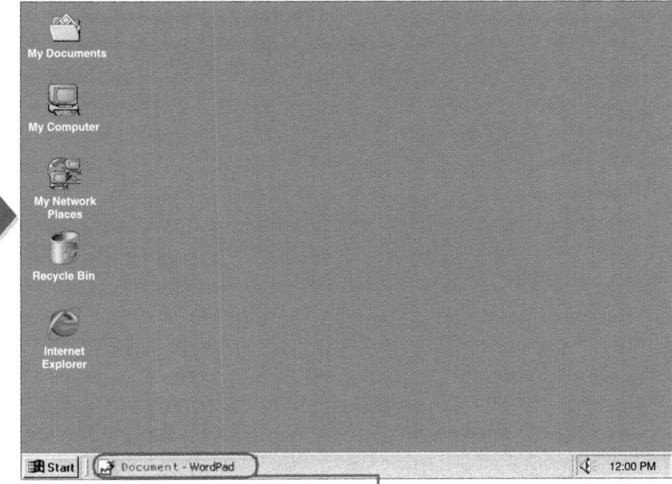

MINIMIZE A WINDOW

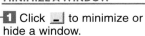

1 Click ▁ to minimize or hide a window.

■ The window disappears, but the taskbar button stays on the taskbar.

■ To redisplay the window, click its button on the taskbar.

MOVE A WINDOW

You can move any window to a different location on the desktop. This lets you work with programs in a way that feels most comfortable for you.

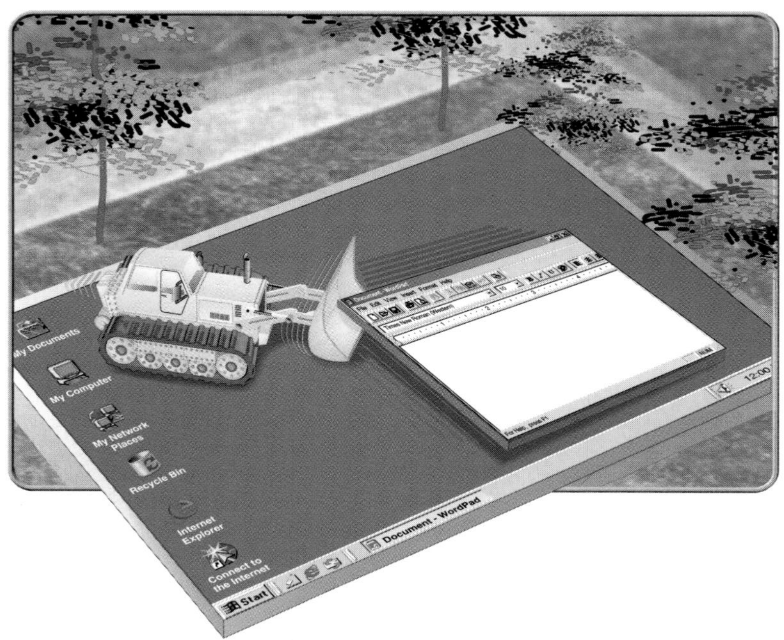

MOVE A WINDOW

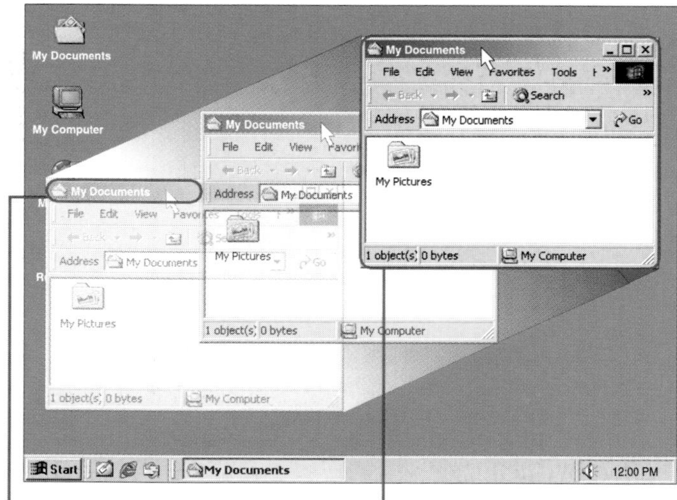

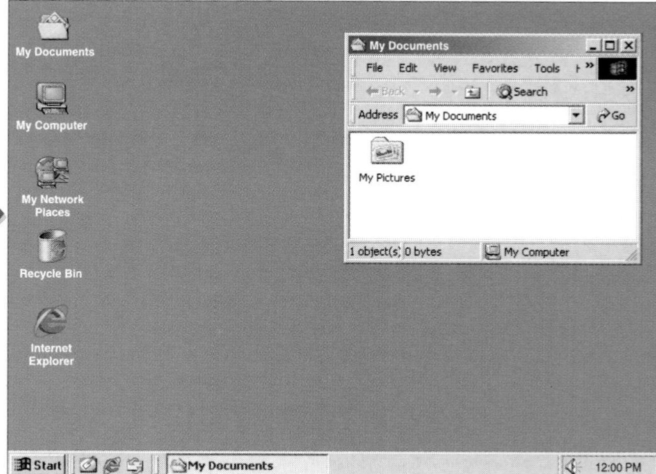

1 Move the mouse cursor over a window's title bar.

2 Drag the mouse to move the window to its new location.

■ The window moves along with your mouse to its new location.

RESIZE A WINDOW

You can easily change a window's size using your mouse.

RESIZE A WINDOW

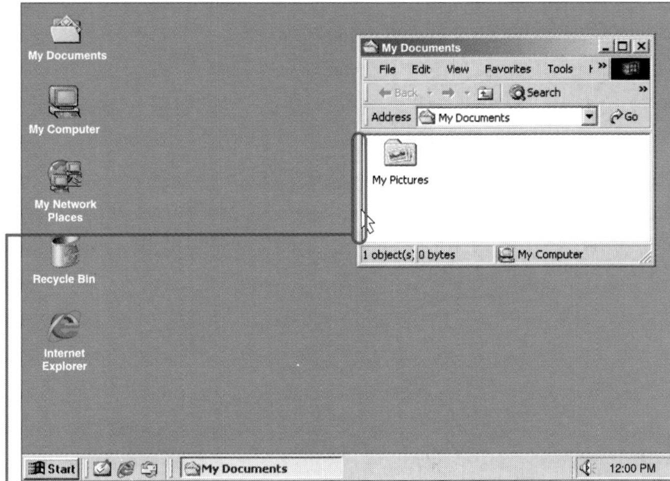

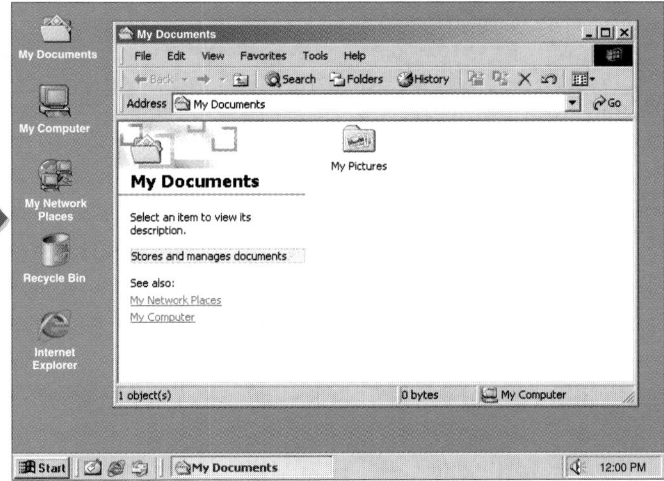

1 Move the mouse cursor over a window edge (↖ changes to ↕, ↔, ⤡ or ⤢).

2 Drag the double-headed mouse arrow until the window changes to the size you want.

■ The window keeps the new size.

SWITCH BETWEEN WINDOWS

You can have several program windows open at a time, and switch between them whenever you want.

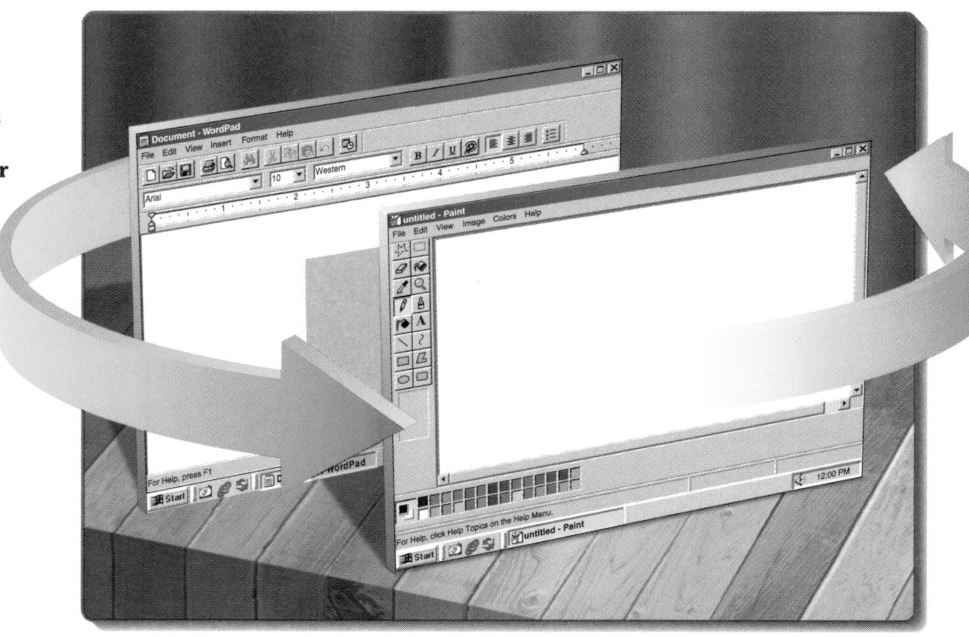

SWITCH BETWEEN WINDOWS

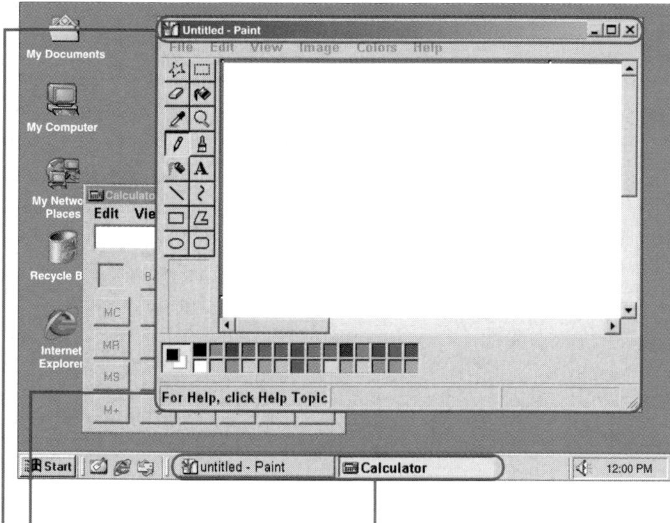

■ The window you are working in (example: **Paint**) will appear on top of the other windows. This is called the *active window*.

■ The active window will display a blue title bar.

■ The taskbar will have a button for each open window.

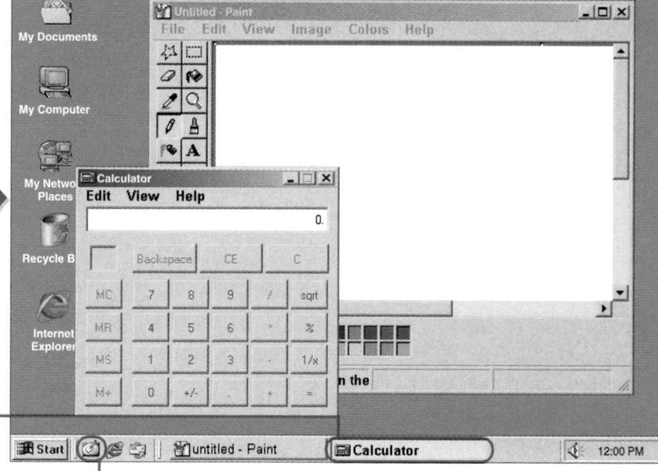

1 Click the task bar button for the window you want to work with (example: **Calculator**).

■ The window appears in front of all other windows and its title bar turns blue. It is now the active window.

■ To clear all windows from the screen, click .

■ You can bring all the windows back to their original size and place by clicking again.

CLOSE A WINDOW

When you no longer need a window or its information, you can close the window and remove it from your screen.

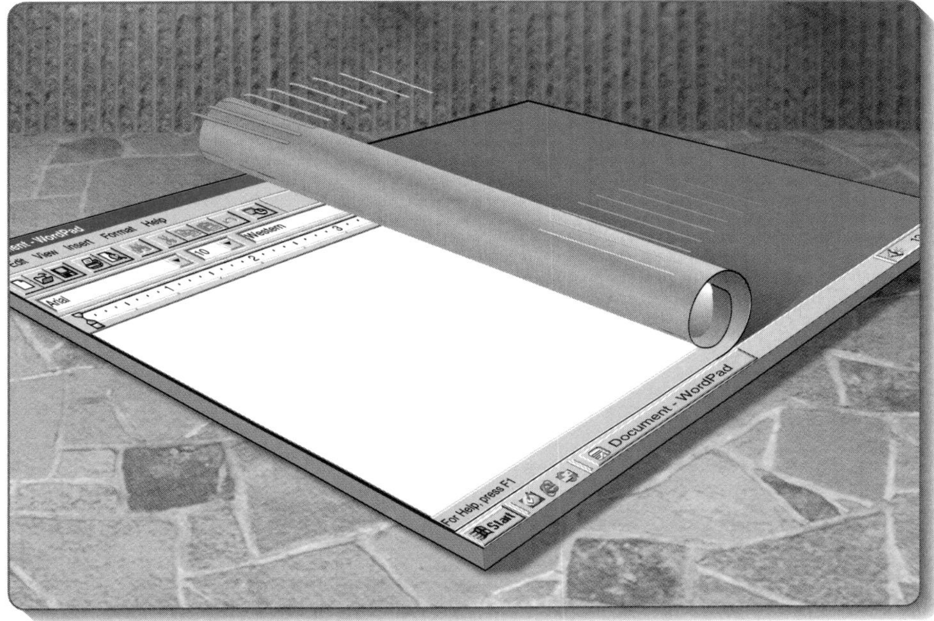

CLOSE A WINDOW

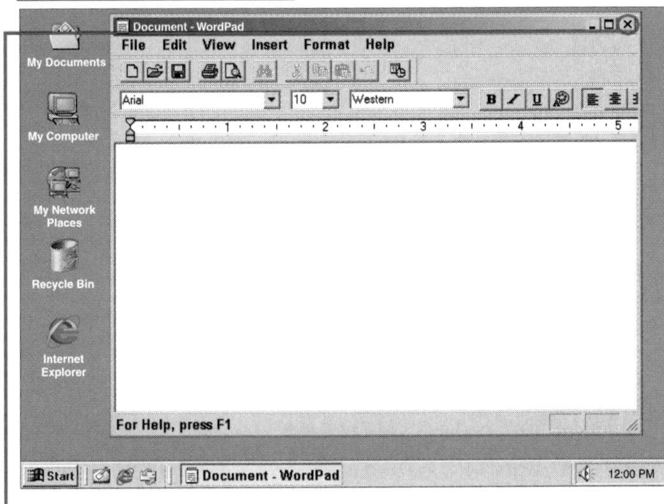

1 Click ✕.

■ The window disappears.

■ The taskbar button disappears from the taskbar.

CHANGE THE DATE AND TIME

Your server needs to have the correct date and time on it. Windows 2000 uses the date and time to manage your network and to manage information stored on your server.

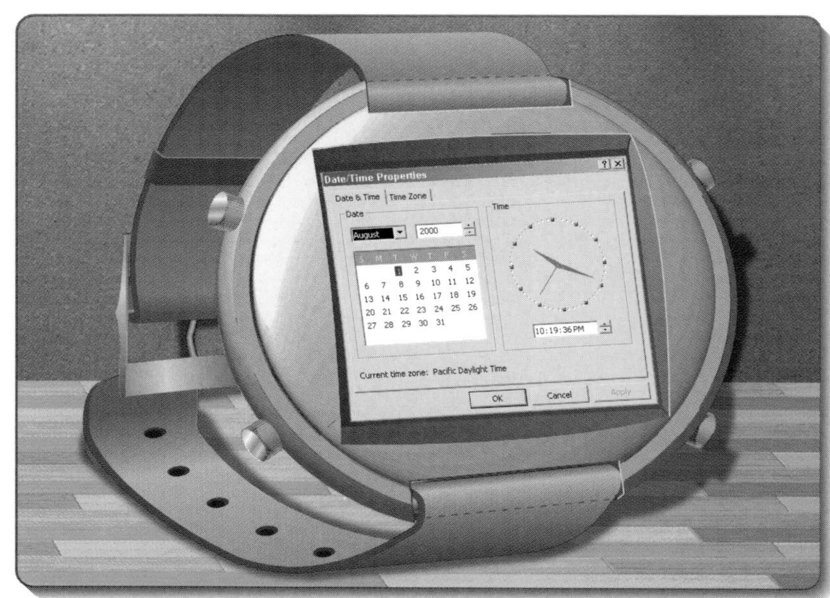

CHANGE THE DATE AND TIME

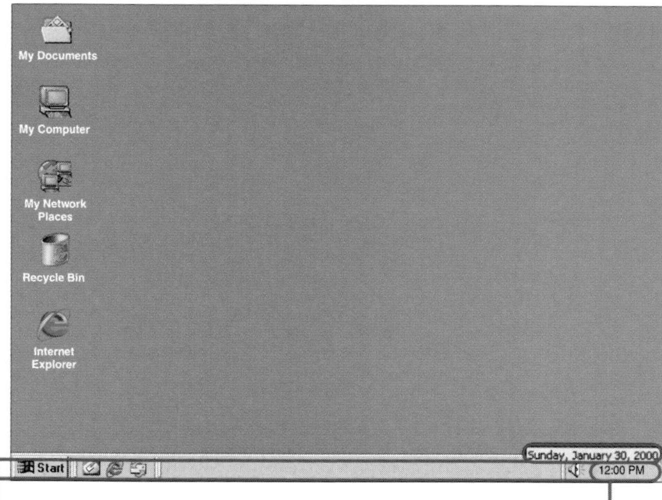

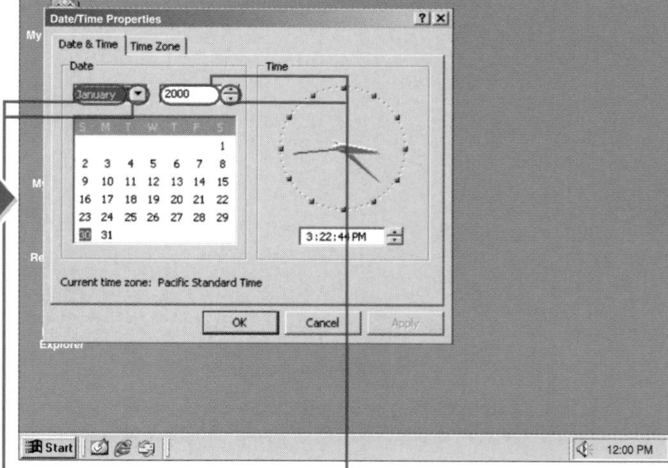

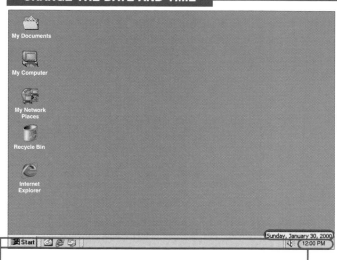

CHANGE THE DATE

1 You can see the date by positioning the mouse over the time display.

■ A box that looks like a yellow sticky note shows the date.

2 To change the date or time, double-click this area with your mouse.

■ The Date/Time Properties dialog box appears.

■ This area displays the current month.

3 To change the month, click ▼ and click the correct month.

■ This area displays the year.

4 Change the year by clicking ▲ or ▼ until the correct year appears.

Do I have to reset the date and time every time I start my computer?

No, the computer will remember the date and time. Your computer has a built-in clock that keeps track of the date and time even when you turn off your computer.

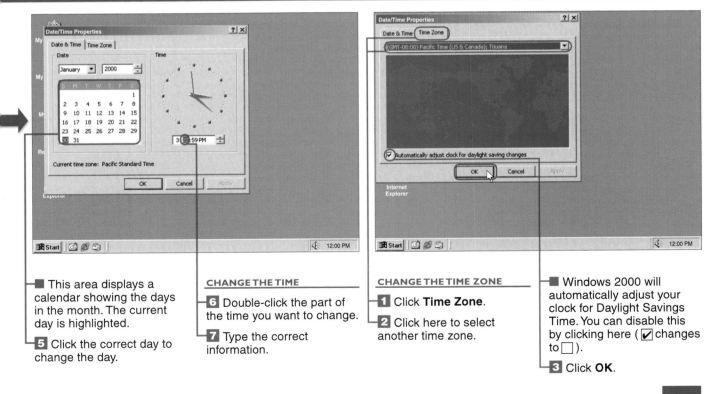

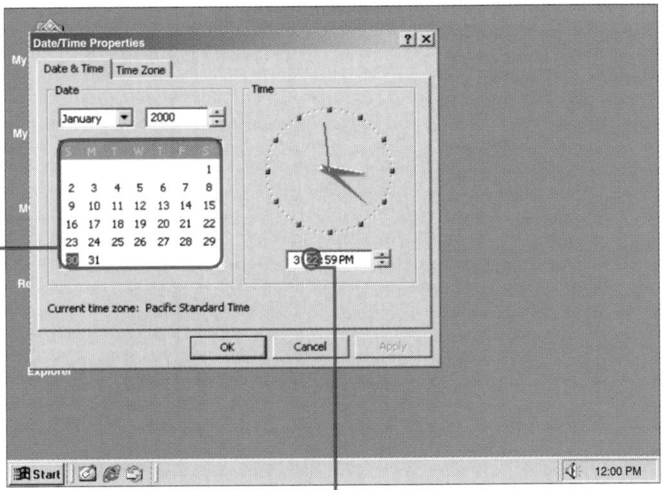

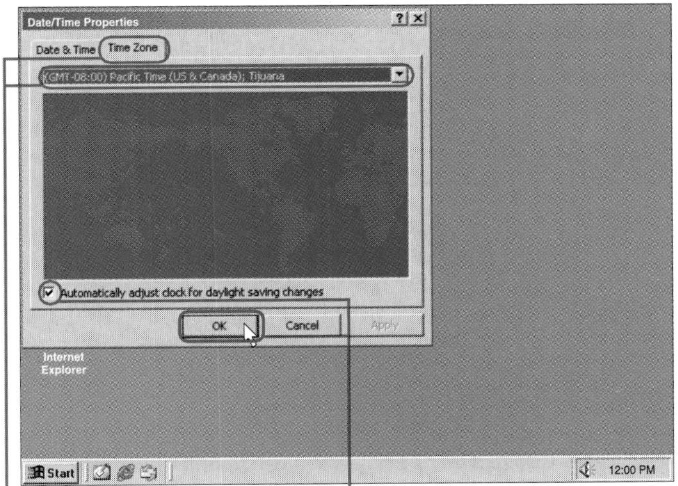

■ This area displays a calendar showing the days in the month. The current day is highlighted.

5 Click the correct day to change the day.

CHANGE THE TIME

6 Double-click the part of the time you want to change.

7 Type the correct information.

CHANGE THE TIME ZONE

1 Click **Time Zone**.

2 Click here to select another time zone.

■ Windows 2000 will automatically adjust your clock for Daylight Savings Time. You can disable this by clicking here (☑ changes to ☐).

3 Click **OK**.

You can decorate your desktop by adding wallpaper. You can display a company logo, family photos, or images from the Internet.

ADD WALLPAPER

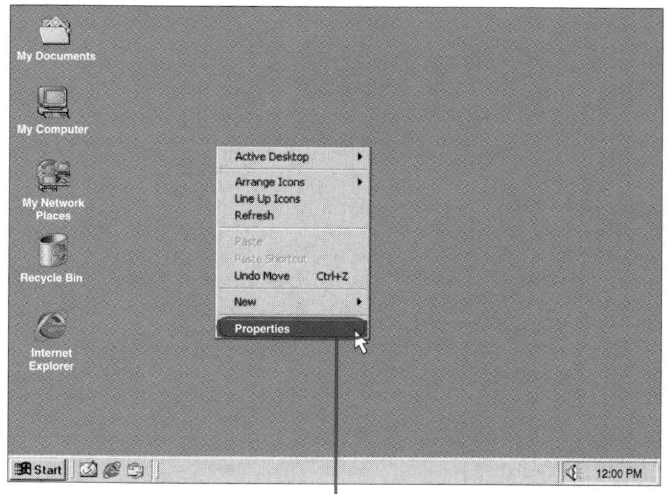

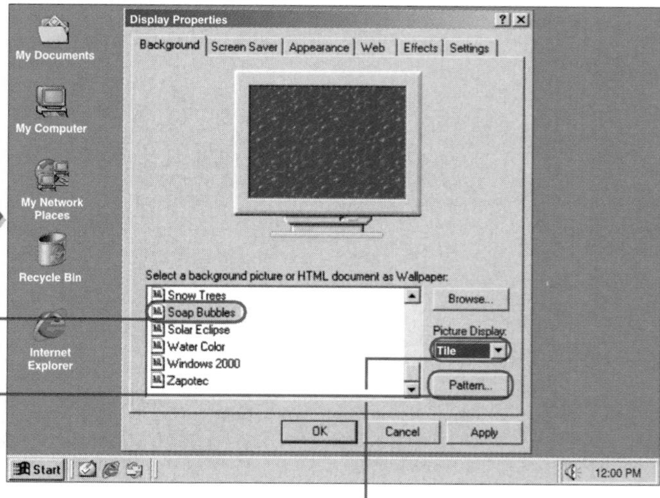

1 Right-click a blank area on your desktop.

■ A pop-up menu appears.

2 Click **Properties**.

■ The Display Properties dialog box appears.

3 Click the wallpaper you want to use.

4 Click this area to change the way the wallpaper fits on your desktop.

5 Click the way you want to display the wallpaper.

Note: For more information on these choices, see the top of the next page.

What are the different ways I can display wallpaper on my desktop?

Center: Places the wallpaper in the middle of the desktop. This is useful for pictures or company logos.

Tile: Repeats the wallpaper until it fills your desktop. This is useful for small patterns.

Stretch: Stretches the wallpaper to fill your desktop. This is a good way to make pictures fit the whole desktop.

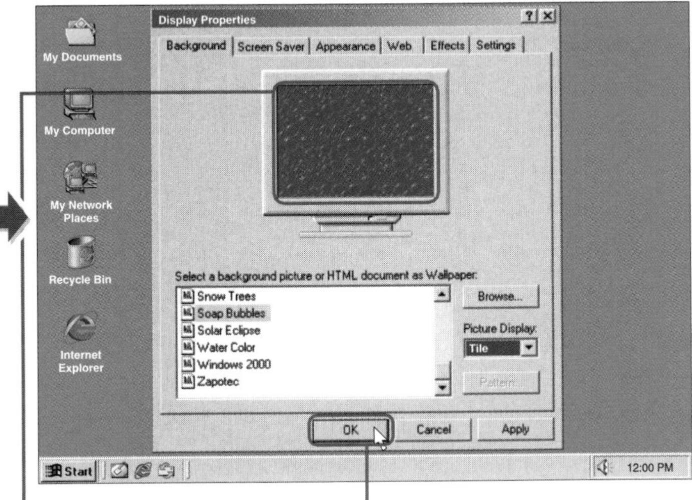

■ This is a preview area, where you can see how your wallpaper will look on your desktop.

6 Click **OK** to add the wallpaper to your desktop.

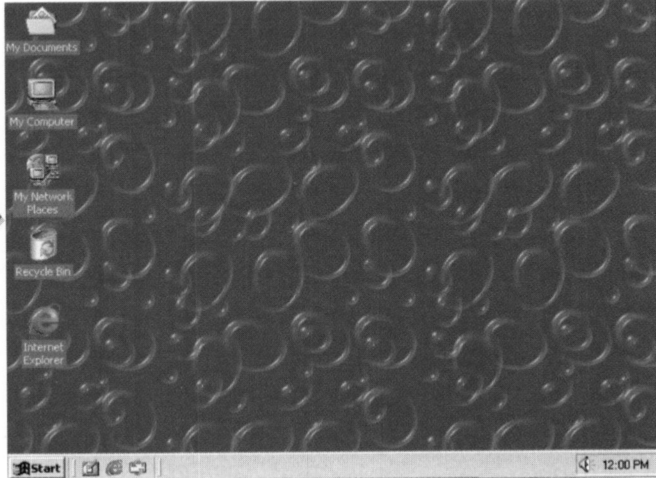

■ The wallpaper appears on your desktop.

■ To remove wallpaper from your desktop, perform steps 1 through 3, clicking **(None)** in step 3. Then perform step 6.

SET UP A SCREEN SAVER

A screen saver blanks out your desktop and replaces it with a picture or pattern. It appears when you do not use your computer for a period of time.

SET UP A SCREEN SAVER

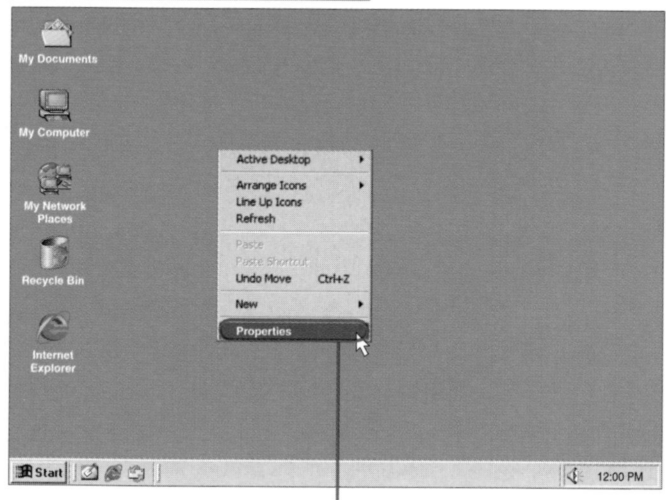

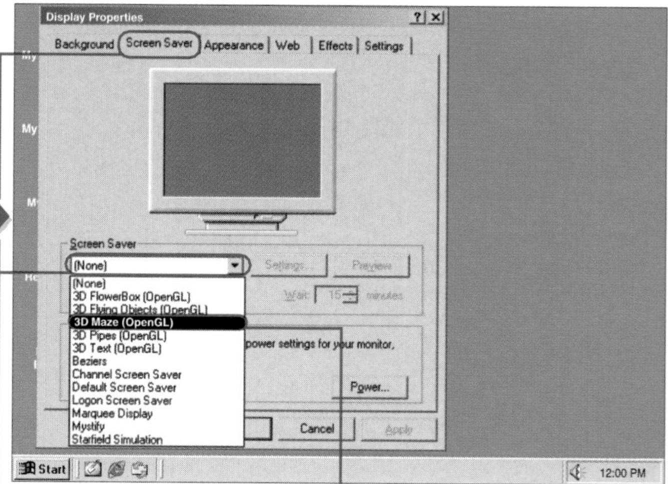

1 Right-click a blank area on your desktop.

■ A pop-up menu appears.

2 Click **Properties**.

■ The Display Properties dialog box appears.

3 Click **Screen Saver**.

4 Click this area to display a list of the available screen savers.

5 Click the screen saver you want to use (example: **3D Maze (OpenGL)**).

Is it a good idea to use a screen saver?

Screen savers are a good way to hide your desktop if you will be away from your computer for a while. That way you don't need to close your applications and log off. Screen savers can also be used to leave a message for others, such as "I'll be right back." Most screen savers are used either for security or for their entertainment value.

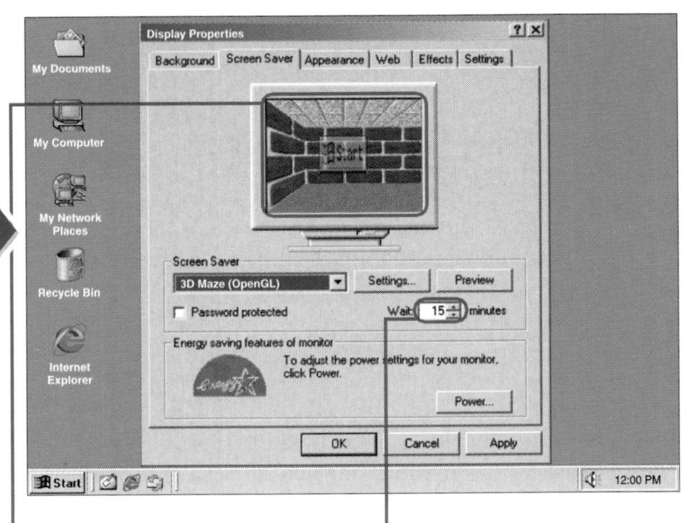

■ The preview area shows you how the screen saver will look.

■ The screen saver will start when you do not use your computer for a certain amount of time.

6 Click ▲ or ▼ to adjust the number of minutes of inactivity before the screen saver starts.

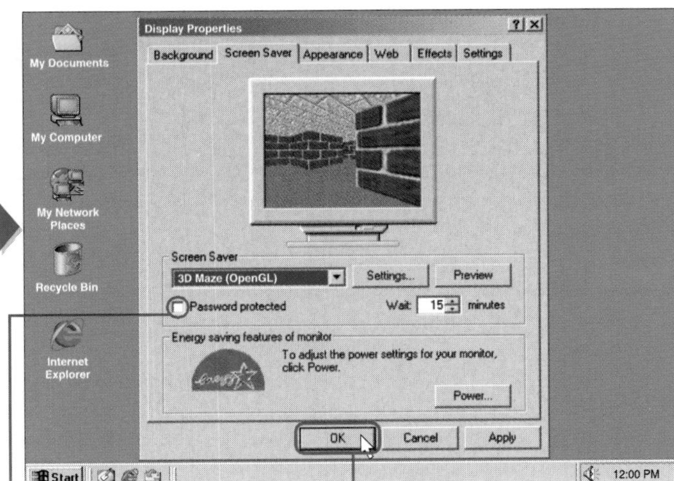

7 Click **Password Protected** to require a password to regain access to your desktop (☐ changes to ☑).

■ The reentry password is the same as the user's logon password.

8 Click **OK** to turn the screen saver on.

■ When the screen saver appears on your screen, you can move the mouse or press a key on your keyboard to remove the screen saver.

START A COMMAND PROMPT WINDOW

The Command Prompt window lets you work with older MS-DOS commands and programs that you may have on your computer.

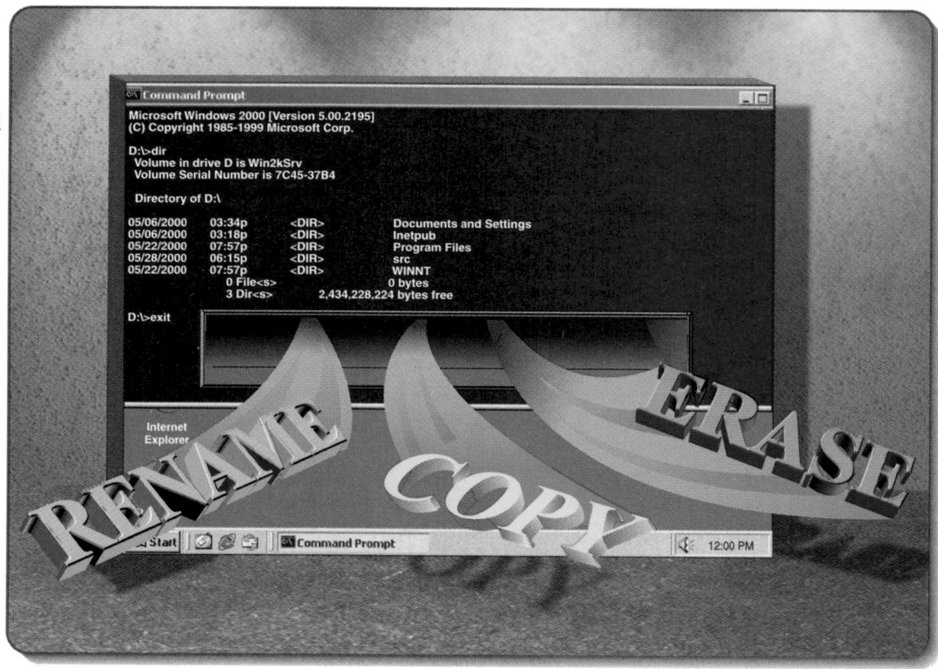

Some older MS-DOS programs, especially games, will not work with Windows 2000. Whenever possible, you should work with programs written specifically for Windows 95, Windows 98, Windows NT, or Windows 2000.

START A COMMAND PROMPT WINDOW

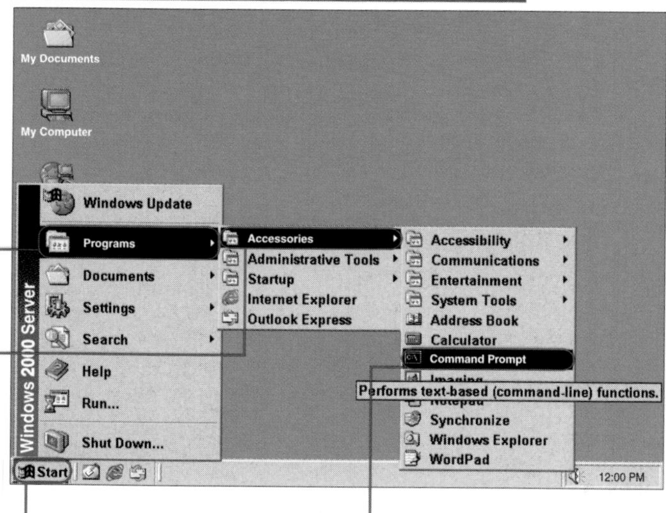

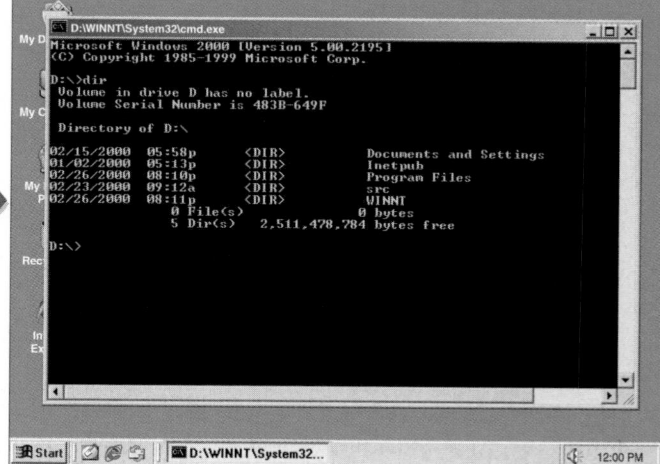

1 Click **Start**.

2 Click **Programs**.

3 Click **Accessories**.

4 Click **Command Prompt**.

■ The Command Prompt window appears.

■ You can use MS-DOS commands and start MS-DOS programs in this window.

■ For example, the `dir` command lists the contents of the current directory.

Note: You can maximize the window by holding down **Alt** *and pressing* **Enter**.

How can I tell what older MS-DOS commands are available in Windows 2000?

In the Command Prompt window, type **help** and then press Enter to display a list of MS-DOS commands that you can use.

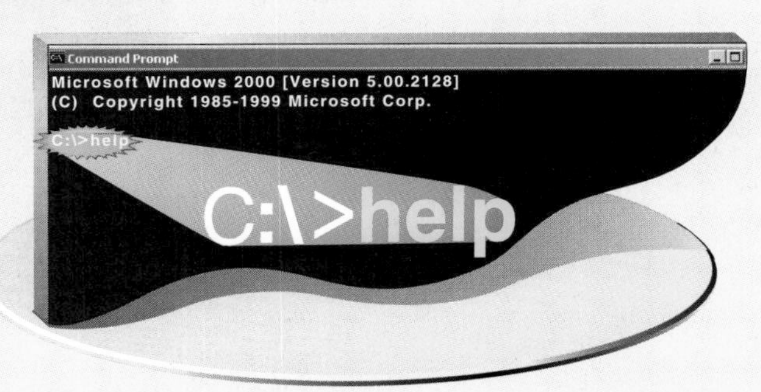


```
Microsoft Windows 2000 [Version 5.00.2195]
(C) Copyright 1985-1999 Microsoft Corp.

D:\>dir
 Volume in drive D is Win2kSrv
 Volume Serial Number is 7C45-3784

 Directory of D:\

05/06/2000  03:34p      <DIR>          Documents and Settings
05/06/2000  03:18p      <DIR>          Inetpub
05/22/2000  07:57p      <DIR>          Program Files
05/28/2000  06:15p      <DIR>          src
05/22/2000  07:57p      <DIR>          WINNT
               0 File(s)              0 bytes
               5 Dir(s)   2,434,228,224 bytes free

D:\>
```

```
D:\WINNT\System32\cmd.exe
Microsoft Windows 2000 [Version 5.00.2195]
(C) Copyright 1985-1999 Microsoft Corp.

D:\>dir
 Volume in drive D has no label.
 Volume Serial Number is 483B-649F

 Directory of D:\

02/15/2000  05:58p      <DIR>          Documents and Settings
01/02/2000  05:13p      <DIR>          Inetpub
02/26/2000  08:10p      <DIR>          Program Files
02/23/2000  09:12a      <DIR>          src
02/26/2000  08:11p      <DIR>          WINNT
               0 File(s)              0 bytes
               5 Dir(s)   2,511,478,784 bytes free

D:\>exit
```

MINIMIZE THE COMMAND PROMPT WINDOW

1 Hold down Alt and then press Enter again to return the screen to a window.

■ The Command Prompt returns to a window.

EXIT THE COMMAND PROMPT WINDOW

1 When you finish using the Command Prompt window, type **exit** and then press Enter to close the window.

■ You return to Windows 2000.

PROGRESS
INSTALLING
Battery

CHAPTER 3

Exploring the Control Panel

This chapter shows you how to manage software and hardware on your server through the Control Panel.

INSTALL NEW HARDWARE

You can install new hardware on your server. Windows 2000 will help you install the necessary software that works with your new hardware.

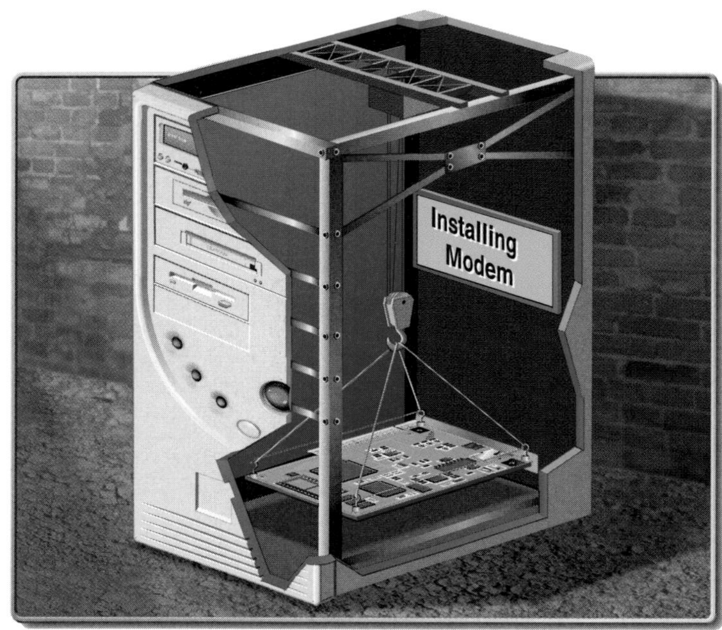

Warning: Never add or remove hardware inside your computer while it is turned on; you could injure yourself or damage your computer equipment. Always follow the manufacturer's instructions for adding or removing hardware. If you are not comfortable doing this, ask a computer professional to help you.

INSTALL NEW HARDWARE

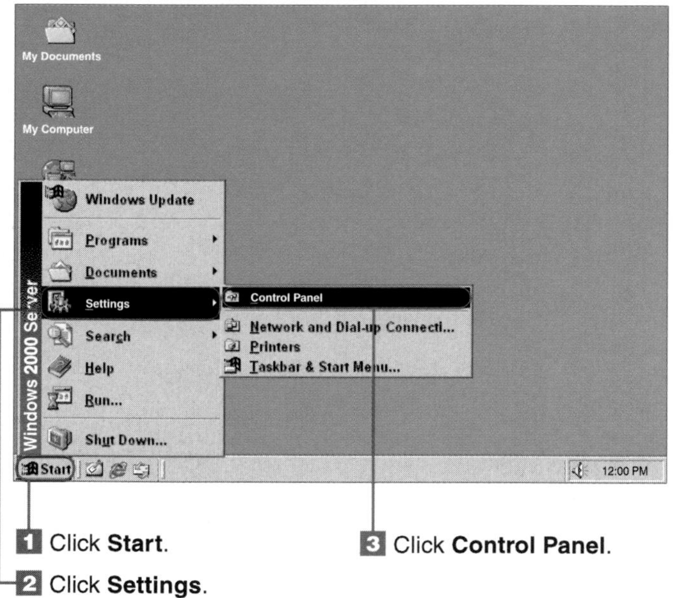

1 Click **Start**.

2 Click **Settings**.

3 Click **Control Panel**.

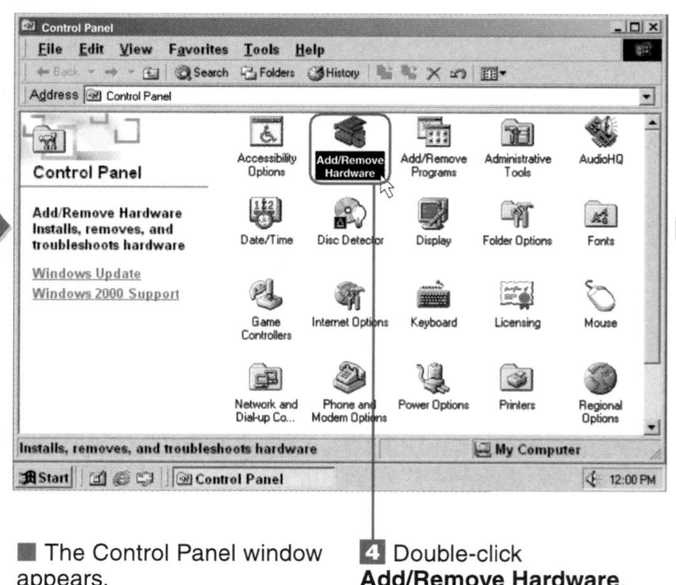

■ The Control Panel window appears.

4 Double-click **Add/Remove Hardware**.

How can I tell if my new hardware will work with my server?

Microsoft maintains a Hardware Compatibility List, or HCL, that lists all of the components that have been successfully tested with Windows 2000. Check this list on Microsoft's Web site at www.microsoft.com/windows2000/upgrade/compat/default.asp before buying new hardware for your computer.

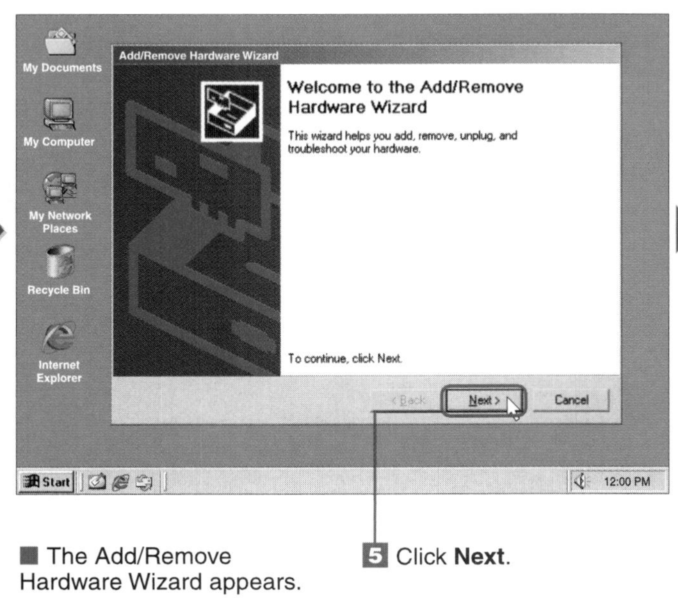

■ The Add/Remove Hardware Wizard appears.

Note: You should make sure all other programs are closed before continuing.

5 Click **Next**.

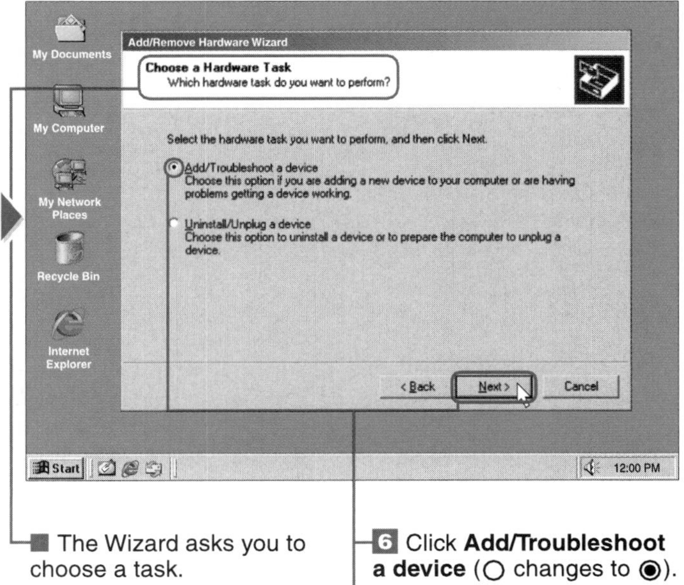

■ The Wizard asks you to choose a task.

6 Click **Add/Troubleshoot a device** (○ changes to ◉).

7 Click **Next**.

CONTINUED

INSTALL NEW HARDWARE

The Wizard will guide you through the steps needed to properly install your hardware. Some hardware is smart enough to install and configure itself when you turn on the computer.

INSTALL NEW HARDWARE (CONTINUED)

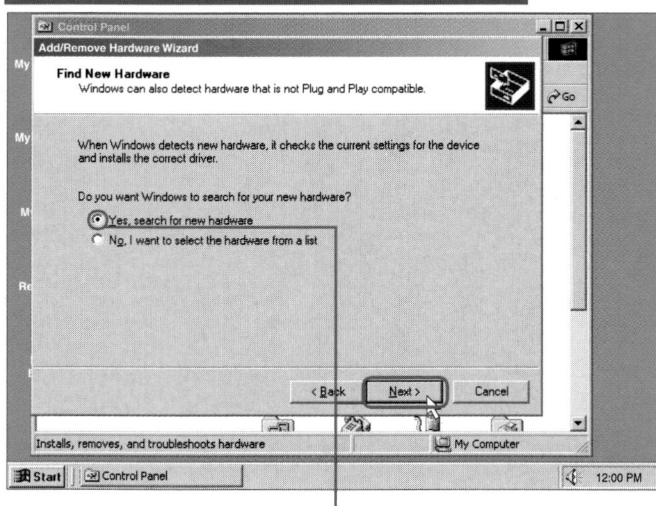

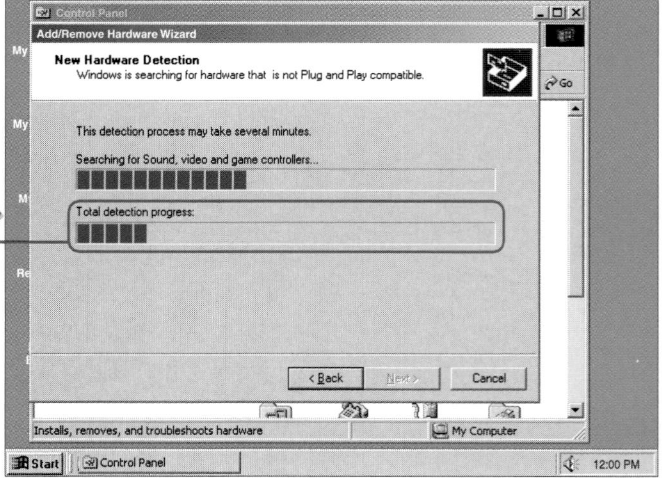

■ If a Plug and Play device is detected, Windows will install the software.

8 Click **Yes, search for new hardware** (○ changes to ◉).

9 Click **Next**.

■ The search may take several minutes.

■ This area displays the search progress.

*Note: You can click **Cancel** to stop the search at any time.*

What is Plug and Play?

Plug and Play is technology that makes it easy to install new hardware. It requires a computer that knows how to detect Plug and Play devices and that will let themselves be configured automatically by the computer.

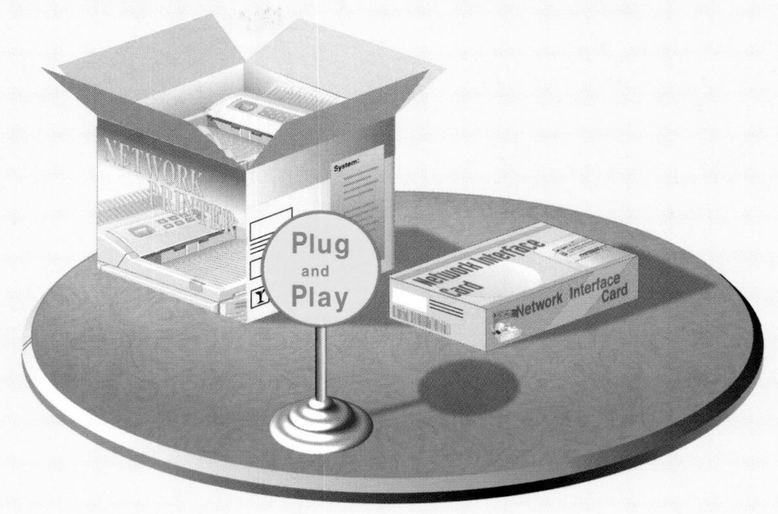

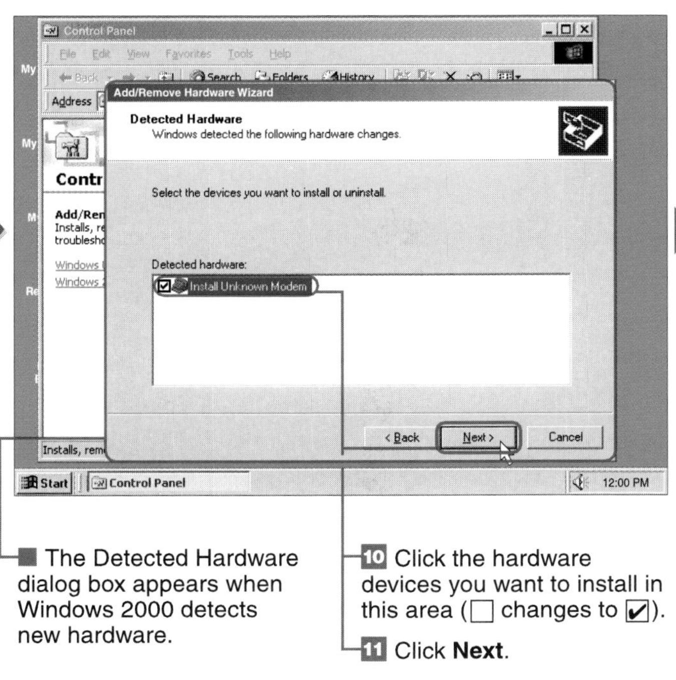

■ The Detected Hardware dialog box appears when Windows 2000 detects new hardware.

10 Click the hardware devices you want to install in this area (☐ changes to ☑).

11 Click **Next**.

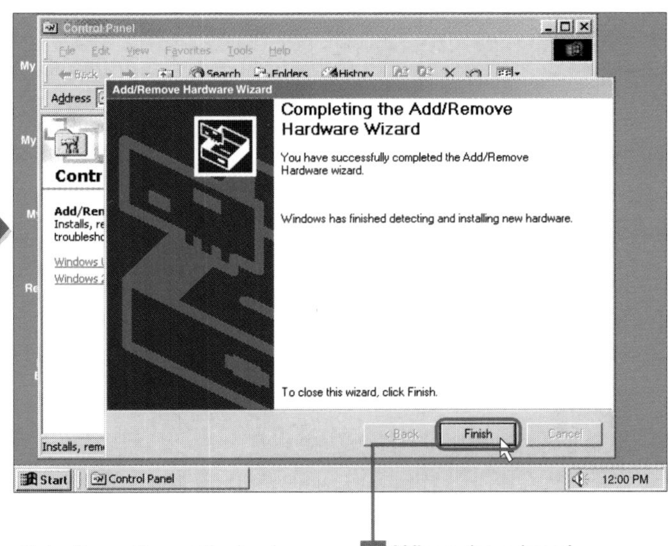

Note: Depending on the hardware, you may be asked to select other options or install a floppy disk or CD with device drivers. Follow the manufacturer's instructions.

12 When the wizard completes the installation, click **Finish**.

Note: You may need to restart your computer before using your new hardware.

ADD PROGRAMS

You can add new programs to your server. New programs can include word processors, graphics programs, and mail programs.

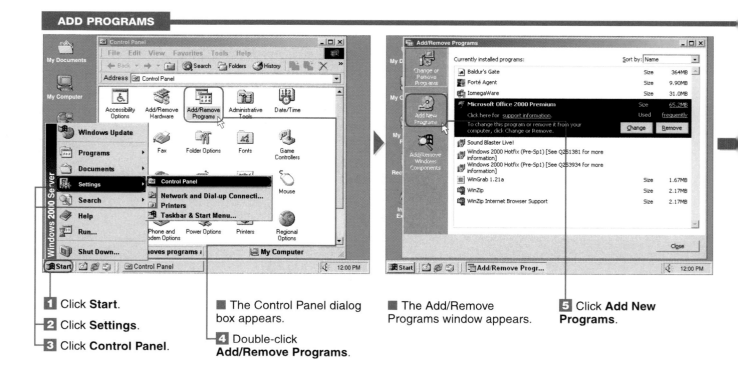

ADD PROGRAMS

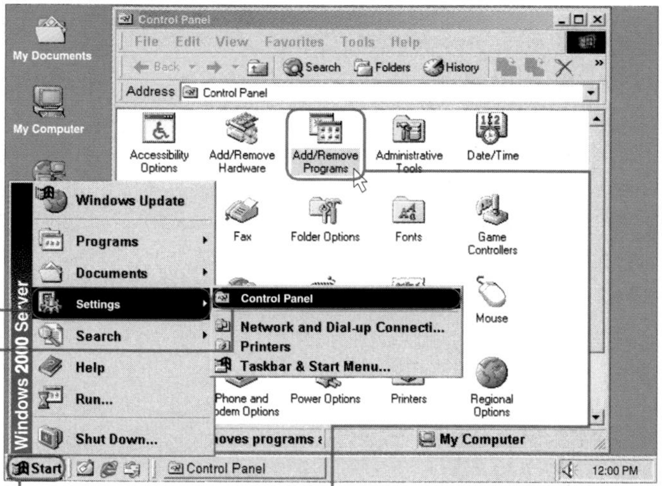

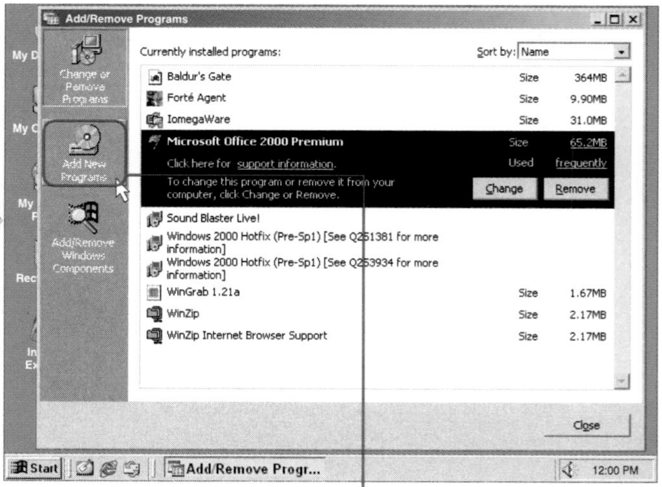

1 Click **Start**.

2 Click **Settings**.

3 Click **Control Panel**.

■ The Control Panel dialog box appears.

4 Double-click **Add/Remove Programs**.

■ The Add/Remove Programs window appears.

5 Click **Add New Programs**.

Why do some programs install themselves automatically?

Newer programs on CD-ROM use AutoPlay, which launches a setup program when you put the disk in the computer. Older programs, and those on diskettes, don't use AutoPlay and must be installed manually.

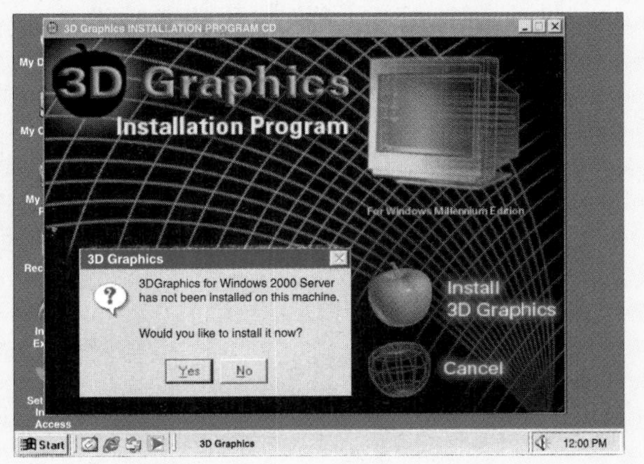

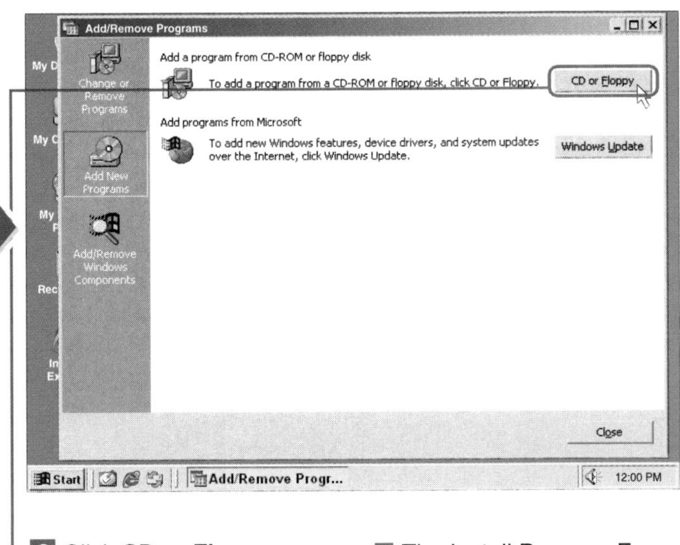

6 Click **CD or Floppy**.

■ The Install Program From Floppy Disk or CD-ROM dialog box appears.

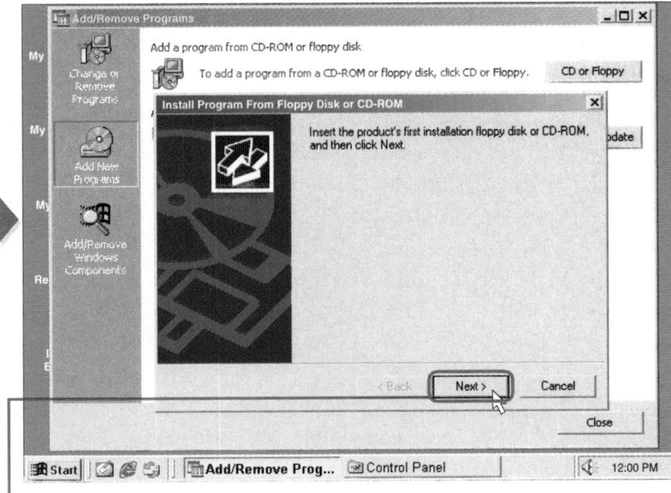

■ Insert your CD-ROM or floppy installation disk into the computer.

7 Click **Next**.

■ Follow the installation instructions from your Setup program.

REMOVE WINDOWS PROGRAMS

If you do not use a program any more, you can remove it from your computer. This will free up disk space and remove the program from your Start menu.

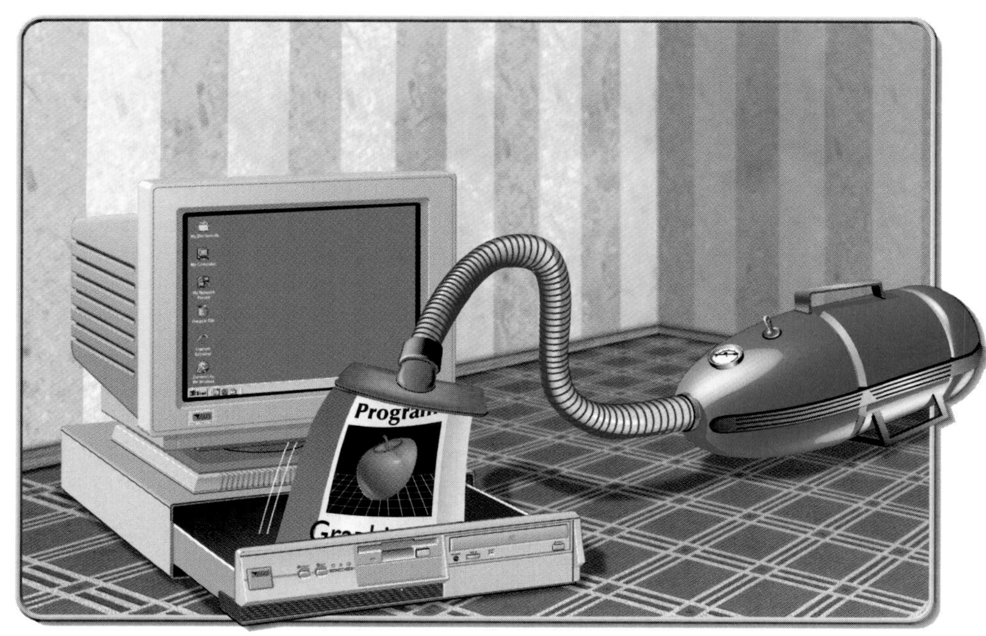

REMOVE WINDOWS PROGRAMS

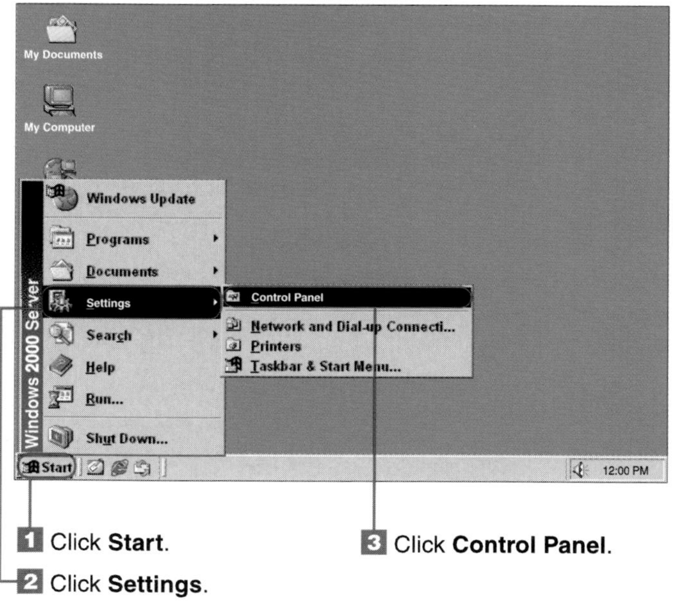

1 Click **Start**.

2 Click **Settings**.

3 Click **Control Panel**.

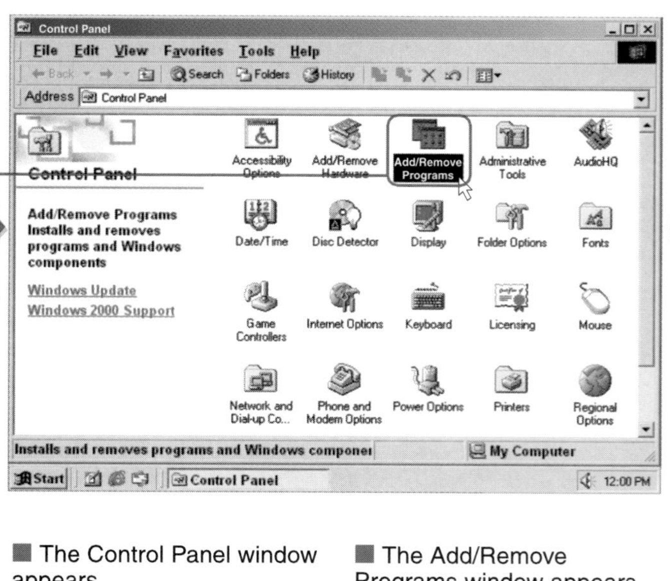

■ The Control Panel window appears.

4 Double-click **Add/Remove Programs**.

■ The Add/Remove Programs window appears.

Can I uninstall a program by deleting the files myself from my hard drive?

When a program is installed, it makes many changes to Windows 2000's system files. Deleting program files does not remove the system file changes; instead, your system may become unstable or crash. It is much safer to uninstall programs using the procedure in this section.

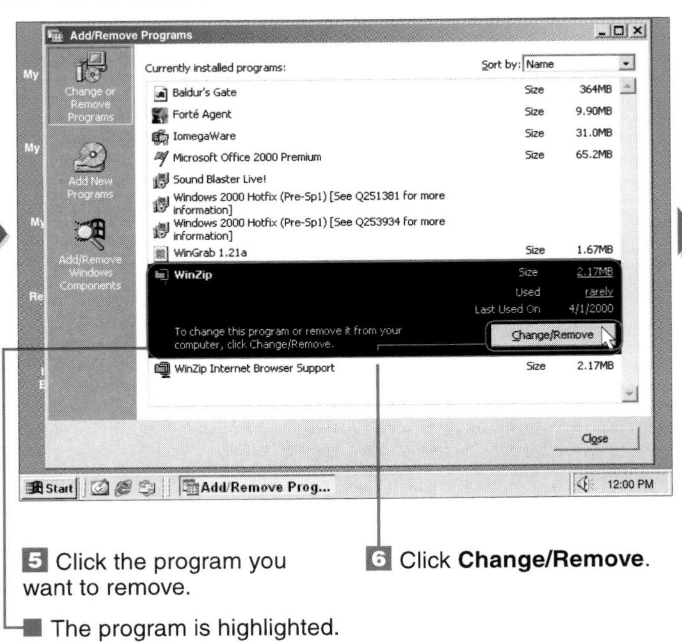

5 Click the program you want to remove.

■ The program is highlighted.

6 Click **Change/Remove**.

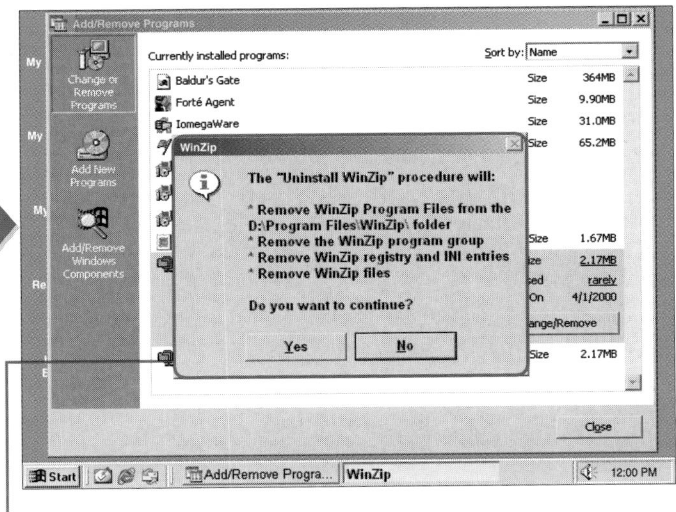

■ The program's uninstall dialog box appears.

7 Follow the program's uninstall instructions. Each program uses different steps to remove itself from your computer.

SET THE ACCESSIBILITY OPTIONS

Windows 2000 lets you change the way the keyboard, monitor, mouse, and sounds work. People with different physical needs can adjust the system to compensate for those needs.

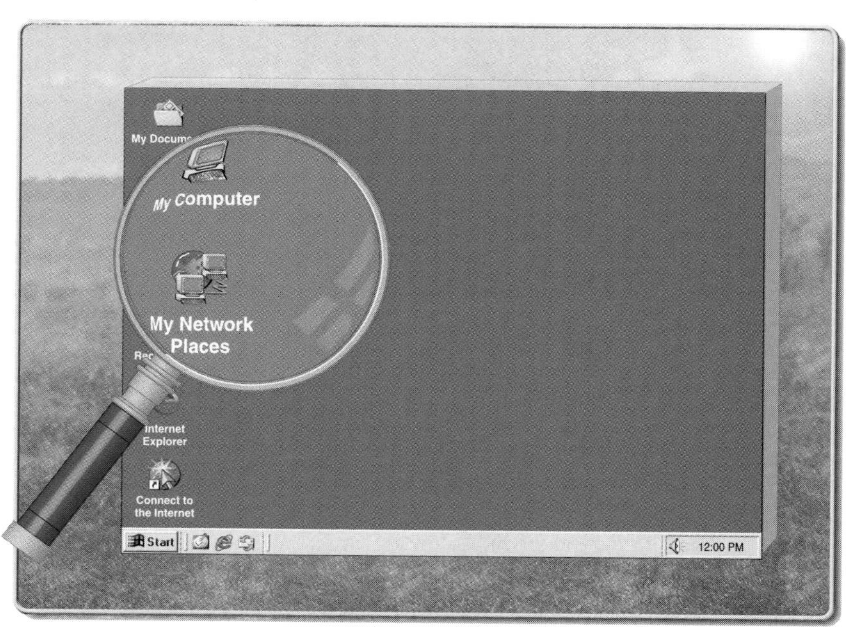

SET THE ACCESSIBILITY OPTIONS

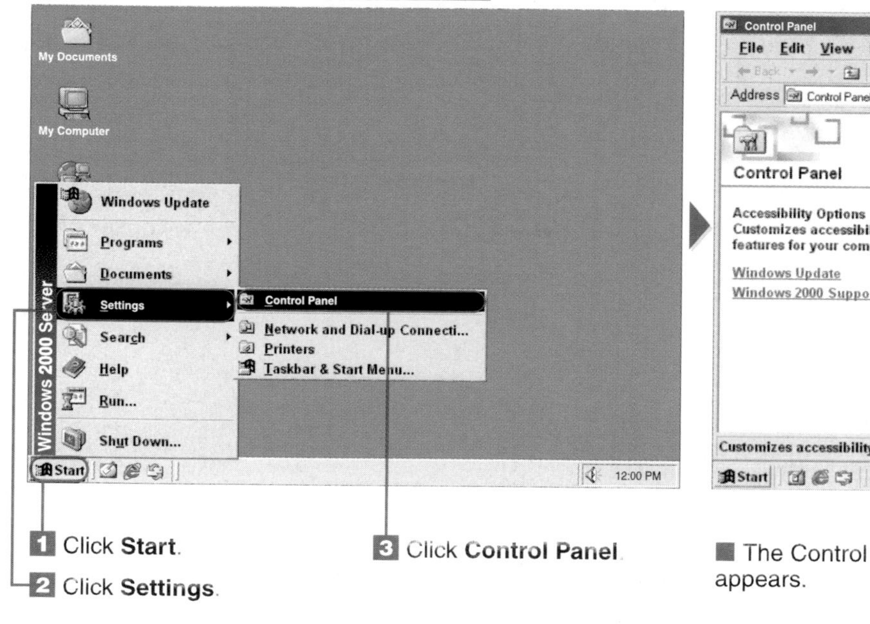

1 Click **Start**.

2 Click **Settings**.

3 Click **Control Panel**.

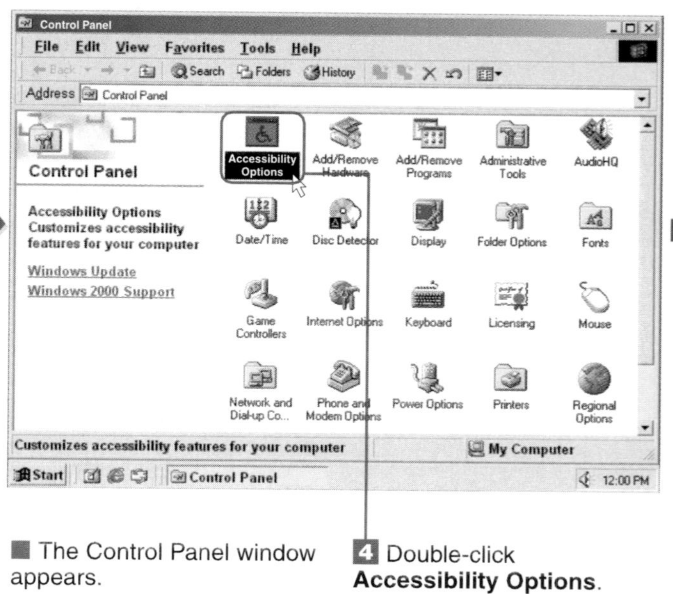

■ The Control Panel window appears.

4 Double-click **Accessibility Options**.

Are these the only tools to help people with different physical needs?

Windows 2000 has other applications available, including the Magnifier and the Narrator. The Accessibility Options affect only basic system operation. For more information, see the Help file, or use the Accessibility Wizard by clicking **Start, Programs,** and then **Accessories**.

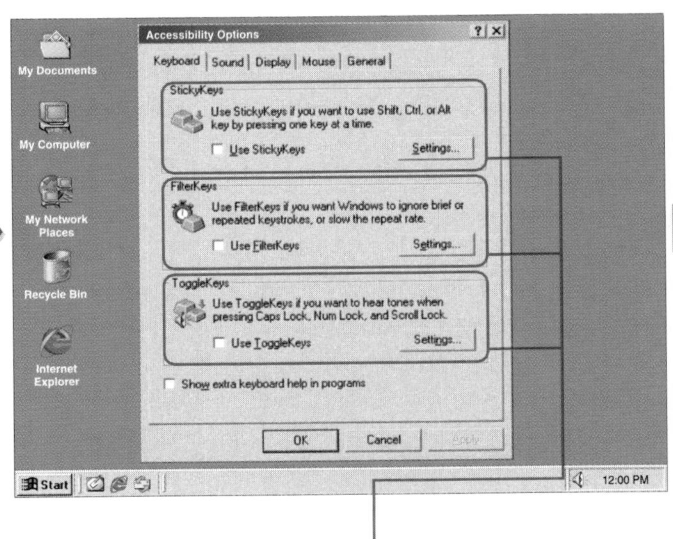

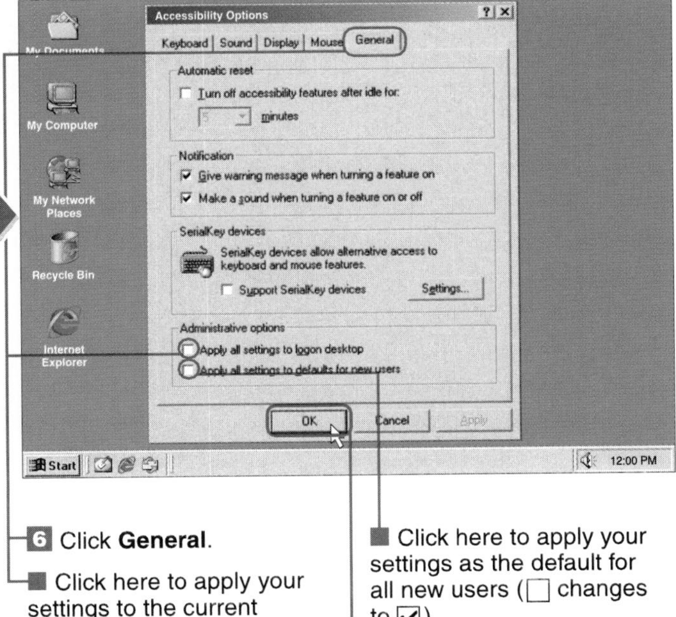

■ The Accessibility Options dialog box appears.

■ You can change the way your keyboard, mouse, and monitor work by using these options.

5 Click the options that suit you (☐ changes to ☑).

6 Click **General**.

■ Click here to apply your settings to the current desktop (☐ changes to ☑).

■ Click here to apply your settings as the default for all new users (☐ changes to ☑).

7 Click **OK**.

SET POWER OPTIONS

Your server uses power options to manage its power usage.

SET POWER OPTIONS

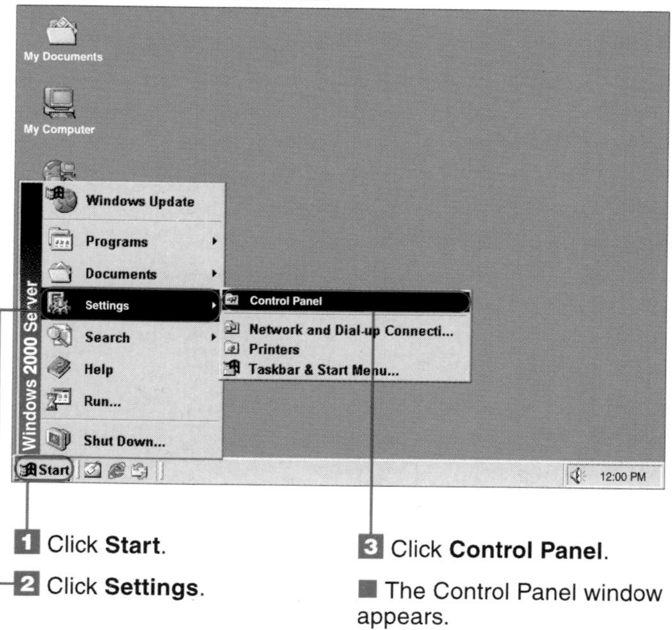

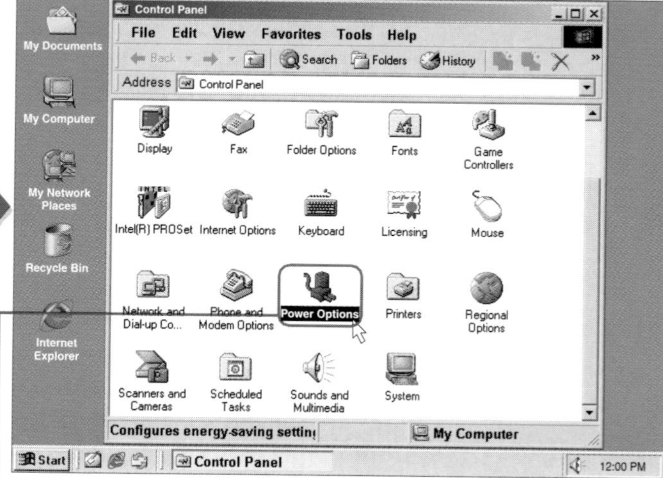

1 Click **Start**.

2 Click **Settings**.

3 Click **Control Panel**.

■ The Control Panel window appears.

4 Double-click **Power Options**.

■ The Power Options Properties dialog box appears.

What does a UPS do?

An uninterruptible power supply (UPS) provides your server with power should your electricity fail. If you want your server available all the time, even when the power fails, consider investing in a UPS.

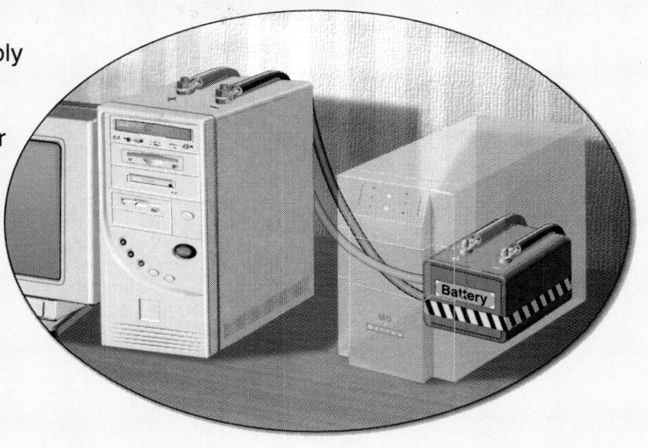

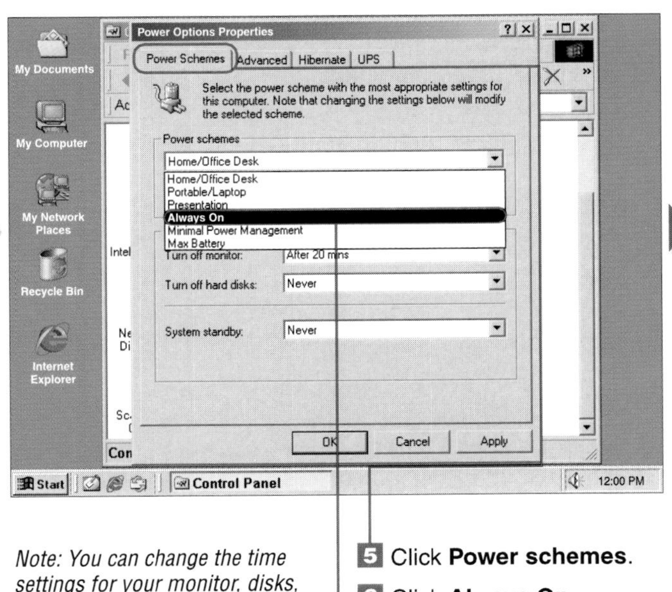

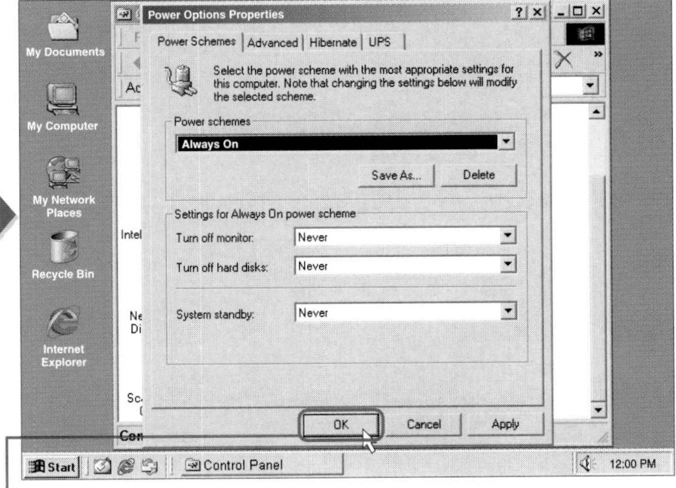

Note: You can change the time settings for your monitor, disks, and system standby.

5 Click **Power schemes**.

6 Click **Always On**.

7 Click **OK**.

CONFIGURE AN UNINTERRUPTIBLE POWER SUPPLY

Windows 2000 Server contains support for various UPS systems and lets you configure them for your particular situation. You can set up the UPS service directly in Windows and use it to automatically inform network users of power failure alerts and other important messages.

CONFIGURE YOUR UPS

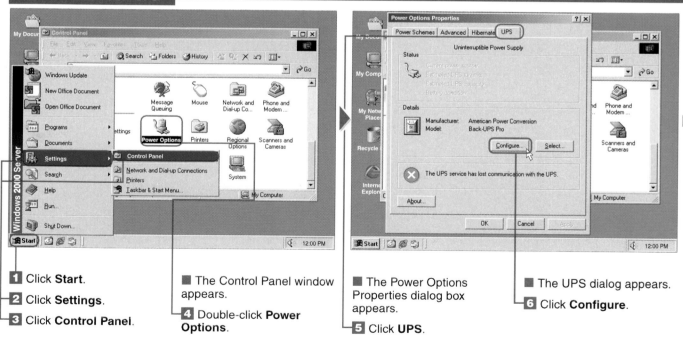

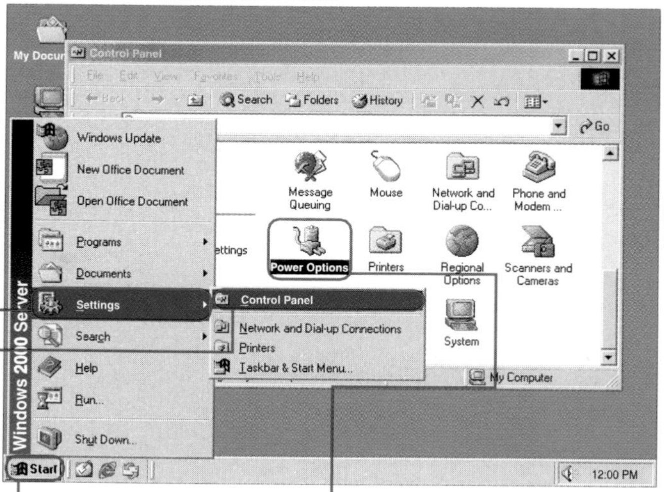

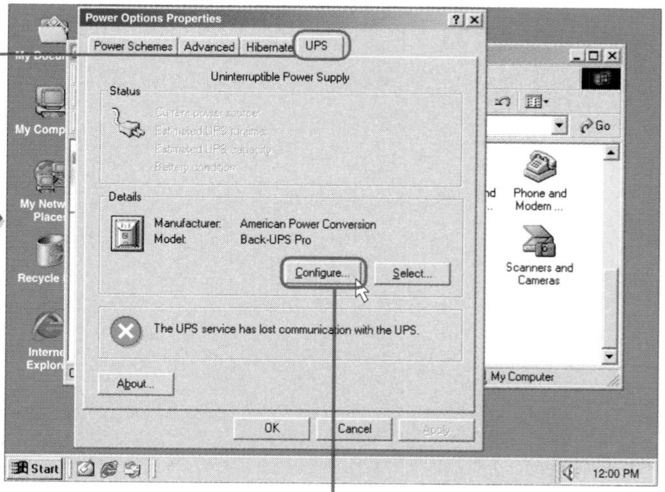

1. Click **Start**.
2. Click **Settings**.
3. Click **Control Panel**.

■ The Control Panel window appears.

4. Double-click **Power Options**.

■ The Power Options Properties dialog box appears.

5. Click **UPS**.

■ The UPS dialog appears.

6. Click **Configure**.

Can I use any UPS with Windows 2000 Server?

Check the Windows Hardware Compatibility List at the Microsoft Web site and check the Web site of your UPS manufacturer to see if your UPS is compatible. If your UPS is not compatible, you may not be able to use it with Windows 2000.

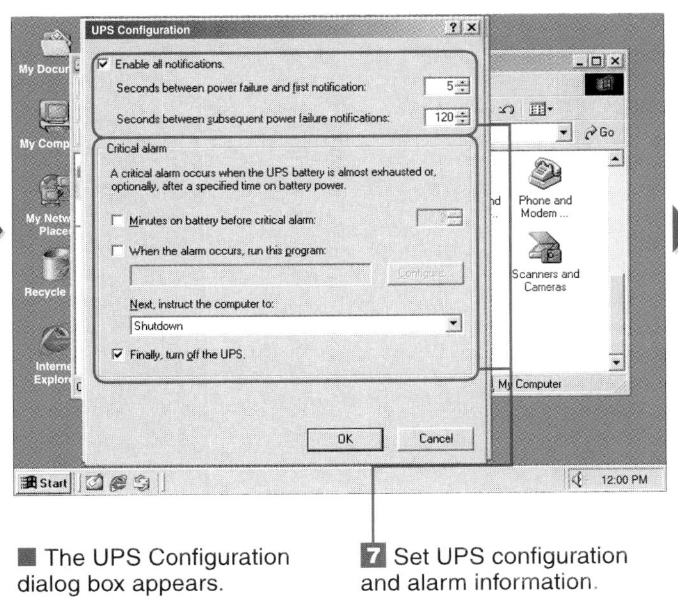

■ The UPS Configuration dialog box appears.

7 Set UPS configuration and alarm information.

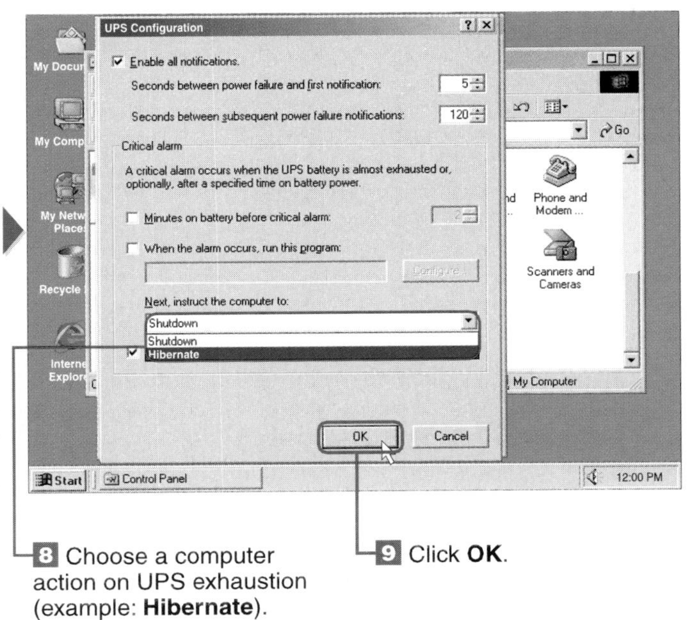

8 Choose a computer action on UPS exhaustion (example: **Hibernate**).

9 Click **OK**.

zip
TRAVAN

CHAPTER 4

Setting Up Network Services

Network Services are the backbone of your business. In this chapter you will see how to install and configure the different types of services you may need.

A network is made up of computers connected together. This makes it easy to share information and to manage the flow of information between people.

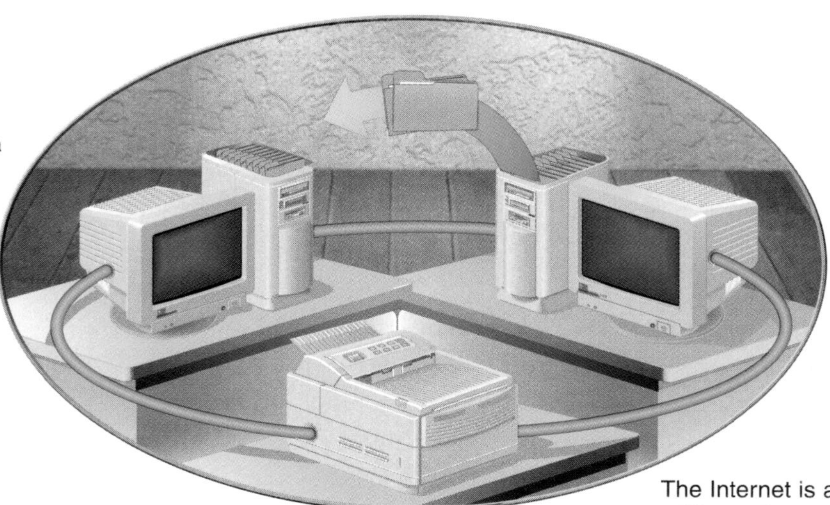

The Internet is a network of millions of computers, all sharing information with one another. It is sometimes called a "network of networks."

EASY TO MANAGE

People usually belong to a common organization at work, such as Sales or Accounting. Networks make it easier to organize information and resources for people in these groups.

COST EFFECTIVE

People can share a printer on a network rather than having to have a printer for each person in your office.

SHARE INFORMATION

Networks make it easy to share information within a group or between groups. This is more effective than walking copies of reports from desk to desk.

UNDERSTANDING NETWORK HARDWARE

All networks require special hardware to communicate.

COMPUTER

You need at least two computers to have a network. These can be of different types, such as Intel, Macintosh, and Sun.

NETWORK INTERFACE CARD

Each computer must have a network interface card (NIC), or network adapter. A NIC physically connects each computer to the network.

TRANSMISSION MEDIUM

Most networks use a special type of cable to connect a computer to a network, such as twisted pair cable. Some small network systems use wireless or infrared waves instead.

HUB

A hub provides a central location for connecting all network cables together. Hubs can come with four, eight, sixteen, or even more ports for network cabling.

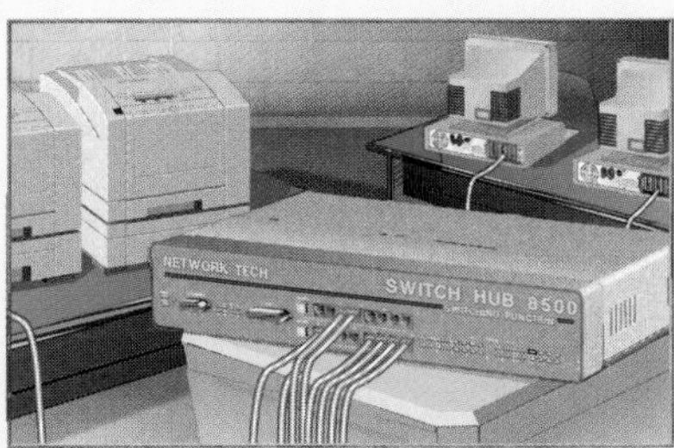

ROUTER, BRIDGE, OR MODEM

Routers, bridges, and modems are used to connect one network with another. Nearly all networks use one of these to connect to the Internet.

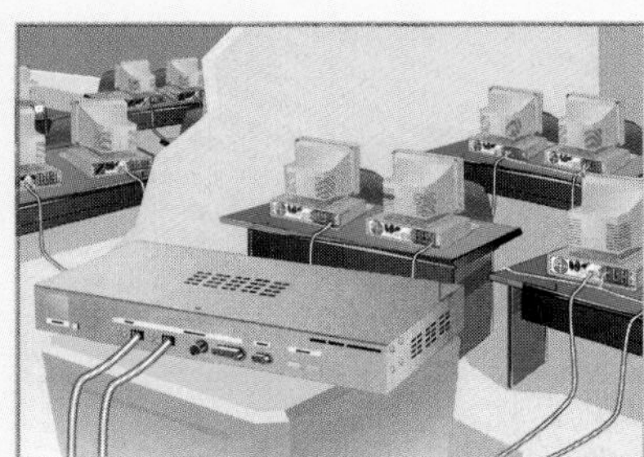

IDENTIFY NETWORK COMPONENTS

Windows 2000 requires four components that allow you to create a network.

ADAPTER

An adapter provides the electrical signal that allows computers to communicate. Examples of adapters include Ethernet card or a modem.

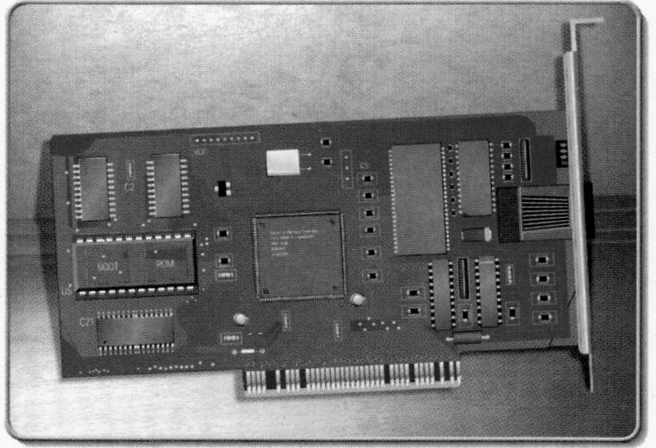

PROTOCOL

A network protocol is a language that is used on a network. Two computers must use the same protocol or they won't be able to communicate with each other.

SERVICE

A network service is something that one computer can do for another computer, such as share files or share a printer.

CLIENT

A network client is used to gain access to network servers. For example, a NetWare client is needed to connect to a NetWare server.

TYPES OF DOMAIN STRUCTURES

Depending on how your network is set up, the computers will be grouped into one of the following domain structures.

WORKGROUP

A workgroup is also called a peer-to-peer network. Each computer is responsible for maintaining its own information, users, and programs. Workgroups are not centrally managed, and they are best for networks with ten or fewer computers in the same office.

DOMAIN

A domain is a Microsoft term for a group of computers that are managed together as a group. User names, passwords, shared printers, and access to files are controlled from a network server called a domain controller.

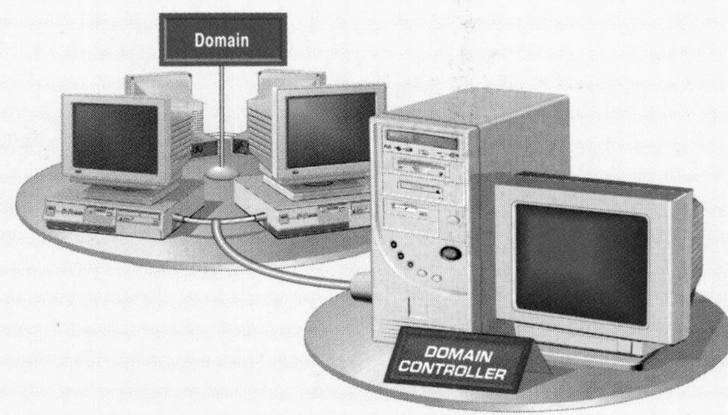

ORGANIZATIONAL UNIT

Organizational units are new with Windows 2000. They are a way of breaking domains down into smaller, more manageable units. An example would be the Sales organization within the MyBigCo domain.

You must collect important information about your network before you can begin installing any network services. Contact your network administrator or Internet service provider if you are not sure about your network's information – do not make any of it up!

If you are positive that you will never connect to another network or the Internet, you can accept the default values that Windows 2000 suggests.

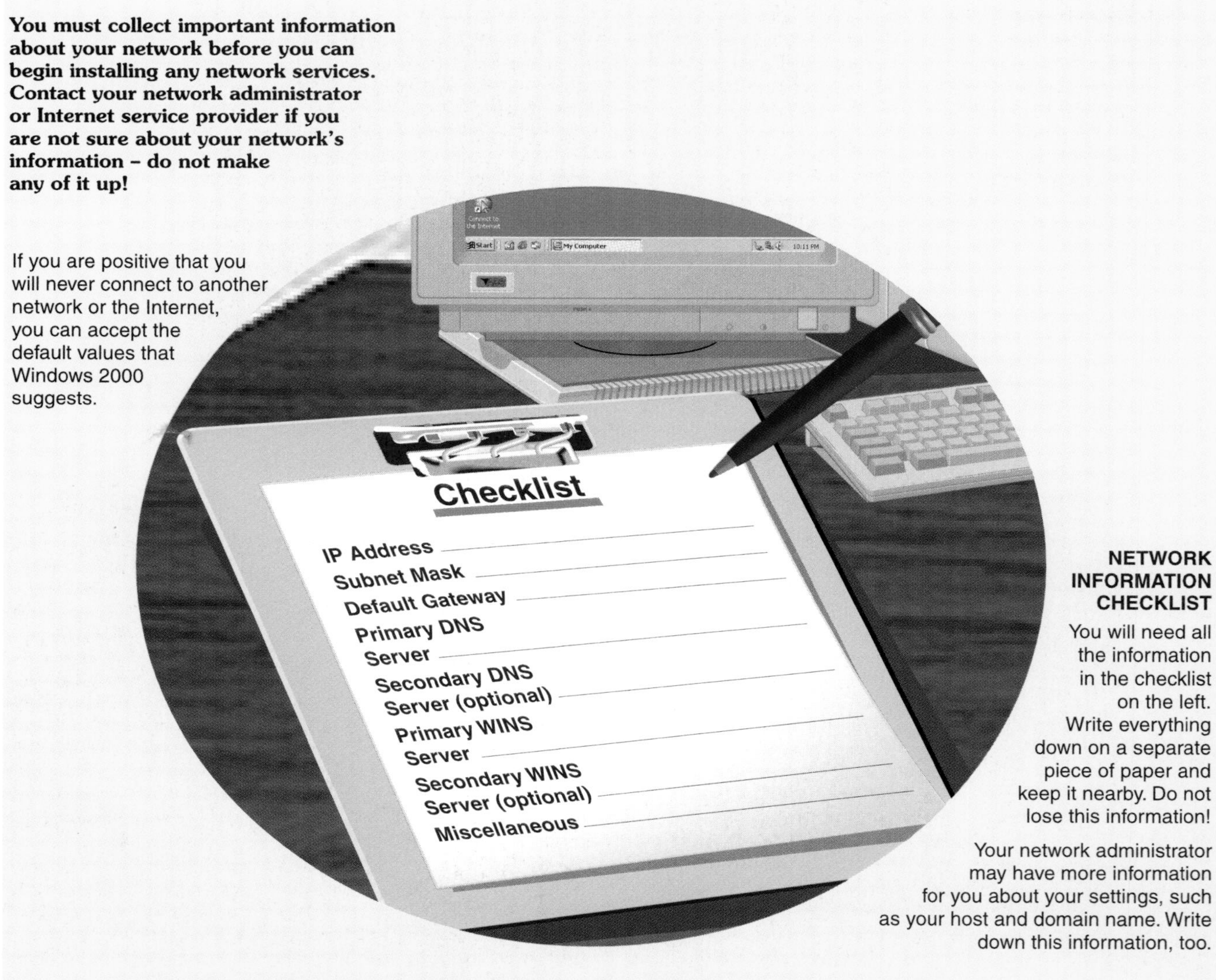

NETWORK INFORMATION CHECKLIST

You will need all the information in the checklist on the left. Write everything down on a separate piece of paper and keep it nearby. Do not lose this information!

Your network administrator may have more information for you about your settings, such as your host and domain name. Write down this information, too.

LAUNCH THE CONFIGURE YOUR SERVER WIZARD

The Configure Your Server Wizard helps you install and configure a variety of services on your server. The wizard asks you for information and will set up the services based on the answers you provide.

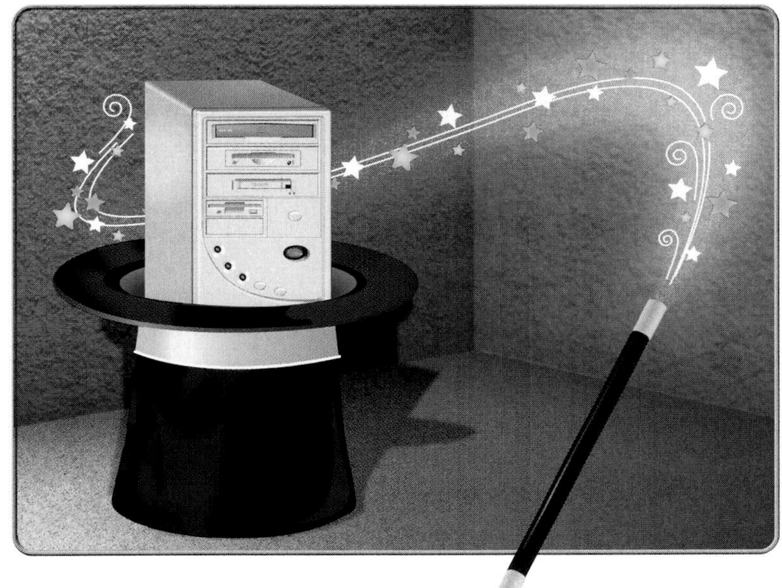

LAUNCH THE CONFIGURE YOUR SERVER WIZARD

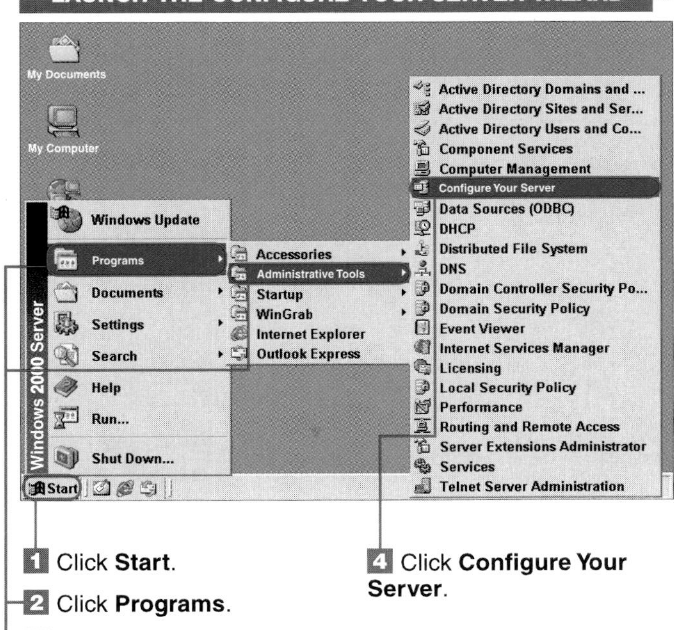

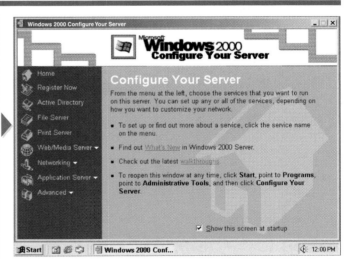

1 Click **Start**.

2 Click **Programs**.

3 Click **Administrative Tools**.

4 Click **Configure Your Server**.

■ The Configure Your Server window appears.

■ Many of the tasks in this chapter and configurations you can make in Windows 2000 are available through the Configure Your Server Wizard.

VIEW TCP/IP

Transmission Control Protocol/Internet Protocol (TCP/IP) allows computers to communicate with one another. Most networks use TCP/IP, including all computers on the Internet.

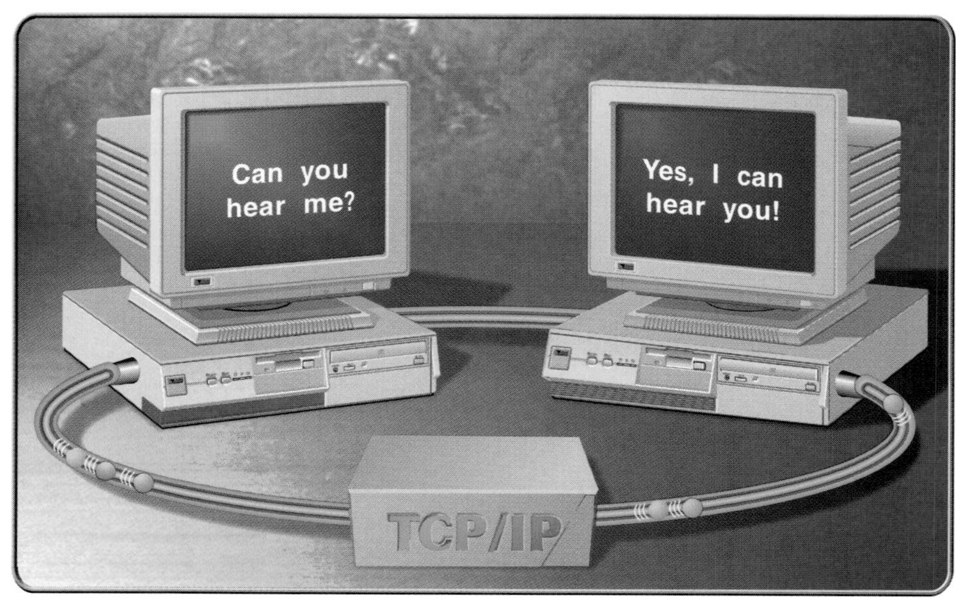

VIEW TCP/IP

1 Click **Start**.

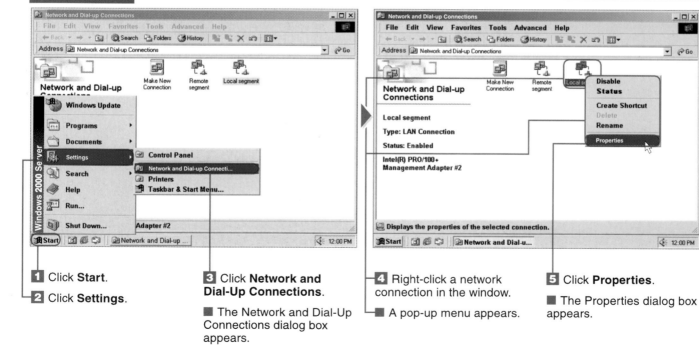

2 Click **Settings**.

3 Click **Network and Dial-Up Connections**.

■ The Network and Dial-Up Connections dialog box appears.

4 Right-click a network connection in the window.

■ A pop-up menu appears.

5 Click **Properties**.

■ The Properties dialog box appears.

Do I need to change any of the settings?

If your computer is already connected to the network and is working, you do not need to change any settings. It would be a good idea to write down the settings you see here just in case you need to reconfigure your server.

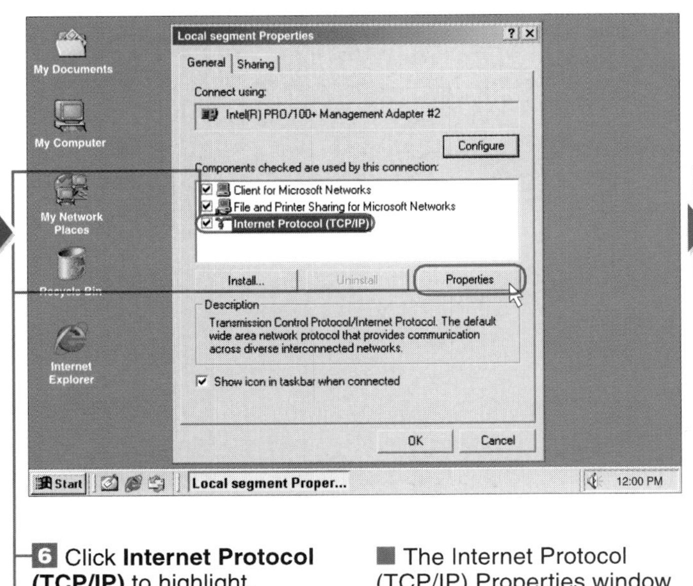

6 Click **Internet Protocol (TCP/IP)** to highlight.

7 Click **Properties**.

■ The Internet Protocol (TCP/IP) Properties window appears.

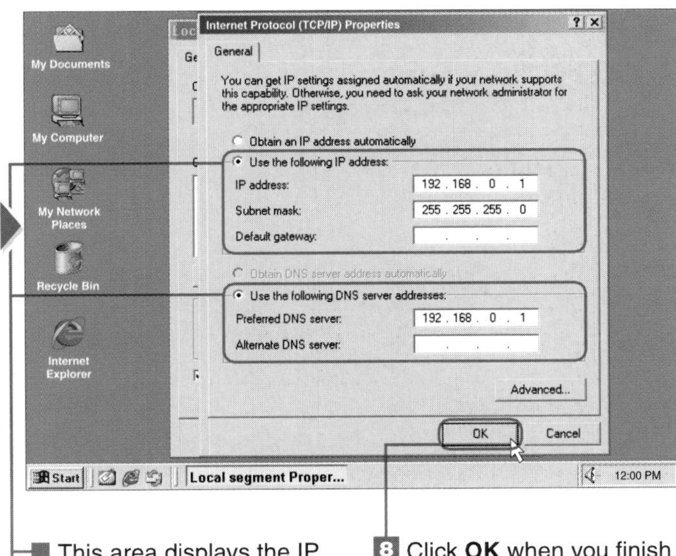

■ This area displays the IP address information.

■ This area displays the DNS server address.

8 Click **OK** when you finish viewing your settings.

INSTALL DHCP

Dynamic Host Configuration Protocol (DHCP) is a service that provides IP addresses and network information to other computers on your network. This makes it easy to maintain other computers without having to visit each one.

In order to run DHCP, you need to have a fixed IP address for your network adapter.

INSTALL DHCP

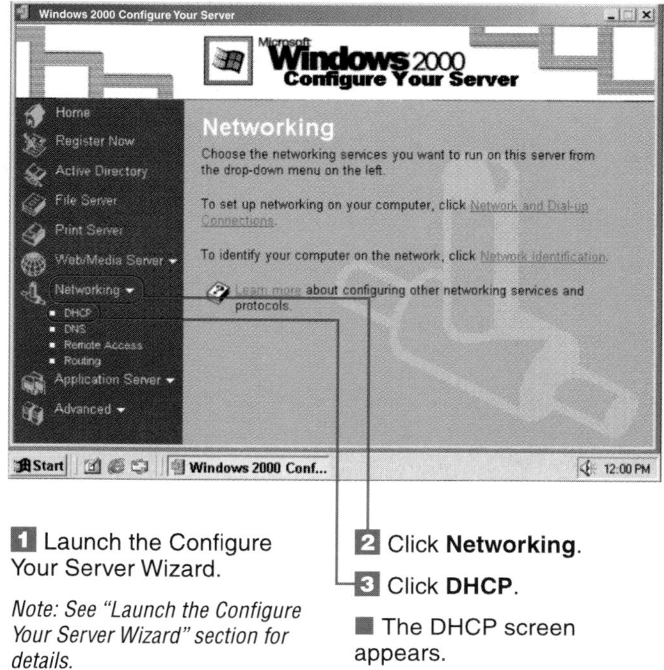

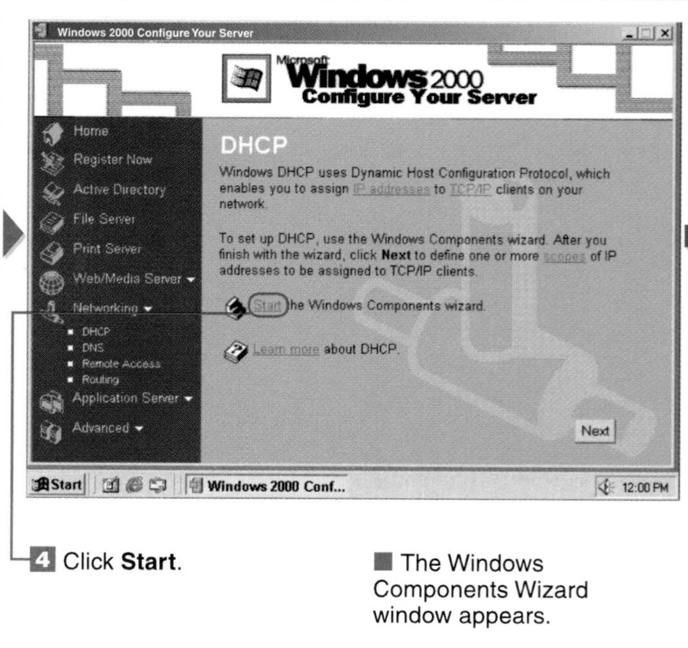

1 Launch the Configure Your Server Wizard.

Note: See "Launch the Configure Your Server Wizard" section for details.

2 Click **Networking**.

3 Click **DHCP**.

■ The DHCP screen appears.

4 Click **Start**.

■ The Windows Components Wizard window appears.

Do I need to set up DHCP on my server?

Check with your administrator to see if you should run DHCP for your network. You can also use Internet Connection Sharing (ICS), which is a much simpler way to provide addresses to computers than DHCP. See Chapter 6 for information on ICS.

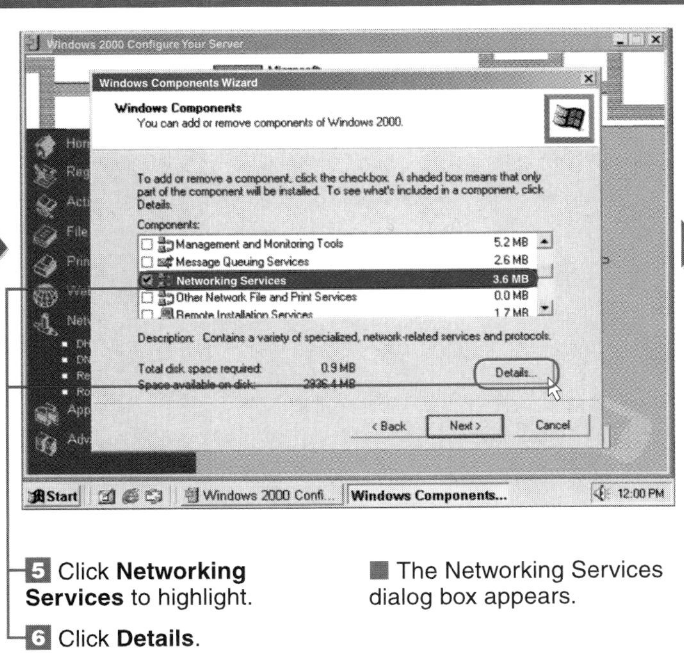

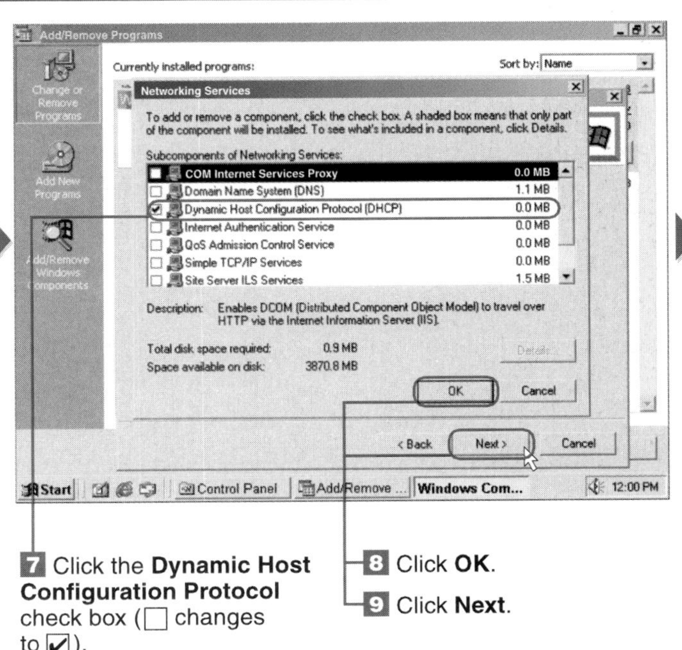

5 Click **Networking Services** to highlight.

6 Click **Details**.

■ The Networking Services dialog box appears.

7 Click the **Dynamic Host Configuration Protocol** check box (☐ changes to ☑).

8 Click **OK**.

9 Click **Next**.

CONTINUED

INSTALL DHCP

You will need the following information for a scope. Check with your network administrator for the settings.

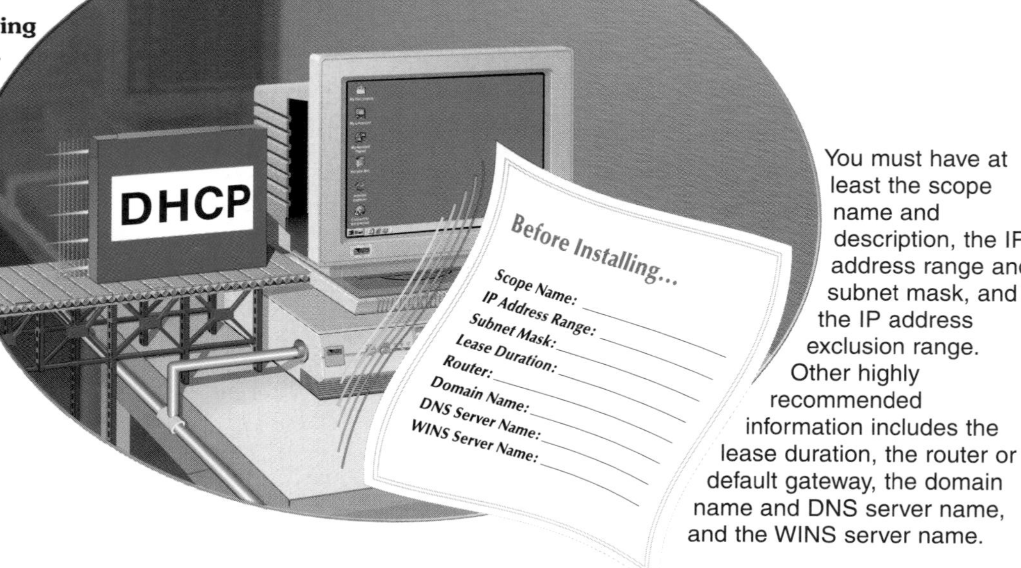

You must have at least the scope name and description, the IP address range and subnet mask, and the IP address exclusion range. Other highly recommended information includes the lease duration, the router or default gateway, the domain name and DNS server name, and the WINS server name.

INSTALL DHCP (CONTINUED)

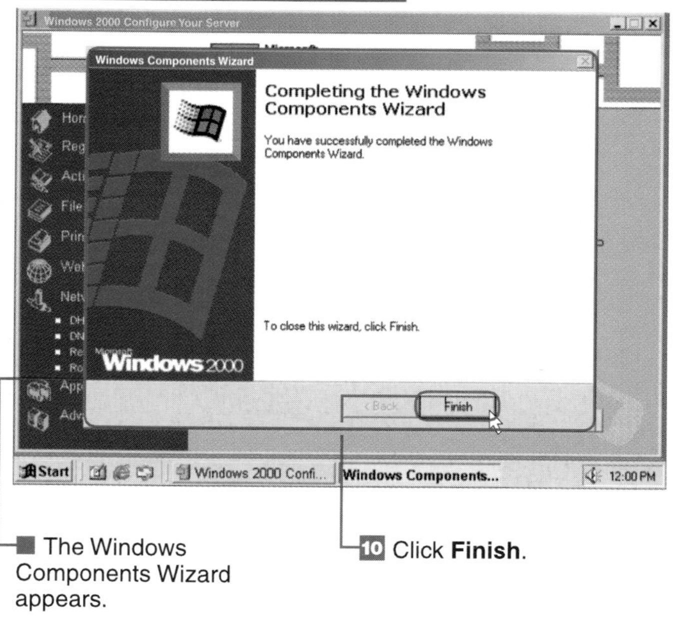

■ The Windows Components Wizard appears.

10 Click **Finish**.

CREATE A DHCP SCOPE

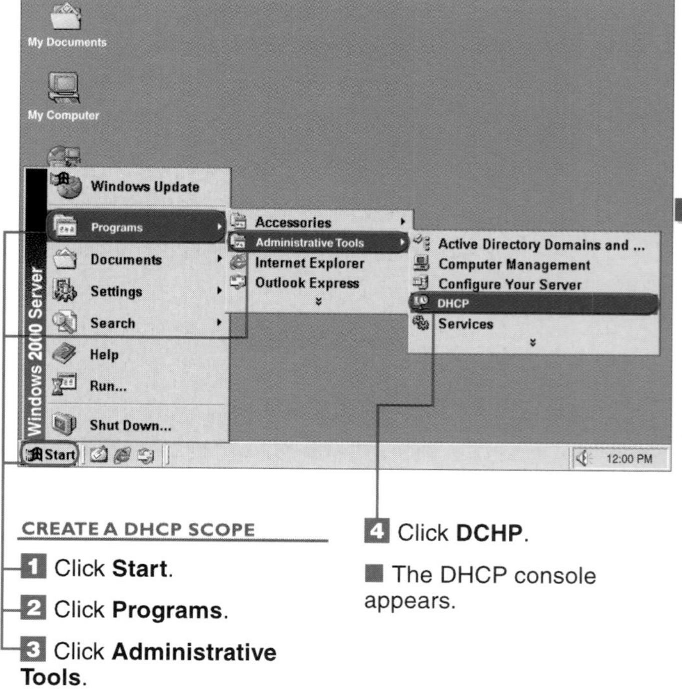

CREATE A DHCP SCOPE

1 Click **Start**.

2 Click **Programs**.

3 Click **Administrative Tools**.

4 Click **DCHP**.

■ The DHCP console appears.

What does a scope do?

DHCP scopes are used to group addresses and network information together. This makes it easy to use a common group of settings for groups of computers on a network.

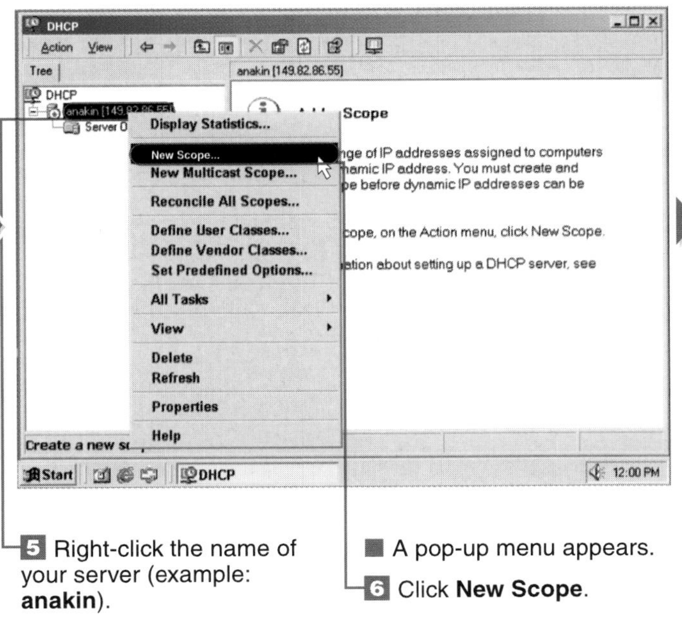

5 Right-click the name of your server (example: **anakin**).

■ A pop-up menu appears.

6 Click **New Scope**.

■ The New Scope Wizard appears.

7 Click **Next**.

CONTINUED

TCP/IP addresses are always four sets of numbers that range from 0 to 255, with each set separated by periods. An example is 192.168.1.254.

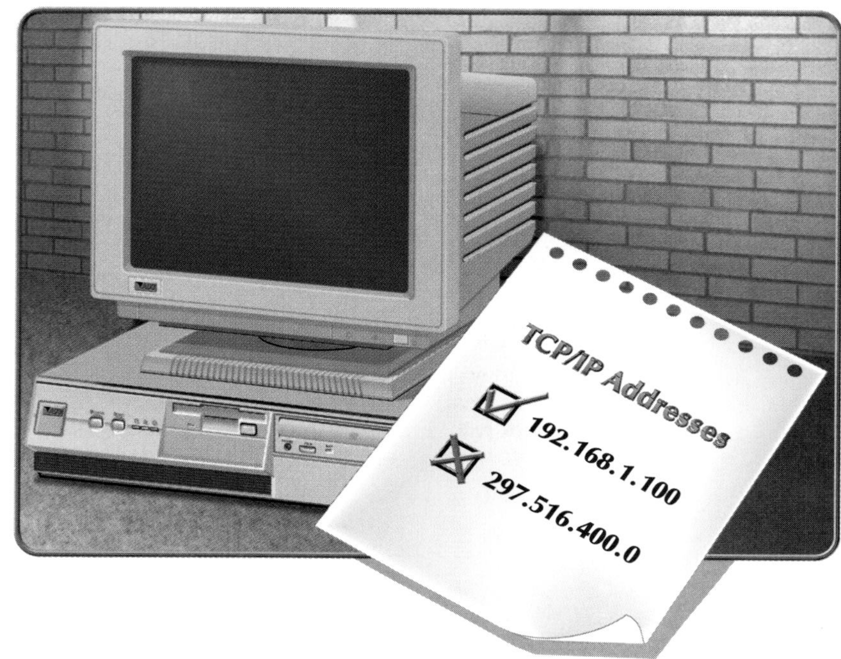

You should avoid using 0 or 255 as any of the numbers unless you have been instructed to do so by your network administrator. Those numbers are often used for special purposes on the network and should not be used by computers or servers.

CREATE A DHCP SCOPE (CONTINUED)

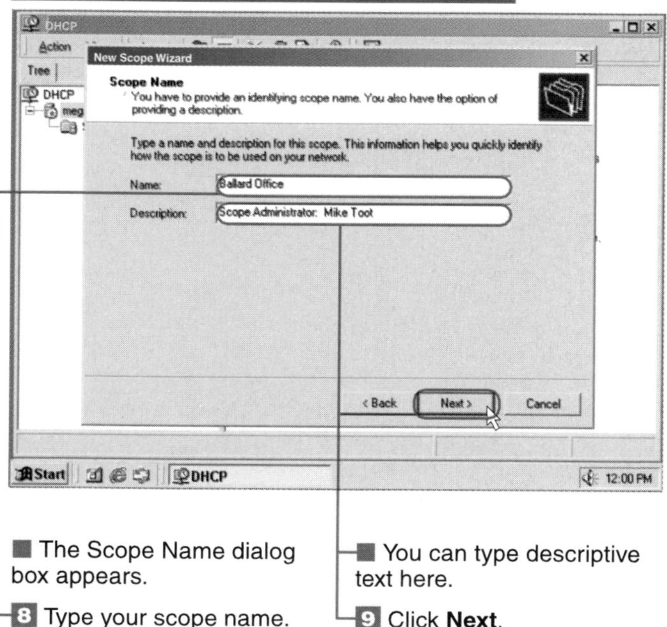

■ The Scope Name dialog box appears.

8 Type your scope name.

■ You can type descriptive text here.

9 Click **Next**.

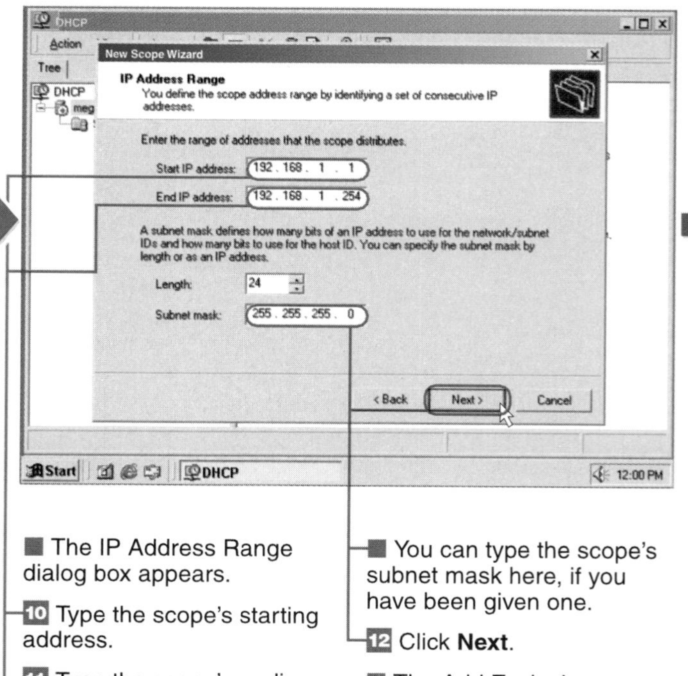

■ The IP Address Range dialog box appears.

10 Type the scope's starting address.

11 Type the scope's ending address.

■ You can type the scope's subnet mask here, if you have been given one.

12 Click **Next**.

■ The Add Exclusions dialog box appears.

What IP addresses should I exclude from the DHCP scope?

You should exclude the IP addresses for any devices with static IP addresses that provide networking services, such as your DHCP server, your router or gateway, your DNS server, and your domain controller. You may have others, such as printers, that meet this requirement; check with your network administrator for details.

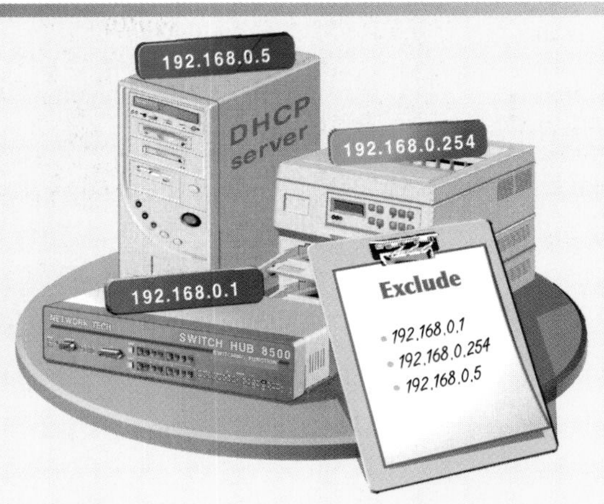

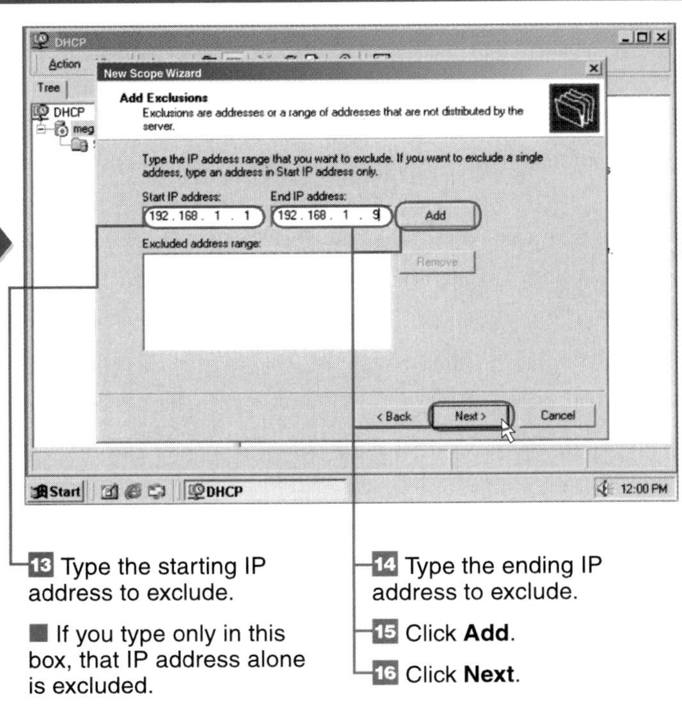

13 Type the starting IP address to exclude.

■ If you type only in this box, that IP address alone is excluded.

14 Type the ending IP address to exclude.

15 Click **Add**.

16 Click **Next**.

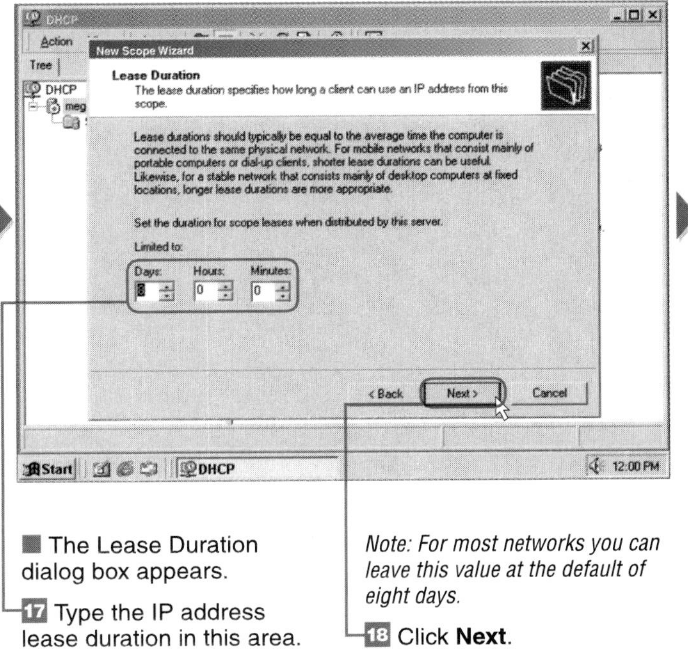

■ The Lease Duration dialog box appears.

17 Type the IP address lease duration in this area.

Note: For most networks you can leave this value at the default of eight days.

18 Click **Next**.

CONTINUED

DHCP provides important network information to computers on your network. This information helps your users log on to your network, locate resources such as servers and printers, and gain access to the Internet.

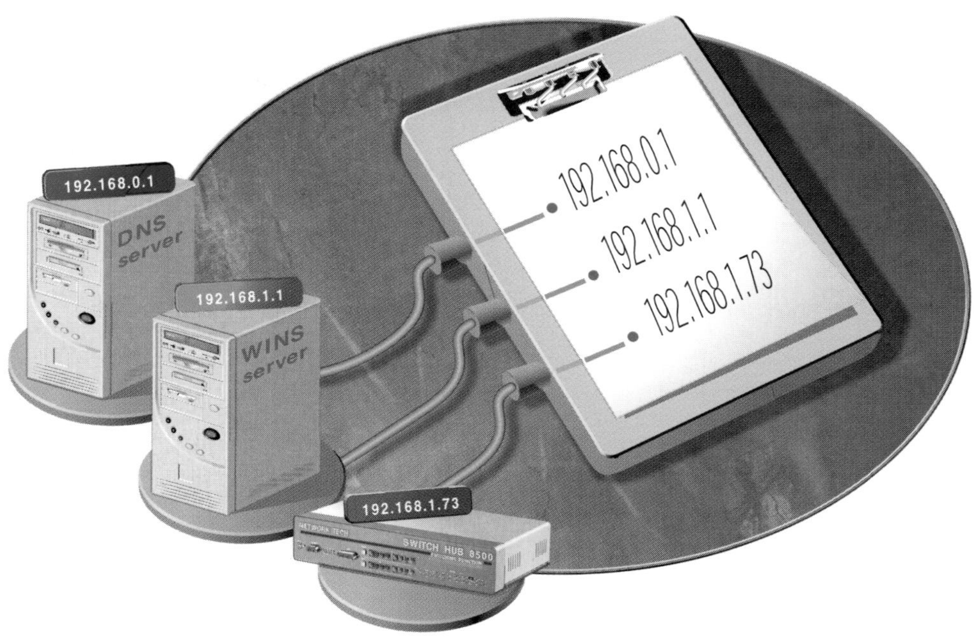

CREATE A DHCP SCOPE (CONTINUED)

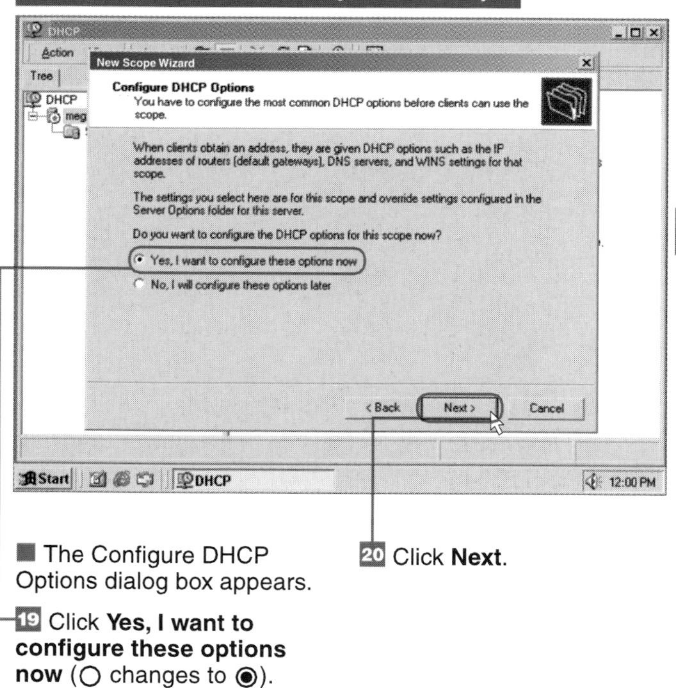

■ The Configure DHCP Options dialog box appears.

19 Click **Yes, I want to configure these options now** (○ changes to ◉).

20 Click **Next**.

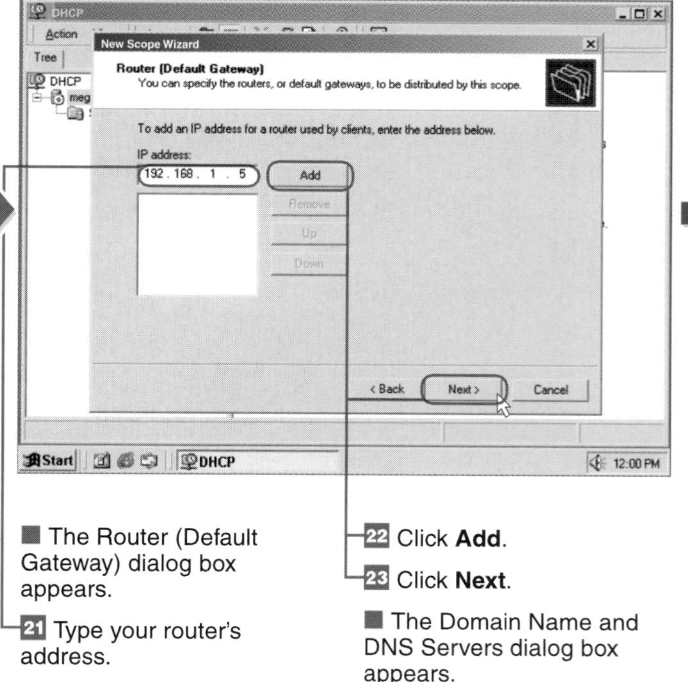

■ The Router (Default Gateway) dialog box appears.

21 Type your router's address.

22 Click **Add**.

23 Click **Next**.

■ The Domain Name and DNS Servers dialog box appears.

Do I need to have both DNS and WINS servers on my network?

You will need a DNS server in nearly all cases; you will need a WINS server if you have non–Windows 2000 computers on your network. The servers do not need to be on separate machines — many smaller networks run DHCP, DNS, and WINS on one domain controller. But if you have more than fifty users, you should install some of these services on another server.

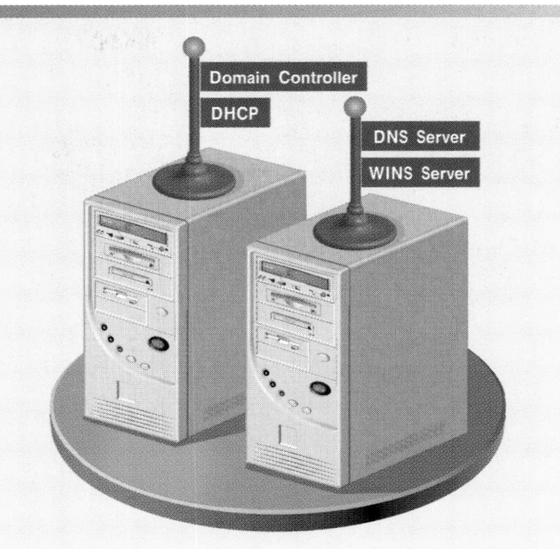

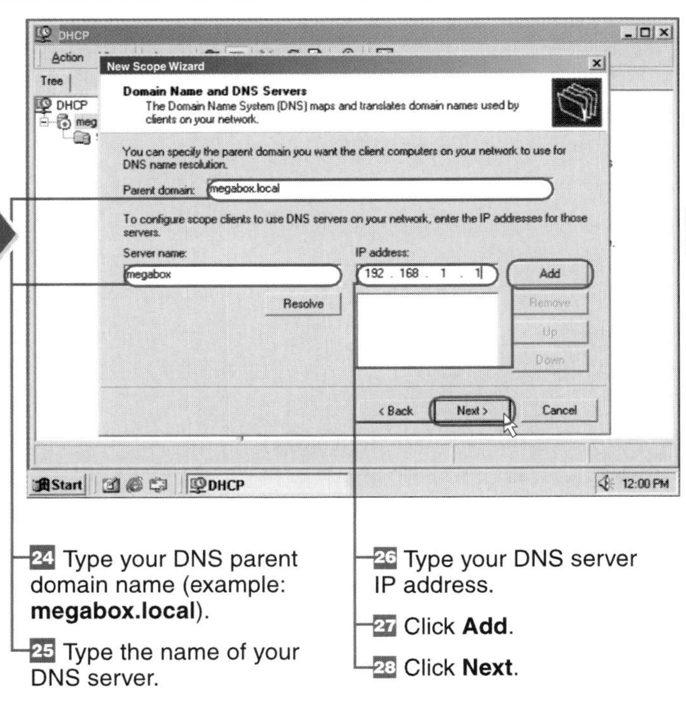

24 Type your DNS parent domain name (example: **megabox.local**).

25 Type the name of your DNS server.

26 Type your DNS server IP address.

27 Click **Add**.

28 Click **Next**.

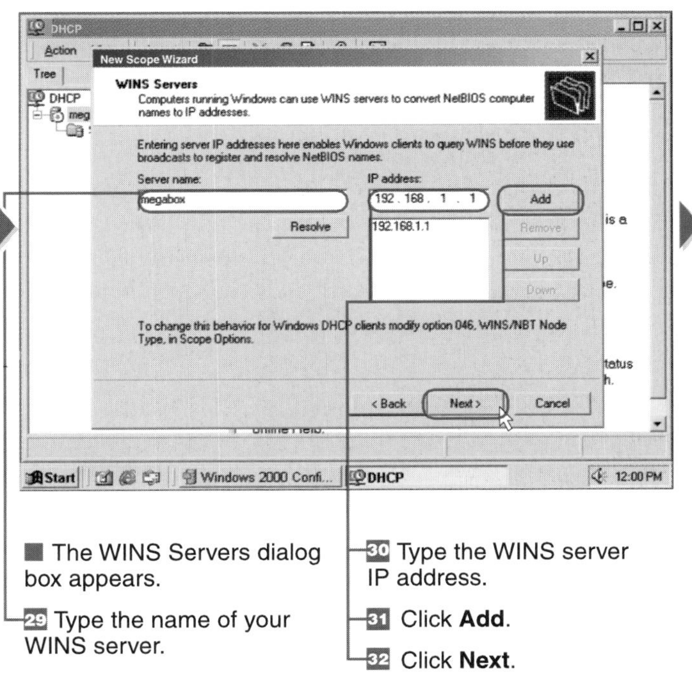

■ The WINS Servers dialog box appears.

29 Type the name of your WINS server.

30 Type the WINS server IP address.

31 Click **Add**.

32 Click **Next**.

CONTINUED

Before your server can hand out IP addresses, you must authorize your server. If you're running Active Directory, you must be a member of the Enterprise Administrators to do this.

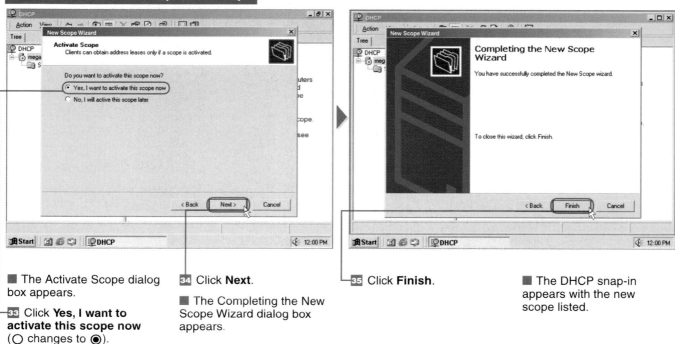

CREATE A DHCP SCOPE (CONTINUED)

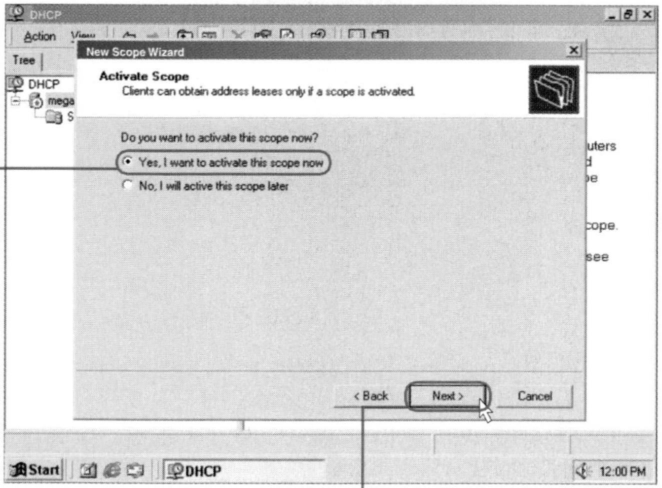

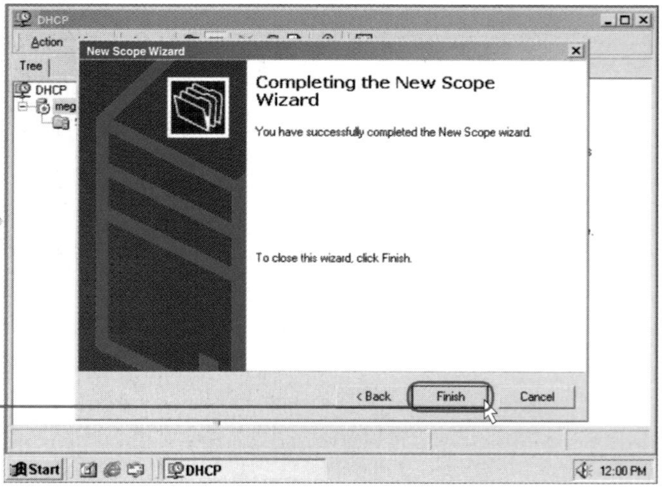

■ The Activate Scope dialog box appears.

33 Click **Yes, I want to activate this scope now** (○ changes to ◉).

34 Click **Next**.

■ The Completing the New Scope Wizard dialog box appears.

35 Click **Finish**.

■ The DHCP snap-in appears with the new scope listed.

How do I authorize my DHCP Server?

If you are running Active Directory, you need to click **Action** and then **Authorize** in the menu. If you are not running Active Directory, press the F5 key to refresh your display. The server should show a green upward-pointing arrow.

VIEW DHCP SETTINGS

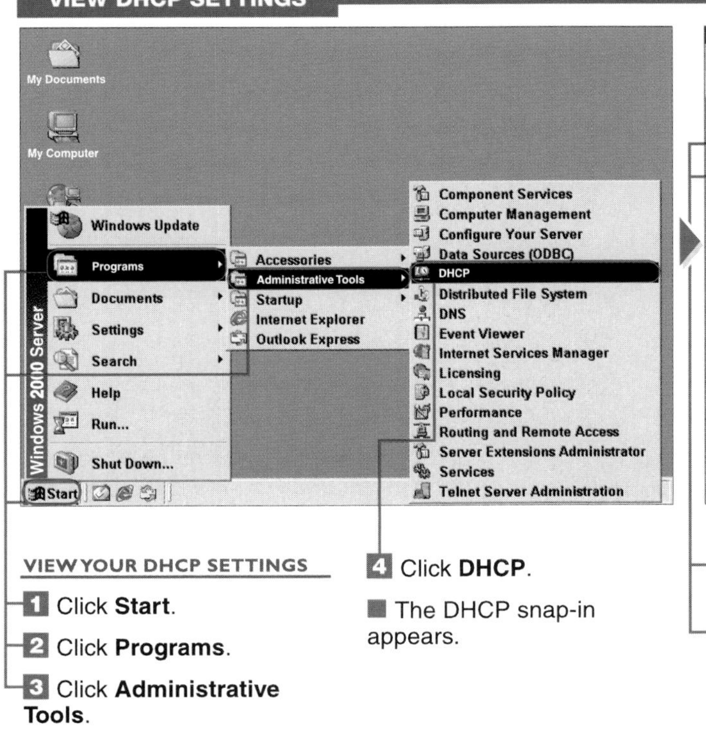

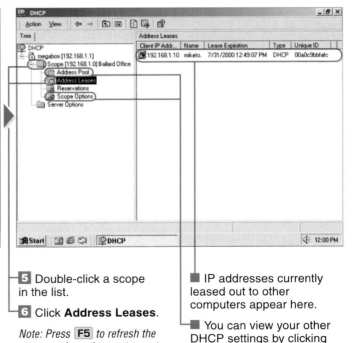

VIEW YOUR DHCP SETTINGS

1 Click **Start**.

2 Click **Programs**.

3 Click **Administrative Tools**.

4 Click **DHCP**.

■ The DHCP snap-in appears.

5 Double-click a scope in the list.

6 Click **Address Leases**.

Note: Press F5 to refresh the screen and see the most recent updates.

■ IP addresses currently leased out to other computers appear here.

■ You can view your other DHCP settings by clicking **Address Pool** and **Scope Options**.

INSTALL DNS

Domain Name Service (DNS) is used to provide names and IP addresses for computers on the Internet.

DNS works just like calling a telephone operator who provides you with a person's phone number if you know their name, and vice versa.

INSTALL DNS

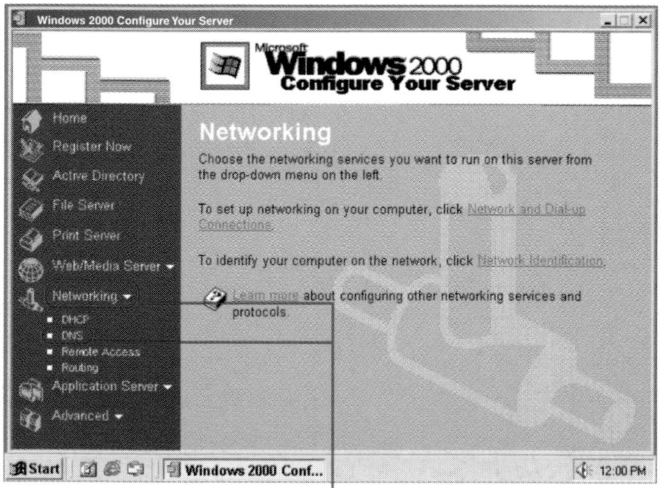

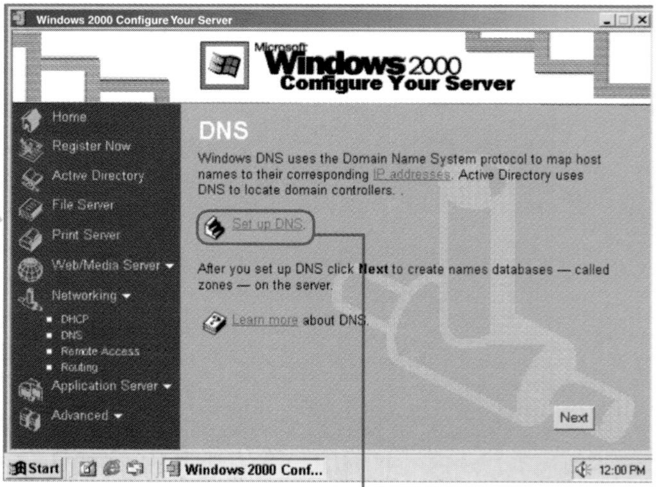

1 Launch the Configure Your Server Wizard.

Note: See "Launch the Configure Your Server Wizard" section for details.

■ The Configure Your Server window appears.

2 Click **Networking**.

3 Click **DNS**.

■ The DNS dialog box appears.

4 Click **Set up DNS**.

Do I need to run DNS on my server?

Maybe. If you plan on running Active Directory, you will need a DNS server somewhere on your network. You may need a DNS server if you plan on connecting to the Internet. Check with your ISP to see if you can use their DNS server instead of configuring and running one yourself.

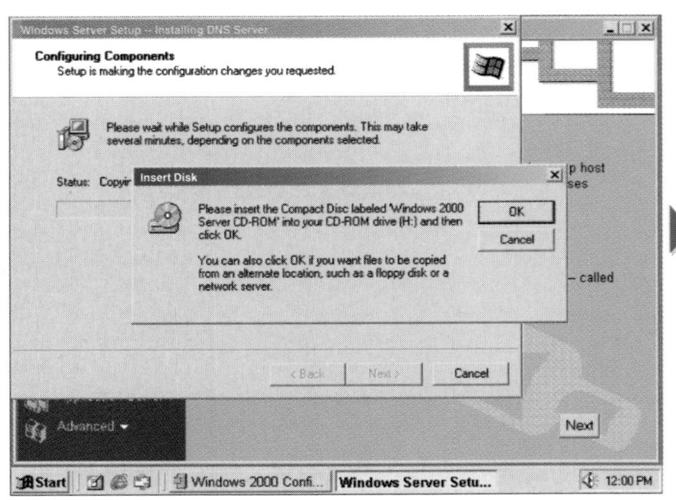

*Note: If the Insert Disk dialog box appears, put your Windows 2000 Server CD in your CD-ROM drive and click **OK**.*

■ After files are copied to your drive, the DNS dialog box appears again.

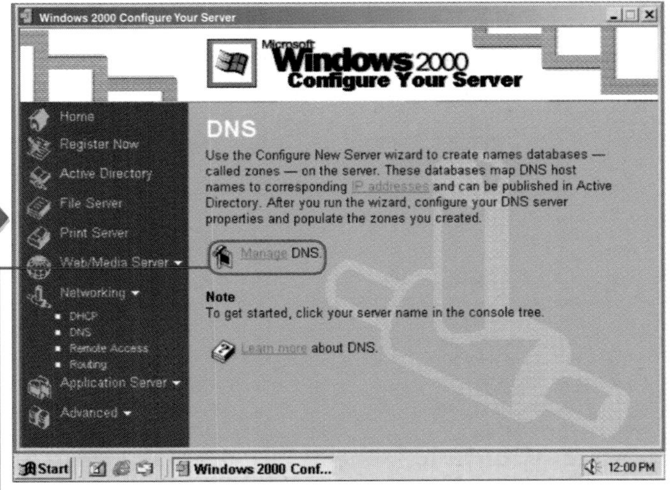

5 Click **Manage** DNS.

CONTINUED

Domain name resolution can be complex, especially when there are other DNS servers in your environment. This task configures the simplest form of DNS for a small network.

Consult with a network professional or your network administrator before setting up DNS on your network. There may be special settings you will need for your server for it to function properly.

INSTALL DNS (CONTINUED)

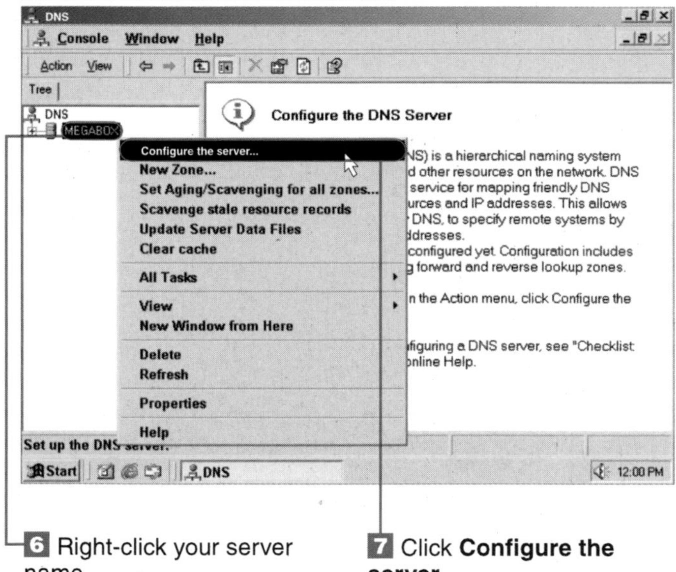

6 Right-click your server name.

■ A pop-up menu appears.

7 Click **Configure the server**.

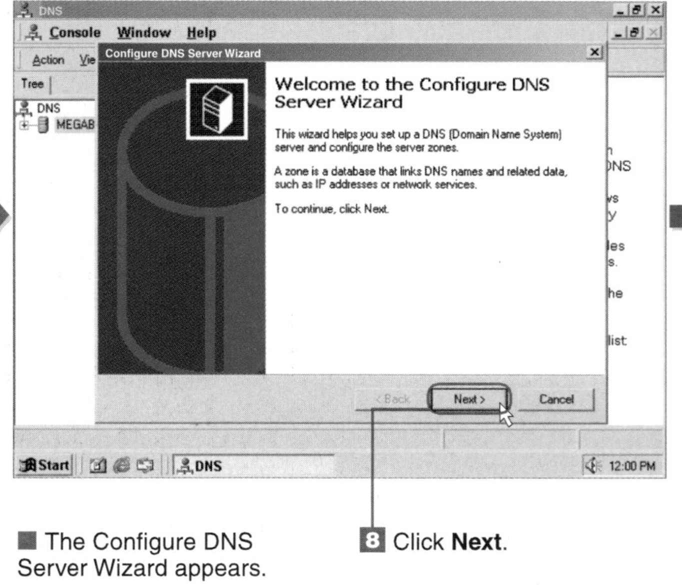

■ The Configure DNS Server Wizard appears.

8 Click **Next**.

What is the difference between forward lookup zones and reverse lookup zones?

Forward lookup zones help resolve domain names into IP addresses, such as www.mybigco.com into 192.168.1.1. Reverse lookup zones help resolve IP addresses into names, such as 192.168.1.10 into miketo.mybigco.com. Both are used to help find machines and services on the Internet and on local networks.

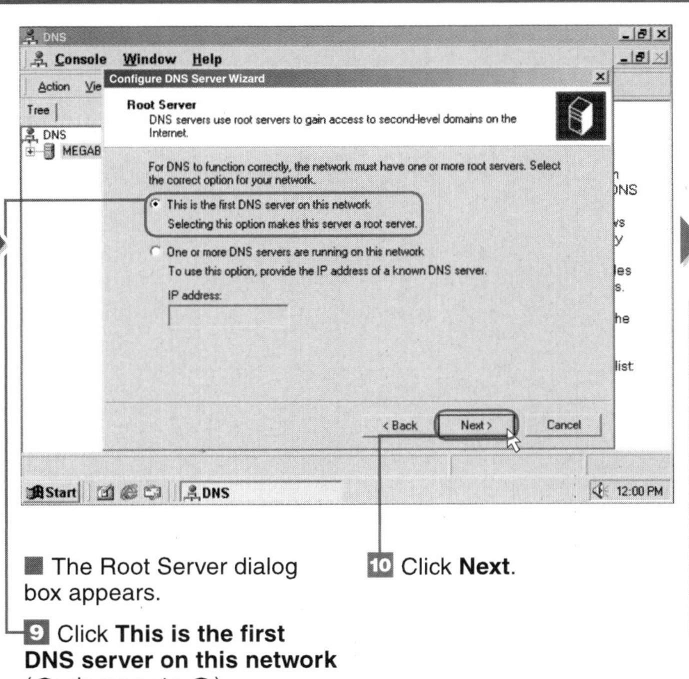

■ The Root Server dialog box appears.

9 Click **This is the first DNS server on this network** (○ changes to ◉).

10 Click **Next**.

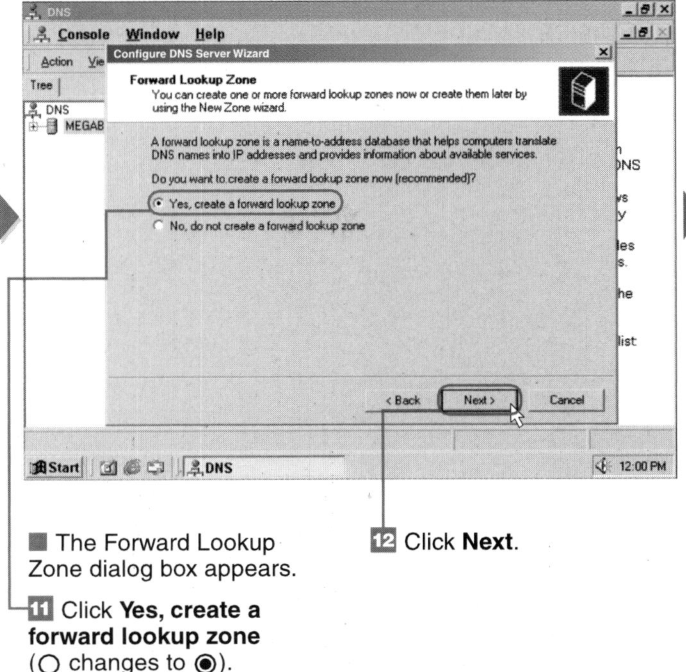

■ The Forward Lookup Zone dialog box appears.

11 Click **Yes, create a forward lookup zone** (○ changes to ◉).

12 Click **Next**.

CONTINUED

DNS works by maintaining lists of servers and corresponding IP addresses.

INSTALL DNS (CONTINUED)

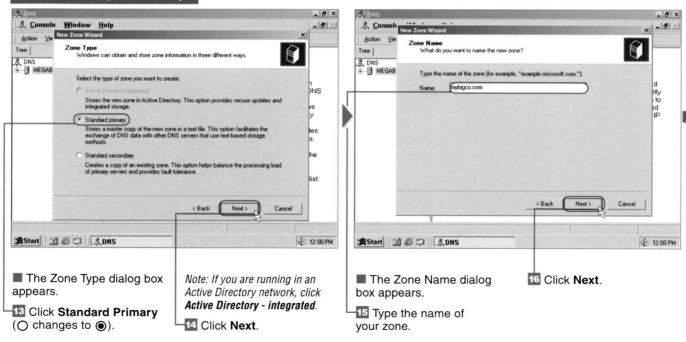

■ The Zone Type dialog box appears.

13 Click **Standard Primary** (○ changes to ◉).

Note: If you are running in an Active Directory network, click ***Active Directory - integrated****.*

14 Click **Next**.

■ The Zone Name dialog box appears.

15 Type the name of your zone.

16 Click **Next**.

What should I call my DNS zone?

If you are setting up DNS for a small office that will connect to the Internet, use your domain name as the zone name — for example, **mybigco.com**. Otherwise, you should use a zone name that you have been given by your network administrator.

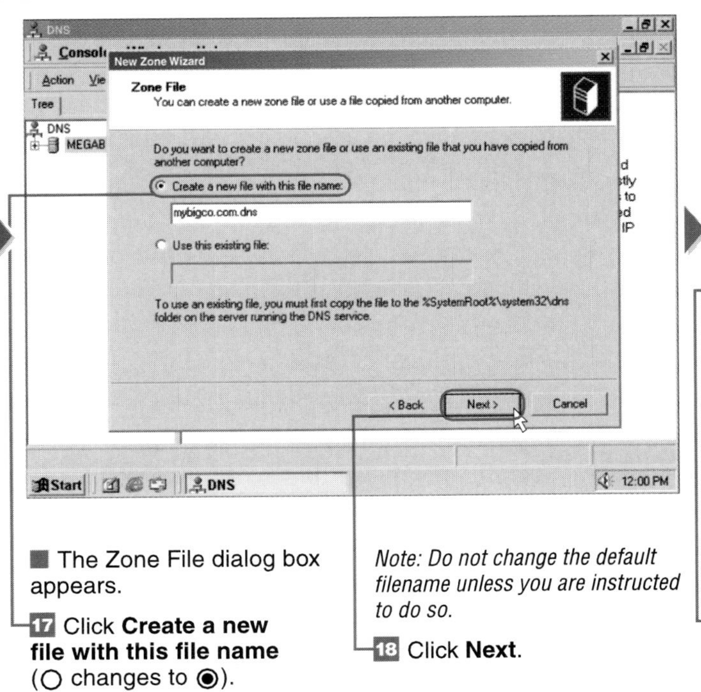

■ The Zone File dialog box appears.

17 Click **Create a new file with this file name** (○ changes to ◉).

Note: Do not change the default filename unless you are instructed to do so.

18 Click **Next**.

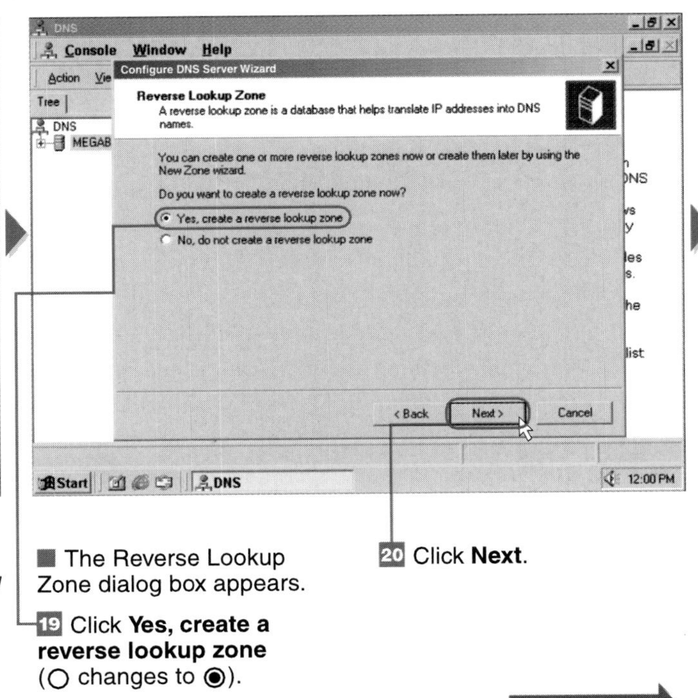

■ The Reverse Lookup Zone dialog box appears.

19 Click **Yes, create a reverse lookup zone** (○ changes to ◉).

20 Click **Next**.

CONTINUED

DNS also helps you find computers on your local network. Frequently accessed resources are manually added in so they are always available.

INSTALL DNS (CONTINUED)

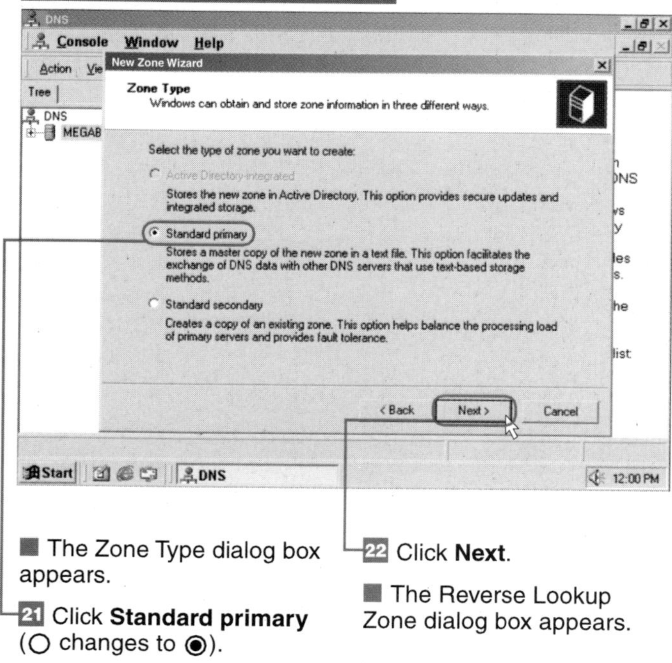

■ The Zone Type dialog box appears.

21 Click **Standard primary** (○ changes to ◉).

*Note: If you are running in an Active Directory network, click **Active Directory - integrated**.*

22 Click **Next**.

■ The Reverse Lookup Zone dialog box appears.

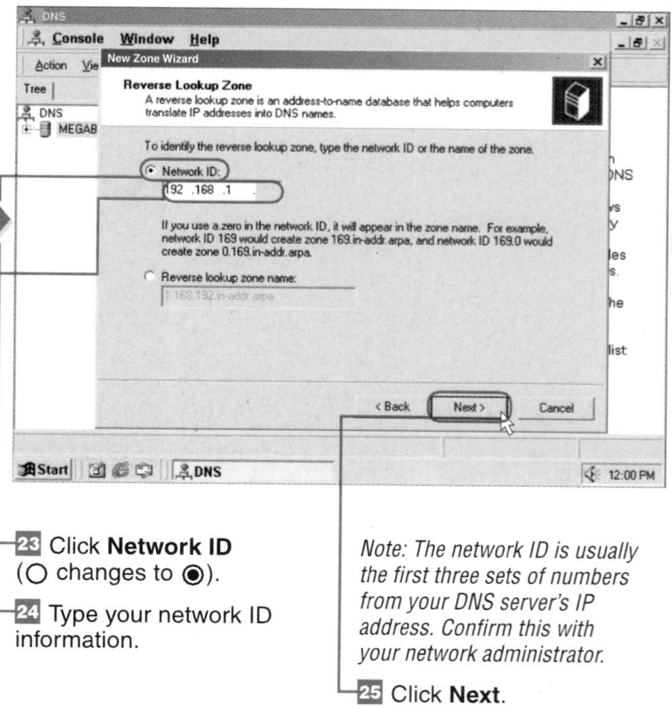

23 Click **Network ID** (○ changes to ◉).

24 Type your network ID information.

Note: The network ID is usually the first three sets of numbers from your DNS server's IP address. Confirm this with your network administrator.

25 Click **Next**.

I'm finding all this very confusing; is there somewhere I can go for more information?

The Windows 2000 Server help files contain a lot of useful information on general concepts, setup checklists, best practices, and troubleshooters. Check the help file under Networking and DNS for more information.

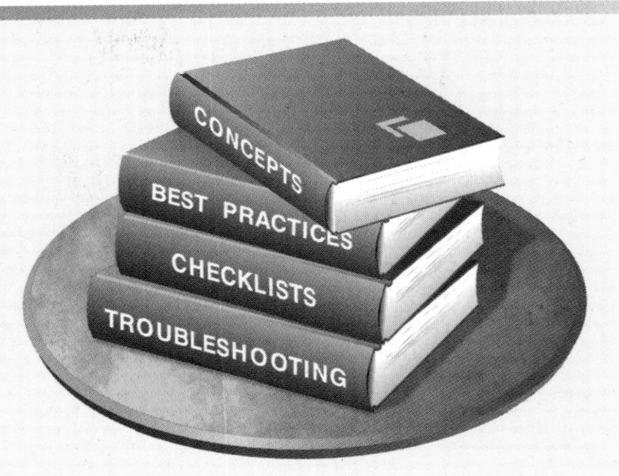

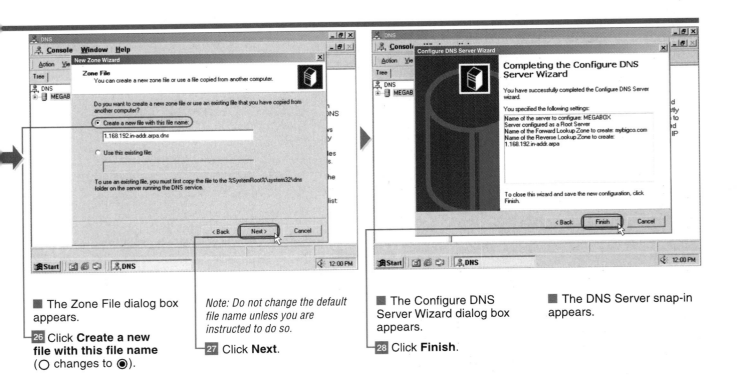

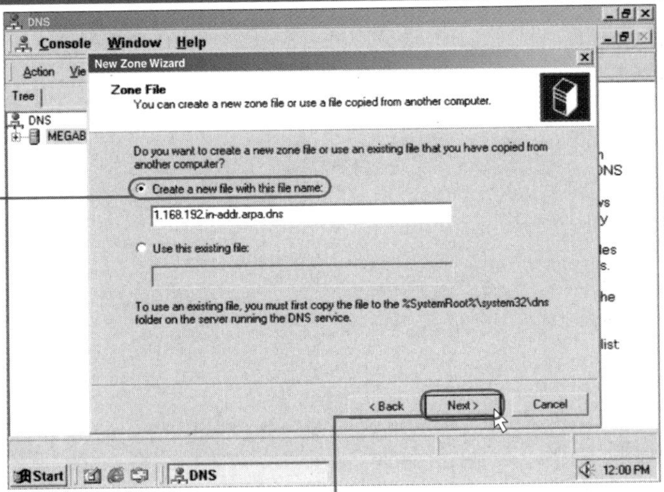

■ The Zone File dialog box appears.

26 Click **Create a new file with this file name** (○ changes to ◉).

Note: Do not change the default file name unless you are instructed to do so.

27 Click **Next**.

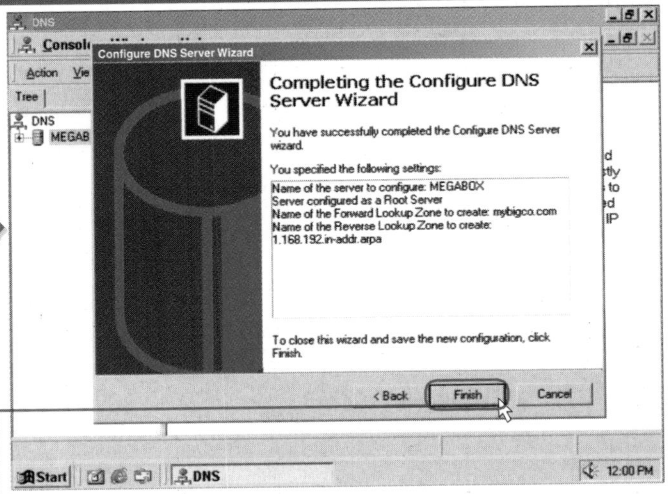

■ The Configure DNS Server Wizard dialog box appears.

28 Click **Finish**.

■ The DNS Server snap-in appears.

INSTALL WINS

Windows Internet Naming Service (WINS) is similar to DNS. It provides names and IP addresses to computers running older versions of networking software.

You only need to install WINS if you have older versions of Windows on your network, like Windows 98 or Windows NT.

INSTALL WINS

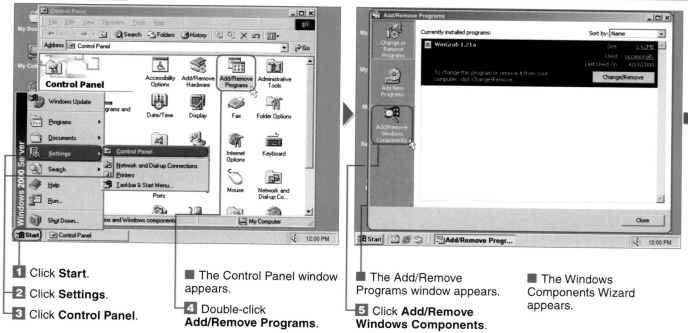

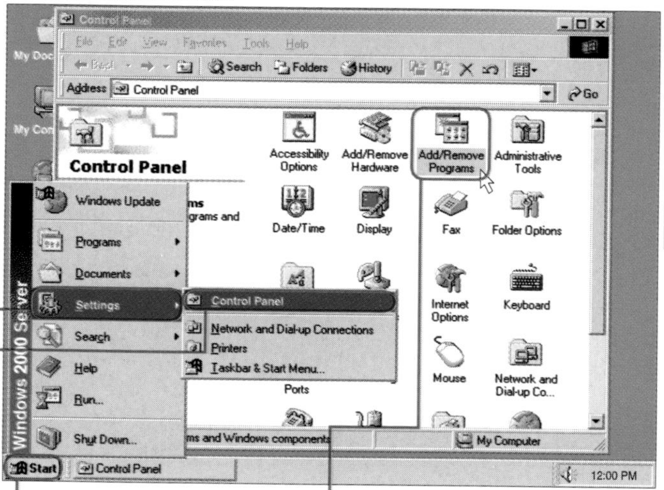

1 Click **Start**.

2 Click **Settings**.

3 Click **Control Panel**.

■ The Control Panel window appears.

4 Double-click **Add/Remove Programs**.

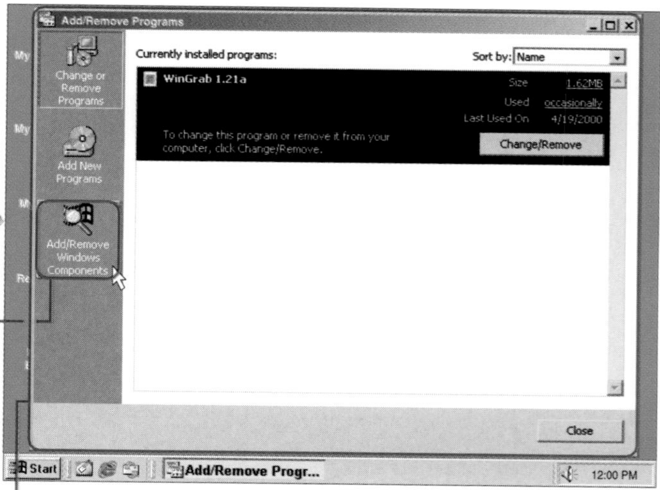

■ The Add/Remove Programs window appears.

5 Click **Add/Remove Windows Components**.

■ The Windows Components Wizard appears.

How does WINS differ from DNS?

WINS uses a different type of network protocol to resolve names than does DNS. WINS uses the NetBIOS protocol. NetBIOS was used on early networks with fewer numbers of computers. Today's larger networks need more powerful services like DNS to handle thousands of client requests.

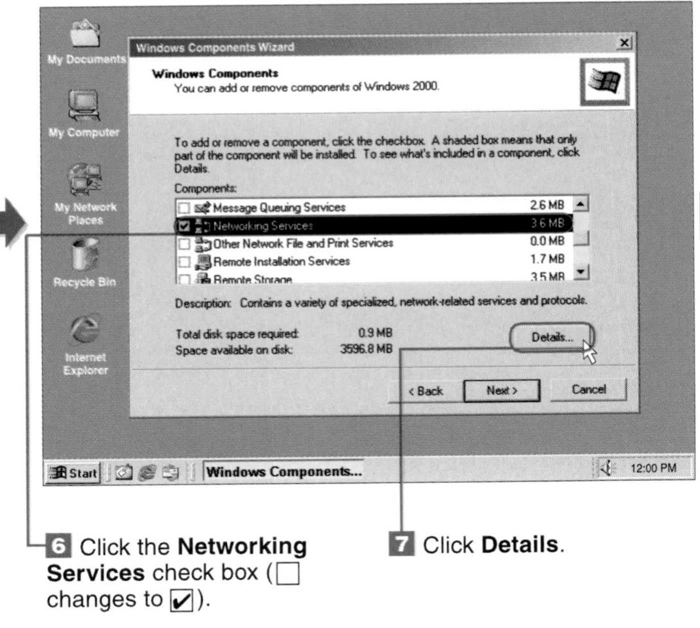

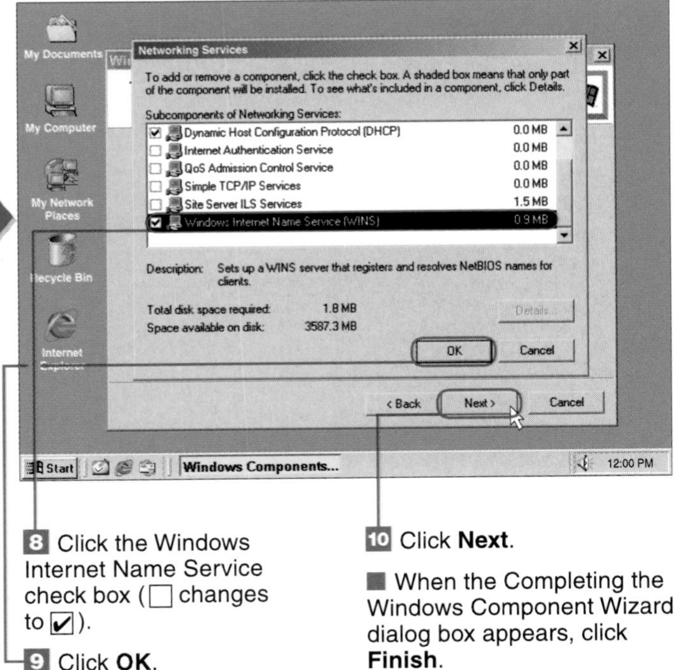

6 Click the **Networking Services** check box (☐ changes to ☑).

7 Click **Details**.

8 Click the Windows Internet Name Service check box (☐ changes to ☑).

9 Click **OK**.

10 Click **Next**.

■ When the Completing the Windows Component Wizard dialog box appears, click **Finish**.

INSTALL ACTIVE DIRECTORY

Active Directory is an industrial-strength directory service for large networks. It lets people find resources on the network—computers, printers, even other people.

Important: Active Directory is quite complex and requires advanced administrative knowledge. Unless you have been told that you must have Active Directory at your site, you probably do not need to install it on your network.

INSTALL ACTIVE DIRECTORY

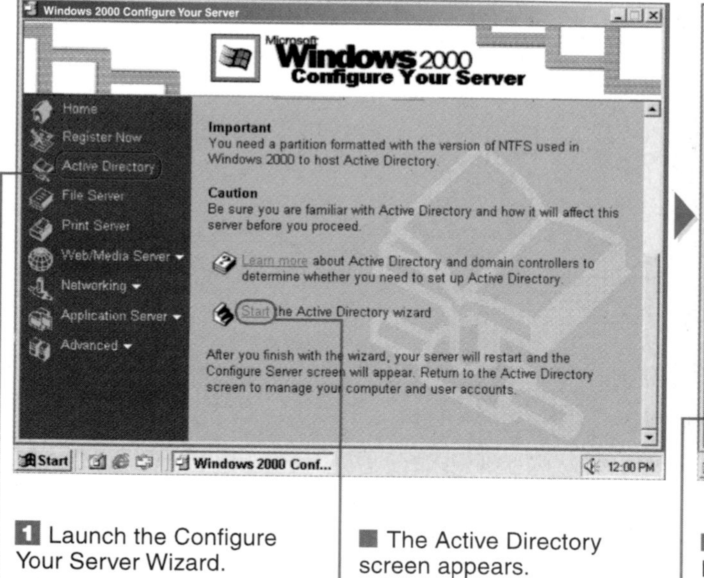

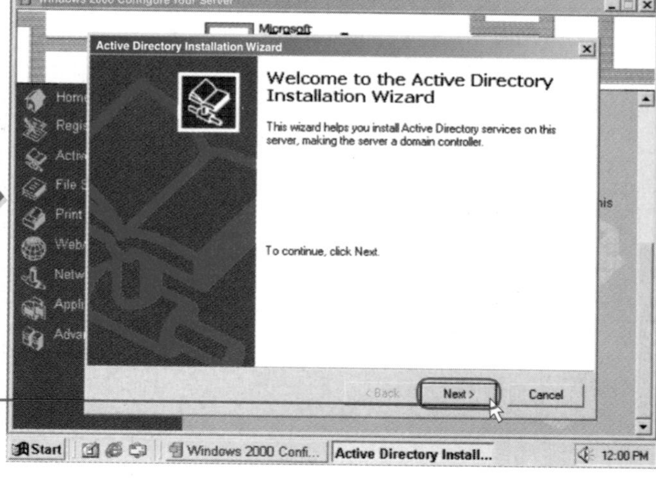

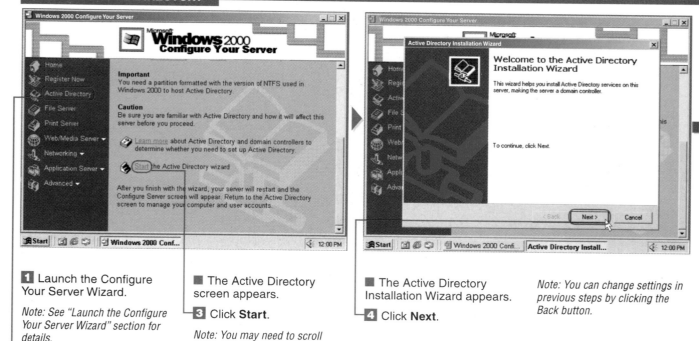

1. Launch the Configure Your Server Wizard.

Note: See "Launch the Configure Your Server Wizard" section for details.

2. Click **Active Directory**.

■ The Active Directory screen appears.

3. Click **Start**.

Note: You may need to scroll down to see the link.

■ The Active Directory Installation Wizard appears.

4. Click **Next**.

Note: You can change settings in previous steps by clicking the Back button.

What do I have to do before I install Active Directory?

You must do a lot of planning before you add Active Directory. You must identify and set up your Windows 2000 network; determine your organizational setup and people's access to the network; then construct your domain tree in Active Directory.

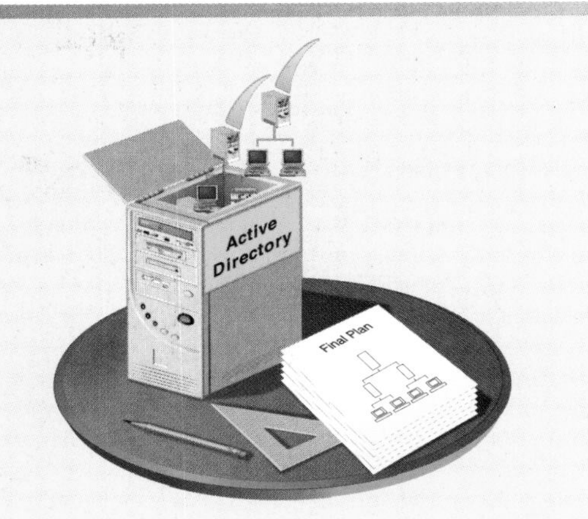

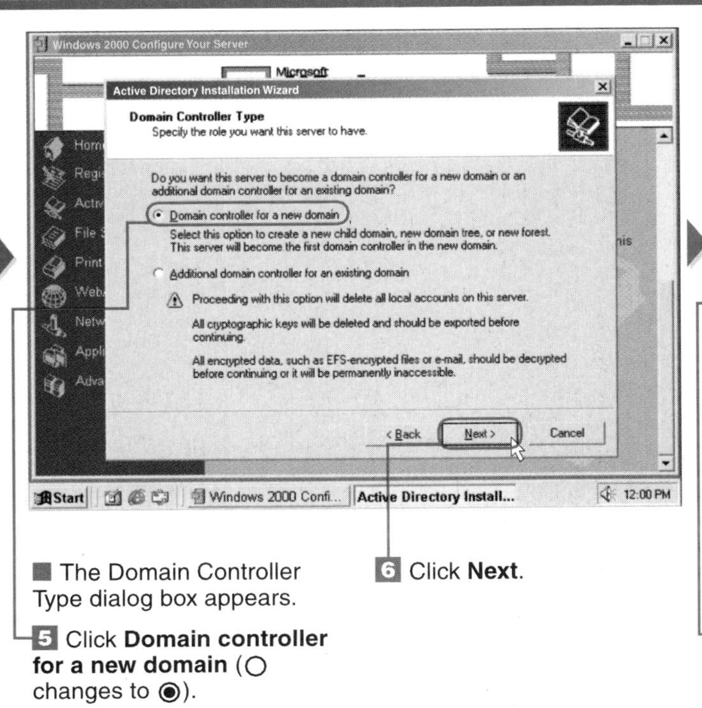

■ The Domain Controller Type dialog box appears.

5 Click **Domain controller for a new domain** (○ changes to ◉).

6 Click **Next**.

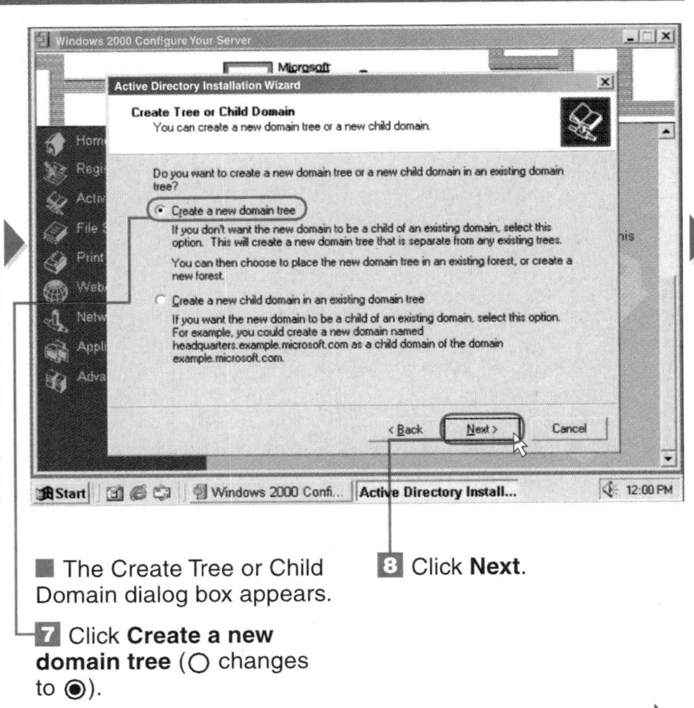

■ The Create Tree or Child Domain dialog box appears.

7 Click **Create a new domain tree** (○ changes to ◉).

8 Click **Next**.

CONTINUED

Active Directory is used to store computer and resource information from DNS. You may be asked to install DNS before you install Active Directory.

INSTALL ACTIVE DIRECTORY (CONTINUED)

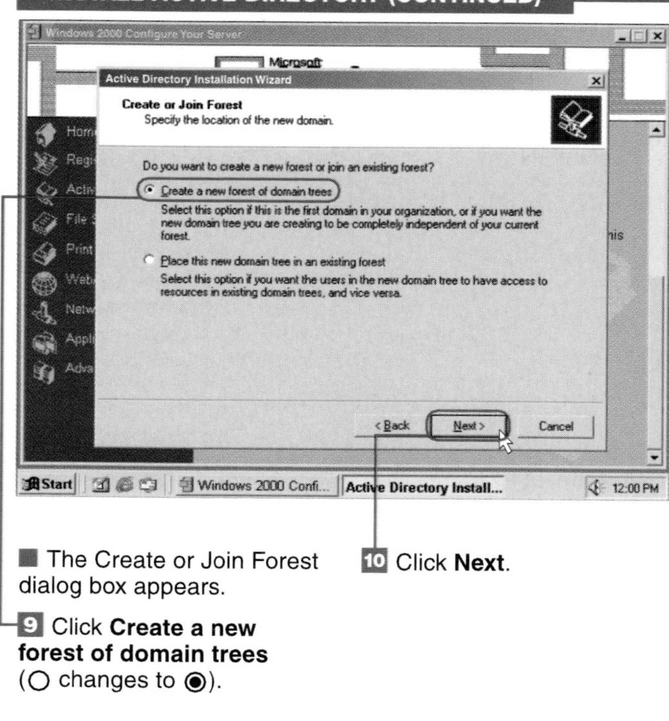

■ The Create or Join Forest dialog box appears.

9 Click **Create a new forest of domain trees** (○ changes to ◉).

10 Click **Next**.

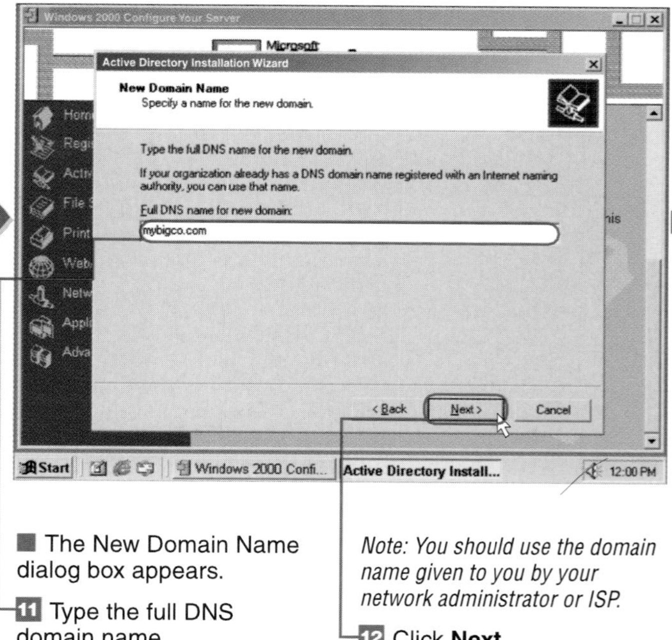

■ The New Domain Name dialog box appears.

11 Type the full DNS domain name.

Note: You should use the domain name given to you by your network administrator or ISP.

12 Click **Next**.

Why does Active Directory need to know so much about my organization?

In order to locate, manage, and organize resources, you need to give the directory a picture of how you plan to run your business. Defining how all the parts connect can be a difficult task, but the benefits are worth it.

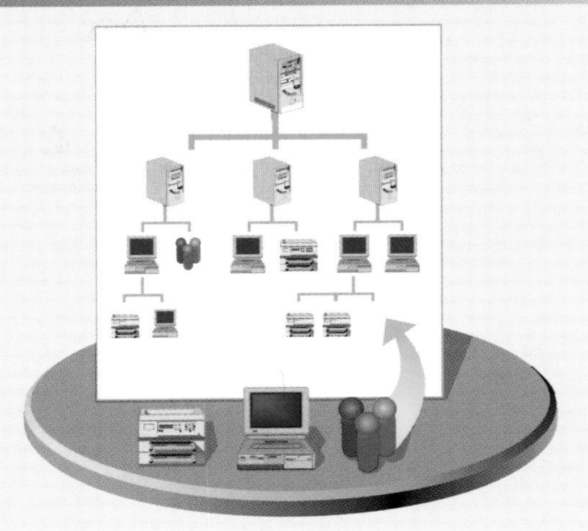

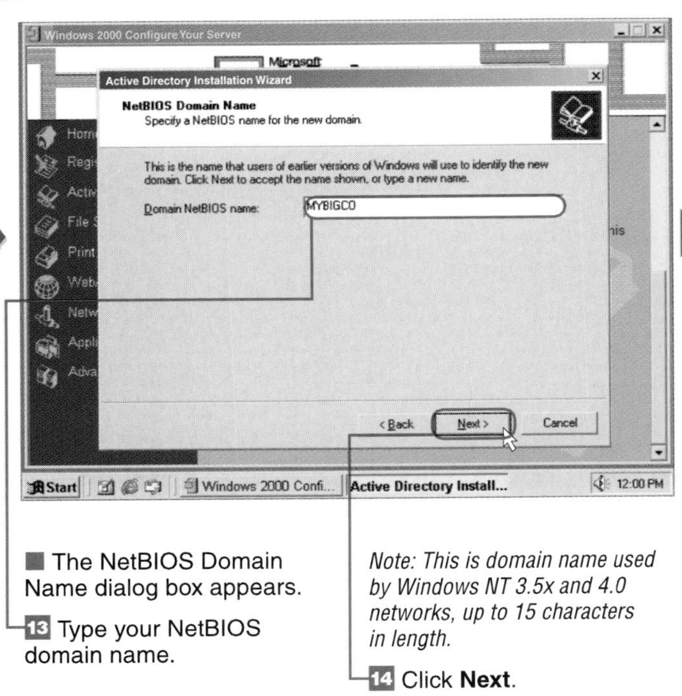

■ The NetBIOS Domain Name dialog box appears.

13 Type your NetBIOS domain name.

Note: This is domain name used by Windows NT 3.5x and 4.0 networks, up to 15 characters in length.

14 Click **Next**.

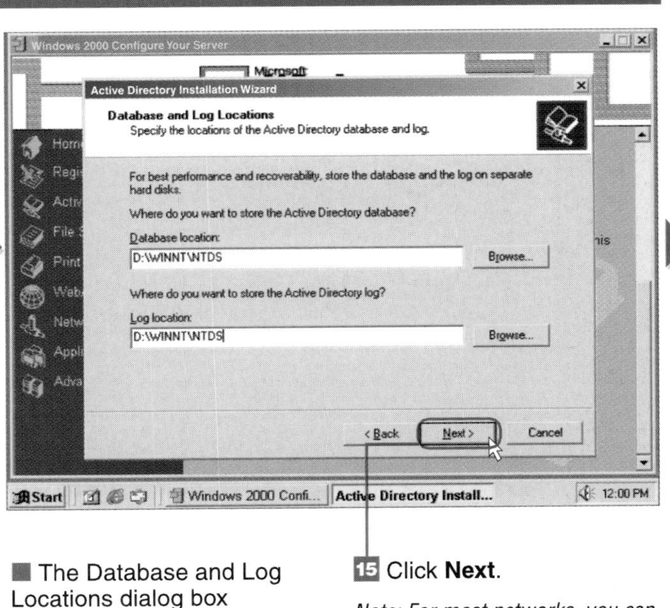

■ The Database and Log Locations dialog box appears.

15 Click **Next**.

Note: For most networks, you can accept the default locations.

CONTINUED

You can find more information about Active Directory to help you with your planning. You can purchase books on Active Directory planning and migration at your local bookstore or from an online book seller.

INSTALL ACTIVE DIRECTORY (CONTINUED)

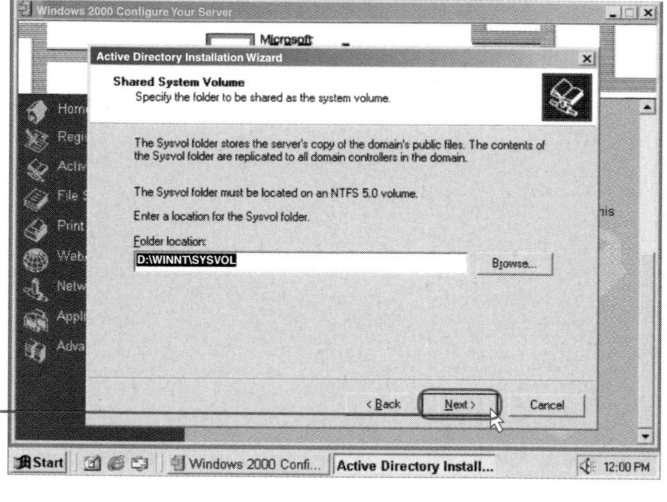

■ The Shared System Volume dialog box appears.

16 Click **Next**.

Note: For most networks, you can accept the default folder location.

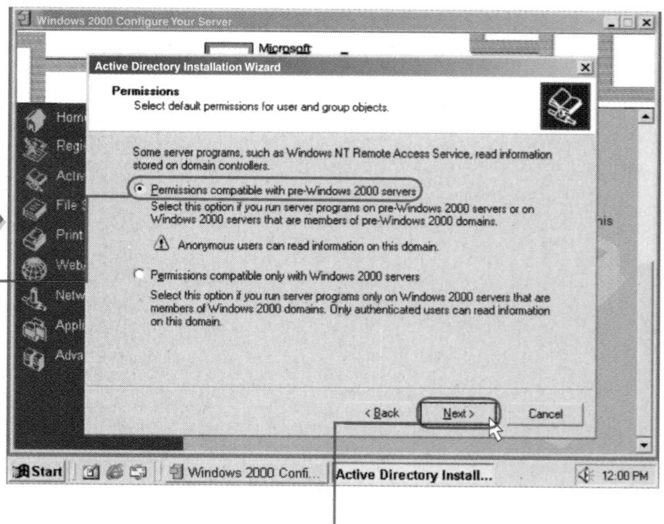

■ The Permissions dialog box appears.

17 Click **Permissions compatible with pre-Windows 2000 servers** (○ changes to ◉).

*Note: You should click **Permissions compatible only with Windows 2000 servers** if you are running only Windows 2000 servers on your network.*

18 Click **Next**.

Will Active Directory work with my Windows NT–based domains?

Active Directory can coexist with Windows NT domains. However, there are migration and interoperability issues to consider if you are moving to Active Directory. You should purchase a book on Active Directory if you are moving from Windows NT to Active Directory.

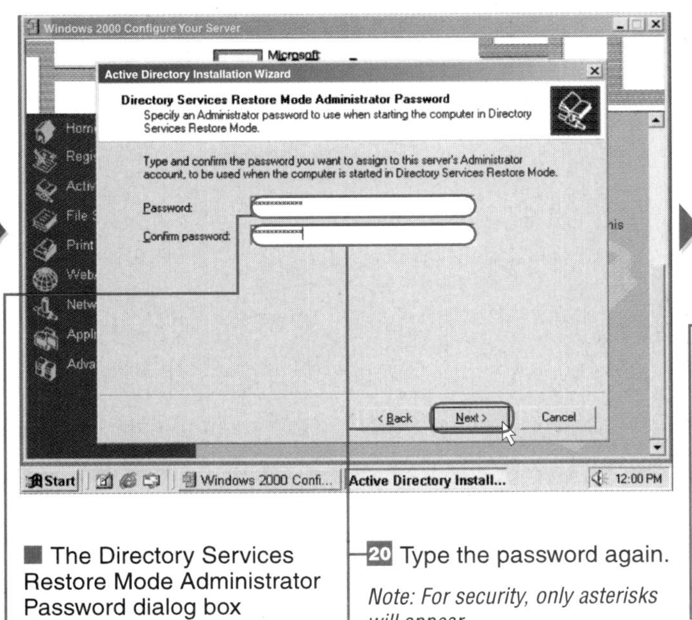

■ The Directory Services Restore Mode Administrator Password dialog box appears.

19 Type an administrator password.

20 Type the password again.

Note: For security, only asterisks will appear.

21 Click **Next**.

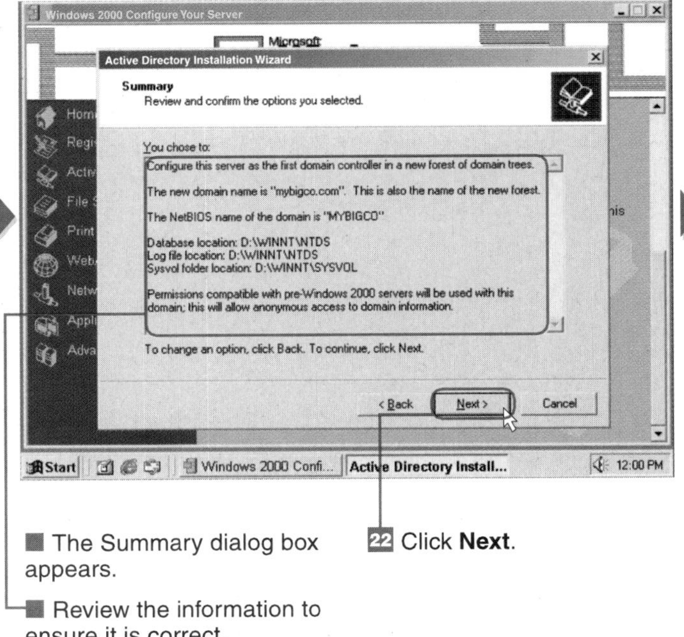

■ The Summary dialog box appears.

■ Review the information to ensure it is correct.

22 Click **Next**.

CONTINUED

You can manage Active Directory by using three different snap-ins: Active Directory Domains and Trusts, Active Directory Sites and Services, and Active Directory Users and Computers.

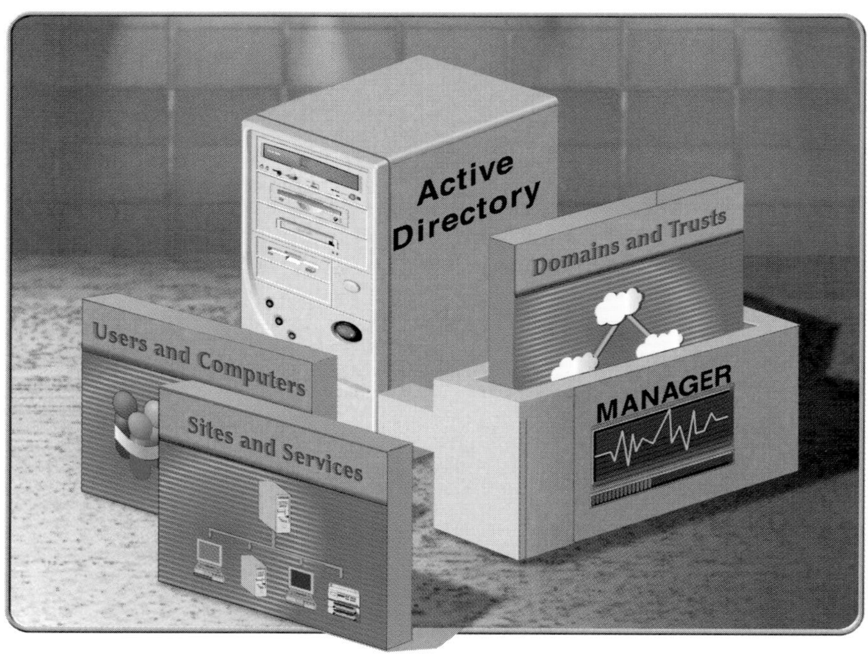

You will learn more about these tools in upcoming tasks and chapters.

INSTALL ACTIVE DIRECTORY (CONTINUED)

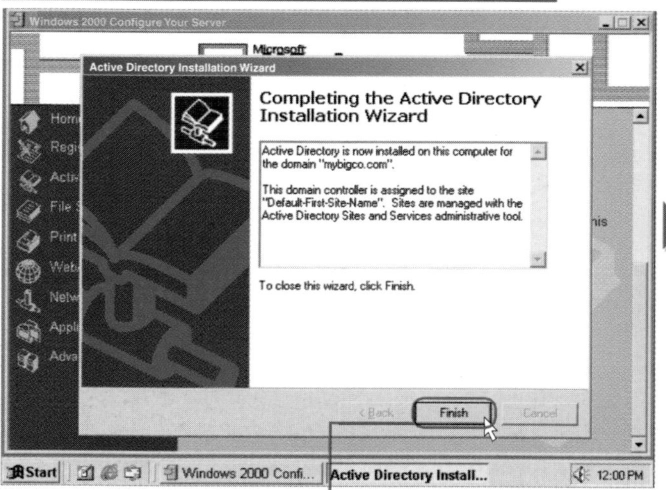

Note: Active Directory installs and configures itself. This process may take several minutes; do not stop or restart your server while it works.

■ The Completing the Active Directory Installation Wizard dialog box appears.

23 Click **Finish**.

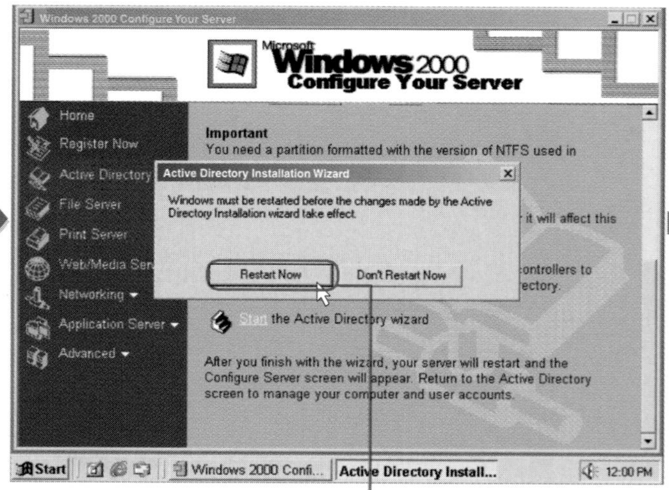

■ A dialog box appears, prompting you to restart your server.

24 Click **Restart Now**.

Do I need Active Directory for a small business?

If you have fewer than 20 computers on your network, you probably do not need Active Directory.

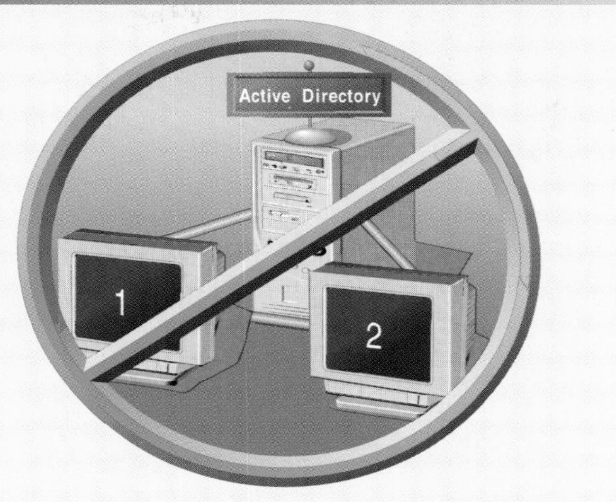

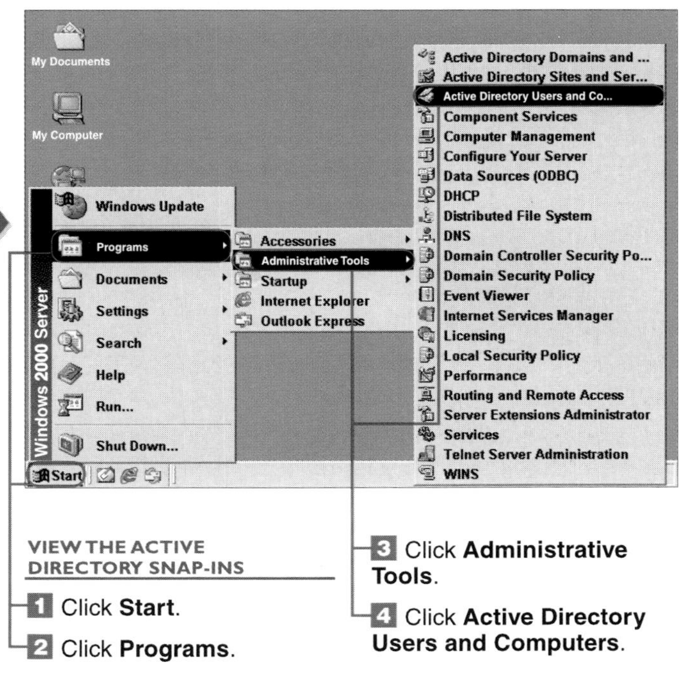

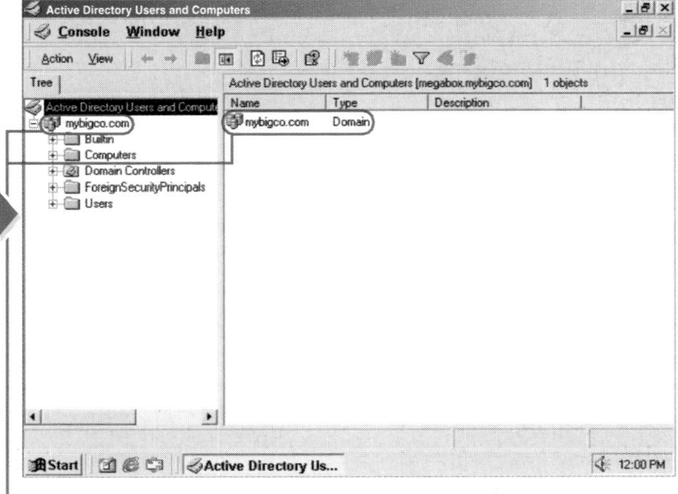

VIEW THE ACTIVE DIRECTORY SNAP-INS

1 Click **Start**.

2 Click **Programs**.

3 Click **Administrative Tools**.

4 Click **Active Directory Users and Computers**.

■ The Active Directory Users and Computers snap-in appears.

CONFIGURE ACTIVE DIRECTORY SERVER SETTINGS

After you install Active Directory, you can make changes to your server without reinstalling.

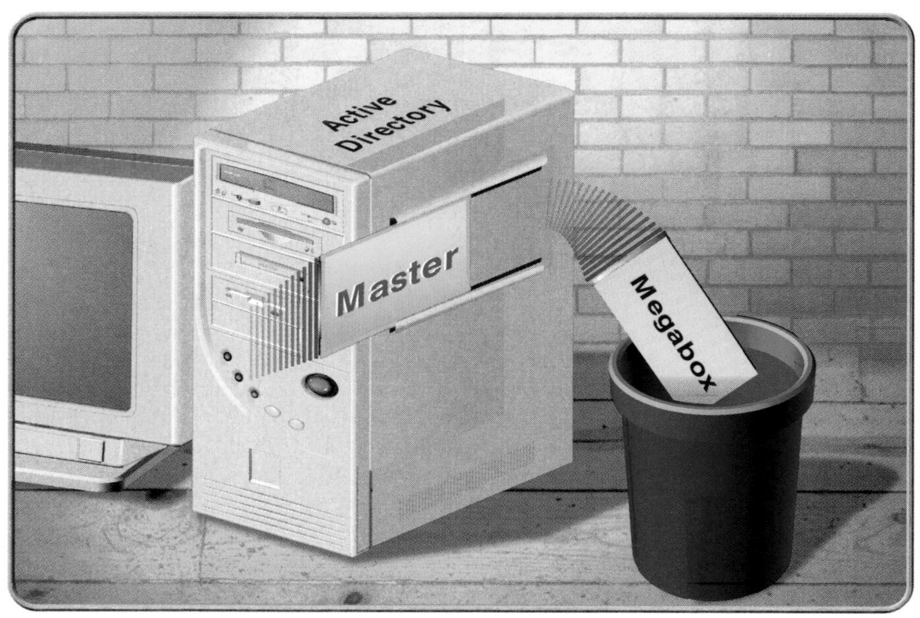

CONFIGURE ACTIVE DIRECTORY SERVER SETTINGS

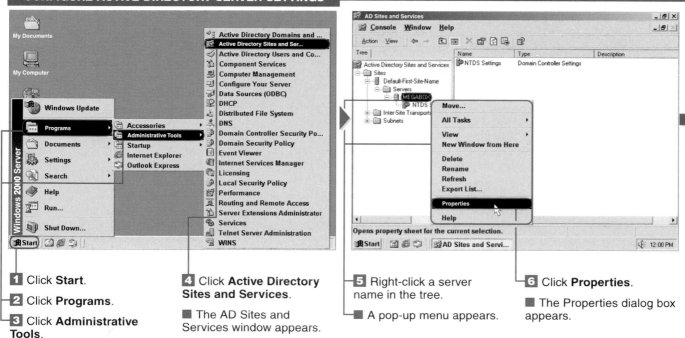

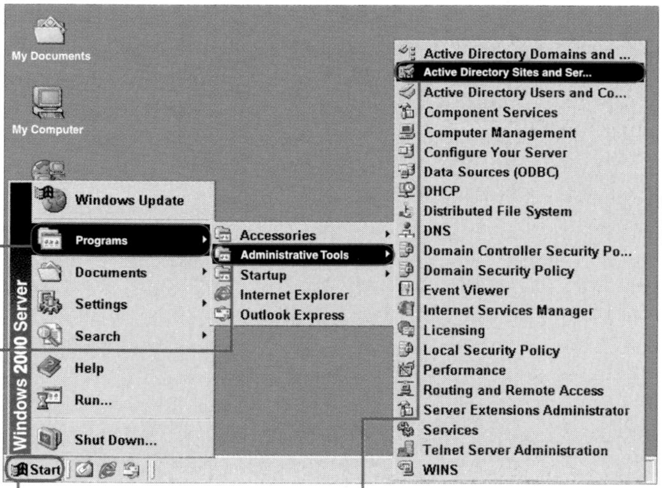

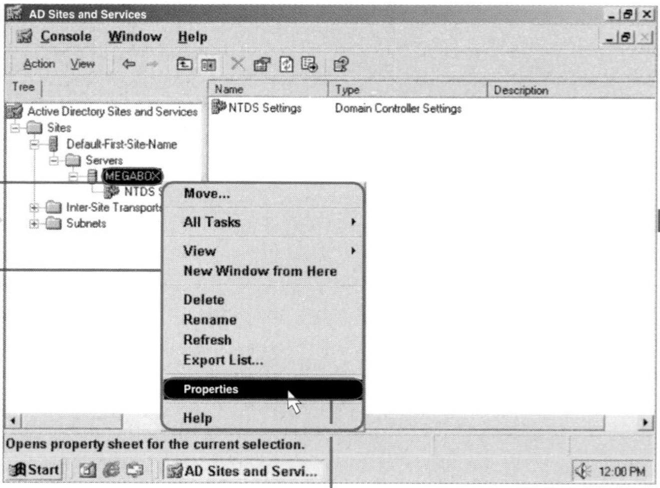

1 Click **Start**.

2 Click **Programs**.

3 Click **Administrative Tools**.

4 Click **Active Directory Sites and Services**.

■ The AD Sites and Services window appears.

5 Right-click a server name in the tree.

■ A pop-up menu appears.

6 Click **Properties**.

■ The Properties dialog box appears.

Can I change the server settings for a particular domain controller?

Yes. You can change the domain controller in Active Directory Sites and Services so you can change the server settings. Active Directory Sites and Services only configure the settings for the selected domain controller.

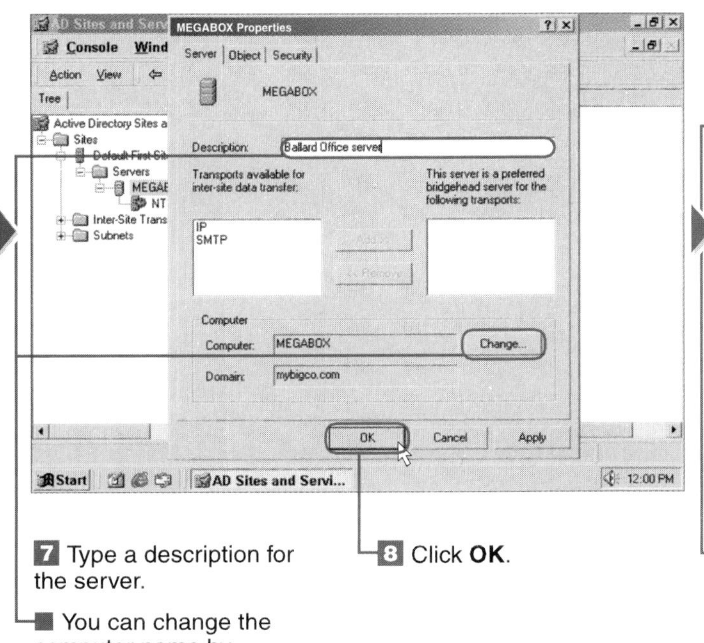

7 Type a description for the server.

■ You can change the computer name by clicking **Change**.

8 Click **OK**.

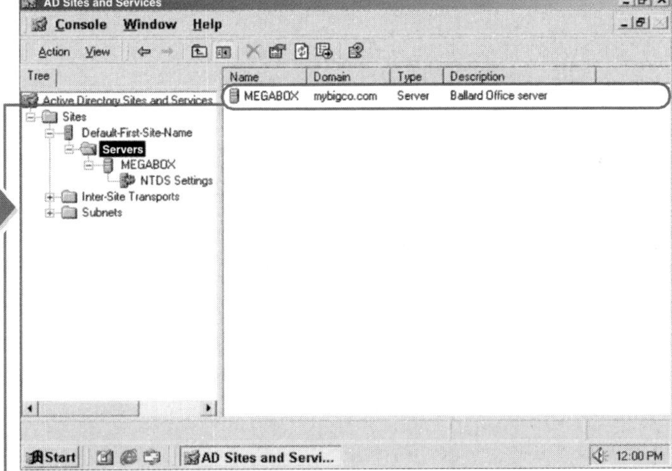

■ The Servers list displays your description and name changes, if any.

INTEGRATE GATEWAY SERVICES FOR NETWARE

Gateway Services for NetWare (GSNW) allows you to access Novell NetWare servers in your network.

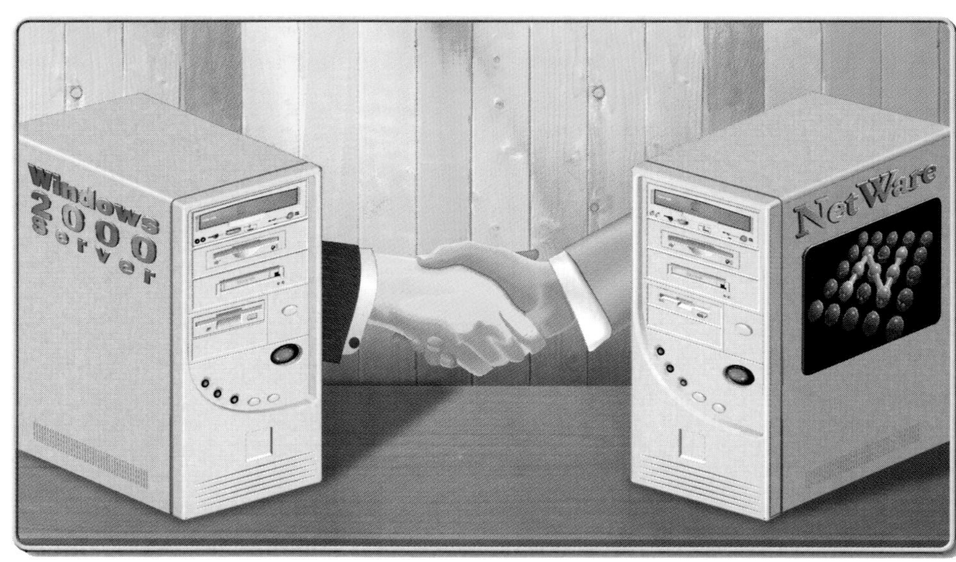

You only need to install GSNW if you need access to NetWare file servers or print servers.

INTEGRATE GATEWAY SERVICES FOR NETWARE

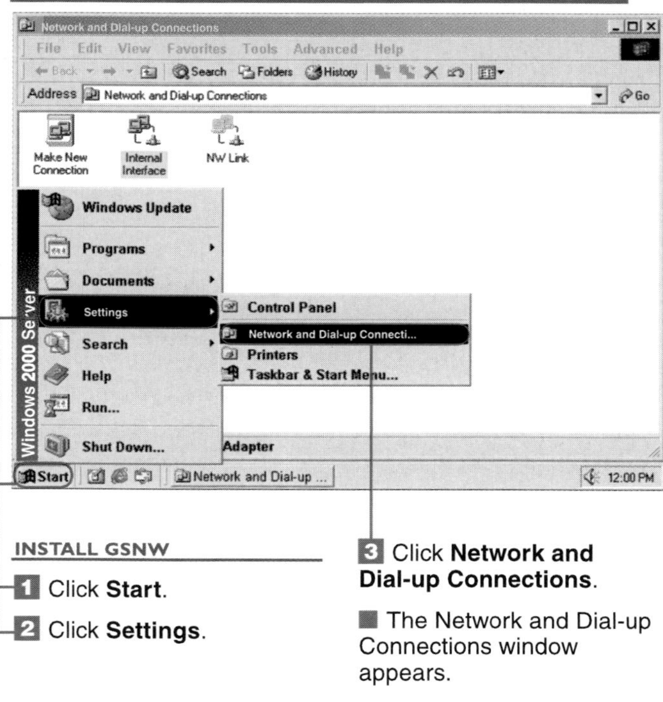

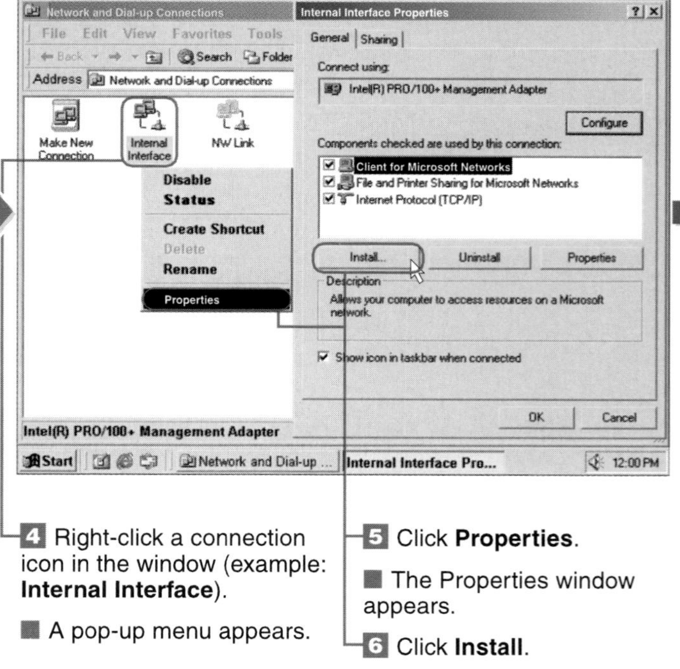

INSTALL GSNW

1 Click **Start**.

2 Click **Settings**.

3 Click **Network and Dial-up Connections**.

■ The Network and Dial-up Connections window appears.

4 Right-click a connection icon in the window (example: **Internal Interface**).

■ A pop-up menu appears.

5 Click **Properties**.

■ The Properties window appears.

6 Click **Install**.

Do I have to install GSNW on all my computers?

No. Because GSNW acts as a gateway to NetWare services, you do not need to install NetWare on other computers in your network.

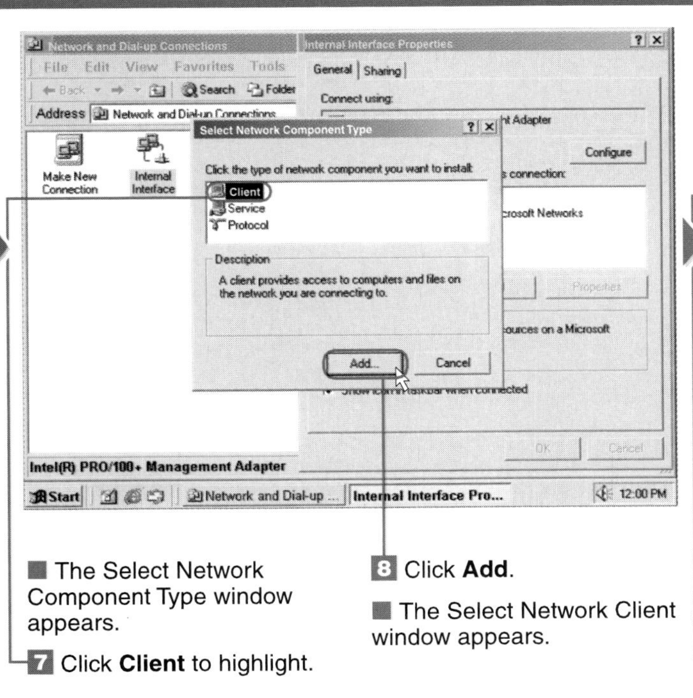

■ The Select Network Component Type window appears.

7 Click **Client** to highlight.

8 Click **Add**.

■ The Select Network Client window appears.

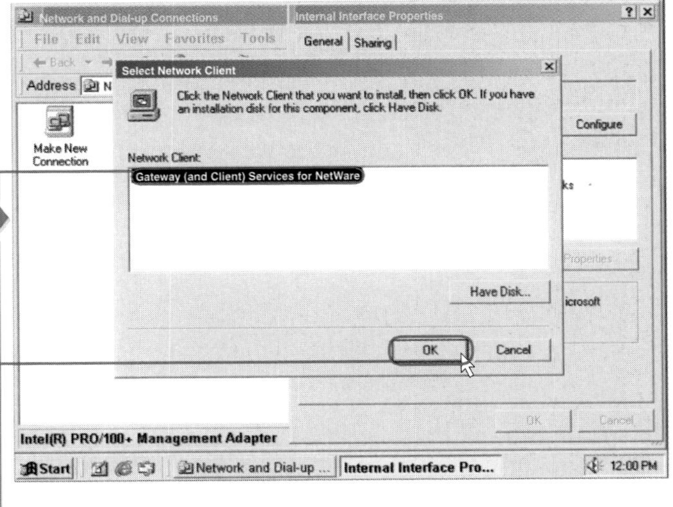

9 Click **Gateway (and Client) Services for NetWare** to highlight.

10 Click **OK**.

■ The Gateway (and Client) Services for NetWare component appears in the Properties dialog box.

Note: You must restart Windows 2000 Server to complete the installation.

INTEGRATE AN APPLETALK NETWORK

AppleTalk provides network services for Apple computers. Computers such as the Macintosh, G3, and PowerBook use AppleTalk to communicate with each other.

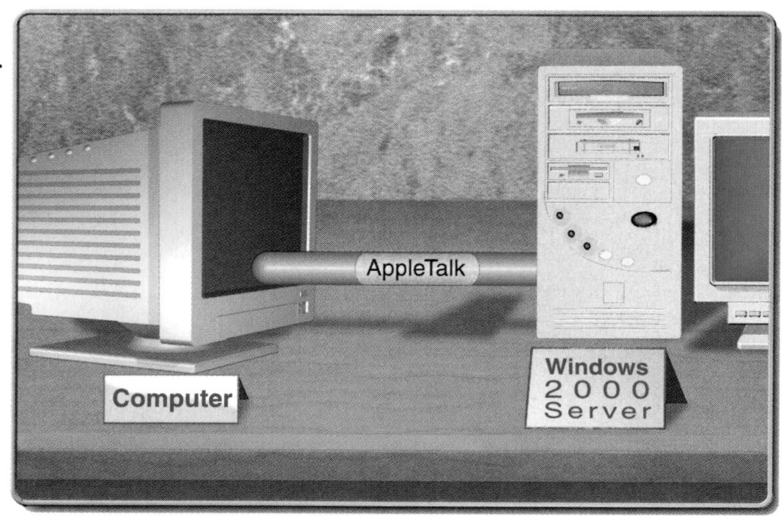

If you do not have any Apple computers on your network, you do not need to install AppleTalk.

INTEGRATE AN APPLETALK NETWORK

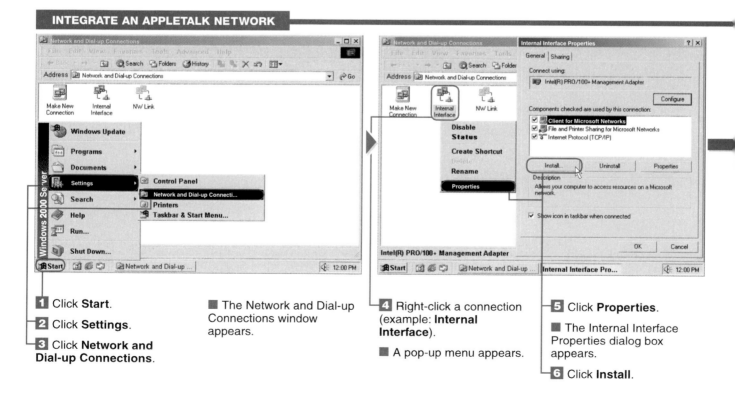

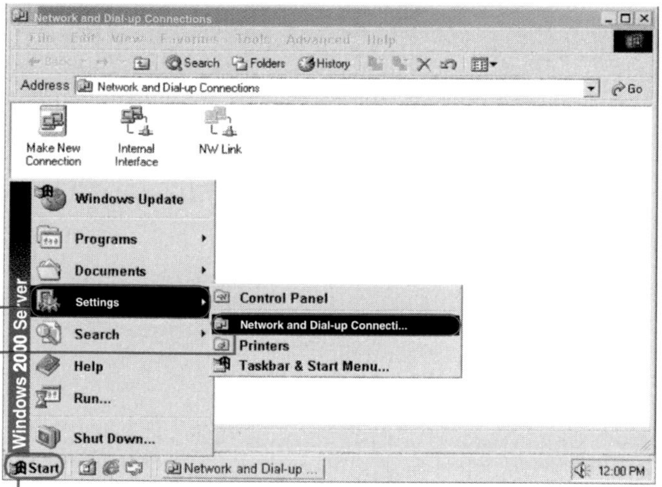

1 Click **Start**.

2 Click **Settings**.

3 Click **Network and Dial-up Connections**.

■ The Network and Dial-up Connections window appears.

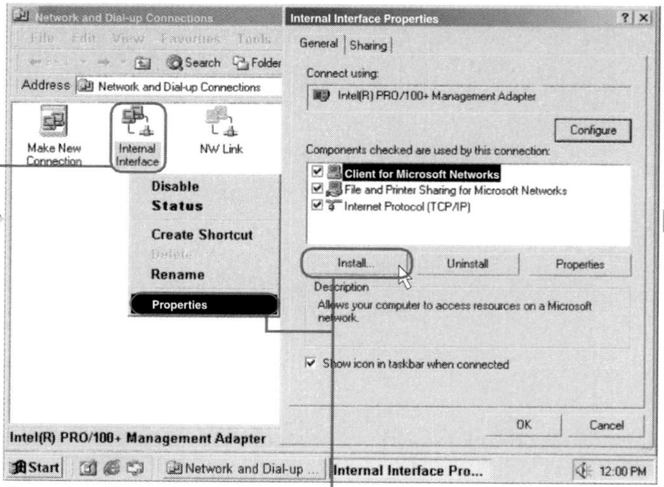

4 Right-click a connection (example: **Internal Interface**).

■ A pop-up menu appears.

5 Click **Properties**.

■ The Internal Interface Properties dialog box appears.

6 Click **Install**.

Can I add Macintosh file and print services?

Yes. You can add AppleTalk file and AppleTalk print services separately in the New Components Wizard.

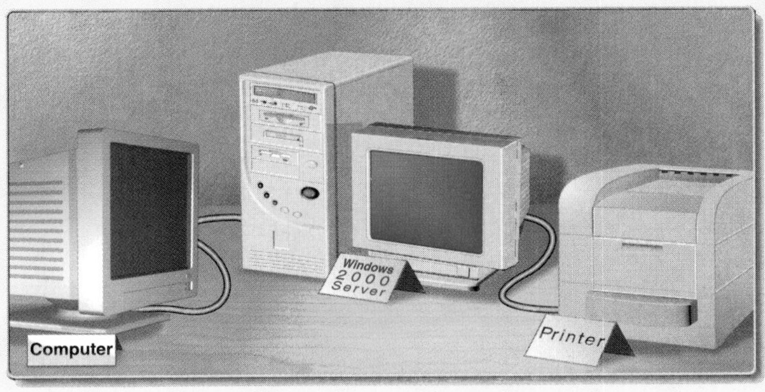

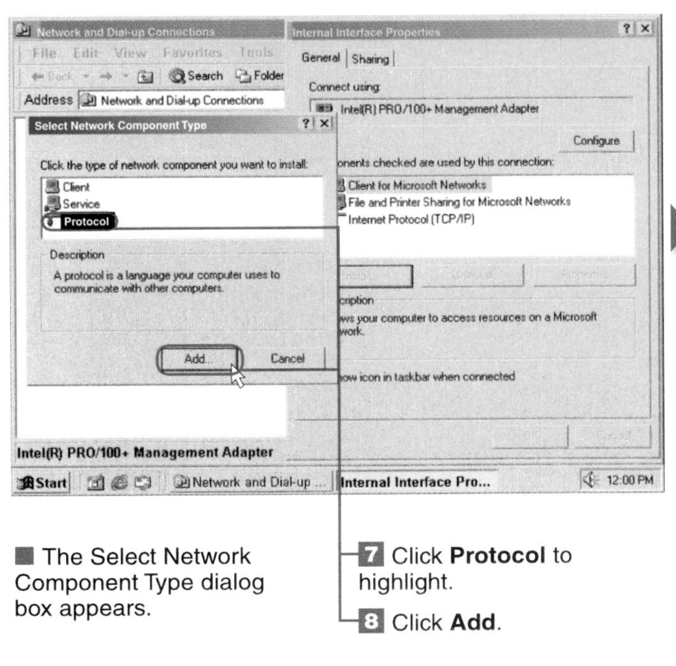

■ The Select Network Component Type dialog box appears.

7 Click **Protocol** to highlight.

8 Click **Add**.

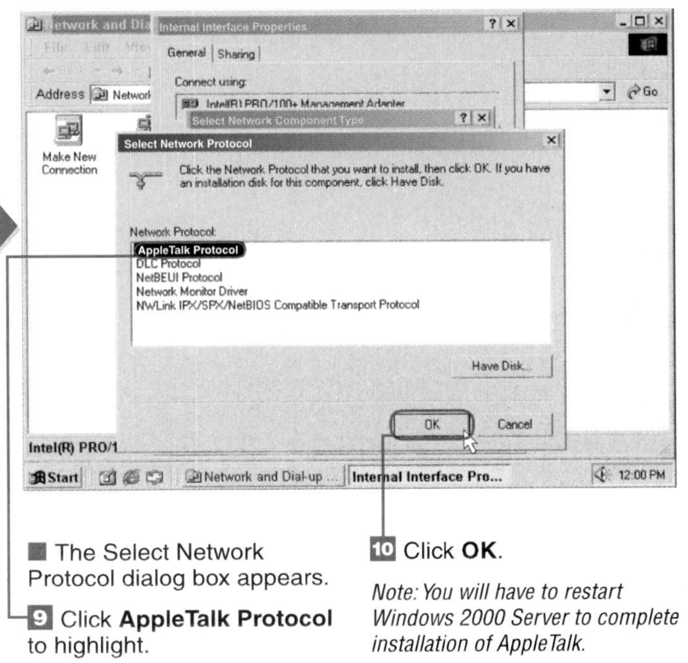

■ The Select Network Protocol dialog box appears.

9 Click **AppleTalk Protocol** to highlight.

10 Click **OK**.

Note: You will have to restart Windows 2000 Server to complete installation of AppleTalk.

CDRW 3000
WRITING
SECURI
TEMPLA

Security can be used to relax or tighten up access to your network, depending on your business needs. This chapter shows you how to analyze and change the security of your server to match your needs.

START SECURITY CONFIGURATION AND ANALYSIS

The Security Configuration and Analysis snap-in can help you analyze security for your server and provide you with suggestions for improving your server's security.

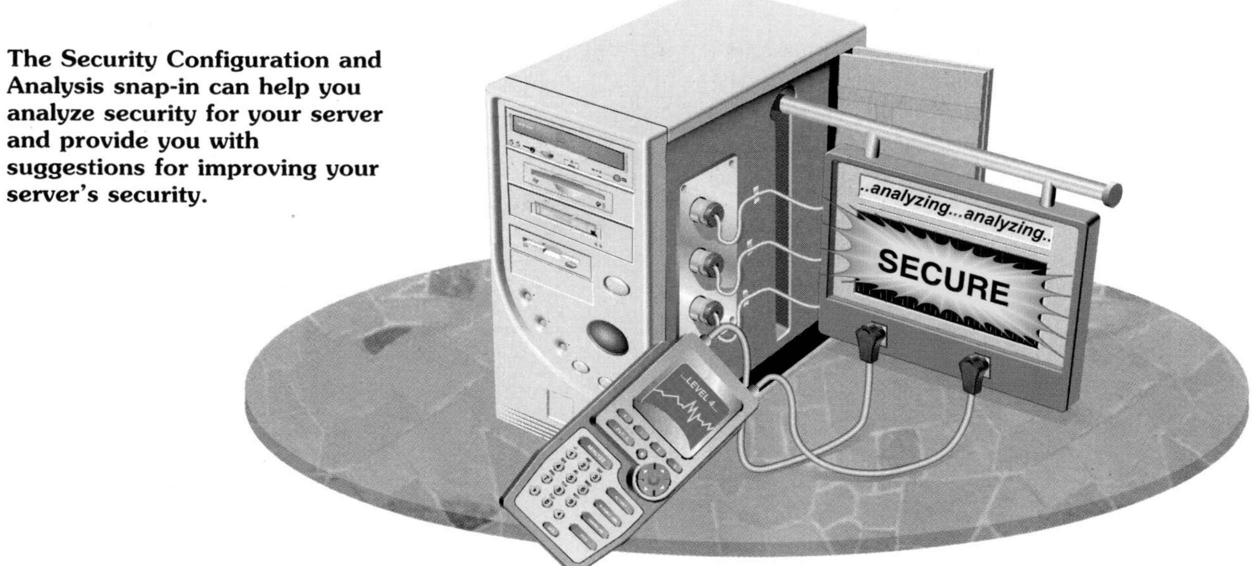

START SECURITY CONFIGURATION AND ANALYSIS

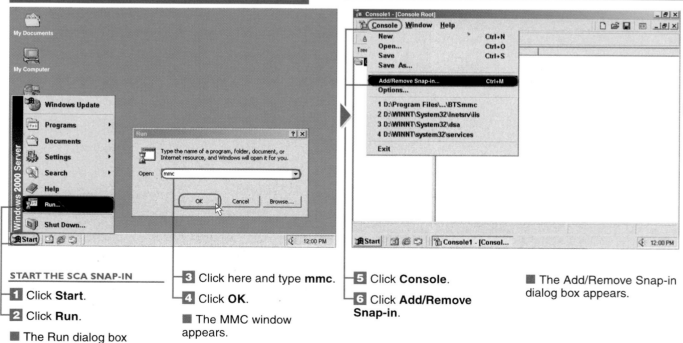

START THE SCA SNAP-IN

1 Click **Start**.

2 Click **Run**.

■ The Run dialog box appears.

3 Click here and type **mmc**.

4 Click **OK**.

■ The MMC window appears.

5 Click **Console**.

6 Click **Add/Remove Snap-in**.

■ The Add/Remove Snap-in dialog box appears.

What is the difference between the Security Configuration and Analysis snap-in and the Security Templates snap-in?

You use the Security Configuration and Analysis snap-in to do most of the security analysis management on your server. The Security Templates snap-in provides a quick way to view and compare all the templates and their settings but does not provide any analysis.

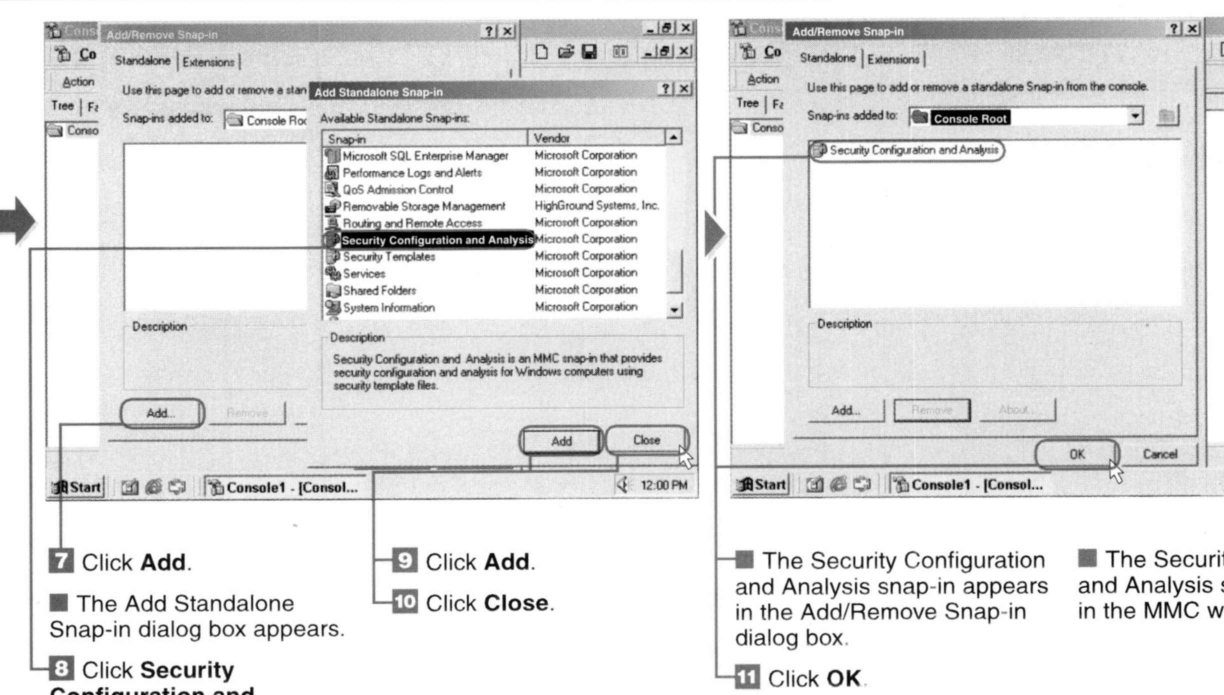

7 Click **Add**.

■ The Add Standalone Snap-in dialog box appears.

8 Click **Security Configuration and Analysis** to highlight.

9 Click **Add**.

10 Click **Close**.

■ The Security Configuration and Analysis snap-in appears in the Add/Remove Snap-in dialog box.

11 Click **OK**.

■ The Security Configuration and Analysis snap-in appears in the MMC window.

CREATE A SECURITY ANALYSIS DATABASE

The Security Configuration and Analysis snap-in maintains its own database of templates and settings. You need to create a database before you can analyze your security settings.

CREATE A SECURITY ANALYSIS DATABASE

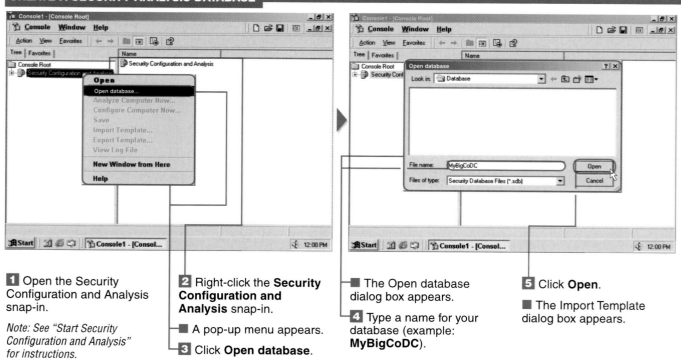

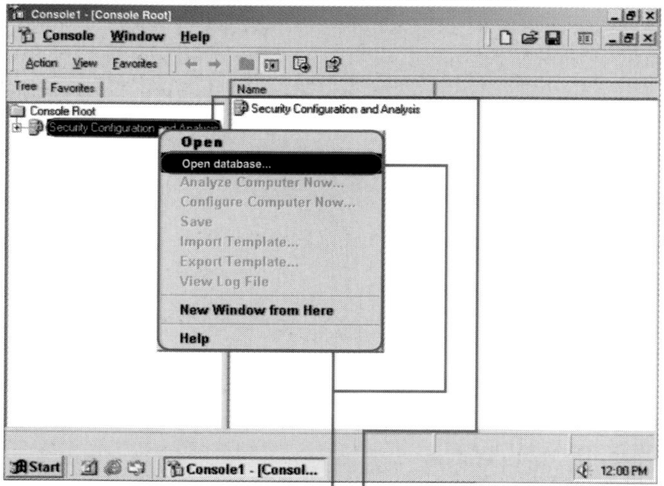

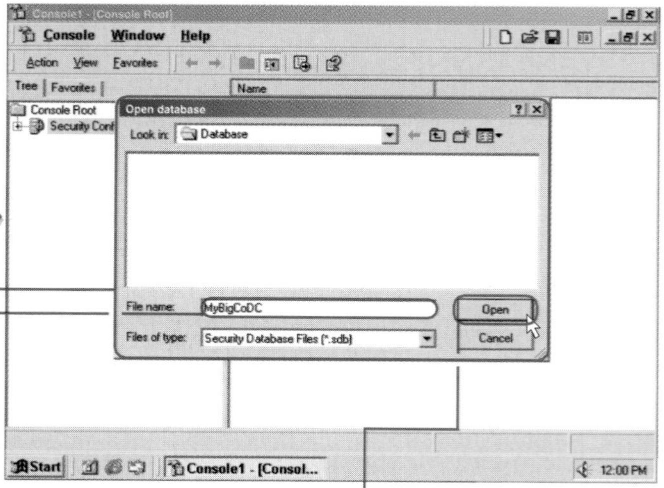

1 Open the Security Configuration and Analysis snap-in.

Note: See "Start Security Configuration and Analysis" for instructions.

2 Right-click the **Security Configuration and Analysis** snap-in.

■ A pop-up menu appears.

3 Click **Open database**.

■ The Open database dialog box appears.

4 Type a name for your database (example: **MyBigCoDC**).

5 Click **Open**.

■ The Import Template dialog box appears.

What are all the different templates listed in the window?

The templates contain suggested settings for workstations and servers depending on the role. For example, `basicdc` contains the default domain controller settings, while `hisecdc` contains suggested settings for a highly secure domain controller. A highly secure domain controller provides extensive logging limited access.

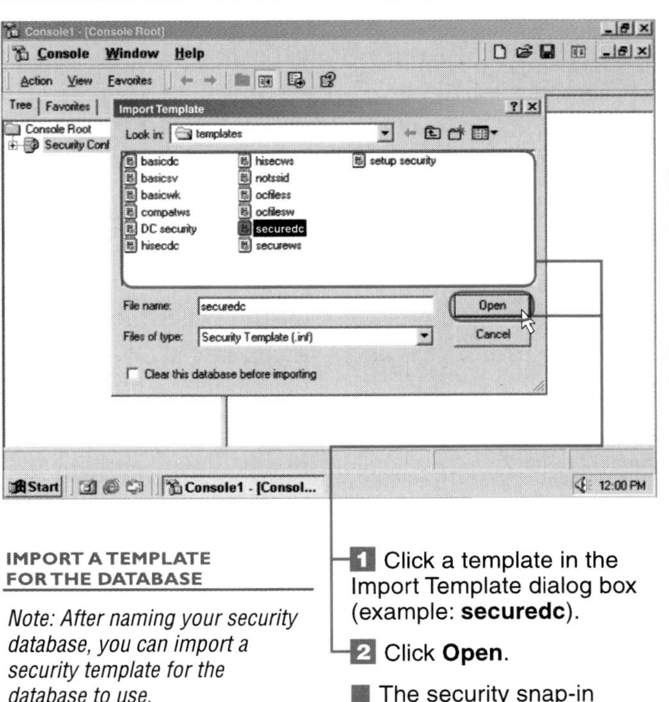

IMPORT A TEMPLATE FOR THE DATABASE

Note: After naming your security database, you can import a security template for the database to use.

1 Click a template in the Import Template dialog box (example: **securedc**).

2 Click **Open**.

■ The security snap-in reappears.

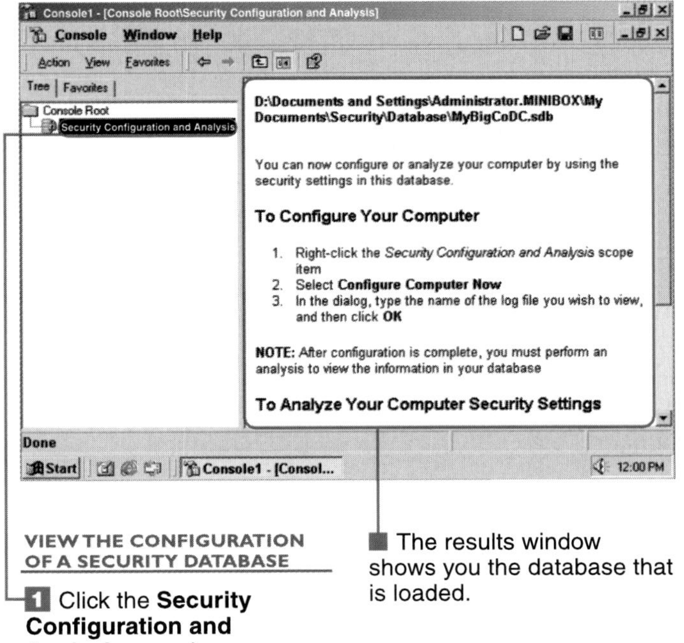

VIEW THE CONFIGURATION OF A SECURITY DATABASE

1 Click the **Security Configuration and Analysis** snap-in.

■ The results window shows you the database that is loaded.

ANALYZE YOUR SERVER

After you have imported a template, you can compare the template's security settings with those on your server.

ANALYZE YOUR SERVER

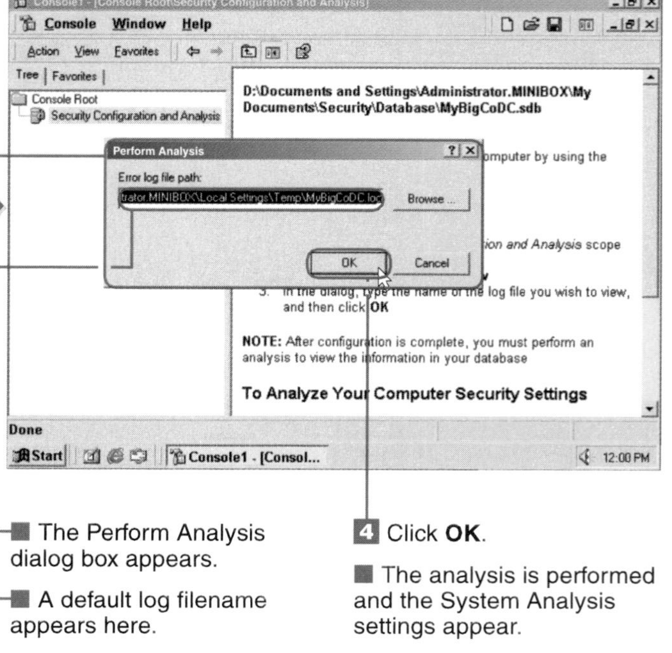

1 Open the Security Configuration and Analysis snap-in and ensure that a template has been imported.

Note: See "Create a Security Analysis Database" for details.

2 Right-click **Security and Configuration Analysis**.

3 Click **Analyze Computer Now**.

■ The Perform Analysis dialog box appears.

■ A default log filename appears here.

4 Click **OK**.

■ The analysis is performed and the System Analysis settings appear.

Why do I need a separate database for security settings?

The Security Configuration and Analysis database actually contains a copy of your computer's security settings. Having these settings separate lets you create custom templates for other computers without affecting the settings on your server.

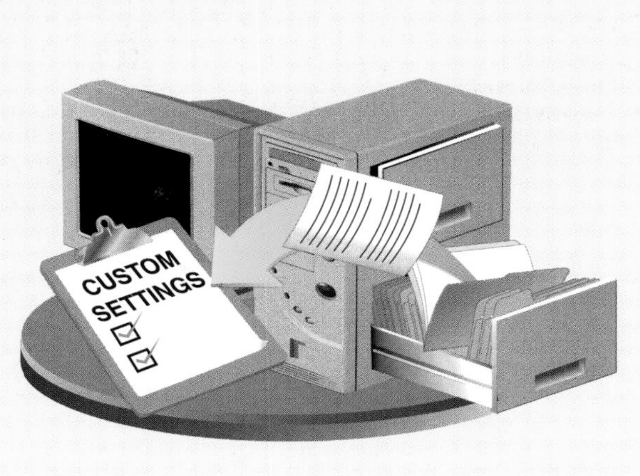

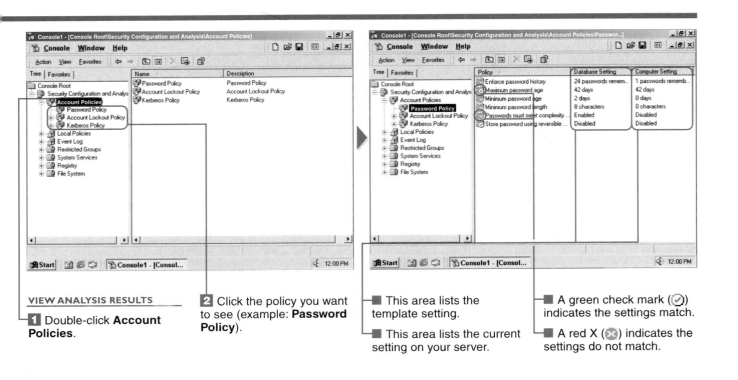

VIEW ANALYSIS RESULTS

1 Double-click **Account Policies**.

2 Click the policy you want to see (example: **Password Policy**).

- This area lists the template setting.
- This area lists the current setting on your server.
- A green check mark (✓) indicates the settings match.
- A red X (✗) indicates the settings do not match.

EDIT AND APPLY THE RECOMMENDED SETTINGS

You can edit the template settings and then apply them to your server. This makes it easy to configure your server's security settings.

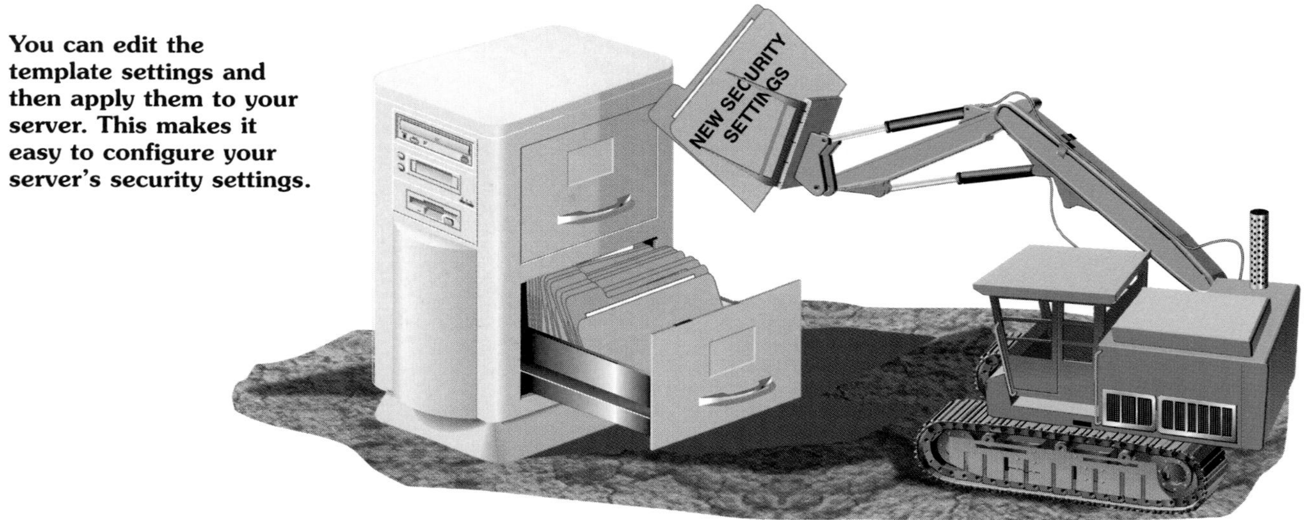

EDIT AND APPLY THE RECOMMENDED SETTINGS

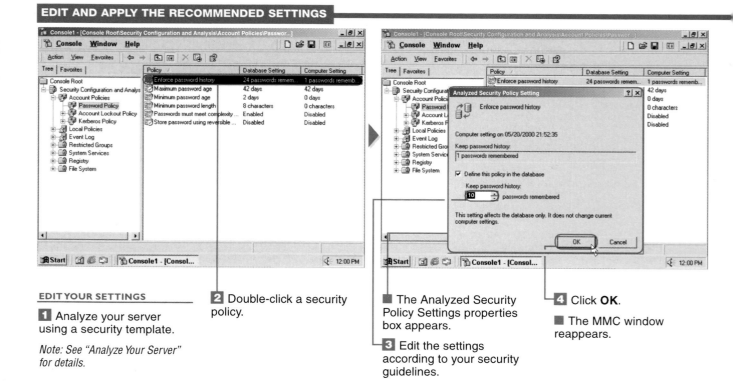

EDIT YOUR SETTINGS

1 Analyze your server using a security template.

Note: See "Analyze Your Server" for details.

2 Double-click a security policy.

■ The Analyzed Security Policy Settings properties box appears.

3 Edit the settings according to your security guidelines.

4 Click **OK**.

■ The MMC window reappears.

Can I customize the template settings if I want to change some settings?

You can change any or all of the template settings, depending on what your security policy will be. If you do this, it is strongly recommended you export the template to another file, keeping the original template unchanged.

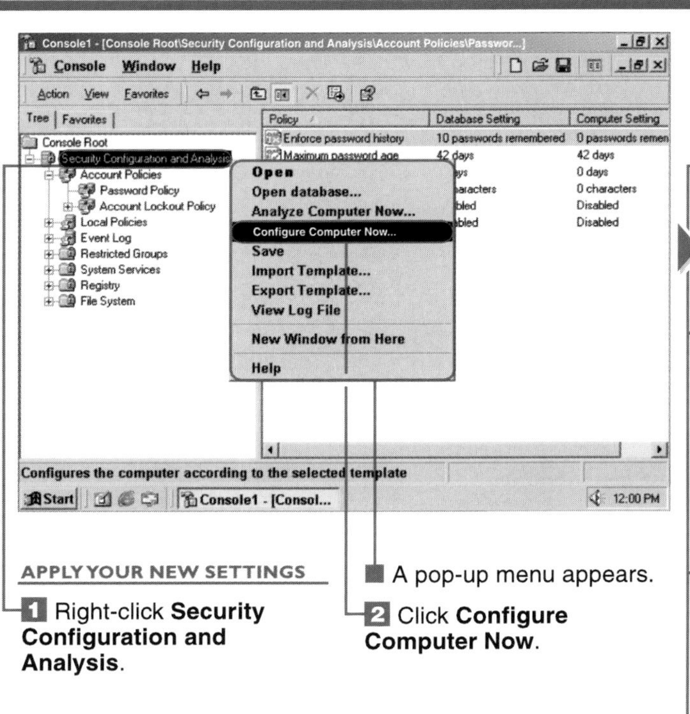

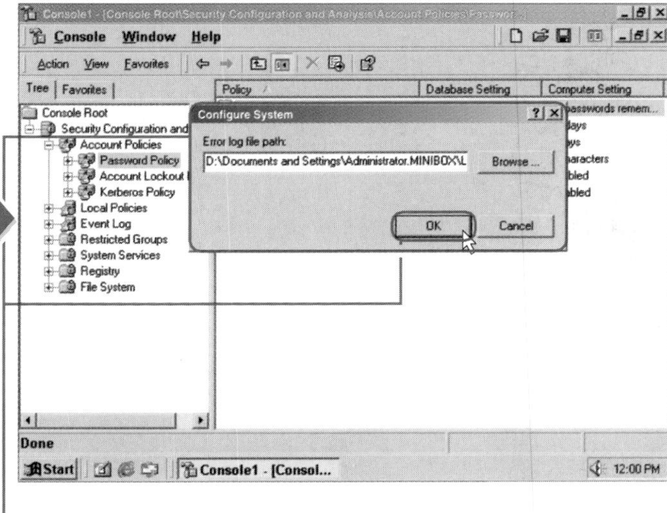

APPLY YOUR NEW SETTINGS

1 Right-click **Security Configuration and Analysis**.

■ A pop-up menu appears.

2 Click **Configure Computer Now**.

■ The Configure System dialog box appears, prompting for a log filename.

Note: The log file saves to your Temp directory by default.

3 Click **OK**.

■ The template is applied to your server and the settings changed to reflect the template.

Note: See "Analyze Your Server" for details on viewing the new settings.

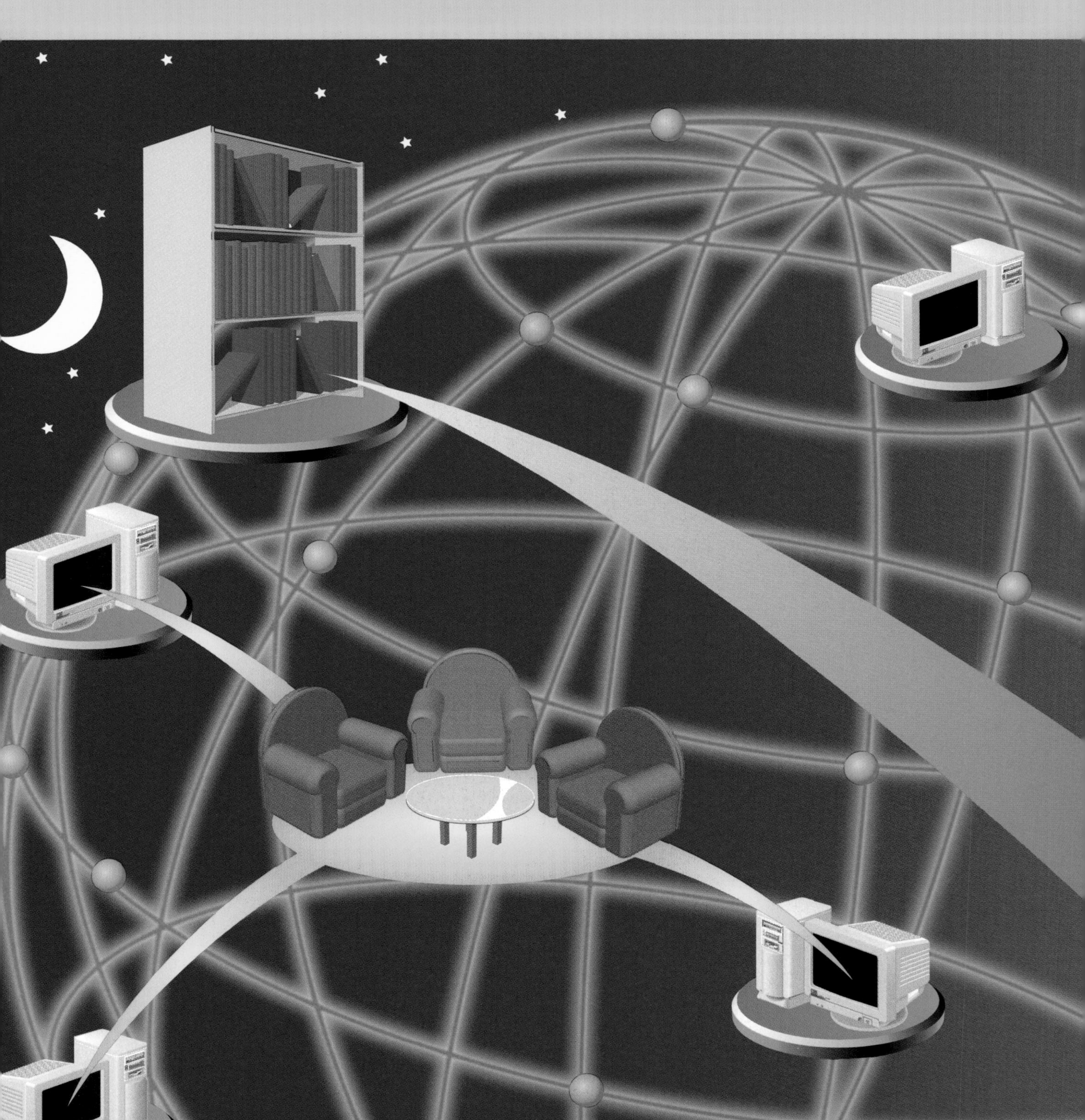

CHAPTER 6

Connecting to the Internet

In this chapter you will discover how to connect your server and your users to the Internet.

INTRODUCTION TO THE INTERNET

The Internet is a worldwide group of computers connected together by a network. Though the Internet consists of more than just Web sites, it is frequently called *the Web*, or World Wide Web.

WEB PAGE

A Web page is a document on the Internet. The documents can contain text, pictures, animations, graphics, or even live movies.

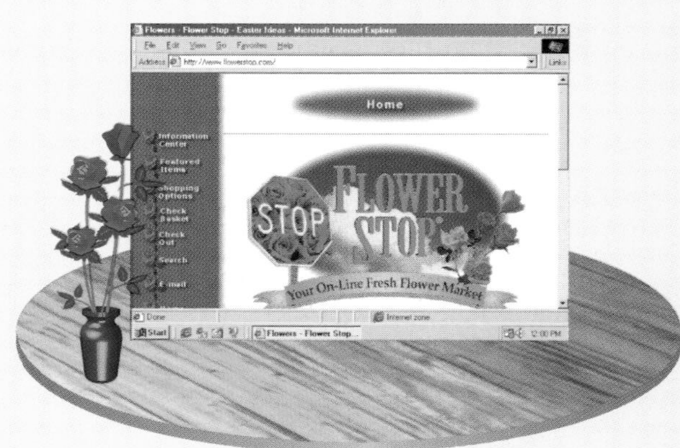

WEB SITE

A Web site is a group of Web pages that can be found at the same Internet address. The same person, business, or organization usually maintains the site.

SURF THE WEB

The World Wide Web is made up of an ever-expanding collection of documents, pictures, audio clips, and live video cameras. Originally created as a way for universities to conduct research, the Web now provides information, services, and content to anyone who wants to use it. You can order groceries, read international newspapers, or see pictures of your family in distant cities.

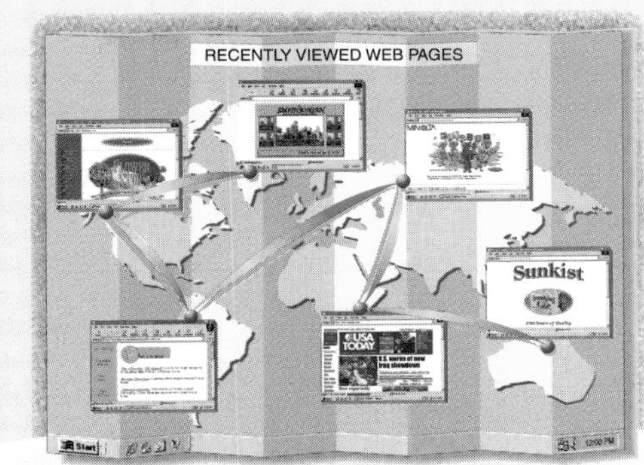

SEND AND RECEIVE E-MAIL

Electronic mail, or e-mail, is perhaps the single most popular use of the Internet. It works just like regular mail: You write a letter, address it to someone, and send it off to an electronic post office. The e-mail system takes care of getting your letter to the correct person and sending their mail back to you. One big benefit over regular mail: delivery usually.

EXCHANGE FILES

People also use the Internet for exchanging files with one another. The files transferred can be of nearly any size, from the smallest note to immense files that contain billions of bits of data. You can pick up the latest copy of a shareware program, give a video file to someone, or swap collections of electronic baseball cards with your best friend.

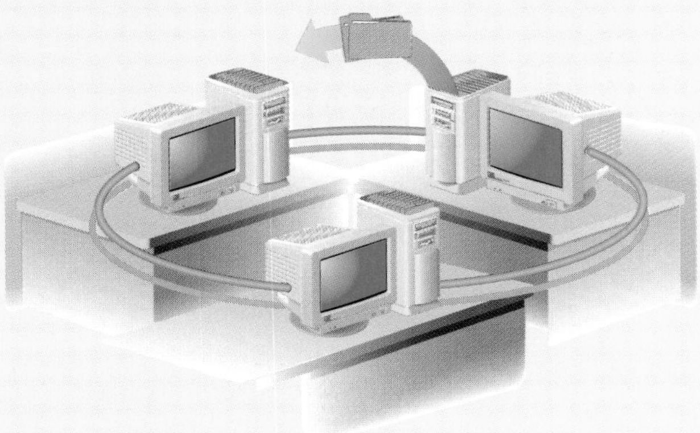

SET UP DIAL-UP NETWORKING

If you are using a modem to connect to an Internet Service Provider (ISP), you need to set up Dial-up Networking for your Internet connection.

SET UP DIAL-UP NETWORKING

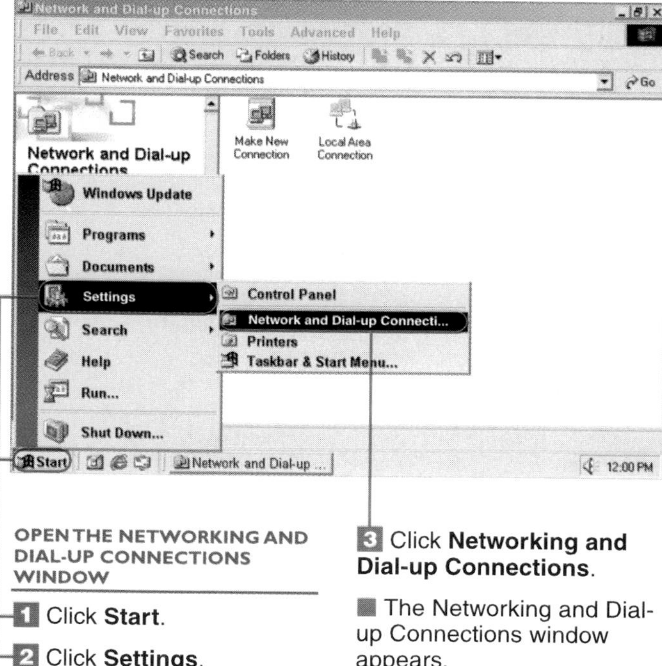

OPEN THE NETWORKING AND DIAL-UP CONNECTIONS WINDOW

1 Click **Start**.

2 Click **Settings**.

3 Click **Networking and Dial-up Connections**.

■ The Networking and Dial-up Connections window appears.

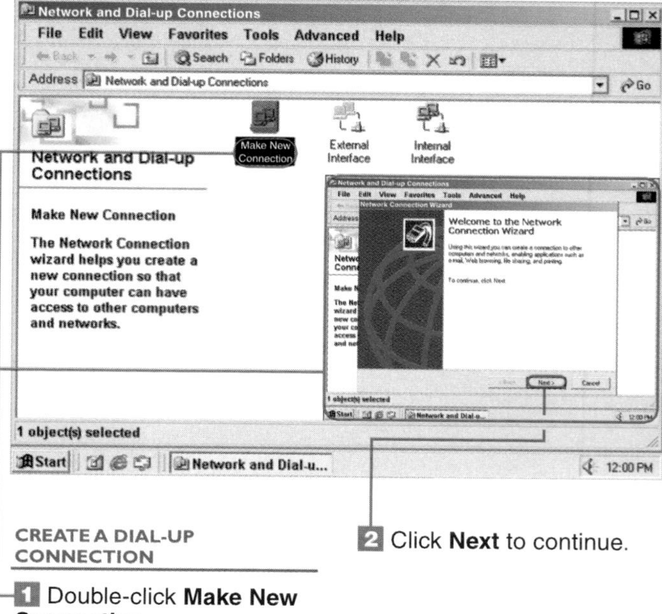

CREATE A DIAL-UP CONNECTION

1 Double-click **Make New Connection**.

■ The Welcome to the Network Connection Wizard screen appears.

2 Click **Next** to continue.

What do I need to know from my ISP before I connect to the Internet?

You will need to know Internet address information, such as the default gateway and DNS server. Your ISP will have all this information for you.

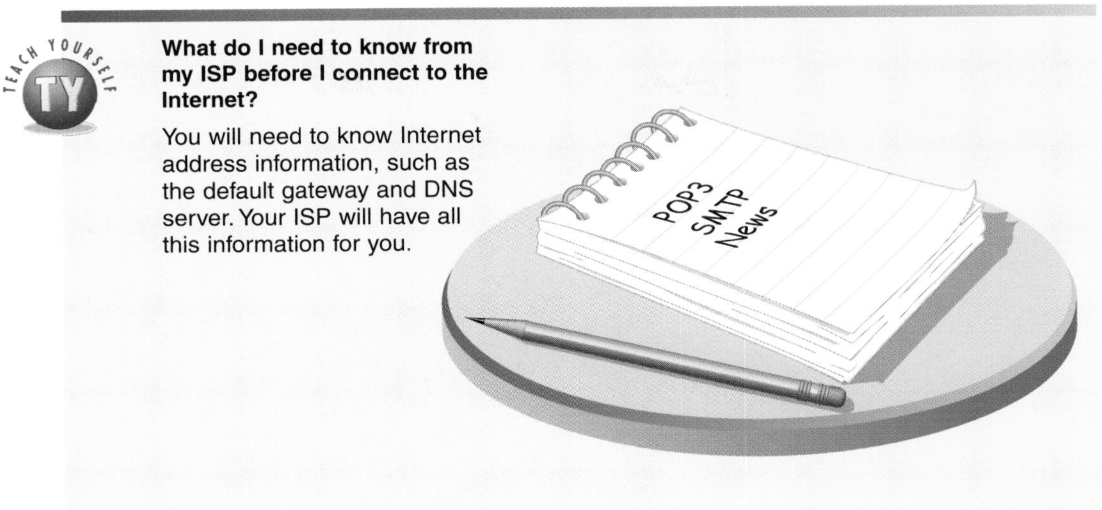

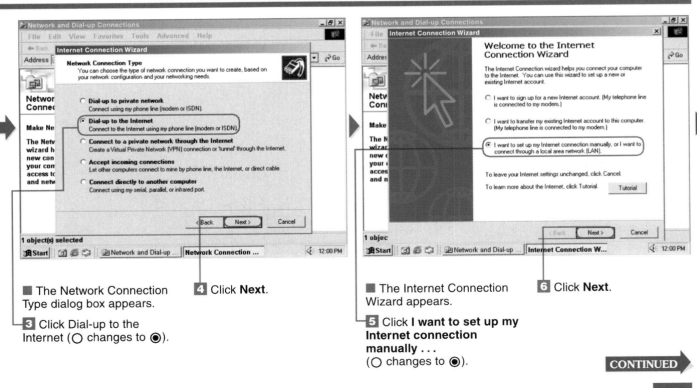

■ The Network Connection Type dialog box appears.

3 Click Dial-up to the Internet (○ changes to ◉).

4 Click **Next**.

■ The Internet Connection Wizard appears.

5 Click **I want to set up my Internet connection manually . . .** (○ changes to ◉).

6 Click **Next**.

CONTINUED

SET UP DIAL-UP NETWORKING

Dial-up networking is used to connect two computers using regular phone lines rather than a network.

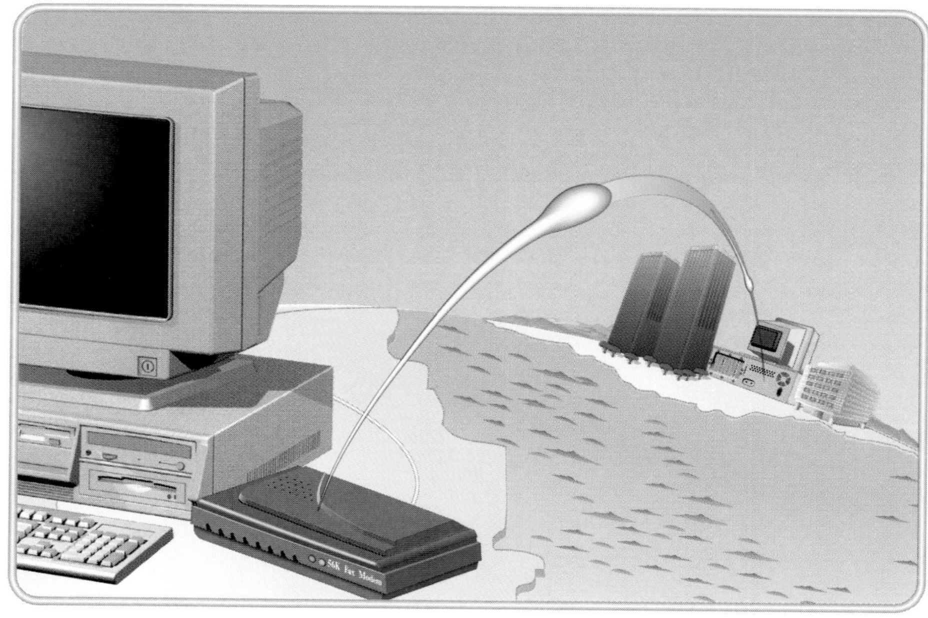

SET UP DIAL-UP NETWORKING (CONTINUED)

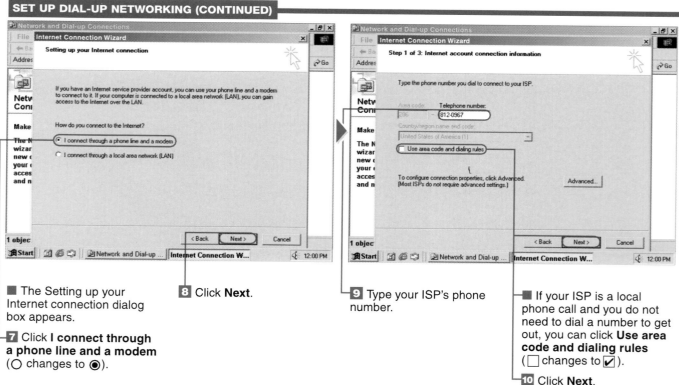

■ The Setting up your Internet connection dialog box appears.

7 Click **I connect through a phone line and a modem** (○ changes to ◉).

8 Click **Next**.

9 Type your ISP's phone number.

■ If your ISP is a local phone call and you do not need to dial a number to get out, you can click **Use area code and dialing rules** (☐ changes to ☑).

10 Click **Next**.

Do I have to set up networking every time I want to connect to the Internet?

You only need to set up the connection once. After that, you can dial in to the Internet at any time.

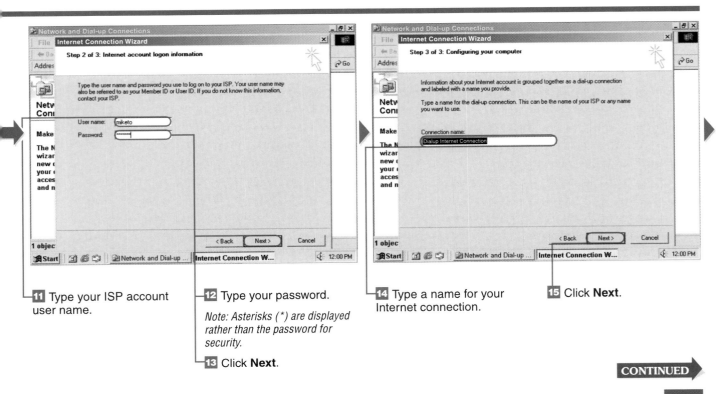

11 Type your ISP account user name.

12 Type your password.

Note: Asterisks (*) are displayed rather than the password for security.

13 Click **Next**.

14 Type a name for your Internet connection.

15 Click **Next**.

CONTINUED

SET UP DIAL-UP NETWORKING

Before you plug your modem into your office phone system, check with your network administrator or ISP. Many office phone systems use digital signals instead of analog and can permanently damage your modem.

SET UP DIAL-UP NETWORKING (CONTINUED)

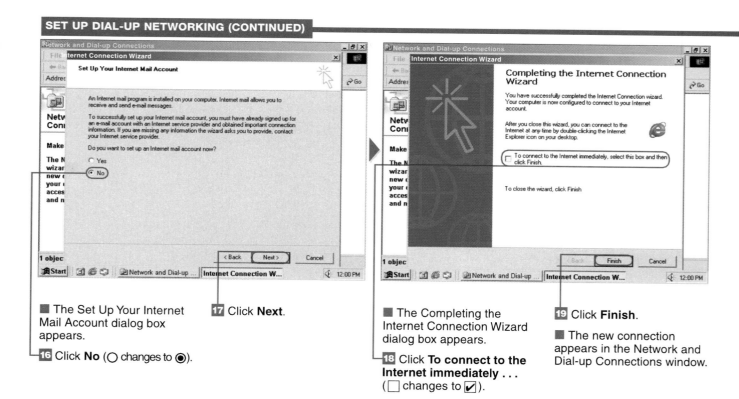

■ The Set Up Your Internet Mail Account dialog box appears.

16 Click **No** (○ changes to ◉).

17 Click **Next**.

■ The Completing the Internet Connection Wizard dialog box appears.

18 Click **To connect to the Internet immediately . . .** (☐ changes to ☑).

19 Click **Finish**.

■ The new connection appears in the Network and Dial-up Connections window.

What is Internet Connection Sharing?

Internet Connection Sharing, or ICS, lets several computers in your office use just one connection to your ISP for Internet access.

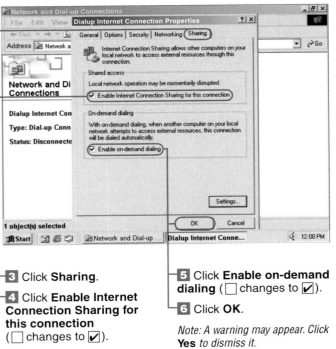

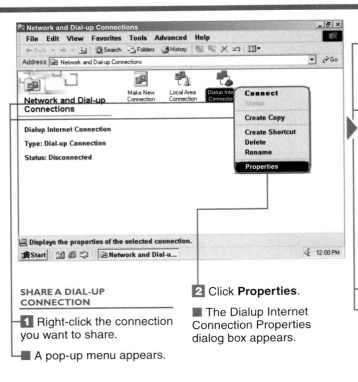

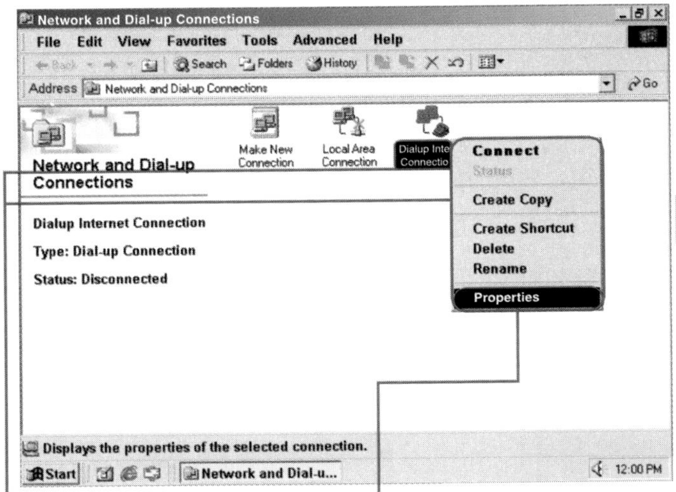

SHARE A DIAL-UP CONNECTION

1 Right-click the connection you want to share.

■ A pop-up menu appears.

2 Click **Properties**.

■ The Dialup Internet Connection Properties dialog box appears.

3 Click **Sharing**.

4 Click **Enable Internet Connection Sharing for this connection** (☐ changes to ☑).

5 Click **Enable on-demand dialing** (☐ changes to ☑).

6 Click **OK**.

Note: A warning may appear. Click **Yes** *to dismiss it.*

Before you can send or receive e-mail, you need to set up your account information. You can do this when you run the Internet Connection Wizard, or the first time you run Outlook Express.

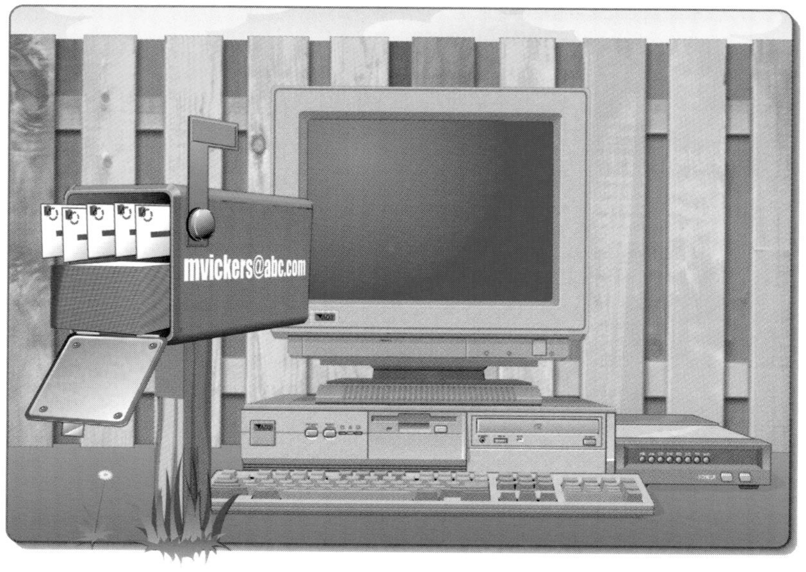

You will need an e-mail account with your ISP, and you will need the POP3 and SMTP server names and newsgroup server name.

SET UP E-MAIL

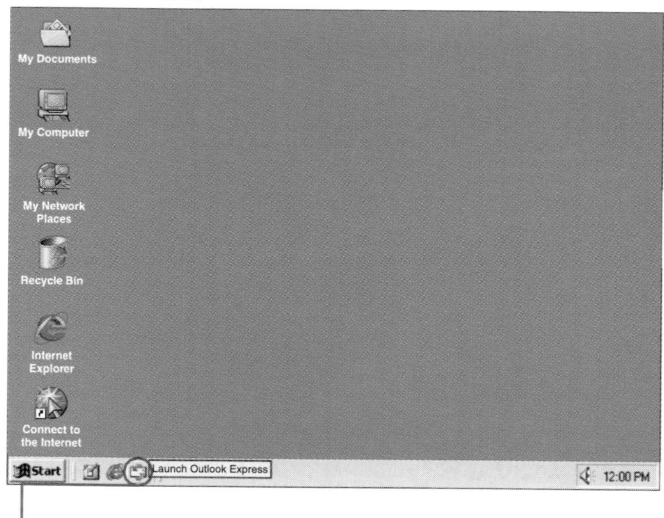

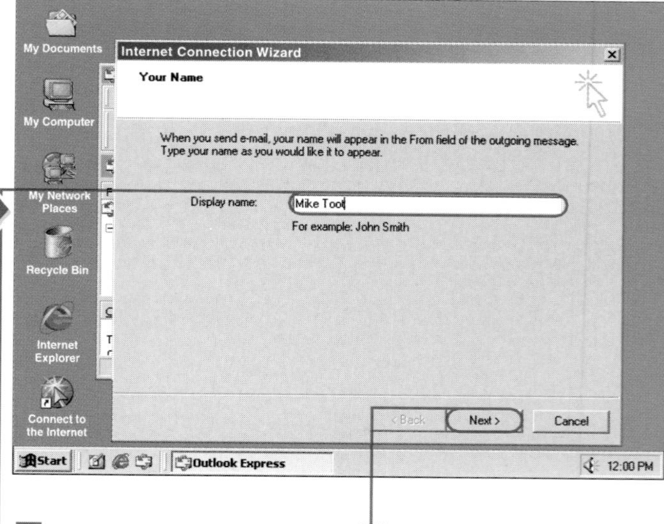

1 Click **Outlook Express**.

■ If your e-mail is not set up, the Internet Connection Wizard appears.

2 Type your name.

3 Click **Next**.

■ The Internet E-mail Address dialog box appears.

What are SMTP and POP3?

SMTP and POP3 are e-mail protocols for sending and receiving e-mail, respectively. They are used to store mail until you can pick it up with an e-mail program. Your ISP will tell you which ones to use and what settings you need for your e-mail program.

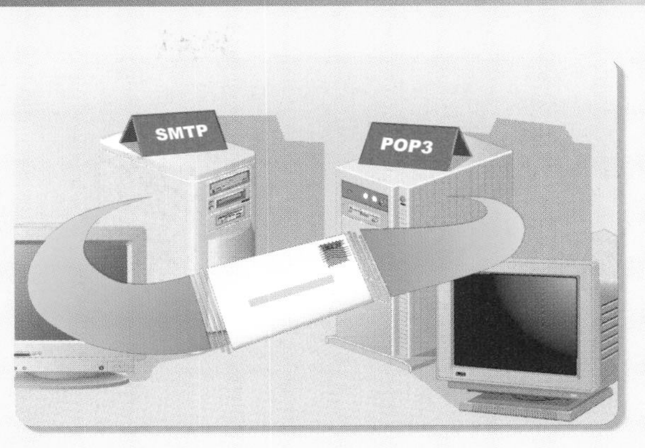

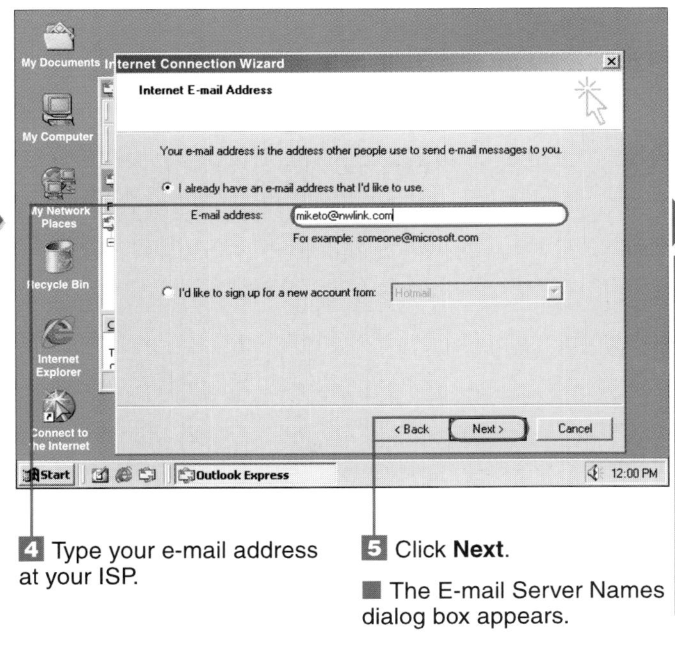

4 Type your e-mail address at your ISP.

5 Click **Next**.

■ The E-mail Server Names dialog box appears.

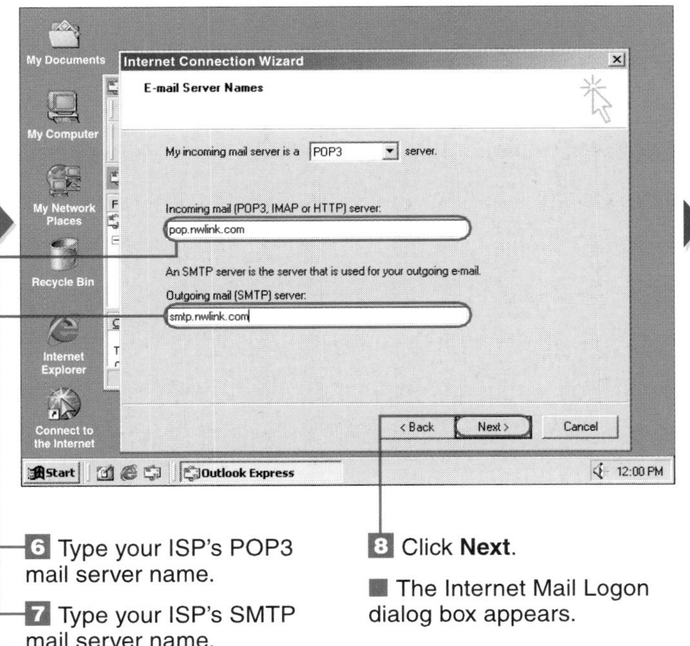

6 Type your ISP's POP3 mail server name.

7 Type your ISP's SMTP mail server name.

8 Click **Next**.

■ The Internet Mail Logon dialog box appears.

CONTINUED

It's common for businesses to have a single account with an ISP but many e-mail addresses for their employees. For example, employees would all use the MyBigCo account, but each person would have their own e-mail address.

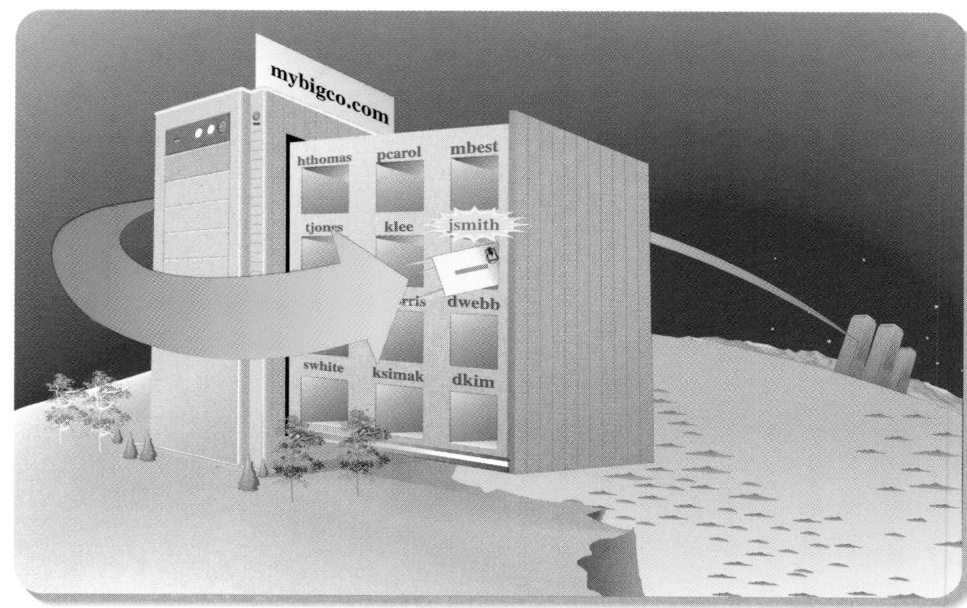

SET UP E-MAIL (CONTINUED)

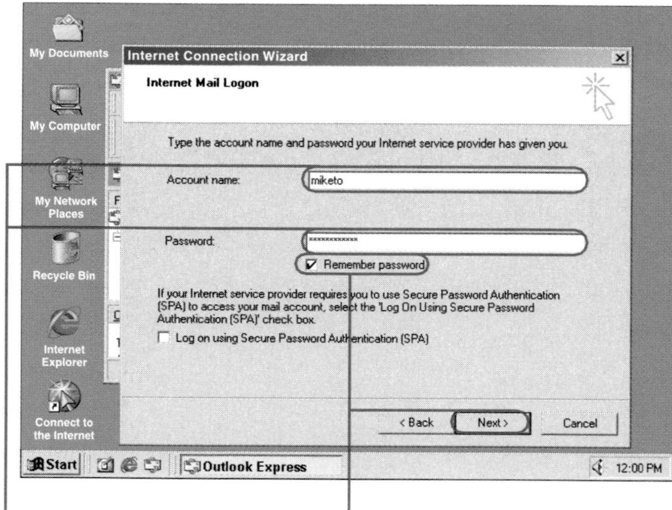

9 Type your ISP user name.

10 Type your password.

Note: Asterisks (*) are displayed rather than your password for security.

■ Click **Remember password** (☐ changes to ☑) if you want the software to remember your password for you.

11 Click **Next**.

■ The Congratulations dialog box appears.

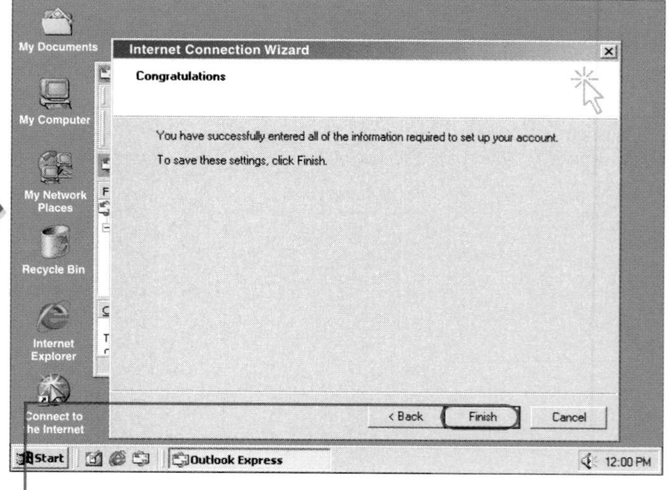

12 Click **Finish**.

Is it possible to have our own e-mail server?

Yes, you could have your own e-mail server in your business. Because e-mail servers are complex, you should ask a computer professional to help you install and configure e-mail server software.

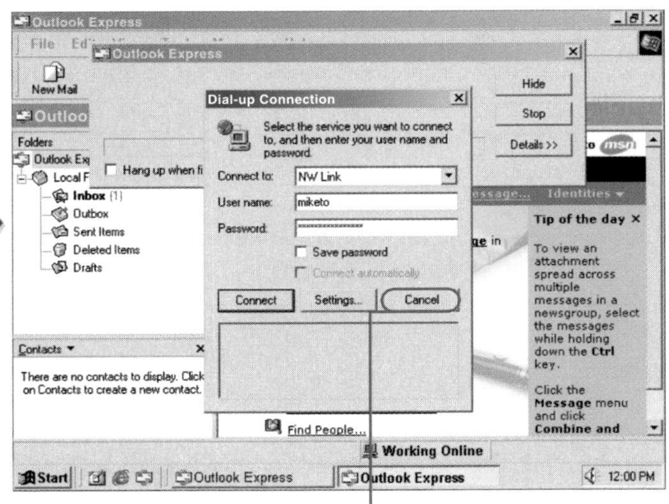

■ A Dial-up Connection dialog box may appear.

13 Click **Cancel**.

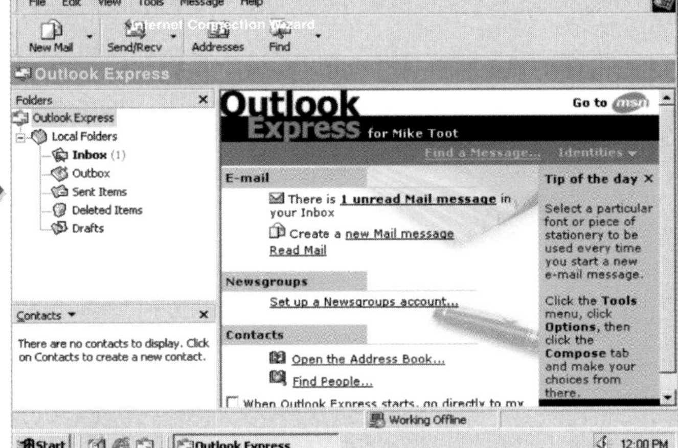

■ Outlook Express appears.

Note: For more information on using Outlook Express, see Chapter 12.

SPREADSHEET
SPREADSHEET
SPREADSHEET
WORD PROCESSOR
Create Professional Documents
ESSOR
fessional Documents
Database
Database
base
INTRANET SOFTWARE
INTRANET SOFTWARE

CHAPTER 7

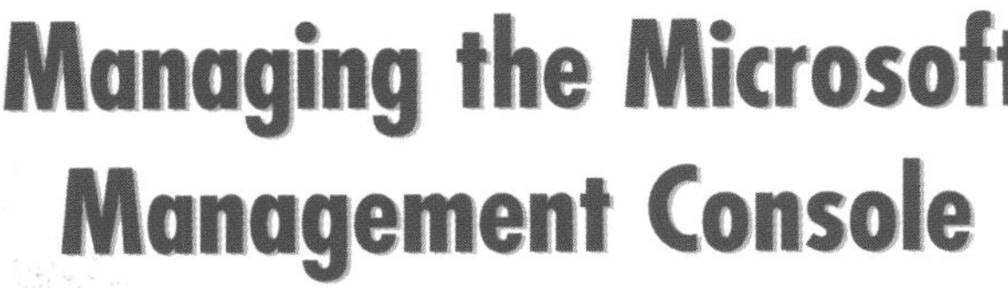
Managing the Microsoft Management Console

Nearly all server management tools are used within the Microsoft Management Console. This chapter introduces you to the console and its snap-ins.

LAUNCH THE MICROSOFT MANAGEMENT CONSOLE

Windows 2000 Server contains several administrative consoles that you can use to maintain software, hardware, and your network. The Microsoft Management Console (MMC) is the place where you can maintain and modify those consoles.

Consoles contain several different items, including console tasks, console monitoring controls, console wizards and documentation, and snap-ins.

LAUNCH THE MICROSOFT MANAGEMENT CONSOLE

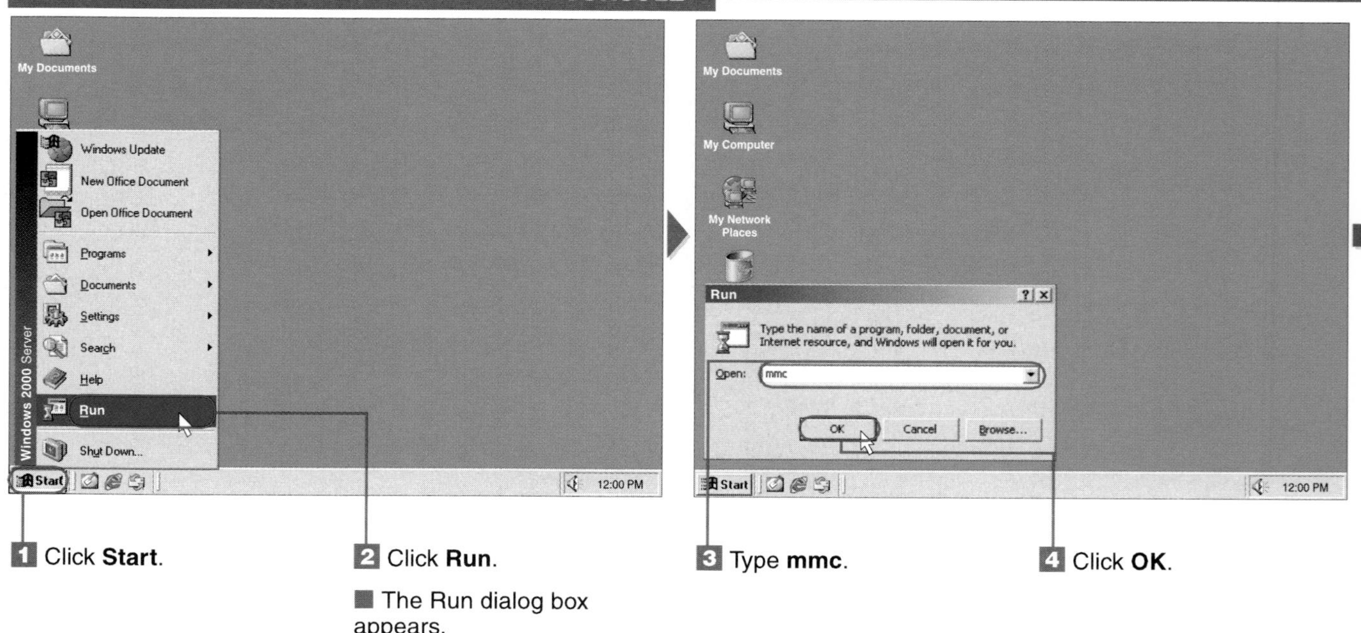

1 Click **Start**.

2 Click **Run**.

■ The Run dialog box appears.

3 Type **mmc**.

4 Click **OK**.

Can I open these consoles from a location other than the MMC?

Yes. You can access these consoles from the Start menu. Click the Start button, then click Control Panel, then double-click the Administrative Tools icon.

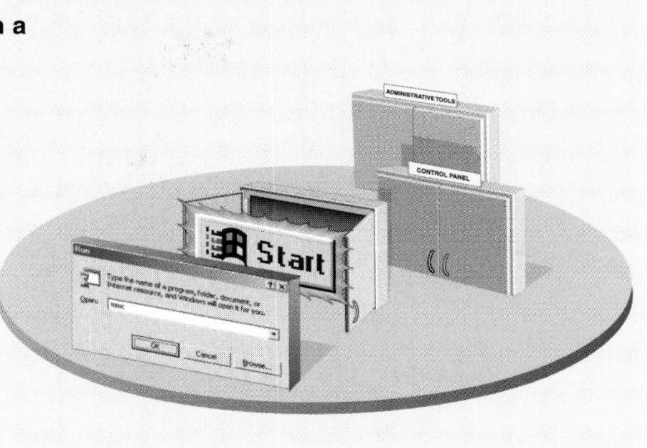

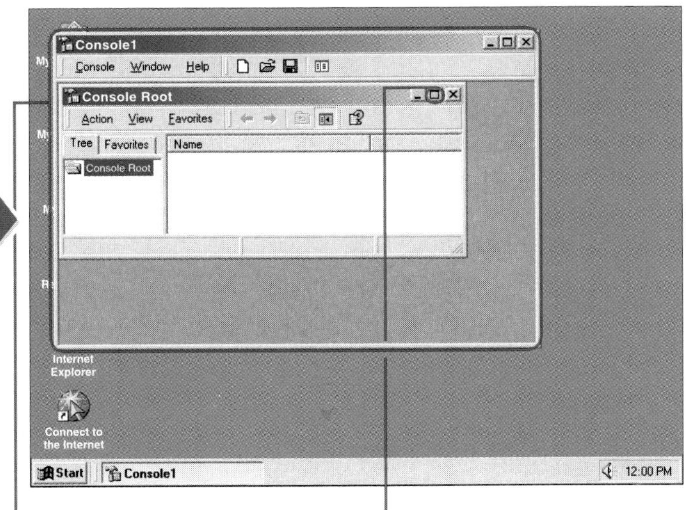

■ The Microsoft Management Console window appears.

■ You can click ▢ to maximize the console window in the MMC window.

■ The console window expands to fill the MMC window.

ADD AN MMC SNAP-IN

The MMC contains dozens of predefined consoles called snap-ins. These snap-ins provide many management functions for your computer and network.

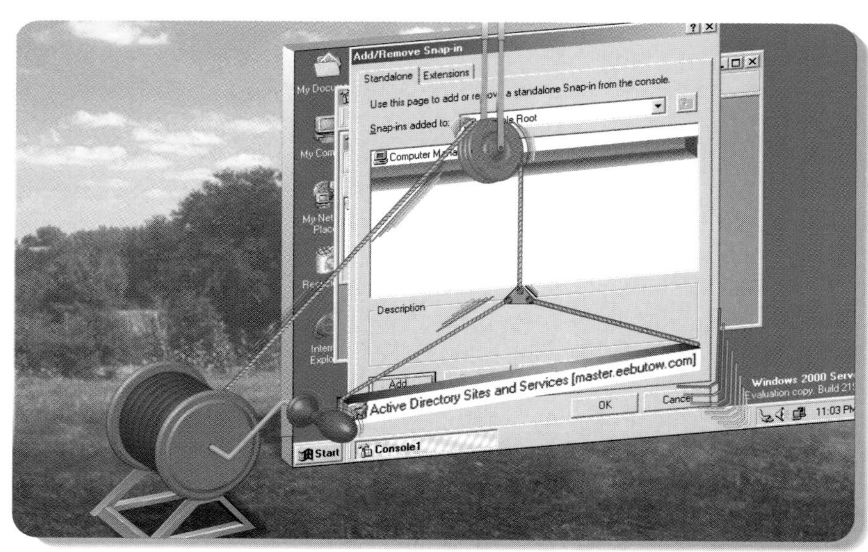

Other snap-ins may come with software that you load on your computer.

ADD AN MMC SNAP-IN

1 Click **Start**.

2 Click **Run**.

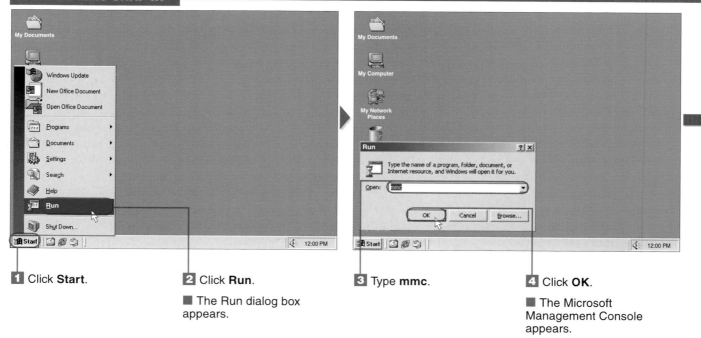

■ The Run dialog box appears.

3 Type **mmc**.

4 Click **OK**.

■ The Microsoft Management Console appears.

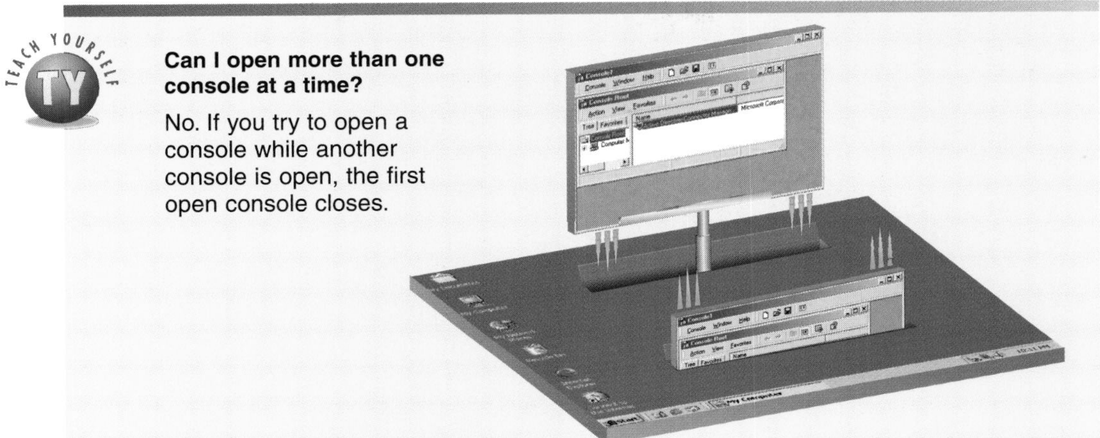

TEACH YOURSELF

Can I open more than one console at a time?

No. If you try to open a console while another console is open, the first open console closes.

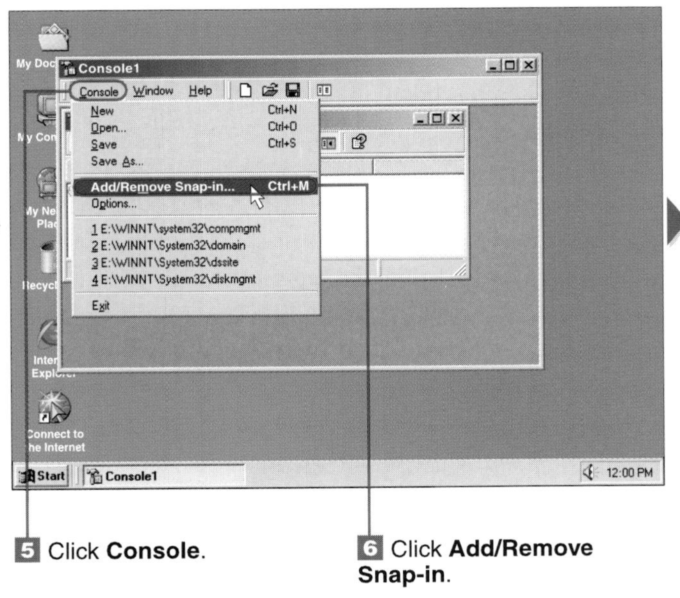

5 Click **Console**.

6 Click **Add/Remove Snap-in**.

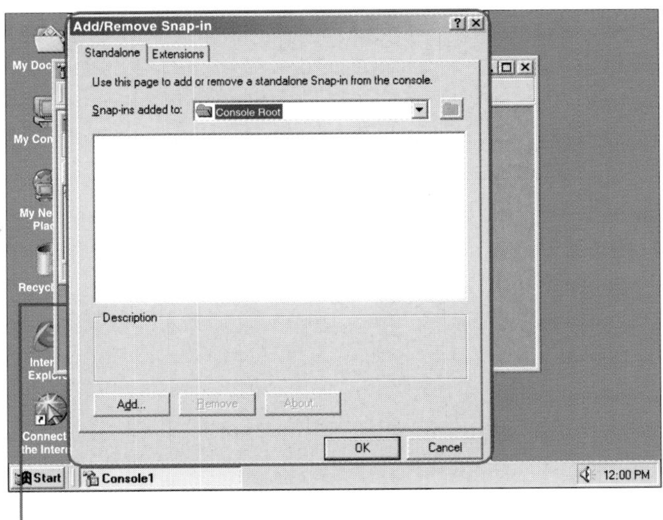

■ The Add/Remove Snap-in dialog box appears.

CONTINUED

ADD AN MMC SNAP-IN

You can create sets of snap-ins that help you manage your network efficiently. One way is to group them by theme — user account management in one MMC, server management in another, and so forth.

ADD AN MMC SNAP-IN (CONTINUED)

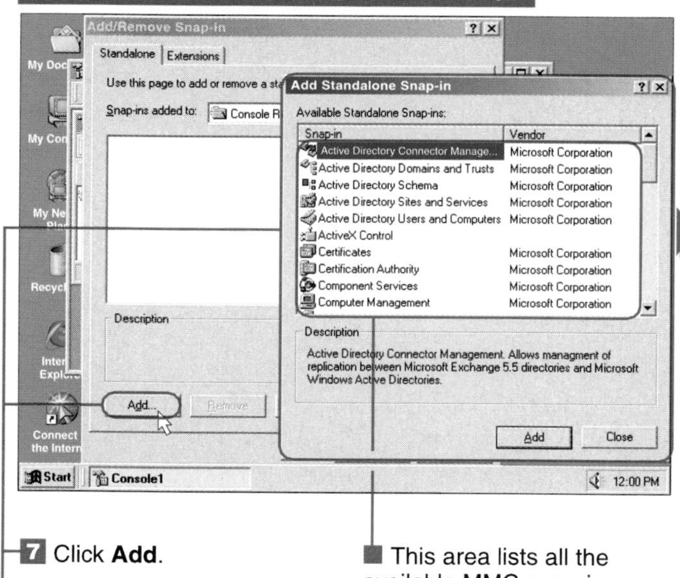

7 Click **Add**.

■ The **Add Standalone Snap-in** dialog box appears.

■ This area lists all the available MMC snap-ins.

8 Click the snap-in you want to add.

9 Click **Add**.

Note: A window may appear asking you to set some variables for the selected snap-in.

10 Click **Close**.

Where can I get information about an extension?

The Description area on the Extensions tab provides a brief description. You can view the component name and version by clicking the About button below the Description area.

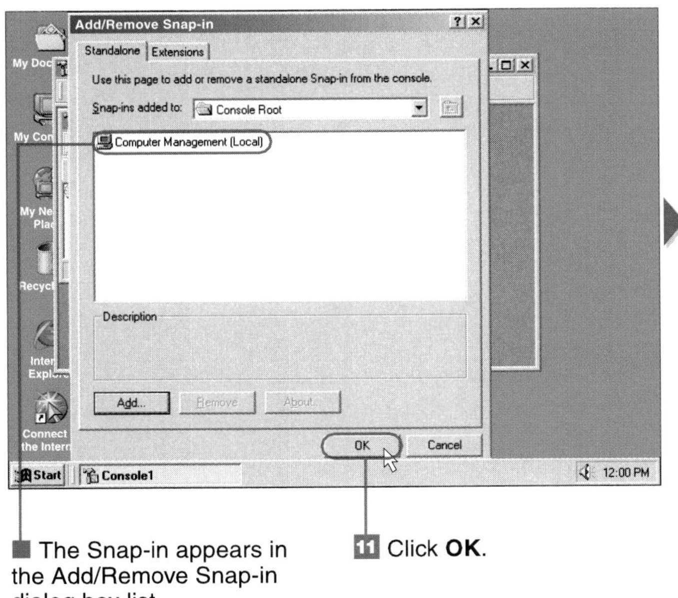

■ The Snap-in appears in the Add/Remove Snap-in dialog box list.

11 Click **OK**.

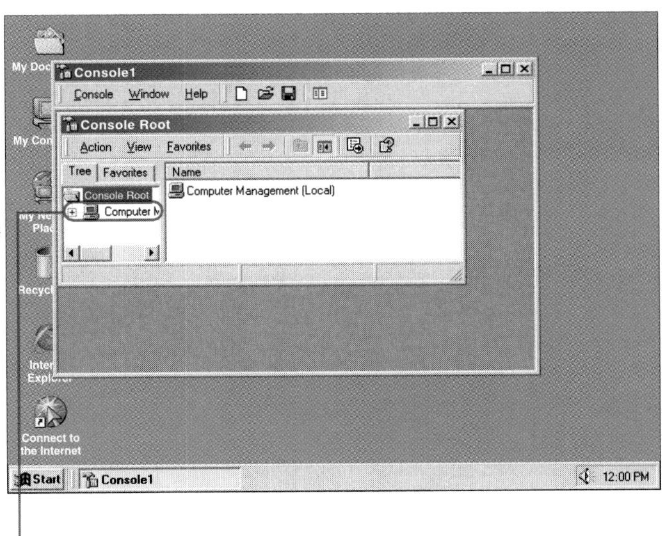

■ The console tree displays the snap-in.

MODIFY MMC ITEMS

You can remove a snap-in or other item from the MMC console.

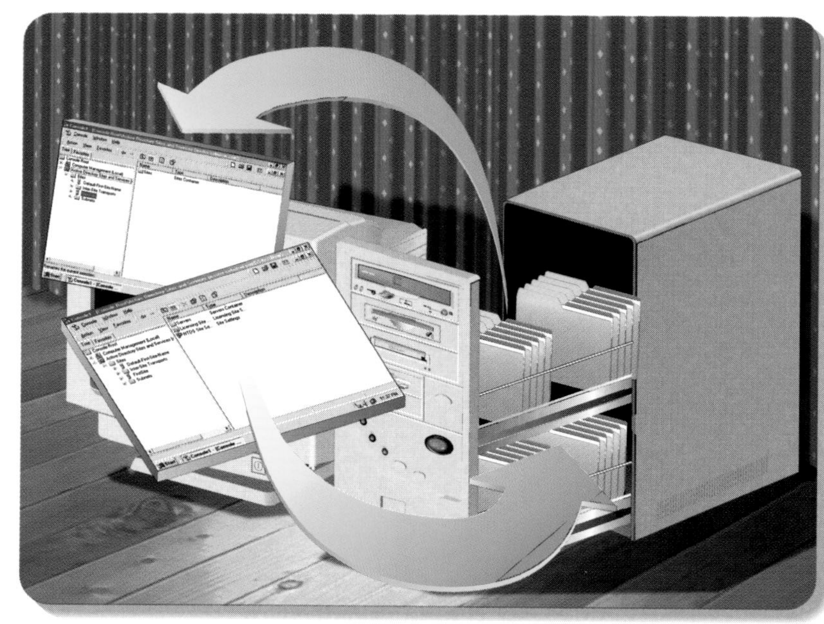

You can also create a new console window from an existing MMC console.

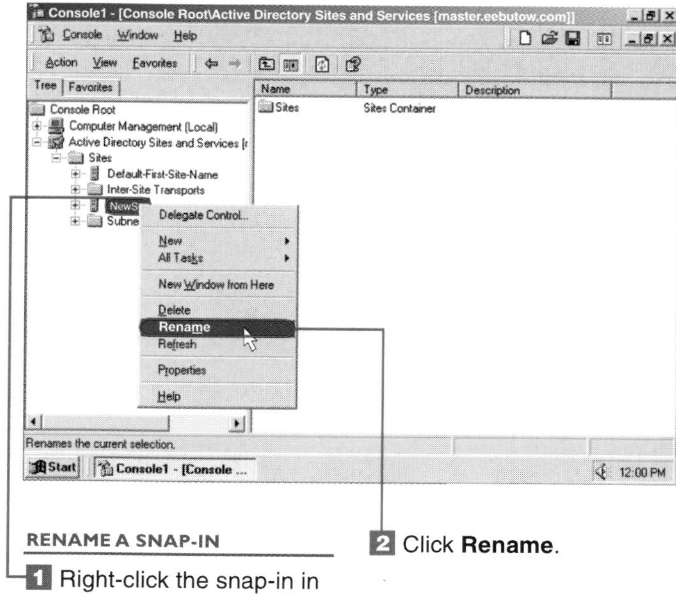

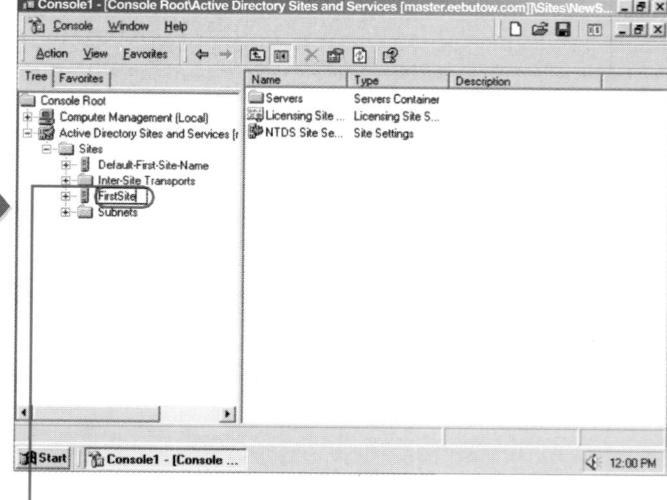

RENAME A SNAP-IN

1 Right-click the snap-in in the tree.

■ A pop-up menu appears.

2 Click **Rename**.

3 Type a new name for the snap-in.

4 Press Enter.

What if I cannot see the Rename command on the pop-up menu?

If you do not see the Rename command on the pop-up menu, then you cannot rename the selected item.

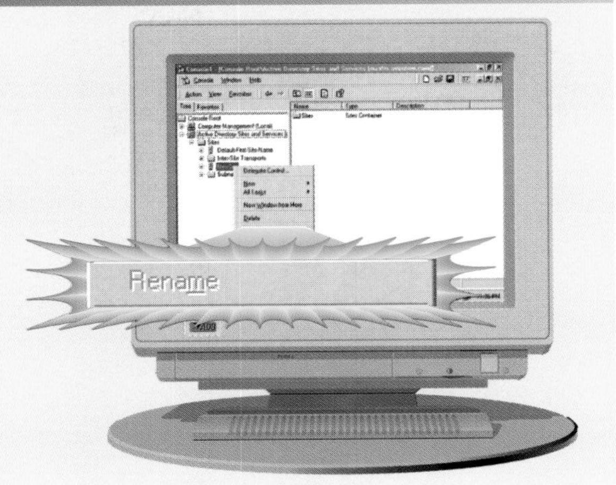

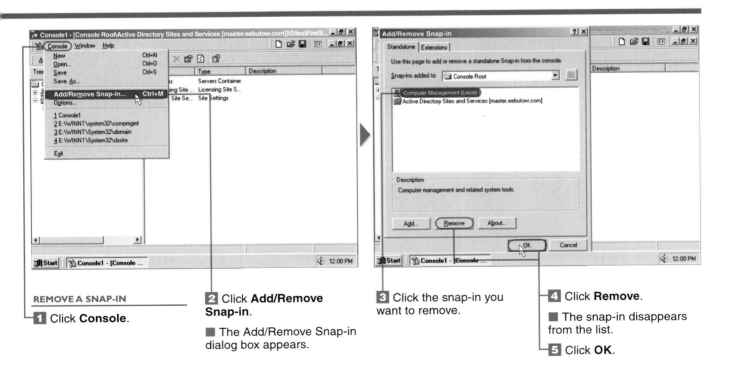

REMOVE A SNAP-IN

1 Click **Console**.

2 Click **Add/Remove Snap-in**.

■ The Add/Remove Snap-in dialog box appears.

3 Click the snap-in you want to remove.

4 Click **Remove**.

■ The snap-in disappears from the list.

5 Click **OK**.

SAVE MMC ITEMS

After you add snap-ins and make any changes, you must save those changes to avoid losing them.

When you save a console, it is automatically saved with an MSC file extension, enabling you to open the console later.

SAVE MMC ITEMS

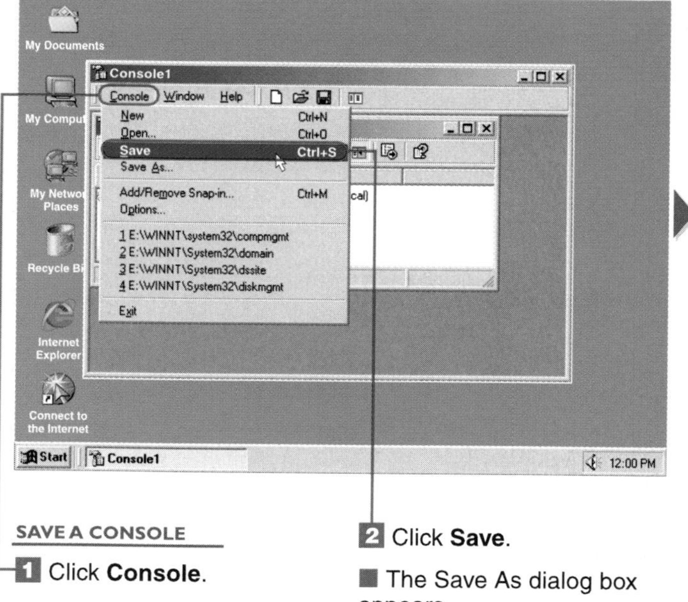

SAVE A CONSOLE

1 Click **Console**.

2 Click **Save**.

■ The Save As dialog box appears.

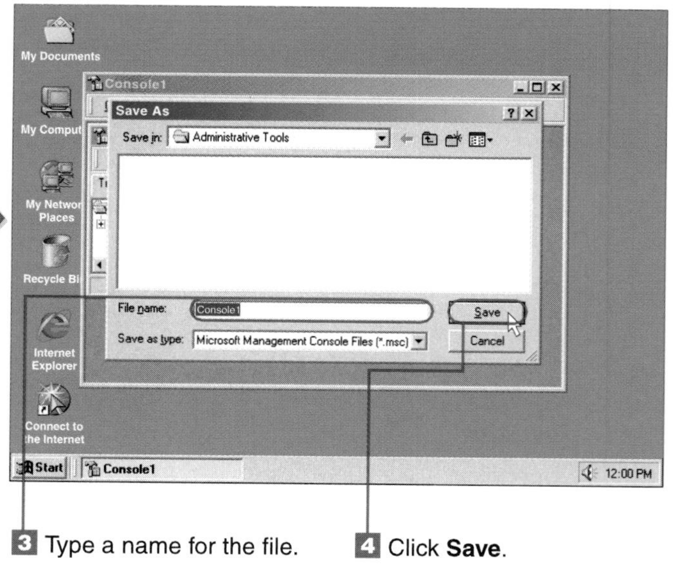

3 Type a name for the file.

4 Click **Save**.

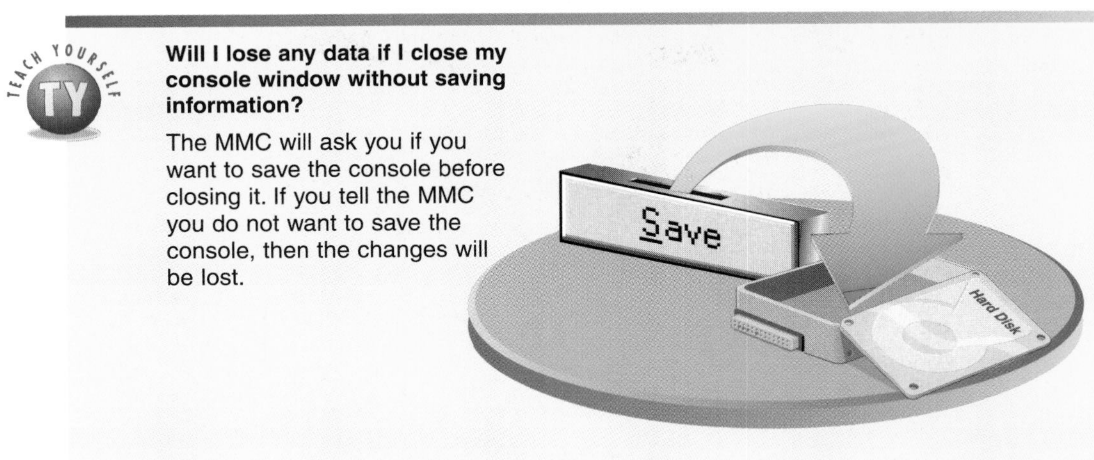

Will I lose any data if I close my console window without saving information?

The MMC will ask you if you want to save the console before closing it. If you tell the MMC you do not want to save the console, then the changes will be lost.

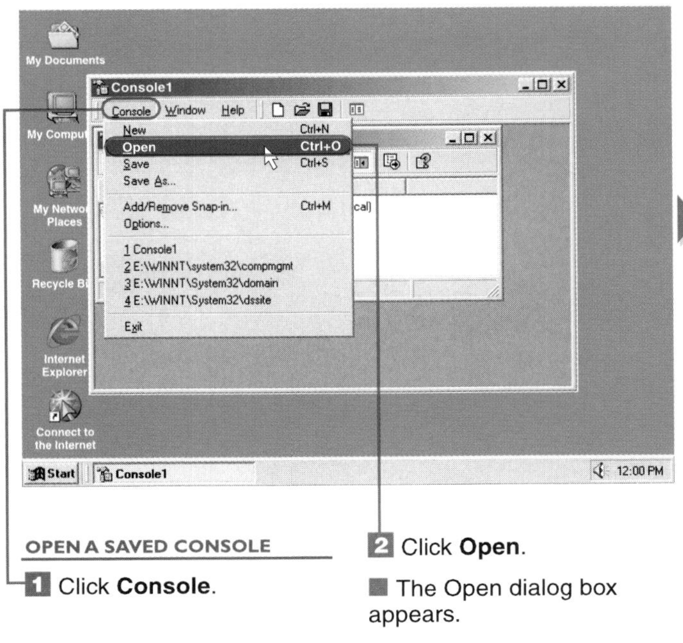

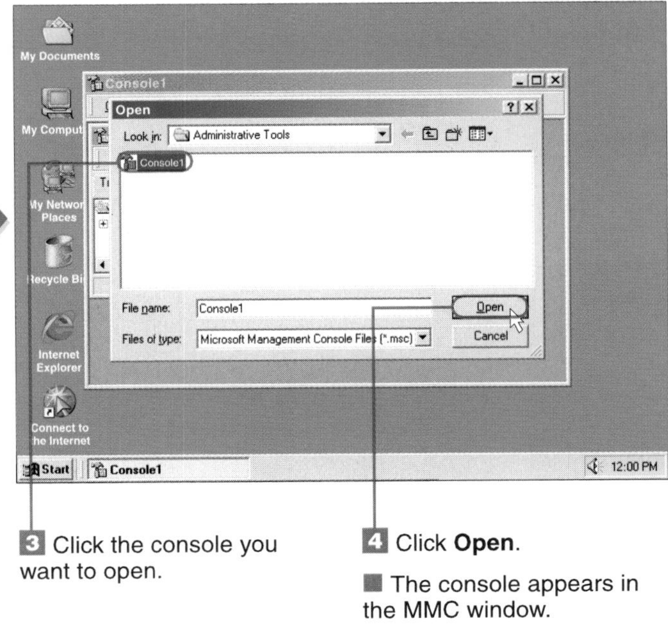

OPEN A SAVED CONSOLE

1 Click **Console**.

2 Click **Open**.

■ The Open dialog box appears.

3 Click the console you want to open.

4 Click **Open**.

■ The console appears in the MMC window.

CDRW 3000
WRITING
OPEN
CLOSE
GROUP
USER ACCOUNT
NEW ACCOUNT

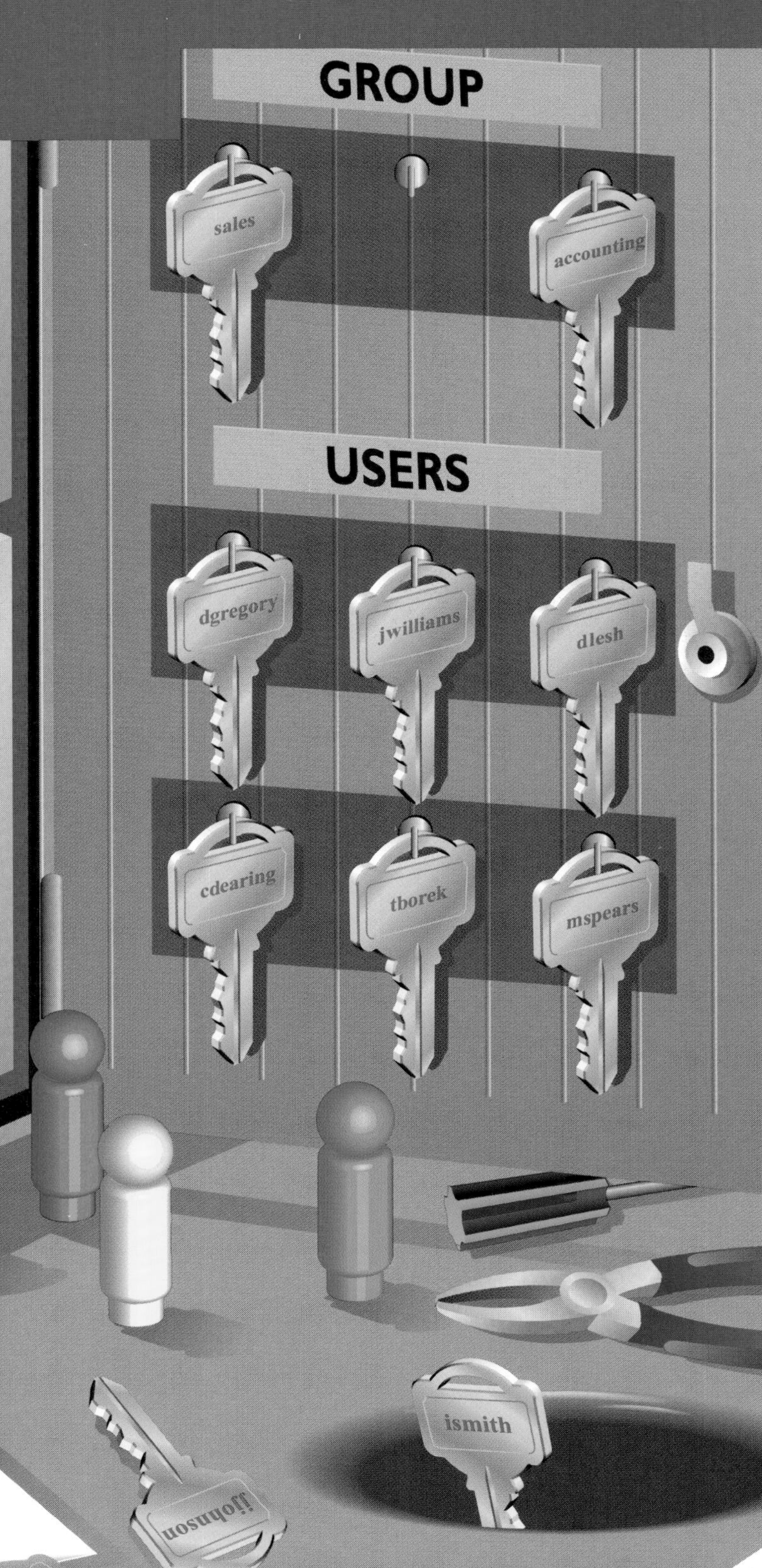

CHAPTER 8

Managing People and Groups on Your Network

In this chapter you will learn how to work with user accounts, user profiles, groups, and group policies. These are the key components for managing your users quickly and efficiently.

ADD A USER ACCOUNT

You can create user accounts for your Windows 2000 Server computer and all other servers and clients on your network using Active Directory Users and Computers.

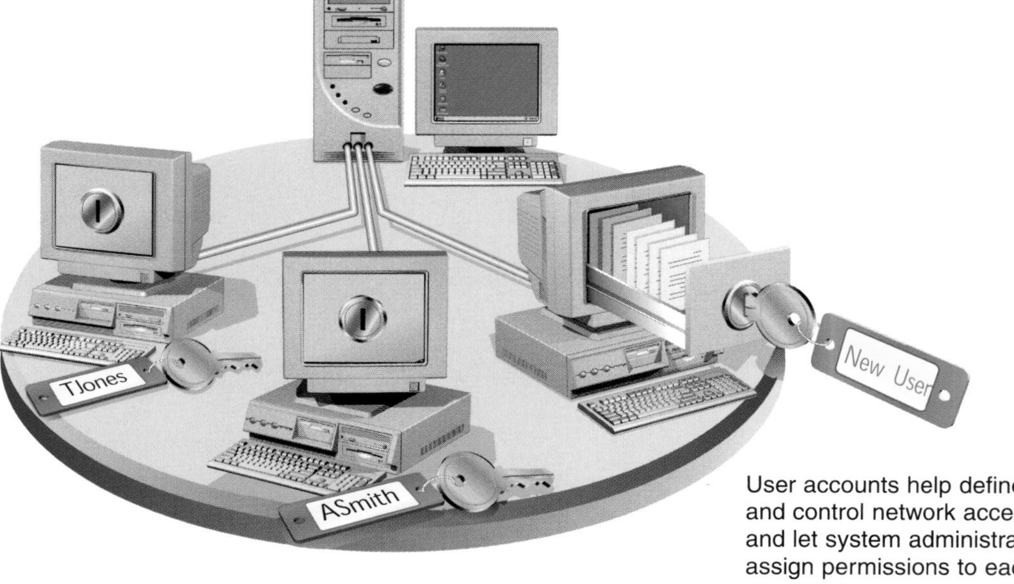

User accounts help define and control network access, and let system administrators assign permissions to each user on the network.

ADD A USER ACCOUNT

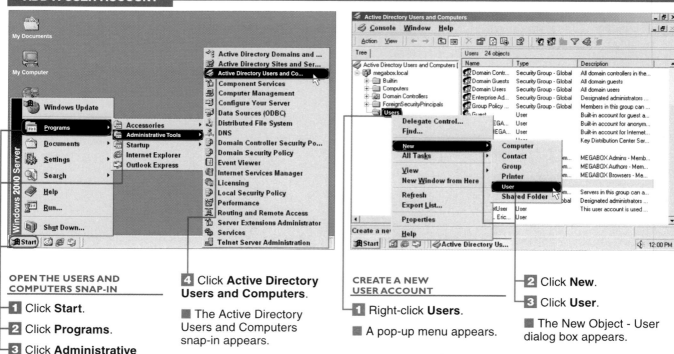

OPEN THE USERS AND COMPUTERS SNAP-IN

1 Click **Start**.

2 Click **Programs**.

3 Click **Administrative Tools**.

4 Click **Active Directory Users and Computers**.

■ The Active Directory Users and Computers snap-in appears.

CREATE A NEW USER ACCOUNT

1 Right-click **Users**.

■ A pop-up menu appears.

2 Click **New**.

3 Click **User**.

■ The New Object - User dialog box appears.

Can I add a user to Active Directory by copying a previously created user account?

Yes. Copy a previously created user account by right-clicking the user account and clicking **Copy**. Then update the account with your new user information.

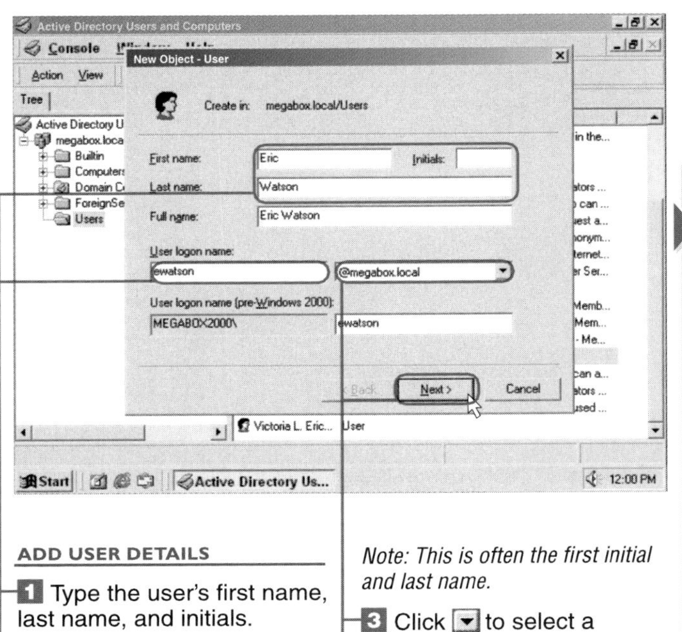

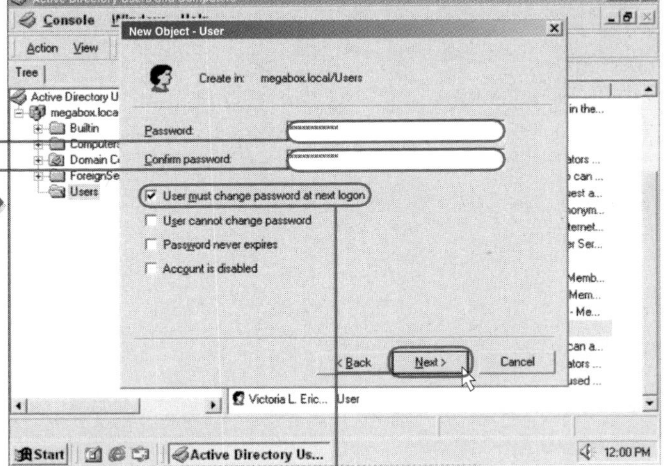

ADD USER DETAILS

1 Type the user's first name, last name, and initials.

2 Type the user's logon name.

Note: This is often the first initial and last name.

3 Click ▾ to select a domain name that the user will belong to.

4 Click **Next**.

5 Type a password.

■ Asterisks (*) will appear as you type instead of the password as a security measure.

6 Type the password again.

7 Click **User must change password at next logon** (☐ changes to ☑).

■ This forces users to change the password the next time they log on.

8 Click **Next**.

CONTINUED

ADD A USER ACCOUNT

When you create a new user account, make sure to use a secure password for the new account.

Secure passwords are ones that cannot be guessed easily (your spouse's name or children's names or significant dates like birthdays *can* be guessed easily). The best passwords use words that are not found in dictionaries, combinations of letters and numbers, or use unusual keyboard letters.

ADD A USER ACCOUNT (CONTINUED)

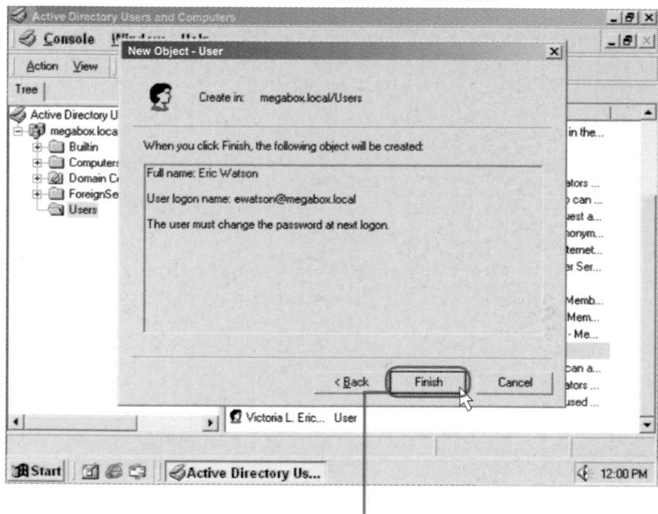

■ A confirmation dialog box appears, showing your selections.

9 Click **Finish**.

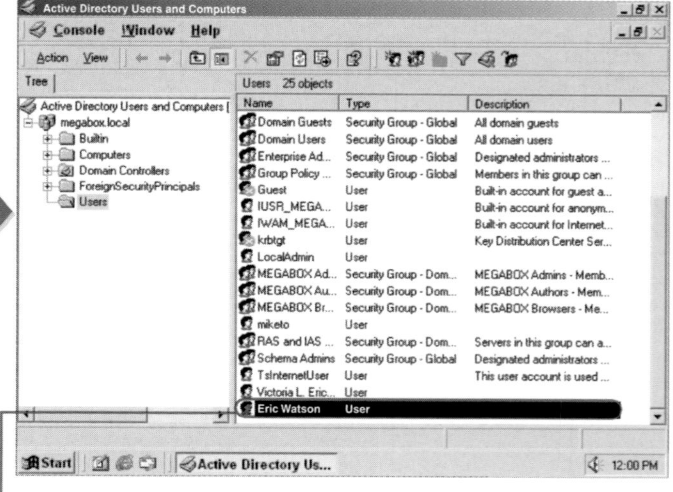

■ The new user appears in the snap-in.

How do I add accounts if I don't have Active Directory Users and Computers on my server?

You can add a user account if you do not have Active Directory installed by following the procedure on this page. This is common on networks that use Windows NT domains or workgroups.

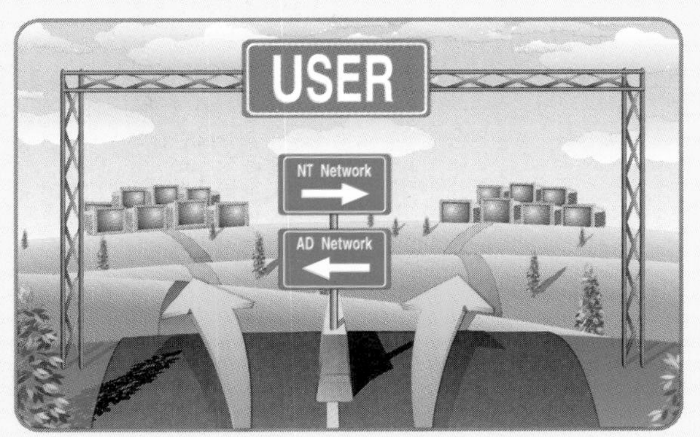

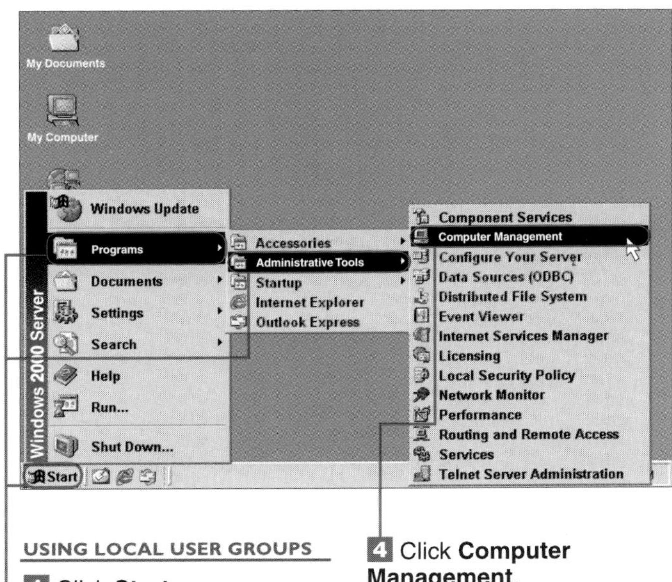

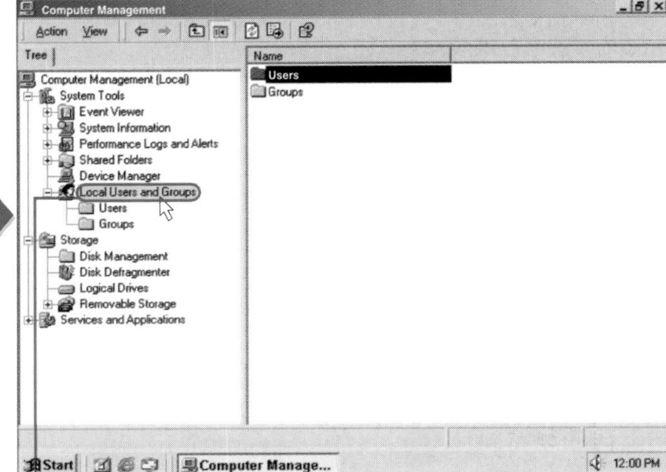

USING LOCAL USER GROUPS

1 Click **Start**.

2 Click **Programs**.

3 Click **Administrative Tools**.

4 Click **Computer Management**.

■ The Computer Management window appears.

5 Click **Local Users And Groups**.

Note: See "Add a User Account" using Active Directory for details.

SECURE A USER ACCOUNT

Two things identify your users: the user name and password. The user password is the key to establishing identity. Windows 2000 allows you to place limits or restrictions on passwords to make them difficult to guess or break.

PASSWORD RESTRICTIONS

Your user passwords should be ones that cannot be easily guessed. You can use Windows 2000 to restrict passwords to be a certain minimum length, or use a mix of letters, numbers, and symbols.

If the passwords are too complex or lengthy, people will write them down near their computers for easy access. This provides an easy way for others to defeat your security.

PASSWORD DURATION

Passwords can last forever, or you can require users to change their passwords after a certain number of days. If you have high turnover in a group, you should require password changes more frequently for members of that group.

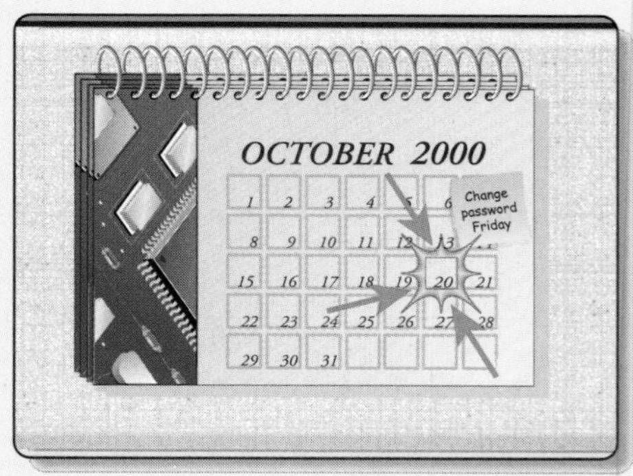

ACCOUNT LOCKOUT

You will want to select how many times your users can try to log on with a bad user name or password before locking the account. This will help keep unauthorized users from repeatedly trying name and password combinations.

DISABLED ACCOUNT

You can disable an account when an employee leaves the company, or if you have seasonal help or contractors who work at your company.

This allows you to re-enable a disabled account when the contractors return. This way, you do not have to recreate the account's policies and permissions.

BACKUP TO TAPE

You can assign a temporary password to a new employee's account at your company. The first time the user logs on, the system will automatically prompt the employee to change the temporary password.

This helps keep the new account secure, and keeps new account information secure from others in your company.

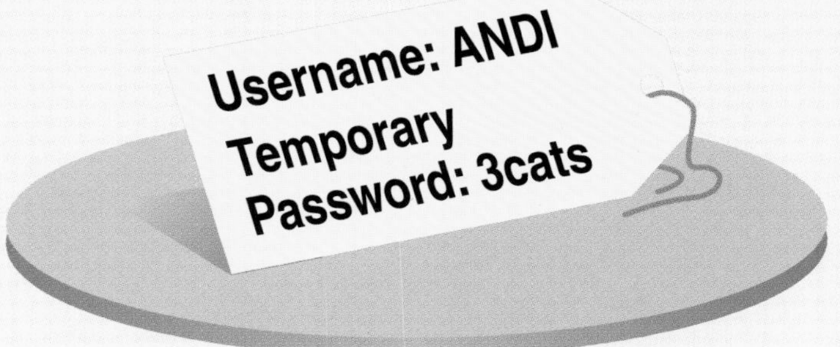

VIEW USER ACCOUNT PROPERTIES

User account properties help manage your users. These properties are used to determine group membership, provide home directories for network file storage, and enable or disable network access.

VIEW USER ACCOUNT PROPERTIES

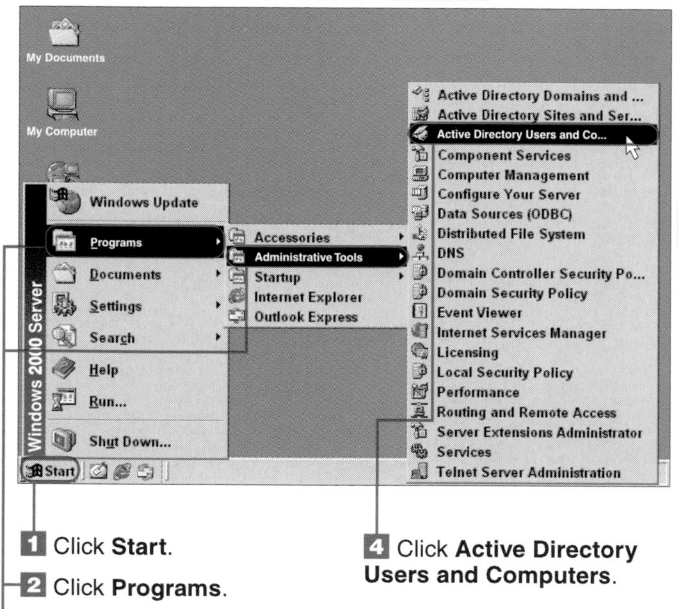

1 Click **Start**.

2 Click **Programs**.

3 Click **Administrative Tools**.

4 Click **Active Directory Users and Computers**.

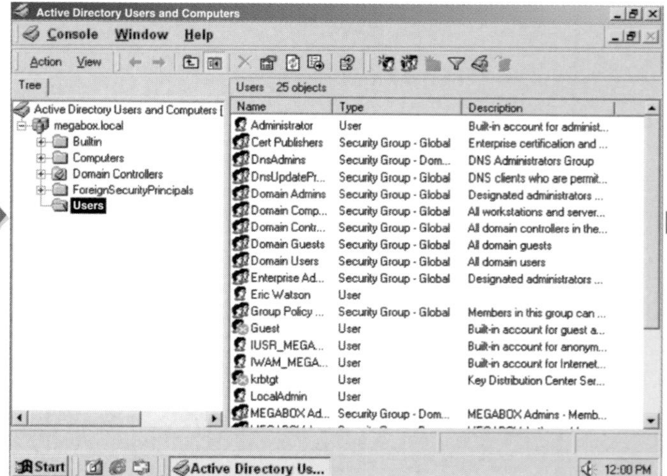

■ The Active Directory Users and Computers snap-in appears.

How can I find a user account in Active Directory?

You can easily find a user by right-clicking a domain or organizational units in the Active Directory tree and then clicking **Find**. You can then enter the name of the user you want to find.

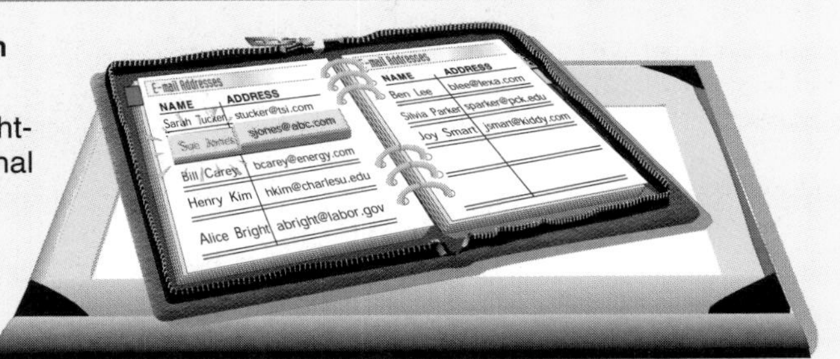

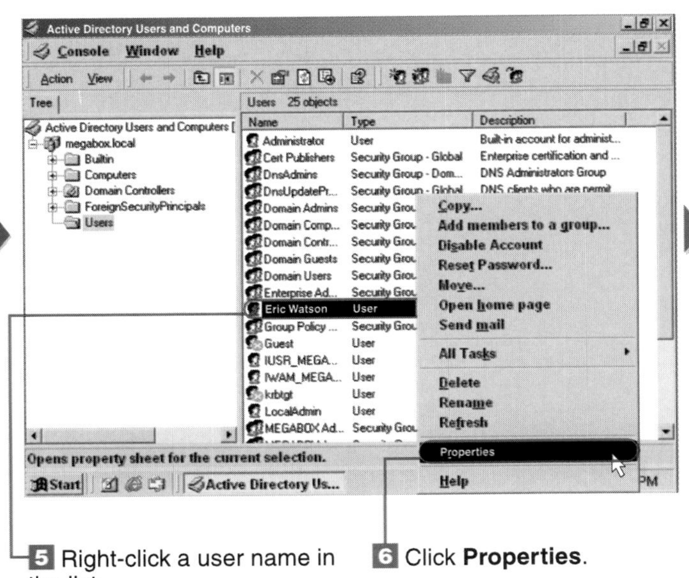

5 Right-click a user name in the list.

Note: An X in a red circle appearing in the User's list means that the user's account is disabled.

6 Click **Properties**.

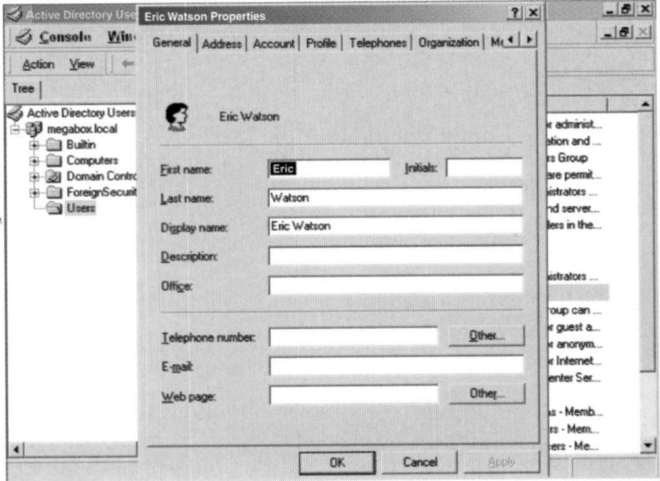

■ The Properties dialog box appears.

Note: You can add or modify the user's information on the different tabs as necessary.

ADD A USER TO A GROUP

You can add users to groups in your network. This makes it easier to assign settings to groups of users, rather than to each user individually.

ADD A USER TO A GROUP

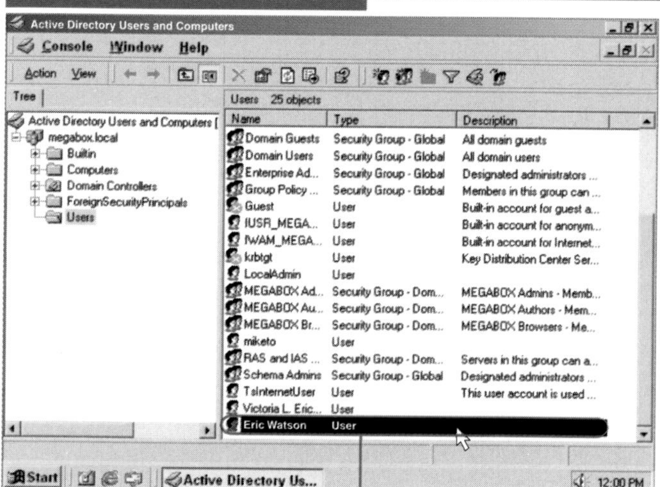

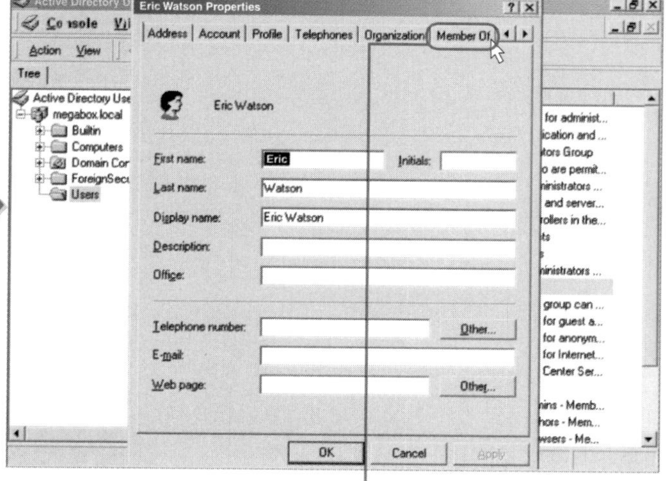

1 Open the Active Directory Users and Groups snap-in.

Note: See "View User Account Properties" for details.

2 Double-click a user name (example: **Eric Watson**).

■ The user's Properties dialog box appears.

3 Click the **Member Of** tab.

What is the difference between a user and a group?

A user is an individual on your network. A group is several users who use the same equipment or need access to the same information.

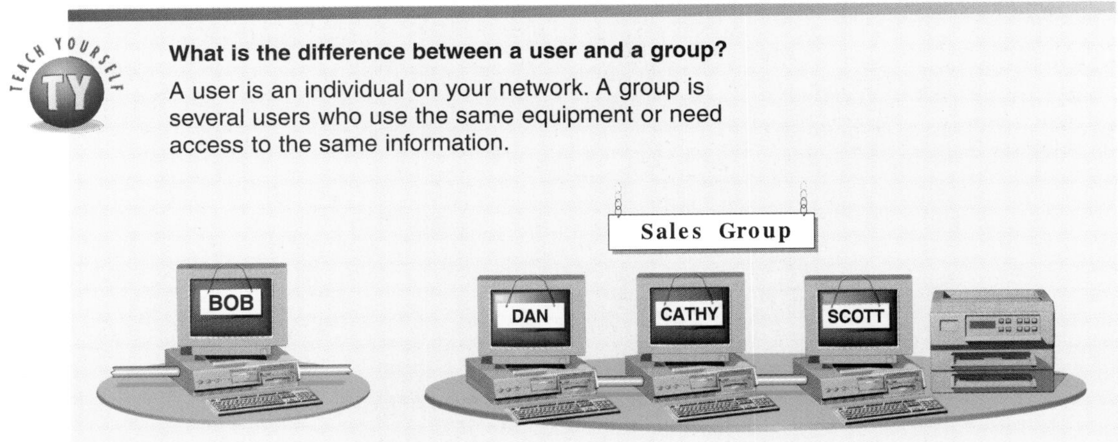

4 Click **Add**.

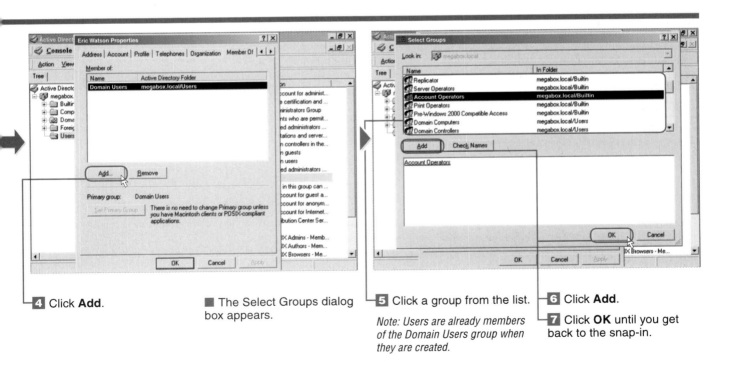

■ The Select Groups dialog box appears.

5 Click a group from the list.

Note: Users are already members of the Domain Users group when they are created.

6 Click **Add**.

7 Click **OK** until you get back to the snap-in.

ADD A HOME DIRECTORY

Home directories provide a convenient location to back up and manage user profiles and user documents.

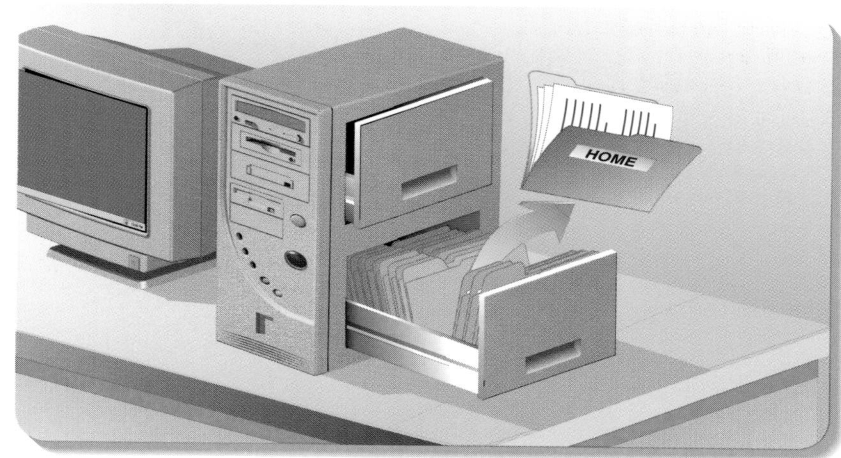

Windows 2000 Server lets you set up the home directory for the server computer and all client computers in the network.

ADD A HOME DIRECTORY

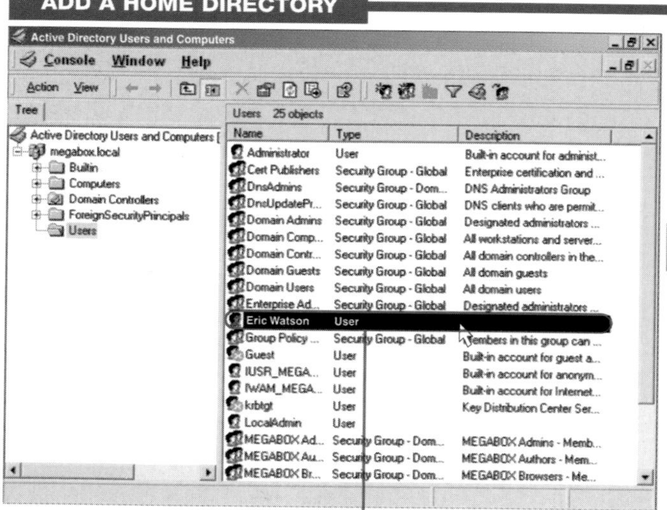

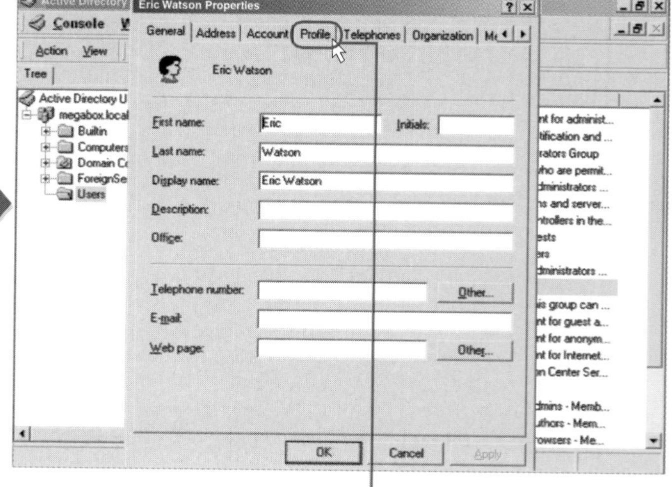

1 Open the Active Directory Users and Computers snap-in.

Note: See "Add a User Account" for details.

2 Double-click a user name in the list (example: **Eric Watson**).

■ The user's Properties dialog box appears.

3 Click the **Profile** tab.

What happens if I don't specify a home directory?

Windows 2000 Server will use the home directory on the user's computer. This means the user will not be able to use roaming or mandatory profiles.

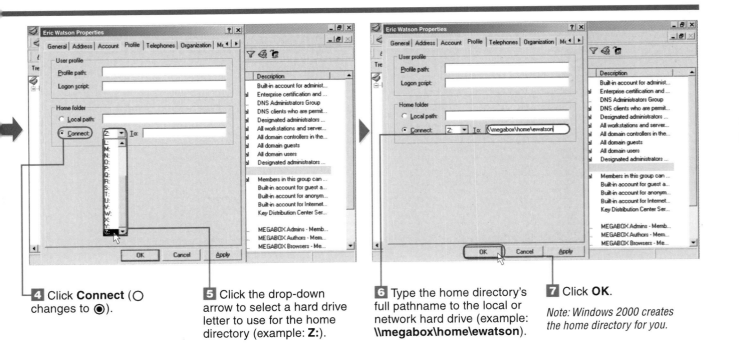

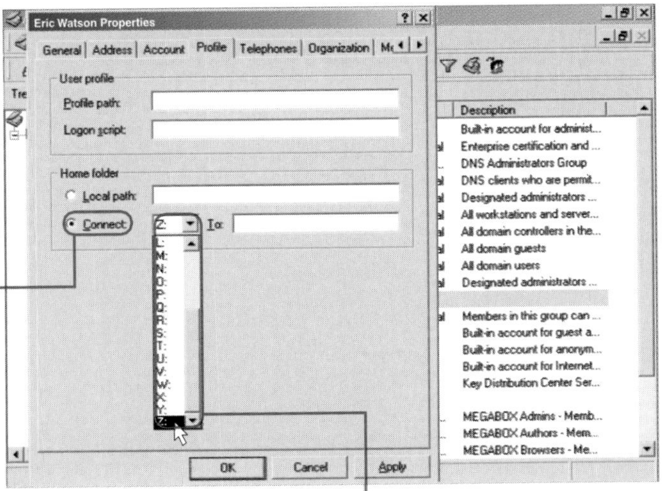

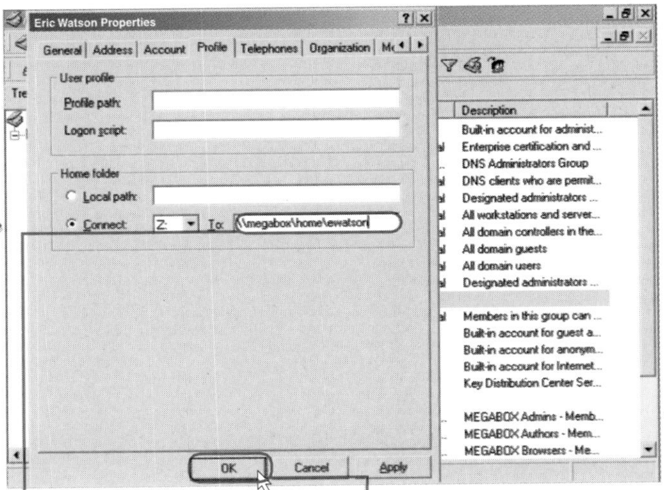

4 Click **Connect** (○ changes to ◉).

5 Click the drop-down arrow to select a hard drive letter to use for the home directory (example: **Z:**).

6 Type the home directory's full pathname to the local or network hard drive (example: **\\megabox\home\ewatson**).

7 Click **OK**.

Note: Windows 2000 creates the home directory for you.

COPY A USER PROFILE TO THE SERVER

You can copy a user profile to your server. This lets you assign an existing profile to a specific user or assign a default profile to all your users.

These profiles will only work with Windows 2000 or Windows NT; they will not work with Windows 95 or Windows 98.

COPY A USER PROFILE TO THE SERVER

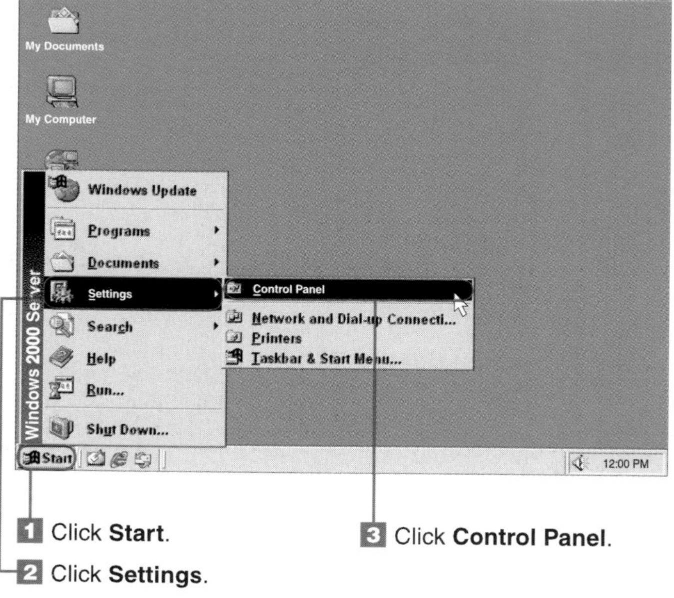

1 Click **Start**.

2 Click **Settings**.

3 Click **Control Panel**.

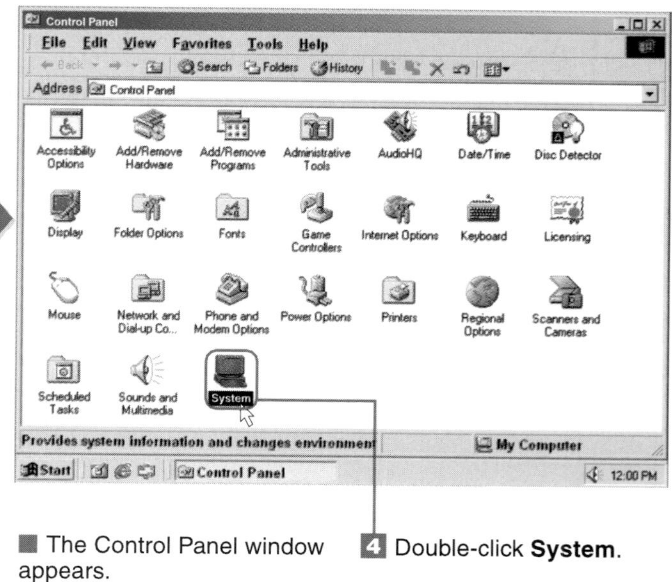

■ The Control Panel window appears.

4 Double-click **System**.

Why can I not copy user profiles?

You must be logged on as an administrator to the computer that has the local profiles stored on it before you can copy the profiles.

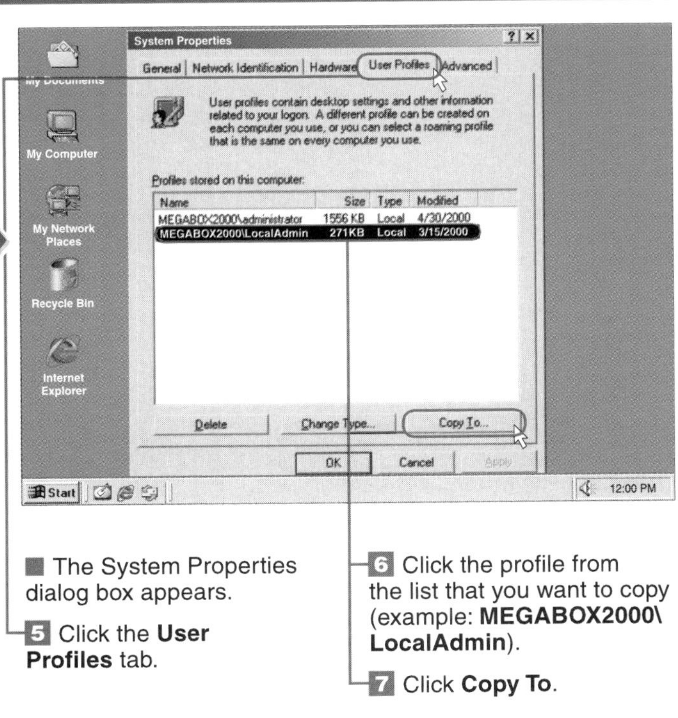

■ The System Properties dialog box appears.

5 Click the **User Profiles** tab.

6 Click the profile from the list that you want to copy (example: **MEGABOX2000\LocalAdmin**).

7 Click **Copy To**.

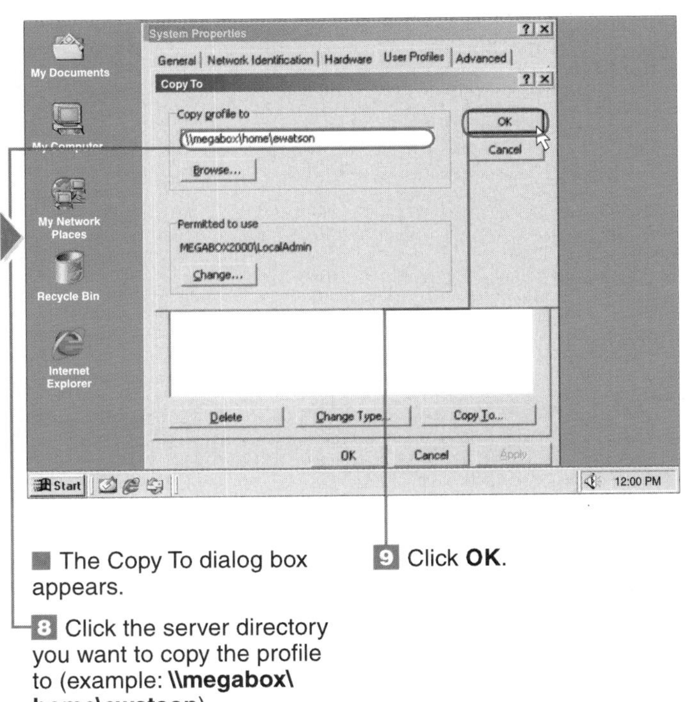

■ The Copy To dialog box appears.

8 Click the server directory you want to copy the profile to (example: **\\megabox\home\ewatson**).

9 Click **OK**.

CREATE A ROAMING USER PROFILE

Roaming user profiles "follow" your users no matter which workstation they log on to. This lets users keep their familiar settings for the desktop.

The profile is kept on a server so it is always available to users logging on to any Windows 2000 or Windows NT 4.0 workstation.

CREATE A ROAMING USER PROFILE

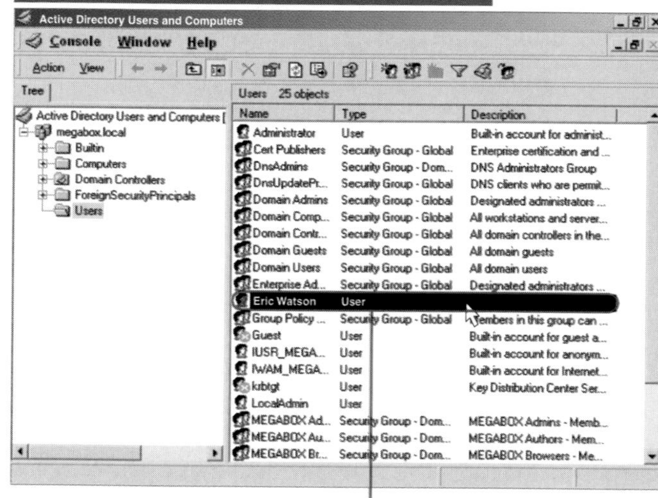

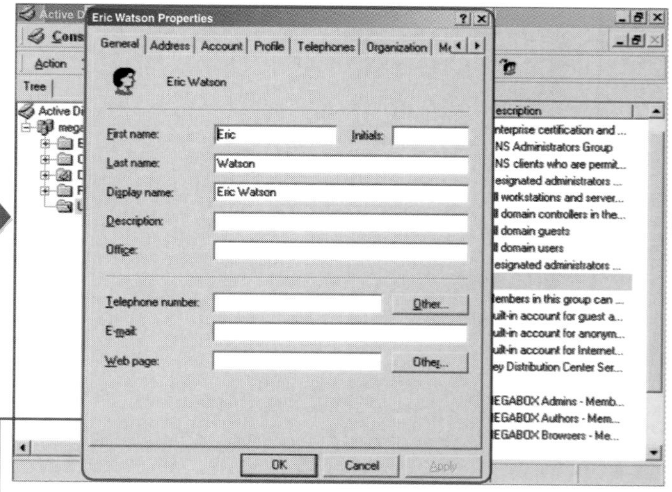

1 Open the Active Directory Users and Computers snap-in.

Note: See "Add a User Account" for details.

2 Double-click a user's name (example: **Eric Watson**).

■ The user's Properties dialog box appears.

Can I assign the same roaming user profile to more than one user account?

Yes. You must first create a profile, copy the profile to the server, and then modify each user's properties to use that profile. See "Copy a User Profile to the Server" for more information about copying profiles.

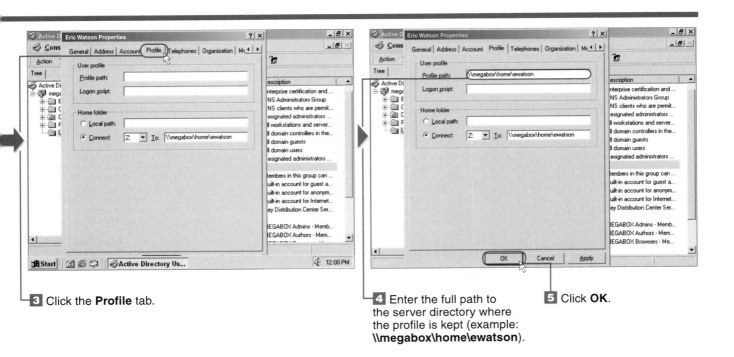

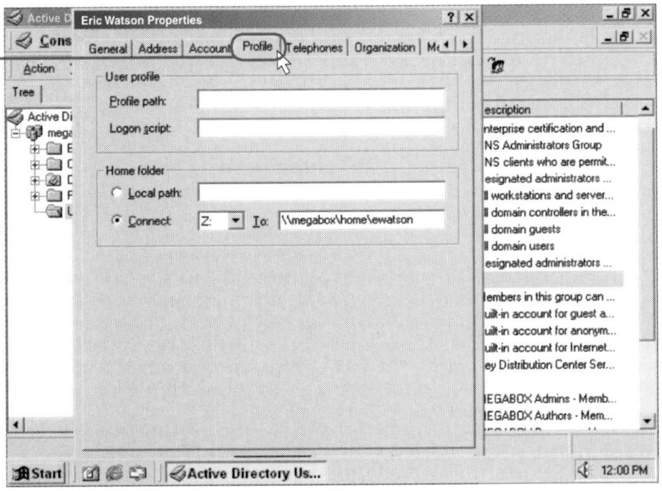

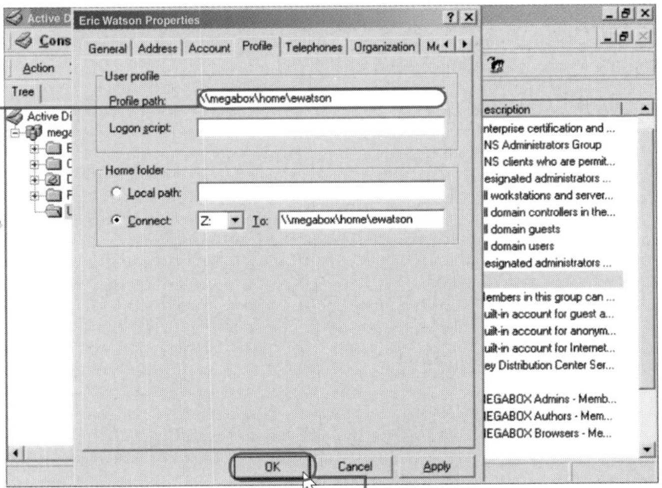

3 Click the **Profile** tab.

4 Enter the full path to the server directory where the profile is kept (example: **\\megabox\home\ewatson**).

5 Click **OK**.

CREATE A MANDATORY USER PROFILE

Mandatory user profiles are used to give the same settings to each user. This makes it easy to have a fixed desktop with the same settings for all your users.

However, users cannot make permanent changes to the mandatory user profile. Any changes they make disappear when they log off.

CREATE A MANDATORY USER PROFILE

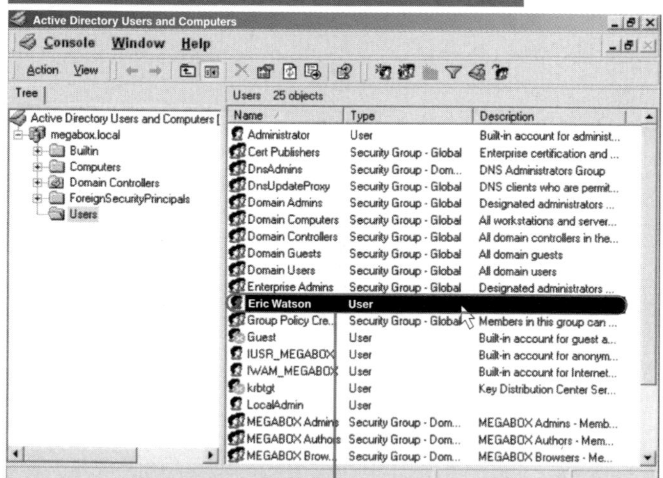

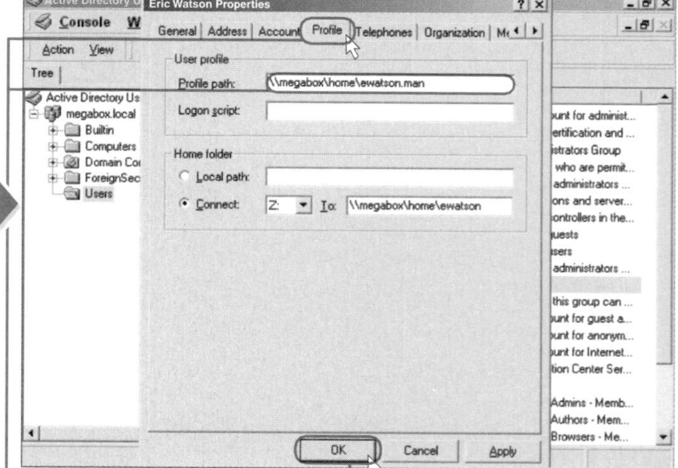

Note: You must create a shared folder on the server and assign proper permissions before using mandatory profiles.

1 Open the Active Directory Users and Computers snap-in.

Note: See "Add a User Account" for details.

2 Double-click a user name in the list (example: **Eric Watson**).

■ The user's Properties dialog box appears.

3 Click **Profile** tab.

4 Type the full path to the server directory where the mandatory profile is kept, ending in .man (example: **\\megabox\home\ewatson.man**).

Note: The `.man` extension stands for mandatory.

5 Click **OK**.

DISABLE OR ENABLE USER ACCOUNTS

You can disable a user's account if you do not currently need it but may in the future or if an employee leaves the company.

This lets you keep the account intact so you do not need to re-create the account and its privileges.

DISABLE OR ENABLE USER ACCOUNTS

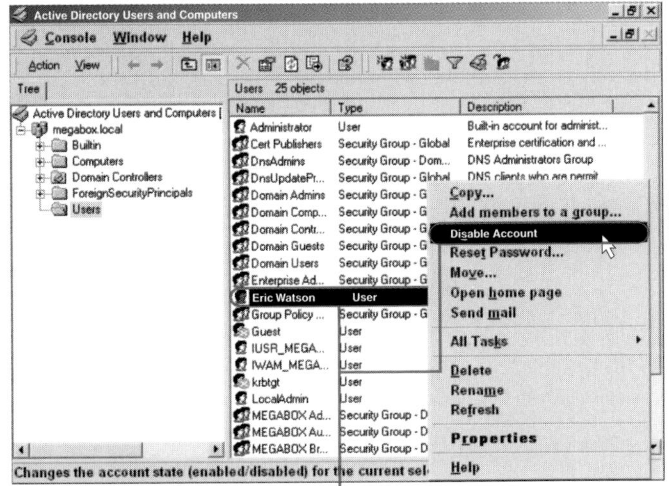

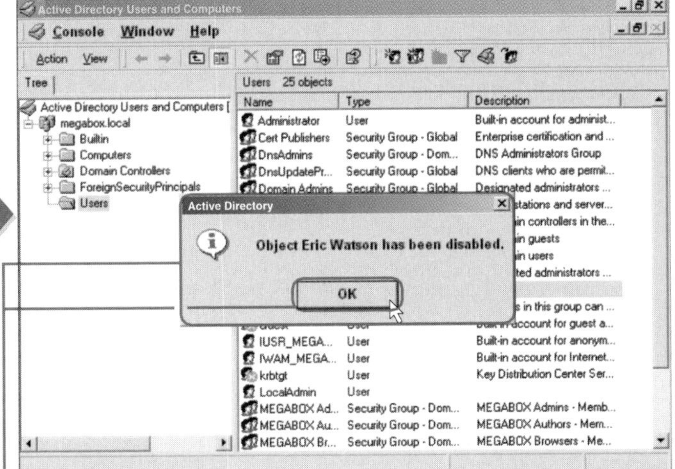

1 Open the Active Directory Users and Computers snap-in.

Note: See "Add a User Account" for details.

2 Right-click a user's name (example: **Eric Watson**).

■ A pop-up menu appears.

3 Click **Disable Account**.

■ A message box appears, stating the account has been disabled.

4 Click **OK**.

*Note: To enable an account, follow steps 1 and 2, and click **Enable Account** in step 3.*

DELETE A USER PROFILE

Deleting profiles lets you remove profiles that you do not use anymore.

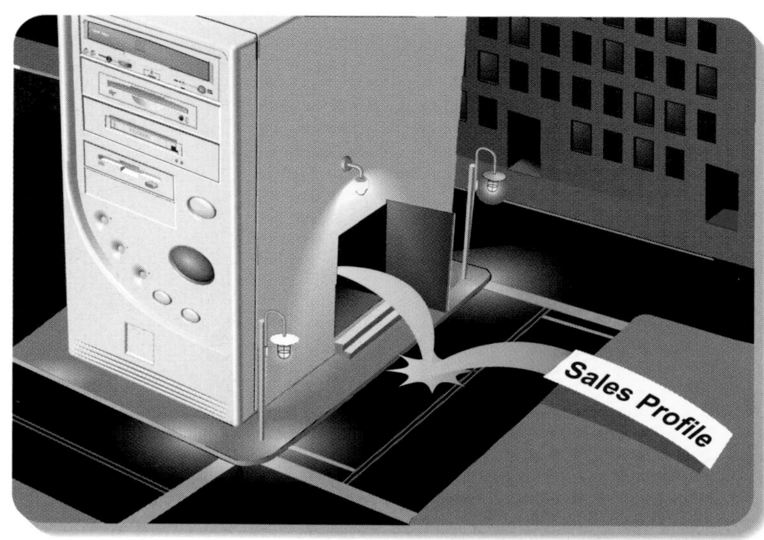

The System Properties dialog box displays the list of available user profiles so you can delete as many profiles as you wish.

DELETE A USER PROFILE

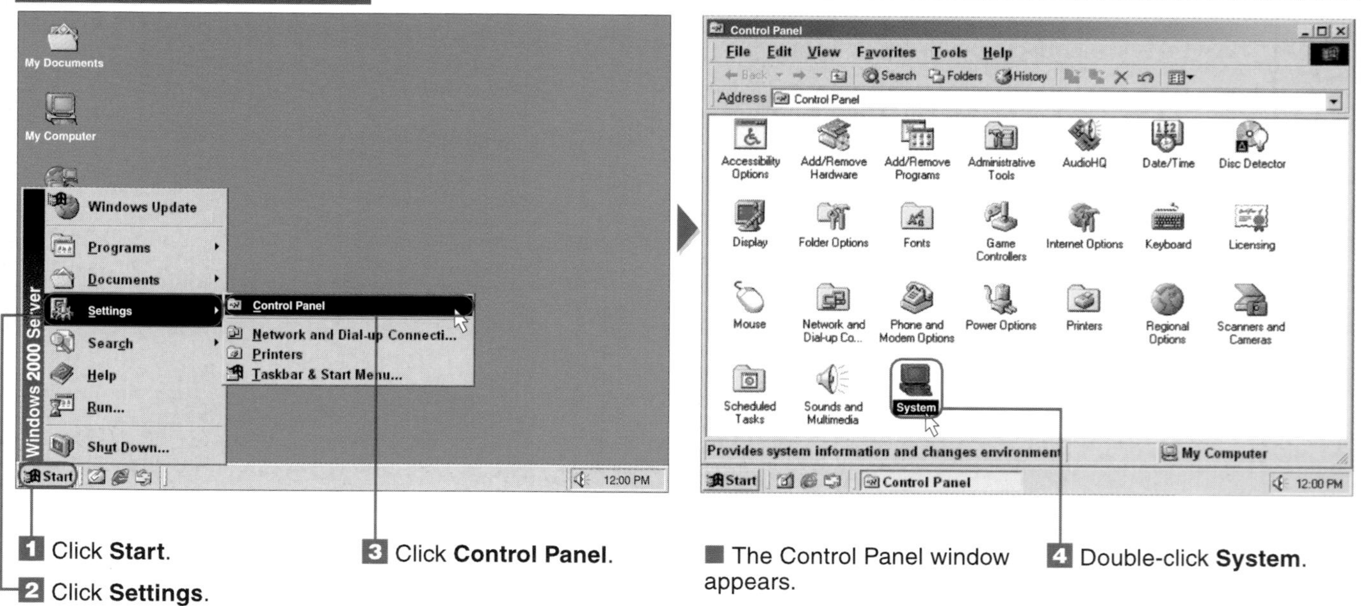

1 Click **Start**.

2 Click **Settings**.

3 Click **Control Panel**.

■ The Control Panel window appears.

4 Double-click **System**.

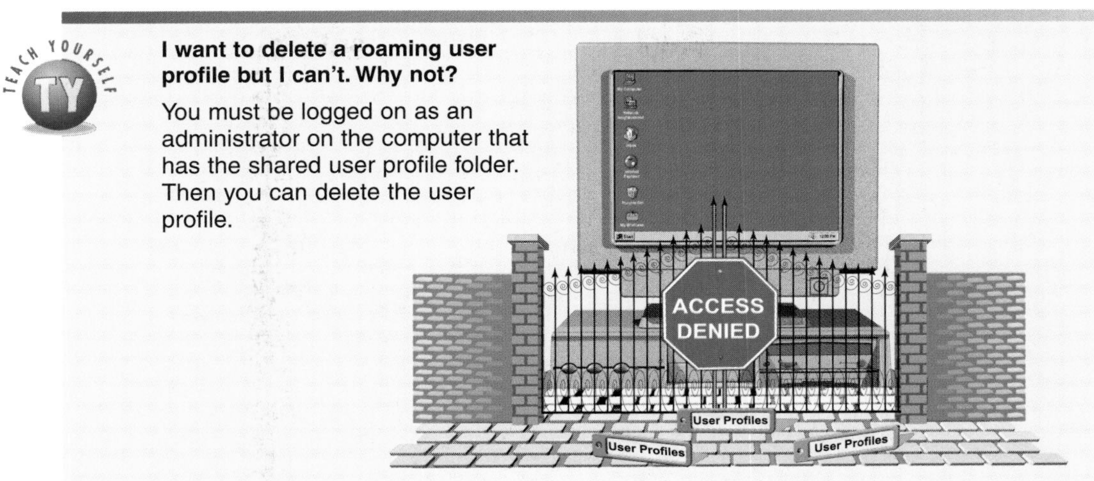

I want to delete a roaming user profile but I can't. Why not?

You must be logged on as an administrator on the computer that has the shared user profile folder. Then you can delete the user profile.

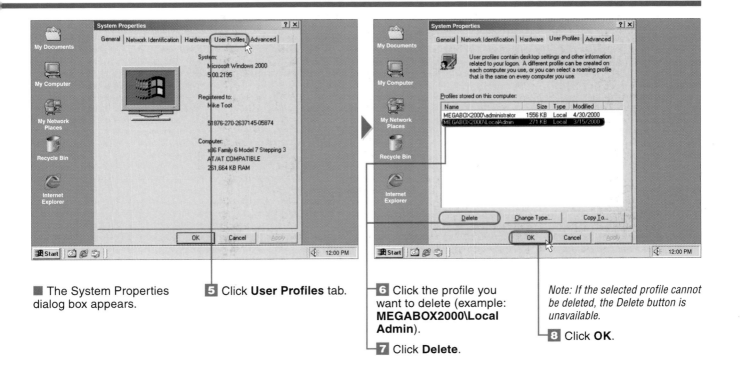

■ The System Properties dialog box appears.

5 Click **User Profiles** tab.

6 Click the profile you want to delete (example: **MEGABOX2000\Local Admin**).

7 Click **Delete**.

Note: If the selected profile cannot be deleted, the Delete button is unavailable.

8 Click **OK**.

ORGANIZE USERS IN GROUPS

User groups make it much easier for the network administrator to manage users. Windows 2000 and Windows NT use groups to keep track of user rights and permissions on the network.

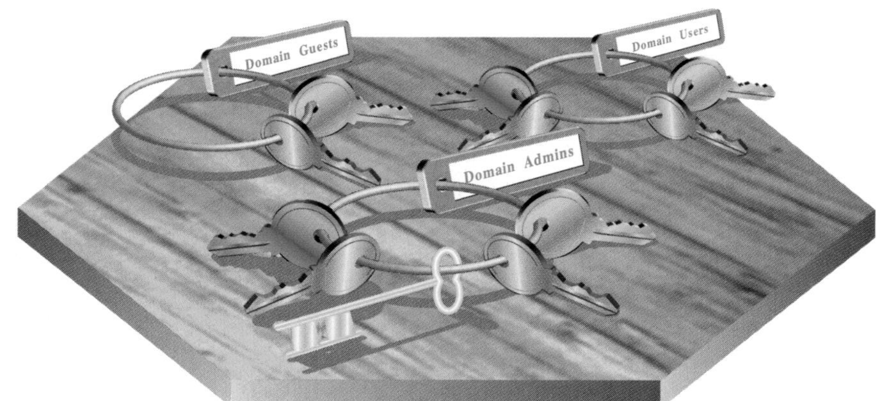

GLOBAL GROUPS

Global groups are ones that apply to the whole domain and can only contain users from that domain. For example, Domain Users is a global group.

LOCAL GROUPS

Local groups are ones that exist only on an individual computer. An example would be {computer name} Admins, where {computer name} is the name assigned to a computer.

UNIVERSAL GROUPS

Universal groups span multiple domains and can contain users from any domain. Unless you are running Windows 2000 exclusively on all your computers, you probably will not use universal groups.

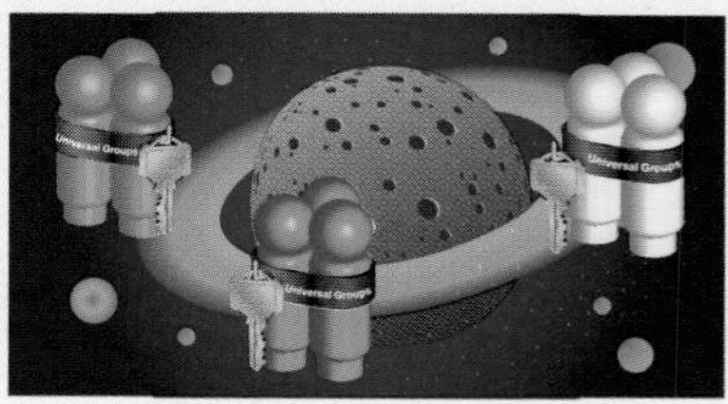

ORGANIZATIONAL UNITS (OU)

Organizational units help group together users in a way that makes sense for your organization. Examples are Marketing or Sales. While you can set up OU's now, you should consult a book on Active Directory for more help with directory design and OU best practices.

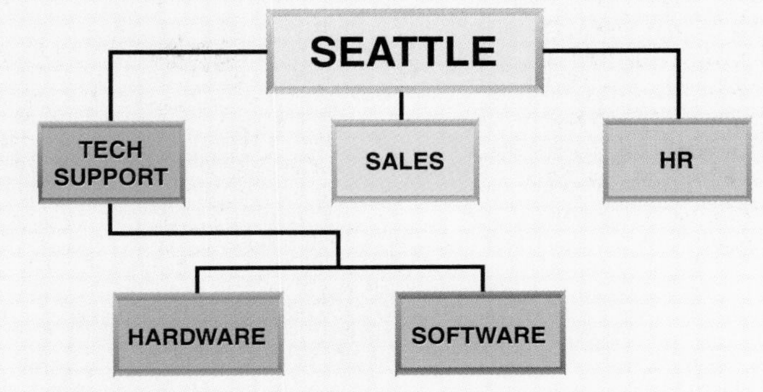

SECURITY GROUPS

Security Groups are used to set rights and permissions for groups. Domain Users is an example of a global Security Group.

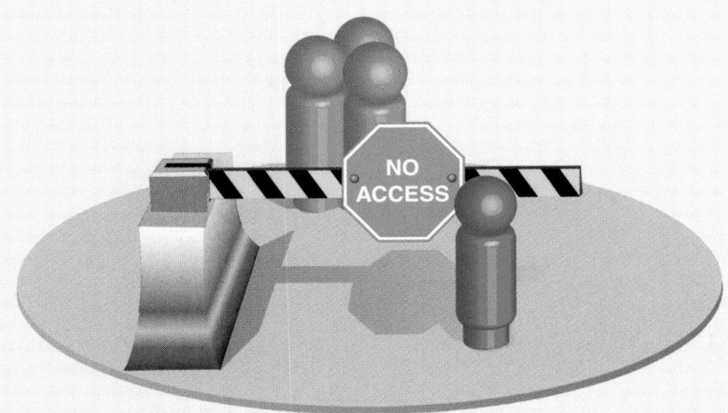

DISTRIBUTION GROUPS

These groups are used when you want to send e-mail to the group. Unless you have a need for this service within Active Directory, you do not need to create this type of group.

DEFINE YOUR GROUPS AND GROUP MEMBERS

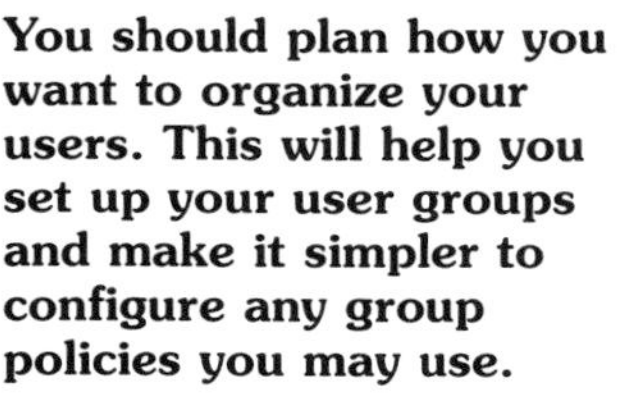

You should plan how you want to organize your users. This will help you set up your user groups and make it simpler to configure any group policies you may use.

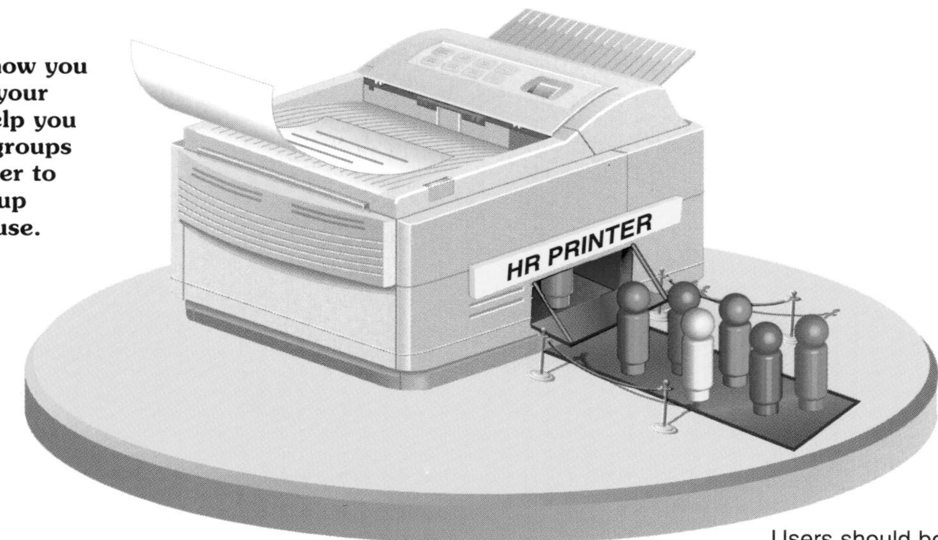

Users should be added to groups that have similar needs or access to the same equipment.

DETERMINE GROUP MEMBERSHIP

Define groups that make sense for your organization, such as Sales, Manufacturing, or Human Resources. Make sure you decide whether the groups should be global or local.

CREATE NEW GROUPS

Use either Active Directory or Local Users and Groups to create your new groups. The next task in this chapter shows you how to create new groups.

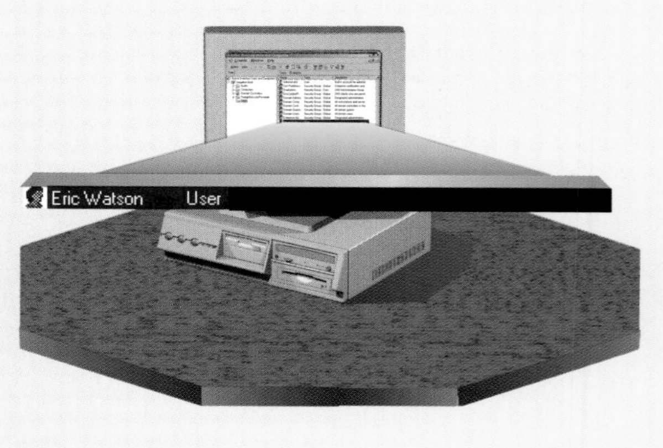

CHANGE GROUP MEMBERSHIP

You can change groups and group members. It is a very good idea, however, to discuss your organizational plan and any changes you want to make with the people involved. That way, you can find out about any special group requirements and adjust your plan accordingly.

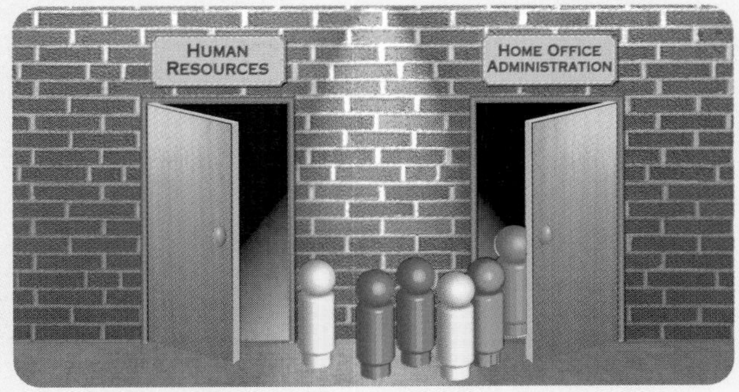

ADD USERS TO GROUPS

Add users to the groups you created. Chapter 9 shows you how to do this.

APPLY POLICIES AND PERMISSIONS

Apply any group-wide settings you want them to have. Group policies are covered in this chapter; permissions for files and printers are covered in Chapters 13 and 14.

CREATE A NEW GROUP

You can use the existing groups in Windows 2000 for your users or you can create a new group.

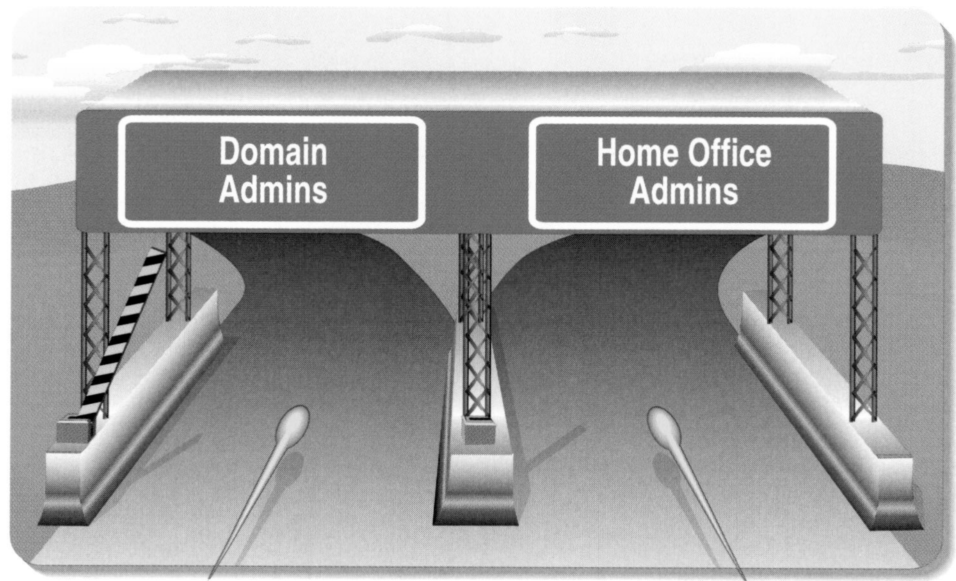

CREATE A NEW GROUP

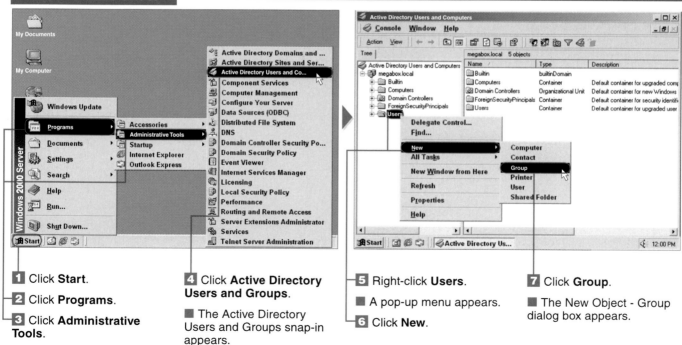

1. Click **Start**.
2. Click **Programs**.
3. Click **Administrative Tools**.
4. Click **Active Directory Users and Groups**.

■ The Active Directory Users and Groups snap-in appears.

5. Right-click **Users**.

■ A pop-up menu appears.

6. Click **New**.
7. Click **Group**.

■ The New Object - Group dialog box appears.

Should I use global or local groups for my users?

Global groups should be used in most cases. Local groups are typically used to hold global groups and to give access to resources to those groups on a particular computer.

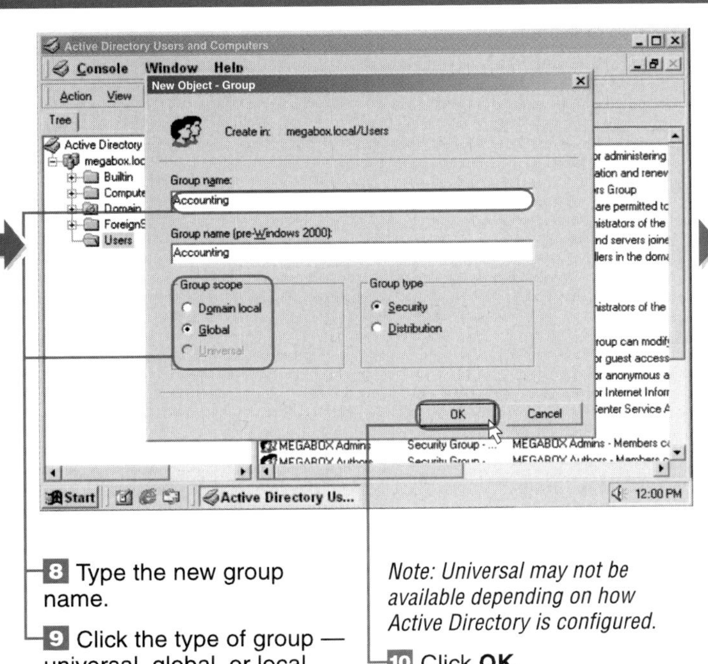

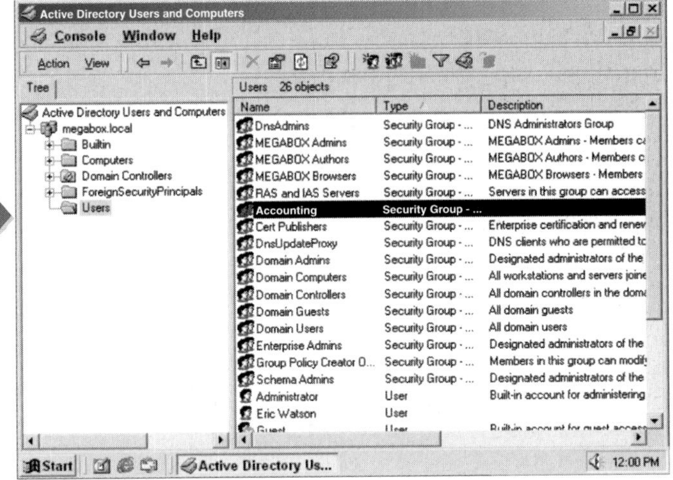

8 Type the new group name.

9 Click the type of group — universal, global, or local (○ changes to ◉).

Note: Universal may not be available depending on how Active Directory is configured.

10 Click **OK**.

■ The new group name appears in the window.

CREATE A NEW GROUP POLICY

Group policies are collections of desktop settings that can be applied to users, groups, and computers. They make it easy to have uniform settings for everyone in your company.

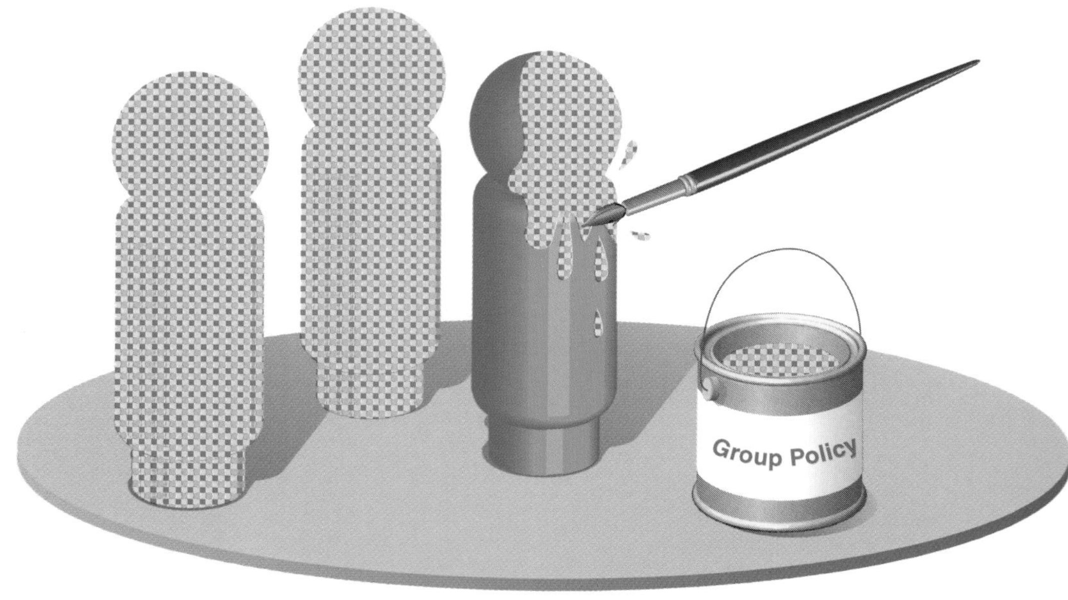

CREATE A NEW GROUP POLICY

1 Click **Start**.

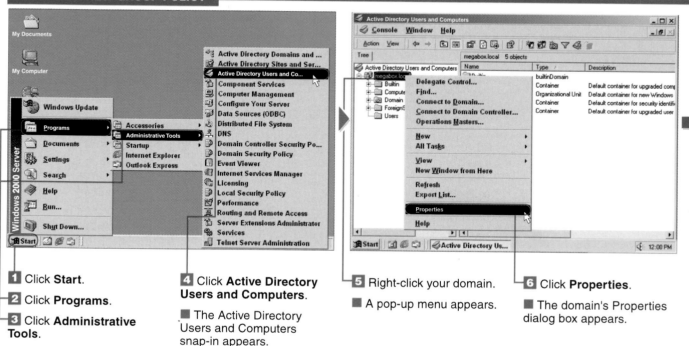

2 Click **Programs**.

3 Click **Administrative Tools**.

4 Click **Active Directory Users and Computers**.

■ The Active Directory Users and Computers snap-in appears.

5 Right-click your domain.

■ A pop-up menu appears.

6 Click **Properties**.

■ The domain's Properties dialog box appears.

Can I use Group Policies with everything on my network?

Only users and Windows 2000 computers receive group policies. If you want to use group policies with Windows NT or Windows 9*x* computers, you must use policy tools that are available for those operating systems.

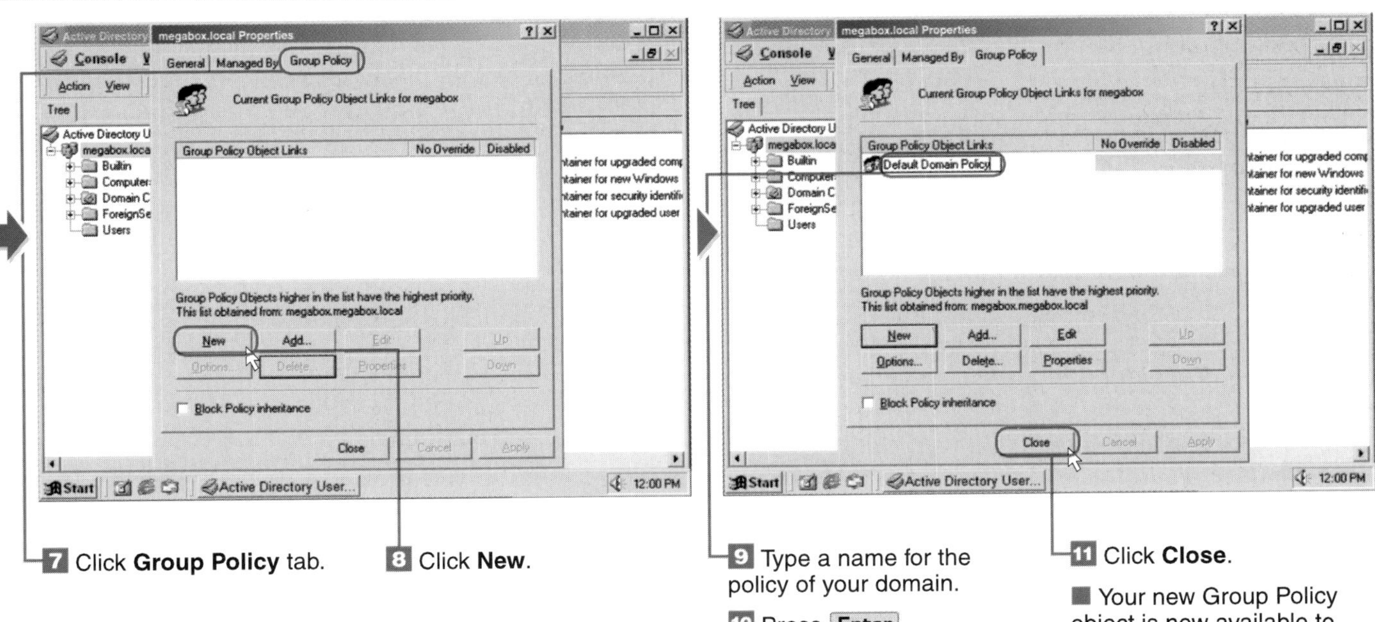

7 Click **Group Policy** tab.

8 Click **New**.

9 Type a name for the policy of your domain.

10 Press **Enter**.

11 Click **Close**.

■ Your new Group Policy object is now available to the domain.

OPEN THE GROUP POLICY EDITOR

The Group Policy Editor snap-in manages your users' desktop components. You can manage settings for users, groups, and computers in a variety of ways.

OPEN THE GROUP POLICY EDITOR

1 Click **Start**.

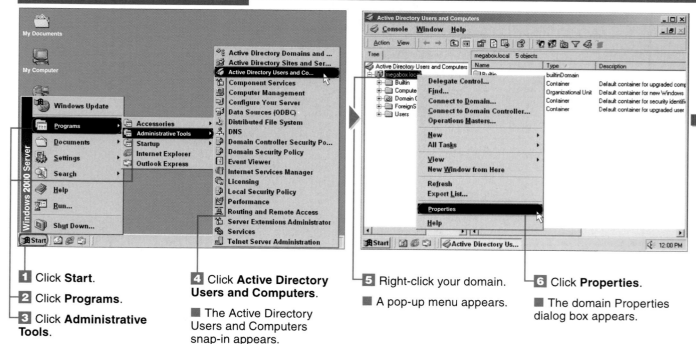

2 Click **Programs**.

3 Click **Administrative Tools**.

4 Click **Active Directory Users and Computers**.

■ The Active Directory Users and Computers snap-in appears.

5 Right-click your domain.

■ A pop-up menu appears.

6 Click **Properties**.

■ The domain Properties dialog box appears.

What is the difference between group policies and user profiles?

User profiles were developed for Windows Nt-based networks. Group profiles are designed for Windows 2000 networks. There is some overlap in features, but group policies are more flexible and powerful.

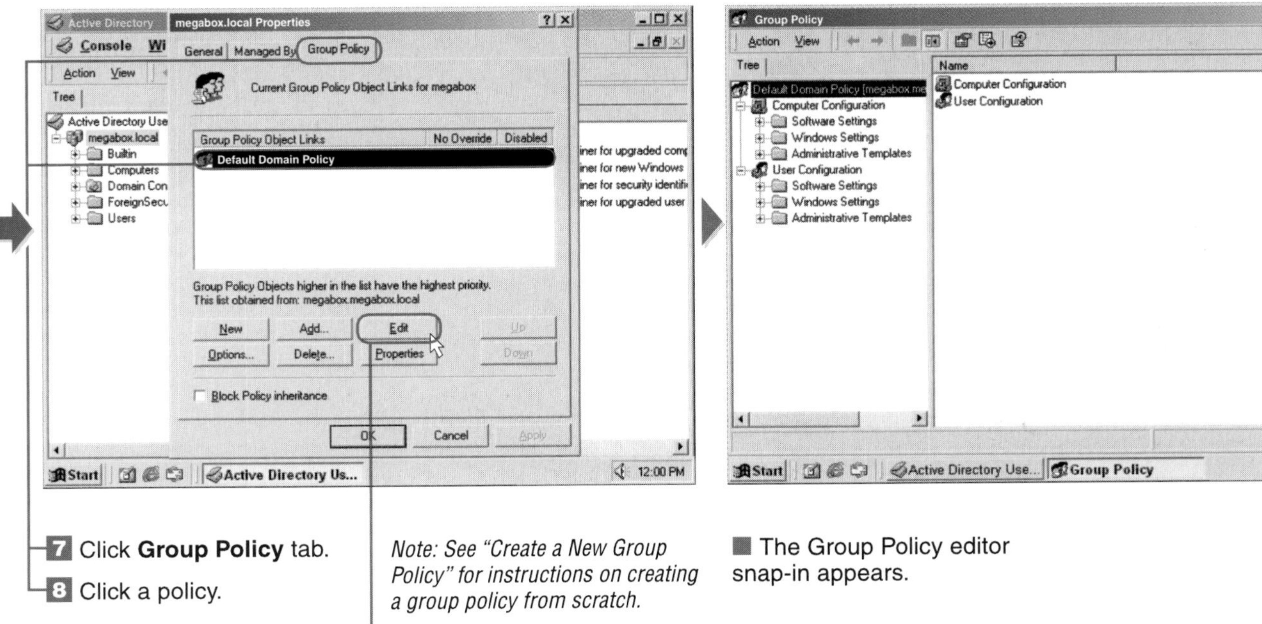

7 Click **Group Policy** tab.

8 Click a policy.

Note: See "Create a New Group Policy" for instructions on creating a group policy from scratch.

9 Click **Edit**.

■ The Group Policy editor snap-in appears.

CONFIGURE AND APPLY GROUP POLICIES

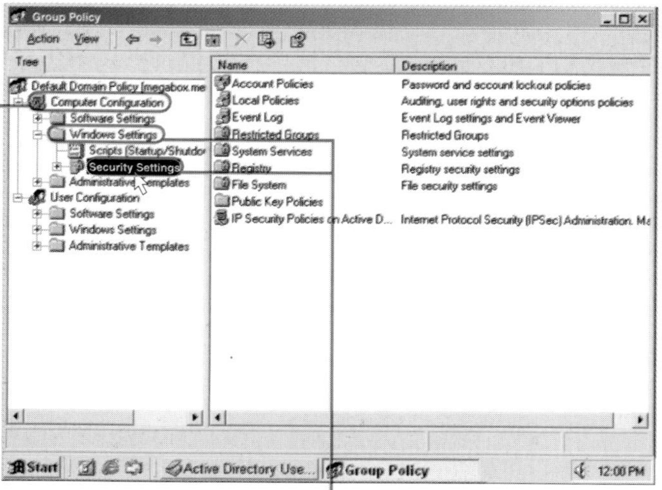

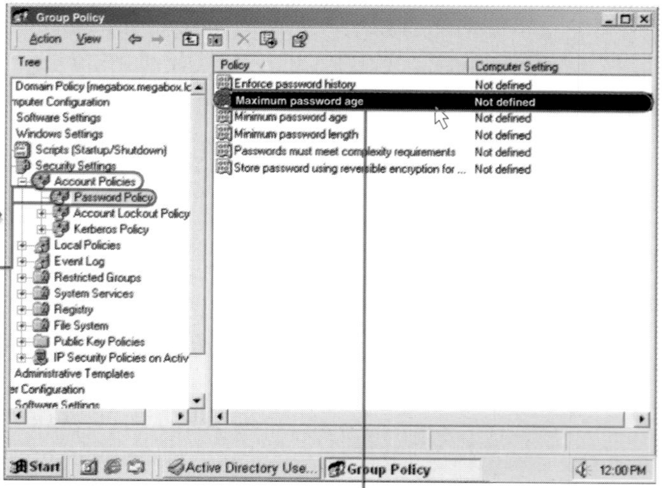

You configure a group policy and apply it using the Group Policy Editor. The policy will apply to everything in the group.

CONFIGURE AND APPLY GROUP POLICIES

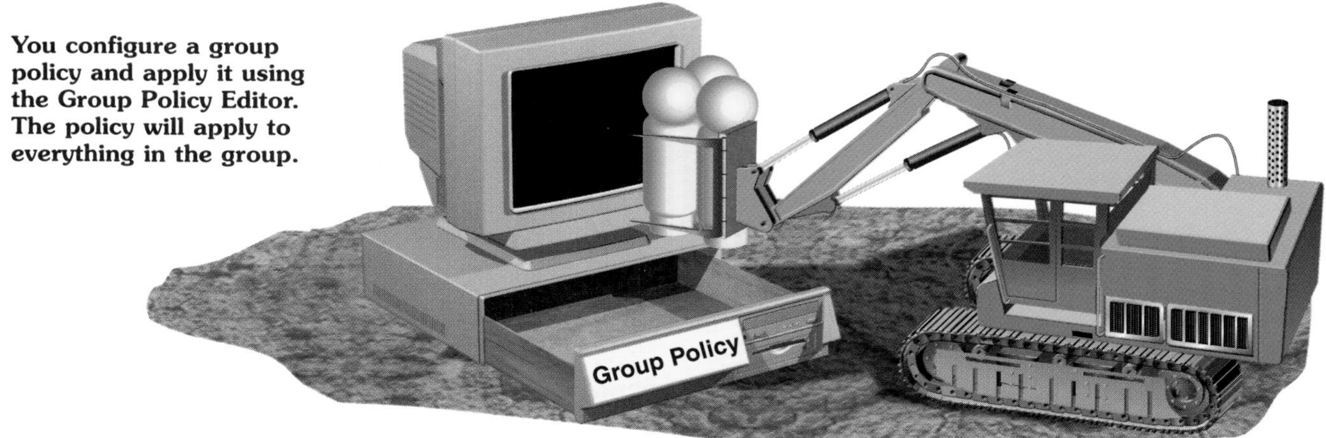

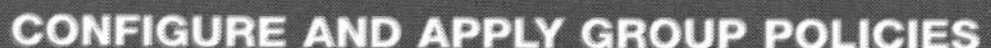

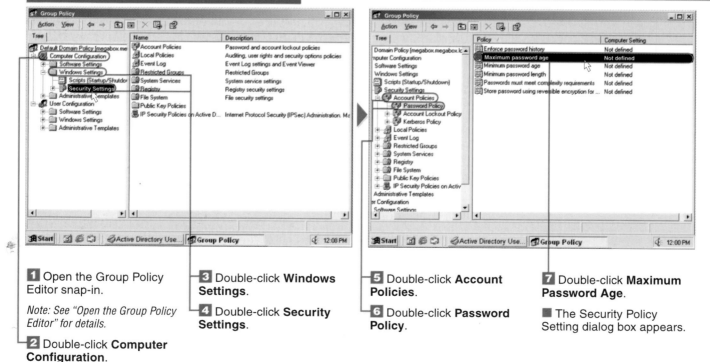

1 Open the Group Policy Editor snap-in.

Note: See "Open the Group Policy Editor" for details.

2 Double-click **Computer Configuration**.

3 Double-click **Windows Settings**.

4 Double-click **Security Settings**.

5 Double-click **Account Policies**.

6 Double-click **Password Policy**.

7 Double-click **Maximum Password Age**.

■ The Security Policy Setting dialog box appears.

What happens if user group policies conflict with computer group policies?

If user group policies and computer group policies conflict with one another, then computer policies take precedence.

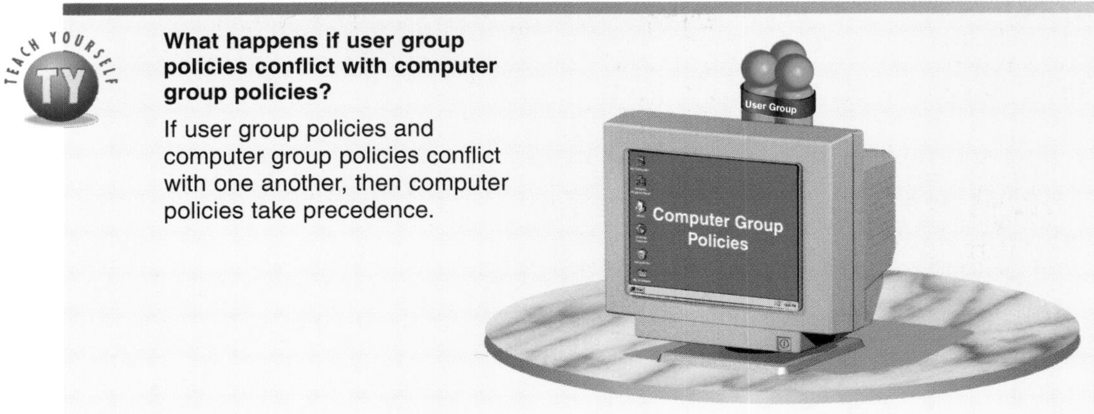

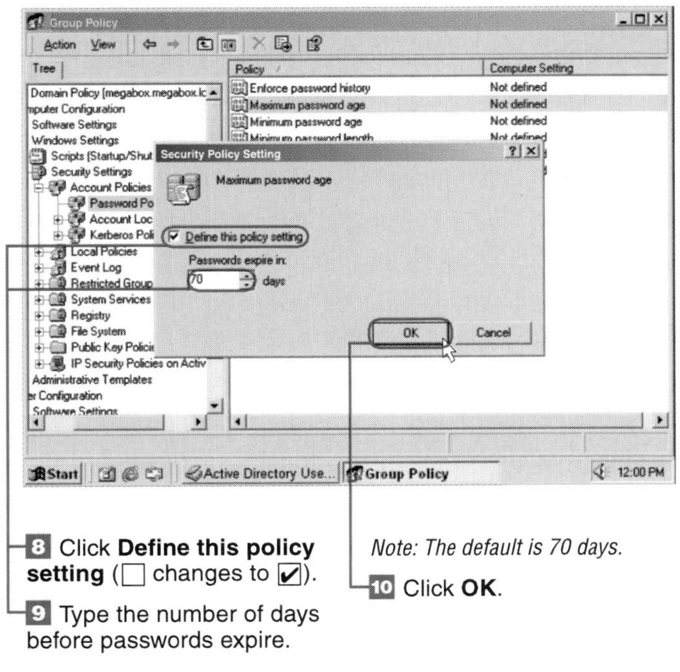

8 Click **Define this policy setting** (☐ changes to ☑).

9 Type the number of days before passwords expire.

Note: The default is 70 days.

10 Click **OK**.

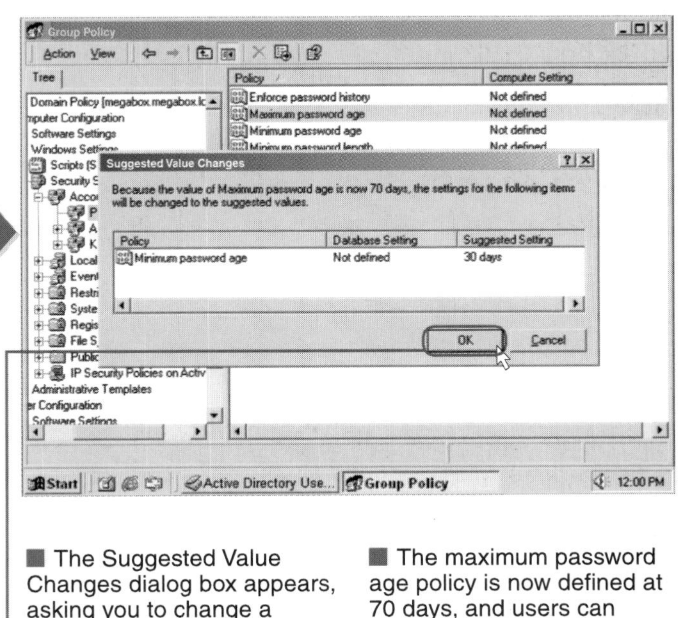

■ The Suggested Value Changes dialog box appears, asking you to change a related setting.

11 Click **OK**.

■ The maximum password age policy is now defined at 70 days, and users can change their passwords after 30 days.

My Documents
My Computer
My Network
Places

CHAPTER 9

Overseeing Computers on Your Network

As an administrator, you will be working with computers and servers on your network. This chapter shows you how to manage them effectively.

VIEW COMPUTER ACCOUNTS

Every computer in your domain running Windows 2000 or Windows NT must have a computer account. Computer accounts help determine access to information and resources in your domain.

VIEW COMPUTER ACCOUNTS

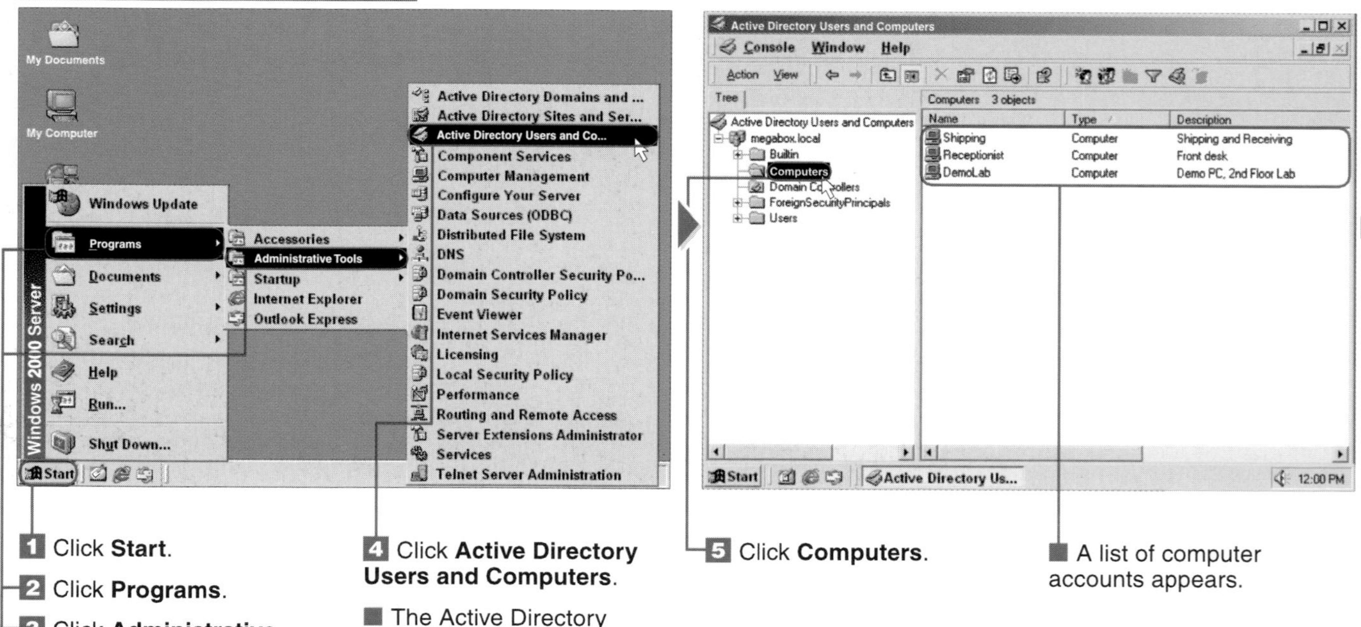

1 Click **Start**.

2 Click **Programs**.

3 Click **Administrative Tools**.

4 Click **Active Directory Users and Computers**.

■ The Active Directory Users and Computers snap-in appears.

5 Click **Computers**.

■ A list of computer accounts appears.

Can two computers have the same account name?

No. Each computer account name must be unique within your domain, including those computers that you bring in from other domains.

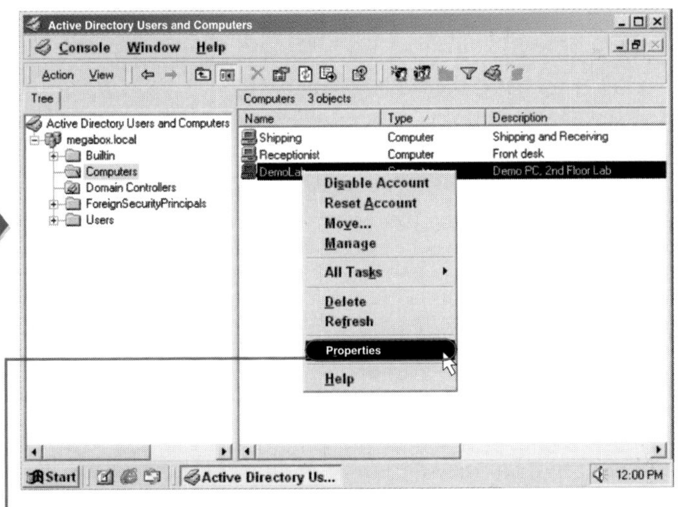

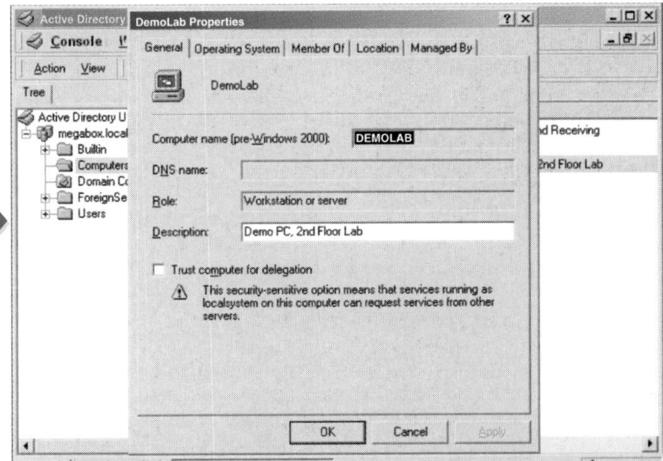

6 Right-click a computer account.

7 Click **Properties**.

■ The Computer Account Properties window appears.

■ The Computer Properties window provides details about the computer name, membership in any groups, its location, and management information.

ADD A COMPUTER ACCOUNT

Before you can access network resources from a Windows 2000 or Windows NT workstation, you must add a computer account to the domain for that workstation.

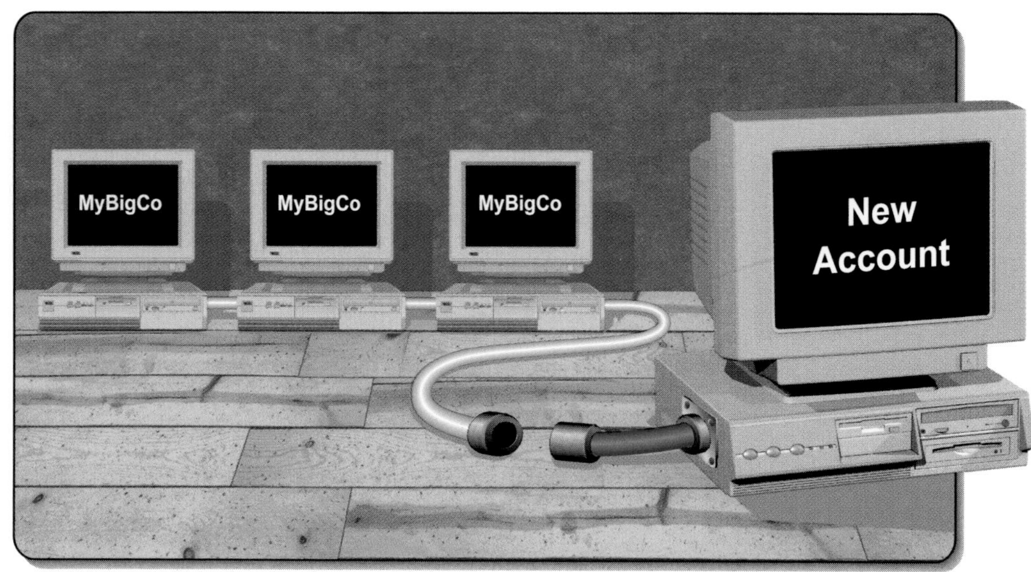

ADD A COMPUTER ACCOUNT

1 Click **Start**.

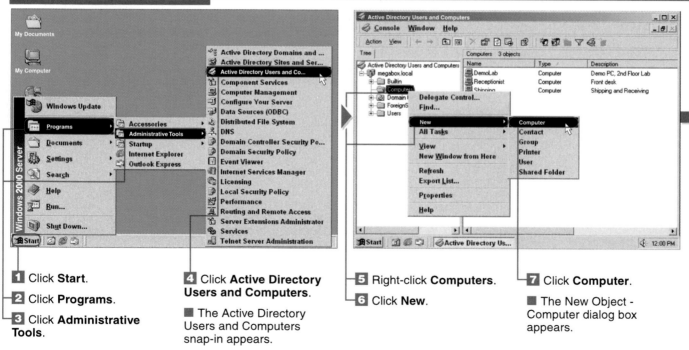

2 Click **Programs**.

3 Click **Administrative Tools**.

4 Click **Active Directory Users and Computers**.

■ The Active Directory Users and Computers snap-in appears.

5 Right-click **Computers**.

6 Click **New**.

7 Click **Computer**.

■ The New Object - Computer dialog box appears.

Can I assign computer accounts to Windows 95 and 98 computers?

If you run Windows 95 or 98, you cannot assign a computer account to these computers. Windows 95 and 98 lack the necessary security systems to support computer accounts. Users on Windows 95 and 98 can still use their Windows 2000 user accounts to participate in the domain.

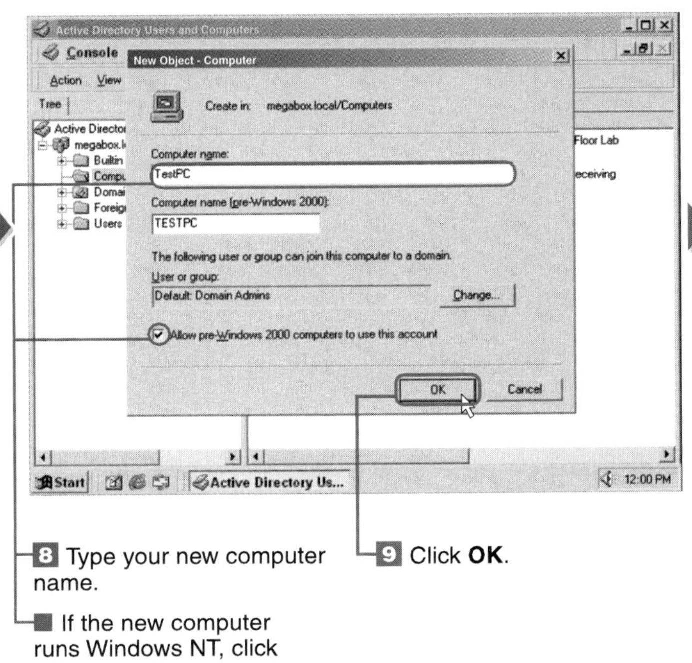

8 Type your new computer name.

■ If the new computer runs Windows NT, click **Allow pre-Windows 2000 computers to use this account** (☐ changes to ☑).

9 Click **OK**.

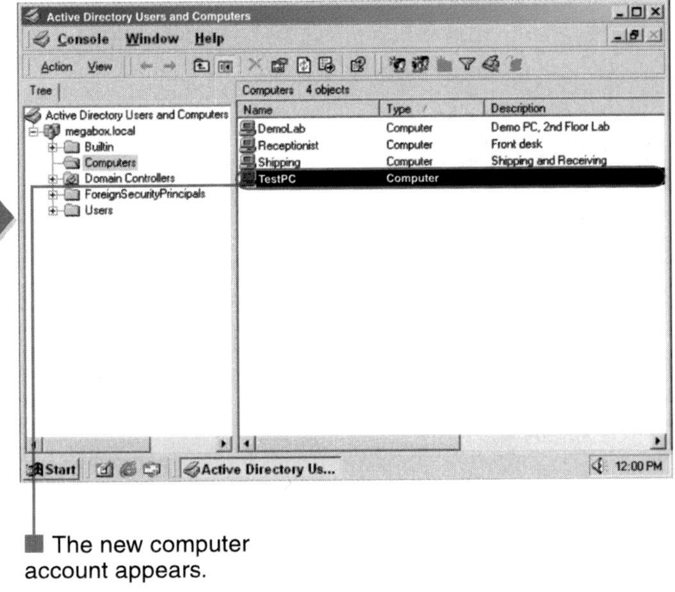

■ The new computer account appears.

You can manage a wide variety of Windows 2000 features and services from within the Computer Management snap-in. It provides a single location for frequently accessed consoles, such as Shared Folders management, Device Manager, and Services.

MANAGE YOUR SERVER

1 Click **Start**.

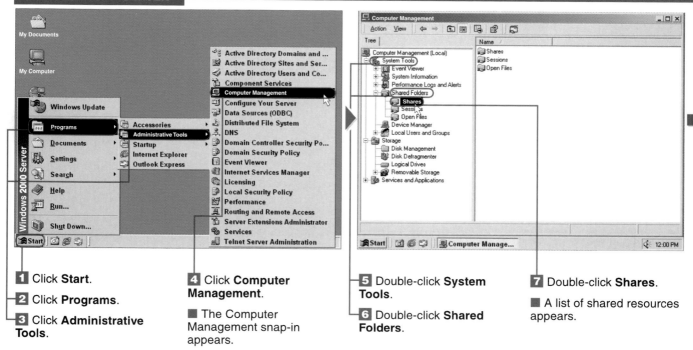

2 Click **Programs**.

3 Click **Administrative Tools**.

4 Click **Computer Management**.

■ The Computer Management snap-in appears.

5 Double-click **System Tools**.

6 Double-click **Shared Folders**.

7 Double-click **Shares**.

■ A list of shared resources appears.

Do I need to know how to manage all the different services and features?

Most of your server's functions work just fine without any adjustment. This book covers the important ones; if you are curious about the others, you can get more information from the Windows Help file on each device or service you see here.

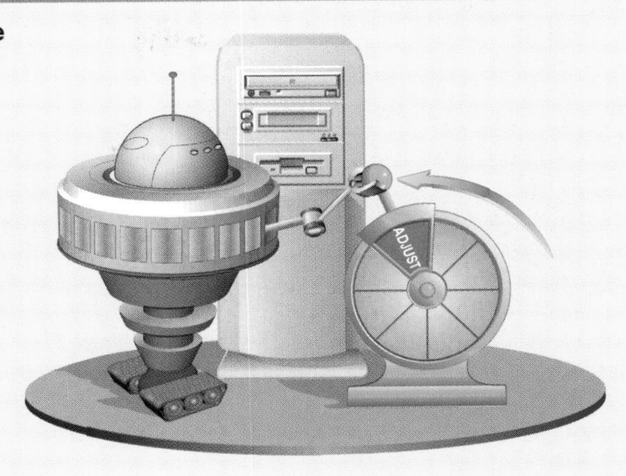

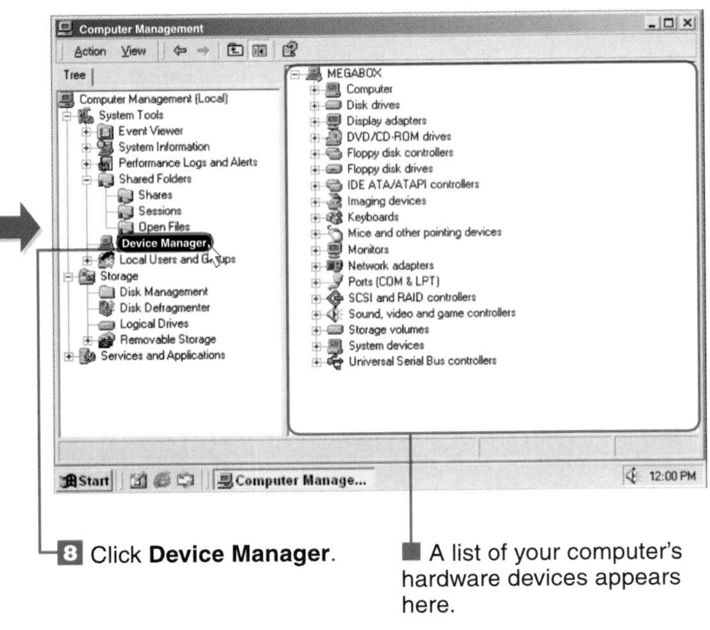

8 Click **Device Manager**.

■ A list of your computer's hardware devices appears here.

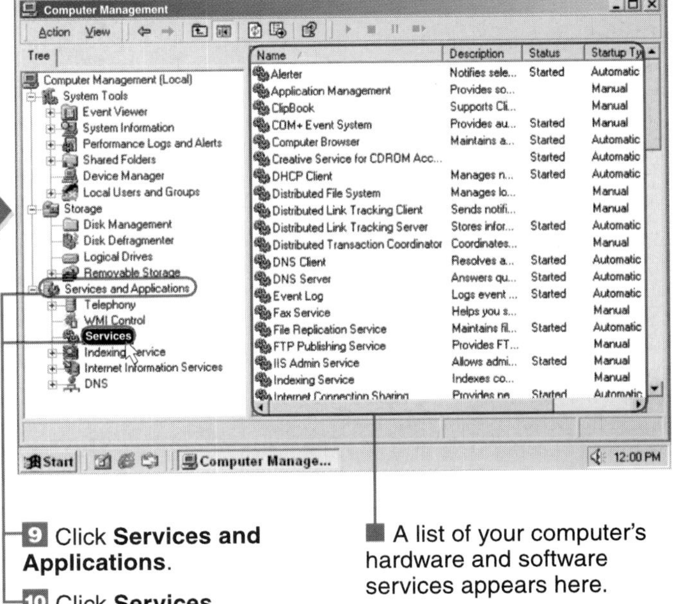

9 Click **Services and Applications**.

10 Click **Services**.

■ A list of your computer's hardware and software services appears here.

MANAGE OTHER COMPUTERS REMOTELY

You can manage other computers without physically going to that computer.

MANAGE OTHER COMPUTERS REMOTELY

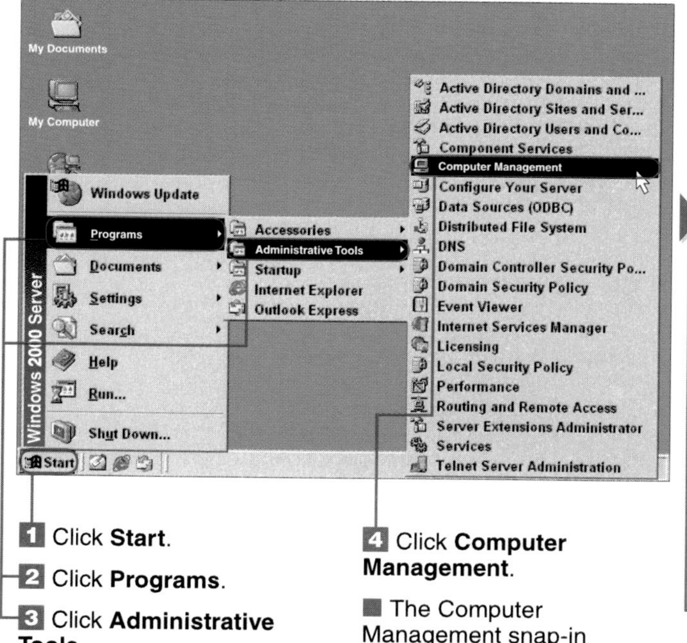

1 Click **Start**.

2 Click **Programs**.

3 Click **Administrative Tools**.

4 Click **Computer Management**.

■ The Computer Management snap-in appears.

5 Right-click **Computer Management (Local)**.

6 Click **Connect to another computer**.

■ The Select Computer dialog box appears.

Can anyone manage other computers remotely?

No. A user must be a member of the Domain Admins global group, which must be a member of the local machine's Administrators local group. Administrators local groups are set up automatically when you install Windows 2000, but you must determine which users go into the Domain Admins group.

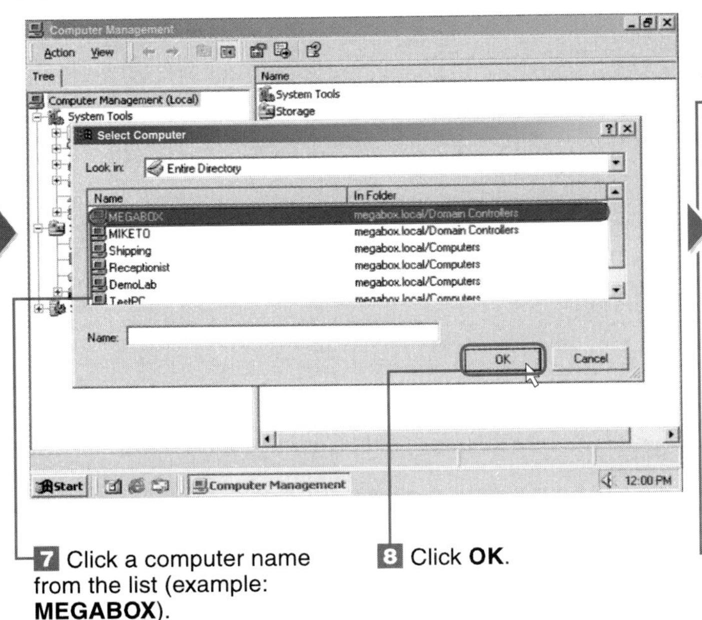

7 Click a computer name from the list (example: **MEGABOX**).

8 Click **OK**.

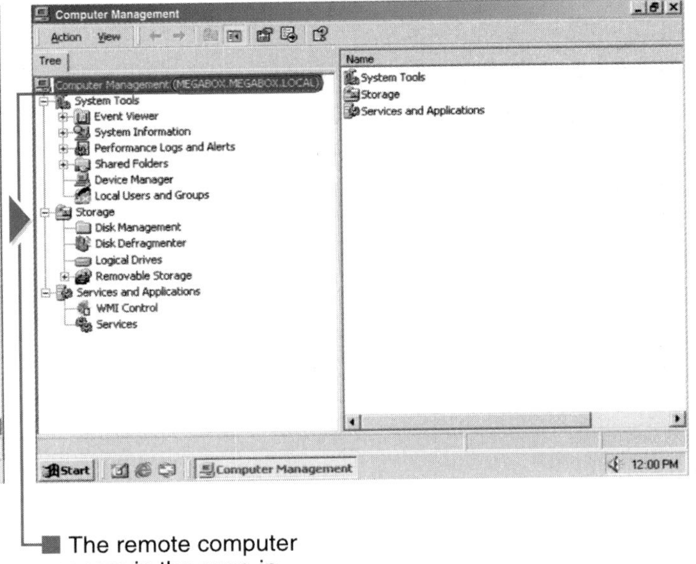

■ The remote computer appears in the snap-in.

BUILD A TRUST

Your domain will likely have to communicate and share information with other domains. Windows 2000 Server lets you do this by building a trust with the other domain.

When you *trust* another domain, you share your resources with it. If another domain trusts you, then its resources are available to you.

BUILD A TRUST

1 Click **Start**.

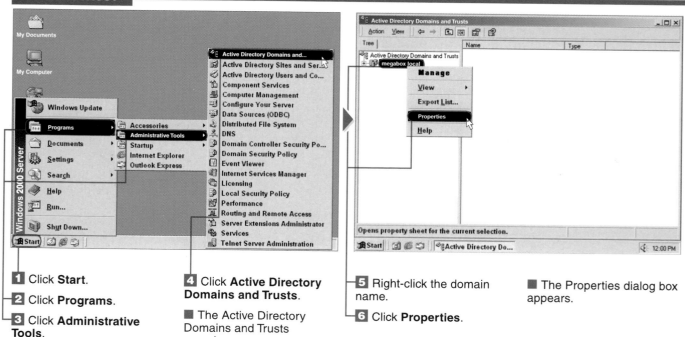

2 Click **Programs**.

3 Click **Administrative Tools**.

4 Click **Active Directory Domains and Trusts**.

■ The Active Directory Domains and Trusts snap-in appears.

5 Right-click the domain name.

6 Click **Properties**.

■ The Properties dialog box appears.

Do I create trusts or does Active Directory create them automatically?

Active Directory automatically creates trusts between controllers in your domain. You can manually create explicit trusts to another domain outside your domain.

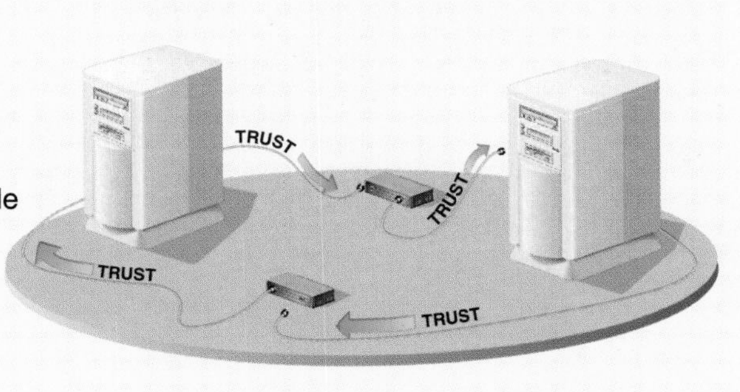

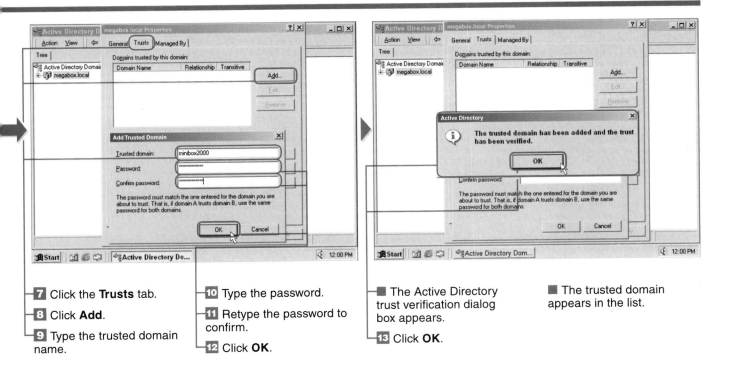

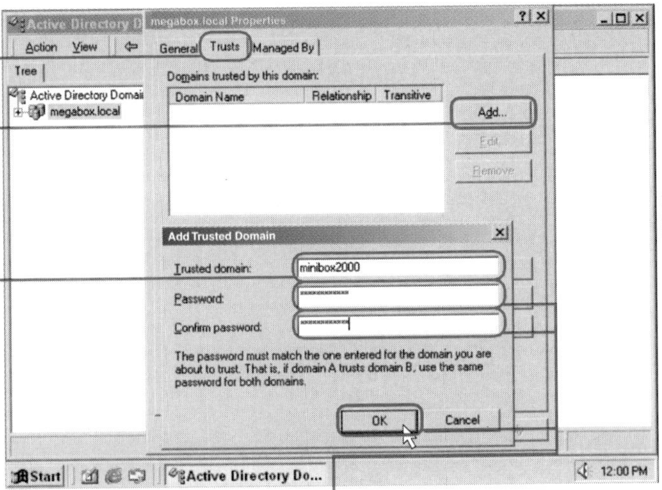

7 Click the **Trusts** tab.

8 Click **Add**.

9 Type the trusted domain name.

10 Type the password.

11 Retype the password to confirm.

12 Click **OK**.

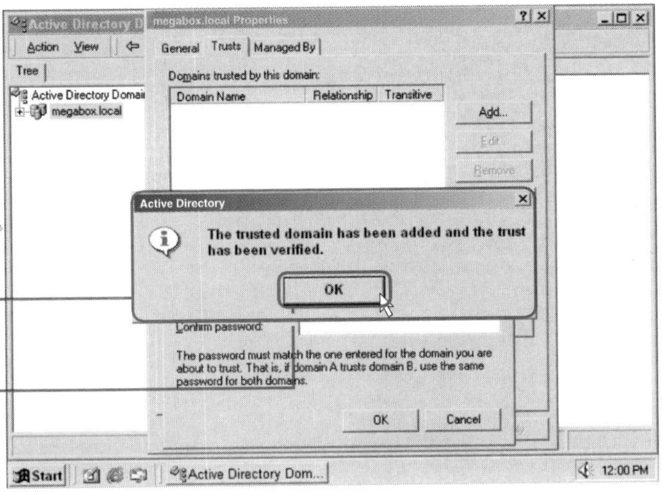

■ The Active Directory trust verification dialog box appears.

13 Click **OK**.

■ The trusted domain appears in the list.

SHARED
SH
NOT
SHARED
Company Picnic
Announcement
Date: Saturday, October 21, 2000
Time: 10:30 AM - 6:00 PM
Venue: Garden Gate Park

CHAPTER 10

Managing Files and Disks

Information storage and access is the most frequently-used server function. You will learn how to manage files and hard drives, how to share information, and how to change permissions for sensitive data.

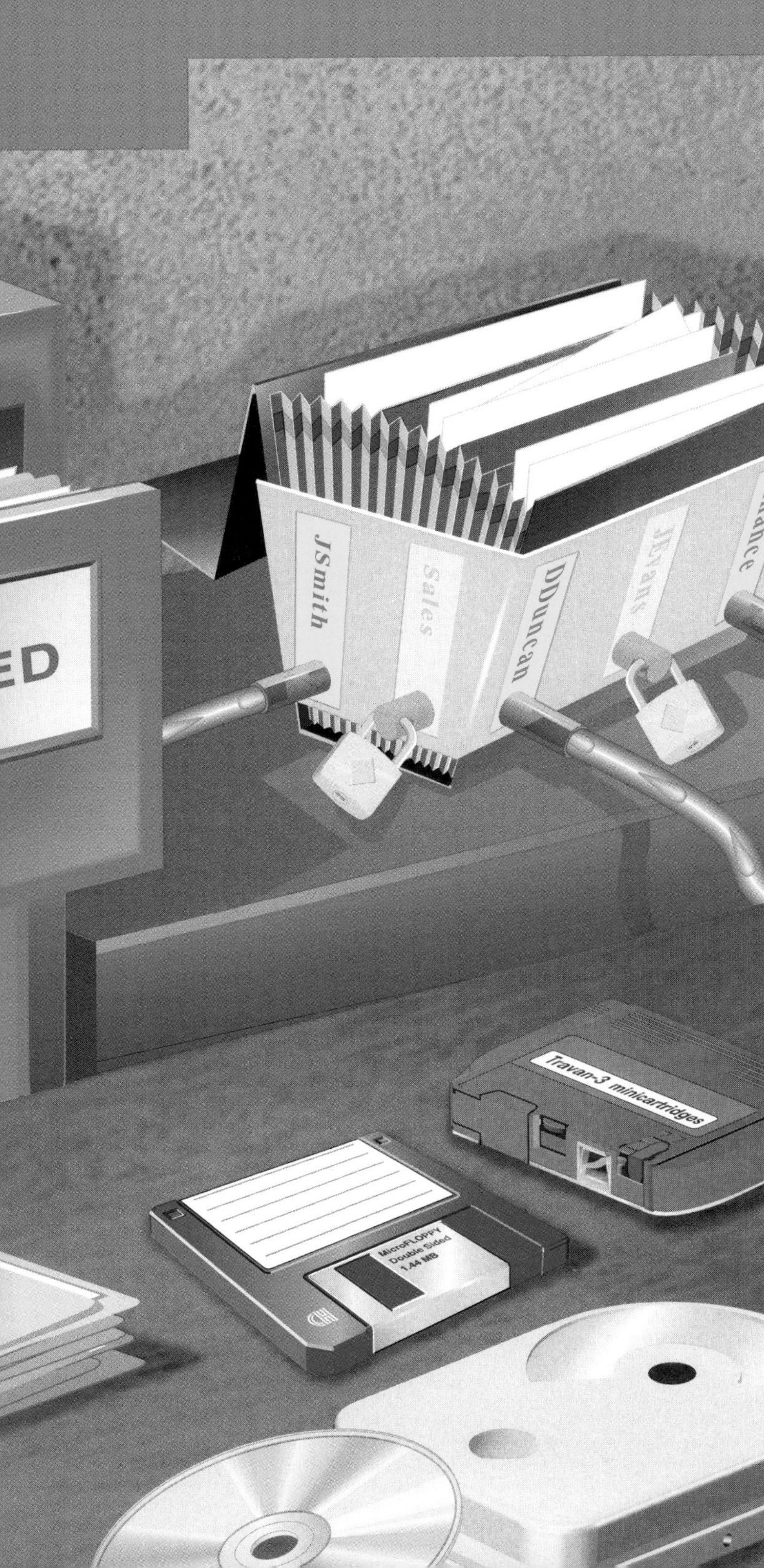

LAUNCH WINDOWS EXPLORER

You use Windows Explorer to manage files and folders anywhere on your computer or on your network. Windows Explorer can find any file you want and help you keep your files in order.

LAUNCH WINDOWS EXPLORER

1 Click **Start**.

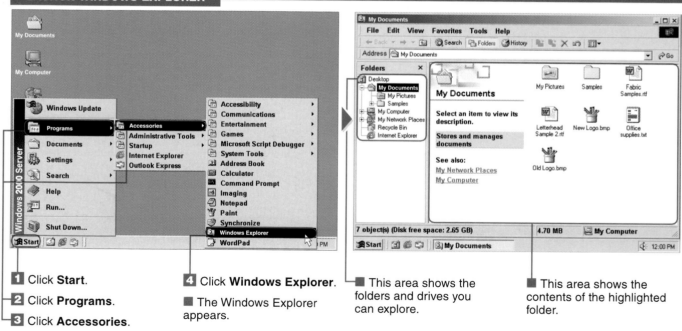

2 Click **Programs**.

3 Click **Accessories**.

4 Click **Windows Explorer**.

■ The Windows Explorer appears.

■ This area shows the folders and drives you can explore.

■ This area shows the contents of the highlighted folder.

How can I tell if a folder contains other folders?

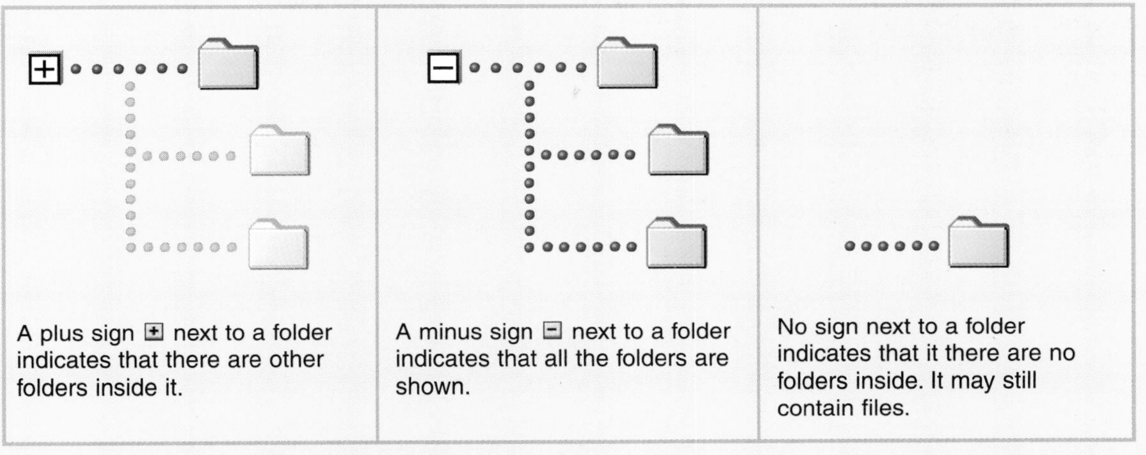

A plus sign ⊞ next to a folder indicates that there are other folders inside it.

A minus sign ⊟ next to a folder indicates that all the folders are shown.

No sign next to a folder indicates that it there are no folders inside. It may still contain files.

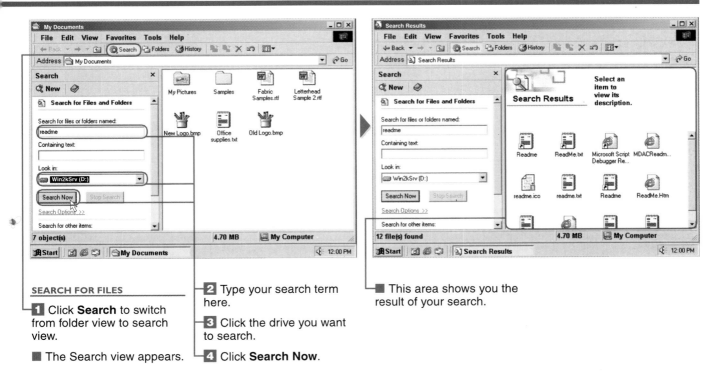

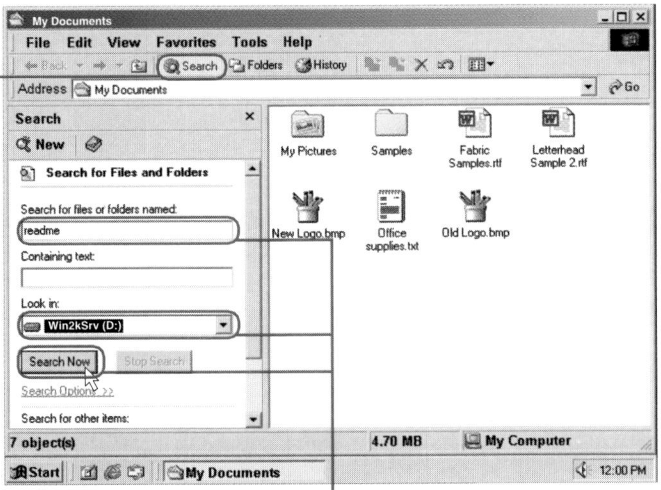

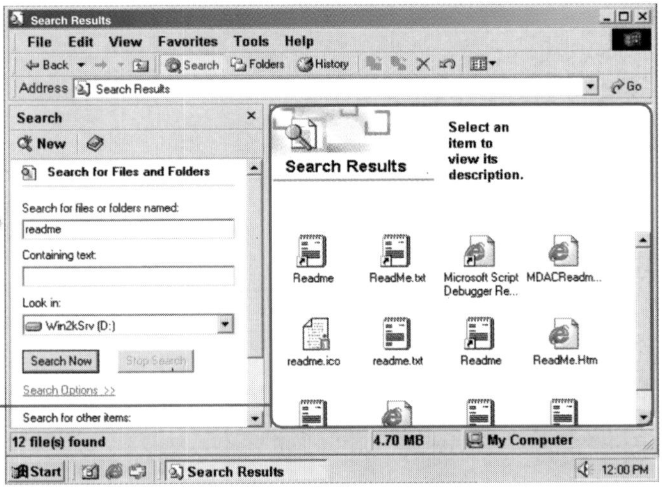

SEARCH FOR FILES

1 Click **Search** to switch from folder view to search view.

■ The Search view appears.

2 Type your search term here.

3 Click the drive you want to search.

4 Click **Search Now**.

■ This area shows you the result of your search.

SELECT FILES

When working in Windows Explorer, you must select the files you want to work with.

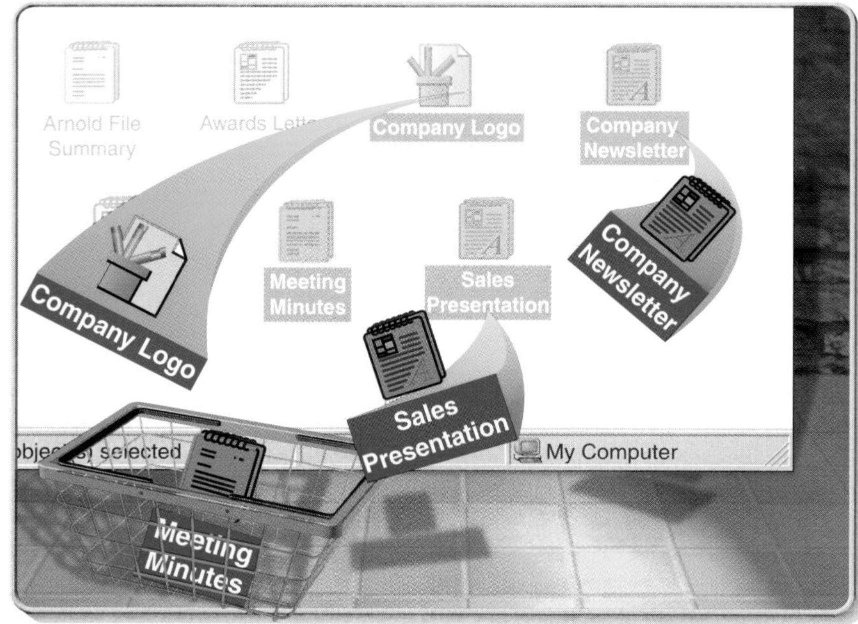

SELECT FILES

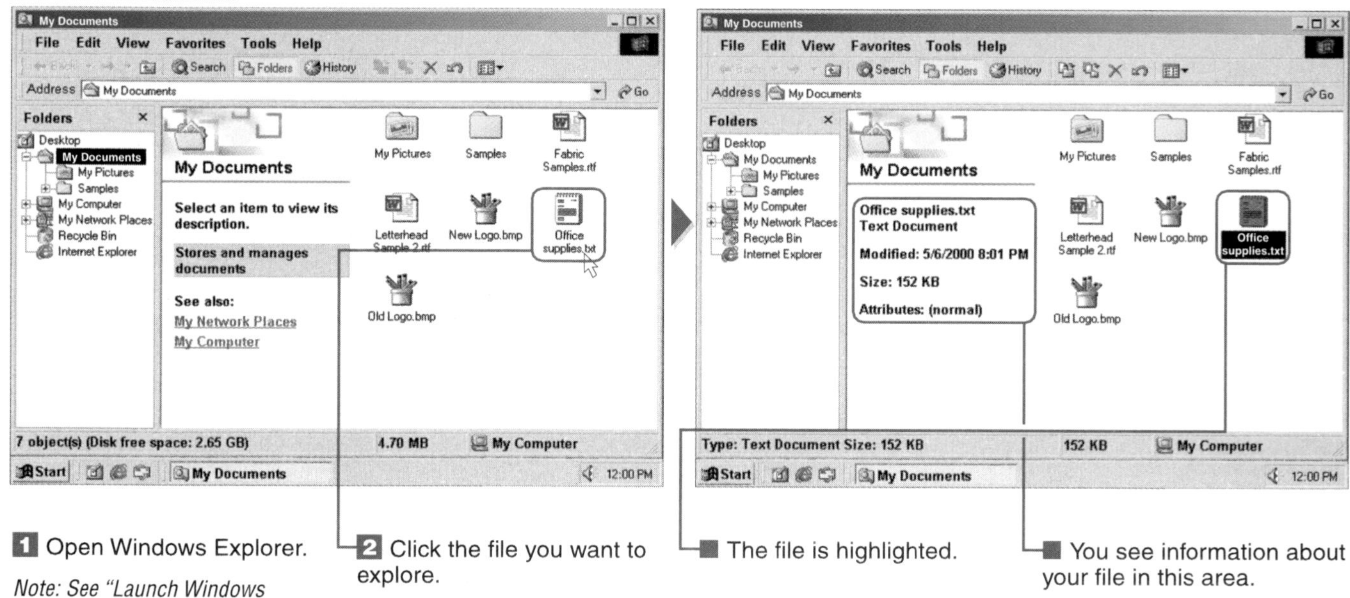

1 Open Windows Explorer.

Note: See "Launch Windows Explorer" for more information.

2 Click the file you want to explore.

■ The file is highlighted.

■ You see information about your file in this area.

How do I deselect files?

To cancel all the files you have selected, click in a blank area in the window. You can deselect a single file by holding down **Ctrl** and clicking the file.

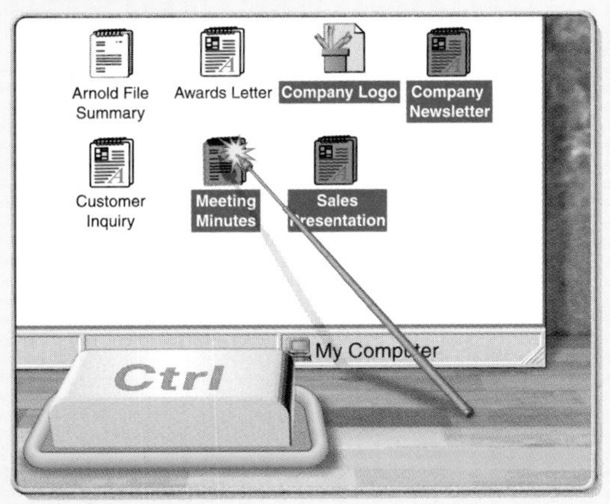

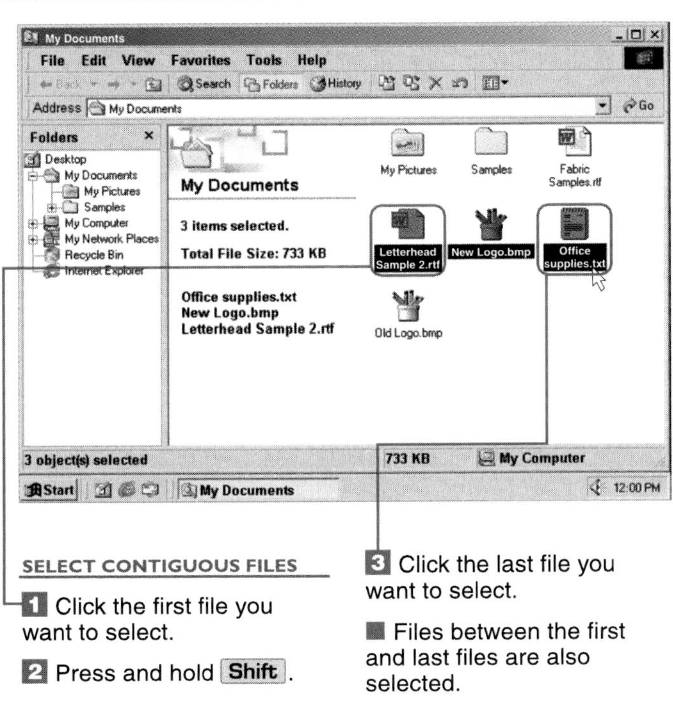

SELECT CONTIGUOUS FILES

1 Click the first file you want to select.

2 Press and hold **Shift**.

3 Click the last file you want to select.

■ Files between the first and last files are also selected.

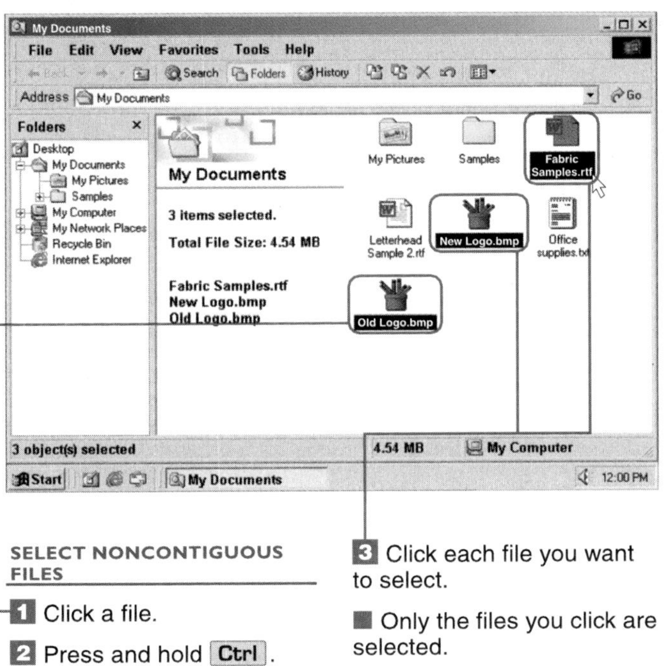

SELECT NONCONTIGUOUS FILES

1 Click a file.

2 Press and hold **Ctrl**.

3 Click each file you want to select.

■ Only the files you click are selected.

COPY OR MOVE FILES

You can use Windows Explorer to copy or move files. You can organize your files much as you would in a file cabinet.

COPY OR MOVE FILES

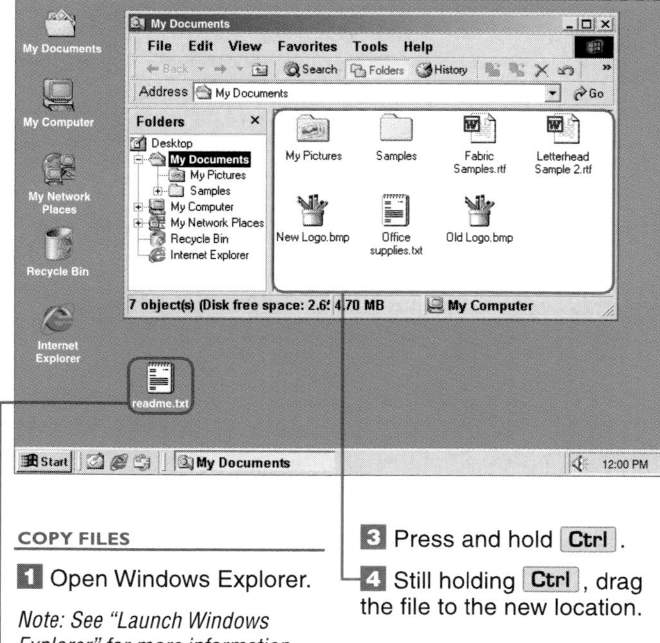

COPY FILES

1 Open Windows Explorer.

Note: See "Launch Windows Explorer" for more information.

2 Click a file to copy.

3 Press and hold **Ctrl**.

4 Still holding **Ctrl**, drag the file to the new location.

■ The file is now in two locations: the old one and the new one.

How is moving different from copying?

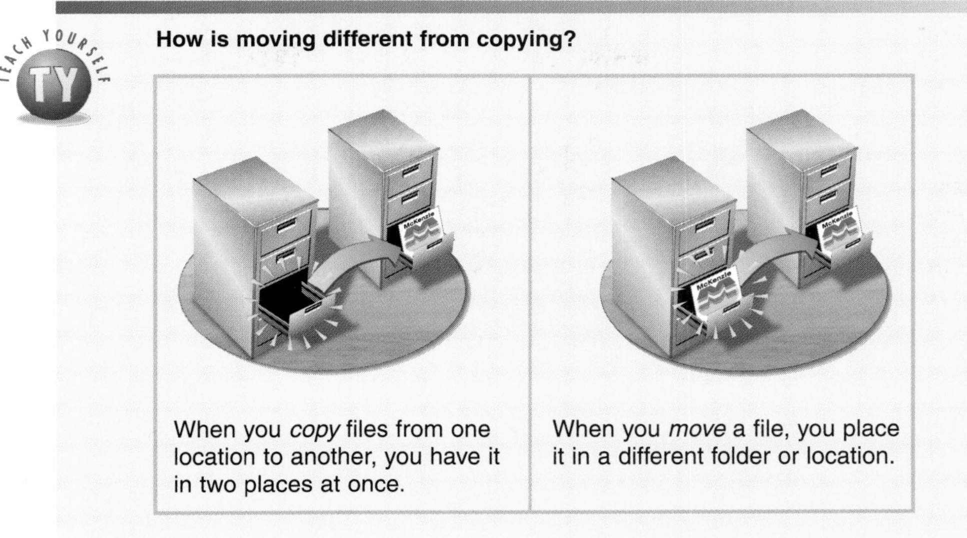

When you *copy* files from one location to another, you have it in two places at once.

When you *move* a file, you place it in a different folder or location.

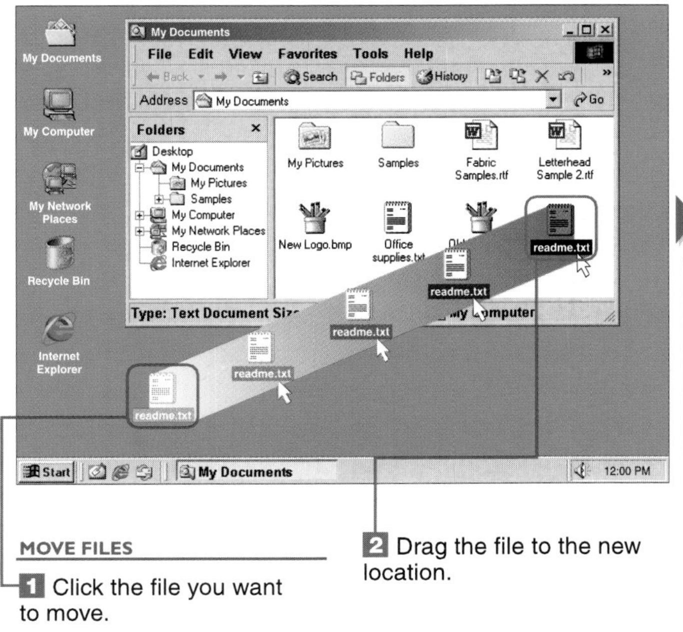

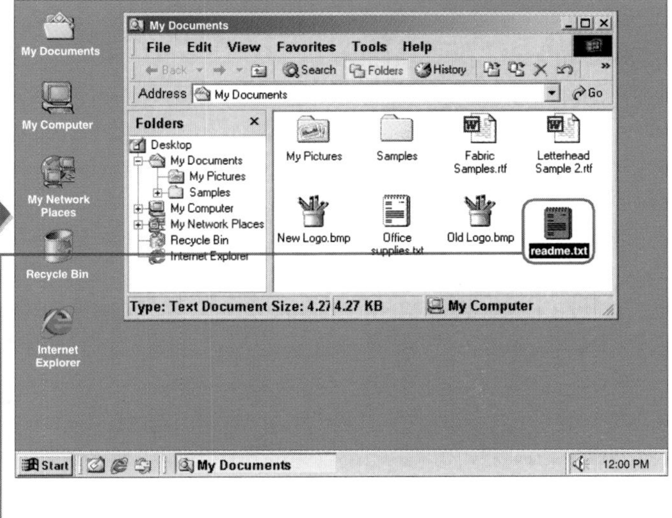

MOVE FILES

1 Click the file you want to move.

2 Drag the file to the new location.

■ The file disappears from the old location and appears in the new location.

RENAME FILES

You can rename files or folders when you want to better describe what the file or folder contains.

RENAME FILES

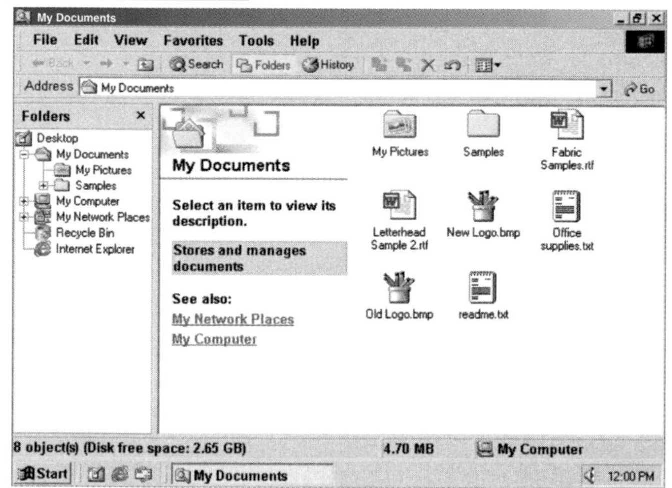

1 Open Windows Explorer.

Note: See "Launch Windows Explorer" for more information.

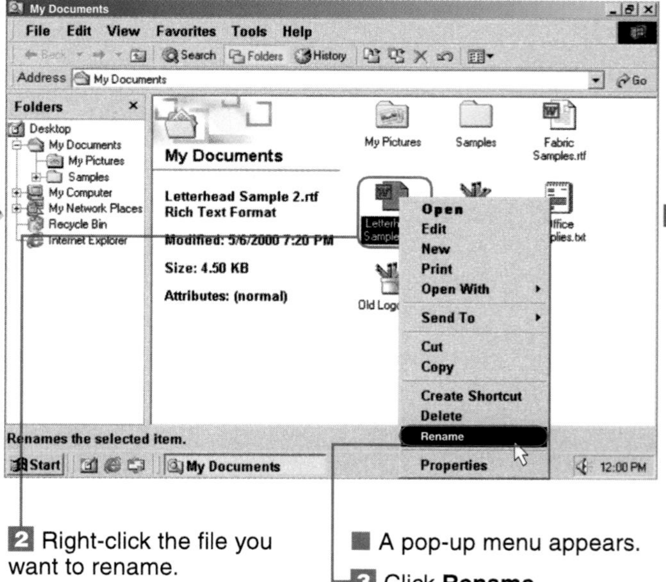

2 Right-click the file you want to rename.

■ A pop-up menu appears.

3 Click **Rename**.

Should I rename a folder?

You should only rename folders that you have created. Windows 2000 and your applications require folders in certain locations with certain names. If you rename one of these folders, you may not be able to start your programs or even your computer.

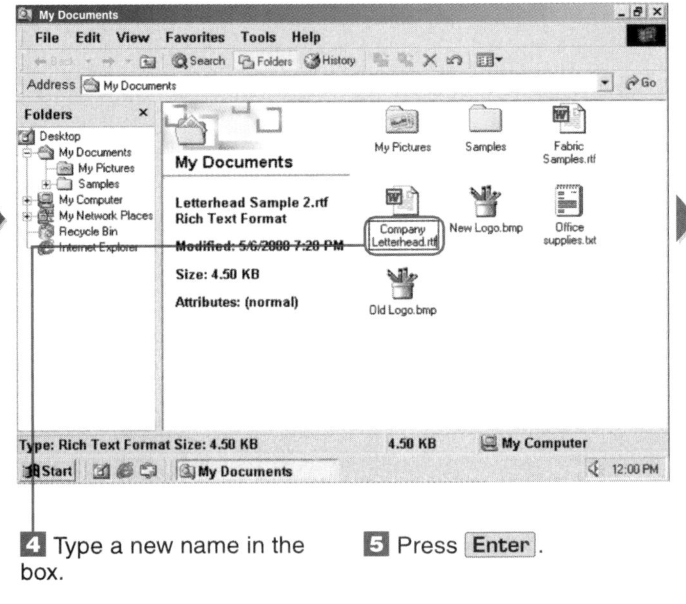

4 Type a new name in the box.

5 Press Enter.

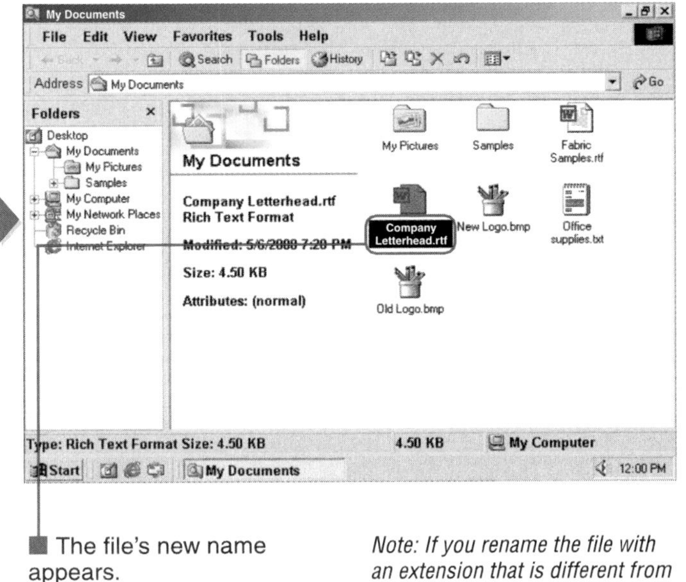

■ The file's new name appears.

Note: If you rename the file with an extension that is different from the previous name, the file may not open properly.

DELETE FILES

If you do not need files anymore, you can delete them from your hard drive.

DELETE FILES

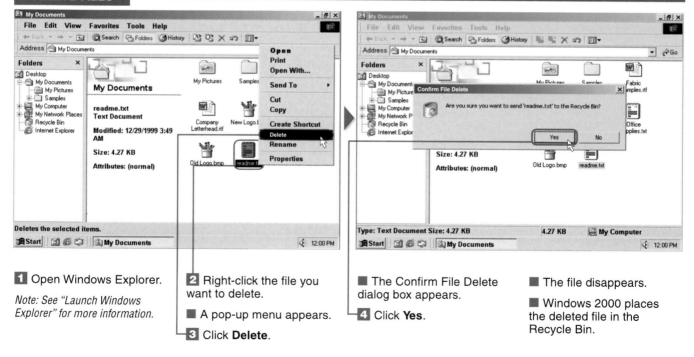

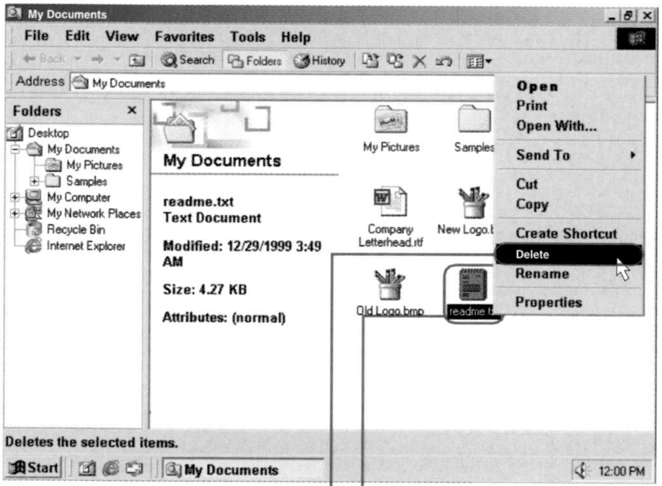

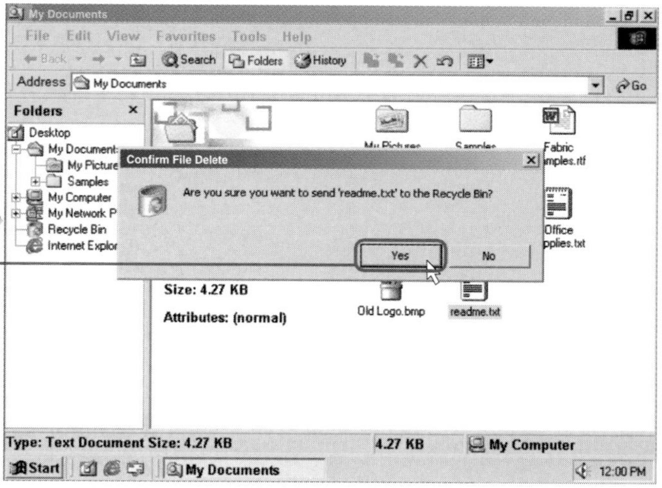

1 Open Windows Explorer.

Note: See "Launch Windows Explorer" for more information.

2 Right-click the file you want to delete.

■ A pop-up menu appears.

3 Click **Delete**.

■ The Confirm File Delete dialog box appears.

4 Click **Yes**.

■ The file disappears.

■ Windows 2000 places the deleted file in the Recycle Bin.

RESTORE FILES

You can restore deleted files from the Recycle Bin back to their original location.

RESTORE FILES

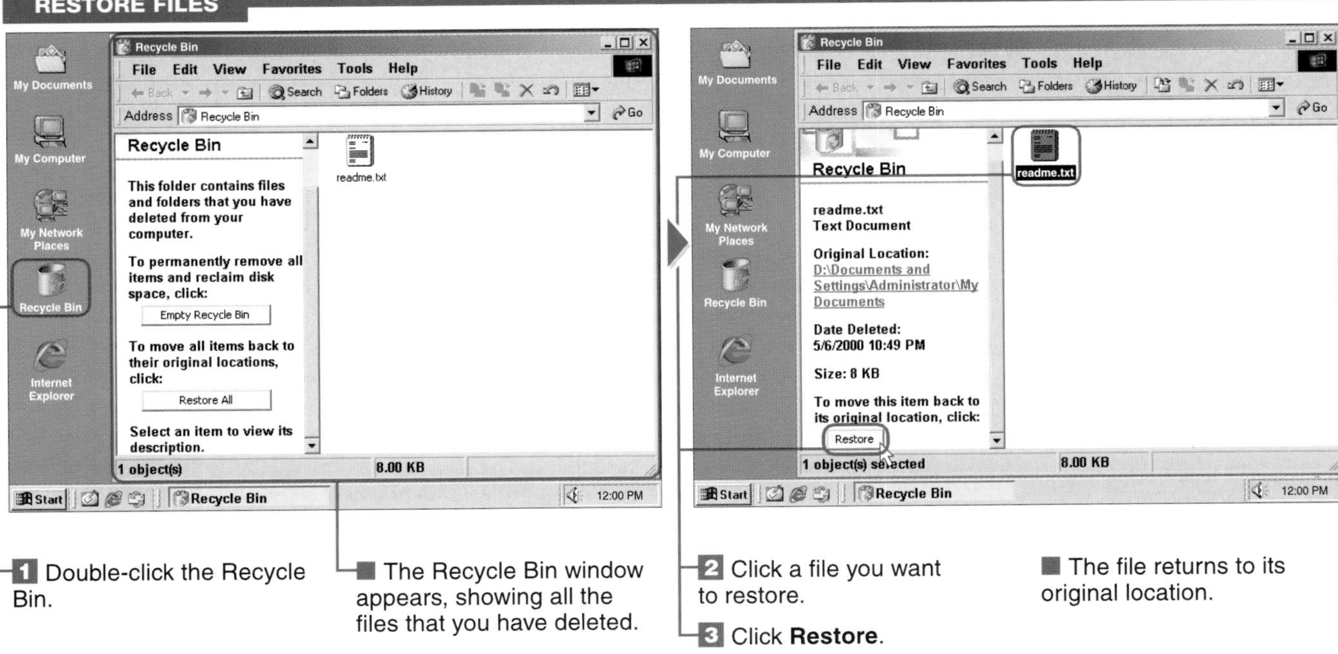

1 Double-click the Recycle Bin.

■ The Recycle Bin window appears, showing all the files that you have deleted.

2 Click a file you want to restore.

3 Click **Restore**.

■ The file returns to its original location.

CREATE A SHARED FOLDER

Windows 2000 makes sharing files and folders with others on your network easy. It also provides security for your information so only authorized users can gain access to your sensitive data.

CREATE A SHARED FOLDER

1 Click **Start**.

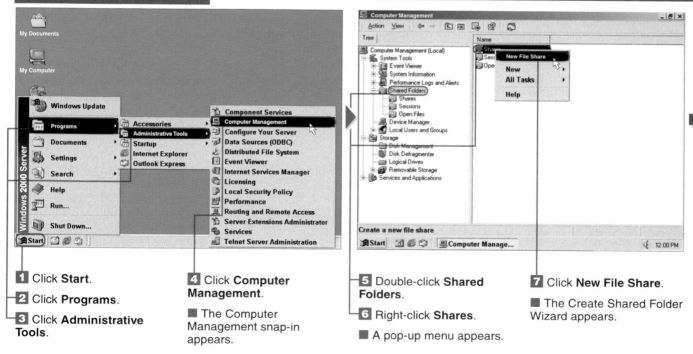

2 Click **Programs**.

3 Click **Administrative Tools**.

4 Click **Computer Management**.

■ The Computer Management snap-in appears.

5 Double-click **Shared Folders**.

6 Right-click **Shares**.

■ A pop-up menu appears.

7 Click **New File Share**.

■ The Create Shared Folder Wizard appears.

How do I tell which folders are shared?

You see an icon in Windows Explorer that looks like a folder with a hand under it. When you see this icon, it means the folder is shared.

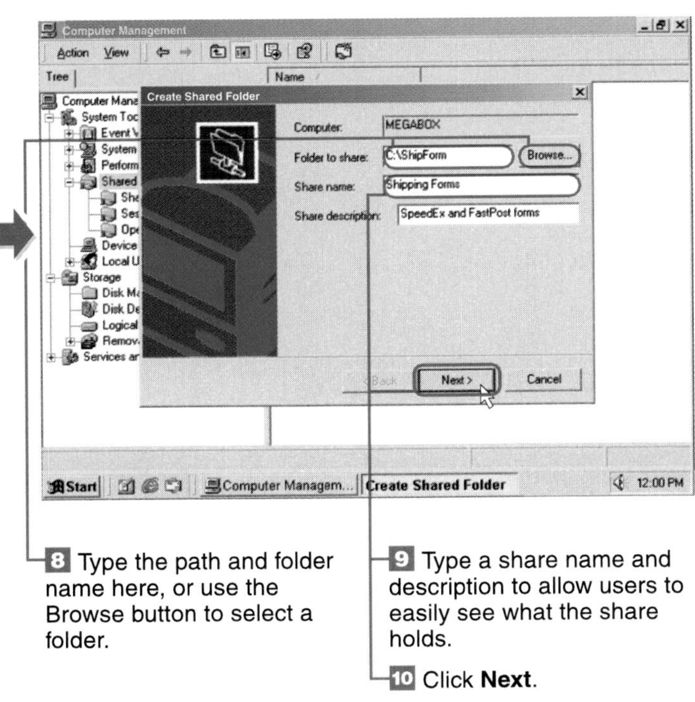

8 Type the path and folder name here, or use the Browse button to select a folder.

9 Type a share name and description to allow users to easily see what the share holds.

10 Click **Next**.

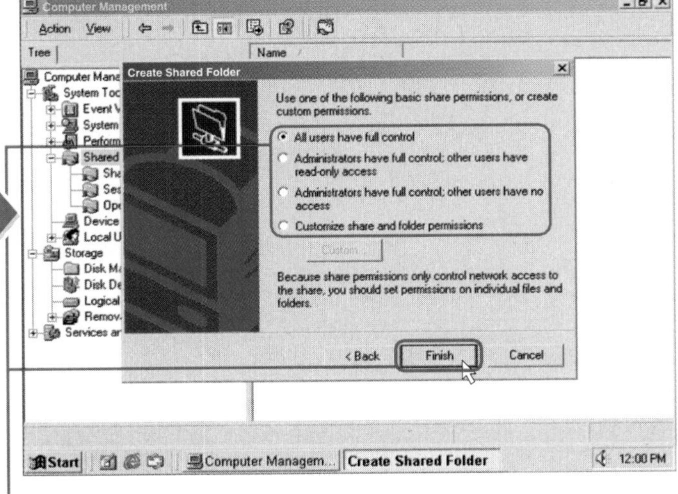

11 Click the type of access you want users to have (○ changes to ◉).

12 Click **Finish**.

■ When asked if you want to make a new share, click **No**.

■ The new share appears in the Shares folder.

CHANGE FOLDER PERMISSIONS

When you add shared folders to your network you can determine who has access to those folders and the files within them by using permissions.

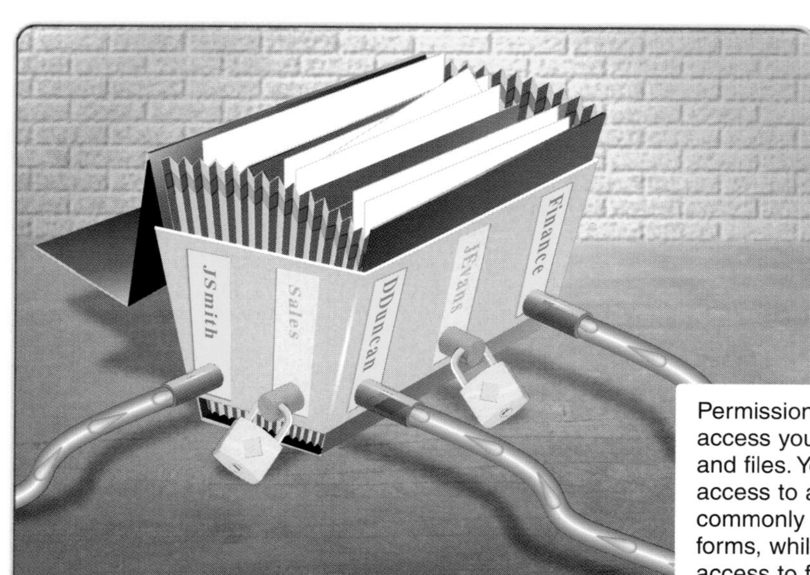

Permissions define the type of access you can have to folders and files. You might give read access to all employees for commonly used business forms, while you would give access to financial data to just a few trusted employees.

CHANGE FOLDER PERMISSIONS

1 Click **Start**.

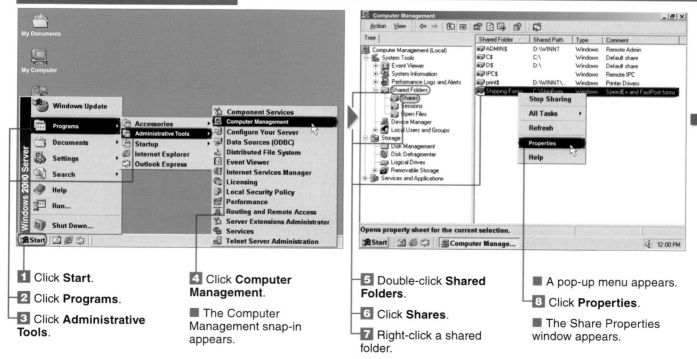

2 Click **Programs**.

3 Click **Administrative Tools**.

4 Click **Computer Management**.

■ The Computer Management snap-in appears.

5 Double-click **Shared Folders**.

6 Click **Shares**.

7 Right-click a shared folder.

■ A pop-up menu appears.

8 Click **Properties**.

■ The Share Properties window appears.

How can I tell if a folder contains other folders?

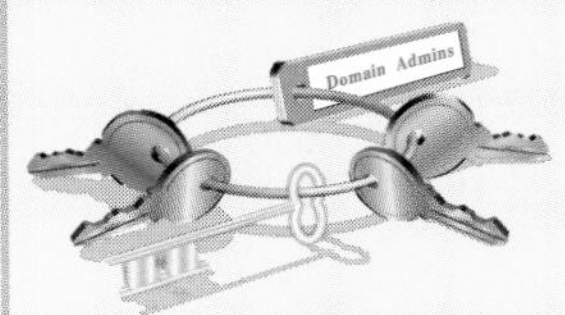 Guests have very limited access to network resources.	 Administrators are the highest level of importance, with access to all functions and areas in the network.	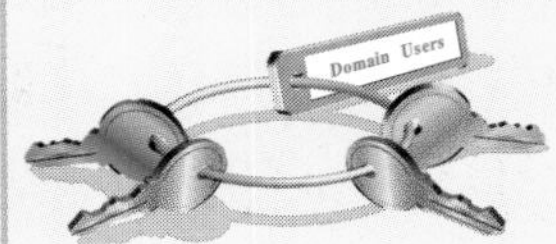 Everyone contains all users in your domain.	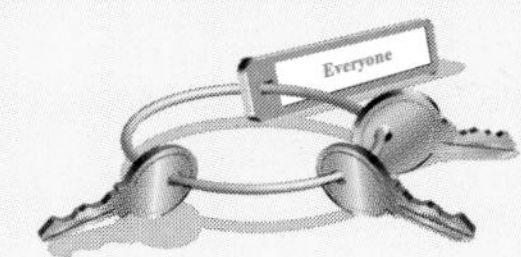 Power Users have access to many functions and network resources.

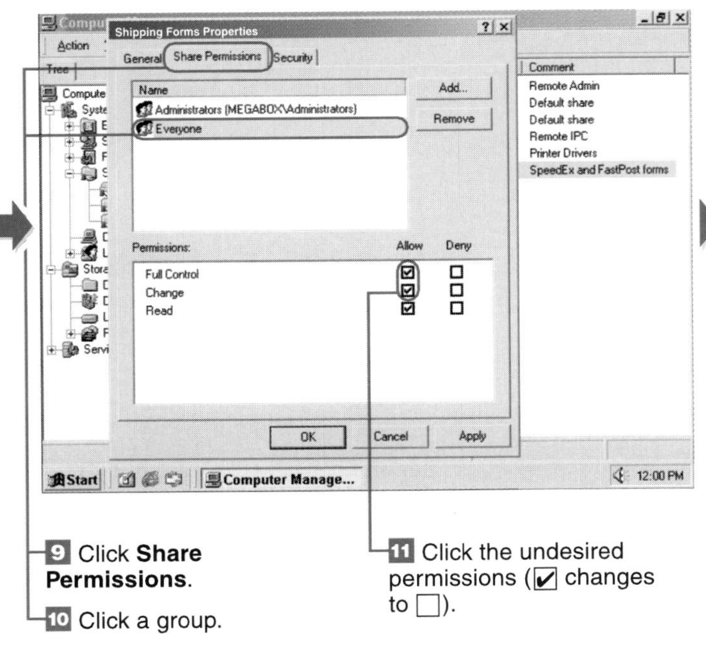

9 Click **Share Permissions**.

10 Click a group.

11 Click the undesired permissions (☑ changes to ☐).

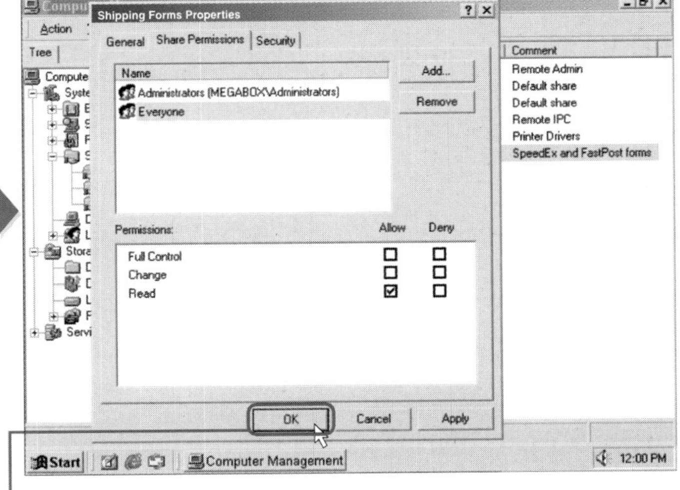

■ The group Everyone now has read-only access to the share.

12 Click **OK**.

■ The Share Properties dialog box disappears.

INTRODUCING DISKS AND STORAGE TYPES

Windows 2000 supports a wide variety of disks and storage types. They have different uses, but serve the same purpose: to store your files and data until you need them.

FLOPPY DISKS AND REMOVABLE DISKETTES

Removable disks include 3 1/2" diskettes, which hold 1.44 megabytes of data, and removable diskettes, which can hold megabytes or gigabytes of data.

HARD DRIVES

Hard drives are the workhorses in every computer. They contain the operating system and program files, and can hold many gigabytes of data.

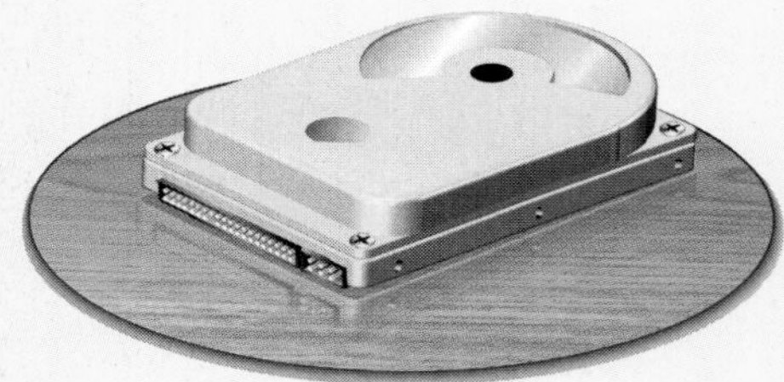

CD AND DVD DISKS

Compact Disks and Digital Video Disks store large amounts of data. You can write data to some types of CD and DVD disks, but most drives are read-only.

TAPE CARTRIDGES

Tape cartridges can hold megabytes or gigabytes of data. They are typically used to make backups of hard drives.

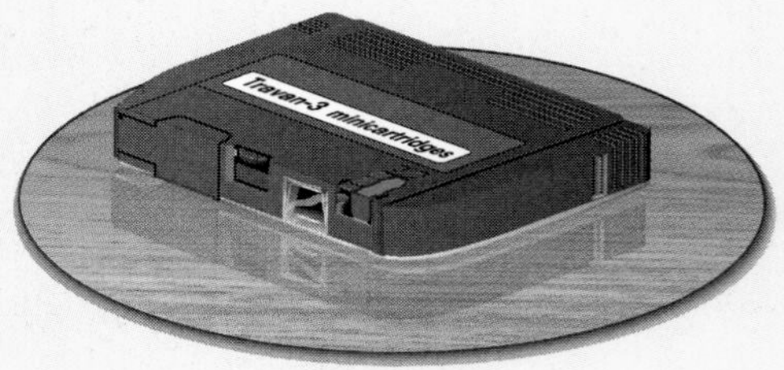

VIEW THE DISK MANAGEMENT SNAP-IN

The Disk Management snap-in enables you to manage all your different disk types from a single window.

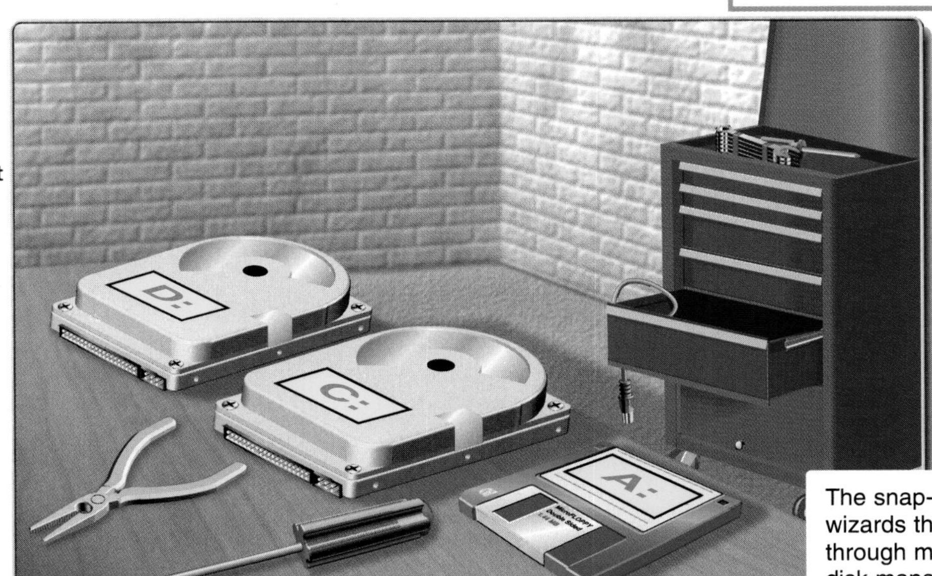

The snap-in includes wizards that guide you through many of the disk management functions.

VIEW THE DISK MANAGEMENT SNAP-IN

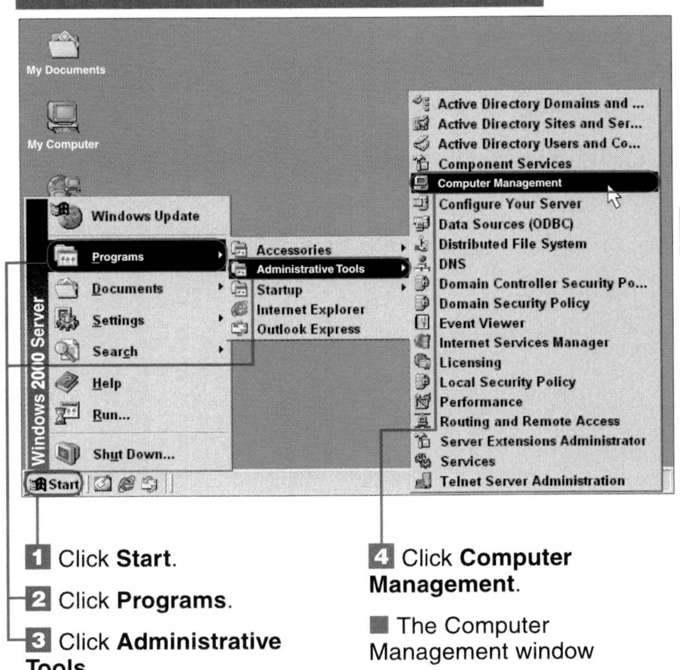

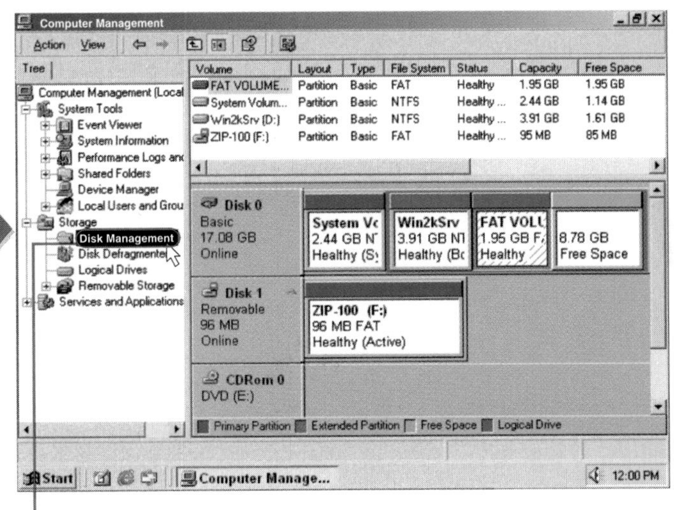

1 Click **Start**.

2 Click **Programs**.

3 Click **Administrative Tools**.

4 Click **Computer Management**.

■ The Computer Management window appears.

5 Click **Disk Management**.

■ The Disk Management snap-in appears.

Note: The Disk Management snap-in may take a few moments to load while it reads your disks.

VIEW DISK PROPERTIES

You can view the properties and current status of all disk types on your system from within the Disk Management snap-in.

VIEW DISK PROPERTIES

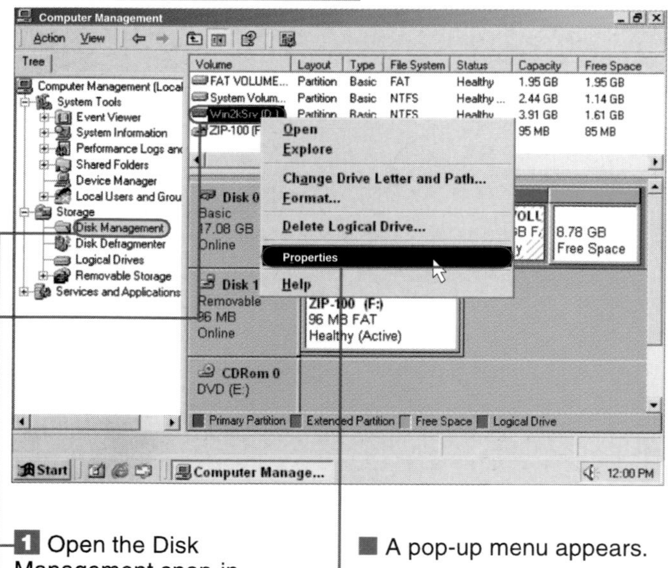

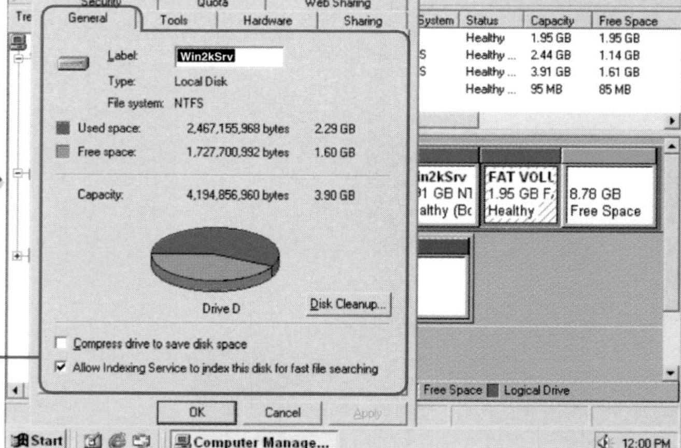

1 Open the Disk Management snap-in.

Note: See "View the Disk Management Snap-In" for more information.

2 Right-click a hard drive in the window.

■ A pop-up menu appears.

3 Click **Properties**.

■ The Properties window appears.

■ The General tab displays the volume table and volume information.

Why am I not able to open the Disk Management snap-in?

You must either be logged on as an administrator or as a user in the Administrators group for you to use Disk Management in the Microsoft Management Console.

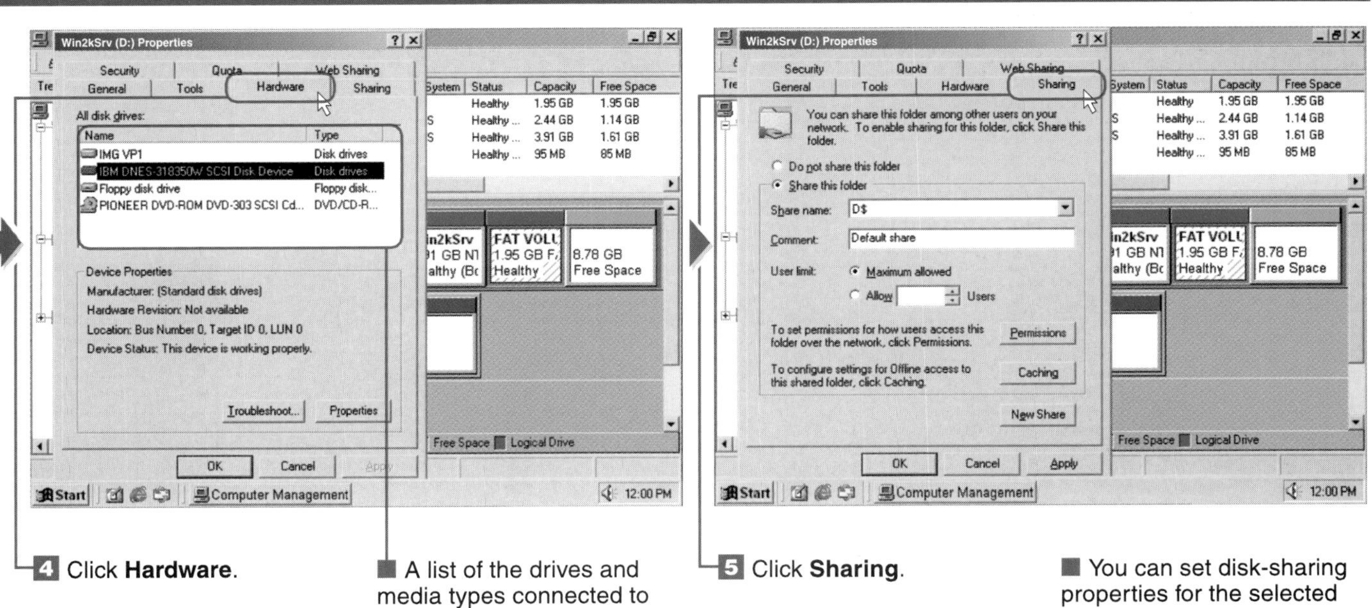

4 Click **Hardware**.

■ A list of the drives and media types connected to the computer appears.

5 Click **Sharing**.

■ You can set disk-sharing properties for the selected volume in this tab.

DEFRAGMENT YOUR DISK

***Disk defragmentation* happens when Windows has to store large files in several different areas on your disk. The Disk Defragmenter rearranges your files so they are stored as single files without fragments.**

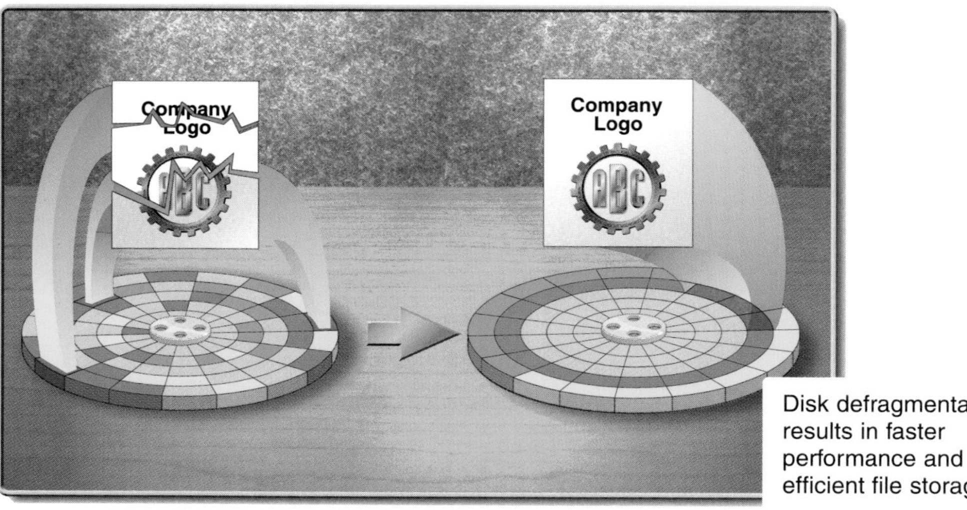

Disk defragmentation results in faster performance and more efficient file storage.

DEFRAGMENT YOUR DISK

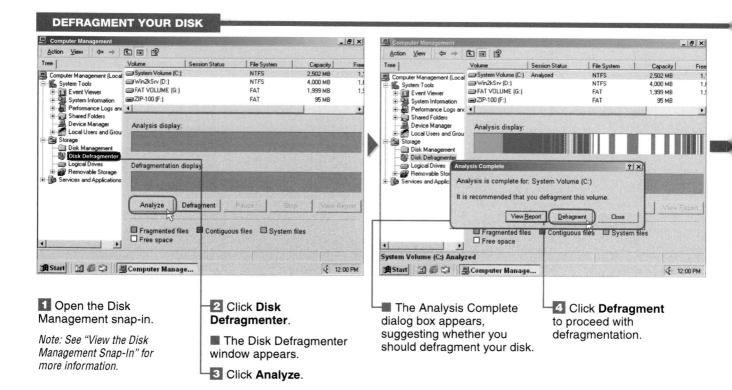

1 Open the Disk Management snap-in.

Note: See "View the Disk Management Snap-In" for more information.

2 Click **Disk Defragmenter**.

■ The Disk Defragmenter window appears.

3 Click **Analyze**.

■ The Analysis Complete dialog box appears, suggesting whether you should defragment your disk.

4 Click **Defragment** to proceed with defragmentation.

How often should I defragment my disks?

If a lot of people use your hard drives, you should defragment frequently, perhaps once a week. Otherwise, once a month should be sufficient.

Note: Defragmentation slows down your computer considerably, so you should defragment drives after work hours.

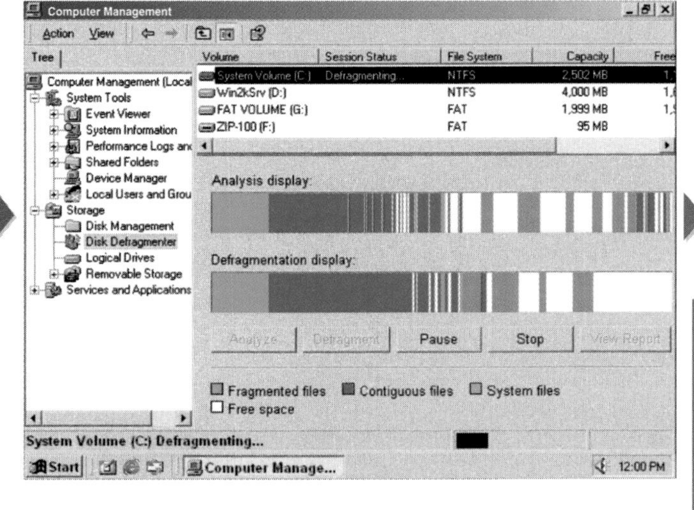

■ The disk defragmenter rearranges your files.

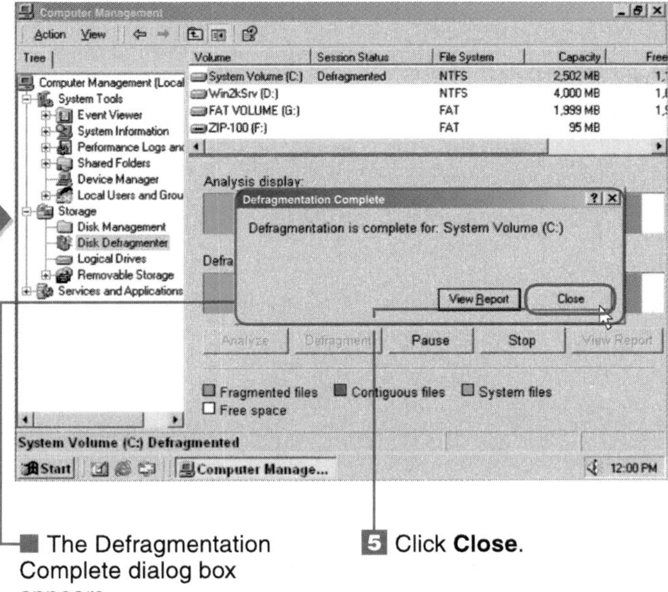

■ The Defragmentation Complete dialog box appears.

5 Click **Close**.

CONVERT DISK FILE SYSTEMS

Windows 2000 supports several different ways to store files, including FAT and NTFS. NTFS supports advanced features such as disk and file security, user quotas, and file encryption.

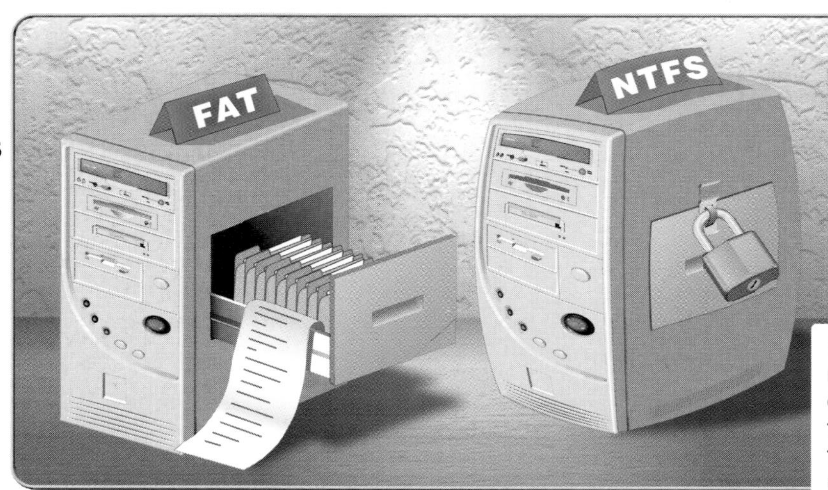

Use NTFS unless you need to run another operating system on the same computer. In that case, you should use FAT.

CONVERT DISK FILE SYSTEMS

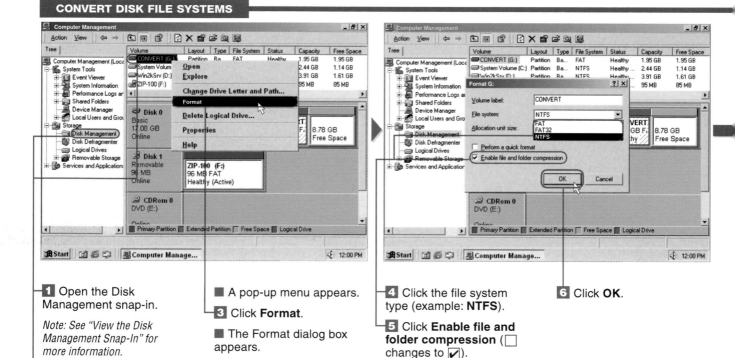

1 Open the Disk Management snap-in.

Note: See "View the Disk Management Snap-In" for more information.

2 Right-click a FAT volume.

■ A pop-up menu appears.

3 Click **Format**.

■ The Format dialog box appears.

4 Click the file system type (example: **NTFS**).

5 Click **Enable file and folder compression** (☐ changes to ☑).

6 Click **OK**.

Will I lose any files if I convert from FAT to NTFS?

Yes. In order to support new features, Windows 2000 must format the partition with the new format; this erases all files. If you want to save your files, copy them to another partition or back up the files. See the section "Copy or Move Files" or Chapter "Backing Up and Restoring Files" for more information.

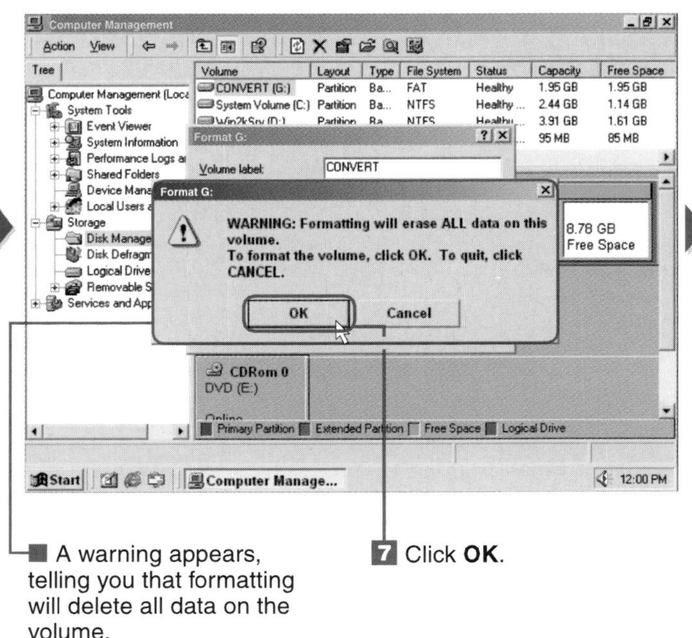

■ A warning appears, telling you that formatting will delete all data on the volume.

7 Click **OK**.

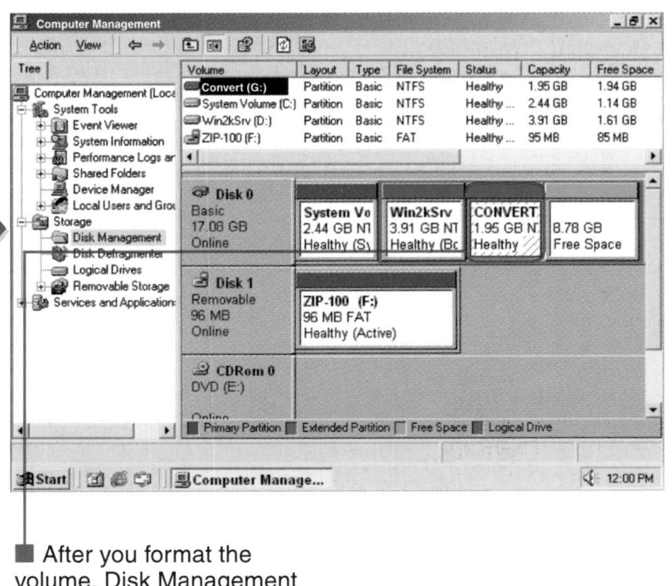

■ After you format the volume, Disk Management reports the new status of your hard drive.

CONFIGURE DISK QUOTAS

***Disk quotas* determine how much hard disk space is available to each user for saving their files, and keep users from overloading your server with their files.**

In order to use disk quotas, you must use network disks that have been formatted with NTFS.

CONFIGURE DISK QUOTAS

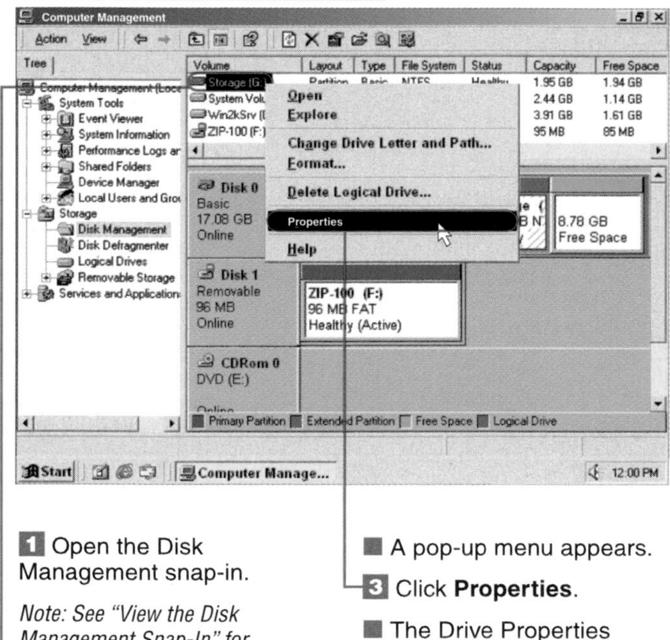

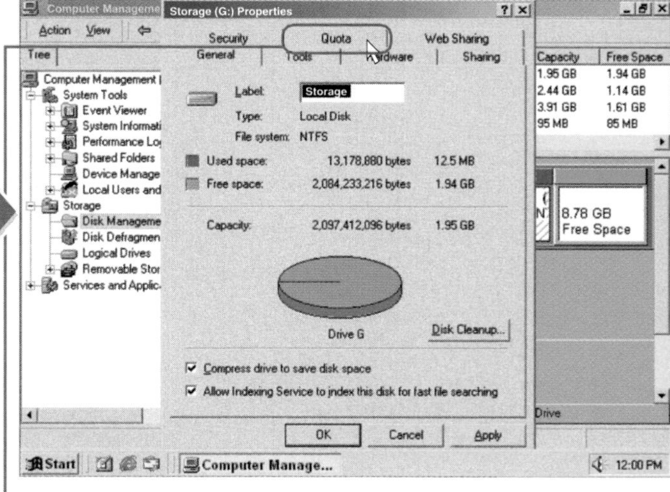

1 Open the Disk Management snap-in.

Note: See "View the Disk Management Snap-In" for more information.

2 Right-click an NTFS volume.

■ A pop-up menu appears.

3 Click **Properties**.

■ The Drive Properties dialog box appears.

4 Click **Quota**.

How restrictive do I have to be when assigning disk quotas?

That depends on the number of users you have, the amount of disk space in each volume, and the amount of information you want to store. Discuss the limits with your users and agree what will work for everyone.

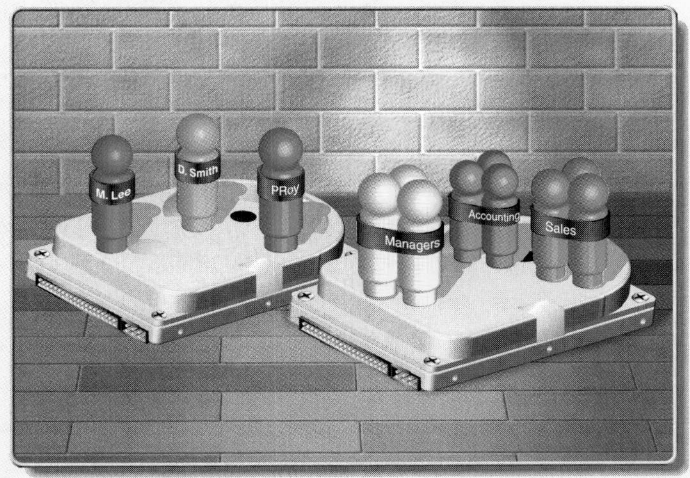

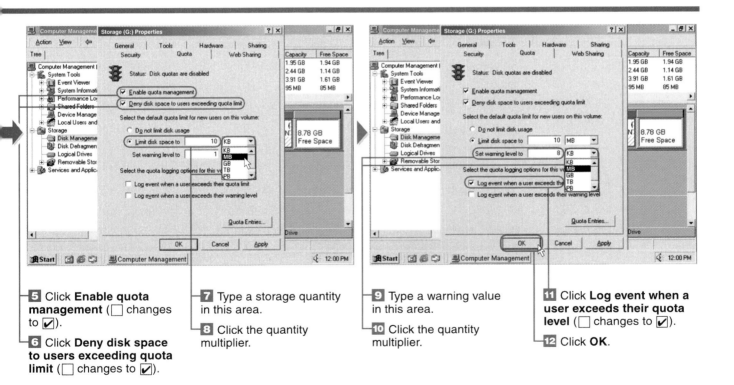

5 Click **Enable quota management** (☐ changes to ☑).

6 Click **Deny disk space to users exceeding quota limit** (☐ changes to ☑).

7 Type a storage quantity in this area.

8 Click the quantity multiplier.

9 Type a warning value in this area.

10 Click the quantity multiplier.

11 Click **Log event when a user exceeds their quota level** (☐ changes to ☑).

12 Click **OK**.

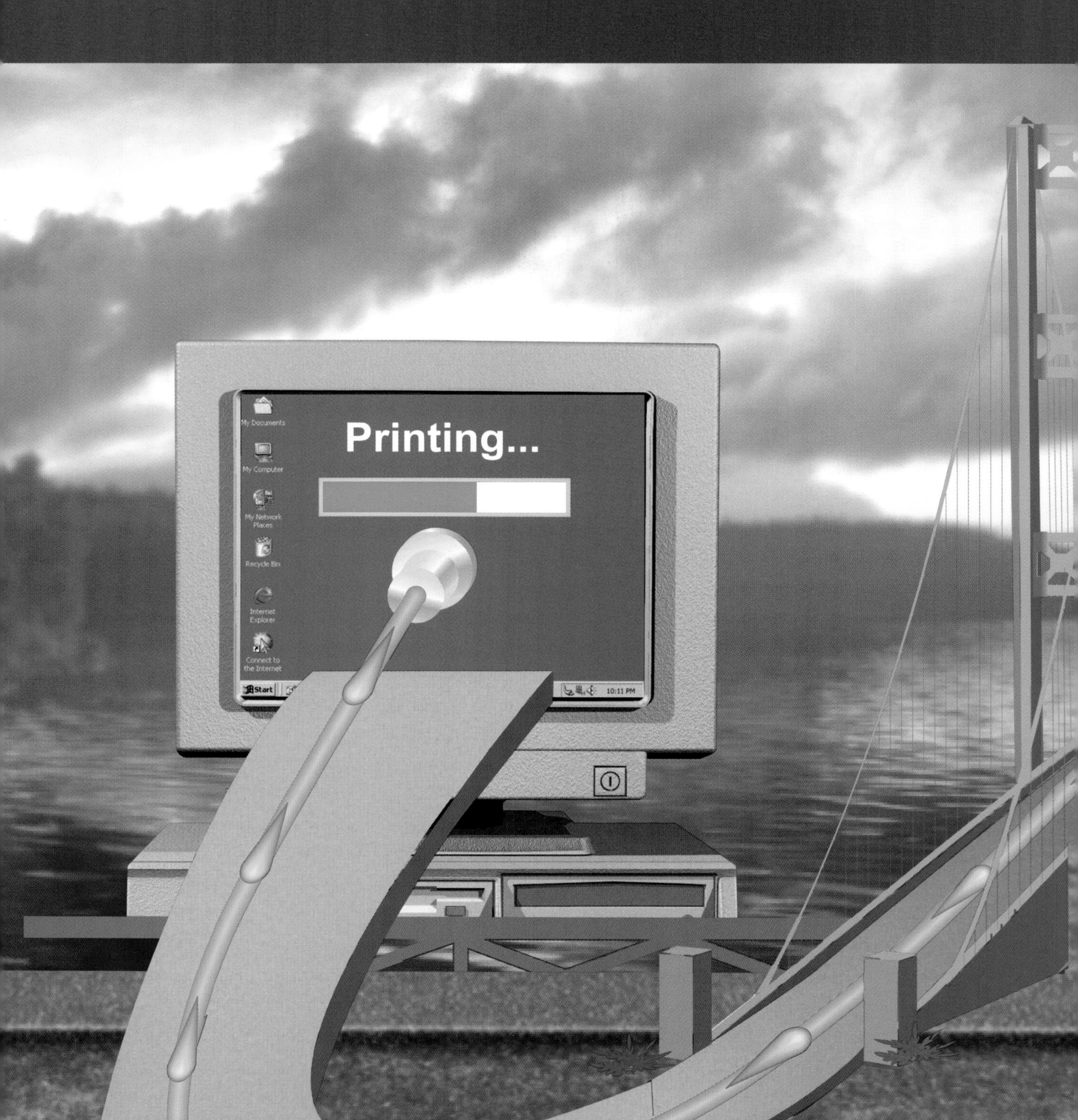

My Documents
Printing...
My Computer
My Network Places
Recycle Bin
Internet Explorer
Connect to the Internet
Start
10:11 PM

CHAPTER 11

Configuring Printers

Most companies share printers on a network so everyone can use them. This chapter shows you how to set up printers and grant printer access to your users.

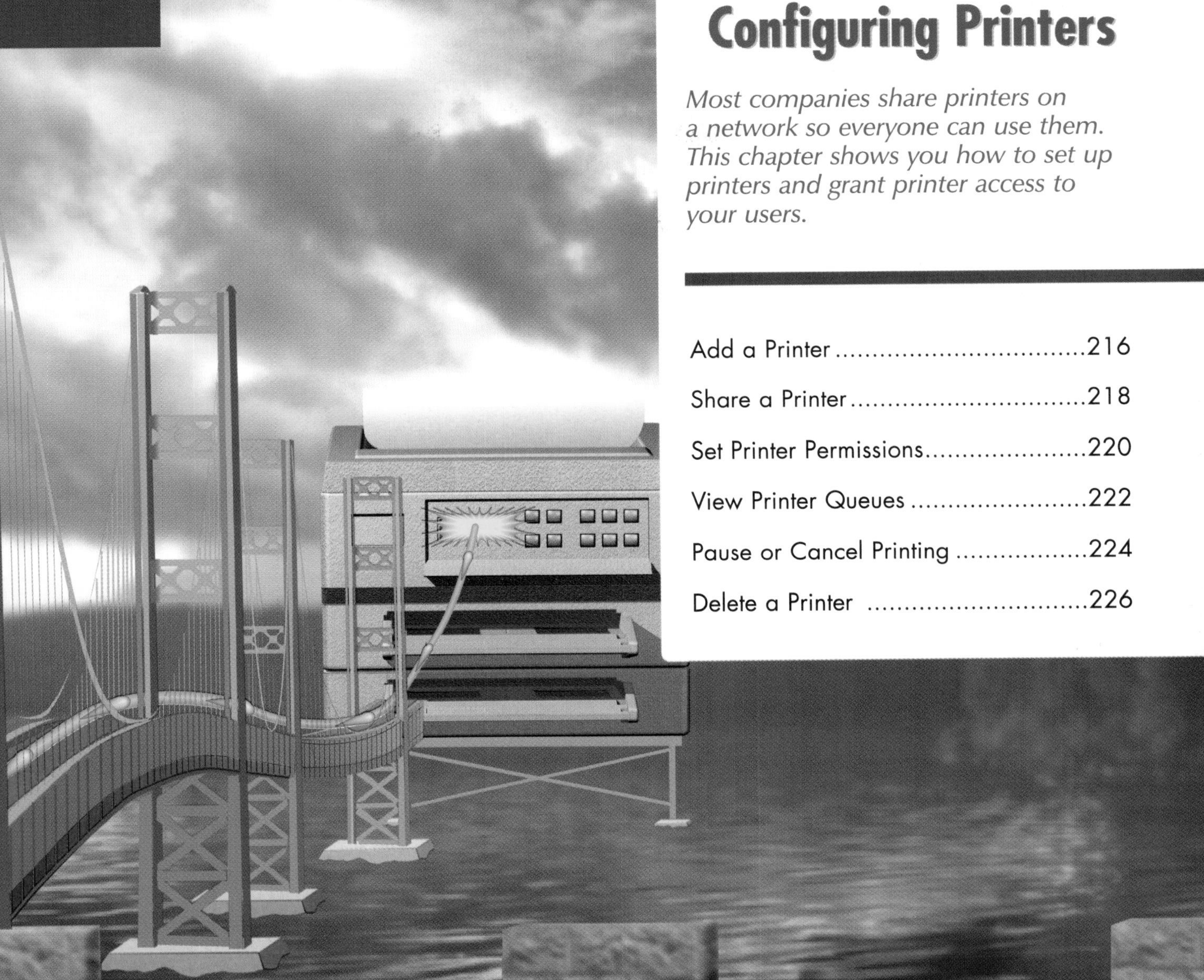

ADD A PRINTER

Windows 2000 makes it easy for you to attach a printer to your computer. The Add Printer Wizard takes you step by step through the process.

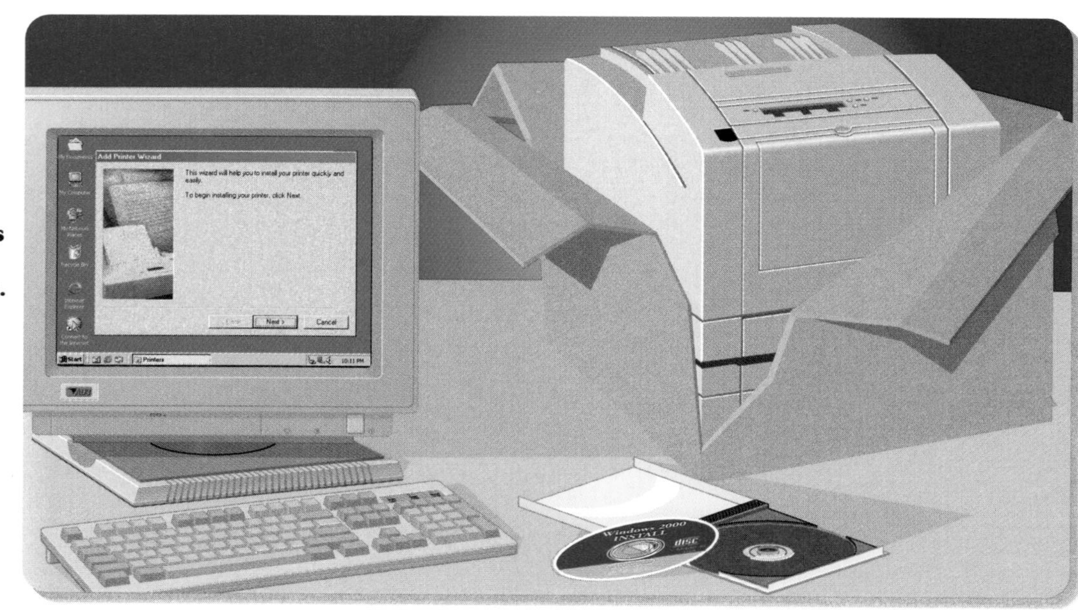

ADD A PRINTER

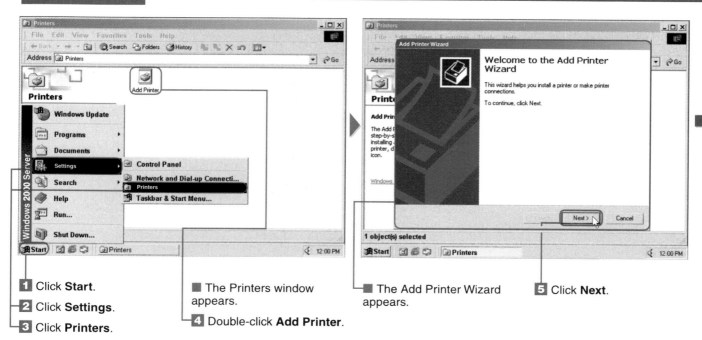

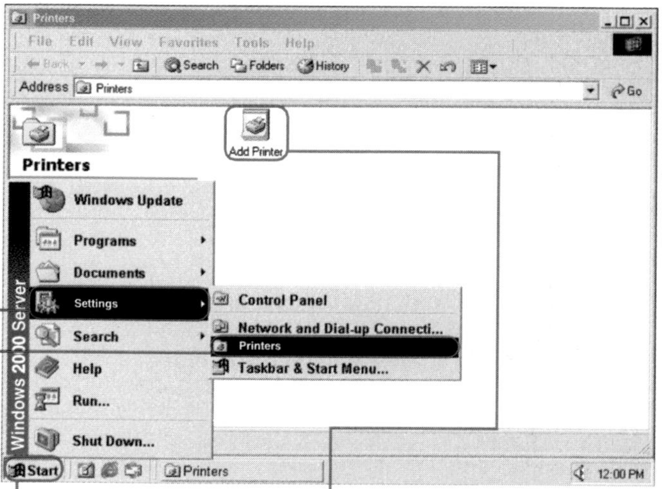

1 Click **Start**.

2 Click **Settings**.

3 Click **Printers**.

■ The Printers window appears.

4 Double-click **Add Printer**.

■ The Add Printer Wizard appears.

5 Click **Next**.

Should I set up a printer on the server or should I use a different computer?

You can set up a local printer or a network printer attached to a computer on the network. Many businesses use a server computer that acts as a print server, particularly if those businesses have a lot of users or print traffic.

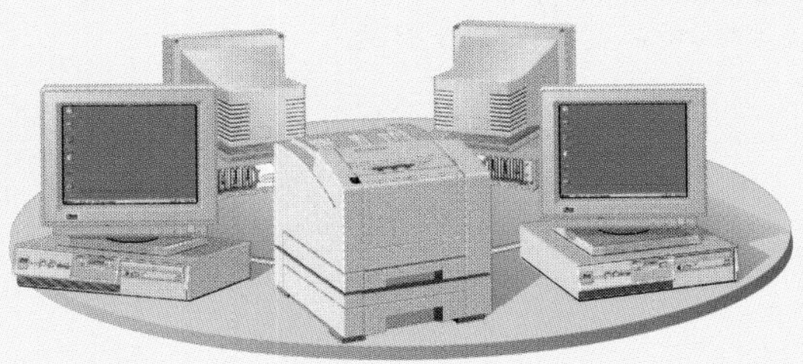

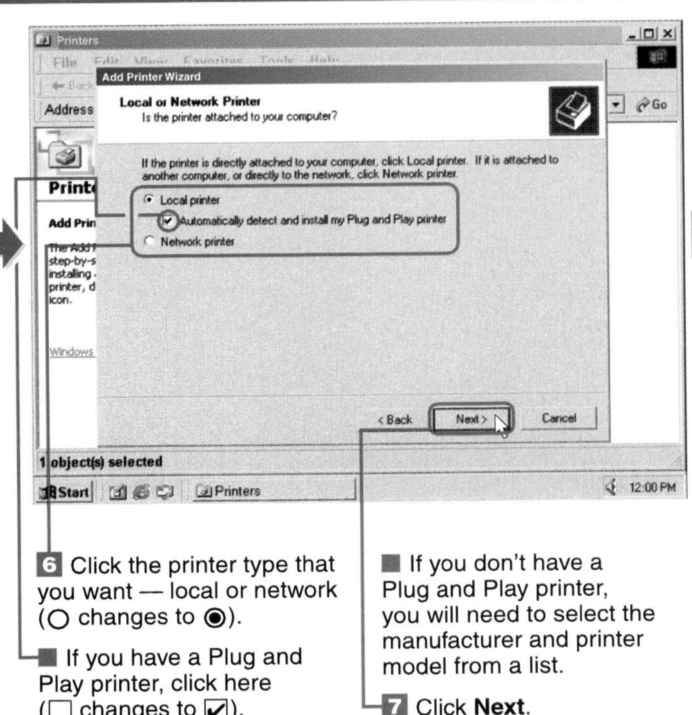

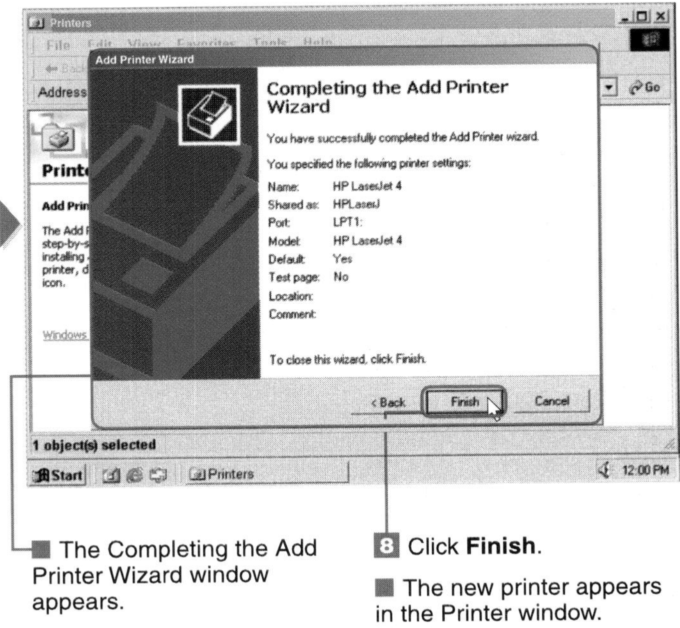

6 Click the printer type that you want — local or network (○ changes to ◉).

■ If you have a Plug and Play printer, click here (☐ changes to ☑).

■ If you don't have a Plug and Play printer, you will need to select the manufacturer and printer model from a list.

7 Click **Next**.

■ The Completing the Add Printer Wizard window appears.

8 Click **Finish**.

■ The new printer appears in the Printer window.

SHARE A PRINTER

After you set up your printer, you can make it available to others on your network. Doing so allows others to print documents on the shared printer.

Before you share a printer, you must have the File and Printer Sharing for Microsoft Networks option installed on your local area connection. This option is turned on by default when you install Windows 2000 Server.

SHARE A PRINTER

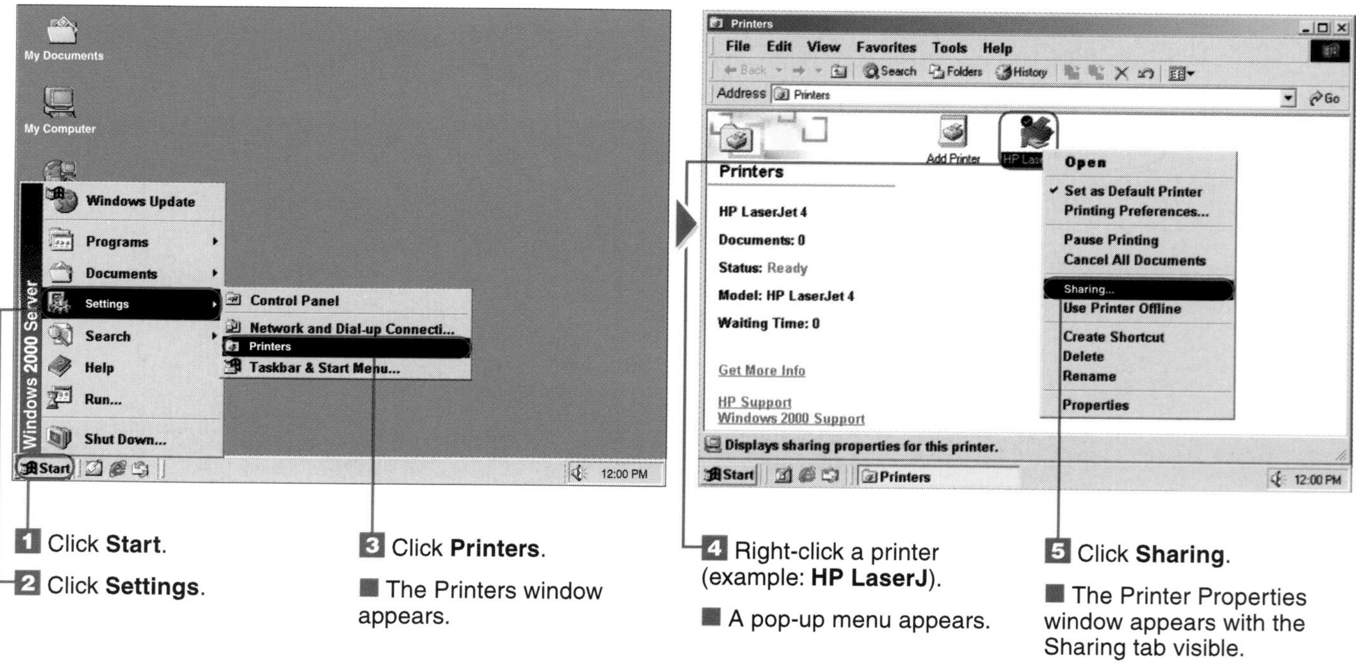

1 Click **Start**.

2 Click **Settings**.

3 Click **Printers**.

■ The Printers window appears.

4 Right-click a printer (example: **HP LaserJ**).

■ A pop-up menu appears.

5 Click **Sharing**.

■ The Printer Properties window appears with the Sharing tab visible.

Do all computers need their own printer driver or do they just use the server driver?

All computers on the network need to have a printer driver installed on their computer. If you install printer drivers on the server, you can make the drivers available to other computers over the network. Some operating systems, such as Windows 2000 and Windows NT, will install the printer drivers automatically; others you must install manually on the client.

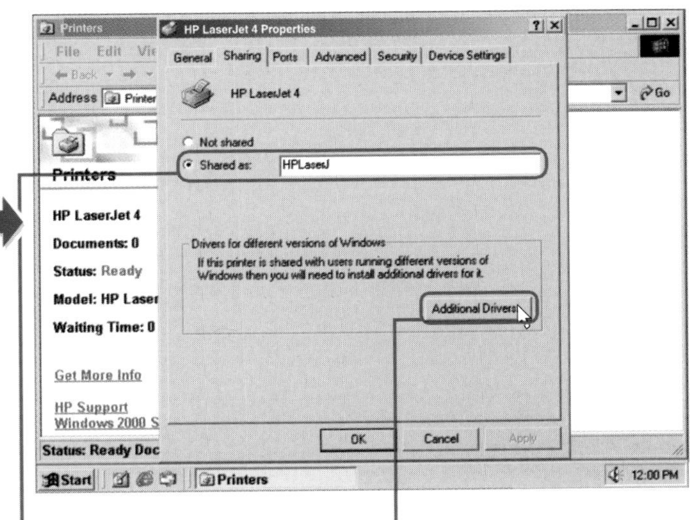

■ When you first install a printer, Windows 2000 Server defaults to sharing the printer.

■ You can stop sharing the printer by clicking **Not Shared**.

6 Click **Additional Drivers** to add support for other operating systems.

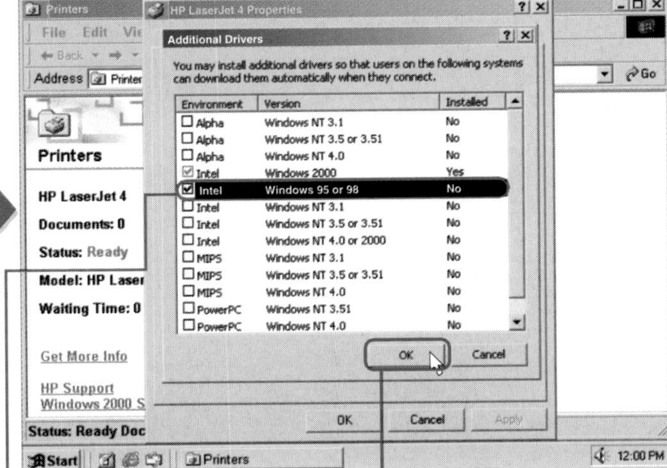

■ The Additional Drivers window appears.

7 Click the check boxes for the operating systems you need to support (example: **Windows 95 or 98**).

8 Click **OK**.

■ Follow the instructions for installing other drivers. You may need a printer driver disk from the manufacturer to do this.

SET PRINTER PERMISSIONS

Printer permissions give users the ability to print to a printer and also determine what tasks a user can perform with that printer.

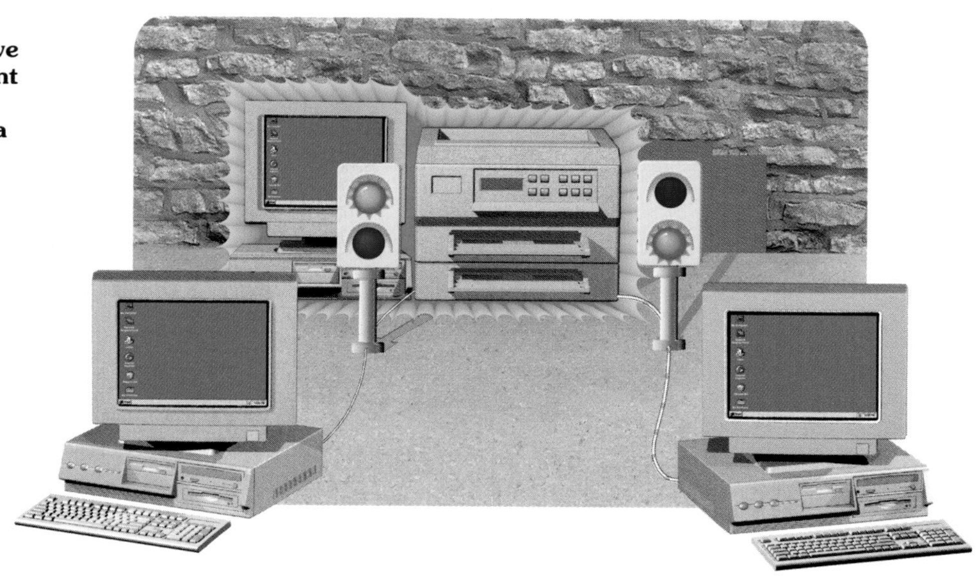

SET PRINTER PERMISSIONS

1 Click **Start**.

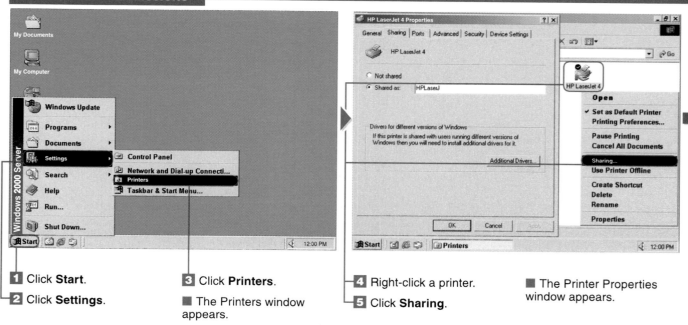

2 Click **Settings**.

3 Click **Printers**.

■ The Printers window appears.

4 Right-click a printer.

5 Click **Sharing**.

■ The Printer Properties window appears.

What types of access can be granted to users?

Print Allows users to print and manage their own documents.

Manage Documents Allows users to manage all documents on the printer.

Manage Printers Gives full access to the printer, including changing printer properties and settings, or deleting the printer.

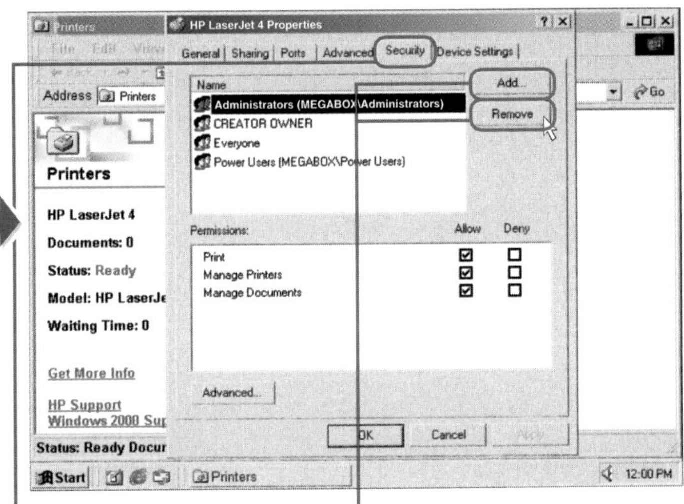

6 Click **Security**.

■ The Security tab appears, listing the groups and their associated printer permissions.

■ Click **Add** to add groups who can access this printer.

■ Click **Remove** to remove groups who can access this printer.

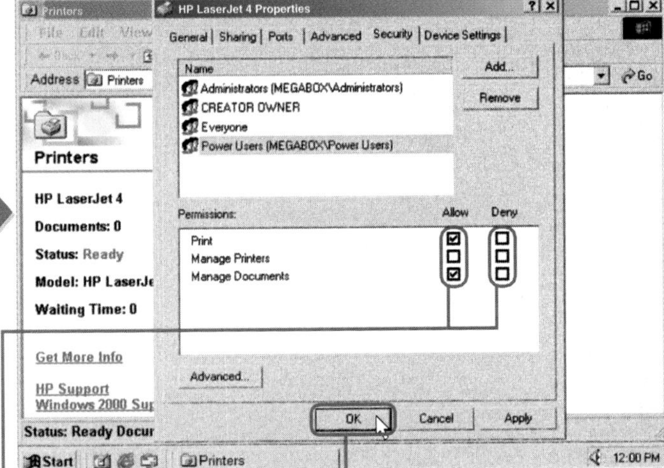

■ You can allow a permission to the selected group by clicking **Allow** (☐ changes to ☑).

■ You can deny a permission to the selected group by clicking **Deny** (☐ changes to ☑).

Note: For more information on printing permissions, see the Windows help file.

7 Click **OK** to close the dialog box.

VIEW PRINTER QUEUES

The print queue shows information about print jobs in the queue. This includes the print job's status, the print job's owner, and the number of pages in the print job.

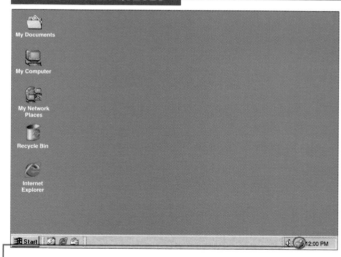

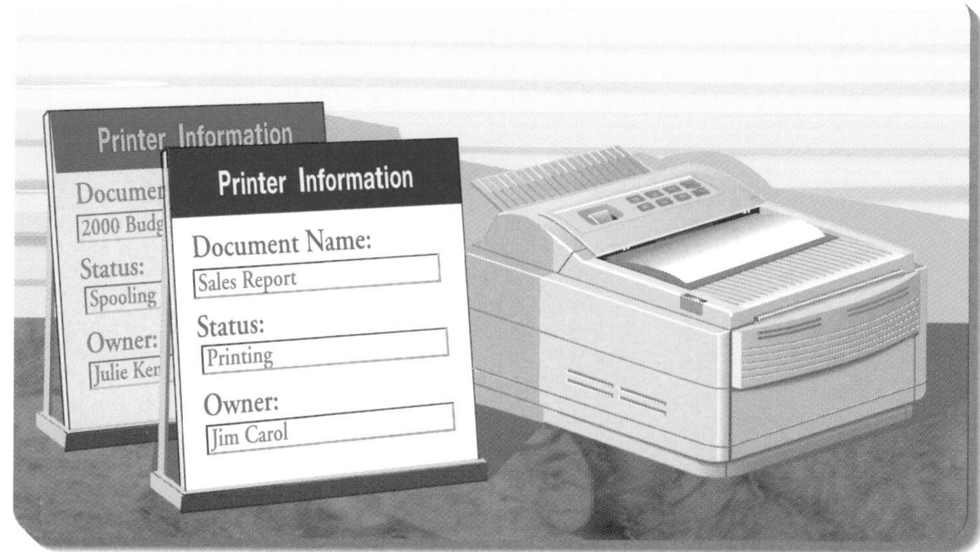

VIEW PRINTER QUEUES

FIND OUT IF YOUR DOCUMENT IS PRINTING

■ When you print a document a printer icon appears in the taskbar to the left of the clock.

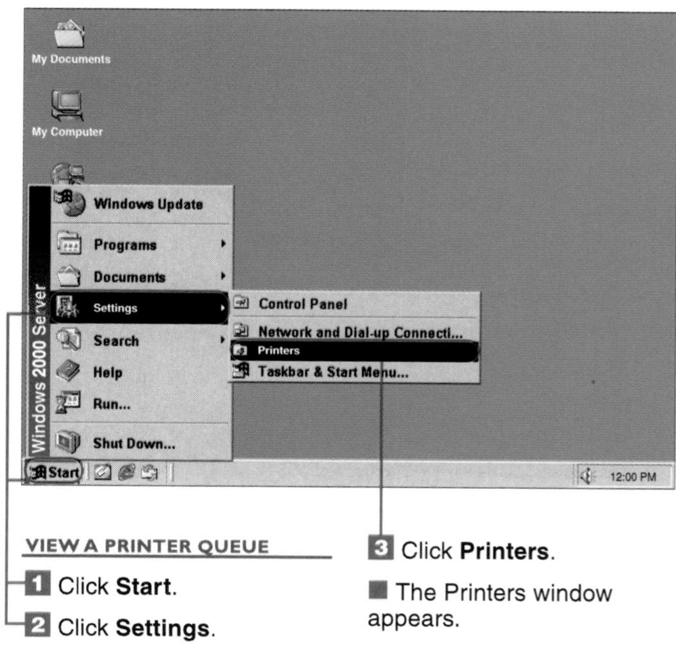

VIEW A PRINTER QUEUE

1 Click **Start**.

2 Click **Settings**.

3 Click **Printers**.

■ The Printers window appears.

Will my server's print queues slow it down?

When your server manages print queues, it spends a lot of its time working with the queued print jobs. As a result, your server will work more slowly, especially if a lot of people send print jobs to your server.

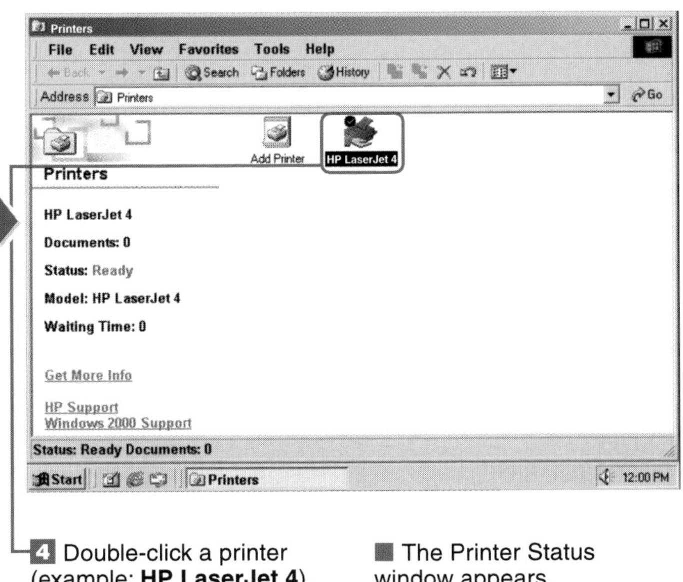

4 Double-click a printer (example: **HP LaserJet 4**).

■ The Printer Status window appears.

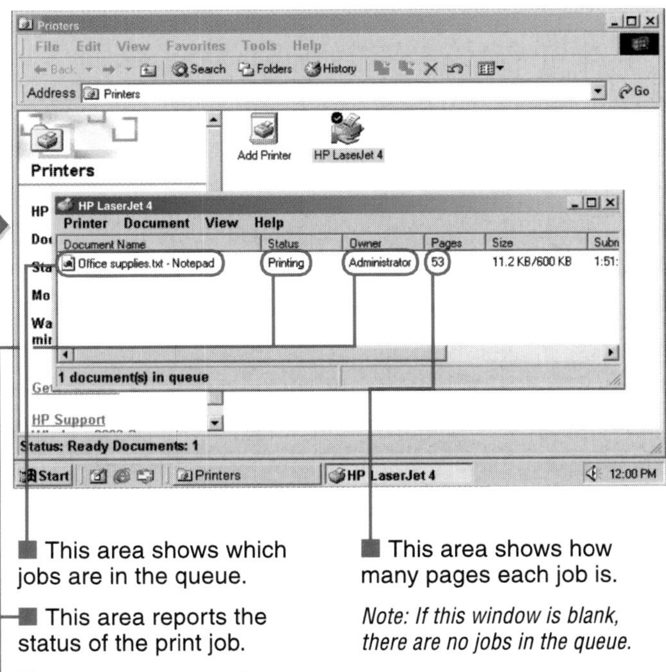

■ This area shows which jobs are in the queue.

■ This area reports the status of the print job.

■ This area shows who sent the job.

■ This area shows how many pages each job is.

Note: If this window is blank, there are no jobs in the queue.

PAUSE OR CANCEL PRINTING

You can also pause or cancel a job in the queue if there is a problem with the document or if printing will take too long.

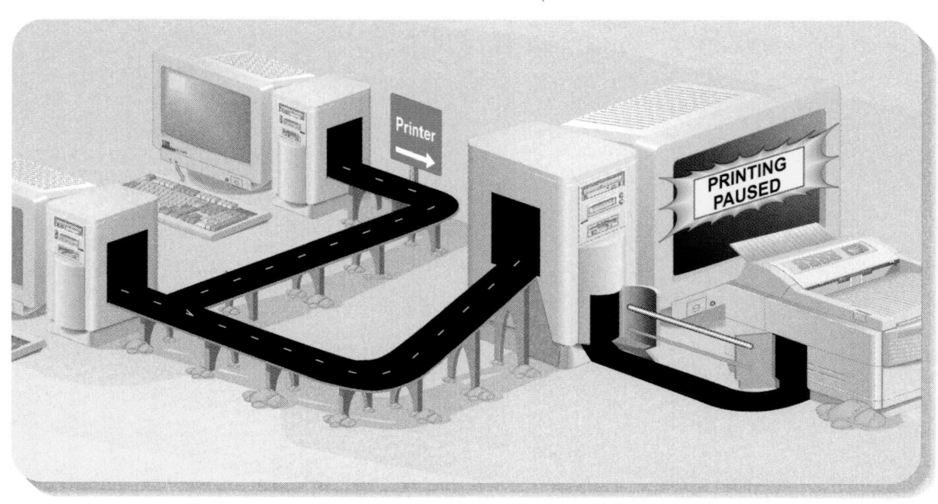

PAUSE OR CANCEL PRINTING

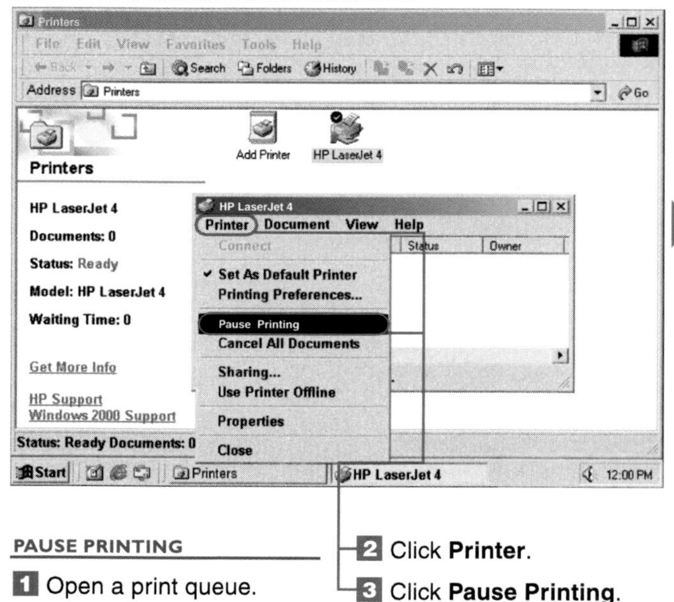

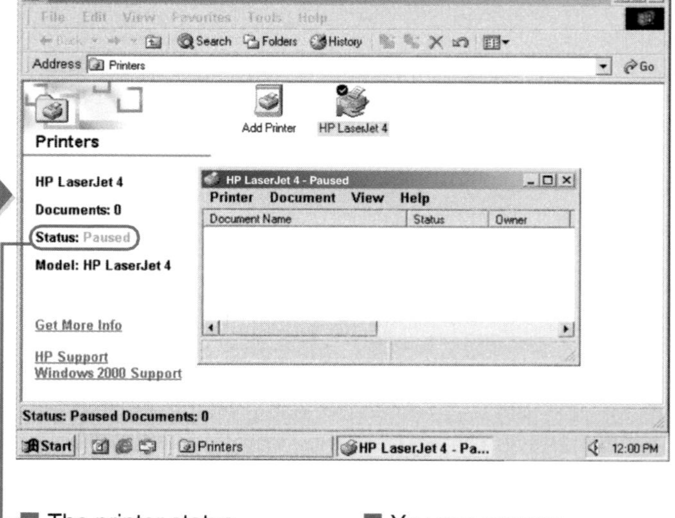

PAUSE PRINTING

1 Open a print queue.

Note: See "View Printer Queues" for details.

2 Click **Printer**.

3 Click **Pause Printing**.

■ The printer status changes to Paused.

■ You can resume printing by repeating steps 1 through 3.

Do I have to cancel all print jobs in order to stop printing?

No. You can select an individual print job in the queue and cancel that job using the same method listed here.

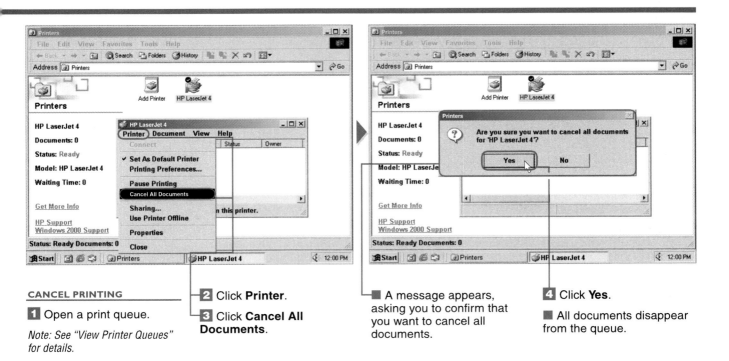

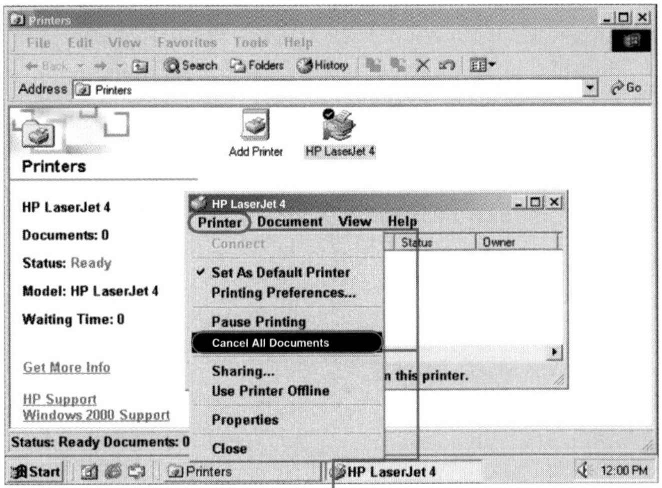

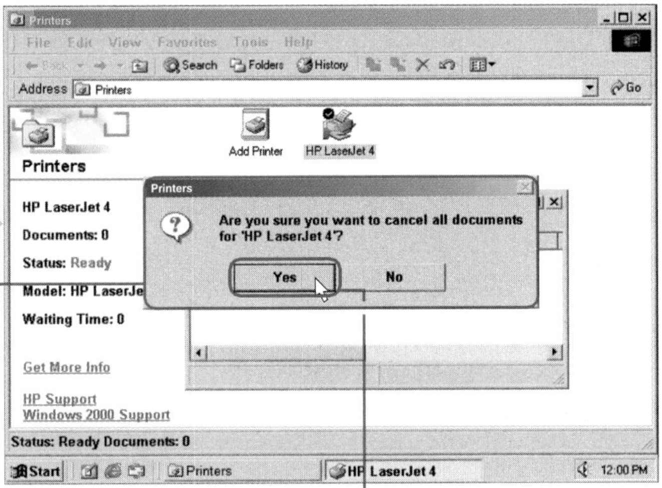

CANCEL PRINTING

1 Open a print queue.

Note: See "View Printer Queues" for details.

2 Click **Printer**.

3 Click **Cancel All Documents**.

■ A message appears, asking you to confirm that you want to cancel all documents.

4 Click **Yes**.

■ All documents disappear from the queue.

DELETE A PRINTER

Windows 2000 Server lets you easily remove a printer. You may need to remove a printer because it no longer exists on your network or because it has become unavailable.

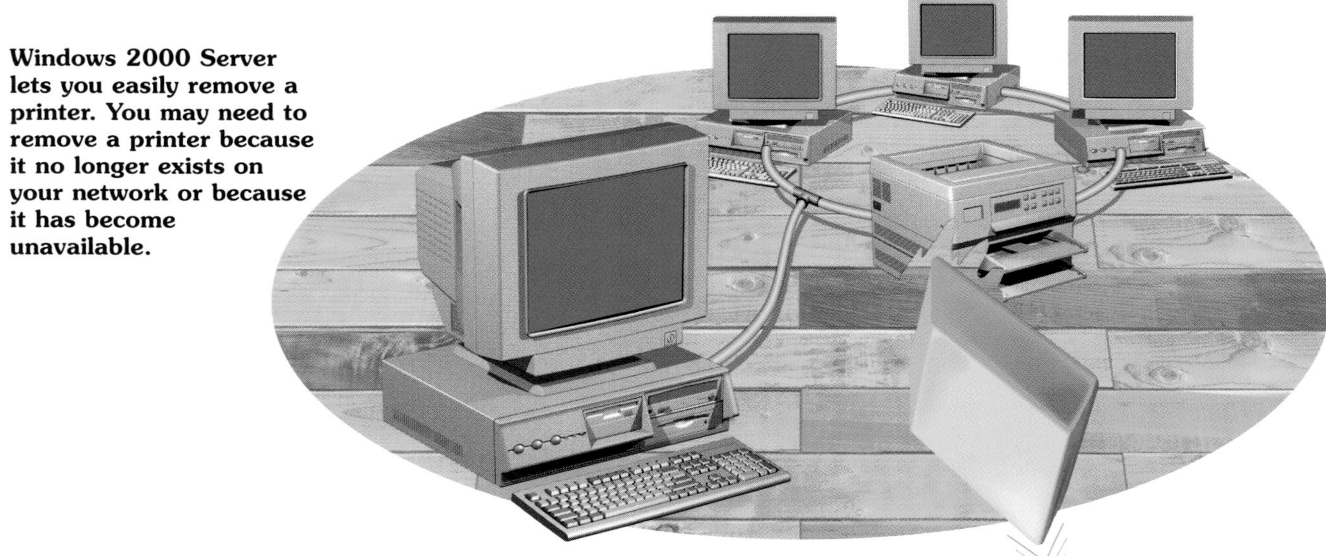

DELETE A PRINTER

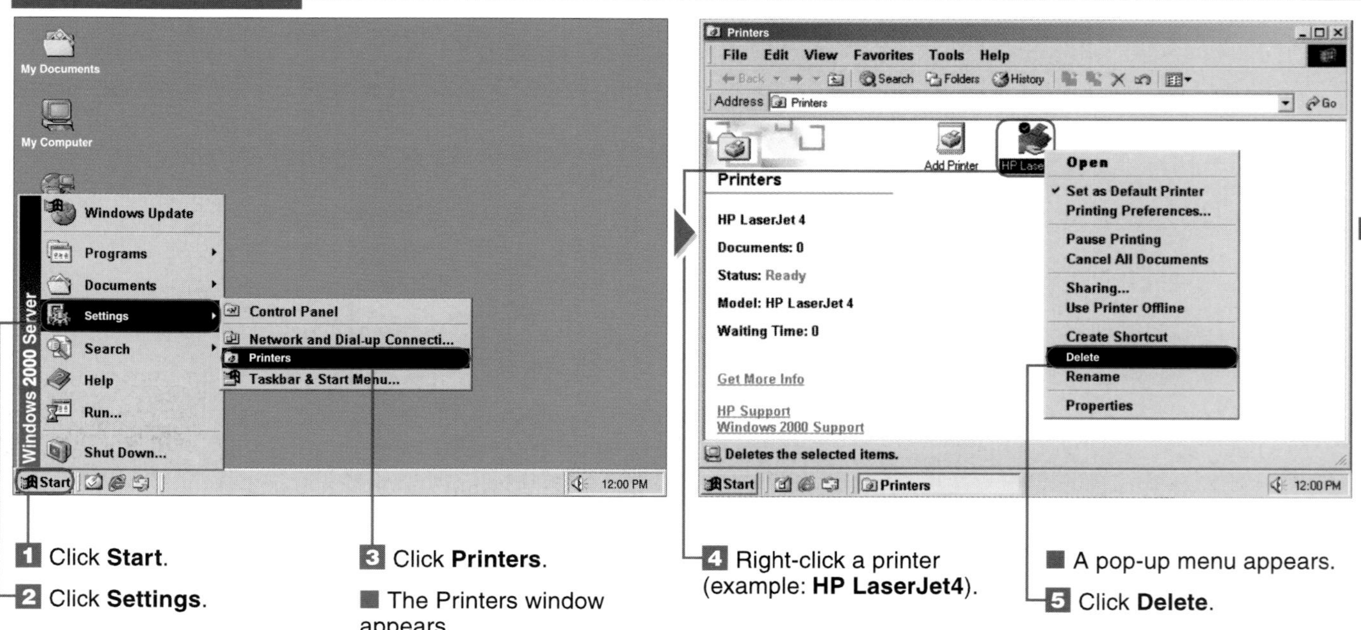

1 Click **Start**.

2 Click **Settings**.

3 Click **Printers**.

■ The Printers window appears.

4 Right-click a printer (example: **HP LaserJet4**).

■ A pop-up menu appears.

5 Click **Delete**.

What happens if I delete the default printer?

When you delete the default printer, Windows 2000 will change the default to another printer you have installed. If you don't have other printers installed, you and your users will not be able to print.

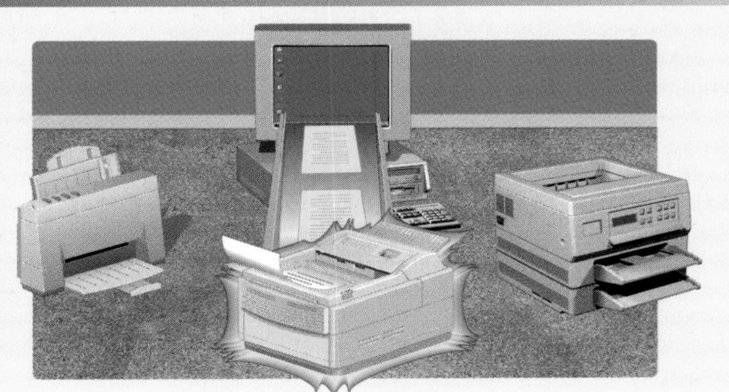

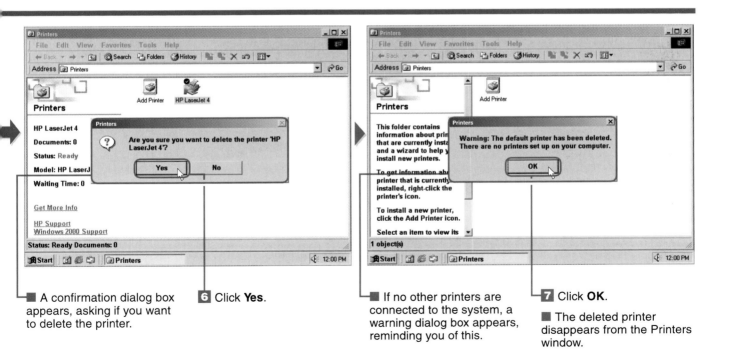

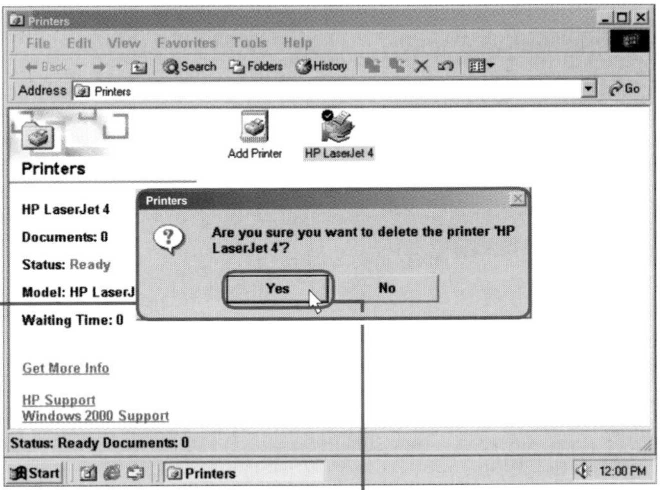

■ A confirmation dialog box appears, asking if you want to delete the printer.

6 Click **Yes**.

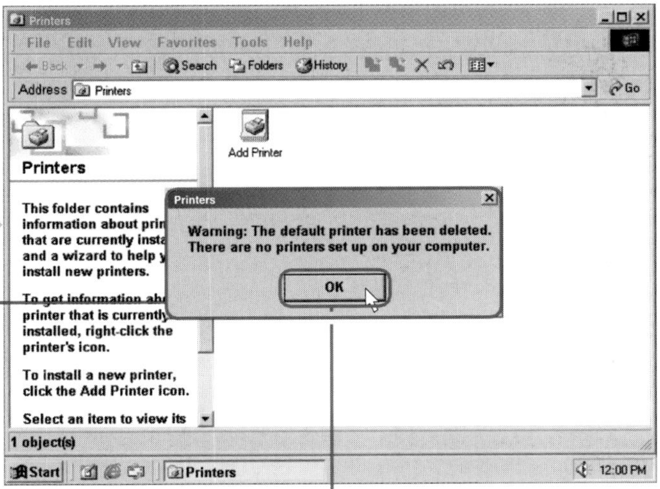

■ If no other printers are connected to the system, a warning dialog box appears, reminding you of this.

7 Click **OK**.

■ The deleted printer disappears from the Printers window.

INTERNET SERVICE PROVIDER
Travel the World
ENTERTAINMENT
NEWS
MUSIC
SPORT
6767

CHAPTER 12

Using Internet Applications

Once you are connected to the Internet, you will want to work with all the information available. In this chapter you will learn the basics of Web browsing and Internet e-mail.

START INTERNET EXPLORER

Internet Explorer is a Web browser that is part of Windows 2000. It lets you view text, graphics, and multimedia over the Internet.

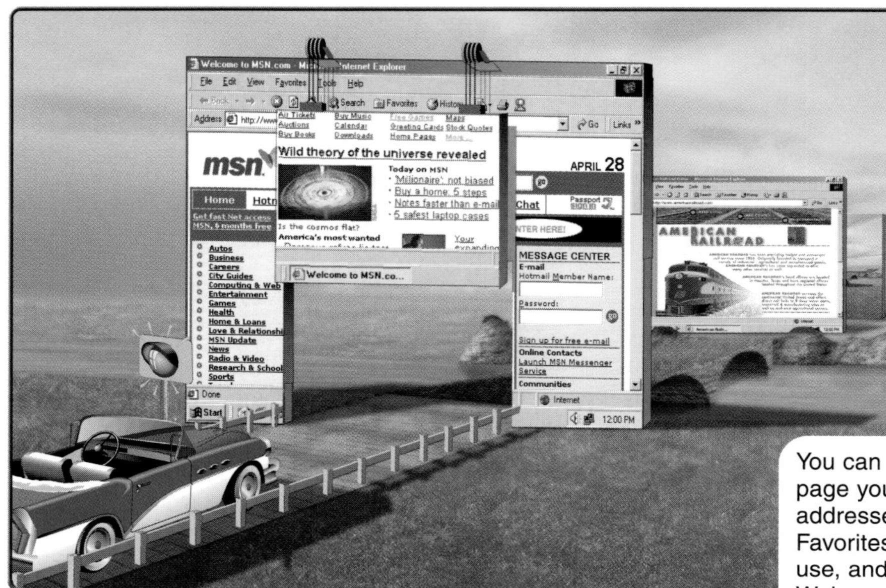

You can view any Web page you want, save addresses into your Favorites list for future use, and search for Web pages of interest.

START INTERNET EXPLORER

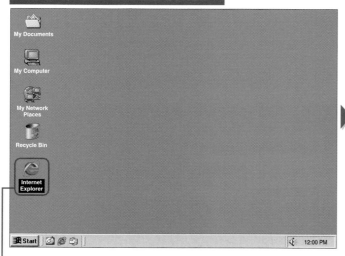

1 Double-click Internet Explorer.

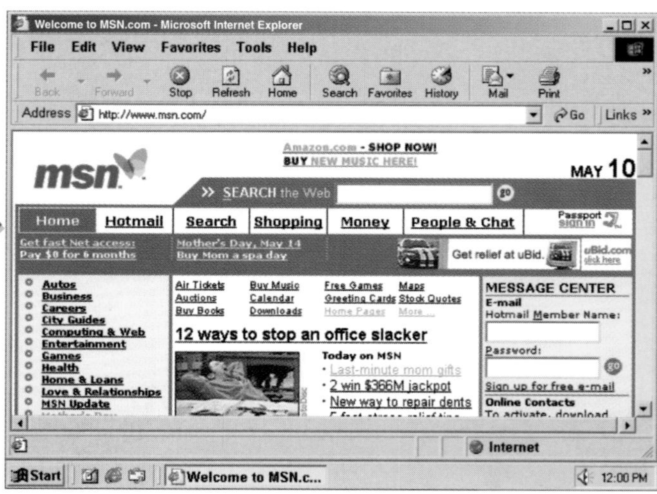

■ The Internet Explorer window appears and displays your home page automatically.

GET AROUND INTERNET EXPLORER

FAVORITES BUTTON

The Favorites button opens a window with a list of the favorite sites you've saved.

MAIL BUTTON

You can launch Outlook Express fromthis button and read your e-mail.

PRINT BUTTON

Use this button to print out the current page you are viewing.

SEARCH BUTTON

The Search button opens a window where you can search for information on the Internet.

HOME BUTTON

The Home button takes you back to your home page.

STOP BUTTON

The Stop button will stop a page from loading if it is taking too long.

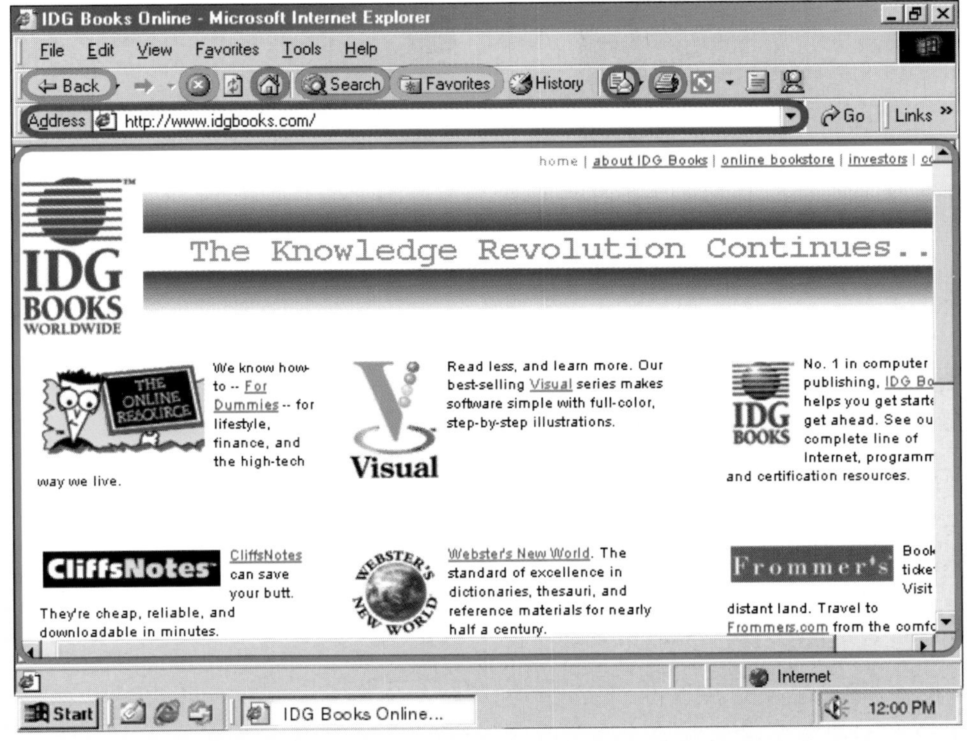

BACK BUTTON

The Back button will take you back one page.

ADDRESS

The address area is where you type in the Web page address you want to visit.

VIEWING AREA

This area is where your Web pages appear.

VIEW A WEB PAGE

You can view a Web page by entering the Web site's address into the browser.

Each Web page has its own address, called a URL, or Uniform Resource Locator.

VIEW A WEB PAGE

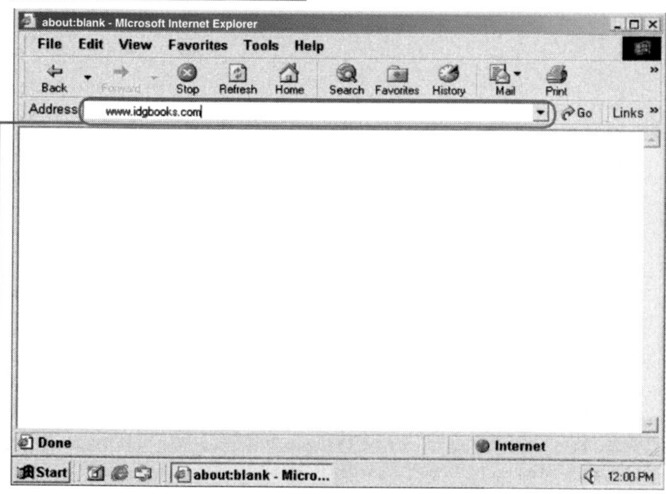

1 Type an address.

2 Press Enter.

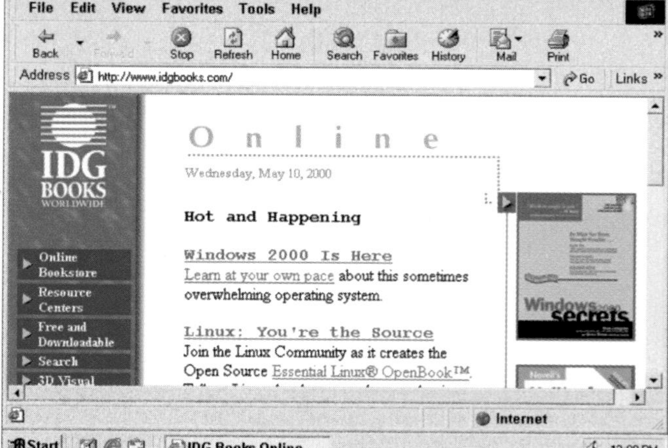

■ The Web page appears.

Note: If you typed the address incorrectly or if the Web page is no longer available, you will get a message to that effect in your browser.

A Web page link connects one page to another page. When you click on the link, you jump to that page.

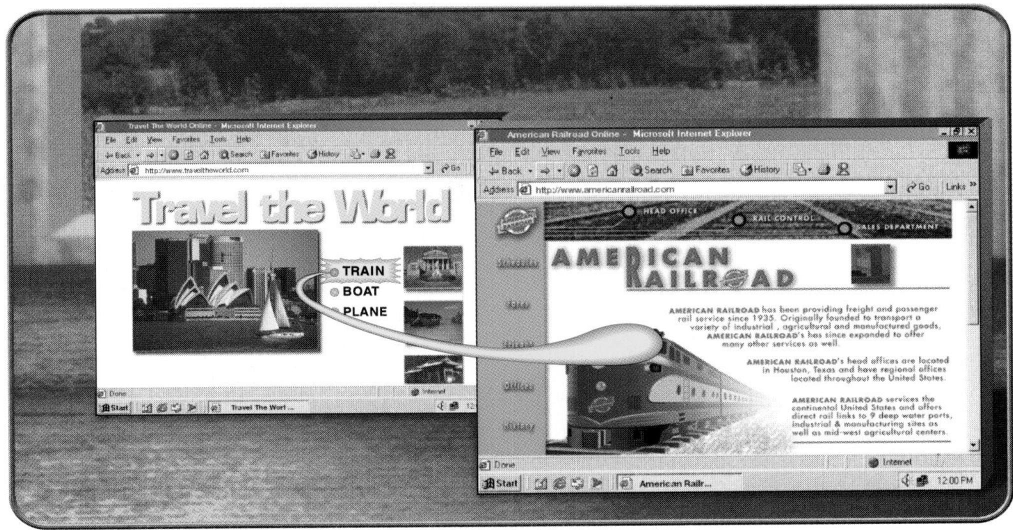

USING WEB PAGE LINKS

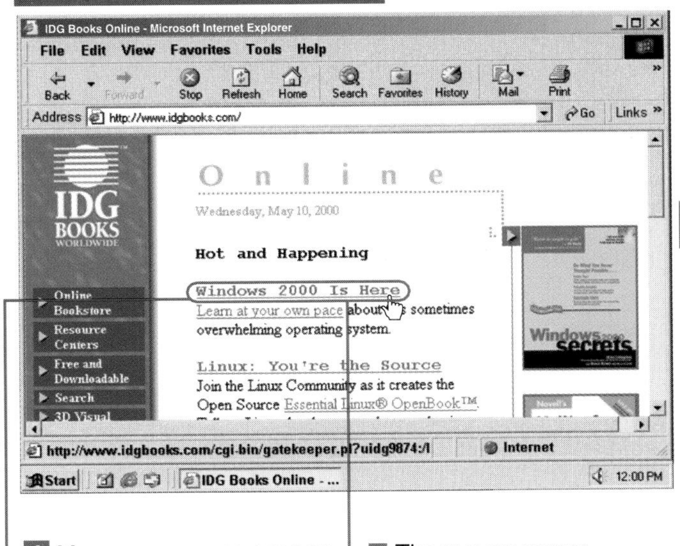

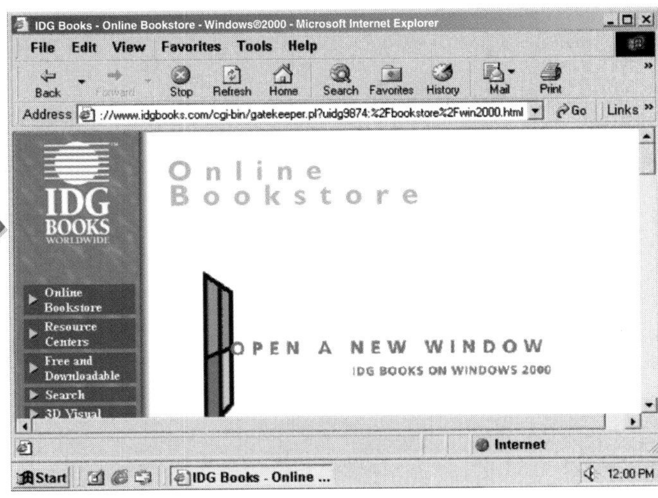

1 Move your mouse over an underlined word or phrase.

■ The mouse cursor changes from an arrow to a hand when you are over a link.

2 Click the link.

■ The new Web page connected to the link appears.

SAVE A FAVORITE WEB PAGE ADDRESS

You can also save favorite Web page addresses in your browser. This makes it easy to find the page again without retyping the whole address.

SAVE A FAVORITE WEB PAGE ADDRESS

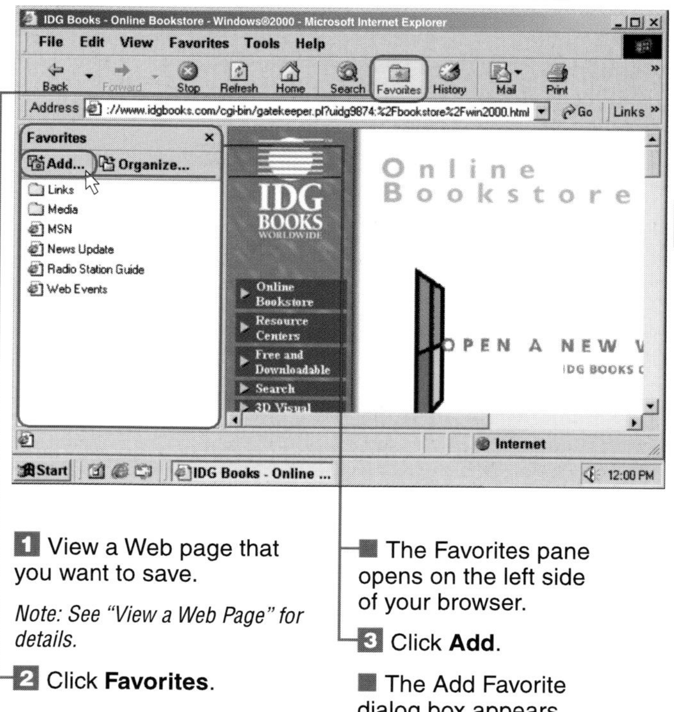

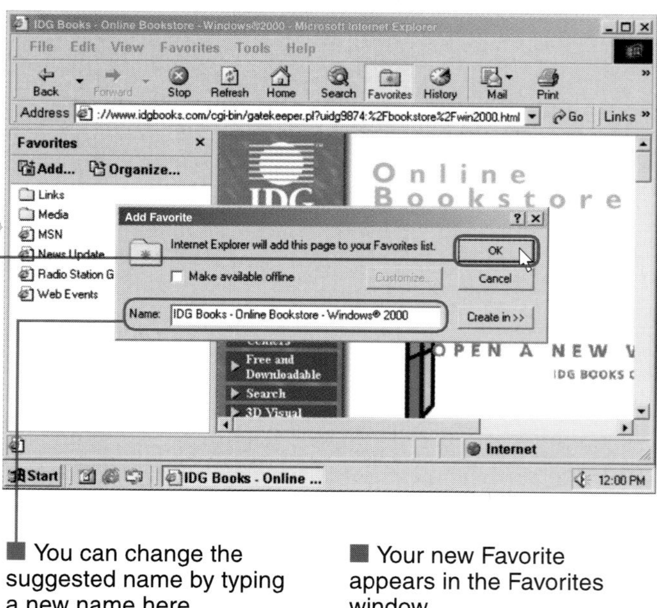

1 View a Web page that you want to save.

Note: See "View a Web Page" for details.

2 Click **Favorites**.

■ The Favorites pane opens on the left side of your browser.

3 Click **Add**.

■ The Add Favorite dialog box appears.

■ You can change the suggested name by typing a new name here.

4 Click **OK**.

■ Your new Favorite appears in the Favorites window.

VIEW A FAVORITE WEB PAGE

You can quickly jump to your favorite Web page by using the Favorites list.

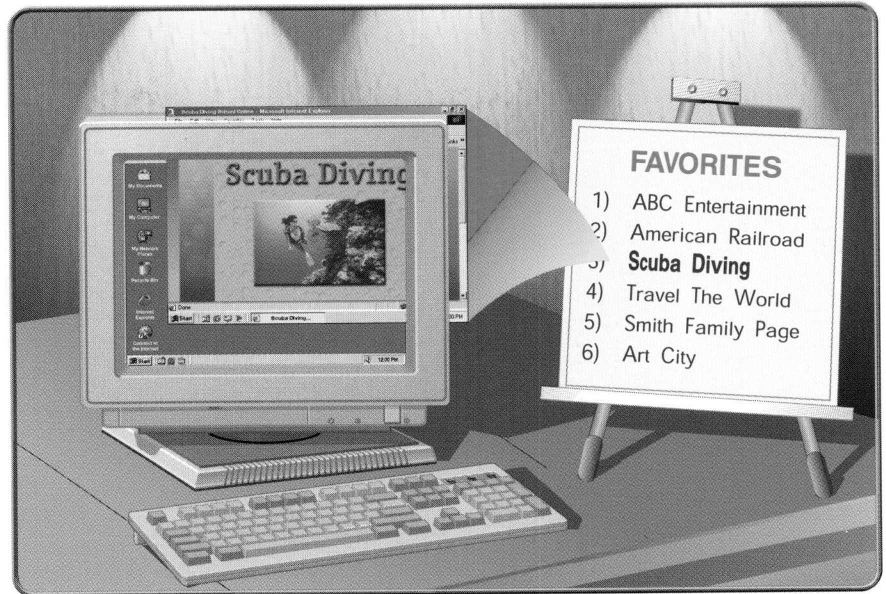

Scuba Diving
FAVORITES
1) ABC Entertainment
2) American Railroad
3) Scuba Diving
4) Travel The World
5) Smith Family Page
6) Art City

VIEW A FAVORITE WEB

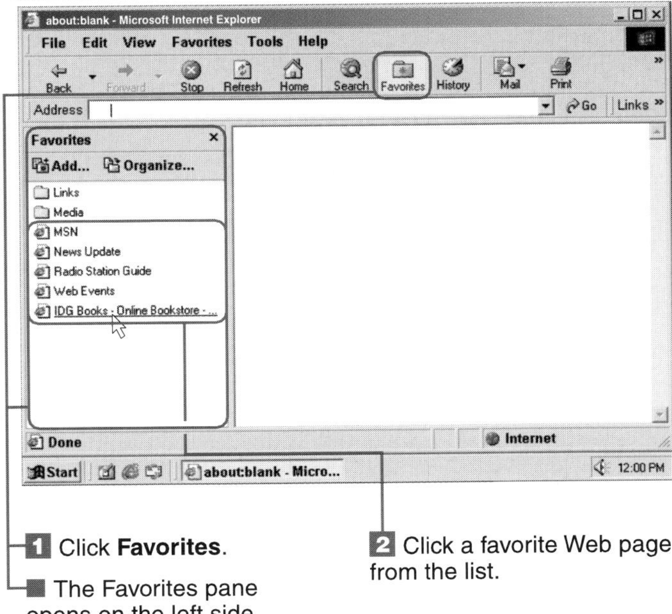

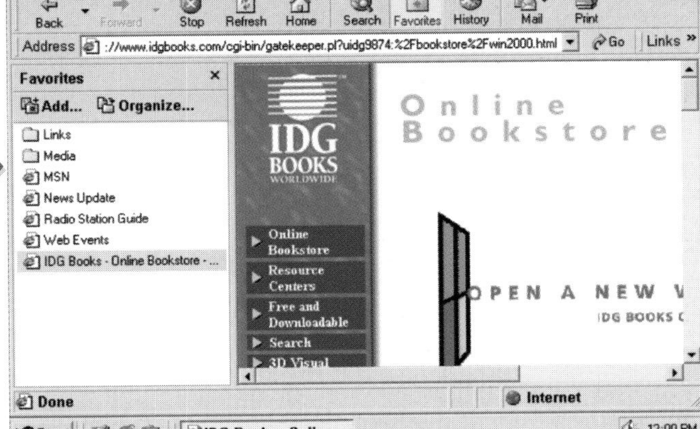

1 Click **Favorites**.

■ The Favorites pane opens on the left side of your browser.

2 Click a favorite Web page from the list.

■ The browser displays your favorite Web page.

You can search the Web for Web sites, Web pages, and information that you find interesting.

SEARCH THE WEB

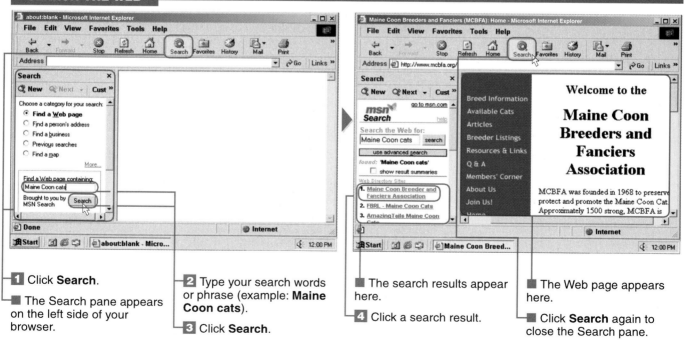

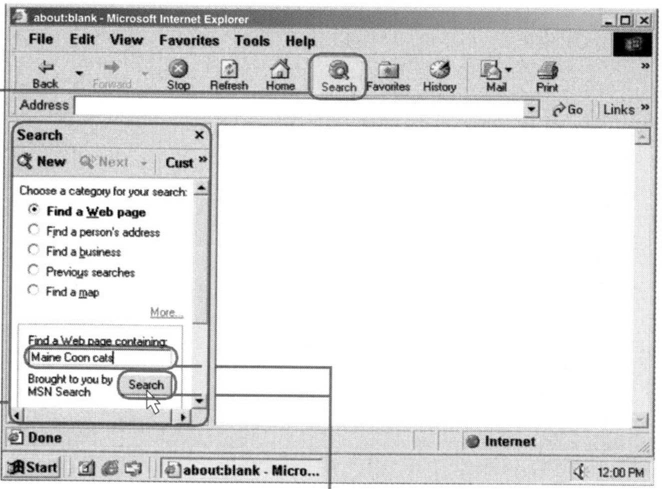

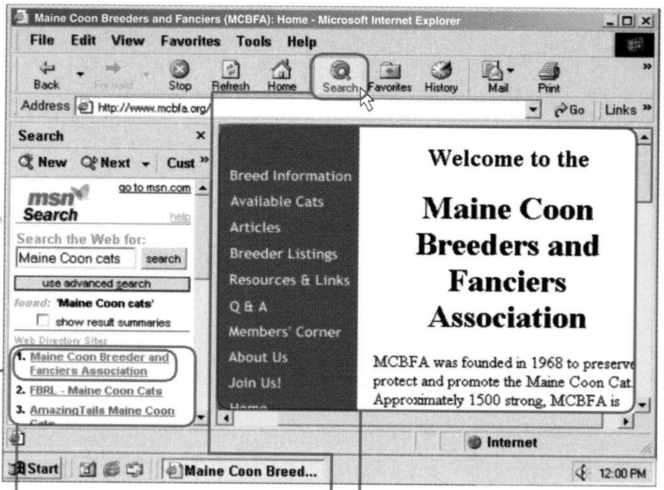

1 Click **Search**.

■ The Search pane appears on the left side of your browser.

2 Type your search words or phrase (example: **Maine Coon cats**).

3 Click **Search**.

■ The search results appear here.

4 Click a search result.

■ The Web page appears here.

■ Click **Search** again to close the Search pane.

PRINT A WEB PAGE

You can send Web pages to your printer if you want a hard copy of Web page information.

You must have a printer available to print Web pages.

PRINT A WEB PAGE

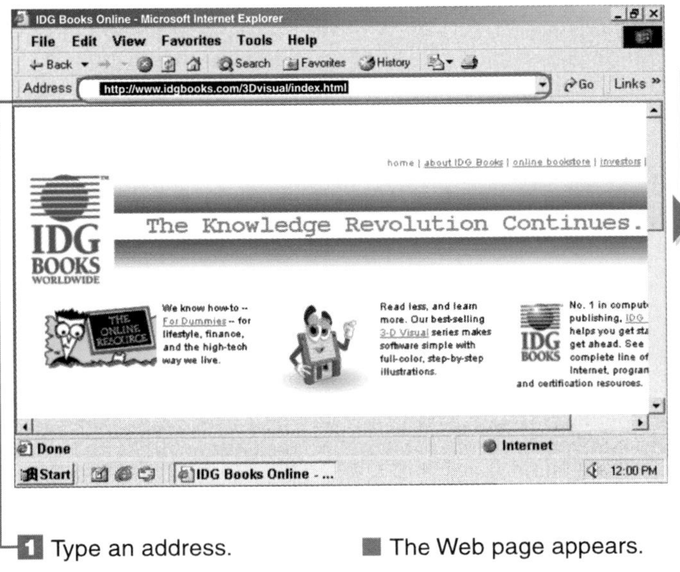

1 Type an address.

2 Press Enter.

■ The Web page appears.

3 Click **Print**.

■ The Web page is printed at your printer.

START OUTLOOK EXPRESS

You can send and receive e-mail using Outlook Express. E-mail is a fast, convenient way to communicate with other people over the Internet.

START OUTLOOK EXPRESS

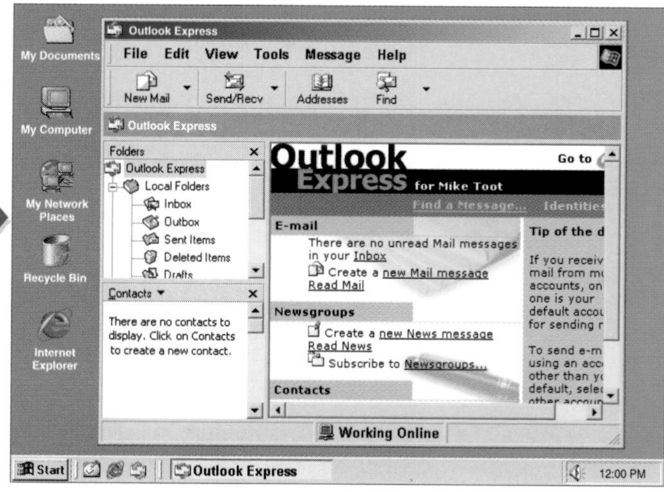

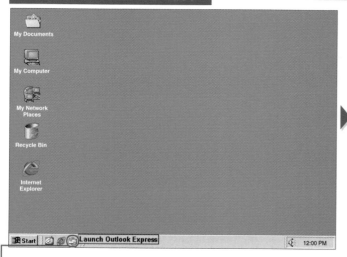

1 Click **Outlook Express**.

■ If the Internet Connection Wizard appears, see Chapter 15.

■ Outlook Express appears.

GET AROUND OUTLOOK EXPRESS

NEW MAIL

The New Mail button lets you compose a new e-mail message.

SEND/RECEIVE

This button connects to your e-mail server, sends your messages, and receives ones addressed to you.

E-MAIL

The E-mail section lets you create a new message or read your mail.

FOLDERS

The Folders pane is where you can organize your e-mail into folders.

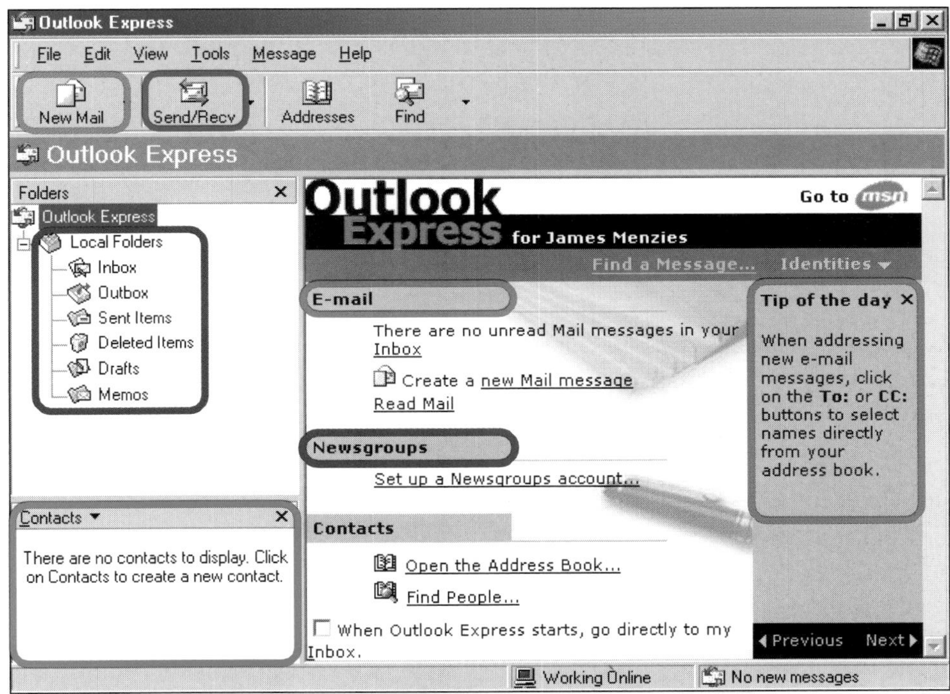

CONTACTS

The Contacts pane shows you a list of people who you can contact.

NEWSGROUPS

The Newsgroups section lets you suscribe to newsgroups and read newsgroups messages.

TIP OF THE DAY

This section gives you a useful tip each day on how to use Outlook Express.

READ YOUR E-MAIL

Outlook Express makes it easy to read your e-mail messages.

READ YOUR E-MAIL

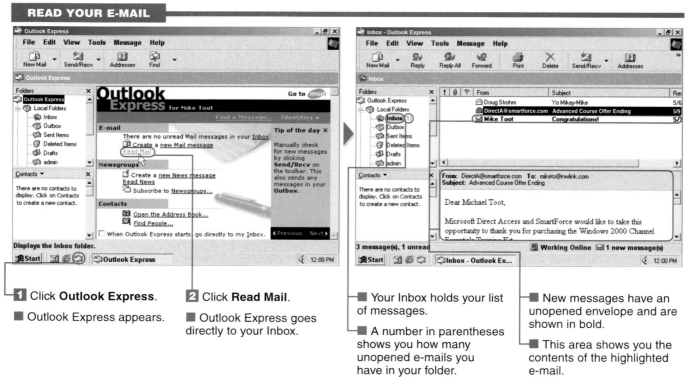

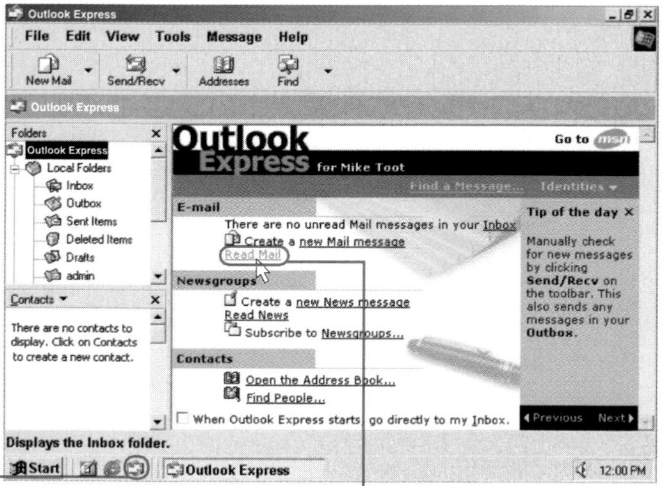

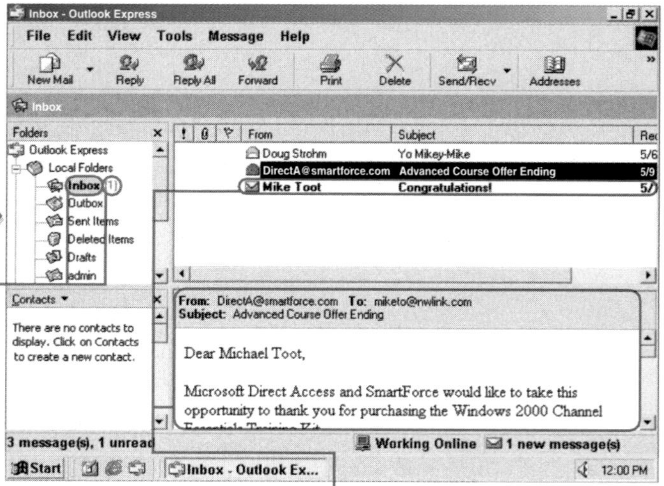

1 Click **Outlook Express**.

■ Outlook Express appears.

2 Click **Read Mail**.

■ Outlook Express goes directly to your Inbox.

■ Your Inbox holds your list of messages.

■ A number in parentheses shows you how many unopened e-mails you have in your folder.

■ New messages have an unopened envelope and are shown in bold.

■ This area shows you the contents of the highlighted e-mail.

COMPOSE AND SEND E-MAIL

It is easy to write e-mail to friends, family, or business acquaintances.

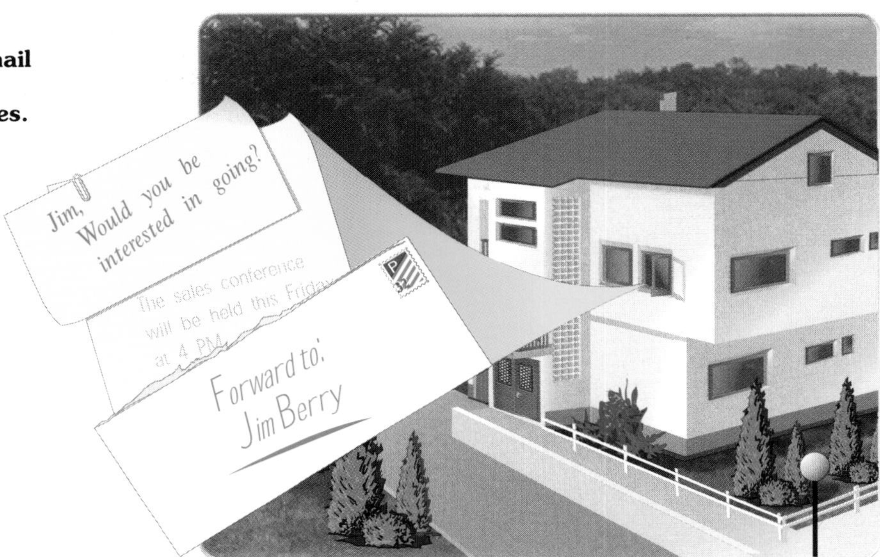

COMPOSE AND SEND E-MAIL

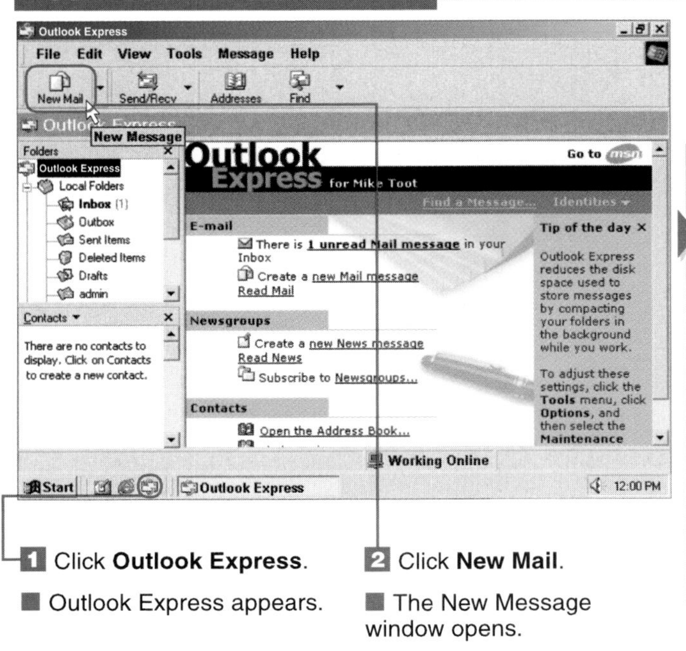

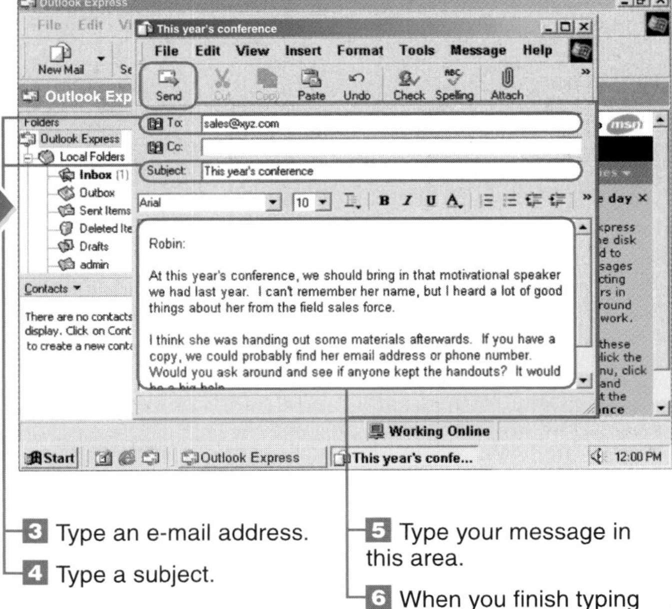

1 Click **Outlook Express**.

■ Outlook Express appears.

2 Click **New Mail**.

■ The New Message window opens.

3 Type an e-mail address.

4 Type a subject.

5 Type your message in this area.

6 When you finish typing your message, click **Send**.

WEB SERVER
WEB SERVER
Welcome To My Web Page!
Bonjour!
Greetings from Paris.
My name is Julie and I'm an avid

CHAPTER 13

Running Your Web Server

This chapter shows you the basics of how to run the Internet Information Server.

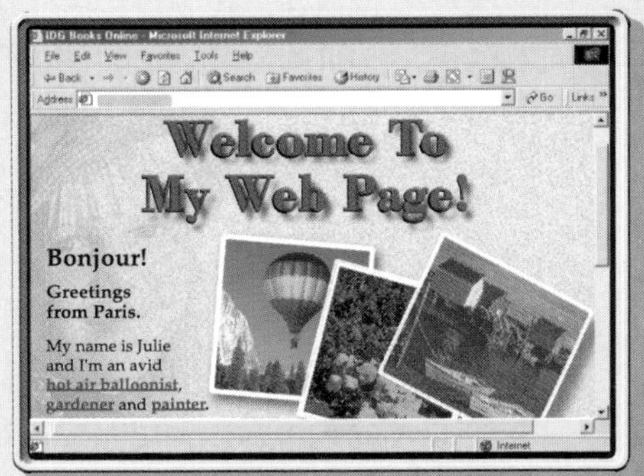

START THE INTERNET SERVICES MANAGER

You can use the Internet Services Manager to set up, configure, and control Web-based services, such as a Web server. It is your starting point for anything Web-related.

START THE INTERNET SERVICES MANAGER

1 Click **Start**.

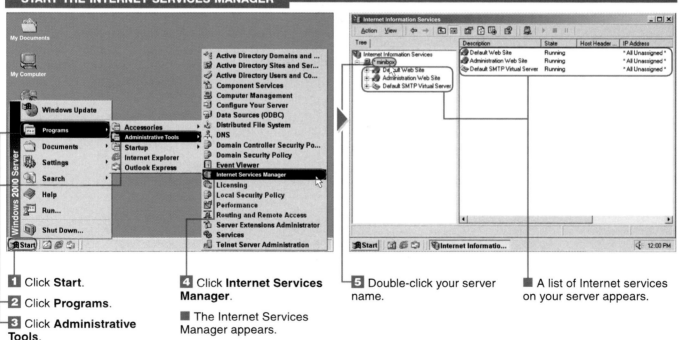

2 Click **Programs**.

3 Click **Administrative Tools**.

4 Click **Internet Services Manager**.

■ The Internet Services Manager appears.

5 Double-click your server name.

■ A list of Internet services on your server appears.

START AND STOP YOUR WEB SERVER

You can start and stop your Web services without shutting down the entire server. This enables you to make the Web site inaccessible so you can perform maintenance or change settings.

START AND STOP YOUR WEB SERVER

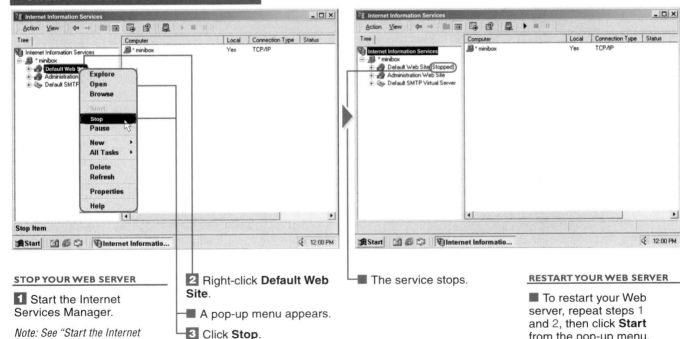

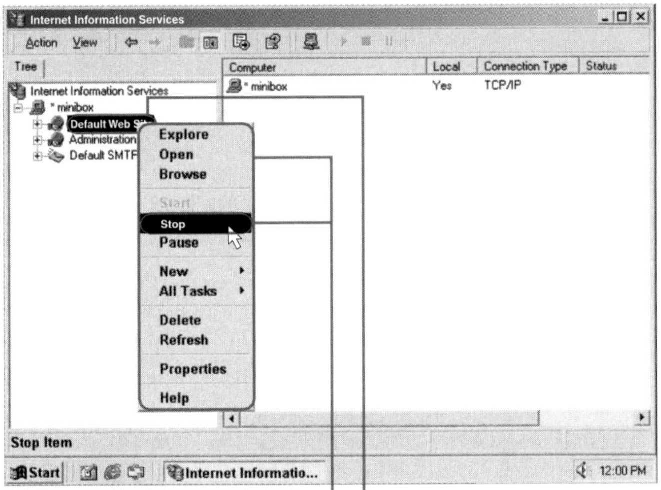

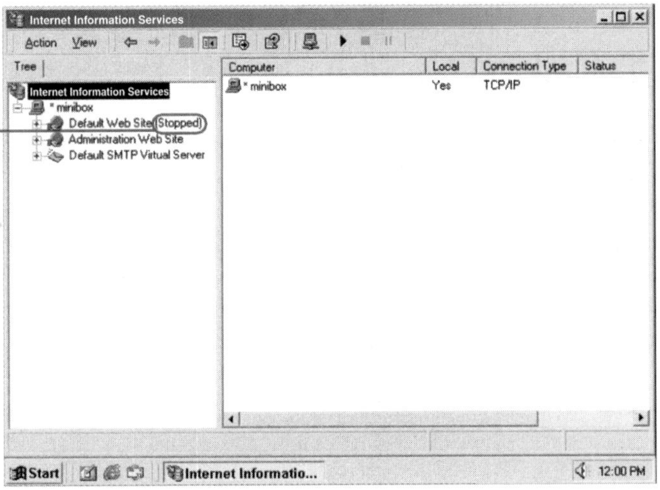

STOP YOUR WEB SERVER

1 Start the Internet Services Manager.

Note: See "Start the Internet Services Manager" for details.

2 Right-click **Default Web Site**.

■ A pop-up menu appears.

3 Click **Stop**.

■ The service stops.

RESTART YOUR WEB SERVER

■ To restart your Web server, repeat steps 1 and 2, then click **Start** from the pop-up menu.

MANAGE ANOTHER WEB SERVER

You can remotely manage Web services on another server in your network by using the Internet Services Manager.

MANAGE ANOTHER WEB SERVER

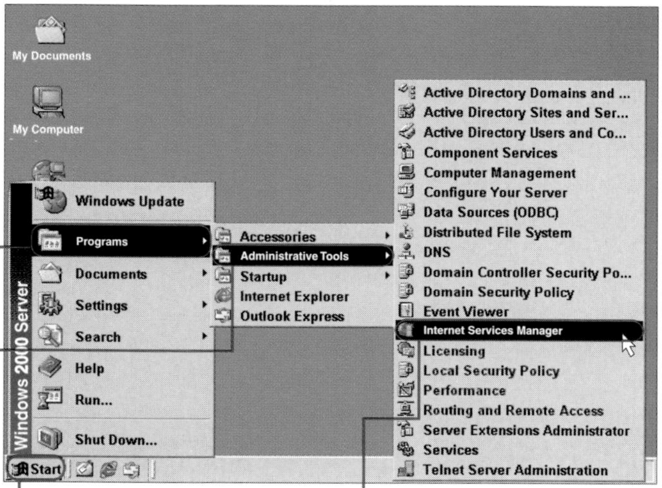

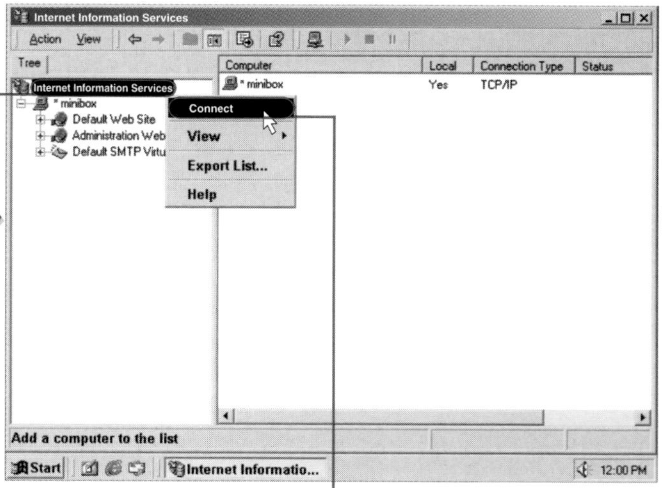

1 Click **Start**.

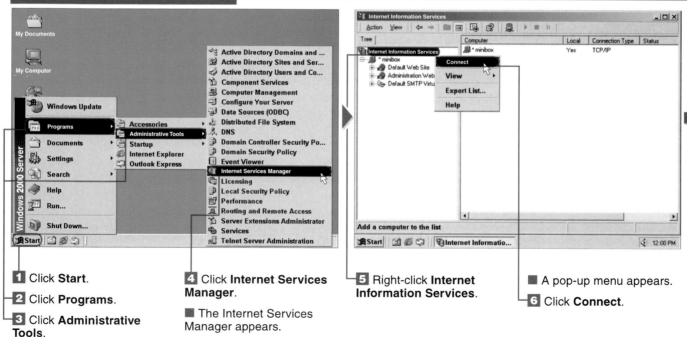

2 Click **Programs**.

3 Click **Administrative Tools**.

4 Click **Internet Services Manager**.

■ The Internet Services Manager appears.

5 Right-click **Internet Information Services**.

■ A pop-up menu appears.

6 Click **Connect**.

What is the Administration Web site in the Internet Services Manager?

The Administration Web site allows you to manage your Web site remotely by using a Web browser rather than the Internet Services Manager. For more information, see the Internet Information Server help file.

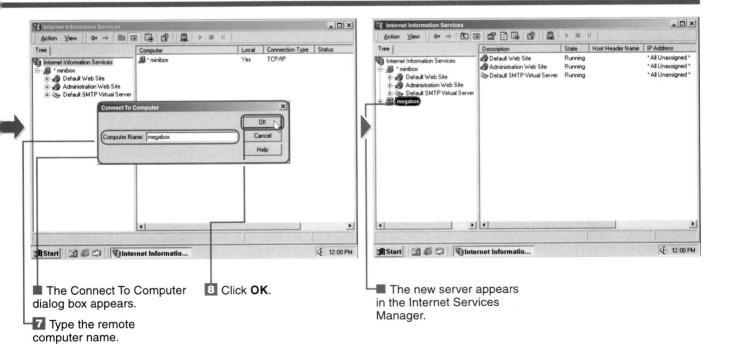

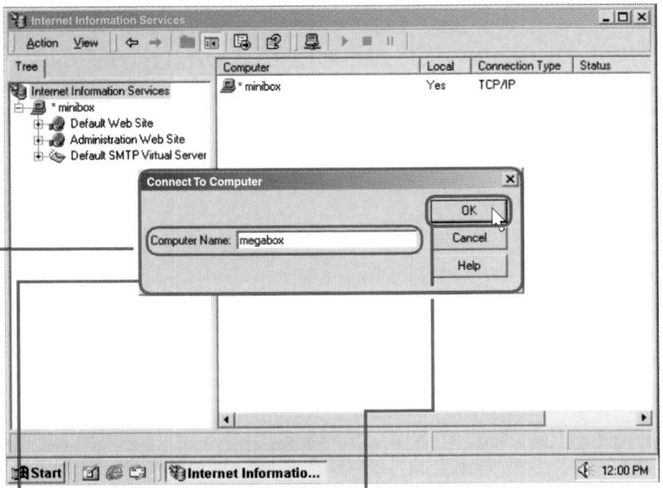

■ The Connect To Computer dialog box appears.

7 Type the remote computer name.

8 Click **OK**.

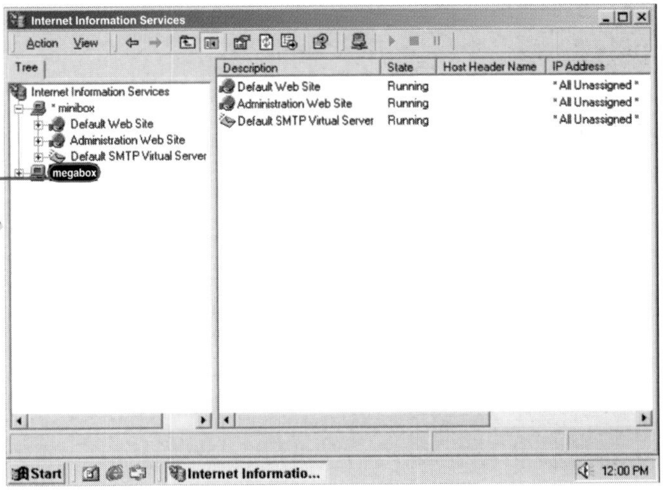

■ The new server appears in the Internet Services Manager.

BROWSE YOUR WEB SERVER

You can connect to your Web server with Internet Explorer to view the Web pages you present to other people.

BROWSE YOUR WEB SERVER

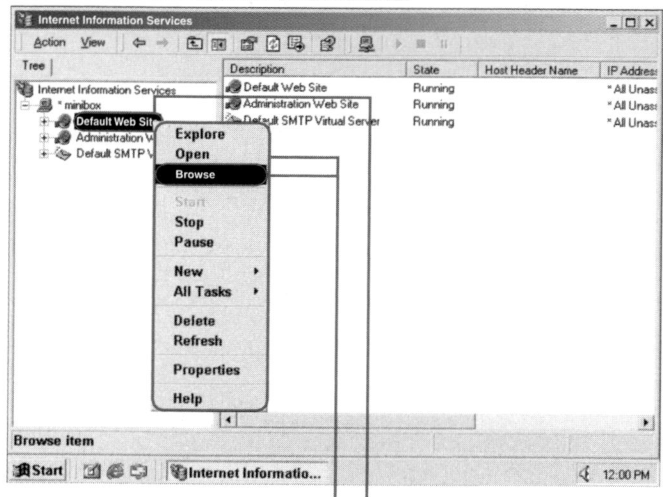

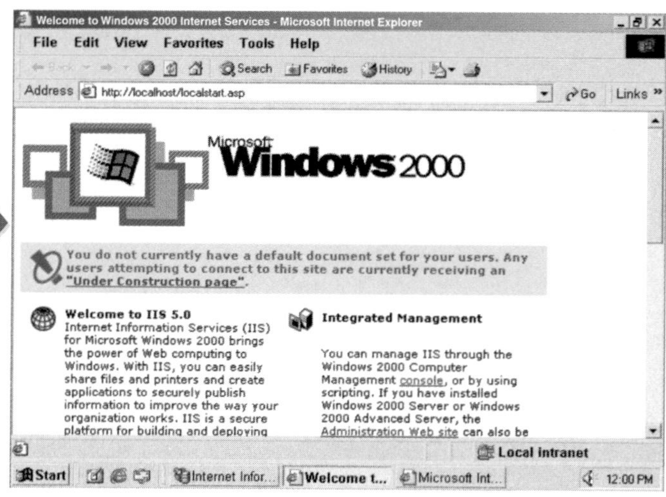

1 Start the Internet Services Manager.

Note: See "Start the Internet Services Manager" for details.

2 Right-click **Default Web Site**.

■ A pop-up menu appears.

3 Click **Browse**.

■ Your server's default Web page appears.

Note: If you do not have a default Web page set up, Windows 2000 displays an introduction Web page and an online help file to get you started.

Web servers are powerful tools to share information between people. You can find out more information from these sources.

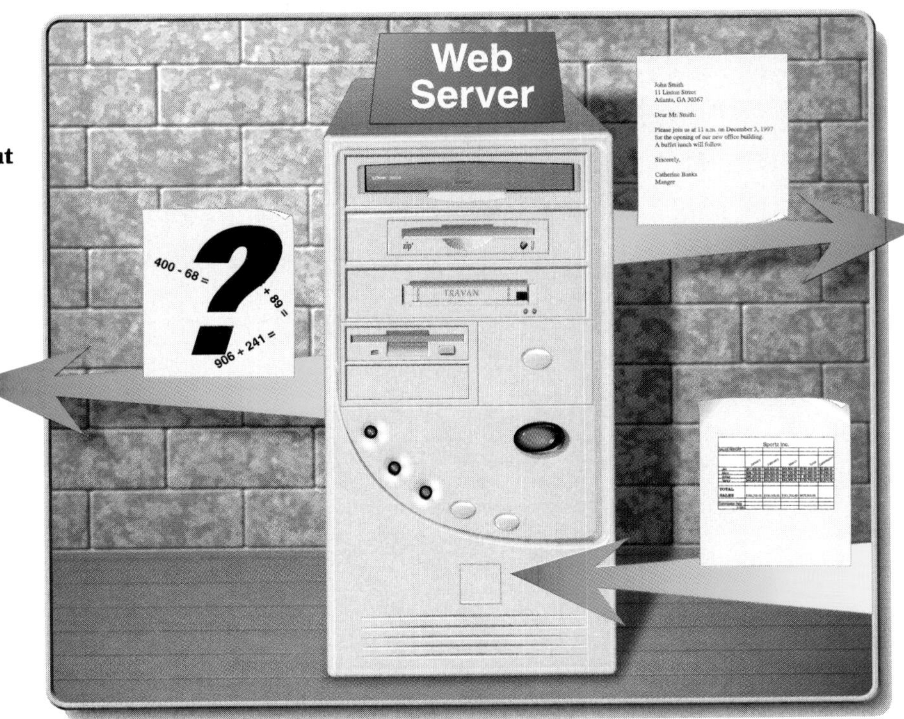

ONLINE HELP FILES

Internet Information Server has extensive online help files and wizards to help you run your Web site. This is the first, best place to check for information.

YOUR LOCAL BOOKSTORE

There are many books on running Web servers and Web design and programming. You can find books for every level of experience to help you get started.

OTHER WEB SITES

There are numerous Web sites on the Internet, including the Microsoft Web site, dedicated to all aspects of running Web servers. You can find answers to all your questions about Web servers and the Internet.

OUT OF ORDER
Boot Disk 1
Boot Disk 2
Boot Disk 3
MicroFLOPPY Double Sided

CHAPTER 14

Using Recovery Tools

When something on the server fails, it is up to you to find out why. This chapter shows you how to use recovery tools as part of your troubleshooting toolkit.

CREATE THE WINDOWS 2000 BOOT DISKS

The Windows 2000 boot disks are used to start the Emergency Repair Disk process. This process is used to repair damaged boot files and Registry settings that keep your server from starting.

CREATE THE WINDOWS 2000 BOOT DISKS

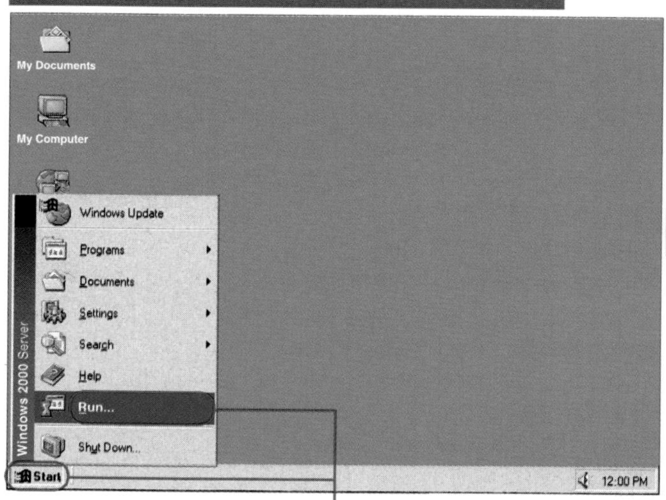

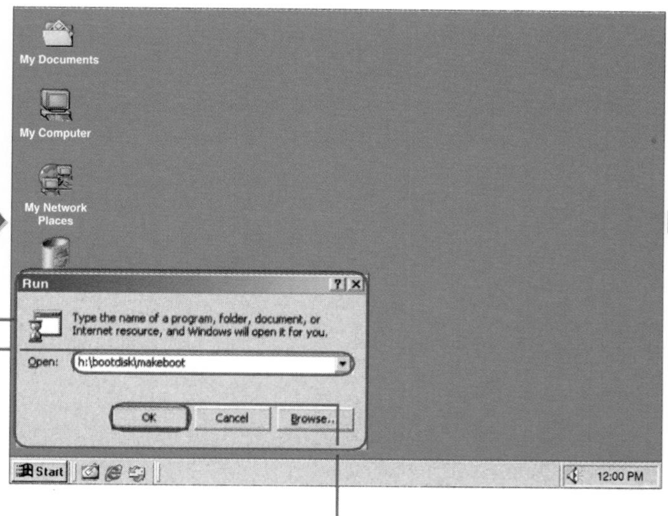

1 Obtain four blank formatted high-density 3.5" floppy disks.

2 Insert the Windows 2000 CD-ROM into your CD-ROM drive.

*Note: If the Microsoft Windows 2000 CD dialog box appears, click **Exit**.*

3 Click **Start**.

4 Click **Run**.

■ The Run dialog box appears.

5 Type **h:\bootdisk\makeboot** in the Open dialog box.

Note: Replace h: with the drive letter for your CD drive, if it is different.

6 Click **OK**.

Can I use the boot disks that came with my Windows 2000 CD?

You can use the boot disks that shipped with your copy of Windows 2000, or you can make your own using this process.

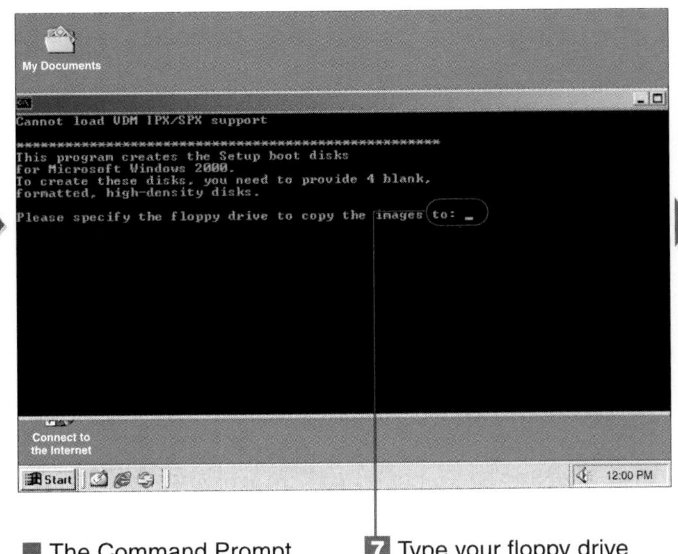

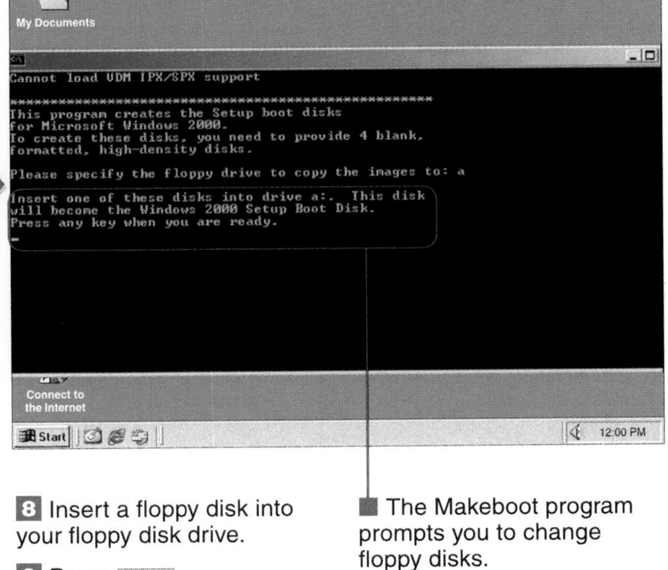

■ The Command Prompt window appears.

7 Type your floppy drive letter at the prompt.

Note: This is usually your a: drive.

8 Insert a floppy disk into your floppy disk drive.

9 Press Enter.

■ The Makeboot program prompts you to change floppy disks.

10 Repeat steps 7 and 8.

CREATE AN EMERGENCY REPAIR DISK

The Emergency Repair Disk contains important information about your hardware, software, applications, and users. You can sometimes use this disk to restore your system without having to reinstall Windows 2000.

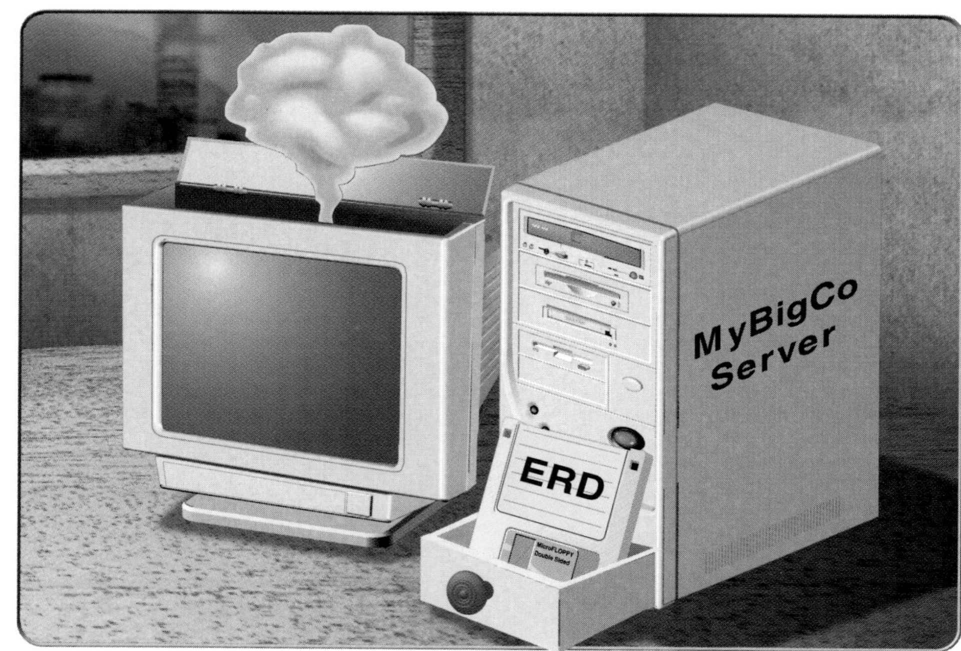

CREATE AN EMERGENCY REPAIR DISK

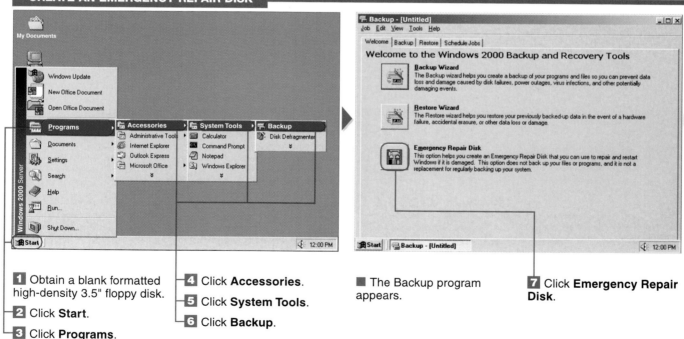

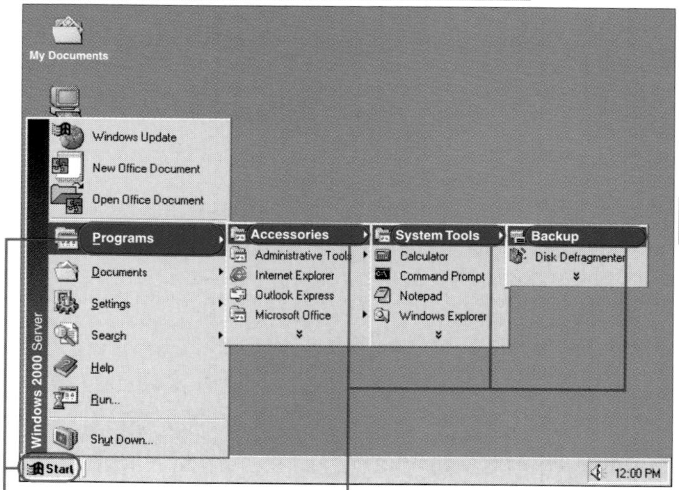

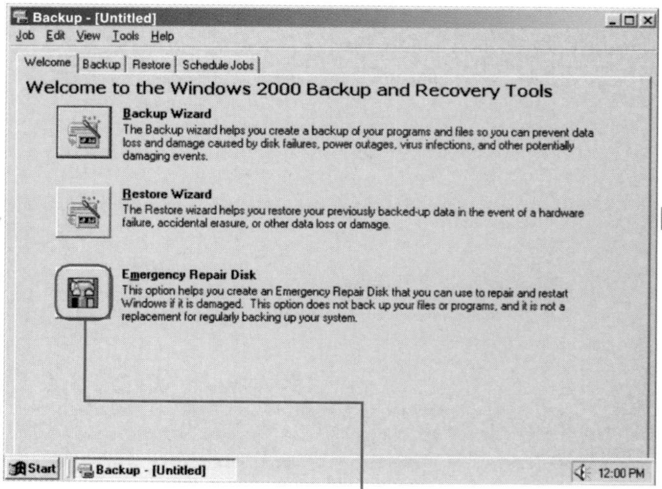

1 Obtain a blank formatted high-density 3.5" floppy disk.

2 Click **Start**.

3 Click **Programs**.

4 Click **Accessories**.

5 Click **System Tools**.

6 Click **Backup**.

■ The Backup program appears.

7 Click **Emergency Repair Disk**.

How often should I make an Emergency Repair Disk?

Make a new repair disk after you install or upgrade services and software, change domains or reorganize your domain structure, or make a large number of changes to users and user rights and privileges. You should consider doing this on a regular basis, such as once a week, along with your regular backups.

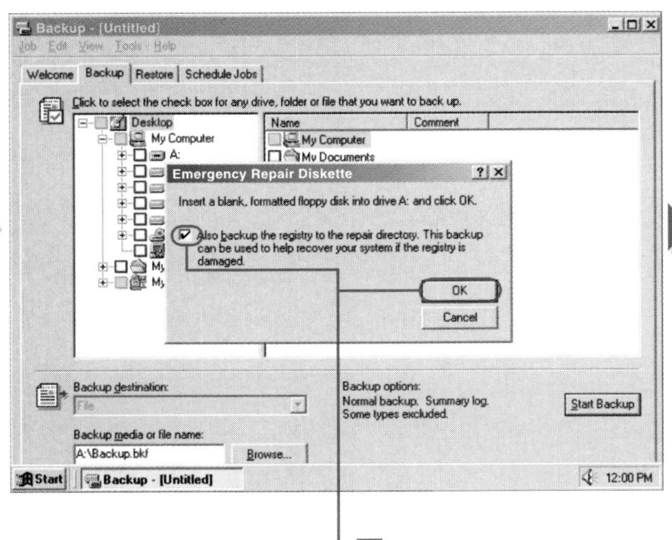

■ The Emergency Repair Diskette dialog box appears.

8 Insert the floppy disk into your floppy drive.

9 Click **Also backup the registry to the repair directory** (☐ changes to ☑).

10 Click **OK**.

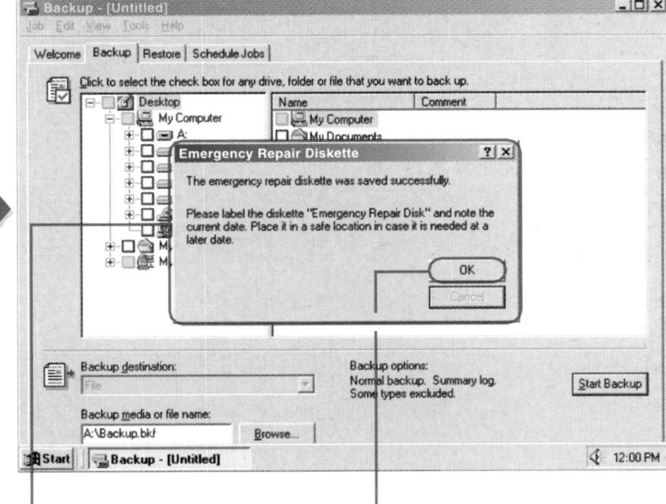

■ A dialog box appears, telling you that the Emergency Repair Disk has been successfully created.

11 Remove the Emergency Repair Disk from the floppy drive.

12 Click **OK**.

Note: You should label the disk clearly and store the disk in a safe location.

START THE EMERGENCY REPAIR PROCESS

You can start the Emergency Repair Process using the four Windows 2000 boot disks and the Emergency Repair Disk. If your server supports booting from a CD-ROM drive, you can start the process using the CD and the Emergency Repair Disk.

Warning: Even if you attempt the repair process, you may still lose all information on your server. Consult a computer professional for other ways to recover data from a server.

START THE EMERGENCY REPAIR PROCESS

```
Windows 2000 Server Setup

  Welcome to Setup.

  This portion of the Setup program prepares Microsoft(R)
  Windows 2000(TM) to run on your computer.

     *  To set up Windows 2000 now, press ENTER.

     *  To repair a Windows 2000 installation, press R.

     *  To quit Setup without installing Windows 2000, press F3.

ENTER=Continue  R=Repair  F3=Quit
```

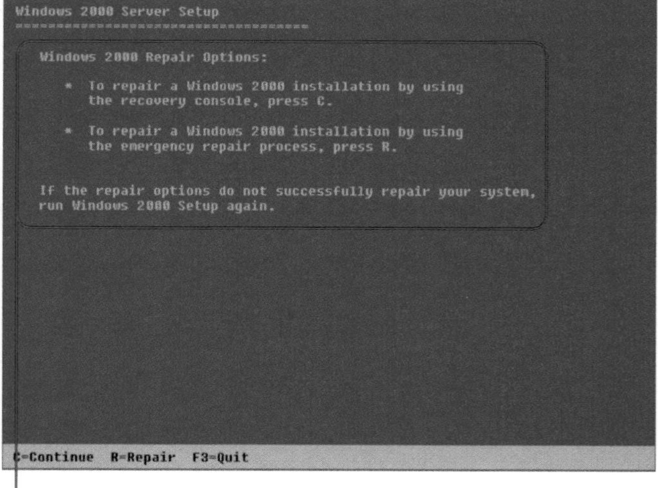

1 Insert Boot Disk #1 into the floppy drive.

2 Restart your server.

3 Insert the floppy disks when prompted.

■ The Windows 2000 Server Setup screen appears.

4 Press R.

■ The Windows 2000 Repair Options screen appears.

5 Press R.

What is the difference between a fast repair and a manual repair?

Fast repair enables you to repair your server and Registry. Manual repair is for users who are familiar with their system and understand the individual repair options.

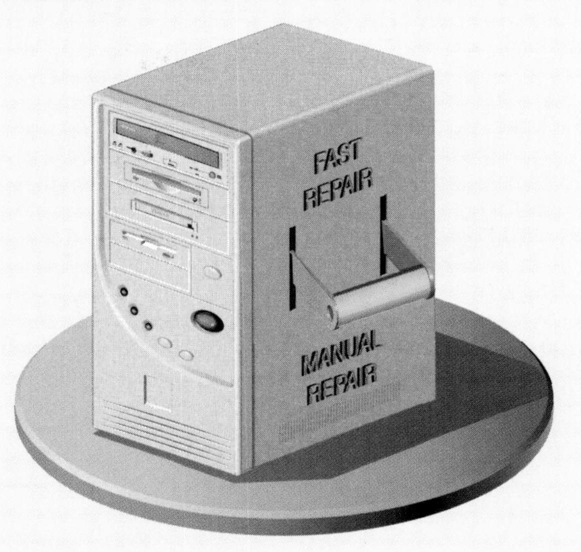


```
Windows 2000 Server Setup
=====================================

  This operation will attempt to repair your Windows 2000 system.
  Depending on the type of damage present, this operation may or
  may not be successful.  If the system is not successfully repaired,
  restart Setup and choose the option to recover a destroyed system
  or system disk

  Select one of the following repair options.

     *  Manual Repair:  To choose from a list of repair options, press M.

     *  Fast Repair:  To perform all repair options, press F.

M=Manual Repair  F=Fast Repair  ESC=Cancel  F3=Quit
```

```
Windows 2000 Server Setup
=====================================

  You need an Emergency Repair Disk for the Windows 2000
  installation you want to repair.
  NOTE:  Setup can only repair Windows 2000 installations.

     *  If you have the Emergency Repair Disk, press ENTER.

     *  If you do not have the Emergency Repair Disk, press L.
        Setup will attempt to locate Windows 2000 for you.

ENTER=Continue  L=Locate  ESC=Cancel  F3=Quit
```

■ The Repair options screen appears.

6 Press F to start the Fast Repair process.

■ The Emergency Repair Disk options screen appears.

7 Press Enter.

8 Insert the Emergency Repair Disk in your floppy drive.

9 Press Enter.

■ The Emergency Repair Disk process checks your computer and reboots when done.

INSTALL THE RECOVERY CONSOLE

The Windows 2000 Server Recovery Console is a command-line program that enables you to recover from problems that prevent you from booting your server.

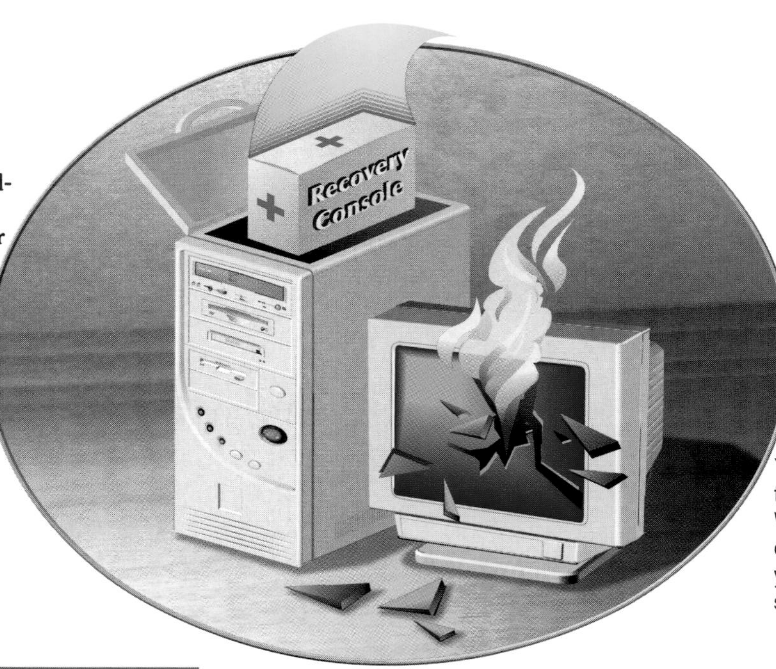

You can use the console to perform repairs to your Windows 2000 installation, or in the worst case, copy your important files off the system.

INSTALL THE RECOVERY CONSOLE

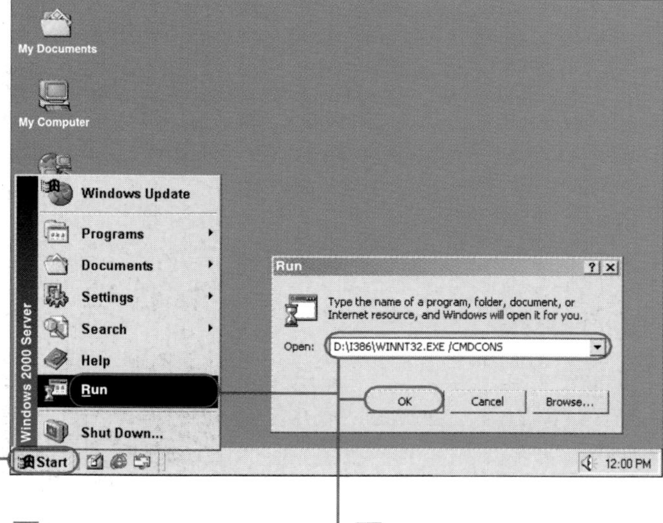

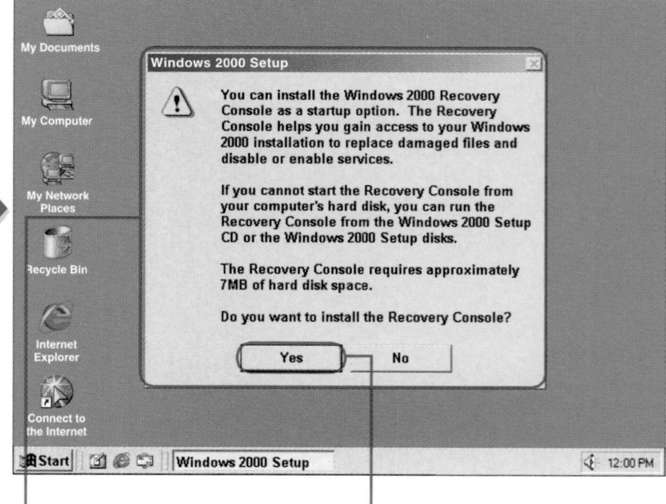

1 Insert the Windows 2000 Server CD into your server's CD-ROM drive.

*Note: If the Microsoft Windows 2000 CD dialog box appears, click **Exit**.*

2 Click **Start**.

3 Click **Run** to display the Run dialog box.

4 Type **d:\i386\winnt32.exe /cmdcons**, where d: is your CD-ROM's drive letter.

5 Click **OK**.

■ The Windows 2000 Setup dialog box appears, asking if you want to install the console.

6 Click **Yes**.

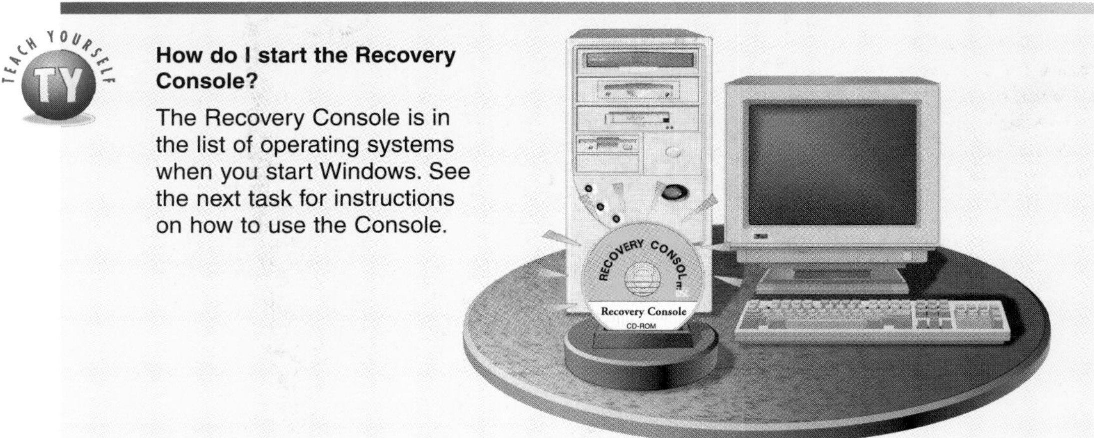

How do I start the Recovery Console?

The Recovery Console is in the list of operating systems when you start Windows. See the next task for instructions on how to use the Console.

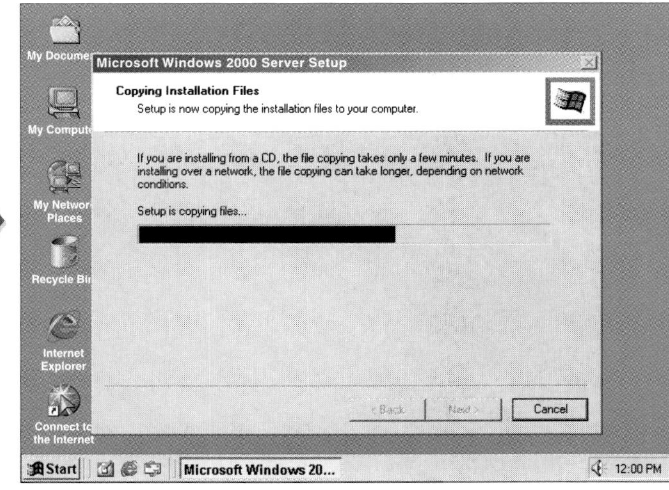

■ The Copying Installation Files dialog box appears.

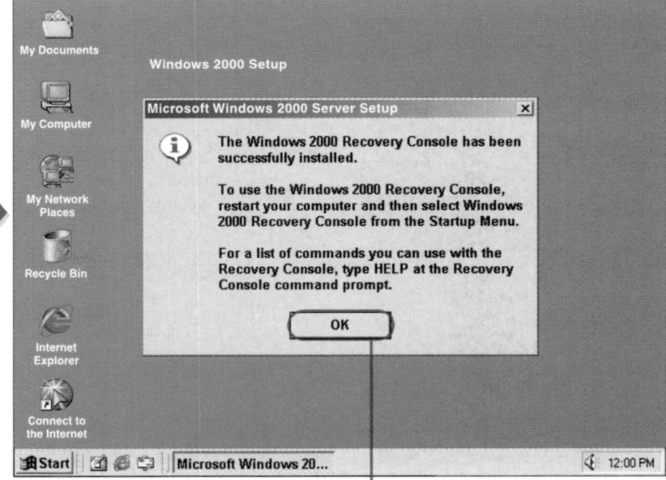

■ When copying is complete, the Microsoft Windows 2000 Server Setup dialog box appears and reports the installation was successful.

7 Click **OK**.

USING THE RECOVERY CONSOLE

The Recovery Console contains many MS-DOS commands that you may already be familiar with, such as Copy and Format.

User Name:
Administrator
Password:
****

Because the Recovery Console is a powerful tool for recovery, you must log on as an administrator when you start the Recovery Console.

USING THE RECOVERY CONSOLE

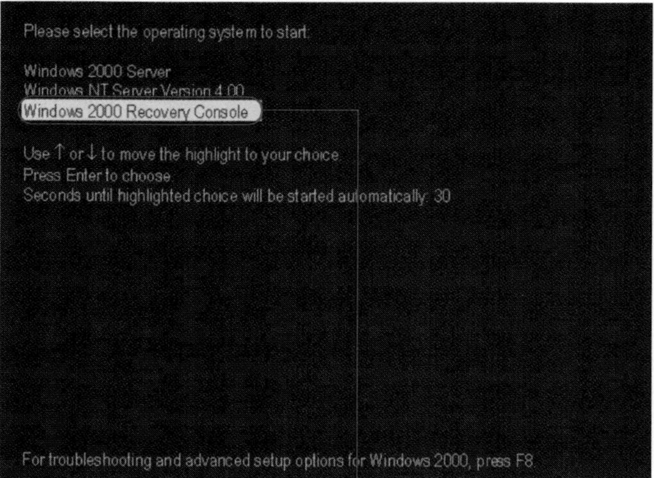
Please select the operating system to start:
Windows 2000 Server
Windows NT Server Version 4.00
Windows 2000 Recovery Console
Use ↑ or ↓ to move the highlight to your choice.
Press Enter to choose.
Seconds until highlighted choice will be started automatically: 30
For troubleshooting and advanced setup options for Windows 2000, press F8.

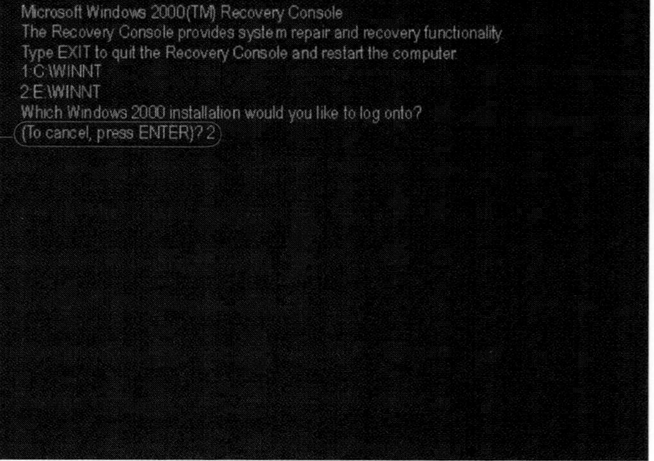
Microsoft Windows 2000(TM) Recovery Console
The Recovery Console provides system repair and recovery functionality.
Type EXIT to quit the Recovery Console and restart the computer.
1: C:\WINNT
2: E:\WINNT
Which Windows 2000 installation would you like to log onto?
(To cancel, press ENTER)? 2

1 Reboot your server.

■ A list of startup options appears.

2 Press ↑ or ↓ to highlight Windows 2000 Recovery Console.

3 Press Enter.

■ The Windows 2000 Recovery Console starts.

4 Type the number of the operating system you want to log on to (example: **2**).

5 Press Enter.

Where can I get a list of Recovery Console commands?

When you start the Recovery Console, type **help** and press Enter. The list of available commands will appear below the command line.

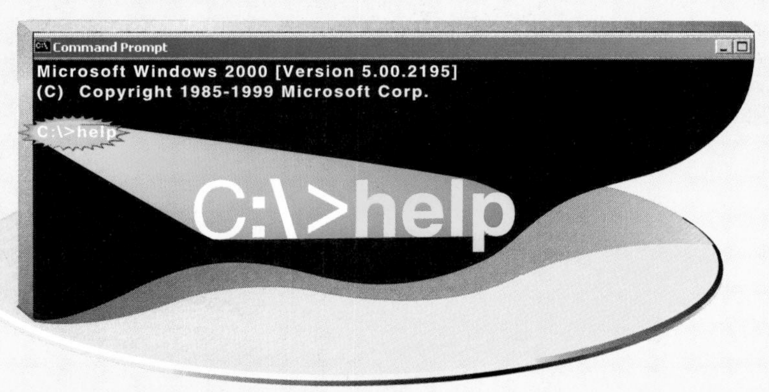


```
Microsoft Windows 2000(TM) Recovery Console
The Recovery Console provides system repair and recovery functionality.
Type EXIT to quit the Recovery Console and restart the computer.
1:C:\WINNT
2:E:\WINNT
Which Windows 2000 installation would you like to log onto?
(To cancel, press ENTER)? 2
Type the administrator password: ********
```

6 Type the administrator password.

■ Asterisks appear rather than the password for security.

7 Press Enter.

```
Microsoft Windows 2000(TM) Recovery Console
The Recovery Console provides system repair and recovery functionality.
Type EXIT to quit the Recovery Console and restart the computer.
1:C:\WINNT
2:E:\WINNT
Which Windows 2000 installation would you like to log onto?
(To cancel, press ENTER)? 2
Type the administrator password: ********
E:\WINNT>
```

■ The command prompt appears and you are logged on to the Recovery Console.

■ You can now type commands at the command prompt to troubleshoot your system.

*Note: You can quit the Recovery Console by typing **EXIT** at the command prompt and pressing* Enter.

START IN SAFE MODE

If you recently installed files or drivers and your computer does not boot, you can start your server in safe mode. Safe mode lets you remove those files or drivers from your system without having to reinstall Windows 2000 Server.

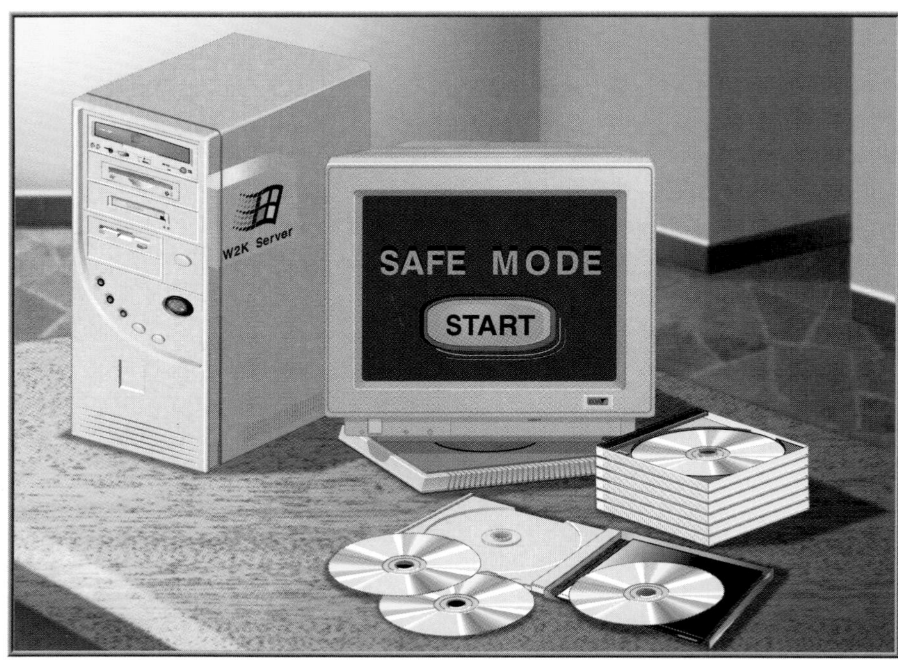

START IN SAFE MODE

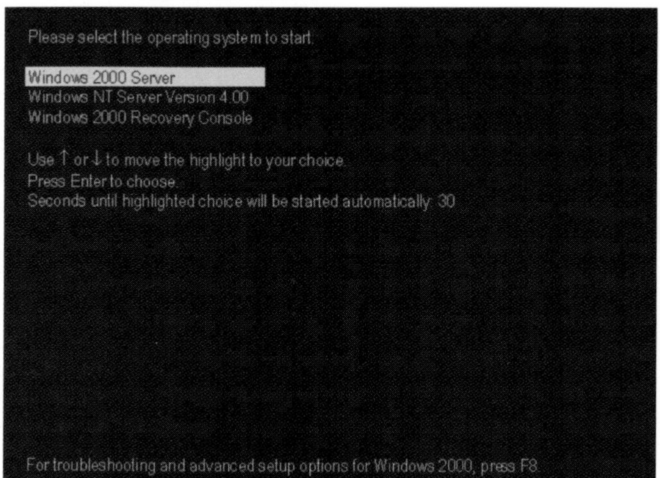

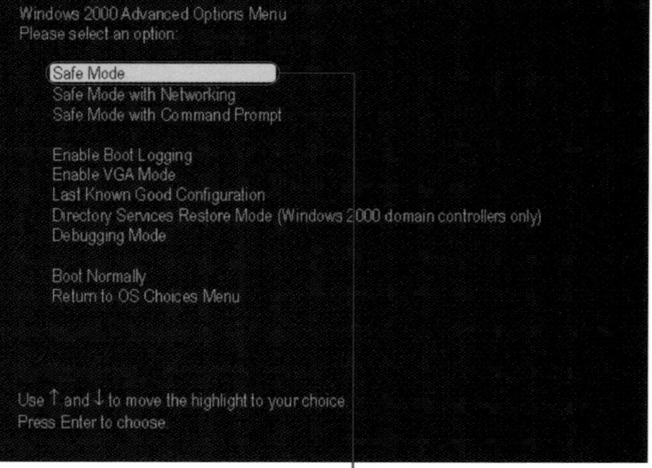

1 Reboot your server.

2 Press the F8 key when the OS Loader appears.

■ The Windows 2000 Advanced Options Menu appears.

3 Press ↑ or ↓ to highlight **Safe Mode**.

4 Press Enter.

What do I do if Safe Mode will not start?

If safe mode does not start, your system files may be corrupted or your hard disk may be damaged. Use the Recovery Console or your emergency boot disks to help find the problem.

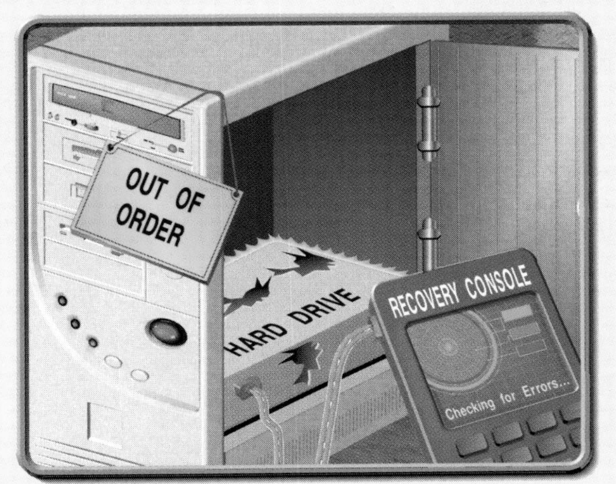

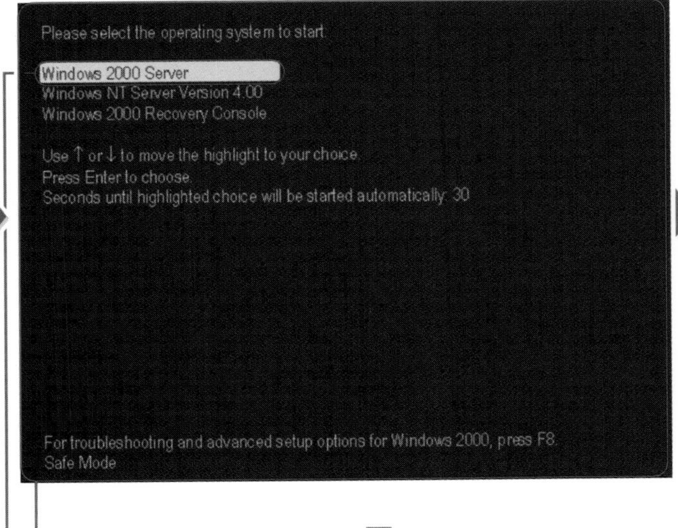

■ The Safe Mode screen appears.

5 Press ↑ or ↓ to highlight **Windows 2000 Server**.

6 Press Enter.

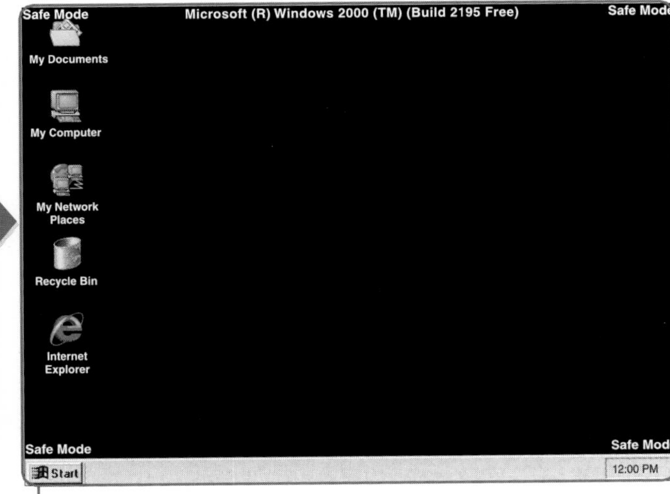

■ Windows 2000 starts in Safe Mode.

START THE SAFE MODE COMMAND PROMPT

When you start the Safe Mode Command Prompt, Windows 2000 Server bypasses the desktop entirely and places you into a full-screen Command Prompt window. You can use the command line to make changes to your system using DOS commands or you can run DOS-based programs.

START THE SAFE MODE COMMAND PROMPT

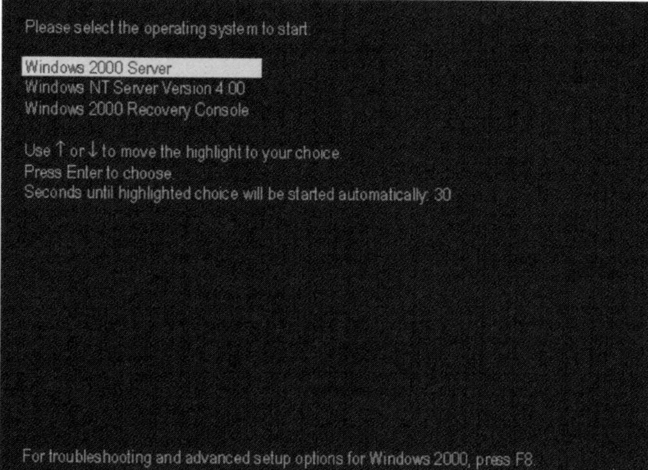

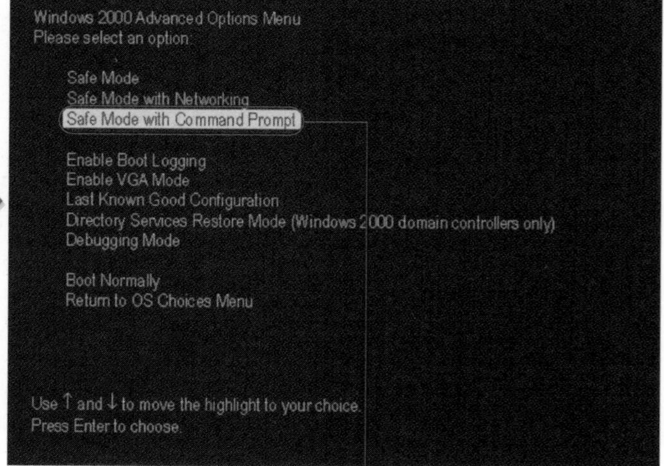

1 Reboot your server.

2 Press F8 when the OS Loader appears.

■ The Windows 2000 Advanced Options Menu appears.

3 Press ↑ or ↓ to highlight **Safe Mode with Command Prompt**.

4 Press Enter.

TEACH YOURSELF
TY

How do I get help for DOS commands if I am not sure what they do?

You can get help for a particular command by typing the command name and **/?**. For example, **dir /?** provides help on the `dir` command.

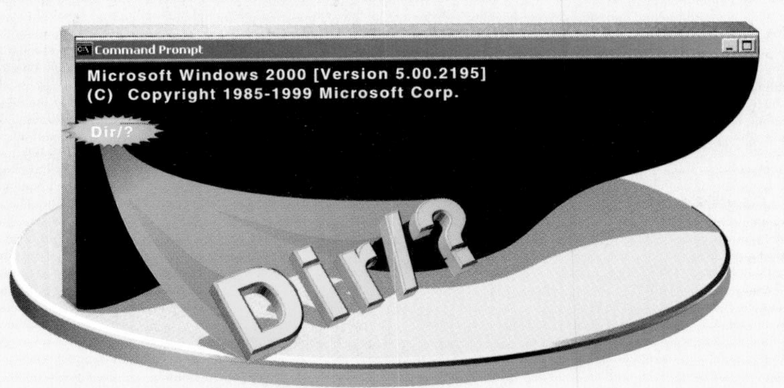
Command Prompt
Microsoft Windows 2000 [Version 5.00.2195]
(C) Copyright 1985-1999 Microsoft Corp.
Dir/?
Dir/?

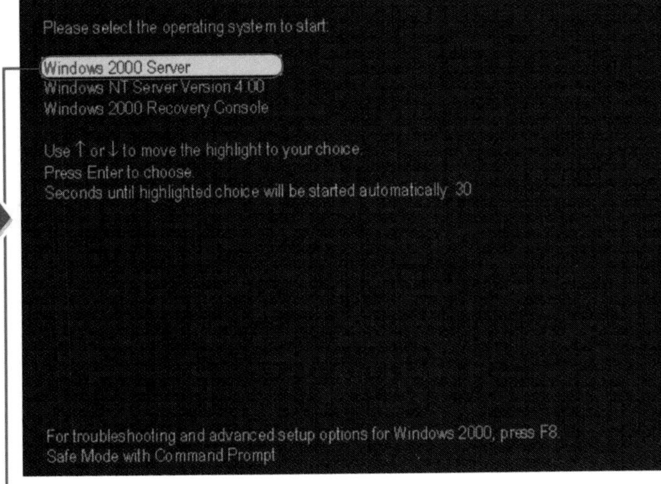
Please select the operating system to start:
Windows 2000 Server
Windows NT Server Version 4.00
Windows 2000 Recovery Console
Use ↑ or ↓ to move the highlight to your choice.
Press Enter to choose.
Seconds until highlighted choice will be started automatically: 30
For troubleshooting and advanced setup options for Windows 2000, press F8.
Safe Mode with Command Prompt

Microsoft Windows 2000 [Version 5.00.2195]
(c) Copyright 1985-1999 Microsoft Corp.
E:\>

5 Press ↑ or ↓ to highlight **Windows 2000 Server** from the Safe Mode OS Loader.

6 Press Enter.

7 Type your Windows 2000 Server user name.

8 Type your password.

■ The command prompt window appears.

■ You can use DOS commands to help in your recovery.

START WITH THE LAST KNOWN GOOD CONFIGURATION

In some cases, a new service, device driver, or program changes the System Registry and causes Windows 2000 Server to either start improperly or to not start at all. When this happens, you can boot your server with the last known good configuration.

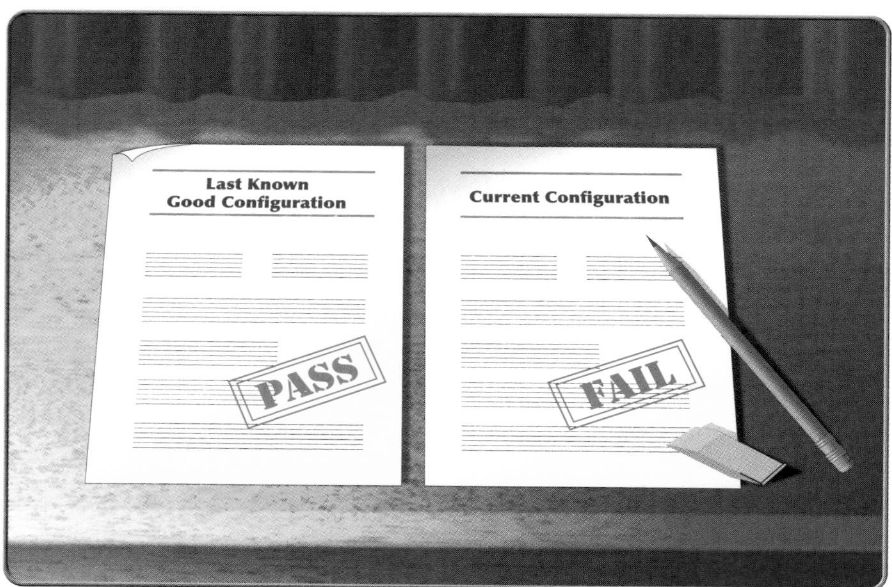

START WITH THE LAST KNOWN GOOD CONFIGURATION

Please select the operating system to start:

Windows 2000 Server
Windows NT Server Version 4.00
Windows 2000 Recovery Console

Use ↑ or ↓ to move the highlight to your choice.
Press Enter to choose.
Seconds until highlighted choice will be started automatically: 30

For troubleshooting and advanced setup options for Windows 2000, press F8.

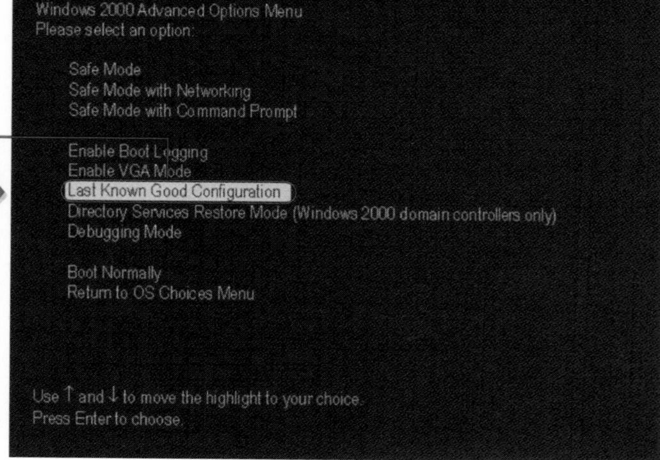

1 Reboot your server.

2 Press F8 when the OS Loader appears.

■ The Windows 2000 Advanced Options Menu appears.

3 Press ↑ or ↓ to highlight **Last Known Good Configuration**.

4 Press Enter.

■ The OS Loader appears.

Can I recover all the settings that have changed since the server saved my last known good configuration?

The Last Known Good Configuration settings are those that were loaded successfully the last time you booted. Any changes you made since that last successful boot were not copied to the Last Known Good Configuration file; you will need to reinstall your software or reenter your changes.

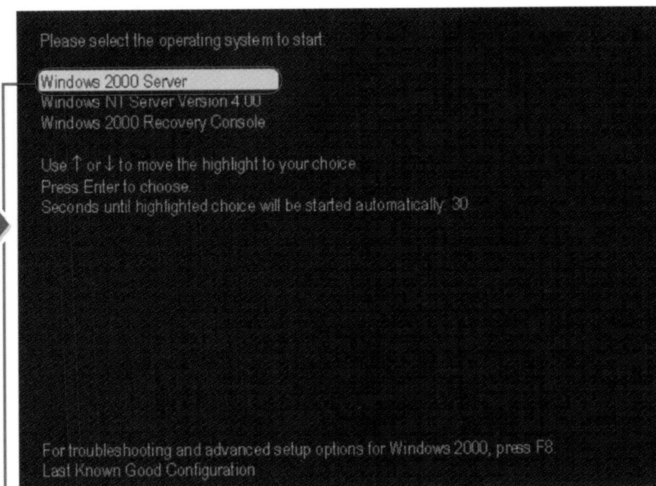

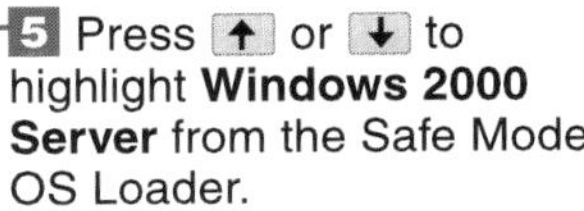

5 Press ↑ or ↓ to highlight **Windows 2000 Server** from the Safe Mode OS Loader.

Note: You may be asked to enter the profile you want to use from the Profile List screen. Press ↑ or ↓ to highlight the hardware profile you want to use and then press Enter.

■ Windows 2000 Server starts up with the profile you selected.

Backup
Program
For DAT drives
version
2.8
DAT
DAT2

CHAPTER 15

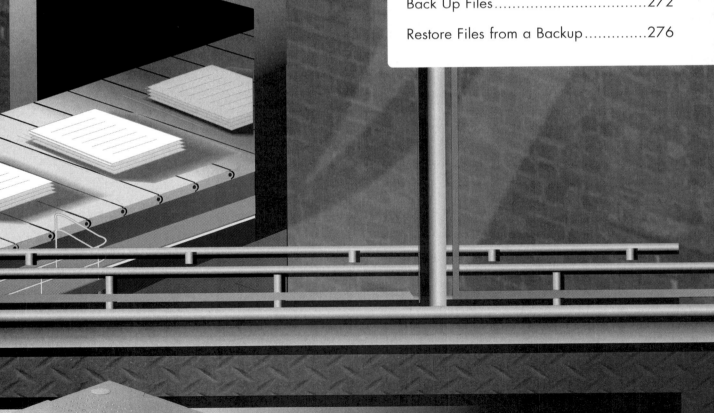

Backing Up and Restoring Files

In case of disaster, how much data can you afford to lose? In this chapter you will learn how to back up and restore your data, so you can restore your files with a minimum of data loss.

Backing up data creates an exact copy that can be restored in case the original files are lost or damaged.

Backing up your server's data is the single most important disaster protection step you can take.

BACKUP DEVICES

You can back up your server's data to a wide variety of devices. Tape backup is the most common system. If you use an external device, you should use the manufacturer's software to back up and restore your data.

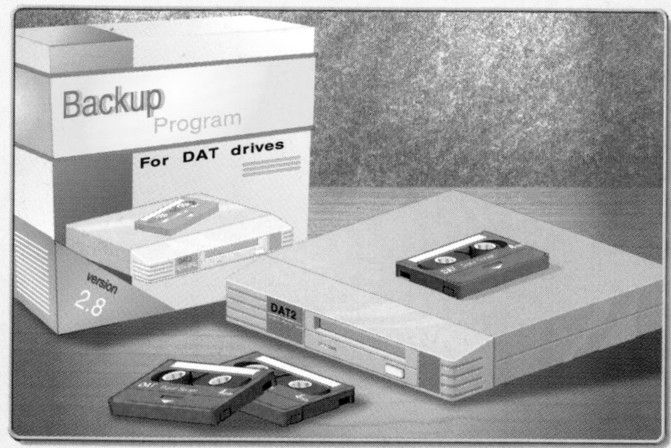

SCHEDULED BACKUPS

Most companies have scheduled backup times to copy server data. This is usually done at night or at low-usage times on the network. Backup frequency is determined by an estimate of how much information you can afford to lose; if you can't afford to lose more than one day's worth of information, back up every day.

What types of information should I back up?

You should back up all information that is useful to running your business. This includes the important things, like financial data or personnel records, and the smaller things, like form banks, company letterhead artwork, and miscellaneous files.

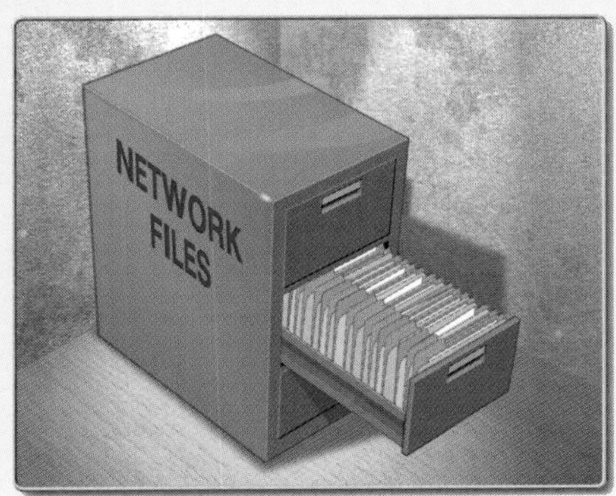

TYPES OF BACKUPS

There are three basic types of backups. A full backup makes a complete copy of the entire volume. Incremental backups copy only files that have changed since the last full backup. Daily backups copy files that have changed that day.

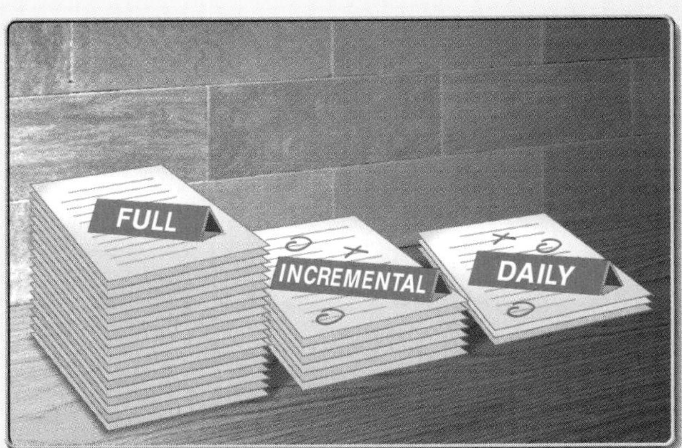

BACKUP STORAGE

Backup tapes or other media should be stored in a safe location. You can use a fireproof box on site, or a locked cabinet. Many businesses use offsite storage for their data, so if something happens to your building, you can recover your undamaged files and data.

BACK UP FILES

Windows 2000 Server lets you back up files on an NTFS-formatted hard disk manually or at a regularly scheduled time.

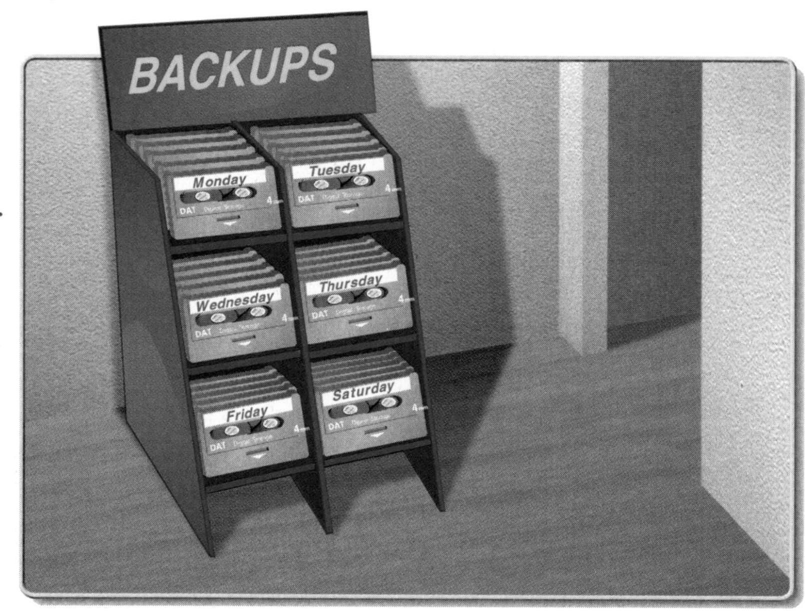

When you back up data regularly, the backup process takes place in the background so you can run Backup unattended.

BACK UP FILES

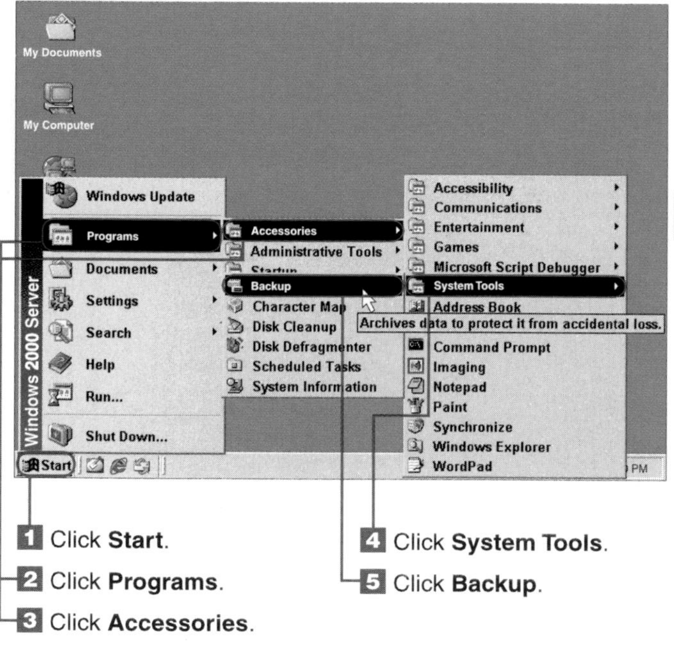

1 Click **Start**.

2 Click **Programs**.

3 Click **Accessories**.

4 Click **System Tools**.

5 Click **Backup**.

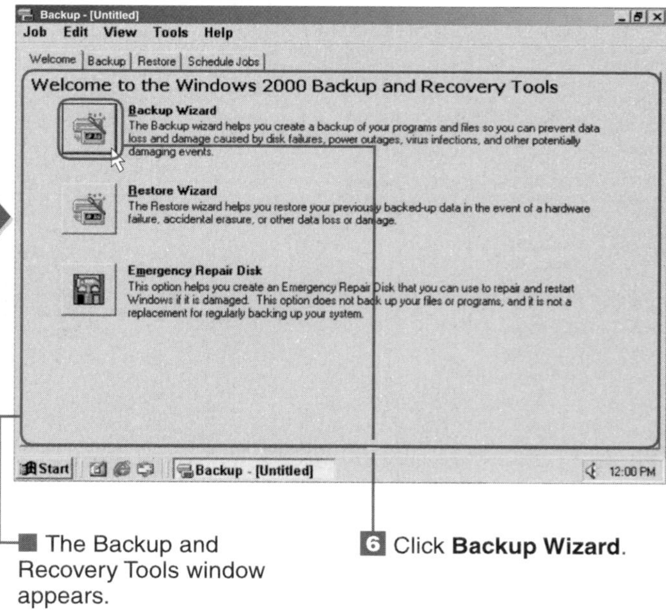

■ The Backup and Recovery Tools window appears.

6 Click **Backup Wizard**.

Why can't I access the Backup program?

You must be a member of the Administrators group or a member of the Backup operators group to back up or restore files.

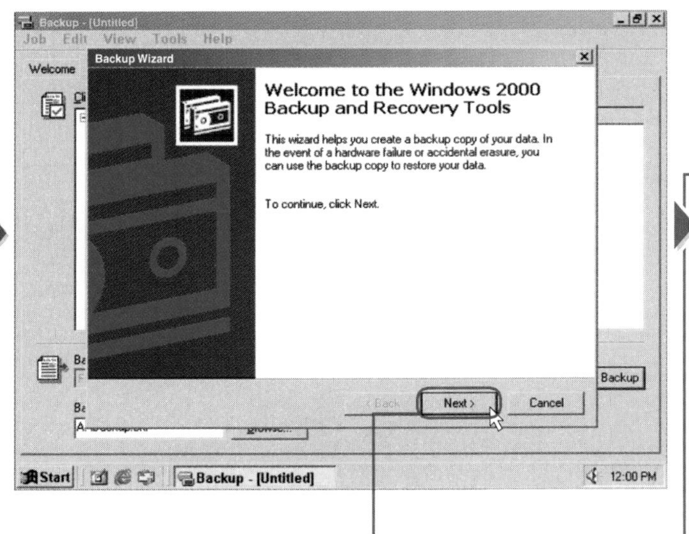

■ The Backup Wizard dialog box appears.

7 Click **Next**.

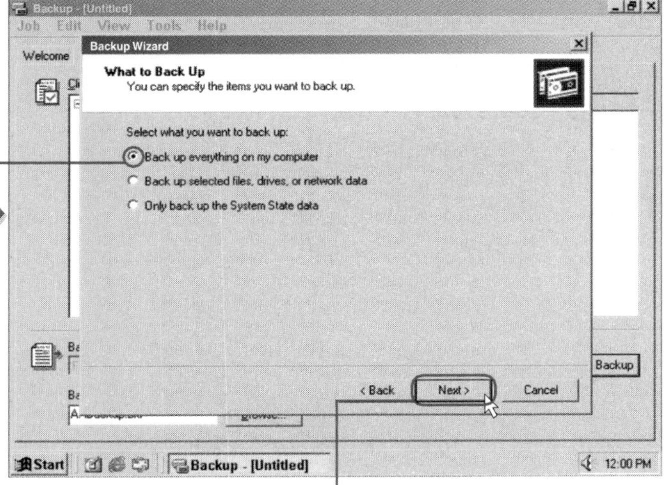

■ The What to Back Up dialog box appears.

8 Click **Back up everything on my computer** (○ changes to ◉).

Note: You can choose instead to click ***Back up selected files, drives, or network data****. Doing so allows you to back up only the files you select.*

9 Click **Next**.

CONTINUED

You can schedule backups using Backup or your backup unit's software. See the Windows help file or your backup software's documentation on how to do this.

BACK UP FILES (CONTINUED)

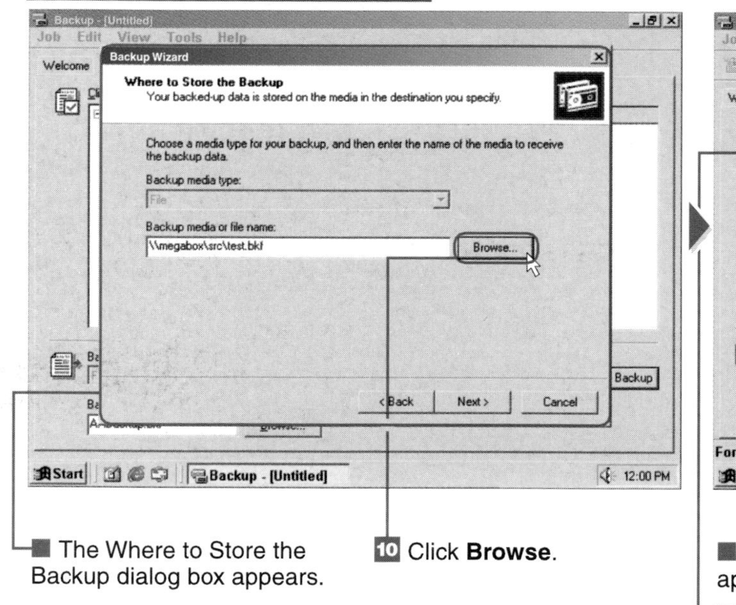

- The Where to Store the Backup dialog box appears.

10 Click **Browse**.

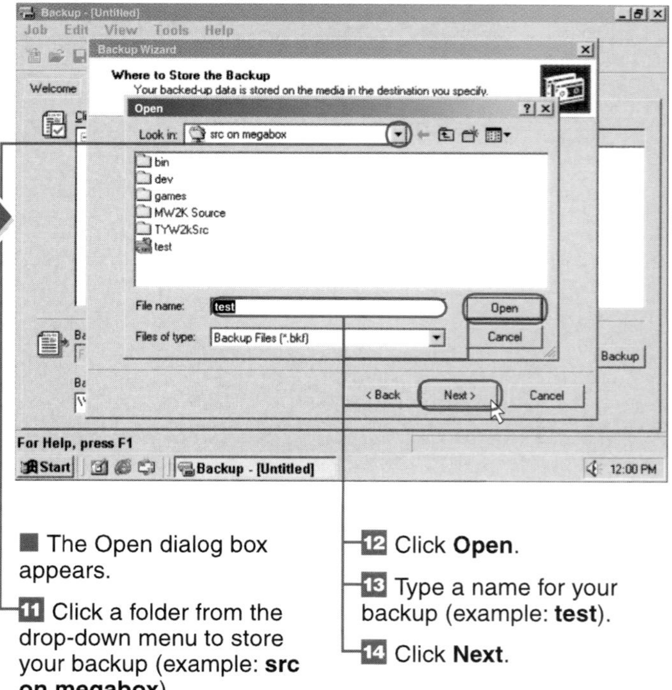

- The Open dialog box appears.

11 Click a folder from the drop-down menu to store your backup (example: **src on megabox**).

12 Click **Open**.

13 Type a name for your backup (example: **test**).

14 Click **Next**.

Are there different types of tape backup systems on the market?

Tape backup systems vary in number of features, amount of data stored, and type of tape. Check with the manufacturer to see what type of tape is recommended for your system.

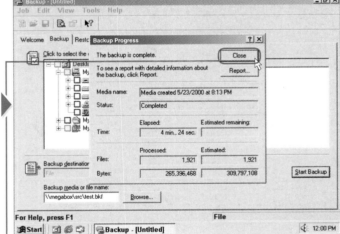

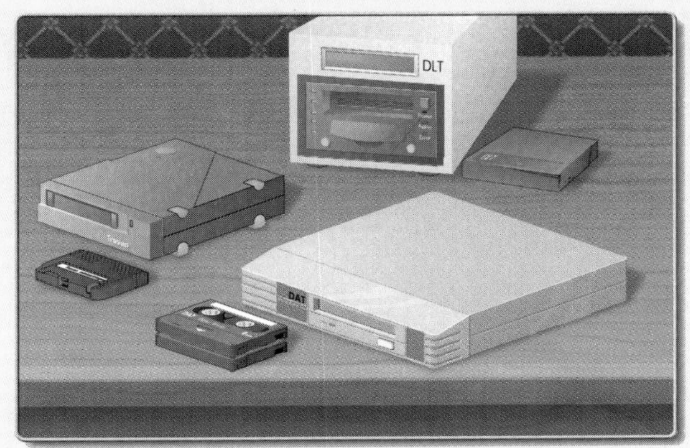

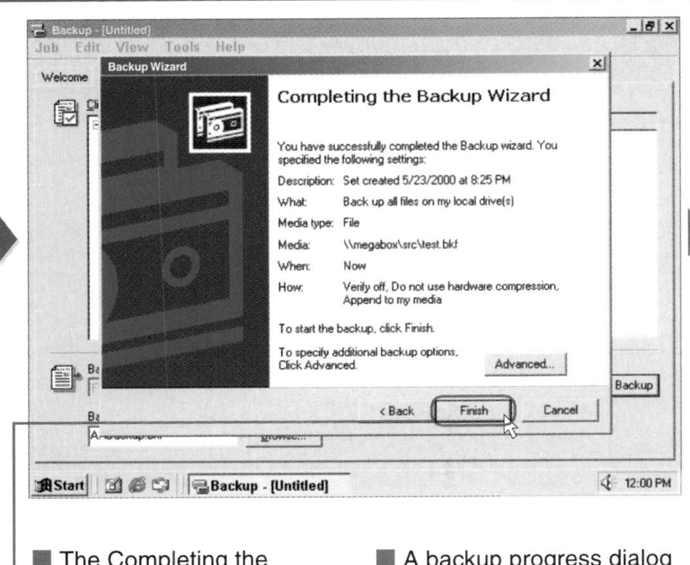

Backup - [Untitled]
Job Edit View Tools Help
Welcome Backup Restore
Backup Progress
The backup is complete.
Close
To see a report with detailed information about the backup, click Report.
Report...
Media name: Media created 5/23/2000 at 8:13 PM
Status: Completed
Time: Elapsed: 4 min., 24 sec. Estimated remaining:
Files: Processed: 1,921 Estimated: 1,921
Bytes: Processed: 265,396,468 Estimated: 309,797,108
Backup destination: File
Backup media or file name: \\megabox\src\test.bkf
Browse...
Start Backup
For Help, press F1
File
Start
Backup - [Untitled]
12:00 PM

■ The Completing the Backup Wizard dialog box appears.

15 Click **Finish**.

■ A backup progress dialog box appears, showing you how many files have been copied and the estimated time to completion.

16 When the backup is complete, click **Close**.

RESTORE FILES FROM A BACKUP

If you are an administrator or a member of the backup operators group, you can restore files from a backup.

RESTORE FILES FROM A BACKUP

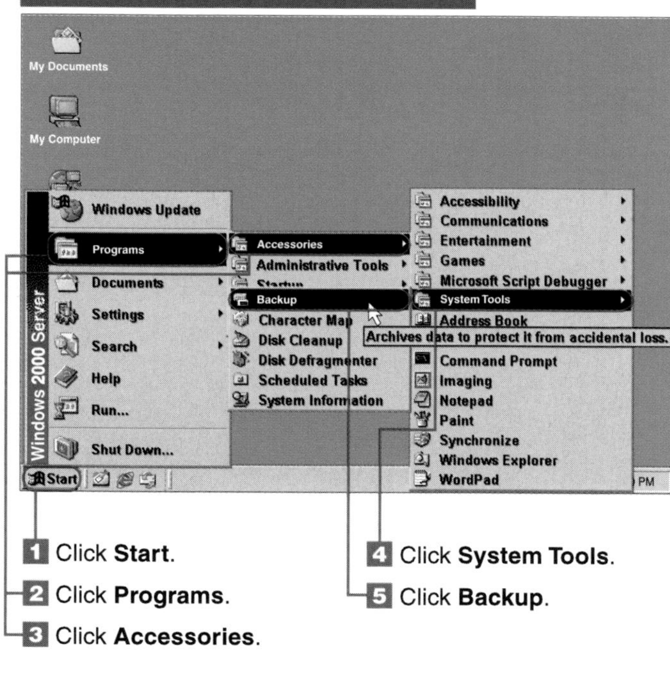

1 Click **Start**.

2 Click **Programs**.

3 Click **Accessories**.

4 Click **System Tools**.

5 Click **Backup**.

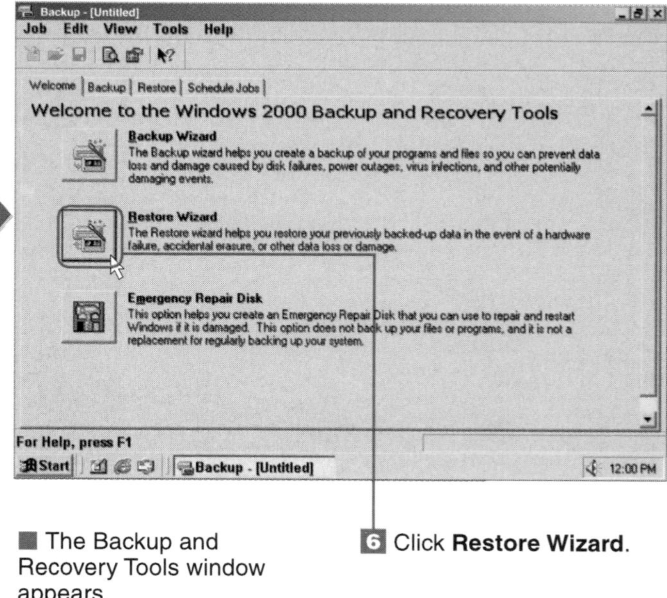

■ The Backup and Recovery Tools window appears.

6 Click **Restore Wizard**.

Can I restore files from an NTFS drive to a FAT drive?

You can, but you can lose data or file permissions if you try this. You should always try to restore to the same format volume as the backup's source.

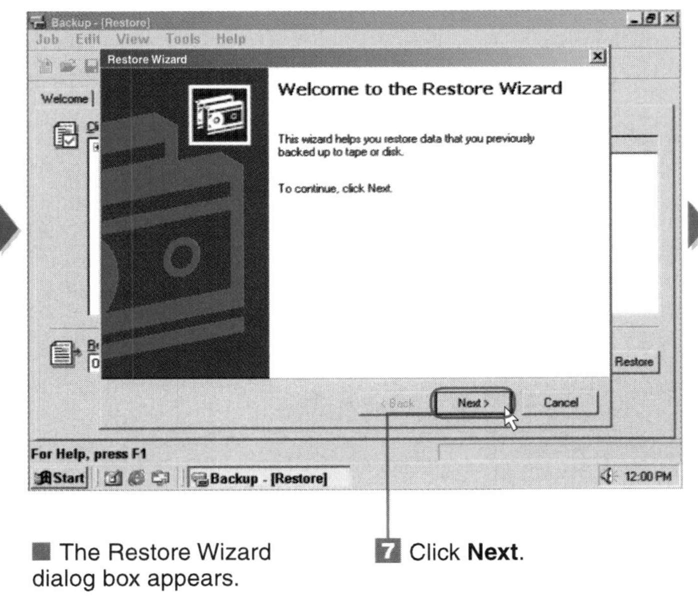

■ The Restore Wizard dialog box appears.

7 Click **Next**.

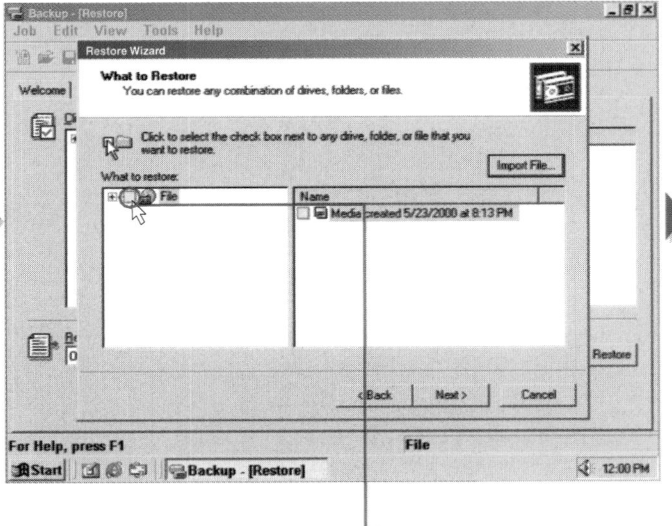

■ The What to Restore dialog box appears.

8 Click the **File** check box.

CONTINUED

RESTORE FILES FROM A BACKUP

Backup will not let you restore files if there is not enough disk space for all the files. You may need to delete some nonessential files to make room, or restore fewer files from Backup.

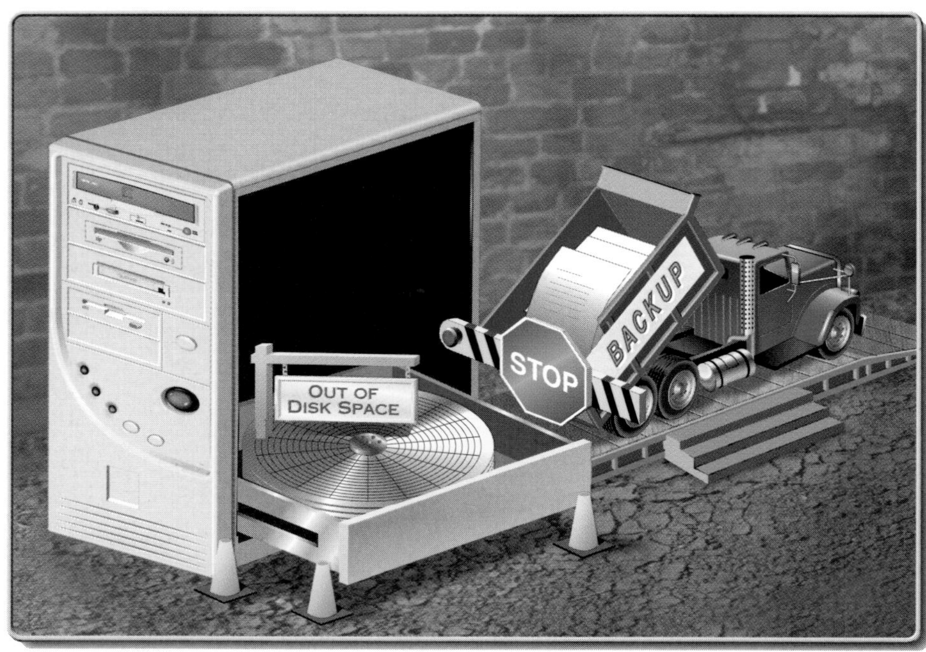

RESTORE FILES FROM A BACKUP (CONTINUED)

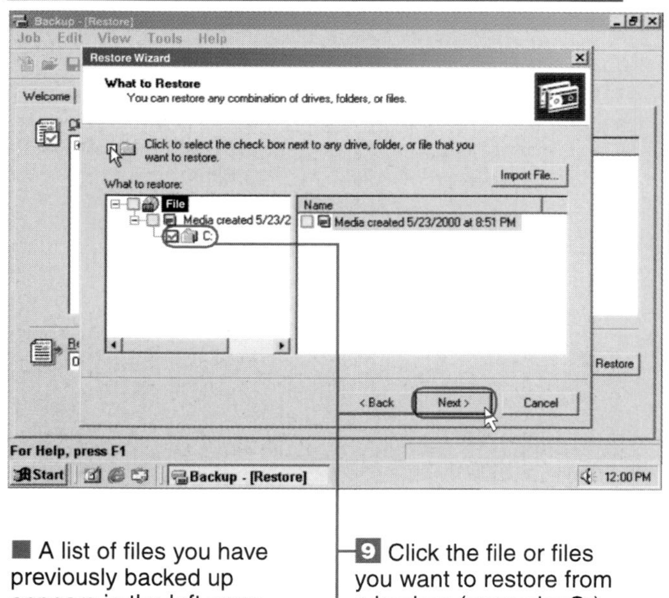

■ A list of files you have previously backed up appears in the left pane.

9 Click the file or files you want to restore from a backup (example: **C:**).

10 Click **Next**.

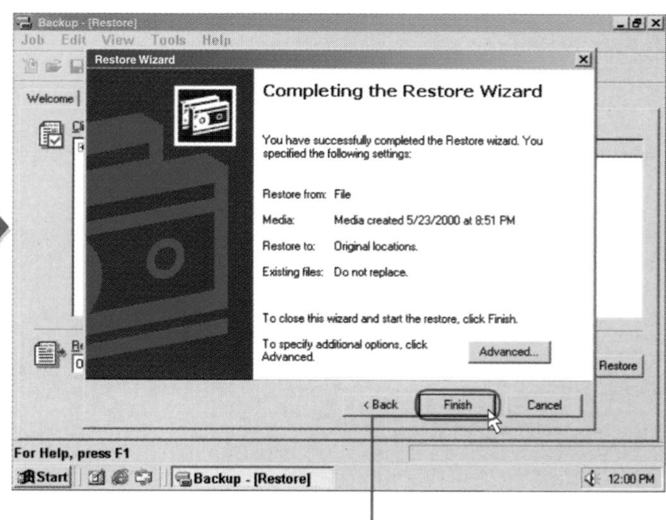

■ The Completing the Restore Wizard dialog box appears.

11 Click **Finish**.

How do I know my backup will work when I need it?

It is always a good idea to have disaster recovery plans that include testing your backup and restore systems. Find a time to do a sample backup and restore of your data to make sure your backups work.

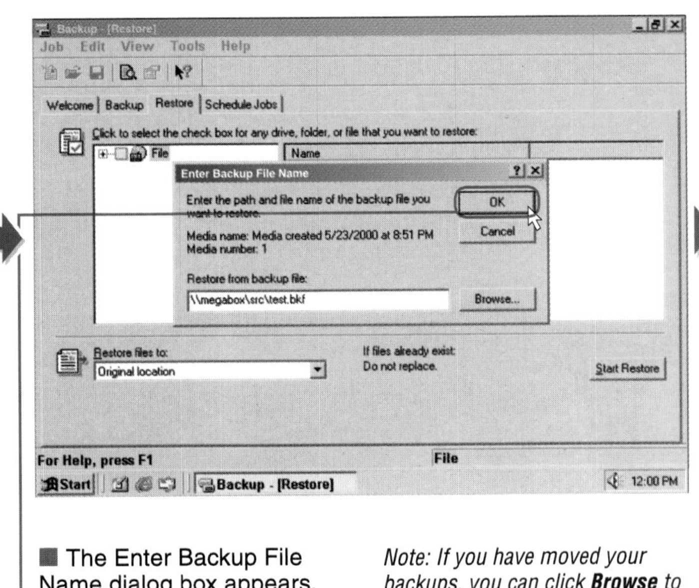

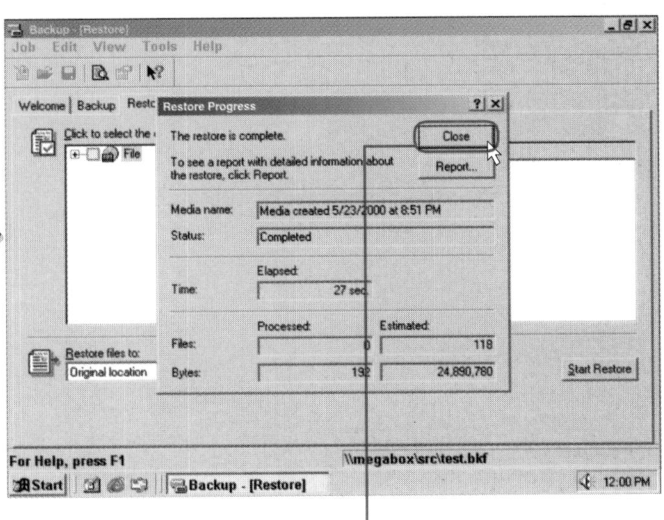

■ The Enter Backup File Name dialog box appears.

12 Click **OK**.

*Note: If you have moved your backups, you can click **Browse** to change to the backup file location.*

■ The Restore Progress dialog box appears.

13 When the restore is complete, click **Close**.

Performance Monitor
MAX
MIN

CHAPTER 16

Monitoring Your Server

Your server may be overloaded, underpowered, or out of disk space. You will learn how to monitor your server's systems and determine whether you need to add to or replace your hardware.

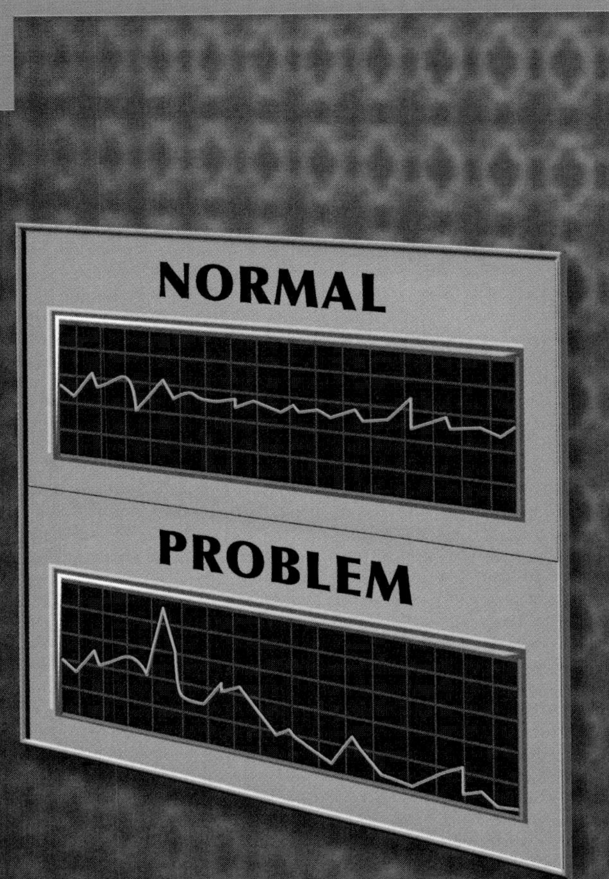

START TASK MANAGER

You can use Task Manager to monitor programs and processes running on your server. It will also help you track CPU and memory use.

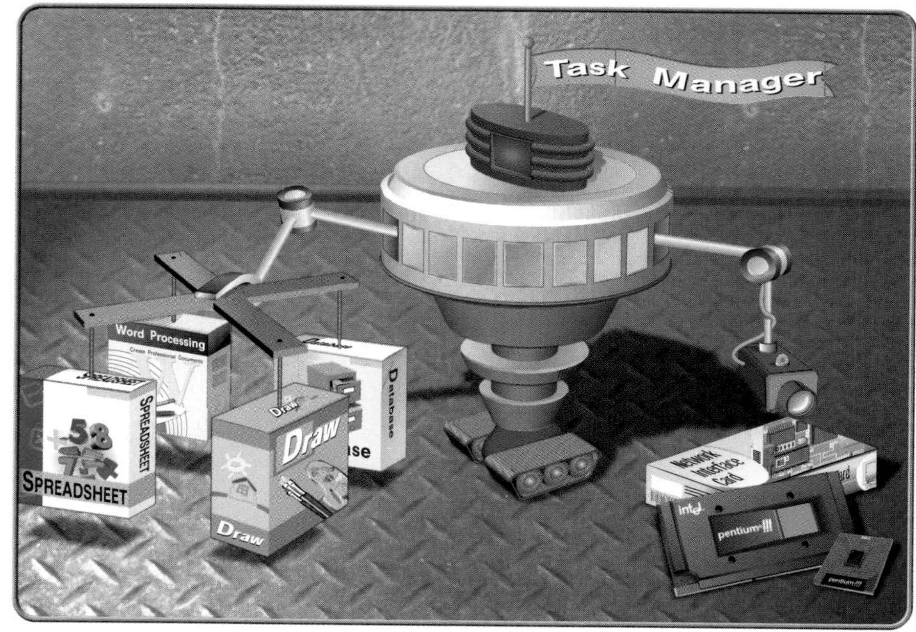

START TASK MANAGER

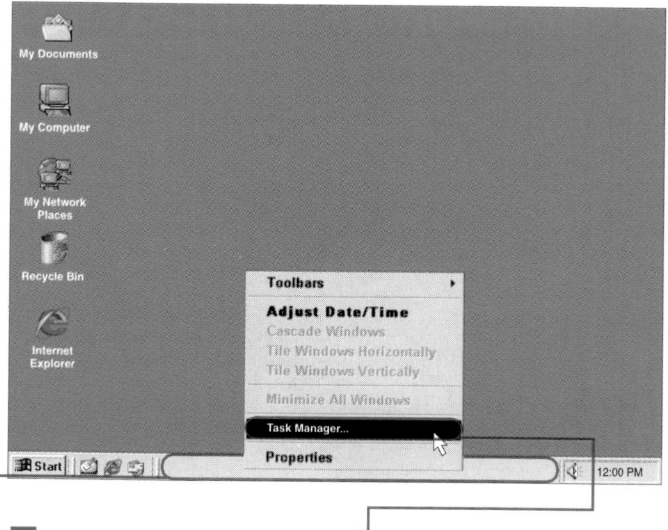

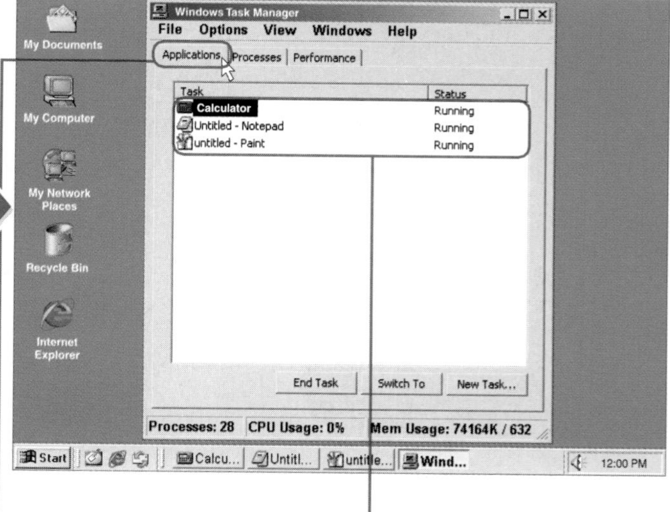

1 Right-click a blank area of the taskbar.

■ A pop-up menu appears.

2 Click **Task Manager**.

■ The Windows Task Manager dialog box appears.

3 Click **Applications**.

■ This area lists applications running on your server.

When should I use Task Manager to close a program?

Sometimes a program is frozen, waiting for a response from another program, or it may have crashed due to a bug. If you have waited several minutes and the program status still reads "Not Responding," you can use Task Manager to close the program by clicking **End Task**.

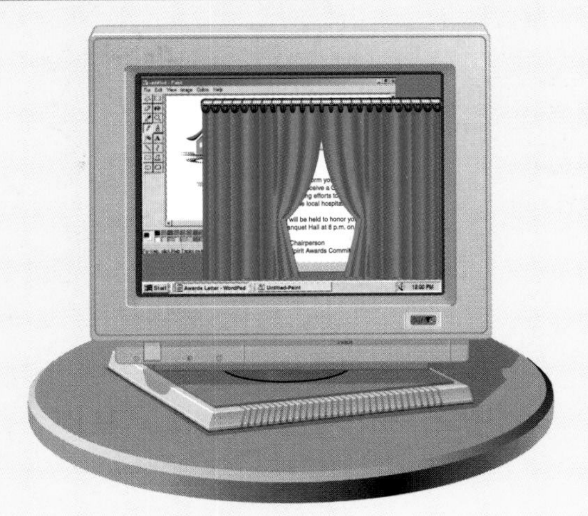

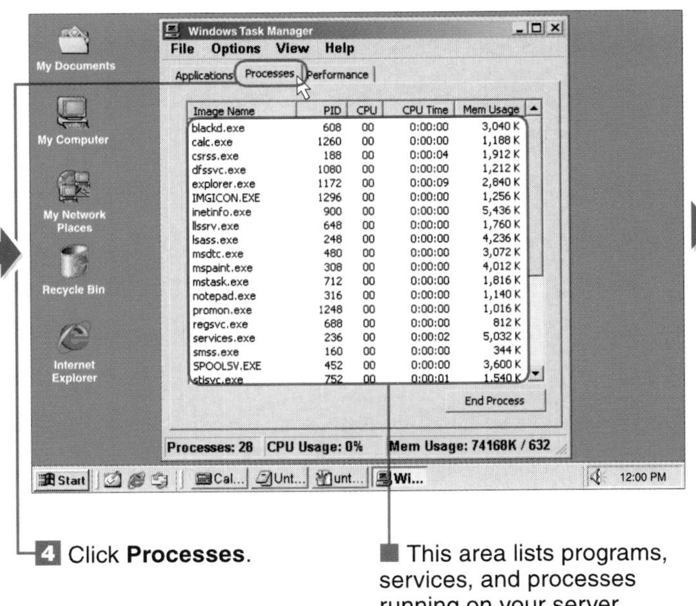

4 Click **Processes**.

■ This area lists programs, services, and processes running on your server.

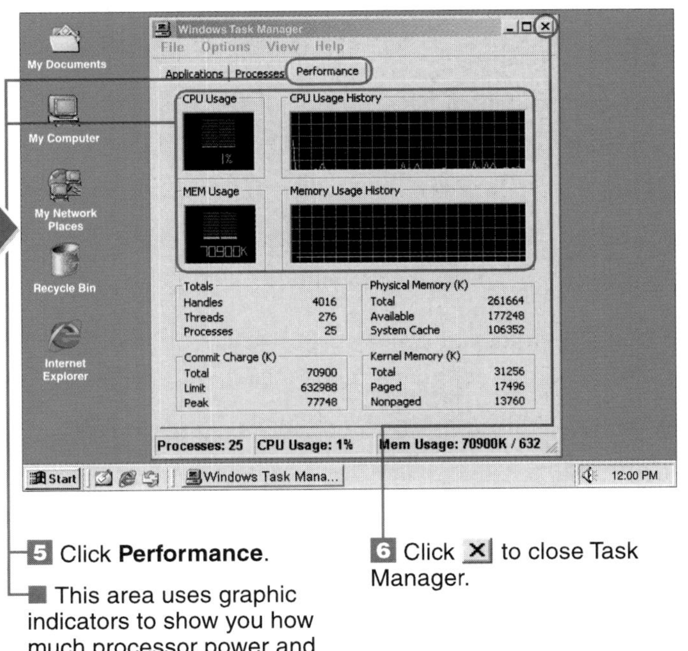

5 Click **Performance**.

■ This area uses graphic indicators to show you how much processor power and memory is being used.

6 Click ✕ to close Task Manager.

SET PERFORMANCE MONITOR

Performance Monitor can show you detailed information about your server's performance. It includes counters to track nearly every aspect of your server's behavior.

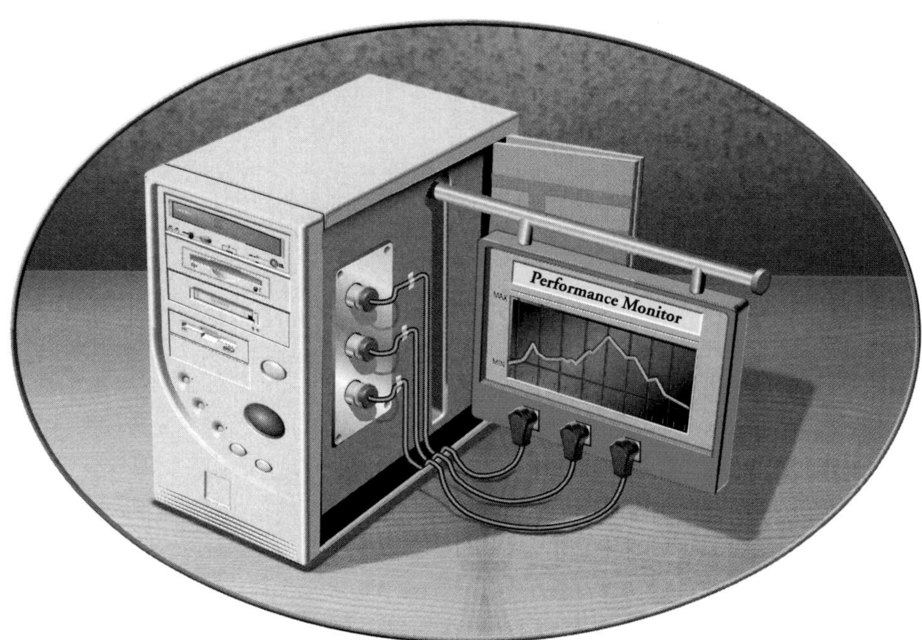

SET PERFORMANCE MONITOR

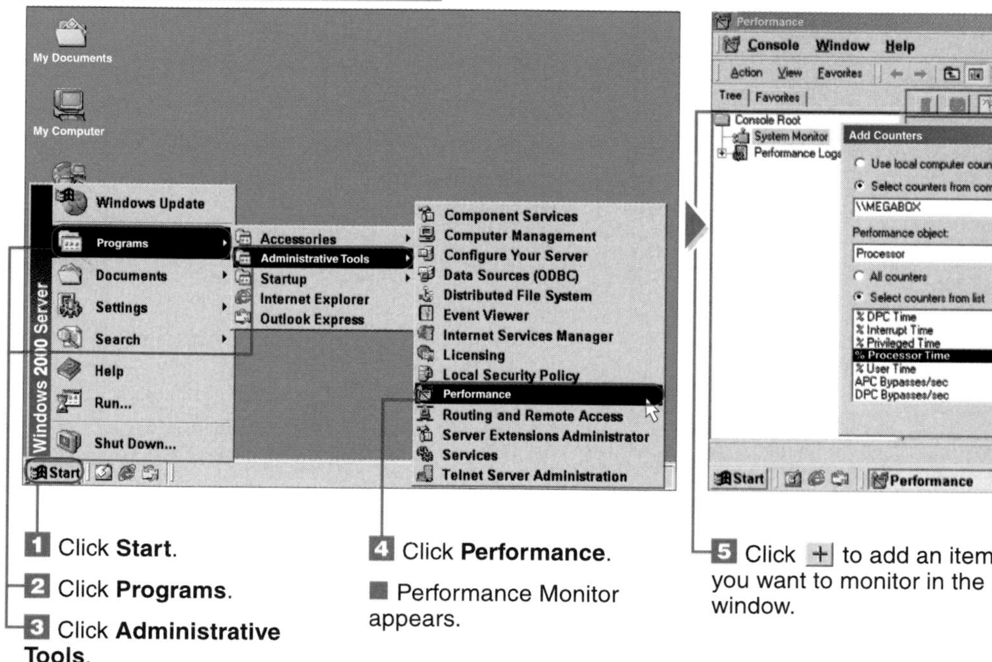

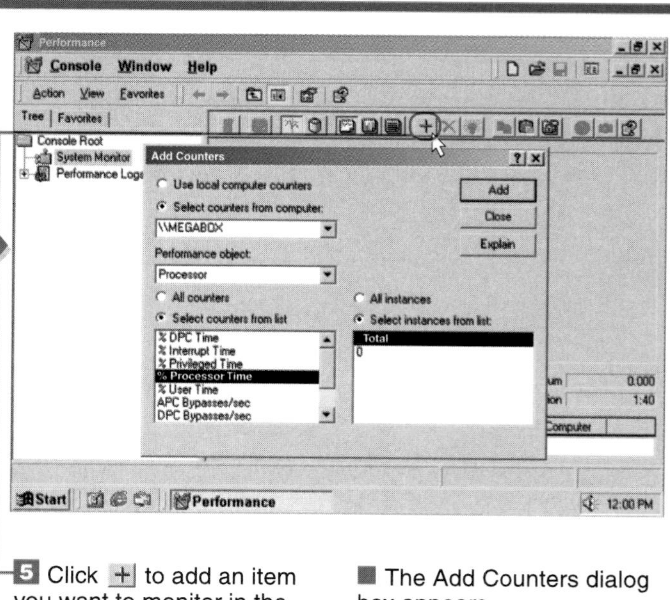

1 Click **Start**.

2 Click **Programs**.

3 Click **Administrative Tools**.

4 Click **Performance**.

■ Performance Monitor appears.

5 Click + to add an item you want to monitor in the window.

■ The Add Counters dialog box appears.

How can I tell whether a graph demonstrates a problem?

Sometimes it is hard to tell when a problem begins. A good idea is to make a baseline recording, which you can then compare to a newer recording to see what kind of problem has appeared.

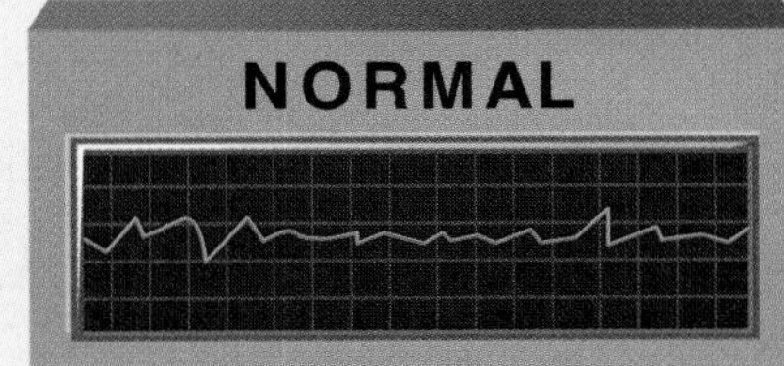

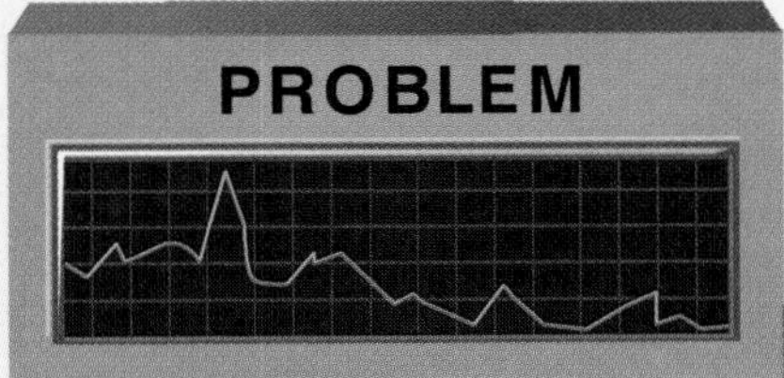

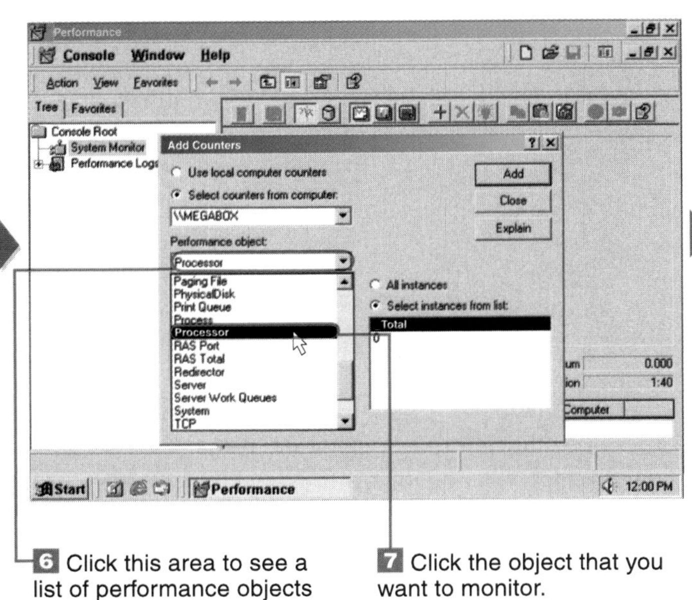

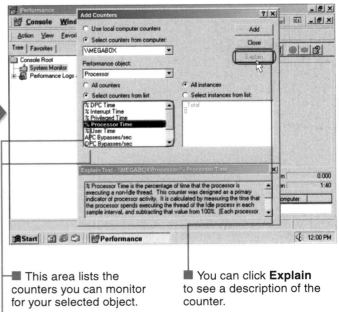

6 Click this area to see a list of performance objects that you can monitor.

7 Click the object that you want to monitor.

■ This area lists the counters you can monitor for your selected object.

8 Click the counter you want to monitor.

■ You can click **Explain** to see a description of the counter.

CONTINUED

SET PERFORMANCE MONITOR

You may need to upgrade or repair your server with new hardware, if the counters are consistently high in comparison to the baseline.

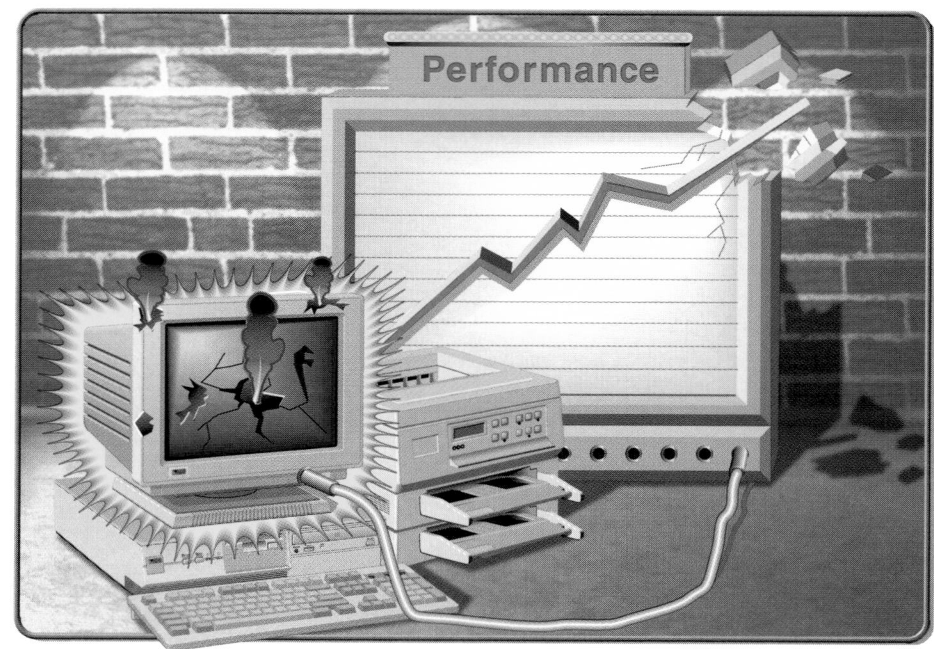

SET PERFORMANCE MONITOR (CONTINUED)

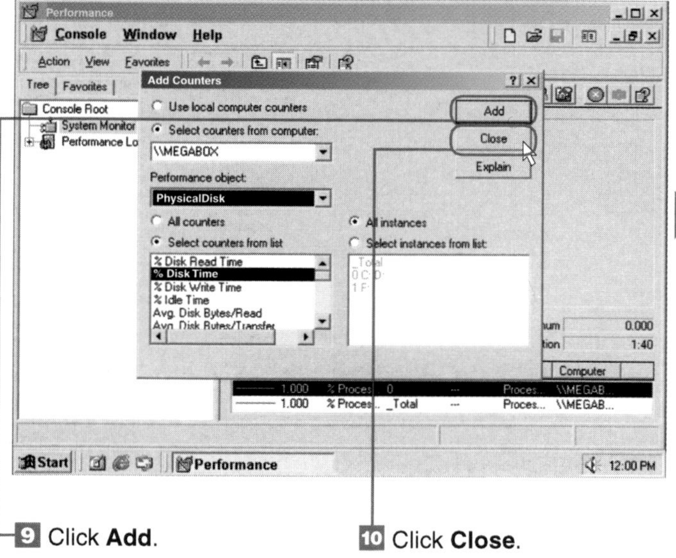

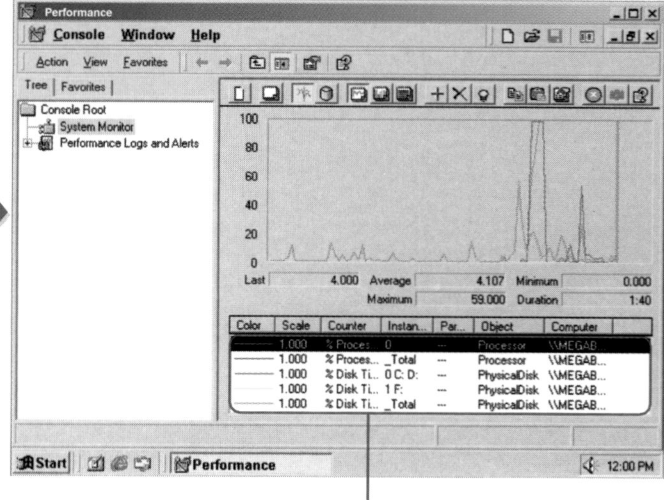

9 Click **Add**.

10 Click **Close**.

Note: To add additional counters to the monitor, repeat steps 6 through 10 for each counter.

■ The object counters appear in the window.

■ This area displays the counters that you are monitoring and the color depicting each in the chart.

Which counters should I monitor?

These two counters provide a basic measurement for server performance.

Object: Processor

Counter: % Processor Time

This counter is a primary indicator of processor activity. If it is consistently over 80%, you should consider upgrading your processor.

Object: Physical Disk

Counter: % Disk Time

This counter measures all hard disk activity. If it is busy more than 90% of the time, you need to add another hard disk or move some applications to another server.

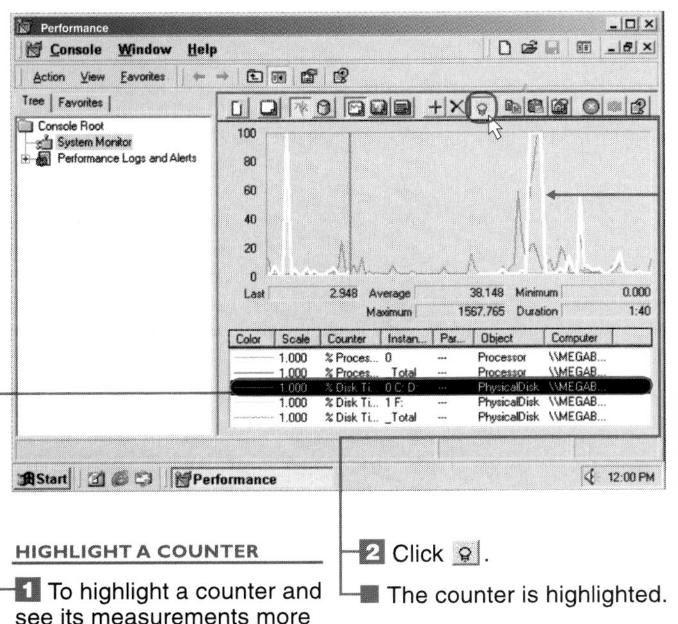

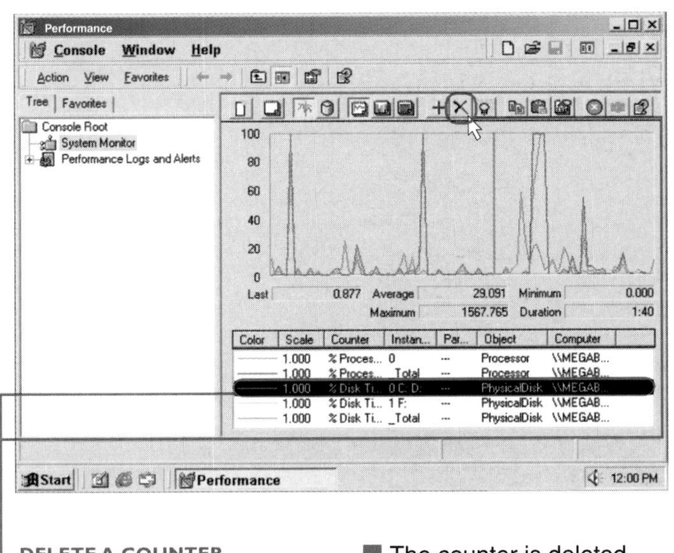

HIGHLIGHT A COUNTER

1 To highlight a counter and see its measurements more clearly, click the counter.

2 Click (highlight icon).

■ The counter is highlighted.

DELETE A COUNTER

1 If you want to remove a counter from the window, click the counter.

2 Click ✕.

■ The counter is deleted from the window.

VIEW EVENTS

You can use the Event Viewer to display the event logs and help diagnose problems with your server.

VIEW EVENTS

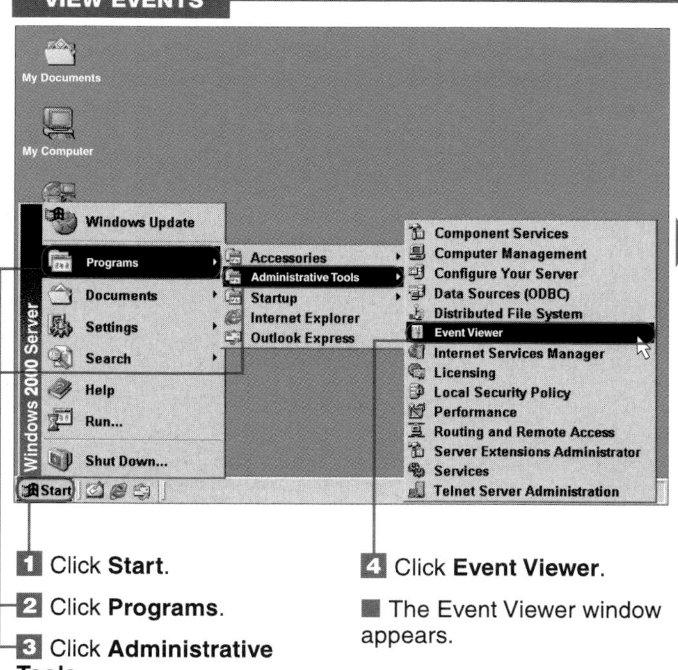

1 Click **Start**.

2 Click **Programs**.

3 Click **Administrative Tools**.

4 Click **Event Viewer**.

■ The Event Viewer window appears.

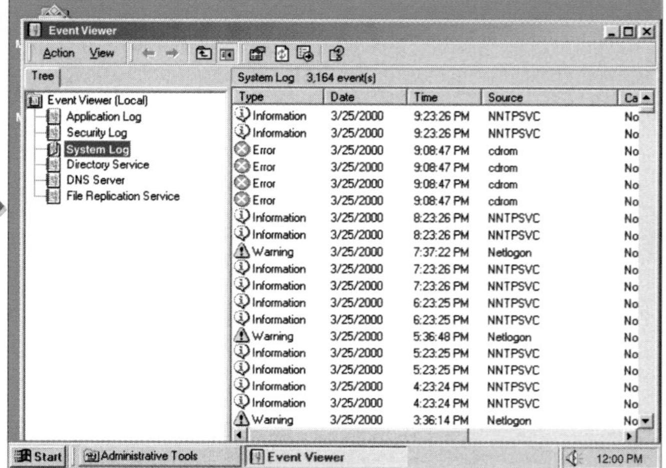

Note: Icons indicate the seriousness of problems with various processes. The ⚠ icon indicates a warning and an ⊗ icon indicates an error.

What type of events can I view?

System

Displays system events, such as services failing to start.

Security

Displays security events, such as successful or failed log on attempts.

Application

Displays application events, such as file backup and restore.

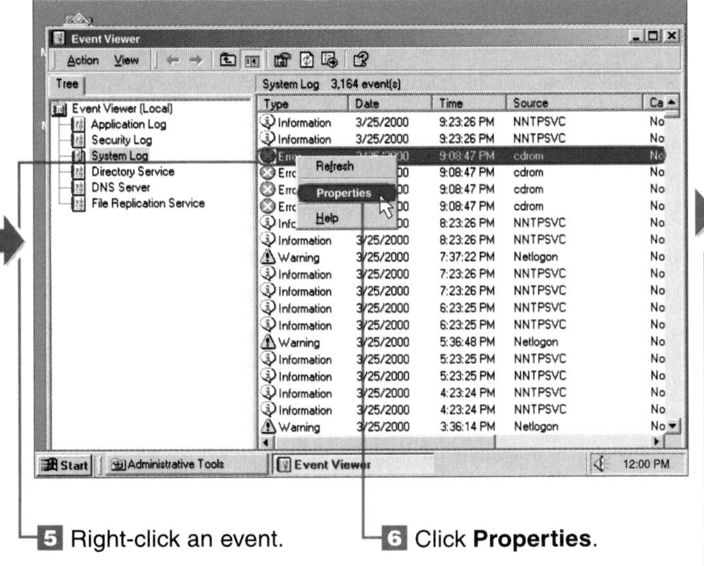

5 Right-click an event.

6 Click **Properties**.

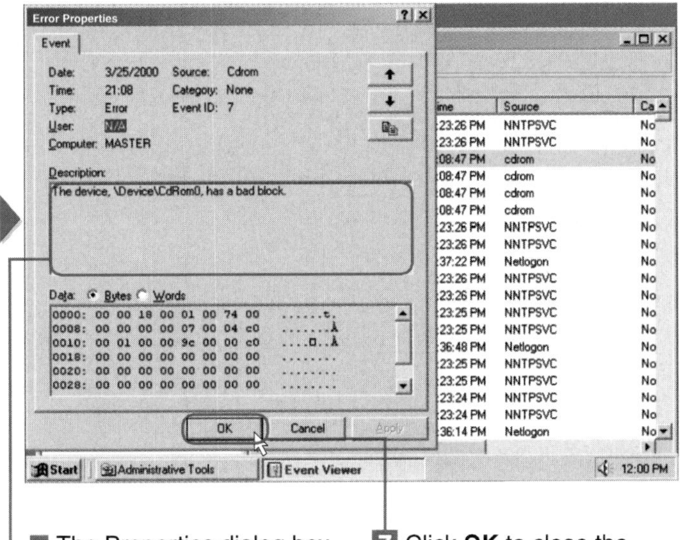

■ The Properties dialog box displays event information.

■ An explanation of error or warning situations appears in this area.

7 Click **OK** to close the Properties dialog box.

VIEW SYSTEM INFORMATION

System Information is a fast way to collect information about your server.

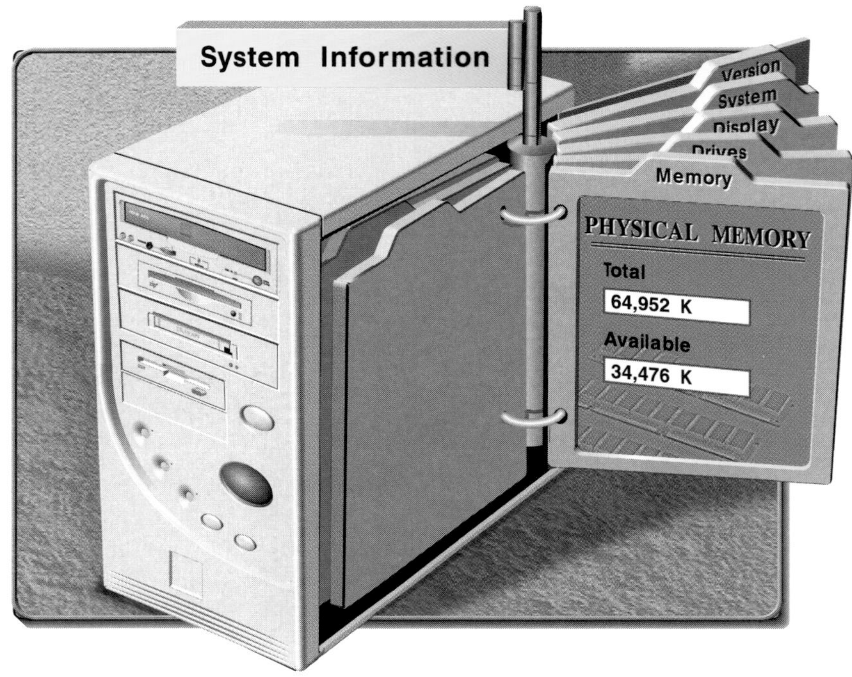

VIEW SYSTEM INFORMATION

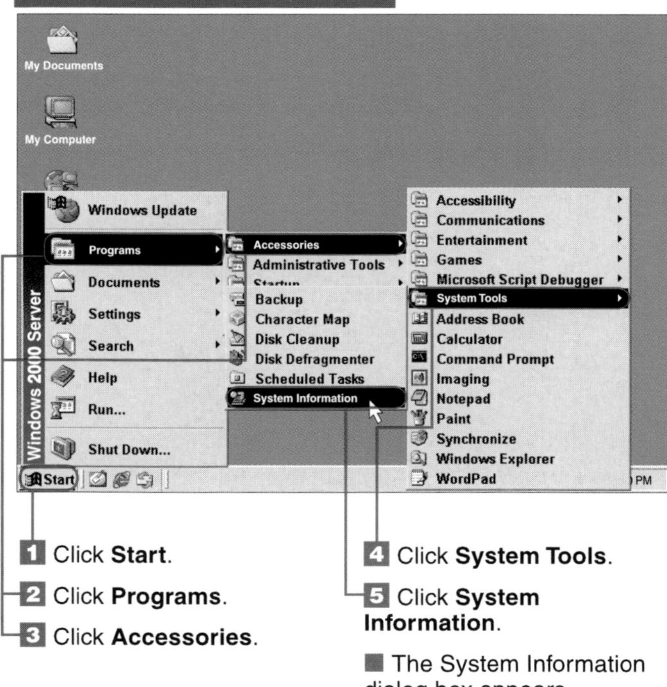

1 Click **Start**.

2 Click **Programs**.

3 Click **Accessories**.

4 Click **System Tools**.

5 Click **System Information**.

■ The System Information dialog box appears.

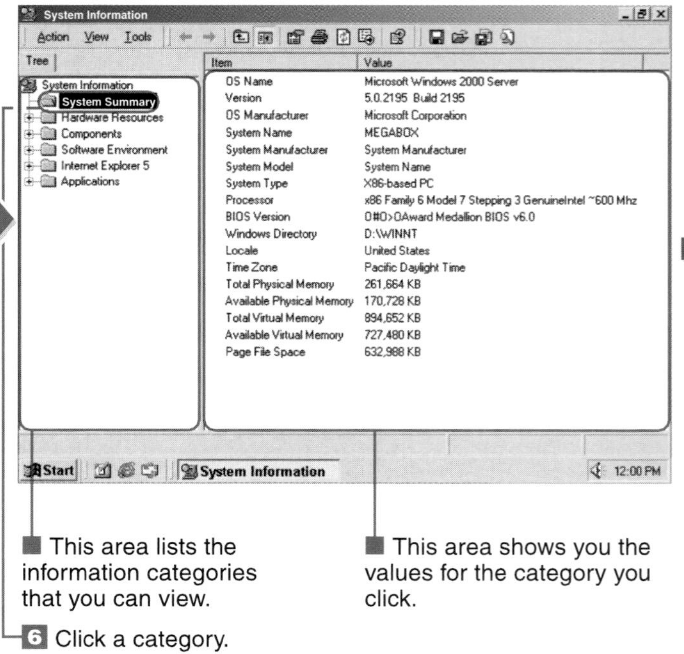

■ This area lists the information categories that you can view.

6 Click a category.

■ This area shows you the values for the category you click.

What information is available about my system?

You can view information about hardware, software, Internet Explorer, and services running on your server.

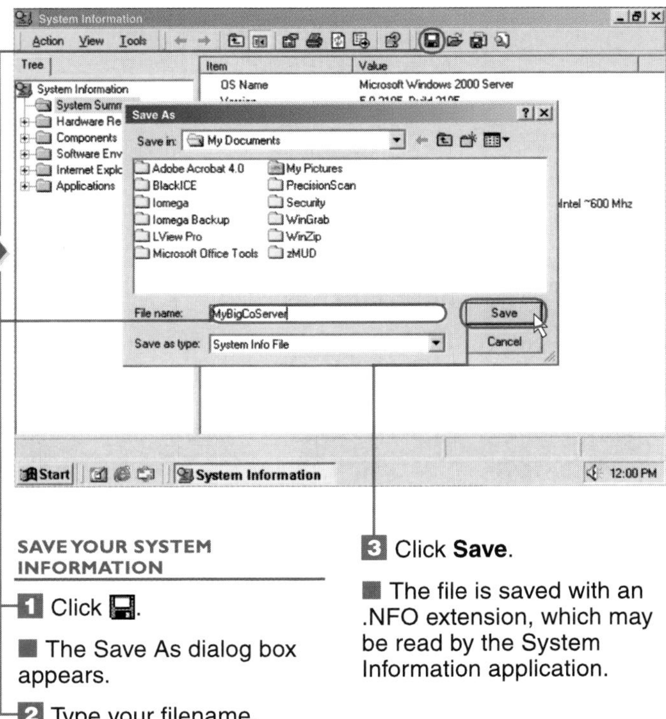

SAVE YOUR SYSTEM INFORMATION

1 Click 💾.

■ The Save As dialog box appears.

2 Type your filename.

3 Click **Save**.

■ The file is saved with an .NFO extension, which may be read by the System Information application.

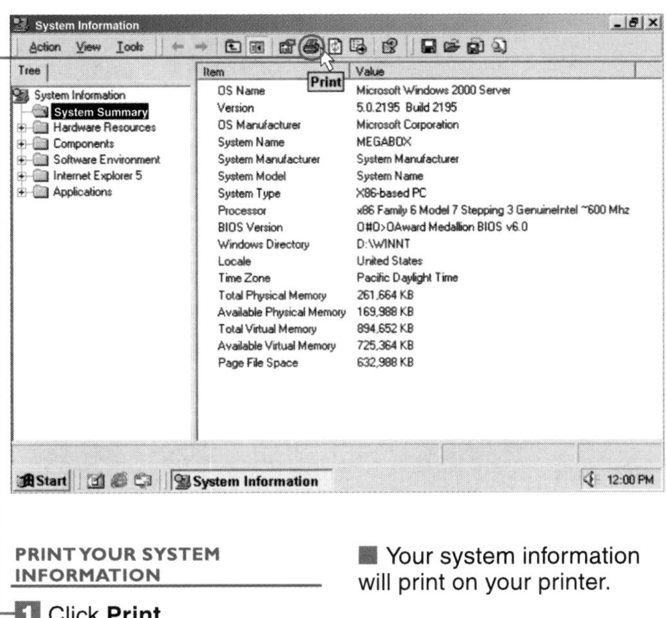

PRINT YOUR SYSTEM INFORMATION

1 Click **Print**.

■ Your system information will print on your printer.

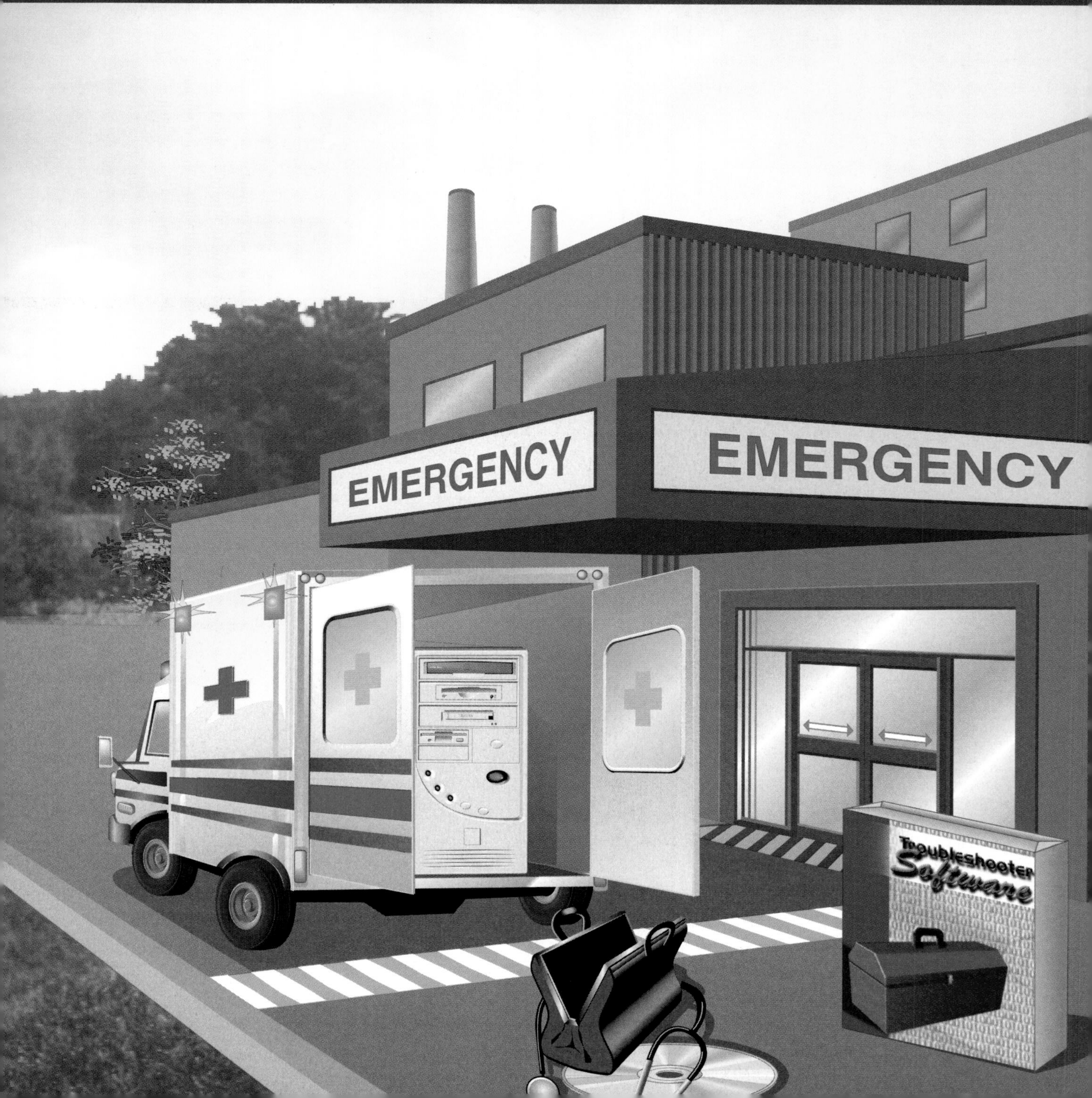

EMERGENCY
EMERGENCY
Troubleshooter
Software

CHAPTER 17

Troubleshooting Your Server

Windows 2000 Server comes with troubleshooters that help you pinpoint problems with your server. This chapter shows you how to use those troubleshooters to get answers for your system.

ACCESS WINDOWS 2000 SERVER TROUBLESHOOTERS

Windows 2000 Server comes with a variety of troubleshooters.

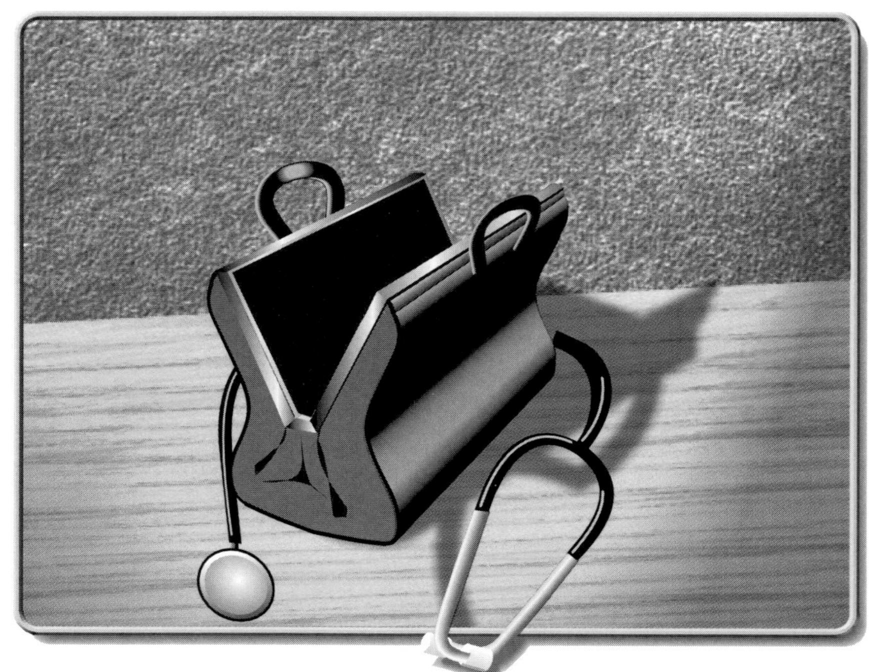

These troubleshooters ask you a series of questions and provide suggestions for solving your problem.

ACCESS WINDOWS 2000 SERVER TROUBLESHOOTERS

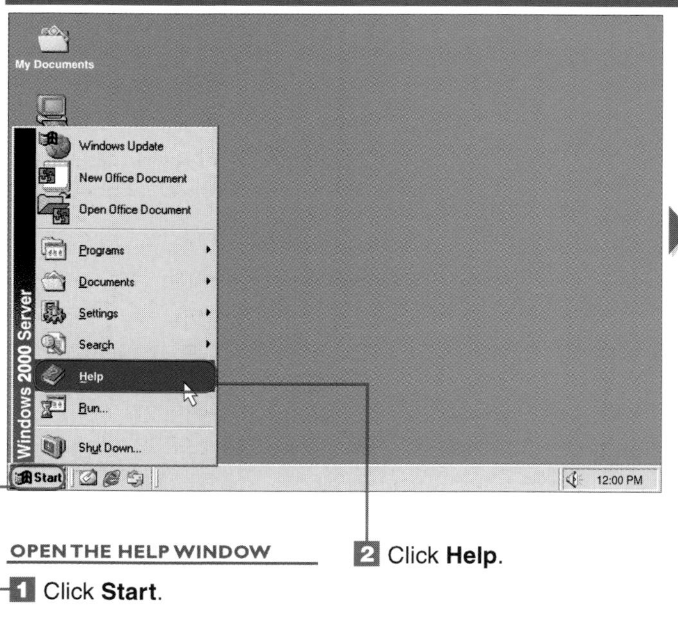

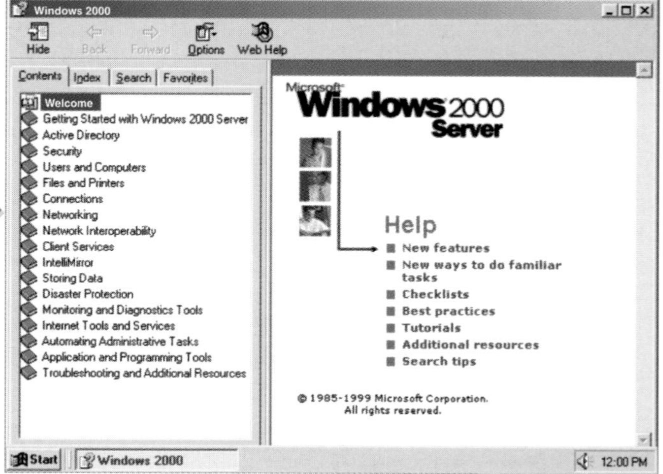

OPEN THE HELP WINDOW

1 Click **Start**.

2 Click **Help**.

■ The Windows 2000 Help window appears.

Can I access troubleshooting information on the Web?

You can access additional troubleshooting information directly from Microsoft's Web site by clicking **WebHelp** on the Windows 2000 Help button bar.

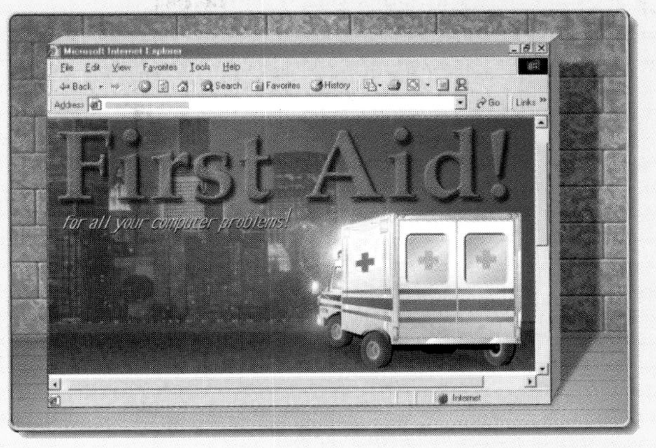

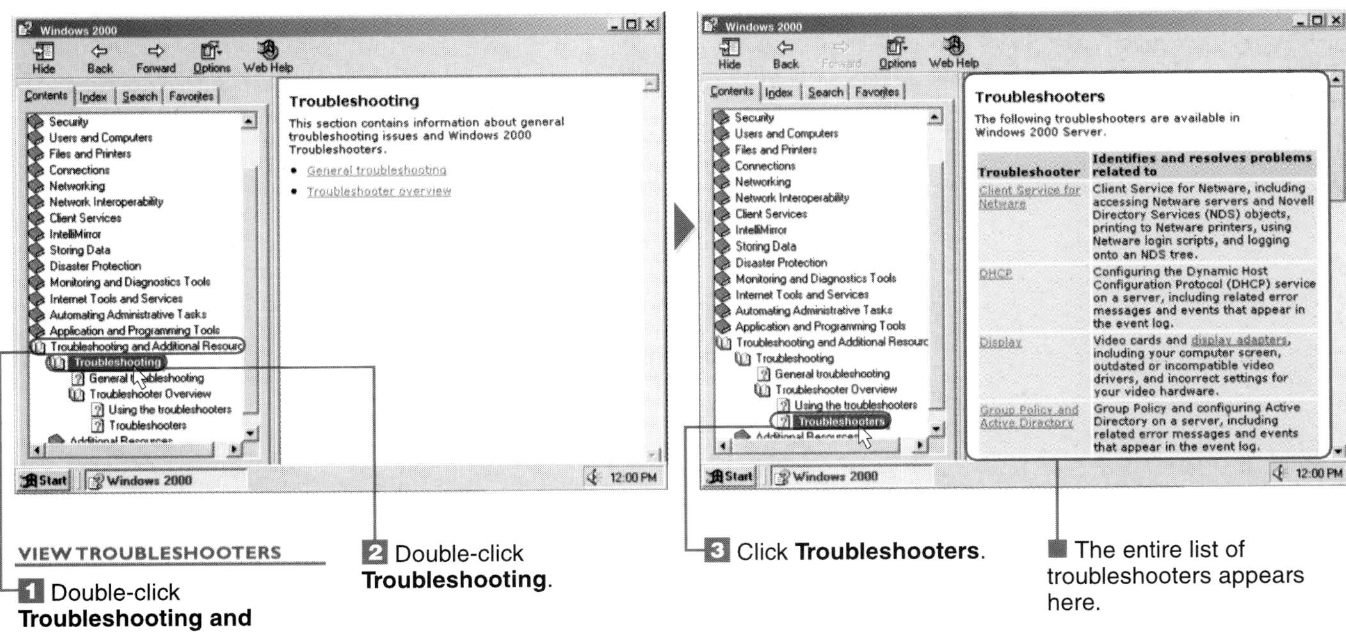

VIEW TROUBLESHOOTERS

1 Double-click **Troubleshooting and Additional Resources**.

2 Double-click **Troubleshooting**.

3 Click **Troubleshooters**.

■ The entire list of troubleshooters appears here.

SOLVE HARDWARE PROBLEMS

The Hardware Troubleshooter provides you with a series of questions about the problem you are having, and each question contains additional information and suggestions to help you solve your problem.

SOLVE HARDWARE PROBLEMS

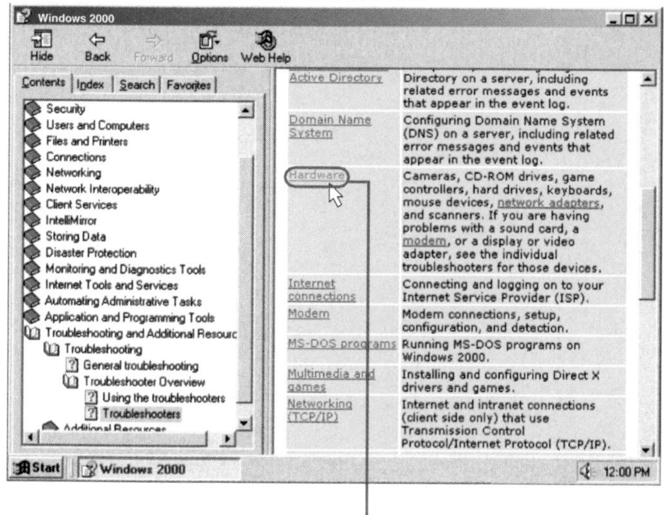

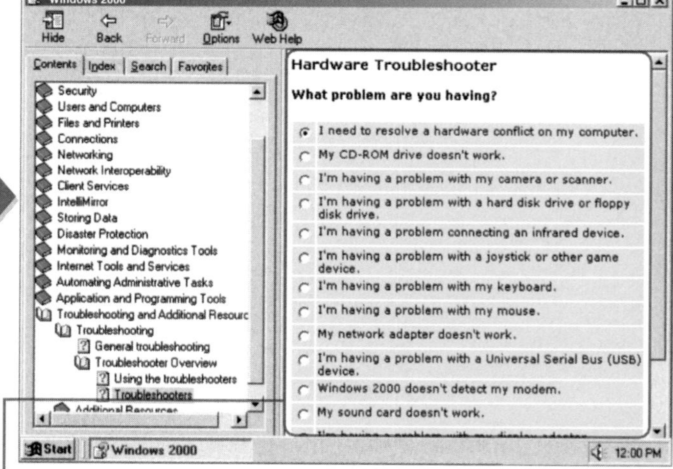

1 Open the Troubleshooters list.

Note: See "Access Windows 2000 Server Troubleshooters" for details.

2 Double-click **Hardware**.

■ The Hardware Troubleshooter appears.

What if none of the Hardware Troubleshooter suggestions help?

You probably have a problem specific to your hardware. Check your hardware manuals, the hardware vendor's Web site, and the Microsoft Web site for help specific to your hardware. (If you have a company IT support desk, you should check with them first.)

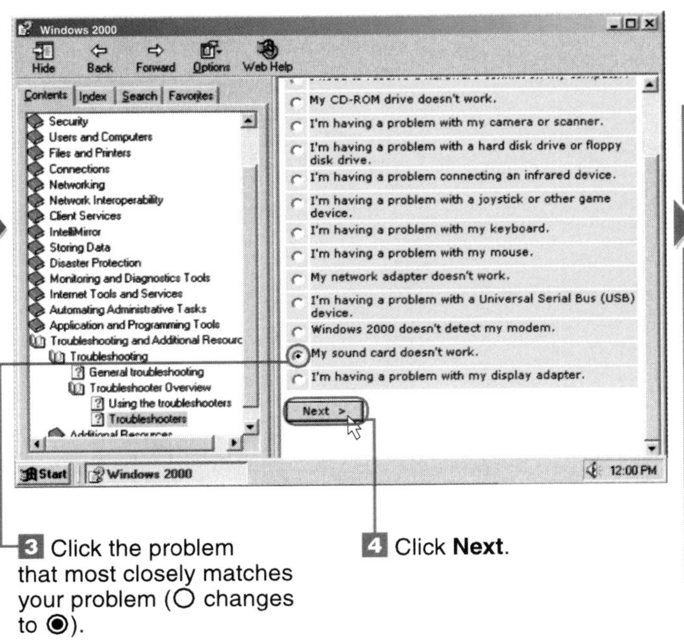

3 Click the problem that most closely matches your problem (○ changes to ◉).

4 Click **Next**.

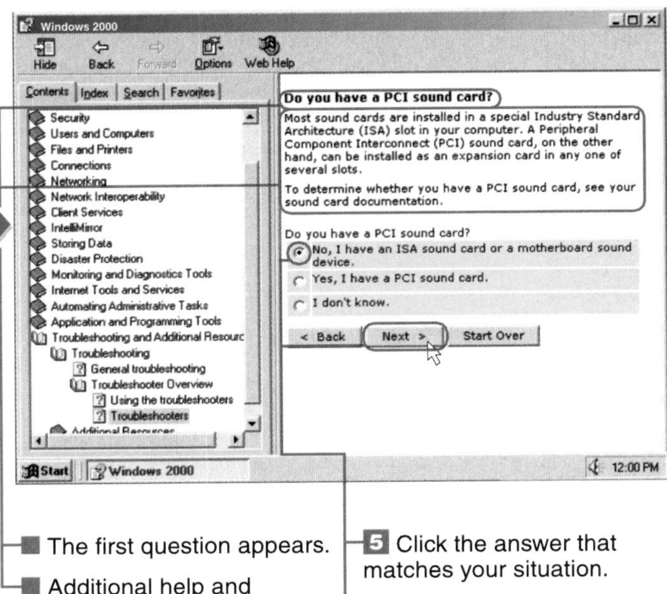

■ The first question appears.

■ Additional help and explanation appears below.

Note: You can back up by clicking ***Back*** *or start over by clicking* ***Start Over****.*

5 Click the answer that matches your situation.

6 Click **Next**.

■ Repeat steps 5 and 6 until the troubleshooter prescribes a solution.

Windows 2000 Server contains a wide variety of software troubleshooters to help you solve your particular problems with getting software to work correctly.

If you have a general software problem, chances are good that Windows 2000 Server provides a troubleshooter for it.

SOLVE SOFTWARE PROBLEMS

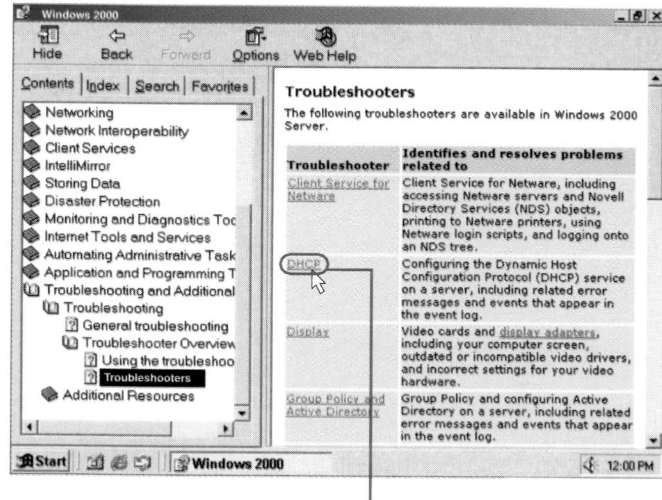

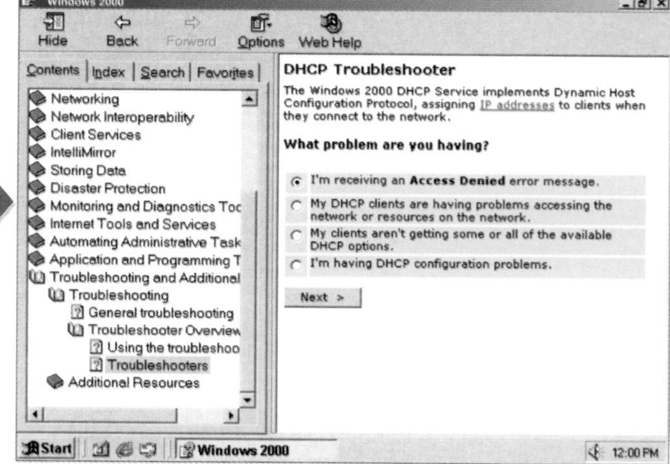

1 Open the Troubleshooters list.

Note: See "Access Windows 2000 Server Troubleshooters" for details.

2 Click the software troubleshooter you need (example: **DHCP**).

■ The DHCP Troubleshooter appears.

When I run a software troubleshooter, I do not see my problem. What should I do?

If you don't see the specific problem you're having in the troubleshooter, then you should contact the company that produced the software for support and any other information you could use to fix your problem.

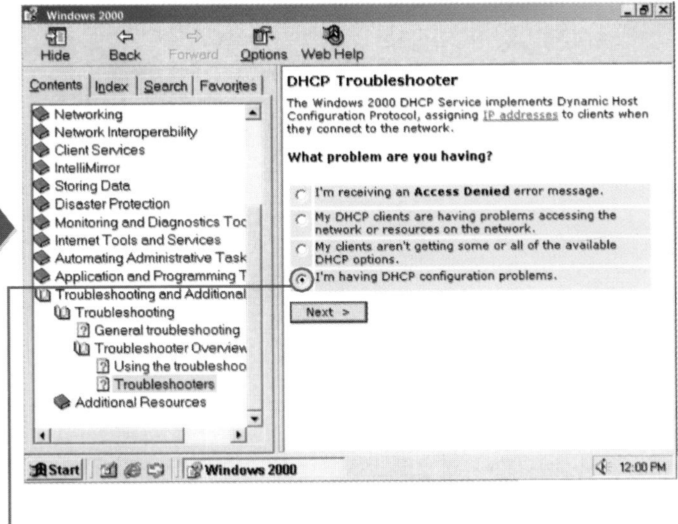

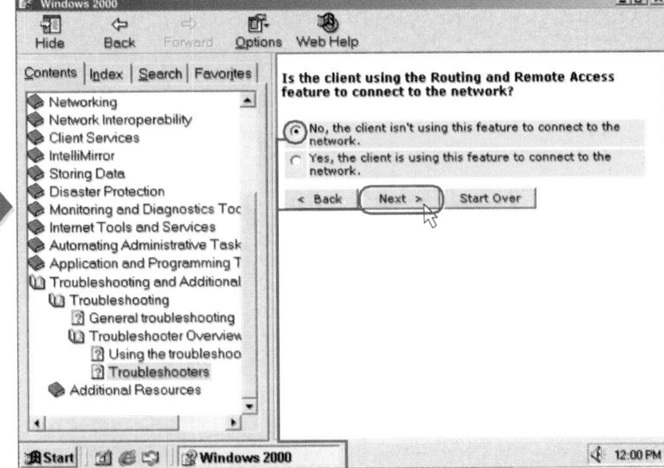

3 Click the problem that most closely matches your problem (○ changes to ◉).

4 Click **Next**.

■ The first question appears.

■ Additional help and explanation appears below.

5 Click the answer that matches your situation.

6 Click **Next**.

■ Repeat steps 5 and 6 until the troubleshooter prescribes a solution.

USING NETWORK TROUBLESHOOTERS

You can choose from a variety of network troubleshooters if you find that you are having networking problems.

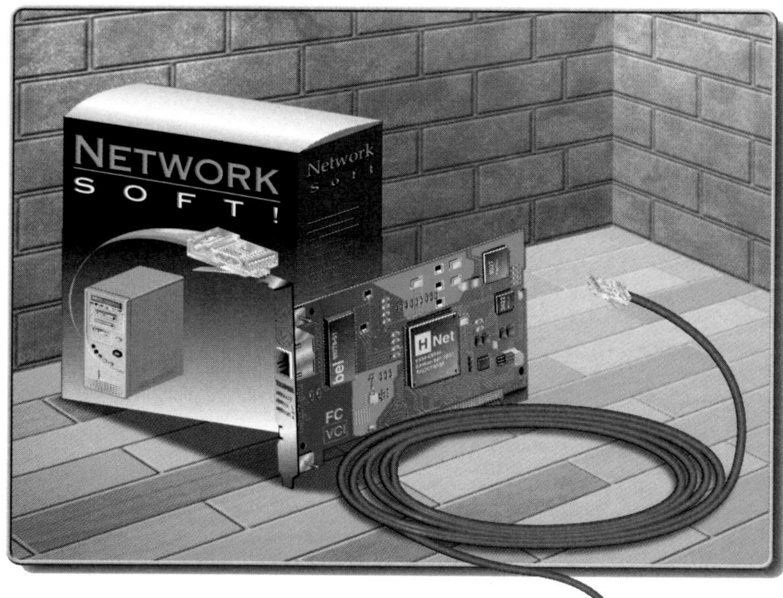

These network troubleshooters provide error messages and suggestions for solving your problems so you can diagnose the most common networking problems.

USING NETWORK TROUBLESHOOTERS

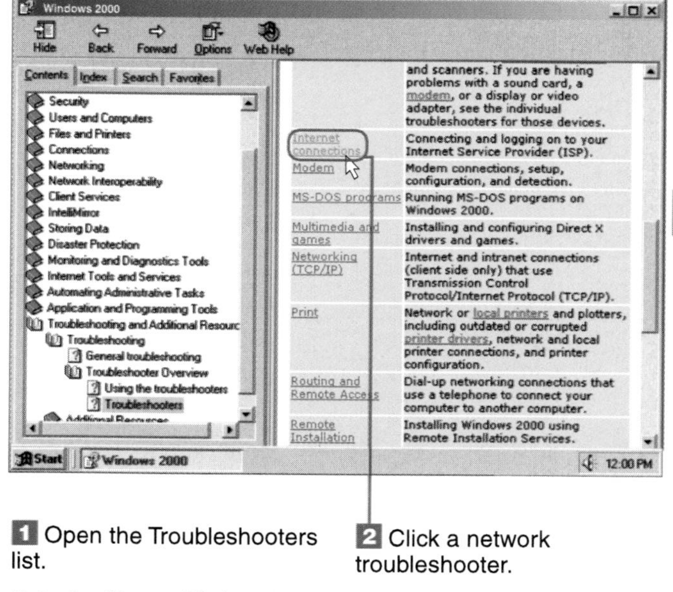

1 Open the Troubleshooters list.

Note: See "Access Windows 2000 Server Troubleshooters" for details.

2 Click a network troubleshooter.

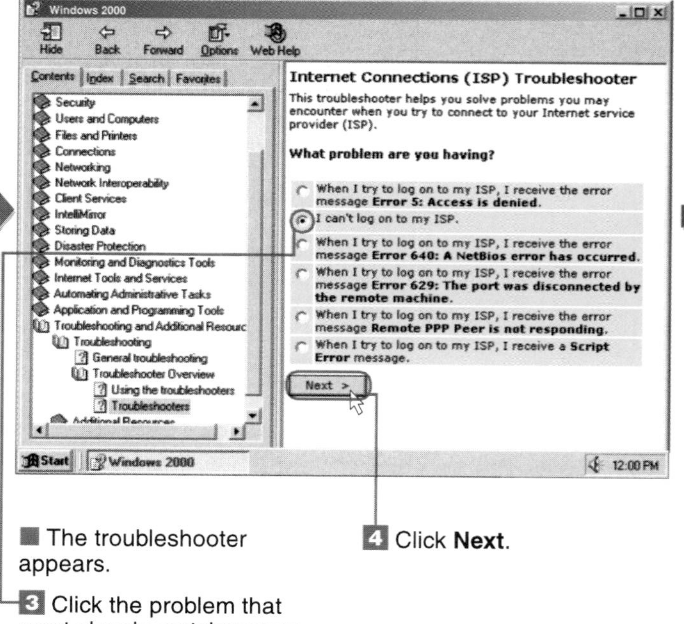

■ The troubleshooter appears.

3 Click the problem that most closely matches your problem.

4 Click **Next**.

What should I do if the troubleshooter cannot fix my Internet connection?

If the troubleshooter cannot solve your Internet connection problems, contact your Internet service provider (ISP) for assistance. Be sure to write down exactly what you have done to solve the problem before calling your ISP.

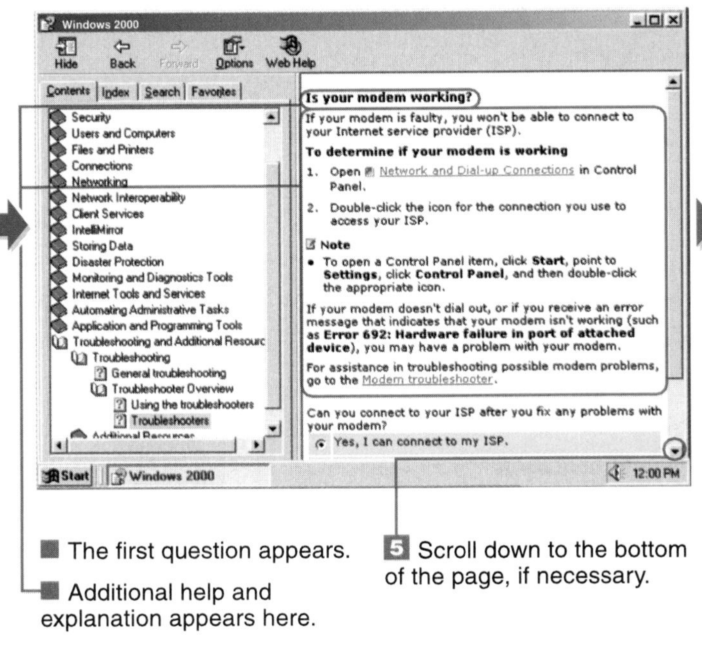

- The first question appears.
- Additional help and explanation appears here.

5 Scroll down to the bottom of the page, if necessary.

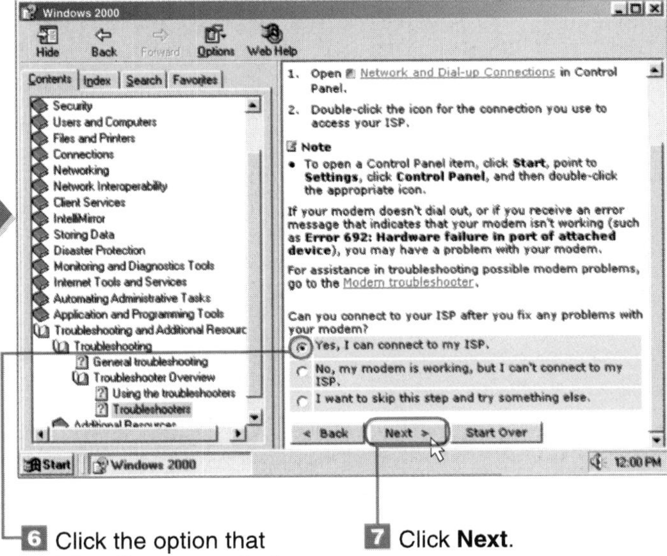

6 Click the option that matches the answer to the question.

*Note: You can go back by clicking **Back** or start over by clicking **Start Over**.*

7 Click **Next**.

8 Repeat steps 6 and 7 until the troubleshooter prescribes a solution.

FIND ADDITIONAL RESOURCES

The most immediate type of help you can get is through documentation. *Teach Yourself VISUALLY Windows 2000 Server* provides a great way to get started, but Windows 2000 also provides additional resources for you to use.

FIND ADDITIONAL RESOURCES

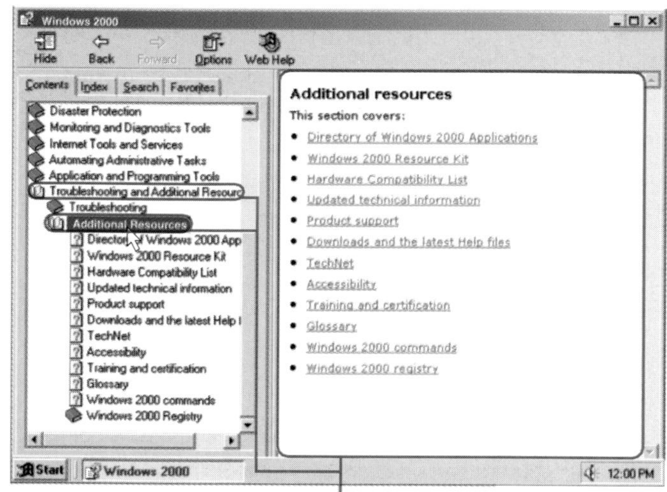

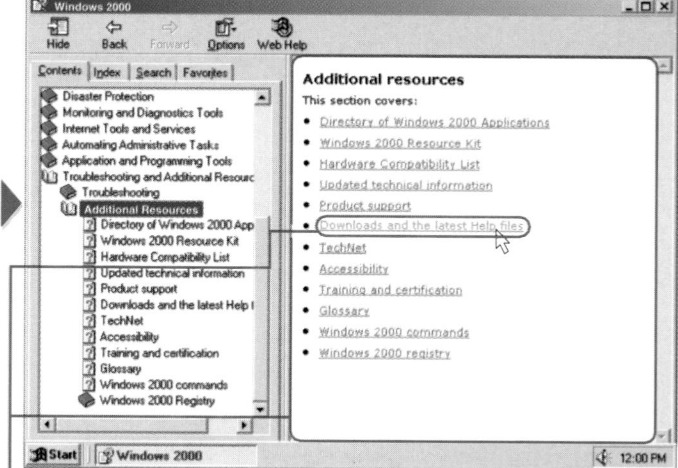

DOWNLOAD A HELP FILE

1 Open the Windows 2000 Help window.

Note: See the first task in "Access Windows 2000 Server Troubleshooters" for instructions.

2 Double-click **Troubleshooting and Additional Resources**.

3 Double-click **Additional Resources**.

■ The Additional Resources page appears.

4 Click **Downloads and the latest Help files**.

■ The downloads and help files information appears here.

5 Click a file to download it from the Internet.

How can I get additional help from Microsoft?

You can choose from the following support methods from Microsoft:

TechNet Web site
www. microsoft.com/technet/ default.asp is a free service that contains listings of known problems, software patches, and up-to-date product information.

Telephone support
In the US and Canada, is available at (800) 936-4900. You will be charged a $245 fee per call for using these services.

Microsoft Special Support programs
support. microsoft.com/directory/ overview.asp is a subscription service requiring that you pay a fee.

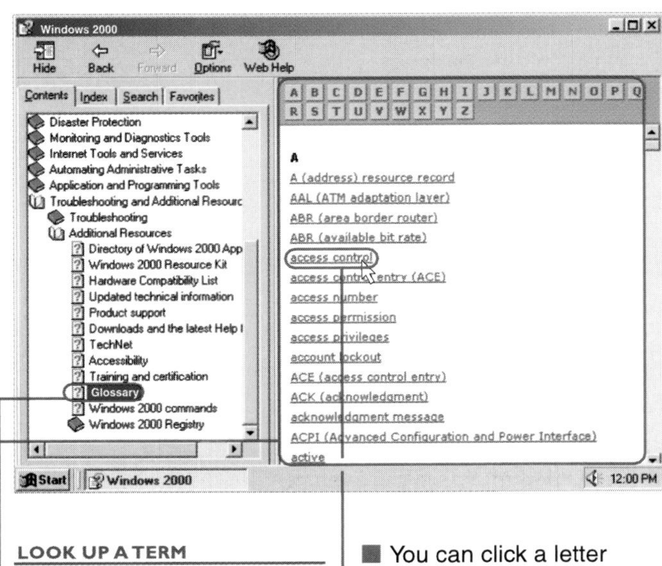

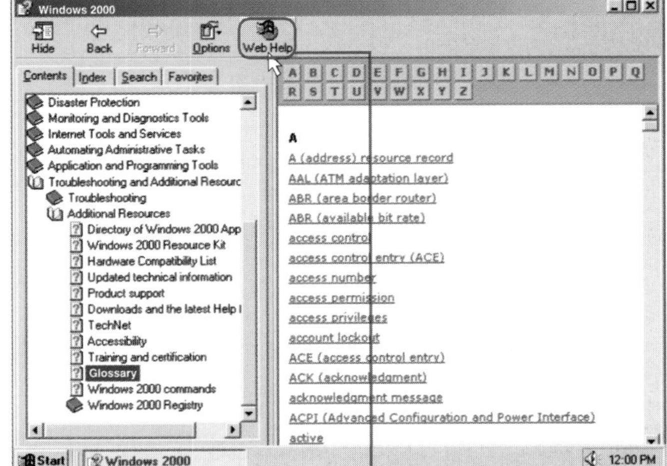

LOOK UP A TERM

1 Perform steps 1 through 3 of the task on the opposite page.

2 Click **Glossary**.

■ The glossary appears.

■ You can click a letter button (example: A) to go to that section of the alphabet.

3 Click on a term to see its definition (example: **access control**).

GET HELP FROM THE WEB

1 Open the Windows 2000 Help window.

Note: See the first task of "Access Windows 2000 Server Troubleshooters" for details.

2 Click **Web Help**.

■ Windows will dial your Internet connection and take you to the Windows 2000 Help Web page.

My Computer
Network Neighborhood
Inbox
Internet Explorer
Recycle Bin
My Briefcase
Start
DECEMBER
S M T W T F S
1 2 3 4 5 6
7 8 9 10 11 12 13
14 15 16 17 18 19 20
21 22 23 24 25 26 27
28 29 30 31
Windows 2000

Installing Windows 2000 Server

This appendix shows you how to install Windows 2000 Server or upgrade to Windows 2000 Server from an earlier version of Windows.

Before you install Windows 2000 Server, you need to determine if your system meets the minimum hardware requirements.

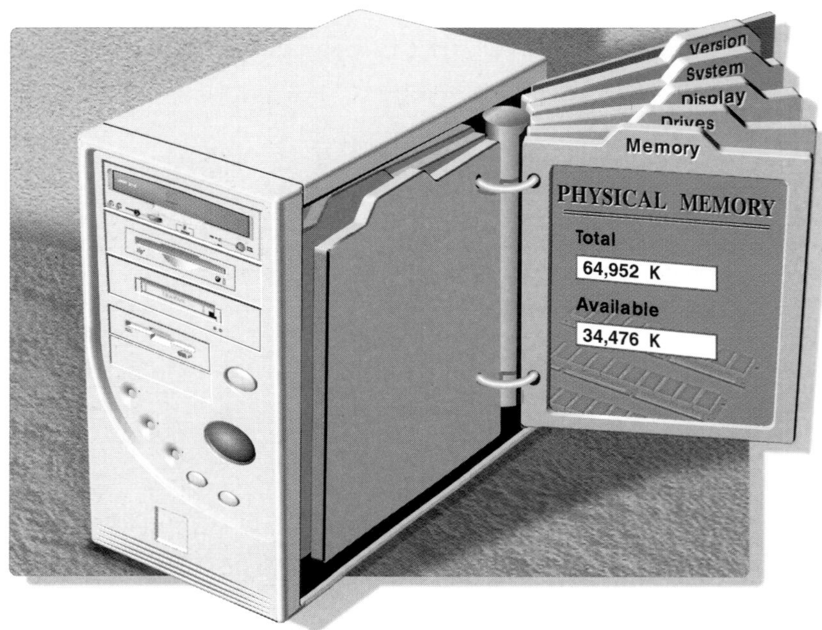

PENTIUM-CLASS PROCESSOR

At a minimum, you will need a Pentium processor that runs at 133 MHz or greater. You will get better performance if you invest in a processor running at 300 MHz or greater.

RANDOM ACCESS MEMORY (RAM)

Windows 2000 Server requires a minimum of 128 megabytes of RAM. However, you will get much better performance if you have at least 256 megabytes of RAM in your server.

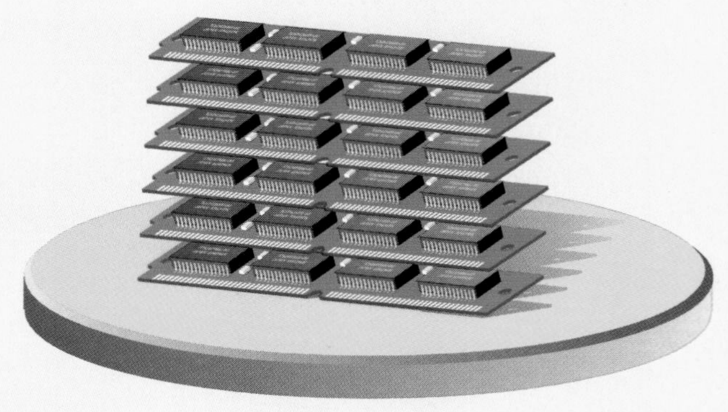

HARD DISK SPACE

You should plan on having at least 1 gigabyte (GB) of free disk space before you install Windows 2000 Server. You can free up space by backing up files to a tape drive; you can restore them after you have finished your installation.

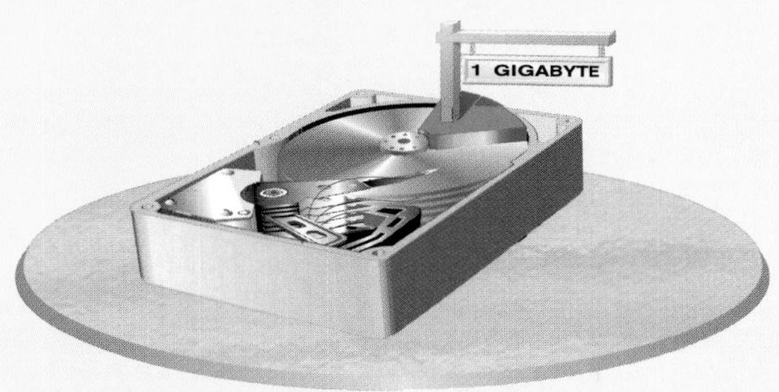

CD-ROM DRIVE

A CD-ROM drive is a necessity for server installations and is used to get files from your setup disk onto your hard drive.

ALL HARDWARE ON HCL

All hardware — disk drives, network cards, video adapters, modems, and so on — must be on the Hardware Compatibility List (HCL). The most up-to-date list can be found at www.microsoft.com/hwtest/hcl/.

BOOT FROM CD-ROM (OPTIONAL)

If you have a newer computer with an up-to-date BIOS, you can boot from your CD-ROM drive. Check with your server manufacturer to see if this is available.

CHECK YOUR OS VERSION

Before you install Windows 2000 Server, you must determine whether you can upgrade your current version of Windows to Windows 2000 Server.

If you don't have another operating system on your server, you can skip this task.

CHECK YOUR OS VERSION

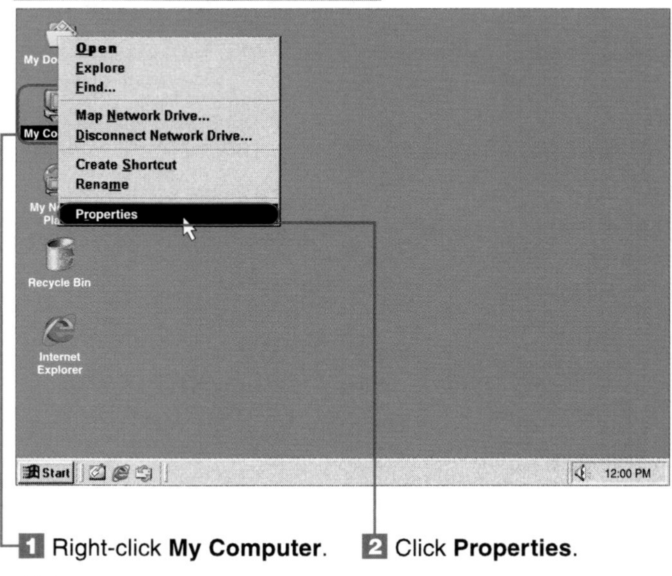

1 Right-click **My Computer**.

■ A pop-up menu appears.

2 Click **Properties**.

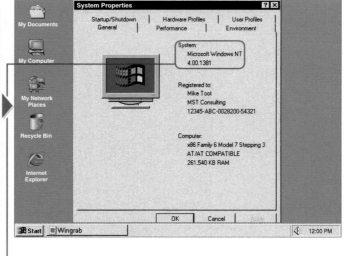

■ The System Properties dialog box appears.

■ The operating system version is listed here.

Note: You can also watch your computer boot; a splash screen appears showing you which OS you are using.

DECIDE WHETHER YOU CAN UPGRADE

WINDOWS 9X OR WINDOWS NT WORKSTATION 4.0

You cannot upgrade to Windows 2000 Server, nor will you be able to keep any applications or data. You will need to do a clean install on your server.

WINDOWS NT SERVER 4.0

You can upgrade your Windows NT Server 4.0. The installation process takes care of converting all your files and security settings to Windows 2000 Server.

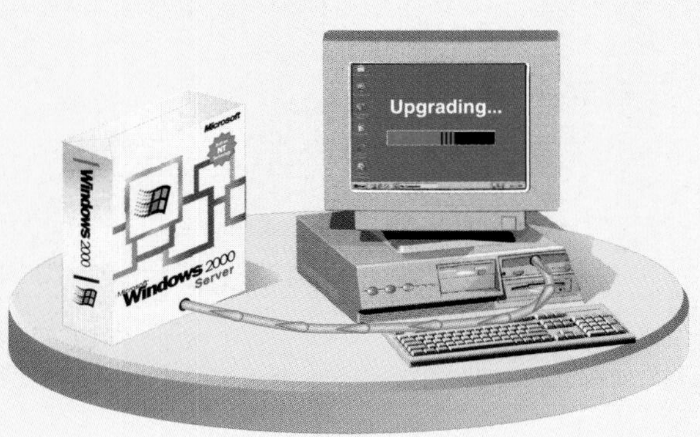

Windows 2000 Server works best with hardware and software that meets Microsoft's design requirements. A list of approved software and hardware is available at www.microsoft.com/windows2000/upgrade/compat/default.asp.

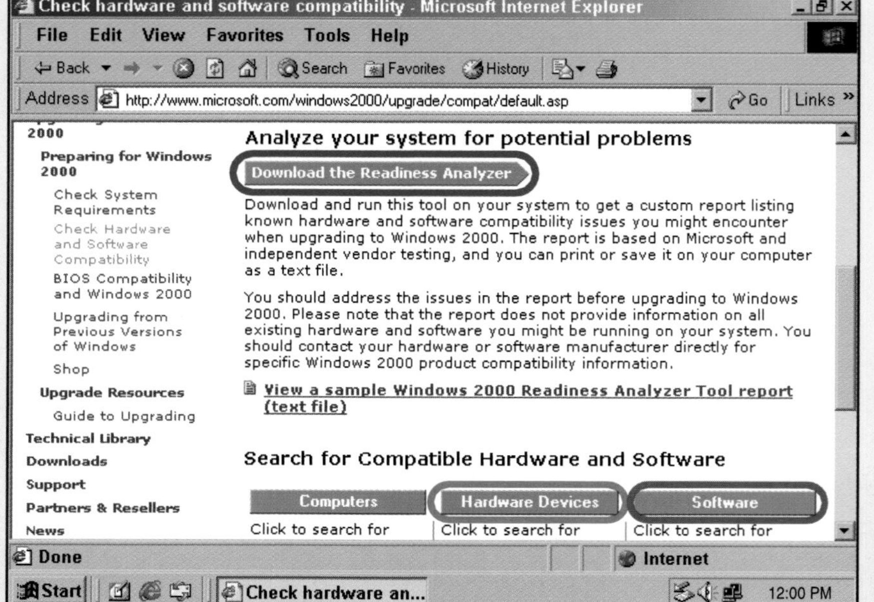

Although you can sometimes use older hardware and software, you should plan on collecting hardware and software that is approved before you install Windows 2000.

Download the Readiness Analyzer

The Readiness Analyzer is a program that you can download and run on your Windows system to check whether existing hardware and softward components are compatible with Windows 2000.

Check Hardware Compatibility

This section lets you search for compatible hardware.
You should also check the vendor's home page to see if any new updates or drivers are available for your hardware.

Check Software Compatibility

The Software Compatibility section lets you search for software that will run on Windows 2000.
You should also check the vendor's home page for new versions or product updates that will work with Windows 2000.

PREPARE YOUR SERVER

Before you install Windows 2000 Server, you need to prepare your computer based on the information from the previous tasks.

BACK UP DATA

If you are upgrading from another operating system, you should back up any data that is needed to run your business. Use a backup program or copy files to another computer, hard disk, tape backup, or floppy disk.

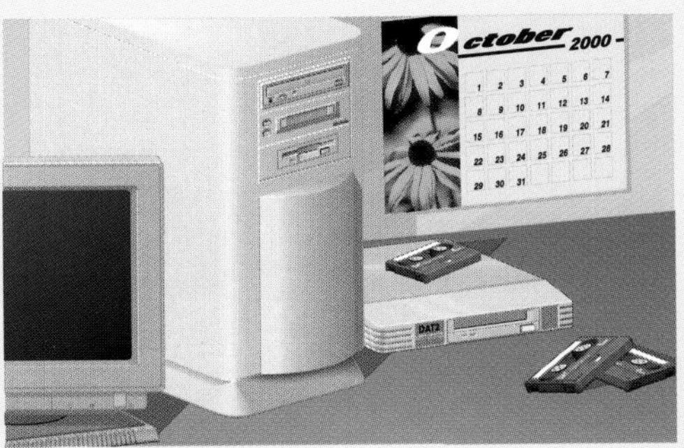

INSTALL NEW HARDWARE

Install any new hardware that you will use in your new server. Follow the manufacturer's instructions to install new hardware.

Warning: Make sure that the power is off before installing hardware. If you are not comfortable doing this, consult a computer professional.

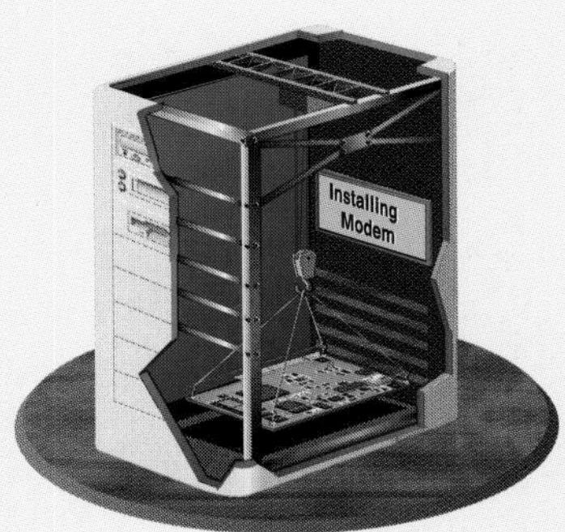

RUN THE SETUP PROGRAM

Windows 2000 Server takes you step by step through the installation process so installing Windows is as painless as possible.

You can start Setup in four different ways, depending on whether you are upgrading or performing a clean install.

RUN THE SETUP PROGRAM

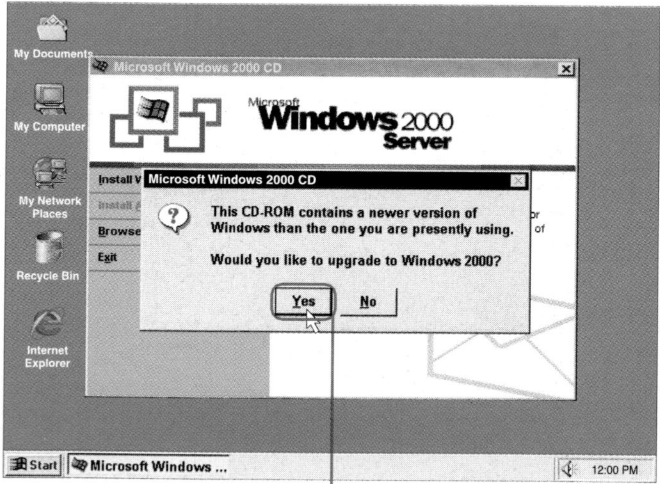

RUN SETUP TO UPGRADE YOUR CURRENT OS

1 Insert the Windows 2000 Server CD-ROM in your CD drive.

■ The Microsoft Windows 2000 CD dialog box appears.

2 Click **Yes**.

■ The installation process begins.

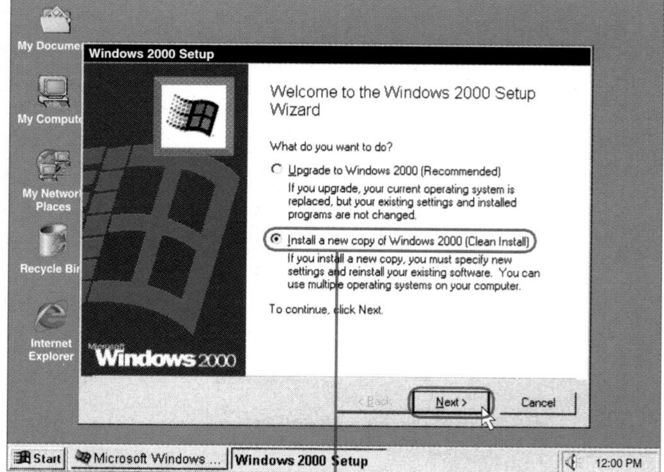

RUN SETUP TO INSTALL A NEW OS

1 Insert the Windows 2000 Server CD-ROM in your CD drive.

■ The Microsoft Windows 2000 Setup window appears.

2 Click **Install a new copy of Windows 2000 (Clean Install)**. ○ changes to ◉.

3 Click **Next**.

■ The installation process begins.

What if I can't find the boot disks that came with my copy of Windows 2000 Server?

You can make new boot disks using the Windows 2000 Server CD. See Chapter 14 for instructions on making boot disks.

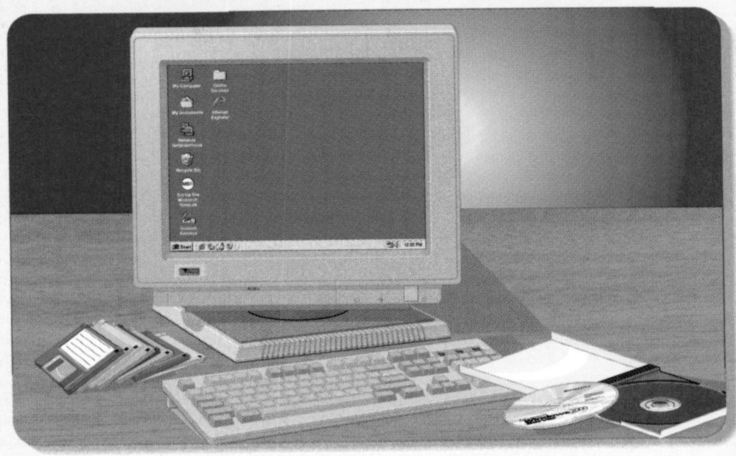

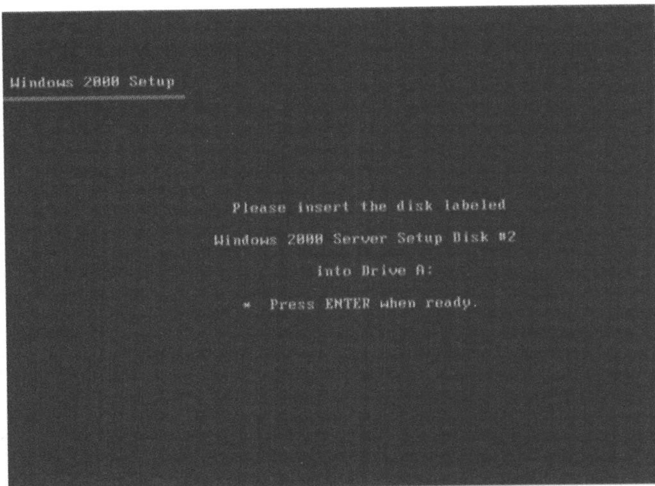

Windows 2000 Server Setup

Welcome to Setup.

This portion of the Setup program prepares Microsoft(R) Windows 2000(TM) to run on your computer.

- To set up Windows 2000 now, press ENTER.
- To repair a Windows 2000 installation, press R.
- To quit Setup without installing Windows 2000, press F3.

ENTER=Continue R=Repair F3=Quit

RUN SETUP FROM THE BOOT DISKS

1 Shut down your computer.

2 Insert Boot Disk #1 in your diskette drive.

3 Turn on your computer.

4 Insert each boot disk and the Windows 2000 Server CD-ROM when instructed and press Enter.

RUN SETUP FROM THE CD-ROM

1 Shut down your computer.

2 Turn on your computer.

3 Immediately insert the Windows 2000 Server CD-ROM into your server.

■ The installation process begins.

Note: Your computer BIOS must support booting from CD to use this method. Check with your manufacturer to see if this is available on your computer.

ACCEPT THE LICENSE AGREEMENT

The Windows 2000 License Agreement contains the terms for your software. Read the license carefully to see how it affects your use of the software.

ACCEPT THE LICENSE AGREEMENT

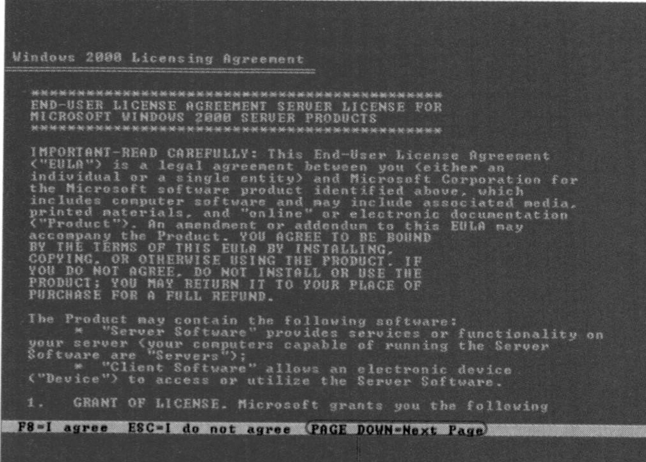

■ After starting the Setup process, the Windows 2000 License Agreement appears.

1 Press Pg Dn until you get to the end of the license agreement.

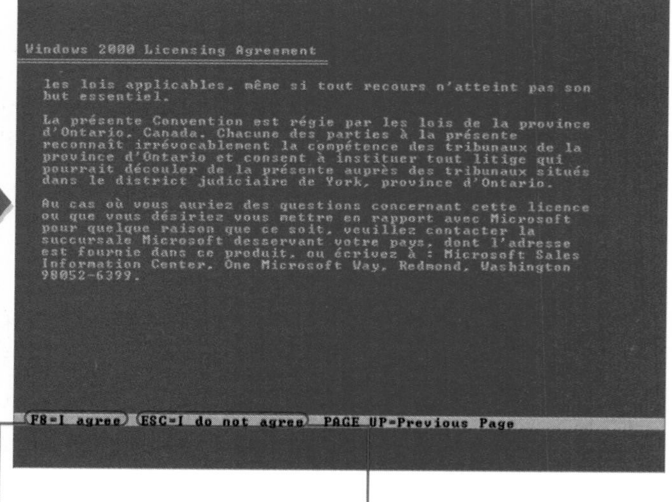

2 Press F8.

■ If you do not agree to the terms, press Esc and the Setup program will quit.

IDENTIFY LICENSING OPTIONS

You need the correct number and types of licenses to get licensed properly. For example, if five Windows workstations connect to a server, you will need a server license, five workstation licenses, and five client access licenses.

SERVER LICENSE

You will need a license for each server you run on a network. The server license allows you to run the software on a single machine only.

WORKSTATION LICENSE

Each workstation will need a license for its operating system. You must have the correct license for each machine; a Windows 9*x* license does not allow you to run Windows 2000 Professional.

CLIENT ACCESS LICENSE

Client Access Licenses allow you to connect workstations to servers. These licenses grant permission to connect to network-based servers or resources.

CREATE THE INSTALL PARTITION

After you agree to the license terms, you need to create the install partition for Windows 2000.

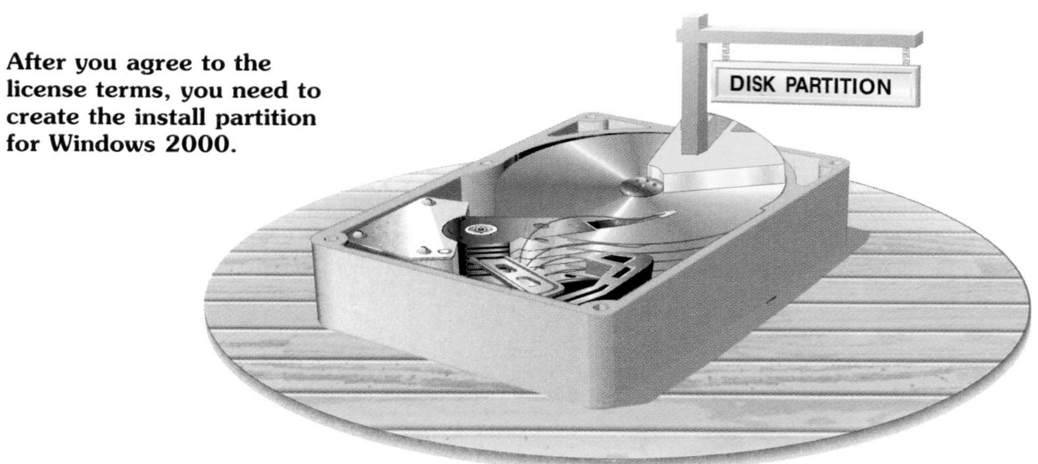

An install partition is an area on the hard disk with enough space for your software.

CREATE THE INSTALL PARTITION

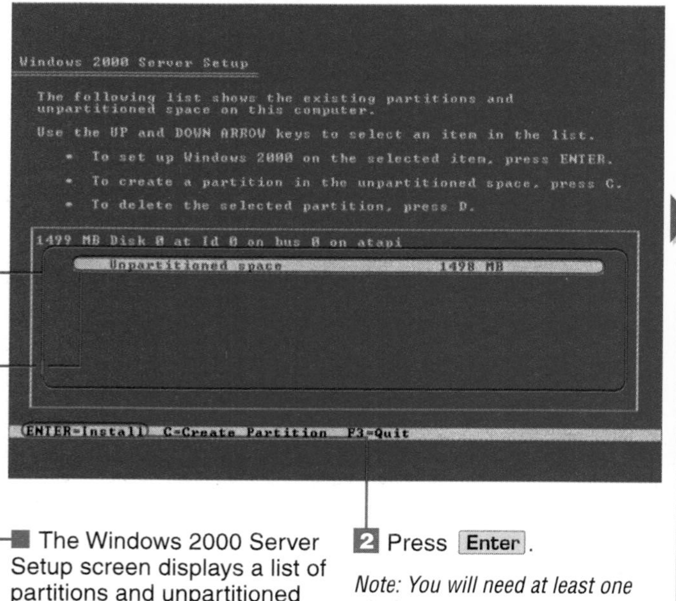

Windows 2000 Server Setup
The following list shows the existing partitions and unpartitioned space on this computer.
Use the UP and DOWN ARROW keys to select an item in the list.
• To set up Windows 2000 on the selected item, press ENTER.
• To create a partition in the unpartitioned space, press C.
• To delete the selected partition, press D.
1499 MB Disk 0 at Id 0 on bus 0 on atapi
Unpartitioned space 1498 MB
ENTER=Install C=Create Partition F3=Quit

■ The Windows 2000 Server Setup screen displays a list of partitions and unpartitioned space on your hard drive.

1 Press ↑ or ↓ to highlight a partition.

2 Press Enter.

Note: You will need at least one gigabyte (1000MB) of free space in a partition.

Windows 2000 Server Setup

A new partition for Windows 2000 has been created on

1499 MB Disk 0 at Id 0 on bus 0 on atapi.

This partition must now be formatted.

From the list below, select a file system for the new partition. Use the UP and DOWN ARROW keys to select the file system you want, and then press ENTER.

If you want to select a different partition for Windows 2000, press ESC.

Format the partition using the NTFS file system
Format the partition using the FAT file system

ENTER=Continue ESC=Cancel

■ The partition format window appears.

3 Press ↑ or ↓ to highlight a formatting option.

Note: NTFS is recommended if you want to use file and folder security, file encryption, and advanced management features.

4 Press Enter.

Can I have more than one partition on my hard drive?

Yes, as long as you leave enough room in each partition for the software and data you expect to have. A common partition scheme is to have your operating system and programs in one partition, and your application data in another partition.

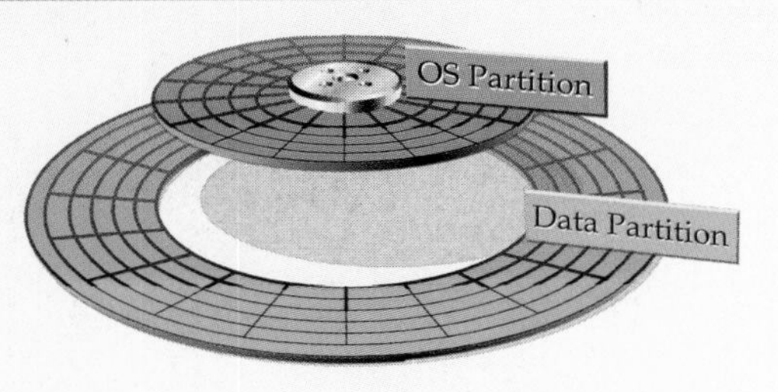

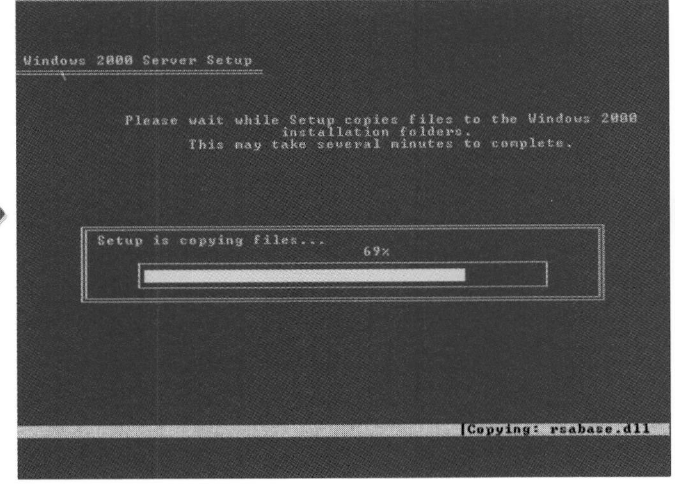

■ The Setup program copies files to your hard drive.

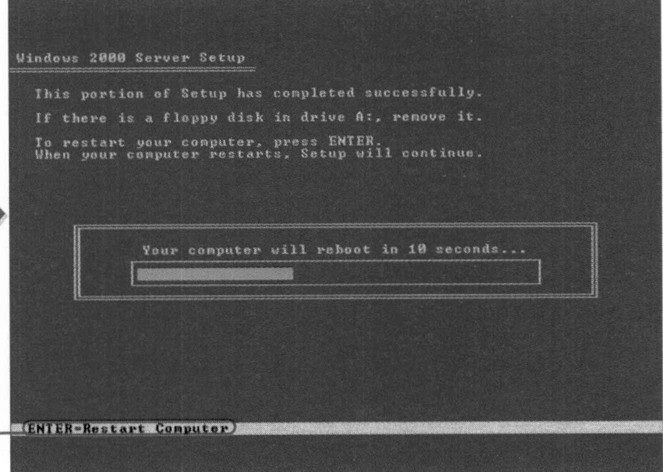

5 When file copying is complete, press Enter to reboot your computer.

■ The server will automatically reboot after 10 seconds.

DETECT HARDWARE DEVICES

After copying your setup files, the Setup program restarts in graphical mode and detects your server's hardware.

DETECT HARDWARE DEVICES

■ The server starts in graphical mode.

■ The Welcome to the Setup Wizard dialog box appears.

1 Click **Next**.

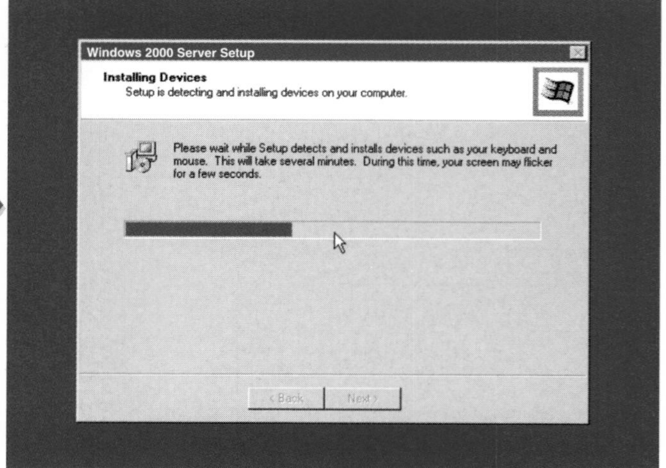

■ The server completes its hardware detection.

CHANGE REGIONAL SETTINGS

You can change system settings such as date and time formats or change keyboard settings if you are using a custom keyboard.

CHANGE REGIONAL SETTINGS

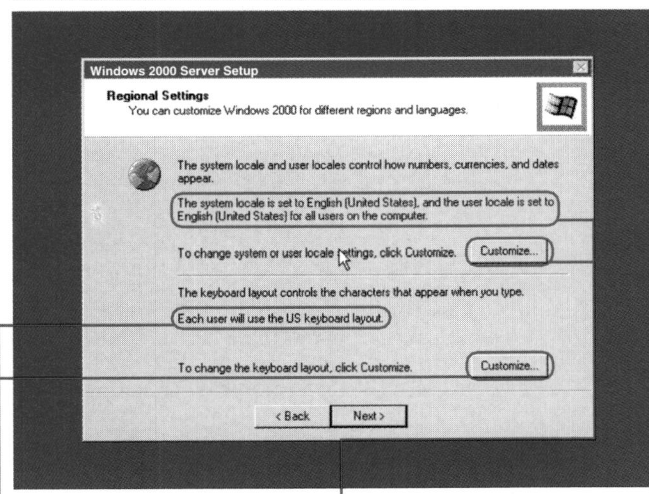

■ The current keyboard settings appear here.

■ You can click **Customize** to choose a different keyboard or layout.

■ The current regional settings appear here.

1 Click **Customize**.

■ The Regional Options dialog box appears.

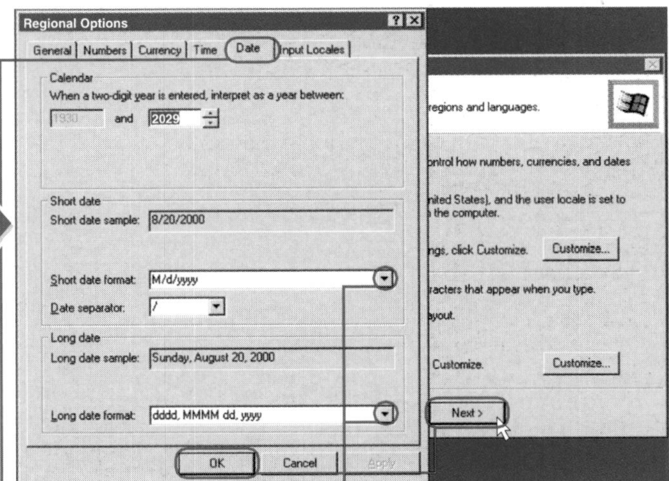

2 Click **Date**.

Note: Change the Short date format and the Long date format settings if you have particular software date requirements for Year 2000 program compatibility.

3 Click ▾ to change the date format.

4 Click **OK**.

5 Click **Next**.

ENTER YOUR NAME AND PRODUCT KEY

You must enter your name and the Microsoft product key in order to use Windows 2000 Server.

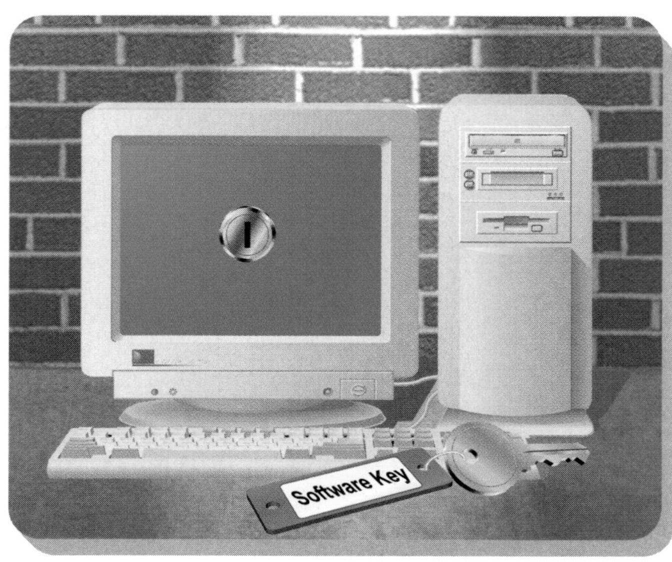

The product key is found on the back of the Windows 2000 Server CD case.

ENTER YOUR NAME AND PRODUCT KEY

Windows 2000 Server Setup

Personalize Your Software

Setup uses the information you provide about yourself to personalize your Windows 2000 software.

Type your full name and the name of your company or organization.

Name: Mike Toot

Organization: MST Consulting

< Back   Next >

Windows 2000 Server Setup

Your Product Key

Your Product Key uniquely identifies your copy of Windows 2000.

The 25-character Product Key appears on the yellow sticker on the back of your Windows 2000 CD case.

Type the Product Key below:

Product Key: 12345 - XXYYZ - Z7890 - EDCBA - 51423

< Back   Next >

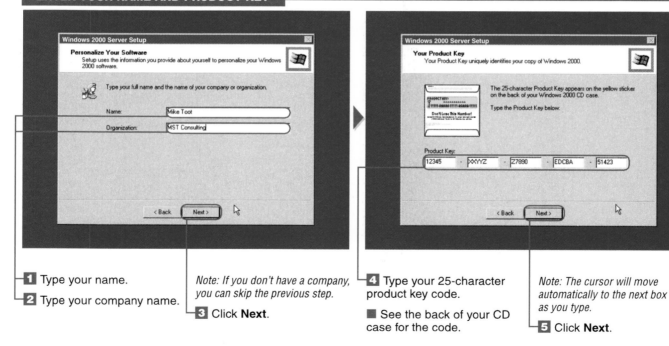

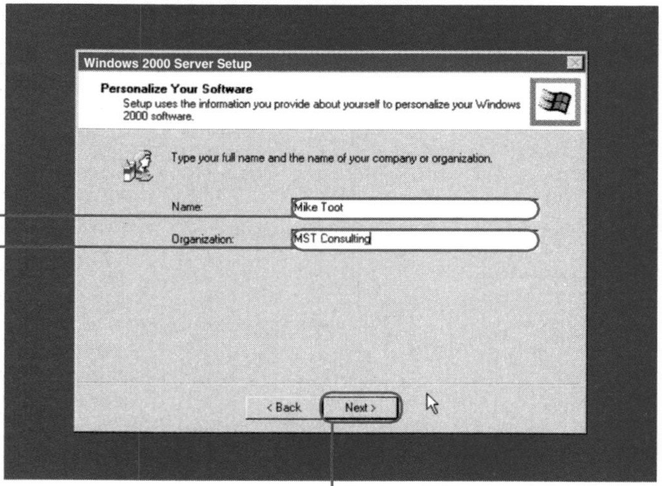

1 Type your name.

2 Type your company name.

Note: If you don't have a company, you can skip the previous step.

3 Click **Next**.

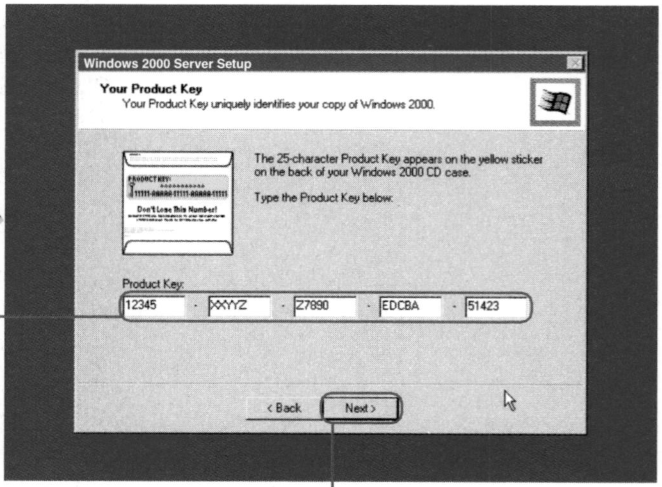

4 Type your 25-character product key code.

■ See the back of your CD case for the code.

Note: The cursor will move automatically to the next box as you type.

5 Click **Next**.

CHOOSE LICENSING MODE AND SERVER NAME

You need to choose a license mode for the workstations that connect to your server.

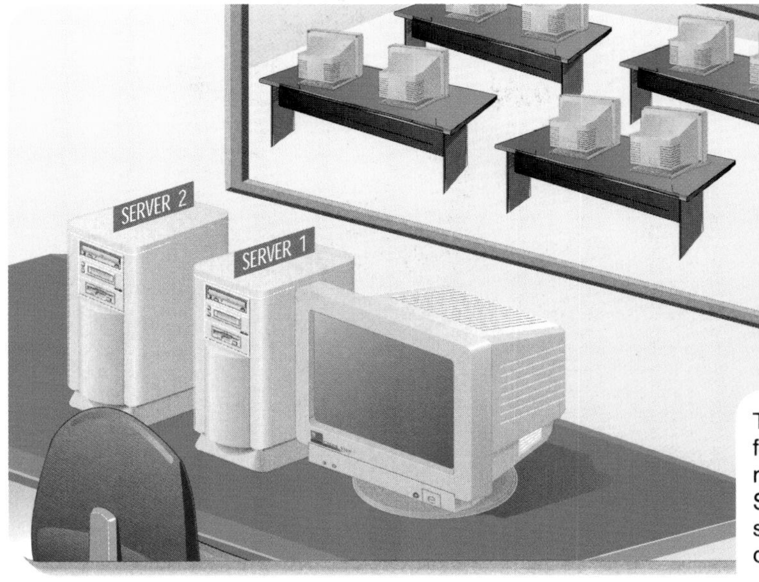

The Per Seat license is best for large networks with many servers; the Per Server license is best for small networks with only one server.

CHOOSE LICENSING MODE AND SERVER NAME

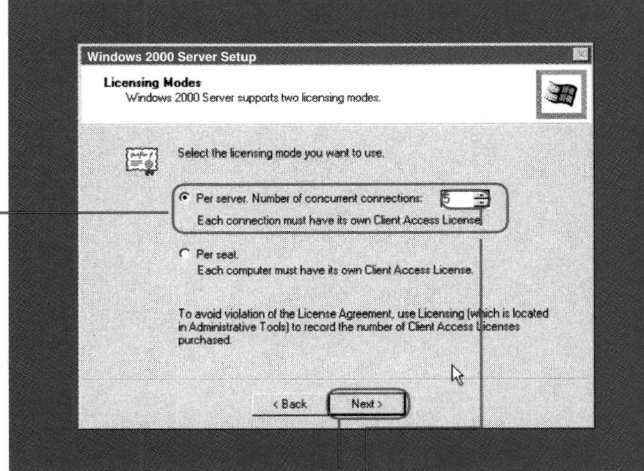

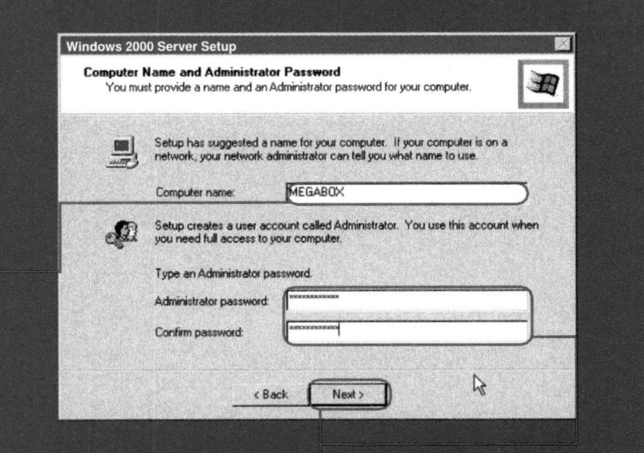

CHOOSE LICENSING MODE

■ The Licensing Mode dialog box appears.

1 Click the licensing mode that you want (○ changes to ◉).

■ If you choose Per server, type the number of workstations in this area.

2 Click **Next**.

CHOOSE SERVER NAME

■ The Computer Name and Administrator Password dialog box appears.

3 Type your server name.

Note: This name must be unique on your domain.

4 Type your administrator password in both areas.

Note: You will need this password to log on to the server later.

5 Click **Next**.

SELECT WINDOWS COMPONENTS

You can choose additional components for your server during setup.

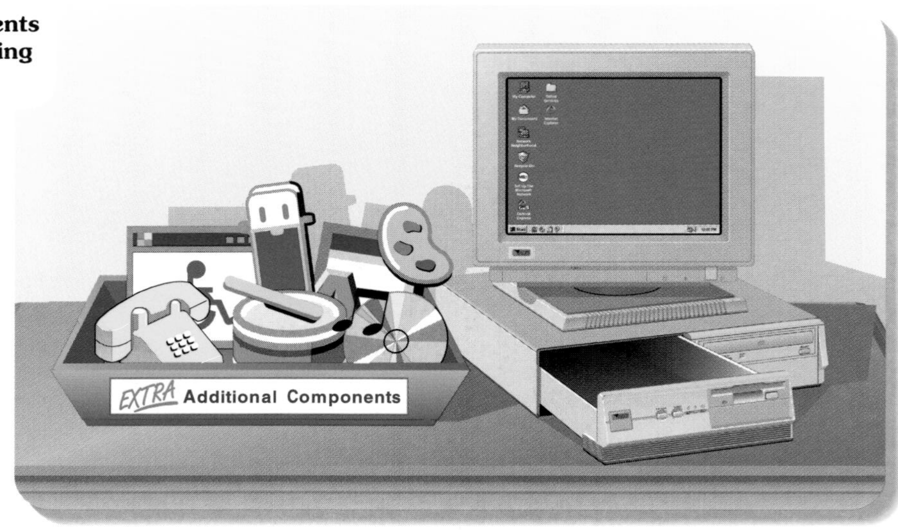

It is also possible to add these components later, after your server has been set up.

SELECT WINDOWS COMPONENTS

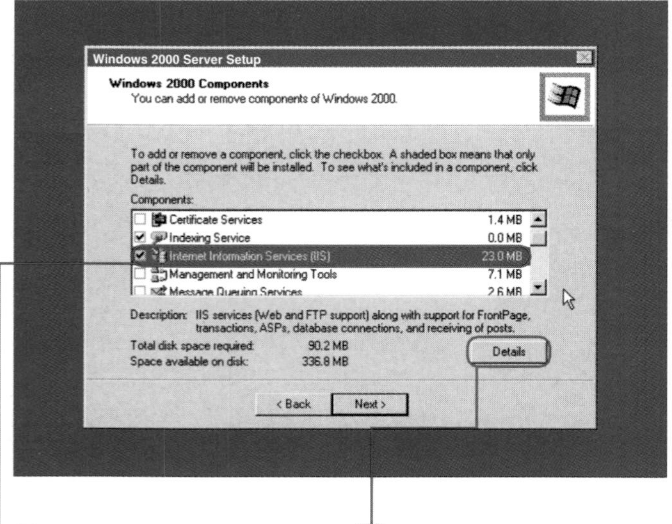

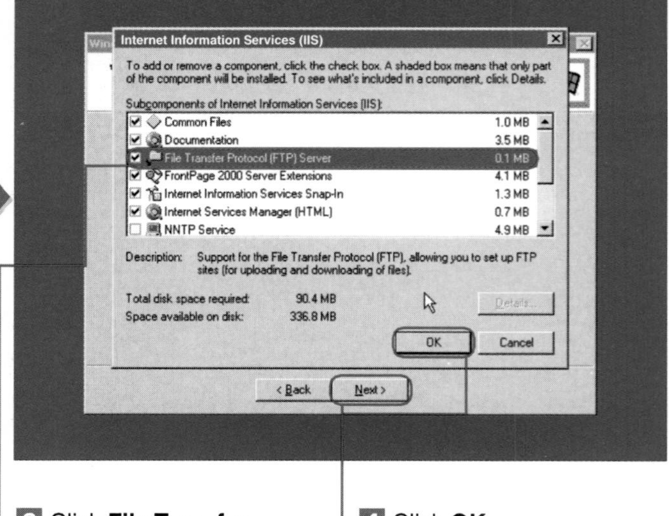

■ The Windows 2000 Components dialog box appears.

1 Click **Internet Information Services (IIS)** to highlight.

2 Click **Details**.

■ The IIS details window appears.

3 Click **File Transfer Protocol (FTP) Server** to highlight.

4 Click **OK**.

5 Click **Next**.

SET DATE AND TIME

During the setup procedure, Windows asks you to set your date, time, and time zone.

SET DATE AND TIME

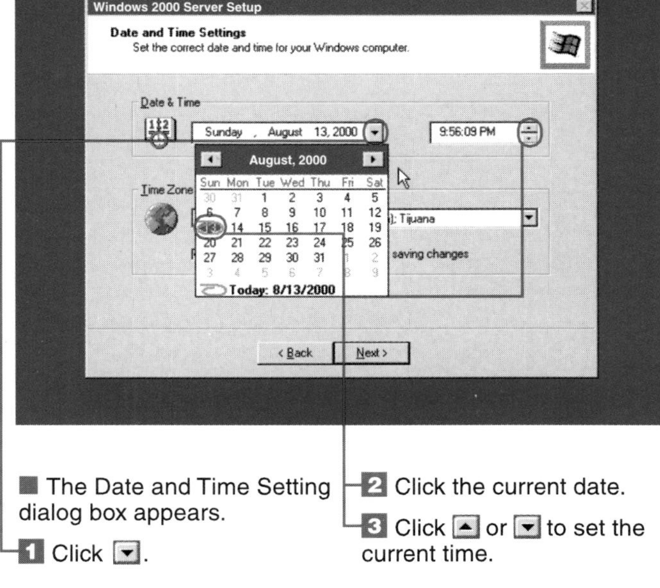

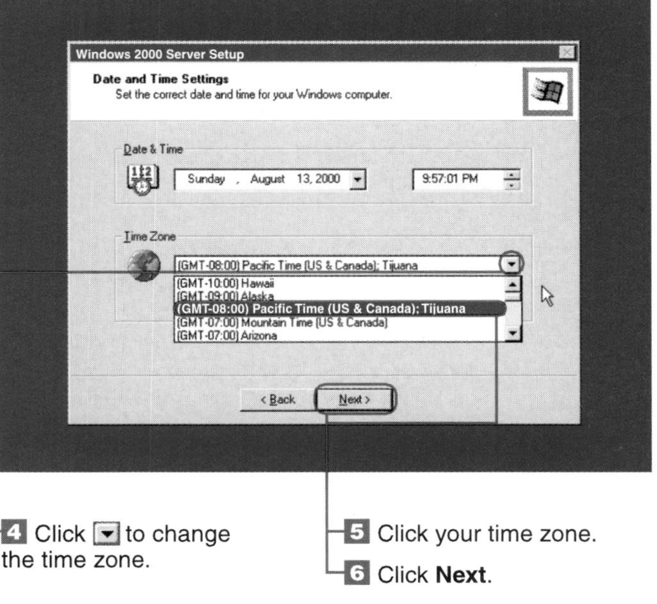

■ The Date and Time Setting dialog box appears.

1 Click ▼.

2 Click the current date.

3 Click ▲ or ▼ to set the current time.

4 Click ▼ to change the time zone.

5 Click your time zone.

6 Click **Next**.

CONFIGURE NETWORKING

You need to configure your server so it can communicate on your network.

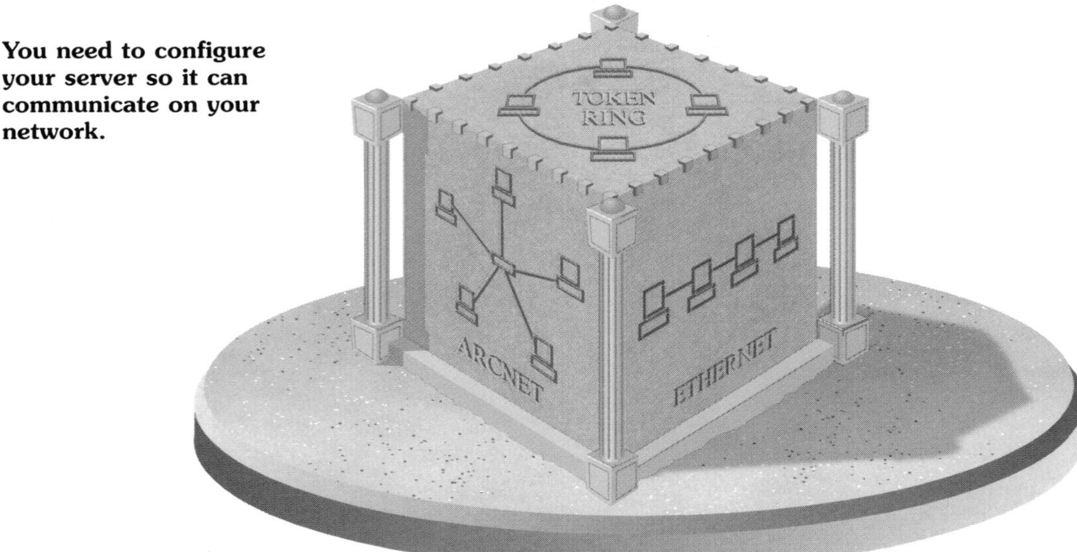

You can accept the default settings during setup. However, read Chapter 4 and check with your network administrator to see if you need custom settings.

CONFIGURE NETWORKING

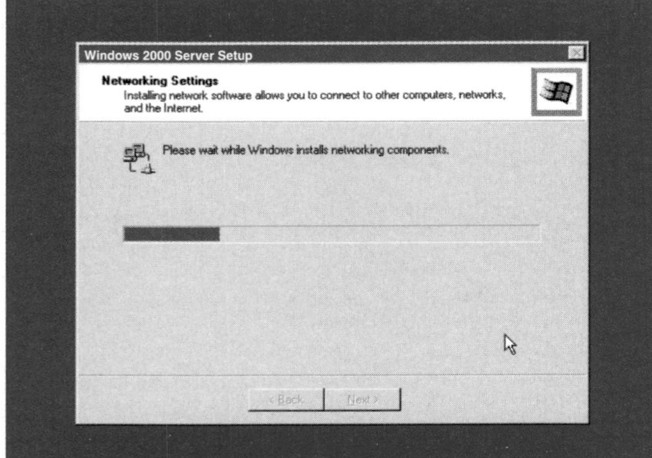

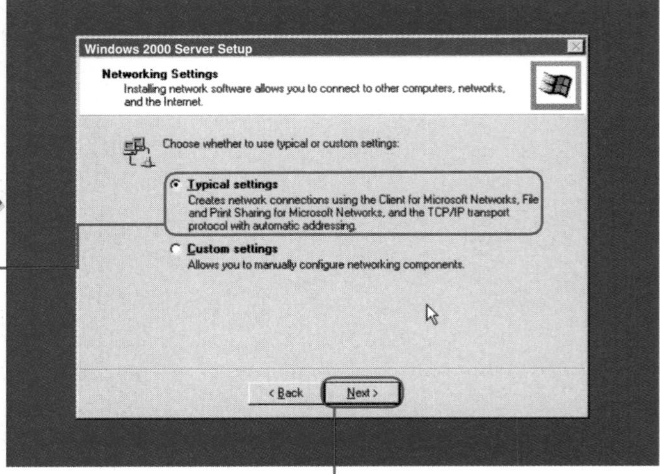

CONFIGURE NETWORK SETTINGS

■ The Networking Settings dialog box appears, showing your network components being installed.

■ When the install is complete, the new Networking Settings dialog box appears.

1 Click the settings you desire (○ changes to ◉).

Note: Typical is recommended.

2 Click **Next**.

What is the difference between workgroups and domains?

A workgroup is a small group of computers that share resources but are not centrally administered. A domain manages groups of computers, resource sharing, and security.

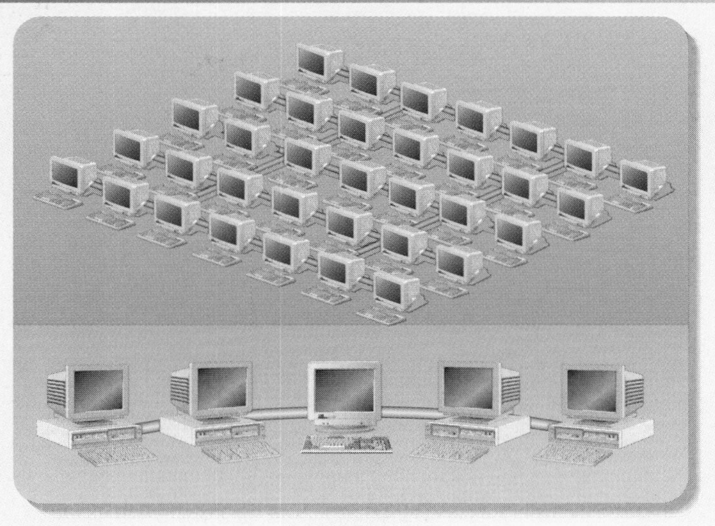

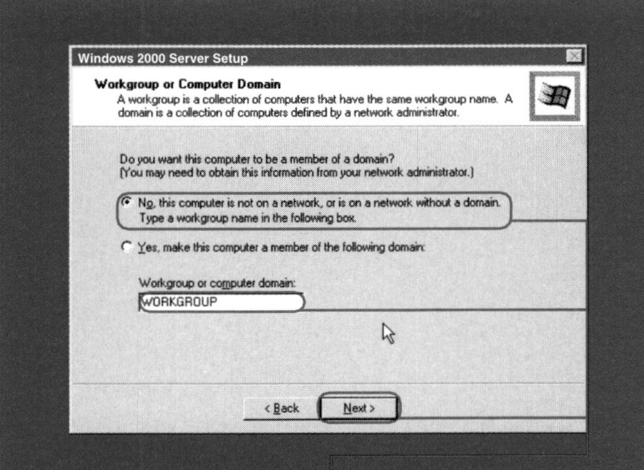

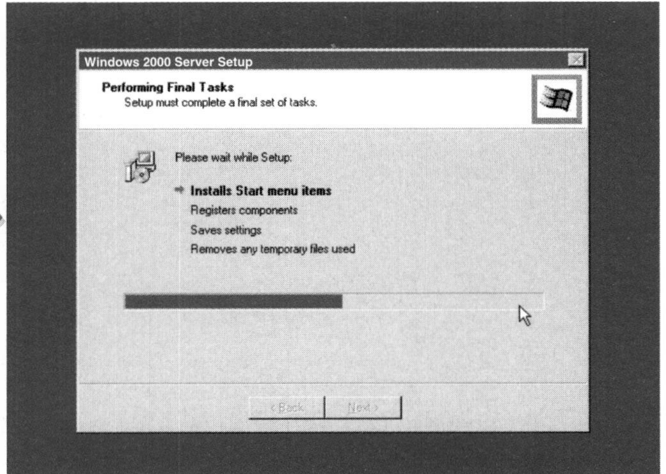

SELECT WORKGROUP OR DOMAIN

■ The Workgroup or Computer Domain dialog box appears, asking whether you want this computer to be part of a domain.

3 Click your choice (○ changes to ◉).

4 Type the name of the workgroup or domain in this area.

5 Click **Next**.

■ The Performing Final Tasks dialog box appears.

FINISH THE INSTALLATION

Windows 2000 Server will complete the installation and take you to the logon screen.

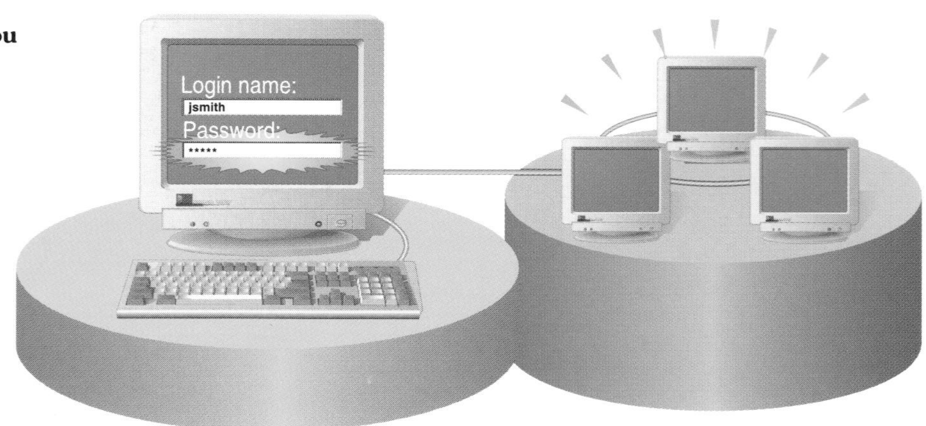

FINISH THE INSTALLATION

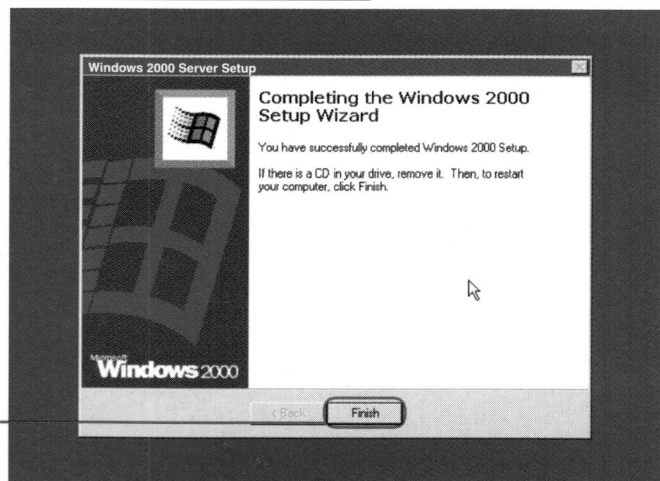

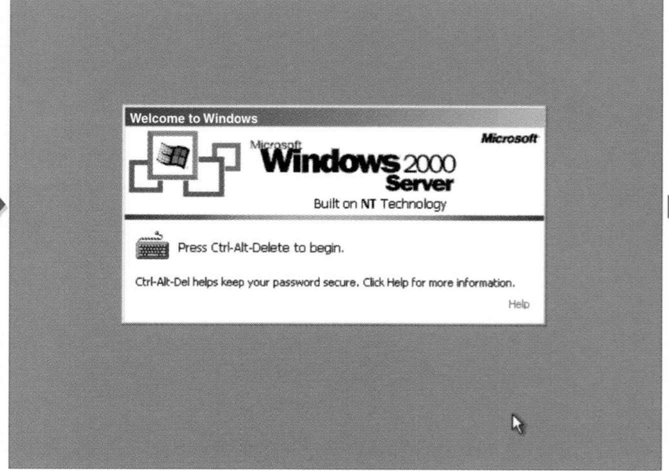

■ The Completing the Windows 2000 Setup Wizard appears.

1 Click **Finish**.

■ The Setup program finishes and the server reboots.

■ The Welcome to Windows dialog box appears.

2 Hold down Ctrl and Alt and then press Delete.

What do I do next?

As the system administrator, you can set up user accounts, share resources, and configure Internet connections. The rest of this book can help you with these tasks.

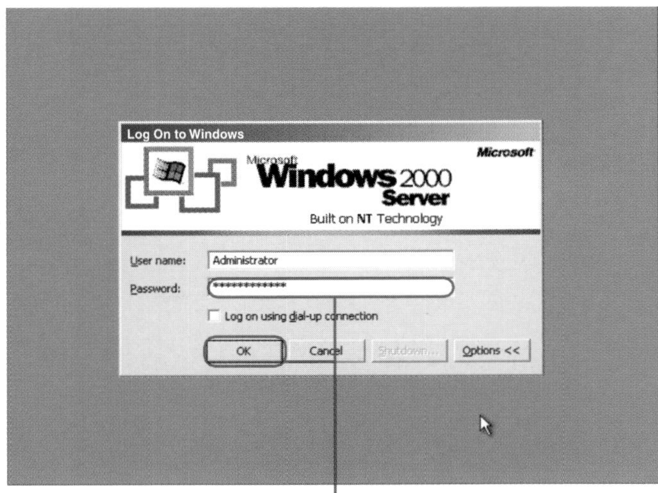

■ The Log On to Windows dialog box appears.

■ The Administrator's account name is already entered.

3 Type the Administrator password you chose in the "Choose Licensing Mode and Server Name" task.

4 Click **OK**.

■ The Windows 2000 desktop appears.

INDEX

E

F

L

M

N

R

S

TRADE & INDIVIDUAL ORDERS

Phone: **(800) 762-2974**
or **(317) 572-3993**
(8 a.m. – 6 p.m., CST, weekdays)
FAX : **(800) 550-2747**
or **(317) 572-4002**

EDUCATIONAL ORDERS & DISCOUNTS

Phone: **(800) 434-2086**
(8:30 a.m.–5:00 p.m., CST, weekdays)
FAX : **(317) 572-4005**

CORPORATE ORDERS FOR 3-D VISUAL™ SERIES

Phone: **(800) 469-6616**
(8 a.m.–5 p.m., EST, weekdays)
FAX : **(905) 890-9434**

Qty	ISBN	Title	Price	Total

Shipping & Handling Charges

	Description	First book	Each add'l. book	Total
Domestic	Normal	$4.50	$1.50	$
	Two Day Air	$8.50	$2.50	$
	Overnight	$18.00	$3.00	$
International	Surface	$8.00	$8.00	$
	Airmail	$16.00	$16.00	$
	DHL Air	$17.00	$17.00	$

Subtotal ______________

CA residents add applicable sales tax ______________

IN, MA and MD residents add 5% sales tax ______________

IL residents add 6.25% sales tax ______________

RI residents add 7% sales tax ______________

TX residents add 8.25% sales tax ______________

Shipping ______________

Total ______________

Ship to:

Name ______________________________

Address ______________________________

Company ______________________________

City/State/Zip ______________________________

Daytime Phone ______________________________

Payment: ☐ Check to IDG Books (US Funds Only)
☐ Visa ☐ Mastercard ☐ American Express

Card # ______________ Exp. __________ Signature ______________________

maranGraphics™